W9-ANG-160

Marketing Management
Strategies and Programs

McGRAW-HILL SERIES IN MARKETING

Marketing Management
Strategies and Programs
Sixth Edition

Joseph P. Guiltinan
University of Notre Dame

Gordon W. Paul
University of Central Florida

Thomas J. Madden
University of South Carolina

The McGraw-Hill Companies, Inc.
New York St. Louis San Francisco Auckland Bogotá
Caracas Lisbon London Madrid Mexico City Milan
Montreal New Delhi San Juan Singapore Sydney
Tokyo Toronto

McGraw-Hill

A Division of The McGraw·Hill Companies

MARKETING MANAGEMENT
Strategies and Programs

Copyright © 1997, 1994, 1991, 1988, 1985, 1982 by The McGraw-Hill Companies, Inc. All rights reserved. Printed in the United States of America. Except as permitted under the United States Copyright Act of 1976, no part of this publication may be reproduced or distributed in any form or by any means, or stored in a data base or retrieval system, without the prior written permission of the publisher.

This book is printed on acid-free paper.

1 2 3 4 5 6 7 8 9 0   DOC   DOC   9 0 3 2 1 0 9 8 7 6

ISBN 0-07-049097-X

The editors were Karen Westover, Dan Alpert, and Richard Mason.
The production supervisor was Michelle Lyon.
The interior design was by Elizabeth Williamson.
The cover design was by Linear Design Group.
The cover illustration was by Tim Clark.
The interior illustrations were by Hadel Studio.
This book was set in Times by GTS Graphics.
This book was printed and bound by R.R. Donnelley and Sons Company.

Library of Congress Cataloging-in-Publication Data
Guiltinan, Joseph P.
  Marketing management: strategies and programs / Joseph P. Guiltinan, Gordon W. Paul, Thomas Madden.—6th ed.
      p. cm.—(McGraw-Hill series in marketing)
  Includes bibliographical references and indexes.
  ISBN 0-07-049097-X
  1. Marketing—Management. I. Paul, Gordon W. II. Madden, Thomas J. III. Title. IV. Series.
HF5415.13.G8 1996
658.8—dc20

96-27233
CIP

International Edition
Copyright © 1997. Exclusive rights by The McGraw-Hill Companies, Inc. for manufacture and export. This book cannot be re-exported from the country to which it is consigned by The McGraw-Hill Companies, Inc. The International Edition is not available in North America.
When ordering this title, use ISBN 0-07-114255-X.

http://www.mhcollege.com

ABOUT THE AUTHORS

JOSEPH P. GUILTINAN is Professor of Marketing at the University of Notre Dame, where he has also served as Chair of the Department of Marketing and as Associate Dean for M.B.A. Programs. Prior to joining the Notre Dame faculty in 1987 he was a member of the faculties of the University of Massachusetts and the University of Kentucky (where he also served as Department Chair). In 1975–76 he was an AACSB Faculty Fellow at the National Aeronautics and Space Administration.

A graduate of the University of Notre Dame with a B.B.A, he holds an M.B.A and a D.B.A from Indiana University. Dr. Guiltinan's research interests are in pricing, marketing strategy, and new product development. His research has appeared in *Journal of Marketing, Journal of Consumer Research, Journal of Product Innovation Management, Social Forces,* and *Journal of Retailing.*

GORDON W. PAUL is Professor of Marketing at the University of Central Florida, where he previously served as Chair of the Department of Marketing. Prior to joining the University of Central Florida, he was a member of the faculties of the University of Massachusetts and Louisiana State University-Baton Rouge. Professor Paul has been a senior Fulbright Scholar on three occasions in Greece and Portugal. In addition, he has been an active consultant, and he is currently involved in a number of business organizations as an officer or partner.

A graduate of the University of Tulsa, he holds an M.B.A from the University of Texas-Austin and a Ph.D. from Michigan State University. He has published in a variety of journals including *Journal of Retailing, Decision Sciences,* and *Journal of Marketing.* Professor Paul has co-authored *Consumer Behavior: An Integrated Approach* (Richard D. Irwin) and *Cases in Marketing Management* (McGraw-Hill).

THOMAS J. MADDEN is Associate Professor of Marketing at the University of South Carolina. Prior to joining the University of South Carolina he was a member of the faculty at the University of Massachusetts-Amherst. Professor Madden is a graduate of the University of Bridgeport with a B.S. and he received his M.B.A from California State University-Fresno. He received his Ph.D. from the University of Massachusetts.

Dr. Madden's research has appeared in *Journal of Marketing, Journal of Marketing Research, Journal of Consumer Research,* and *Journal of Advertising Research.* He is the co-author of *Marketing Research in a Marketing Environment* (Richard D. Irwin) and *Essentials of Marketing Research* (Richard D. Irwin). Dr. Madden has been active in Executive Development Programs both in the U.S. and abroad.

To Our Families

Sharon and Shannon Guiltinan, Joanna McNultz, and Jennifer Urbach

Gloria, Christopher, and Bradley Paul

Priscilla, Michael, and Amy Madden

CONTENTS

PREFACE

This book is specifically designed for advanced undergraduate students and for those M.B.A. students with some previous coursework in marketing. The book originated out of our frustrations with the lack of teaching materials aimed at a middle-management approach to decision making. Our primary objective is to enable students to understand how to make the kinds of decisions they will face in middle-management positions. The book is intended to be used in those courses in which there is an emphasis on the application of marketing concepts, tools, and decision-making processes.

We have conscientiously written this book to accommodate a variety of teaching approaches. For those instructors who favor the lecture or discussion approach, there is ample material and coverage for the course. For those who prefer to use cases, simulations, or other pedagogy, the book provides the basic foundation for such an approach. In addition, practicing managers will find the book useful in providing guidelines for developing marketing plans and programs.

Unlike many marketing management texts, this is not just an introductory text with the addition of cases or additional concepts. As with previous editions, this book presents concepts from a decision-making perspective rather than from a descriptive point of view. As a result, the reader will not find separate chapters on topics such as consumer behavior, marketing research, personal selling, retailing, etcetera. Instead, these topics are covered in the context of their relevance to managers, so that students will gain an appreciation of the importance of the topics in making product, price, distribution, and promotional decisions.

This approach reflects our emphasis on the middle-management marketing decisions that students are most likely to confront in their careers. Accordingly, we make a distinction between top management's strategic decisions and the strategic and operating decisions made by middle managers for a specific product or product line. Additionally, because marketing managers are held accountable for profits as well as sales, we give extensive coverage to the budgetary considerations of marketing decisions. In many cases, top management concludes that marketing overspends, requires a disproportionately high percentage of resources, and does not deliver. Marketers are finding it increasingly necessary to improve their productivity or see their resources steadily diminish, or, worse still, find themselves the victims of corporate cost-cutters. Without the knowledge of profitability and productivity concepts and tools, future managers will be ill-equipped to effectively "sell" their programs to others within the firm and later implement them.

The book has been organized around the **marketing planning process** to clearly delineate the relationships from among marketing decisions. In Part One we present the marketing planning process, and we examine the corporate marketing planning decisions that top management must make to provide direction for middle-management decisions. Part Two presents the analytical tools that middle managers must use in analyzing the situation confronting the products or product lines for which they are responsible. Included in this section are chapters on market analysis (presenting approaches for analyzing the buying process and market segmentation), market measurement, competitive advantage, and profitability and productivity analysis (for budgeting decisions). Part Three presents systematic planning approaches for developing a marketing strategy for a product and for program decisions needed to implement the overall marketing strategy. The programs discussed include product development, pricing, advertising, sales promotion, direct marketing, and sales and distribution. Part Four examines the coordination and control mechanisms available to marketing managers. Included in this section are chapters on organizing and managing marketing and sales activities and on the annual marketing plan.

Users of previous editions will note that in terms of philosophy and perspective, this edition largely follows that of its predecessors. However, we have made some important changes. For one, we have increased our coverage of quality and customer service throughout the book. We have also included more coverage of direct marketing. In both cases we have attempted to incorporate material that reflects and addresses these recent marketing trends. As the importance of international markets continues to expand, marketing managers find they cannot examine multinational concerns as appendages to strategy. As in the previous edition, we have integrated the international dimensions of marketing throughout the text and given emphasis to this important aspect of many marketing decisions.

In addition to these changes, we have added numerous up-to-date examples that illustrate marketing practices as they are applied to a variety of organizations. We have enhanced existing chapters by incorporating new material. In particular, we have made a number of important additions that are useful when defining market segments. We have expanded our discussion of target marketing with an extensive discussion on segmentation and positioning. We have devoted more attention to data collection and analysis as well as evaluating market segments and database segmentation measures. Additionally, we have stressed issues such as category management, strategic alliances, relationship marketing, logistics, changes in distribution, organizational downsizing, and flexibility. Additional emphasis has also been given to services and industrial marketing practices. We have added new end-of-chapter discussion cases and questions to reflect this emphasis as well as to help integrate the international perspective.

To a large extent, the modifications reflect the comments and suggestions of faculty members who have used previous editions as well as the insightful evaluations by several reviewers. For their support and constructive comments we are especially indebted to the following individuals: Sharon E. Beatty, University of Alabama; Cathy Cole, University of Iowa; Edward F. Fern, Virginia Polytechnic Institute and State University; Robert J. Fisher, University of Southern California; Jonathan N. Goodrich, Florida International University; Craig A. Kelley, California State University, Sacramento; Ronald T. Lonsdale, Loyola University of Chicago; Mary Ann McGrath, Loyola University, Chicago; Daryl McKee, Louisiana State University; Kenneth L. Rowe,

Arizona State University; Peter A. Schneider, Seton Hall University; Mark Spriggs, University of Oregon; H. Rao Unnava, Ohio State University; and Larry K. Yarbrough, University of Arkansas.

We continue to be particularly grateful to Sam Gillespie of Texas A&M University who has provided us with constructive suggestions and materials throughout several editions. Our thanks are due, too, to our editor Karen Westover who has been an enthusiastic supporter of the approach we have taken. In addition, Dan Alpert has provided us with many useful suggestions and ensured that deadlines were met. We are most grateful to Richard Mason, Michelle Lyon, and Francis Owens for their substantial editorial, design, and production contributions to this project. Their skill and attention to detail are most appreciated. Finally, we would like to acknowledge the support and suggestions from the adopters of the previous five editions of the book. We have implemented many of these suggestions in this edition.

Joseph P. Guiltinan
Gordon W. Paul
Thomas J. Madden

PART ONE

Middle-Management
Marketing Planning

2

MANAGERIAL PERSPECTIVES ON MARKETING

In today's world it sometimes seems that change is the only constant. Managers of both profit-oriented and not-for-profit organizations face an environment characterized by rapidly changing technology, by competition that is increasingly multinational in scope, and by shifting political and economic forces such as the economic unification of Europe, an international trend toward the deregulation of key industries, and dramatic growth in international trade and foreign investment.

These changes have important implications for marketing decisions in an organization. Decisions on the design of products and services, on prices, and on appropriate promotional methods and distribution systems must be made after considering environmental constraints and opportunities. Because the environment is dynamic and complex, and because the range of marketing decisions, issues, and positions is extensive, organizations must develop processes for coordinating various decisions and activities to ensure a common purpose and direction. This is particularly important at what is generally called the *middle-management* level of an organization. The term *middle management* is generally applied to the vast area between first-line supervisors and vice presidents. In marketing, middle-management personnel include individuals with titles such as product or brand manager, advertising manager, market manager, and sales manager.

This book provides the concepts, tools, and decision-making approaches that prospective middle-level managers need to carry out their specialized job roles and responsibilities. However, each of these job roles represents only one or, at most, a few elements of the total marketing effort. Accordingly, so that a middle manager can fully appreciate and effectively utilize these concepts and tools, it is important to understand the relationship between top-management and middle-management decisions.

In Part 1, which includes Chapters 1 and 2, we examine the broad organizational setting in which the marketing function is performed, and we discuss the ways in which the organization as a whole can attempt to deal with environmental changes. Both of these issues are important to ensure that middle-management activities are integrated and well focused.

Chapter 1 presents the marketing planning process, which serves as the basis for *integrating* the various marketing activities. Chapter 2 discusses the role of top-management decision making, which is to develop a corporate marketing plan that establishes a basic *direction* for middle-management actions.

CHAPTER 1

MARKET ORIENTATION, MARKETING MANAGEMENT, AND THE MARKETING PLANNING PROCESS

Perspectives on what constitutes marketing and on the place marketing holds in the firm have undergone substantial change over the years. In the middle of the twentieth century, the term *marketing* was viewed as more or less equivalent to the term *selling*. Many companies believed that with enough effort and expense, almost any product could be sold by high-powered selling and aggressive advertising. In effect, this "selling concept" implied that marketing's role was to help dispose of whatever goods or services a firm decided to produce.

Make it, someone will buy it.

But as products became more sophisticated, growing personal incomes permitted the purchase of more discretionary items, and competition began to increase, the business environment became increasingly complex. Firms began to place more emphasis on marketing research to learn more about buyers' motives and preferences. Additionally, the pace of new-product development accelerated as more firms sought to satisfy changing market needs and to develop brand and corporate names that would gain the trust and loyalty of customers. But often this approach to business achieved only short-term success. Consider the case of Schwinn.

In the 1960s, one out of every four bicycles sold in the United States was made by Schwinn, a company founded in Chicago in 1895. Schwinn bicycles were sold in the best bicycle shops in the country and the brand was known for its stellar quality. But by 1992, Schwinn's market share had plummeted to a mere 3% and the company was on the brink of bankruptcy. Schwinn's decline began when it ignored the increase in market share going to lower-priced bicycles produced by Huffy and Murray that were being sold in popular mass merchandise stores. Also, Schwinn chose not to develop a product to compete with the new mountain bikes being marketed. In spite of the increasing market acceptance of these bikes Schwinn's management guessed they were a fad. Today, they represent 65% of all bicycle sales. Finally, in an attempt to improve price competitiveness, Schwinn moved production overseas in an effort to reduce its costs. But this move resulted in late deliveries and quality problems. In 1993, the company was purchased by Scott Sports Group which moved the company to Colorado and launched a new product development program. By 1995, Schwinn was able to offer new lines of off-road bikes and kids' bikes, and company sales had reached $250 million.[1]

The problems faced by Schwinn have been shared by many other organizations that experience success. Essentially, management was so convinced of the invincibility of the firm's name and product that it took its success for granted. But in an environment characterized by increasing global competition, a seemingly continuous flow of new technology, and sophisticated customers who expect to get what they want, no firm can presume that it can maintain its standing easily. Unfortunately, managers often spend too little time looking at their environment. One assessment suggests that only 40 percent of a senior executive's time is spent looking outward, and only 30 percent of that time involves thinking at a time horizon of 3 or more years.[2] Managers must realize that regardless of any past success, a firm must understand its customers' needs, its competition, and the broad environment in which it operates to assure long-term success.

In the remainder of this chapter, we examine (1) the nature and causes of customer satisfaction and quality, (2) the importance to a firm of having a "market orientation" in order to deliver quality and thus maintain customer satisfaction and competitive advantage, and (3) how marketing managers use the marketing planning process in implementing a market orientation.

CUSTOMER SATISFACTION AND QUALITY

A buyer's degree of satisfaction with a product is the consequence of the comparison a buyer makes between the level of the benefits *perceived* to have been received after consuming or using a product and the level of benefits *expected* prior to purchase. If, after a given purchase and use occasion a customer believes that a good or service has met expectations, satisfaction results; if not, dissatisfaction results.[3] Repeated satisfactory experiences over time enhance a customer's overall level of satisfaction and enable the customer to develop clear expectations about what to expect in the future. As shown in Figure 1-1, customer satisfaction results in two major benefits to the firm—greater loyalty and positive word-of-mouth communication as customers tell others of their experience.

In order to deliver customer satisfaction, an organization has to offer *quality* in its goods and services. Quality represents all the dimensions of the product offering that result in benefits to the customer. Sometimes the word "value" is used interchangeably with "quality." Typically, value is considered to represent the *relative* quality of an offering taking into account the price of the product.

---

[1]"Hard Pedaling Powers Schwinn Uphill in Sales, toward Profits," *Chicago Tribune,* June 22, 1995, p. C2; and Sandra Atchison, "Pump, Pump, Pump at Schwinn," *Business Week,* Aug. 23, 1993, p. 79.

[2]Gary Hamel and C. K. Prahalad, "Competing for the Future," *Harvard Business Review,* July–August 1994, p. 123.

[3]William Wilkie, *Consumer Behavior,* 3d ed., Wiley, New York, 1994, pp. 541–542.

FIGURE 1-1
Consequences of satisfaction.

The term *quality* is often thought to mean defect-free products. This traditional manufacturing-oriented view of quality has been broadened considerably in recent years. Today, high quality means pleasing customers—going beyond merely protecting them from annoyances. For example, North American automotive manufacturers have nearly eliminated the quality gap between themselves and Japanese firms regarding manufacturing defects. But the Japanese producers have continued to lead in offering fine touches such as computer-driven "active" suspension systems and sets of buttons and levers for controlling lights, stereos, and directional signals, all of which require the exact same pressure to operate. Thus, a truly quality-oriented view of customer satisfaction is one that subscribes to providing a level of benefits that *exceeds* rather than just matches expectations.

In seeking to provide this level of customer satisfaction, organizations can pursue any of eight dimensions of quality.

1. *Performance:* the basic operating characteristics of a product, such as the prompt delivery of an express package or the clarity of a television picture
2. *Features:* the special supplemental characteristics that heighten the use experience, such as free drinks on an airplane trip or optional seat-cover materials in an automobile
3. *Reliability:* the probability of product failure within a given time frame
4. *Conformance:* the degree to which a good or service meets established standards, including the timeliness of an airplane arrival or how close a shirt comes to its stated size
5. *Durability:* the amount of use a product can take before it must be replaced
6. *Serviceability:* the speed and ease of repair, and the courtesy and competence of service personnel
7. *Aesthetics:* how a product looks, feels, sounds, tastes, or smells

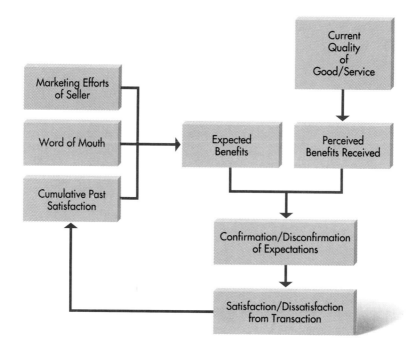

FIGURE 1-2

Satisfaction and quality.

8. *Perceived quality:* the quality that is inferred from a seller's reputation (e.g., Maytag washers, Rolex watches)[4]

The quality of goods or services provided *as perceived by the customer* will determine the customer's perception of performance and, thus, satisfaction, as shown in Figure 1-2.

Quality, Satisfaction, and Performance

The belief that high quality ultimately results in superior business performance is supported by empirical research that shows higher profitability (as measured by a firm's return on investment) is a consequence of higher quality.[5] High quality creates and maintains a high degree of customer satisfaction. As a result (as illustrated in Figure 1-3) quality allows a firm to increase its relative sales position in the market, which is posi-

[4]David Garvin, "Competing on the Eight Dimensions of Quality," *Harvard Business Review,* November–December 1987, pp. 101–109. Researchers who are concerned with measuring the quality of services (as opposed to tangible goods) would note that tangible cues such as facilities and equipment are a potential dimension of quality not covered in Garvin's eight dimensions. See A. Parasuraman, Valerie Zeithaml, and Leonard Berry, "A General Model of Service Quality and Its Implications for Future Research," *Journal of Marketing,* Fall 1985, p. 48.

[5]See Eugene Anderson, Claes Fornell, and Donald Lehmann, "Customer Satisfaction, Market Share, and Profitability: Findings from Sweden," *Journal of Marketing,* July 1994, pp. 53–66; and Lynn Phillips, Dae Chang, and Robert Buzzell, "Product Quality, Cost Position, and Business Performance: A Test of Some Key Hypotheses," *Journal of Marketing,* Spring 1983, pp. 26–43.

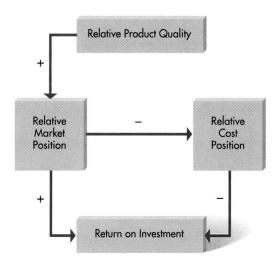

FIGURE 1-3
Quality and profitability. (Adapted from Lynn Phillips, Dae Chang, and Robert Buzzell, "Product Quality, Cost Position, and Business Performance: A Test of Some Key Hypotheses," *Journal of Marketing*, vol. 47, p. 29, Spring 1983.)

tively related to return on investment. Additionally, as a firm's market position grows, it often becomes more competitive on average costs because of economies of scale. Since costs are negatively related to profitability, the lower costs also lead to higher profitability. Another example of how high quality can be associated with low costs leading to higher profitability can be found in the dramatic turnaround at Harley Davidson.

> Honda Motor seized a 44% share of the U.S. heavy motorcycle market when it began production in Ohio. Bikers found Hondas to be lower priced and dramatically more reliable in terms of avoiding breakdowns than the previous market leader, Harley Davidson. At first, Harley Davidson management suspected that Honda had developed some superior manufacturing technology. What they eventually learned, however, was that Honda achieved both lower cost and higher reliability in large part because of its inventory system. Honda and its suppliers were producing parts in small batches every day as needed by manufacturing. If a defective part was discovered, it meant that the problem could be quickly identified and corrected. The system also meant that Honda had very little money tied up in parts inventory. By contrast, Harley Davidson produced parts in large volume batches well in advance of production needs. Not only did this create large, costly inventories but some parts deteriorated by rusting before they could be used, resulting in more defects in the final assembled product. Ultimately, Harley Davidson's management set out to learn how each department could improve its practices in a way that insured greater customer satisfaction, and in five years the company doubled its share of the market and achieved record earnings.[6]

The story of Harley Davidson's turnaround illustrates yet another aspect of the linkage between customer satisfaction and firm performance. As customer satisfaction yields higher growth and profits, the stockholders who own the business will be more

---

[6]Peter Reid, *Well Made in America: Lessons from Harley Davidson,* McGraw-Hill, New York, 1990, pp. 13–19.

FIGURE 1-4

The virtuous circle. (*Source:* Jean-Philippe Deschamps and P. Ranganath Nayak, *Product Juggernauts,* Harvard Business School Press, Boston, 1995, p. 6.)

satisfied as well. Jean-Philippe Deschamps and P. Ranganath Nayak, management consultants with Arthur D. Little, Inc., argue that satisfied owners are then more likely to continue to make investments in human resources and equipment.[7] In turn this enhances employee satisfaction and quality. As Figure 1-4 shows, this results in what they term the *virtuous circle*—a self-reinforcing cycle that can lead to a sustained high level of performance.

In assessing the problems that developed at Schwinn, then, we can see how the company's failure to develop new products and to maintain the high level of quality that customers had come to expect caused an erosion of customer satisfaction. The resulting decline in market share and profitability dissuaded further investment by the former owners that may have turned the firm around. Today, marketing managers and scholars would generally agree that this company's experience could have been avoided by adoption of a *market orientation.*

MARKET ORIENTATION

A market orientation refers to an organizational perspective that encourages (1) the systematic gathering of market intelligence, (2) dissemination of the intelligence across all organizational units, and (3) a coordinated, organizationwide responsiveness to the intelligence.[8] Figure 1-5 portrays the key activities in a market orientation.

[7]Jean-Philippe Deschamps and P. Ranganath Nayak, *Product Juggernauts,* Harvard Business School Press, Boston, 1995, pp. 6–7.

[8]Bernard Jaworski and Ajay Kohli, "Market Orientation: Antecedents and Consequences," *Journal of Marketing,* July 1993, pp. 53–70.

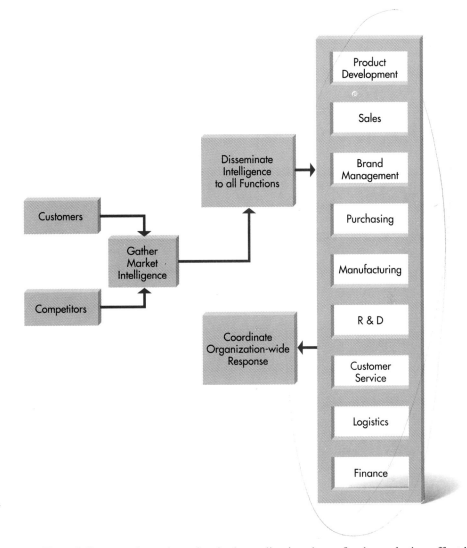

FIGURE 1-5

Market orientation.

Essentially, a market orientation is the realization that a firm's marketing effort is the business of all departments and functions. The well-known business philosophy of *total quality management* offers a similar view. The total quality management approach emphasizes that all departments and employees must commit to and share responsibility for quality—including any of the dimensions discussed above that impact customer satisfaction. Marketing has a lead role in this process in that it is most responsible for identifying clearly the priority needs and concerns of customers. As we will see in Chapter 3, marketing managers have developed methods for summarizing and communicating information on customers' needs and preferences to other units. Without this shared information, units such as purchasing, manufacturing, and research and development will be unable to deliver the quality required for sustained competitive advantage. Eastman Chemical company offers an example of a company that has continually extended its efforts to assure this coordination.

Eastman Chemical manufactures and markets over 400 industrial chemicals, with total sales reaching $4 billion by the mid-1990s. The company first developed a total quality orientation in 1980, but management decided that quality alone would not allow the firm to survive in the long run. The chemical industry was in a wave of consolidations that meant the largest firms would become extremely powerful. Thus, Eastman's management established a goal of reaching $15 billion in sales by the year 2000. The firm's first step toward achieving that goal was to develop multifunctional teams that would identify emerging customer needs. Customers were involved; Eastman invited them to the company's plants to offer insights on its products and processes. The company also implemented a database on customer needs that can be accessed from any point in the organization. By 1994, the company's share of sales from products that were less than five years old was double the industry average.[9]

Achieving the interfunctional coordination necessary to implement the marketing concept is not an easy task. Effective coordination requires that information on buyer needs be known throughout the organization and that each functional department appreciates the constraints faced by other units. Additionally, there must be a strong commitment to the goals of customer satisfaction and profitability.[10] The importance of an organizationwide commitment to the customer cannot be overstated. Firms may need to emulate the actions of Federal Express in developing extensive training programs or other innovative mechanisms for building commitment.

Federal Express (FedEx) completely realigned a large part of its organization to provide a coordinated focus on the customer. Historically, the marketing staff was responsible for direct mail promotion, a distinct pricing group set prices, customer service representatives tracked orders, and finance handled credit and collections. Under the new alignment, the FedEx customer base was divided into segments of similar types, and FedEx created teams from the various functions to manage the accounts in each segment. The company also invested in technical and teamwork training, and created new performance standards to reward teams who enhanced value to the customer and achieved higher repeat business.[11]

Because of the growing recognition of the importance of market orientation, marketing researchers have become interested in how one might measure it. Managers who wish to assess their firms' degree of market orientation may wish to rate their organizations on the list of characteristics in Table 1-1.

A sometimes controversial aspect of being market-oriented revolves around its applicability to not-for-profit organizations such as colleges, arts organizations, political groups, and social-action causes. Hospitals, for example, have begun to recognize that patients expect more than just basic health care. Increasingly, hospitals are emphasizing pleasant "extras": friendly nurses and staff, faster service and attention, nicely decorated rooms, and even gourmet meals in some cases.

---

[9]Jerry Holmes and Gary McGraw, "White Water Ahead: Eastman Chemical Prepares for Turbulent Times," *Research & Technology Management,* September–October 1994, pp. 20–24; and "Eastman Chemical," *Quality,* January 1994, pp. 24–26.

[10]Benson Shapiro, "What the Hell Is Market Oriented?" *Harvard Business Review,* November–December 1988, pp. 119–125.

[11]Alan Grant and Leonard Schlesinger, "Realizing Your Customers' Full Profit Potential," *Harvard Business Review,* September–October 1995, pp. 59–72.

TABLE 1-1	MEASURING MARKET ORIENTATION

The market orientation of a firm is greater to the extent management would agree (A) or disagree (D) with each statement listed.

INTELLIGENCE GENERATION

1. In this business unit, we meet with customers at least once a year to find out what products or services they will need in the future. (A)
2. Individuals from our manufacturing department interact directly with customers to learn how to serve them better. (A)
3. In this business unit, we do a lot of in-house market research. (A)
4. We are slow to detect changes in our customers' product preferences. (D)
5. We poll end users at least once a year to assess the quality of our products and services. (A)
6. We often talk with or survey those who can influence our end users' purchases (e.g., retailers, distributors). (A)
7. We collect industry information through informal means (e.g., lunch with industry friends, talks with trade partners). (A)
8. In our business unit, intelligence on our competitors is generated independently by several departments. (A)
9. We are slow to detect fundamental shifts in our industry (e.g., competition, technology, regulation). (D)
10. We periodically review the likely effect of changes in our business environment (e.g., regulation) on customers. (A)

INTELLIGENCE DISSEMINATION

1. A lot of informal "hall talk" in this business unit concerns our competitors' tactics or strategies. (A)
2. We have interdepartmental meetings at least once a quarter to discuss market trends and developments. (A)
3. Marketing personnel in our business unit spend time discussing customers' future needs with *other* functional departments. (A)
4. Our business unit periodically circulates documents (e.g., reports, newsletters) that provide information on our customers. (A)
5. When something important happens to a major customer or market, the whole business unit knows about it in a short period. (A)
6. Data on customer satisfaction are disseminated at all levels in this business unit on a regular basis. (A)
7. There is minimal communication between marketing and manufacturing departments concerning market developments. (D)
8. When one department finds out something important about competitors, it is slow to alert other departments. (D)

RESPONSE DESIGN

1. It takes us forever to decide how to respond to our competitors' price changes. (D)
2. Principles of market segmentation drive new-product development efforts in this business unit. (A)
3. For one reason or another we tend to ignore changes in our customers' product or service needs. (D)
4. We periodically review our product development efforts to ensure that they are in line with what customers want. (A)
5. Our business plans are driven more by technological advances than by market research. (D)
6. Several departments get together periodically to plan a response to changes taking place in our business environment. (A)
7. The product lines we sell depend more on internal politics than real market needs. (D)

(continued)

RESPONSE IMPLEMENTATION

---

1. If a major competitor were to launch an intensive campaign targeted at our customers, we would implement a response immediately. (A)
2. The activities of the different departments in this business unit are well coordinated. (A)
3. Customer complaints fall on deaf ears in this business unit. (D)
4. Even if we came up with a great marketing plan, we probably would not be able to implement it in a timely fashion. (D)
5. We are quick to respond to significant changes in our competitors' pricing structures. (A)
6. When we find out that customers are unhappy with the quality of our service, we take corrective action immediately. (A)
7. When we find that customers would like us to modify a product or service, the departments involved make concerted efforts to do so. (A)

Source: Bernard Jaworski and Ajay Kohli, "Market Orientation: Antecedents and Consequences," *Journal of Marketing,* July 1993, pp. 65–66.

The primary controversy, however, revolves around the degree to which an organization should focus on customer or client satisfaction when the essential mission of the organization cannot be changed (for example, an antiabortion or environmental group), or where production is based on personal norms and values (as would be the case with arts-based organizations). Although businesses can move across products and markets to satisfy customers and still retain their core purpose of providing economic exchanges, not-for-profit organizations must consider their market orientation within the limits imposed by their purposes.

Market Orientation and Marketing Planning

If a firm is to implement the market-orientation philosophy, it must not only motivate employees to adopt this view; it must provide the analytical tools and decision-making frameworks to generate and process marketing intelligence. Some specific examples of key actions to be taken include

1. Deciding which business opportunities give the firm the best chance to create satisfied customers
2. Analyzing customer decision processes and identifying the various preference patterns in a market
3. Assessing competitive advantages and competitors' positions in a market
4. Measuring market opportunities and assessing the impact of plans for enhancing customer satisfaction or competitive advantage on profitability
5. Applying the knowledge from market intelligence to the design of the market offering

These are the basic actions that, taken together, represent the marketing planning process.

THE MARKETING PLANNING PROCESS

Planning is merely a systematic way for an organization to attempt to control its future. A plan is a statement of *what* the organization hopes to achieve, *how* to achieve it, and *when* it will be achieved. Firms that engage in planning believe that planning

- Encourages systematic thinking about the future
- Leads to improved coordination
- Establishes performance standards for measuring trends
- Provides a logical basis for decision making
- Improves the ability to cope with change
- Enhances the ability to identify market opportunities

Marketing planning is the systematic process for developing and coordinating marketing decisions. Essentially, then, marketing planning provides the framework for implementing a market orientation. It provides the focus for information gathering, the format for information dissemination, and the structure for developing and coordinating the firm's strategic and tactical responses.

As indicated in Table 1-2, it is important that marketing decisions be made at two levels—top management and middle management—so the marketing planning process operates at two levels.

Corporate marketing planning focuses on providing the long-term direction of the organization regarding the markets and needs that will be served. From the perspective of market orientation, the key question this form of planning addresses is "Where can we be most effective at competitively satisfying customers?" It also attempts to set objectives for the various products and businesses it will pursue. Often, firms use the term *strategic business units* (or SBUs) to represent these products and product lines.

TABLE 1-2	**THE TWO LEVELS OF MARKETING MANAGEMENT**		
	THESE PERSONNEL	**AT THIS LEVEL**	**MAKE THESE DECISIONS**
	Chief executive officer	Top management	Markets to be served
	Comptroller		Products to offer
	Vice president of marketing		Product objectives
	Other vice presidents		Allocation of resources
	Marketing managers	Middle management	Product design
	Product and brand managers		Prices
	Sales managers		Advertising
	Advertising managers		Sales promotion
	Promotion managers		Selling and distribution
	Customer service managers		Customer service

FIGURE 1-6

Linking corporate marketing planning to middle-management planning.

Middle-management planning specifies how the corporate marketing plan will be implemented on a product-by-product basis by focusing on the sales and profitability of individual products, brands, or lines of closely related products. While the number of middle-management positions has declined in many firms in recent years, these middle-management functions remain.[12] Indeed, one of the outcomes of the restructuring has been to *increase* the decision-making responsibilities of middle managers. The analyses of customer needs and competitor strengths are a core part of the middle-management marketing planning process. Additionally, it is at this level of planning that detailed actions for product design, advertising, and other strategies for responding to customers and competitors are developed (see Figure 1-6).

It is important to recognize that the two planning levels should be interdependent. Middle-management planning must be consistent with the goals and resource allocation decisions that top management makes in the corporate marketing plan. At the same time, as will be seen in Chapter 2, the corporate marketing planning process must rely on the information provided by middle managers on product and market trends, problems, and opportunities facing the firm.

---

[12]Alex Markels, "Restructuring Alters Middle Management's Role but Leaves It Robust," *Wall Street Journal,* Sept. 25, 1995, pp. A1, A6.

Basic Steps in Planning

Although marketing planning takes place at both the corporate level and the middle-management level, four basic steps are involved at each level (see Figure 1-7).

1. *Conducting a situation analysis.* Before developing any action plan, decision makers must understand the current situation and trends affecting the future of the organization. In particular, they must assess the *problems* and *opportunities* posed by buyers, competitors, costs, and regulatory changes. Additionally, they must identify the *strengths* and *weaknesses* possessed by the firm.
2. *Establishing objectives.* Having completed the situation analysis, the decision makers must then establish specific objectives. Objectives identify the level of performance the organization hopes to achieve at some future date, given the realities of the environmental problems and opportunities and the firm's particular strengths and weaknesses.
3. *Developing strategies and programs.* To achieve the stated objectives, decision makers must develop both strategies (long-term actions to achieve the objectives) and programs (specific short-term actions to implement the strategies).
4. *Providing coordination and control.* Plans that are fairly comprehensive often include multiple strategies and programs. Each strategy and each program may be the responsibility of a different manager. Thus, some mechanism must be developed to assure that the strategies and programs are effectively implemented.

Organizational structures and budgets are the primary means for coordinating actions. Control is also essential because the success of strategies and programs can never be predicted with certainty. The purpose of control is to evaluate the degree to which progress toward an objective is being made and to pinpoint the causes of any failure to achieve objectives so that remedial actions can be taken.

One further point about planning must be noted. Planning is a *process.* Organizations operate in complex and dynamic environments. Therefore, as the situation changes, managers must be prepared to modify objectives and strategies to deal with those changes.

FIGURE 1-7

Basic steps in planning.

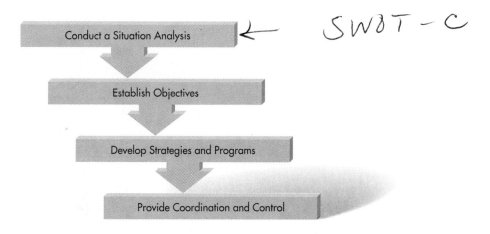

Conduct a Situation Analysis $SWOT - C$

Establish Objectives

Develop Strategies and Programs

Provide Coordination and Control

Marketing Management and the Marketing Planning Process

Marketing management encompasses all the decisions involved in designing and executing marketing plans in order to implement the marketing concept. As we have indicated, marketing decisions are made by top management and by middle managers, and decisions made at these two levels influence one another. Accordingly, both levels will be examined in this book, although our focus is primarily on decision making at the middle-management level.

More specifically, subsequent chapters will examine the kinds of information, concepts, tools, and procedures marketing managers can employ in decision making. As Figure 1-8 indicates, these decision areas are treated within the framework of the

FIGURE 1-8

Marketing management and the marketing planning process: an overview.

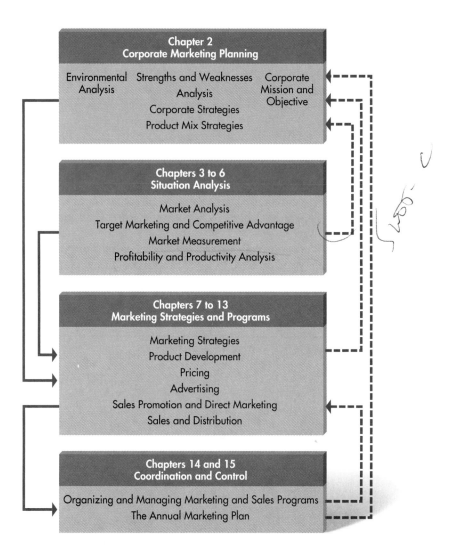

marketing planning process. Chapter 2 examines procedures for developing the situation analysis, objectives, and strategies at the corporate level. Additionally, a major outcome of corporate marketing planning is the development of product objectives that guide decision making at the middle-management level. This is also covered in Chapter 2.

In Chapters 3 to 6 we will examine techniques and procedures for conducting a situation analysis at the individual-product level.

Our primary focus in Chapters 7 to 13 is on developing marketing strategies and programs that will achieve the product objective and that take into account the problems and opportunities uncovered in the situation analysis.

Finally, Chapters 14 and 15 present procedures for coordination and control at both the middle-management and top-management levels.

In examining Figure 1-8 the reader should note the direction of the arrows linking the major sections. That there are arrows going in both directions between two sections reflects two important points. First, in a well-managed organization, top management will use the insights of middle management as an important input to corporate strategy. Information on the situation analysis for a given product and on the feasibility of developing a successful marketing strategy for a product is usually more detailed at the middle-management level and should be communicated to top management.

Second, the control function has a primary purpose of alerting managers to the need for changes in objectives, strategies, or programs.

CONCLUSION

The marketing concept serves as our starting point for examining marketing management because this concept reflects the basic purpose of a business. Without giving effective attention to customer needs, marketing and the other business functions will lack the direction needed for success.

It is important to recognize, however, that a market-oriented organization is one that takes its lead from the *market,* not necessarily from the *marketing department.* Market-oriented firms acquire an understanding of their customers and competitors, determine which customers and needs fit best with the organization's capabilities and profit goals, and develop their responses to the marketplace in a highly coordinated fashion and with a long-term perspective.

Even in a market-oriented organization, however, it is not a simple matter to implement the marketing concept. Organizations are faced with many alternative markets and customers and with a vast array of alternative policies and programs for meeting customer needs. Organizations cannot pursue *all* possible buyers and cannot take *all* possible marketing actions because human and financial resources are usually limited and do not permit such extravagance.

In order to deal with the problems involved in implementing the marketing concept, we have suggested a planning approach. Conducting a situation analysis and setting objectives before developing strategies and programs improve the chances for choosing the best marketing policies. Further, planning really should take place on two levels. At the middle-management level, planning focuses on an individual product or on a line of related products. At the top-management level, planning focuses on the broad question ("What business should we be in?") and on the total mix of products and product lines.

For many firms, the focus on market needs and quality has led to notably outstanding performance. The experiences of these organizations provide valuable lessons for future managers. One such example is Rubbermaid.

RUBBERMAID: DEVELOPING A COMMITMENT TO THE CUSTOMER

The Wooster Rubber Company was founded in Wooster, Ohio, in 1920 as a maker of toy balloons. In 1934 the company made its first dustpan—out of rubber—and began a new direction. The firm adopted its present name in 1957, and today Rubbermaid is almost synonymous with product innovation.

Rubbermaid offers some 5000 products today, almost all made from the petroleum-based polymers known as "resins" (rather than rubber), which are molded into everything from toy cars to garbage cans. To achieve its ambitious goal of having one-third of its sales come from products introduced in the last 5 years, Rubbermaid introduces, on average, one new product each day. At the same time, Rubbermaid products enjoy a strong reputation for quality. Primarily because of these achievements the company was ranked as the most admired company in the United States in surveys conducted by *Fortune* magazine in both 1994 and 1995.

Rubbermaid's emphasis on quality—both in terms of product design and reliability and in terms of attention to customer concerns—has been a hallmark of the company's success. Extensive product testing assures product quality. For example, 32-gallon garbage cans are dropped 6 feet onto concrete floors for durability testing. Rubbermaid believes that such quality allows the firm to charge a 10 percent premium over competing products in most categories. But even with this attention to product durability, Rubbermaid believes it must offer a very liberal refund policy. Refunds are made within 48 hours of a complaint—often even when the product purchased was a competing Rubbermaid look-alike rather than the real thing. Marketing researchers at Rubbermaid have learned that its dissatisfied customers complain to an average of five other people, so the company takes very seriously its obligation to perform to expectations.

The success of Rubbermaid's product-development efforts has been in part ascribed to its use of multifunctional teams. Each division has one set of teams to investigate new product ideas and to allocate funds to the most promising ones. Another set of teams with representation from marketing, finance, manufacturing, and research and development then takes responsibility for developing and introducing the new products. Frequently, large retailers work with these teams to assure that the introductory plans consider retailers' needs with respect to storage and display.

Top management is also involved in the development process at Rubbermaid, but in a different way. Upper-level Rubbermaid managers meet with vice president–level managers of major retail firms to discuss matters that will occur 3 to 4 years into the future such as changing retailer inventory and merchandising policies or major new strategies. For example, such discussions were held to discuss a new Rubbermaid initiative that would create a Rubbermaid "store within a store" selling only Rubbermaid lines. In describing the insights he developed during a stint in research and development, Chief Executive Officer Wolfgang Schmitt commented on the firm's attention to the future by noting: "I can add value in terms of looking out over the horizon, spotting trends, and figuring out how to apply them to our business."

1. What evidence is there that Rubbermaid is market-oriented?

2. Can you see any potential problems resulting from the intense focus on new-product development at Rubbermaid?

3. Describe how middle-management and top-management planning differ at Rubbermaid.

Developed from Lee Smith, "Rubbermaid Goes Thump," *Fortune,* Oct. 2, 1995; "Rubbermaid Turns Trends into Marketing Opportunities, Phenomenal Growth," *Business Dateline,* Apr. 19, 1993; Jean-Phillipe Deschamps and P. Ranganath Nayak, "Fomenting a Customer Obsession," *National Productivity Review,* Sept. 22, 1995, p. 89; Harvey Mackay, "The CEO Hits the Road," *Harvard Business Review,* March–April 1990, p. 32; "Growth Factors: Organizational Learning at Cemex, Rubbermaid, and Banc One," *ASAP,* July 1995.

QUESTIONS AND SITUATIONS FOR DISCUSSION

1. "In market-oriented firms all new products are based on extensive customer research and few new products are not successful." Do you agree or disagree? Explain your answer.

2. Of the eight dimensions of quality, which ones would be most important to an organization that primarily sells services (such as banks, hospitals, or airlines) rather than physical goods?

3. "Repair service is more a function of production than marketing, just as the extension of credit is more a function of finance than marketing." Do you agree or disagree with this statement? Explain.

4. How would you answer the business manager of the local symphony who made the following statement? "At times, I've thought about using marketing more in our affairs, but I simply cannot afford the cost of surveys and advertising campaigns. Anyway, people will always come to hear good music. The quality of our programs is the only important consideration."

5. While some organizations rely on repeat business for the bulk of their customers, others (such as house builders and universities) do not. Is customer satisfaction of less importance to the success of such organizations? Why or why not?

6. The 3M Company has 50,000 products ranging from Scotch tape to heart-lung machines. How would formal marketing planning differ in 3M from a company having only a few products?

7. Consider the following statement: "When a firm selects the customers it desires to serve, it also selects its competitors." How does this statement relate to the concept of market orientation?

8. Develop a list of possible top-management issues that might be considered by the McDonald's Corporation. What middle-management issues would this firm likely deal with?
9. Would marketing planning be more difficult for the Ford Motor Company or for Steelcase (a leading manufacturer of office furniture)? Why? For which company would marketing planning be more important? Taking both answers into consideration, what generalization would you make about the usefulness of planning?

SUGGESTED ADDITIONAL READINGS

Anderson, Eugene W., Claes Fornell, and Donald Lehmann, "Customer Satisfaction, Market Share, and Profitability: Findings from Sweden," *Journal of Marketing,* July 1994, pp. 53–66.

Bonoma, Thomas D., "Marketing Subversives," *Harvard Business Review,* November–December 1986, pp. 113–118.

Day, George, "The Capabilities of Market-Driven Organizations," *Journal of Marketing,* October 1994, pp. 37–52.

Jaworski, Bernard, and Ajay Kohli, "Market Orientation: Antecedents and Consequences," *Journal of Marketing,* July 1993, pp. 53–70.

Levitt, Theodore, "Marketing When Things Change," *Harvard Business Review,* November–December 1977, pp. 107–113.

Payne, Adrian, "Developing a Marketing-Oriented Organization," *Business Horizons,* May–June 1988, pp. 46–53.

Shapiro, Benson, "What the Hell Is Market Oriented?" *Harvard Business Review,* November–December 1988, pp. 119–125.

Slater, Stanley, and John C. Narver, "Market Orientation and the Learning Organization," *Journal of Marketing,* July 1995, pp. 63–74.

Walker, Orville, and Robert Ruekert, "Marketing's Role in the Implementation of Business Strategies: A Critical Review and Conceptual Framework," *Journal of Marketing,* July 1987, pp. 15–33.

CHAPTER 2

CORPORATE MARKETING PLANNING

OVERVIEW

We saw in Chapter 1 that an organization's success ultimately depends on its ability to satisfy its customers profitably. We also noted that, whereas middle managers are primarily responsible for the design and implementation of marketing programs for the various products, top management is responsible for establishing the firm's broader, long-term direction and goals.

Corporate marketing planning is the process by which an organization sets its long-term priorities regarding products and markets in order to enhance the value of the overall company. Two kinds of top-management decisions are involved in corporate marketing planning—*corporate strategy* and *product mix strategy* (see Figure 2-1). In corporate strategy, management identifies the businesses in which the company will be involved in the future by specifying

- The range of markets to be served
- The kinds of products to be offered

In making corporate strategy decisions, the critical question to be answered is, "In what markets will our particular resources be most effective in implementing the marketing concept?"

Once a corporate strategy has been chosen, management must develop a product mix strategy to identify the role each product is expected to play in building the value of the business. In particular, this strategy will usually specify

- The kind of contribution (such as rapid sales growth or high profitability) that each product or product line is expected to make toward increasing the company's value
- The relative share of the firm's resources to be devoted to each product or product line

The product mix strategy provides guidance to middle managers about top management's expectations. As we discuss throughout this book, knowing what role the product is expected to play in the overall corporate picture is essential to the development of marketing strategies and programs.

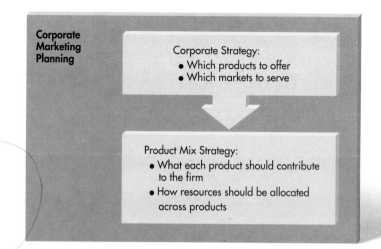

FIGURE 2-1

Elements of corporate marketing planning.

The purpose of this chapter is to identify the various corporate strategies and product mix strategies available to top management and to present procedures and tools for developing a corporate marketing plan. We will also consider the relationship between corporate-level decisions and the marketing planning process at the middle-management level.

CORPORATE STRATEGY

As we indicated at the start of this chapter, corporate strategies are long-range plans designed to select the various businesses a company should be in. They identify the markets to be served (defining them in terms of needs or customers or both) and the product lines and services to be produced on the basis of an assessment of the company's environment, resources, and objectives.

As portrayed in Figure 2-2, corporate strategies should be derived from the analysis of three elements: environmental threats and opportunities, corporate mission and objectives, and organizational strengths and weaknesses. A corporate strategy should be consistent with a company's objectives and achievable with existing (or anticipated) resources and competencies. Further, it should take into account prospective threats and opportunities in the environment.

Environmental Threats and Opportunities

Every organization operates in a dynamic environment that can create a variety of threats or opportunities in the firm's existing or potential markets. Specifically, managers should be aware of the possible impact on their markets of six major environmental forces.

1. *Demographics,* such as the age distribution of the population, birthrates, population growth, regional population shifts, and the percentage of two-worker households
2. *Social and cultural values,* such as attitudes toward health and nutrition, the need for self-expression, materialism, ecological concerns, and product safety
3. *Economic factors,* including inflation and unemployment rates, economic growth, raw materials scarcities, energy costs, interest rates, import duties, and excise taxes
4. *Technology,* particularly developing and anticipated changes that affect the kinds of products available in a market and the kinds of processes (such as automation or the use of synthetic materials) used to produce these products
5. *Legal and regulatory actions,* including regulations on the type of advertising available to a product, product labeling and testing requirements, limitations regarding product contents, pollution control, and restrictions or incentives with respect to imports or exports
6. *Competition,* which to a large extent is a function of the other environmental forces. Specifically, both the *identity* of competitors and the *type of focus* (for example, price-oriented versus technology-oriented) of competition may change because of

- The entry of new firms (especially foreign firms)
- The acquisition of a small competitor by a large, well-financed organization
- Deregulation, changing economic conditions, or new production processes that foster increased price competition
- Changing social and cultural values or new technology that causes buyers to purchase products or services previously considered noncompetitive (such as the renewed popularity of cloth diapers)

Examining these forces is essential to develop corporate strategies because these factors will shape the attractiveness of various businesses. Often such factors will create new opportunities or lead to the rejuvenation of mature markets.

The modern organization must develop *global* assessments of the environment, as trends and developments on these six dimensions are likely to vary around the globe. For example, whereas the population of the United States is aging, in most of Asia young people dominate the population, resulting in huge opportunities for companies such as McDonald's and Coca-Cola on that continent. Similarly, environmental regulations regarding packaging are much more stringent in western Europe than elsewhere.

FIGURE 2-2

Factors influencing corporate strategy.

Strengths and Weaknesses

Because environmental changes result in changing *opportunities* and changing *threats,* they are fundamental considerations in the development of corporate strategies. However, not all firms are equal in terms of their ability to take advantage of an opportunity or to avoid a threatening situation. A second fundamental consideration in selecting a corporate strategy is whether the firm possesses the strengths and weaknesses required to respond to environmental developments. In general, a firm's strengths are analyzed by identifying its *resources* and *competencies.* Managers should pursue those market opportunities that allow it to capitalize on those strengths.

In the broadest sense, resources and competencies include

- Financial resources, such as cash reserves
- Labor and managerial skills, such as the expertise to produce high-technology products or to manage large advertising budgets
- Production capacity and efficient equipment
- Research and development skills and patents
- Control over key raw materials, as in the ownership of energy resources
- Size and expertise of the sales force
- Efficient or effective distribution channels and systems

Too often firms limit their evaluation of resources to the more tangible ones, such as cash and facilities. Yet management and marketing capabilities are often more important. For example, Frito-Lay's success in the snack business is due primarily to effective advertising management and its extensive sales force, which rotates and replenishes the stock in the retail stores. These competencies enhance the company's ability to continue to bring successful new products to the marketplace—a necessity in a market where product variety is important to the buyer. A firm's strongest resource or competency is generally referred to as a *core competency.* Table 2-1 suggests some ways a firm can effectively employ various core competencies.

Often a firm finds that its strategic options are limited unless it can acquire new resources or competencies. In such cases, the firm's strategy may be to form a *strategic alliance* with another firm. A strategic alliance is more than a joint venture. In the case of a joint venture, two firms essentially create a third entity that develops on its own. In a true strategic alliance, two firms collaborate in a far more complete way by *exchanging* some key resources (although new entities may also be formed) that enable both parties to enhance their performance. Typically, alliances involve exchanges of one or more of the resources listed below.

- Access to sales and distribution networks
- New-product technology
- Production technology and capacity[1]

[1]See Kenichi Ohmae, "The Global Logic of Strategic Alliances," *Harvard Business Review,* March–April 1989, pp. 143–149, for a thorough discussion of international strategic alliances.

TABLE 2-1	USING CORE COMPETENCIES		
COMPETENCY	POTENTIAL USE		EXAMPLE
R&D capability	Emphasize high technology in product development		Minnesota Mining & Manufacturing extends imaging technology into medical equipment products
Financial resources	Acquiring other businesses		Philip Morris acquires Kraft
Company reputation for quality	Select markets where reputation is known		Motorola emphasizes markets familiar with its success in electronics
Strong sales force	Select new products that can be sold by same sales force		Frito-Lay division of PepsiCo frequently brings out new snacks
Control over materials and other supplies	Emphasize products that require these resources; compete as low-cost producer		Gallo controls its supply of grapes, glass bottles, and trucking so it can use price to penetrate markets
Distribution system	Emphasize products that would benefit from using same channels		Baxter adds new medical instruments to sell to hospitals served by company's distribution system

In the world of pharmaceuticals, new products are essential to success, but the expansion of biotechnology has made it costly for firms to stay on top of all new developments. Because of the extraordinary costs required for R&D, few firms have the funds available to expand geographically through their own efforts. As a result, many have followed the pattern developed by the British company Glaxo, which trades proprietary drug products with Japanese firms to broaden its product line and generate greater sales volume from its established European sales and distribution network. Case Corporation and GTE have also expanded globally through alliances.

> Case Corp., a Wisconsin-based construction equipment manufacturer, wanted access to the huge Chinese market. So the company has formed a joint venture with Guangxi Liugong Machinery. The two firms will operate a new company that will assemble components made by Case and rely on Guangxi's market expertise for selling.[2]
>
> GTE Corp. and Germany's national phone company Deutsche Telekom AG have formed a strategic alliance in the wireless phone industry. The alliance allows North American GTE customers to travel to Europe and use the Deutsche Telekom network. Similarly, Deutsche Telekom customers can now wander into North America, use GTE services but be billed as if they were at home.[3]

Corporate Mission and Objectives

In most organizations, strategic decisions are guided by statements of corporate mission and/or corporate objectives. A corporate mission describes the broad purposes the organization serves and provides general criteria for assessing *long-run* organizational effectiveness.

[2]"Case Corp.: A Joint Venture in China Creates Access to Market," *Wall Street Journal,* Sept. 22, 1995, p. B4.
[3]John Keller, "GTE Plans a Global and Wireless Drive," *Wall Street Journal,* Oct. 6, 1995, p. B3.

Corporate objectives reflect management's specific expectations regarding organizational performance. Table 2-2 lists some of the more common types of corporate objectives that might be established. Remember that an organization may have more than one objective at a given time. However, there is usually only one primary goal toward which the corporate strategy can be directed.

As the environment changes, organizations often modify their missions and objectives. For example, changes in technology, or the natural extension of existing technology, can create an opportunity for broadening the definition of a business. The regional telephone companies (the so-called Baby Bells) created from American Telephone and Telegraph Corporation's (AT&T's) old telephone monopoly are no longer "telephone companies" but telecommunications firms, doing business in office automation, data systems, cable TV, and a host of other goods and services with related technological bases.

It is important to recognize that there may be built-in conflict when a firm tries to achieve more than one objective. For example, a small business that sets sales growth as a primary goal may find that it must increase working capital and production facilities dramatically to meet rising demand. To acquire the investment funds to support this expansion, the firm may be forced to take on new investors—an action that could conflict with an objective of maintaining family control.

Moreover, a long-range goal for profitability or increased sales may only be achieved if short-run sacrifices are made. For example, Union Pacific Railroad sold its oil and gas exploration and production companies, which represented 17 percent

TABLE 2-2	**COMMON TYPES OF CORPORATE OBJECTIVES**

PROFITABILITY

- Net profit as a percent of sales
- Net profit as a percent of total investment
- Net profit per share of common stock

VOLUME

- Market share
- Percentage growth in sales
- Sales rank in the market
- Production capacity utilization

STABILITY

- Variance in annual sales volume
- Variance in seasonal sales volume
- Variance in profitability

NONFINANCIAL

- Maintenance of family control
- Improved corporate image
- Enhancement of technology or quality of life

of corporate revenues and one-third of corporate profits, in 1995. The sale was expected to generate funds for investing in the company's rail and trucking business which promised higher long-range sales growth opportunities.[4]

In sum, the process of developing a corporate strategy is based on

- Examining environmental threats and opportunities
- Selecting corporate objectives that are consistent with these threats and opportunities, and with the firm's core competencies
- Acquiring any additional competencies required for successful implementation, often through strategic alliances

Although this process appears rather simple, any number of corporate strategies are available to top management. Only by understanding the different types of strategies available can managers effectively select the ones most appropriate for a particular firm's situation.

Types of Corporate Strategy

Organizations have two fundamental directions in which to proceed when selecting a corporate strategy: growth or consolidation. Traditionally, organizations have pursued *growth strategies,* even when sales growth was not the primary corporate objective. Essentially, a growth strategy is one in which sales growth (usually from new products and markets) becomes a vehicle for achieving stability or enhanced profitability.

In recent years, however, both large and small organizations have begun to realize that unbridled and random growth can create as many problems as it solves. *Consolidation strategies,* in which firms seek to achieve current goals (especially enhanced profits) through nongrowth means, have, accordingly, become increasingly popular.

Table 2-3 summarizes the basic types of corporate strategy and shows the specific kinds of strategies in each category.

Growth Strategies for Current Markets

A firm that finds many opportunities and few problems in its present markets is likely to select some form of current-market strategy. Even when problems such as a scarcity of raw materials, new competition, or technological change are encountered, if the current markets are attractive in sales growth, sales stability, or profitability, the corporate strategy may still focus on the current market.

The three strategies that focus on current markets are

- Market penetration
- Product development
- Vertical integration

4Daniel Machalba, "Union Pacific's Davidson Is Appointed Chief Operating Officer: Spinoff Slated," *Wall Street Journal,* July 28, 1995, p. B2.

TABLE 2-3	**BASIC TYPES OF CORPORATE STRATEGY**

GROWTH STRATEGIES

FOR CURRENT MARKETS

- Market penetration
- Product development
- Vertical integration

FOR NEW MARKETS

- Market development
- Market expansion
- Diversification

CONSOLIDATION STRATEGIES

- Retrenchment
- Pruning
- Divestment

MARKET PENETRATION

The term *market penetration* refers to a strategy aimed at increasing sales of existing products in the current markets. Typically, market penetration is achieved by increasing the level of marketing effort (as by increasing advertising or distribution) or by lowering prices.

Indeed, the sales potential of many products goes unrealized because the company is too small to initiate such efforts. As a result, large firms often acquire such products and then engage in the proper market penetration efforts. For example, sales of Gatorade increased dramatically after Quaker Oats acquired the brand in 1983 and sharply expanded advertising and distribution.

Because market penetration requires no change in a firm's products or markets, it is essentially a *status quo* strategy. As long as current performance is sound, and as long as the environment supports growth and provides profit opportunities, a firm may want to stick with its basic business.

> Quaker State Corporation hired a new president whose first corporate strategy was to rebuild the company market share in the $4 billion motor industry because of the sizeable profit potential in that market. Among the actions taken to increase penetration were: a series of aggressive rebates; new colors and lettering for the Quaker State logo and package; and changing the name of the company's Minit-Lube drive-through to Q-Lube to emphasize the brand tie-in.[5]

PRODUCT DEVELOPMENT

Product-development strategies involve the development of new products for existing markets in order to

---

[5]Matt Murray, "How the Man from Campbell Taught Quaker State to Market Oil Like Soup," *Wall Street Journal,* July 14, 1995, pp. B1, B4.

- Meet changing customer needs and wants
- Match new competitive offerings
- Take advantage of new technology
- Meet the needs of specific market segments

Typically, this strategy involves replacing or reformulating existing products or expanding the product line. Usually, product development is appropriate when changing needs and tastes result in the emergence of new segments or when competitive and technological changes motivate firms to modify their product lines.

For example, Toyota and Nissan introduced their Lexus and Infiniti models in large part because of an increase in the relative demand for luxury sedans at the expense of compact cars. Similarly, Gillette introduced Sensor to meet increased demand for high-quality shaving systems. The new razor relied on advanced injection molding technology to offer the benefit of two blades that could move independently.

Often the most important product-development efforts are due to competitive introductions that reach untapped market segments.

While Procter & Gamble's Crest and Colgate-Palmolive's Colgate brands have long dominated the toothpaste market, the competing Arm & Hammer and Mentadent brands beat these giants to the punch with successful baking soda–based products promising whiter teeth. Both Crest and Colgate have since responded with their own versions of baking soda toothpastes which have increased to 30% their share of toothpaste volume in the U.S. But in 1995 Procter & Gamble regained its innovation leadership role to some extent by also introducing Crest Gum Care—the first toothpaste targeted toward solving problems of gingivitis and bleeding gums.[6]

VERTICAL INTEGRATION

To make a firm more efficient in serving existing markets, vertical integration strategies can be selected. Such integration is often accomplished when a firm becomes its own supplier (in *backward integration*) or intermediary (in *forward integration*). As a general rule, these strategies will be most appropriate when the ultimate markets have high-growth potential, because integration requires extensive resources. Some specific types and purposes of vertical integration strategies can be seen in the following examples.

IBM continues to manufacture its own semiconductors, which are vital components of computers, to ensure that it does not become dependent on Japanese producers with respect to prices or access to the latest technology.

Pharmaceutical manufacturers Merck and Eli Lilly have acquired Medco Containment and PCS Health Systems, firms which distribute prescription drugs to participants in company health care plans. These strategic actions should enhance the number of Merck and Lilly drugs that are readily available at competitive prices to employees and retirees of large firms like General Motors.[7]

---

[6]Zachary Schiller, "The Sound and the Fluoride," *Business Week,* Aug. 14, 1995, p. 48.

[7]Bernard Wysocki, "Improved Distribution, Not Better Production Is Key Goal in Mergers," *Wall Street Journal,* Aug. 29, 1995, pp. A1–A2.

In practice, vertical integration is not nearly as simple as other current-market strategies. For example, the managerial and marketing skills required for forward integration into retailing clothing are far different from those involved in manufacturing clothing. Similarly, backward integration may backfire if a firm cannot produce its own supplies efficiently.

Growth Strategies for New Markets

In examining environmental forces and sales trends, top management may conclude that the sales growth, sales stability, or profitability of current markets will be unsatisfactory in the future. Such a conclusion will lead these firms to seek out new markets that will present better opportunities.

In entering new markets, three kinds of corporate strategies can be used.

- Market development
- Market expansion
- Diversification

MARKET DEVELOPMENT

The market-development strategy represents an effort to bring current products to new markets. Typically, management will employ this strategy when existing markets are stagnant or when market-share increases are difficult to achieve because market shares are already very high or because competitors are very powerful. This strategy can be implemented by identifying new uses or new users, as the following examples show.

> Arm & Hammer has long held a dominant market share of the baking soda market. However, this market had been growing very slowly until the company began to promote additional uses of its product (most of which were suggested by regular customers), such as cleaning toilets or deodorizing refrigerators.
>
> VISA has led a movement among credit card firms to expand card usage. The company has initiated a promotional campaign directed at doctors and dentists in an effort to broaden the numbers of medical practices that accept the card. At the same time, to gain wider acceptance by supermarkets, VISA-member banks reduced the fees they charge to supermarkets.

MARKET EXPANSION

A market-expansion strategy involves moving into a new geographic market area. Many firms originate as regional competitors and later move into other areas of the country. For example, Coors beer was sold only in the western part of the nation for many years, and Borden's has recently taken its Creamette's line of pasta products from a midwestern base to nearly national distribution.

In today's business world, companies are likely to expand their markets internationally, and frequently this is the growth strategy most likely to achieve large sales and profit growth.

Amoco Corp., one of the dominant gasoline marketers in the U.S., has announced it will spend over $200 million to build gas station networks in Poland and Romania in search of new growth opportunities. National branding of gasoline is a new phenomenon in those nations. Subsequently, Amoco announced it would build a network of one stop gasoline and fast food service centers in Mexico with the participation of Pemex, the state-owned oil company and Mexican beverage company Fomento Economico Mexicano. The service centers will operate under the name Oxxo Express.[8]

International market expansion can be pursued at three levels: regional strategy, multinational strategy, or global strategy.

A _regional_ strategy implies that a company will concentrate its resources and efforts in one or two areas. Thus, Fiat of Italy has historically competed primarily in Europe and Latin America. This strategy generally is employed when a firm intends to rely primarily on its home base for business.

Multinational strategy involves a commitment to a broad range of national markets including those in Europe, Asia, and the Americas. Such firms organize their businesses around nations or regions so that separate marketing strategies (including decisions on the range of products to offer) are largely left to the local subsidiary. IBM, Nestlé, and Royal Dutch-Shell are among the firms that are considered multinational.

A _global_ strategy is employed when an organization operates in a broad set of markets but with a common set of strategic principles. Put another way, this strategy views the world market as a whole rather than as a series of national markets. Country strategies are thus subordinated to a global framework. Global strategies are most appropriate when a firm's competitors or customers are globalized. For example, Caterpillar competes with Komatsu for earthmoving equipment in virtually every market, and financial institutions like Morgan Guaranty Trust Company work with corporate clients who are themselves global or multinational.

DIVERSIFICATION

A strategy that involves both new products and new markets is termed diversification. This strategy is likely to be chosen when one or more of the following conditions exist.

- No other growth opportunities can be established with existing products or markets.
- The firm has unstable sales or profits because it operates in markets that are characterized by unstable environments.
- The firm wishes to capitalize on a core competence.

Consider, for example, the case of Service Master.

Service Master was founded in 1947 as a rug cleaning firm outside of Chicago. During the next two decades the company expanded by using franchised business persons to provide an increasing variety of maintenance services to business firms. But the growth of two-

[8]Cassey Bukro, "Amoco Plans Convenience in Mexico," _Chicago Tribune,_ Aug. 9, 1995, sec. 3, p. 1.

wage-earner homes has dramatically increased consumer demand for maintenance services. Thus, Service Master added a variety of new branded products (some by acquisition) to serve this market. Among the service products offered are: Tru Green–Chem Lawn, Terminix (pest control), and Merry Maids (housecleaning). Service Master has since struck out in yet another direction, providing management services for long-term care, retirement, and assisted-living facilities which will grow dramatically as the population ages.[9]

When the markets for many of its most successful hardware products (such as drills and chain saws) began to level off, Black & Decker turned its attention to the development of housewares products. Relying on its expertise in cordless-appliance technology, the company achieved success with its Dustbuster vacuum, Spotlighter (a rechargeable flashlight), and the cordless screwdriver. Based on these successes and its ability to manufacture products at low cost, Black & Decker continued its diversification into housewares products by purchasing General Electric's small-appliance business. Within three years, Black & Decker had become the market leader in irons.

Consolidation Strategies

A major strategic development (observable beginning in the mid-1980s) is the increased emphasis on consolidation. Led by large conglomerates, more and more firms are undoing some of their recent growth strategies. Basically, there are three types of consolidation strategies.

- Retrenchment
- Pruning
- Divestment

RETRENCHMENT

Retrenchment is essentially the opposite of market development: A firm reduces its commitment to its existing products by withdrawing from weaker markets. Generally, this strategy is pursued when a firm has experienced uneven performance in different markets. For example, retail firms often decided to concentrate their marketing efforts in those regions of the country where they have the most success. The cost of local advertising and of physically distributing gasoline from refineries to distributors is so high as to make gasoline retailing unprofitable at very low market shares. Consequently, over the past decade Exxon has exited the Los Angeles market, Chevron has given up many locations in the Southeast, and Shell has left parts of the Pacific Northwest.

PRUNING

Pruning occurs when a firm reduces the number of products offered in a market. In effect, pruning is the opposite of product development and occurs when a firm decides that some market segments are too small or too costly to continue to serve.

[9]Culmatta Coleman, "Religious Roots Sprout Divine Results at Service Master," *Wall Street Journal,* Sept. 13, 1995, p. B6.

General Motors decided to drop the Cadillac Fleetwood, Buick Roadmaster, Chevrolet Caprice and Chevrolet Impala SS from its product line at the end of the 1996 model year. Declining demand for these large, rear-wheel-drive cars made it too difficult to generate adequate profits. GM planned to convert much of the capacity freed by this decision to light truck production.[10]

DIVESTMENT

Divestment occurs when a firm sells off a part of its business to another organization. Because this usually means that a firm is taking itself out of a product line and out of a particular market, divestment is essentially the opposite of diversification.

Often, divestment occurs after an organization realizes that a diversification strategy has failed. This is more likely to occur when the business does not fit the organization's competencies or when top management fails to appreciate the kinds of skills central to success in that market. Adolph Coors elected to spin off its nonbeer businesses (including ceramic computer boards, vitamins for animal feed, and auto parts). In explaining the logic of this decision, Chairman Peter Coors said, "The brewery is a consumer operation and all the others are business to business. The mentality and philosophy are quite different."[11]

In other areas, divestment reflects a decision that the business is not an integral part of the firm. According to the chief executive officer, Ralston-Purina spun off its breakfast cereal business because management was too focused on its pet food business to bother spending time on cereal. Viacom International divested its cable TV operations when it decided that business no longer fit the company's long-term mission.[12]

PRODUCT MIX STRATEGY

A corporate strategy provides an organization with a basic direction by establishing the general product and market scope to be pursued. Given this scope, a firm usually elects to divest or prune businesses and products that do not fit the strategy, and to commit resources to those products and businesses that do fit this strategic scope. However, most organizations are involved in a number of products and businesses within the product market scope, and management must have some basis for establishing priorities among those products and businesses.

A product mix strategy helps management solve the problem of establishing priorities. Specifically, a product mix strategy is a plan that specifies, for example,

[10]David Lawder, "GM to End Chevrolet Caprice Model, Other Large Cars," *Reuters Business Report,* May 16, 1995.

[11]Ronald Grover, "Coors Is Thinking Suds 'R US," *Business Week,* June 8, 1992, p. 34; and George Lazarus, "Coors Eyes Spinoff of Non-Beer Units," *Chicago Tribune,* May 15, 1992, sec. 3, p. 4.

[12]Stephanie Forest, Greg Burns, and Gail DeGeorge, "The Whirlwind Breaking Up Companies," *Business Week,* Aug. 14, 1995, p. 44.

- What objectives will be established for each product or business to ensure that corporate objectives will be met
- How various products or businesses will be prioritized for the purpose of allocating scarce resources

Product Portfolio Models

Serious investors usually have a *portfolio* of different kinds of financial investments, each with special characteristics regarding risk, earnings, and growth. Likewise, organizations have a range of products with varying characteristics. Just as an investor attempts to balance the growth, risk, and earnings yields of the various instruments in an investment portfolio, top management should strive to find a desirable balance among alternative products. In seeking this long-run balance, managers must recognize that some products will generate large amounts of cash over and above what is required for operating expenses or for additional investment in production facilities and inventory. However, other products will, at least in the short run, generate far less cash than is needed for operating expenses (including marketing efforts and research and development) and for additional investment.

Portfolio models are methods that managers can use to classify products or business units in order to determine the future cash contributions each can be expected to make and the future cash requirements each product will have. In using a portfolio model, managers usually must examine the competitive strengths of a business unit or a product (or product line) and the threats and opportunities presented by the market in which it competes. That is, empirical research on business success has established that the long-term profit prospects of a product line or business depend on the kinds of forces depicted in Table 2-4. In particular much research has been conducted on the Profit Impact of Market Strategy database (known as PIMS) developed and managed by the Strategic Planning Institute. Covering over 3000 business units in some 450 companies, the PIMS program has succeeded in demonstrating some important relationships among business strategy, competitive position, and market forces. The most pertinent findings are the following.[13]

- Absolute profit levels increase with a firm's relative market share and the growth rate of the market it serves.
- The impact on profitability of extensive efforts at new-product development or product differentiation is positive if the business is already in a strong market position.
- Efforts to increase market share may have a negative *short-run* effect on cash flow even as market share grows.
- Quality (as perceived by the customer) has a favorable effect on market share and profitability.

Such findings lie at the foundation of virtually all product portfolio models. Indeed the earliest models were extremely simple, often considering only market-growth rates and relative market share. For our purposes, we examine the Business Screen (Figure 2-3), which is typical of the most widely known class of portfolio models.

---

[13]Sidney Schoeffler, "Nine Basic Findings on Business Strategy," *PIMS Letter on Business Strategy,* Strategic Planning Institute, Cambridge, Mass., 1977.

TABLE 2-4	EVALUATING COMPETITIVE STRENGTH AND MARKET ATTRACTIVENESS

COMPETITIVE STRENGTH DIMENSIONS

1. Does our market share suggest that we have a strong customer base?
2. Do we have the managerial skills needed to compete?
3. Are our production facilities modern and efficient?
4. Do we possess the technology required to maintain a competitive rate of innovation and product development?
5. Do customers have a positive image of our products?
6. Does our cost structure enable us to be competitive on price while maintaining profitability?
7. Are our distributors well established and supportive?
8. Do we have an adequate number of qualified sales and customer service personnel?
9. Do we have stable and reliable suppliers?

MARKET ATTRACTIVENESS DIMENSIONS

1. Is the industry sales-growth rate high?
2. Is the market size large enough to sustain many competitors?
3. Are industry sales susceptible to cyclical, seasonal, or other fluctuations?
4. Is the rate of product obsolescence high?
5. Does extensive government regulation constrain actions or pose uncertainties?
6. Is the industry demand very low relative to industry capacity?
7. Is there a risk of raw material or component shortages?
8. Are there a large number of well-financed competitors?
9. Do a small number of buyers account for a disproportionately large percentage of industry sales so that we will be heavily dependent on them?
10. Overall, does the industry present a strong potential for profit?
11. Does this industry have a high degree of fit with our corporate strategy?

FIGURE 2-3
The Business Screen. (Adapted from Rick Brown, "Make the Product Portfolio a Basis for Action," *Long-Range Planning,* vol. 24, February 1991, p. 104.)

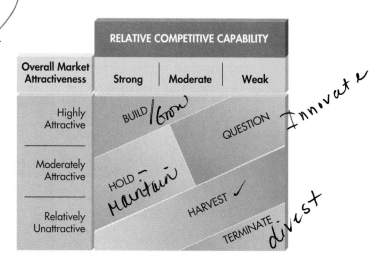

The Business Screen

Like most portfolio models, the Business Screen is a device for categorizing products or business units based on managerial assessments of each unit's relative competitive capabilities and on the attractiveness of the market in which it operates. In a typical application, managers will rate a business on each relevant dimension within Table 2-4, on a scale (perhaps five points ranging from very low to very high). The result will be two composite scores for each business: one on overall market attractiveness, the other on overall competitive strength. The overall rating of market attractiveness allows for a high rating—even if industry sales growth is low—when the overall size, stability, or cost of competing is positive enough to make the market attractive. The overall competitive strength rating reflects the firm's ability to compete successfully in building or maintaining market share. Table 2-5 shows some typical views of the role each type of product should play in the organization's portfolio. According to this model, products rated "build" and "question" should emphasize market-share objectives while those in the "hold" and "harvest" categories should be profit-focused.

These implications should be examined with care, however, because the models are founded on assumptions that are not always appropriate. Managers who use portfolio models should be especially aware of the following considerations.

- Portfolio models implicitly assume that the portfolio must be in cash balance; therefore, there must be a sufficient number of sources of cash to fund products in the build and question categories. In reality, firms may also generate resources through borrowing, and so it may not be necessary to extract all the cash flow from products in lower-growth, less attractive markets just because of high-cash needs in attractive, higher-growth markets.
- Portfolio models suggest products in the hold category can be "milked" with impunity because of their established market position and because they are in mature markets. For this reason, such products are often called "cash cows." In reality, many market-share leaders do experience extensive competitive challenges to their leadership position—especially in large, stable consumer-goods markets. Thus,

TABLE 2-5	**IMPLICATIONS OF THE BUSINESS SCREEN**	
STRATEGIC FOCUS	PRODUCT OBJECTIVE (EXPECTED CONTRIBUTION)	RESOURCE IMPLICATIONS
Build /Grow	Increase volume	Significant reinvestment to defend position or expand market
Hold /Maintain	Maintain cash flow and position	Modest reinvestment as needed
Question /Innovate	Increase share of market	Commit significant additional resources
Harvest	Build cash flow	Gradual withdrawal of resources
Terminate /Divest	None	Divest or liquidate

profitability objectives may have to be subordinated to an objective of market-share maintenance, at least in the short run.

■ Portfolio models indicate that resources should be invested in the "build" and "question" categories in order to enhance the market share of these products. However, there is no assurance that the application of more resources will lead to increases in market share. The ability to maintain or increase market share is dependent not only on having adequate resources but also on the existence of competitive advantage. Thus, managers should invest in high-growth markets only if they can identify a feasible competitive marketing strategy.

■ Because each element of market attractiveness and competitive strength has a different degree of importance in each situation, it is impossible to have a standard method for weighing the importance of the various elements. Additionally, the ratings are somewhat subjective, so different managers may not always rate a particular business the same way on every dimension.

Additionally, portfolio models in general have been attacked for the view that the only interdependencies among the products or businesses in a portfolio are the cash flows. Indeed it has been pointed out that this perspective is part of the reason for the lack of success of so many diversification strategies.[14] In successful diversifications, either the new business should be stronger by virtue of being associated with the parent firm or it should benefit the firm's other businesses by bringing some competitive strength to them (such as new technology or access to broader distribution channels). The term *synergy* is generally applied to such relationships. Synergy means that the whole is worth more than the sum of its parts, that two or more product lines operating in the same firm will be more successful than if they operated in separate organizations because of some commonality in resources employed. Thus, in assessing the role each product line plays in the organization, managers should be careful to identify important synergistic relationships.

THE CORPORATE PLAN AND MIDDLE MANAGEMENT

The corporate marketing plan is important to marketing managers in two respects. First, in most organizations, marketing plays a major role in influencing corporate and product mix strategy. Second, all marketing personnel are responsible in one way or another for developing and implementing the marketing strategies and programs necessary for achieving corporate objectives and product objectives.

Figure 2-4 summarizes the major elements in the corporate marketing planning process and indicates that middle managers can provide two basic kinds of inputs to this process. First, middle managers can provide the most detailed information on each individual product regarding the size of the market, the profitability of the product, and the likely sales results of increasing the marketing expenditures on a product. Second, middle managers must identify the kinds of marketing strategies and programs

[14]Michael Porter, "From Competitive Advantage to Corporate Strategy," *Harvard Business Review,* May–June 1987, pp. 43–59.

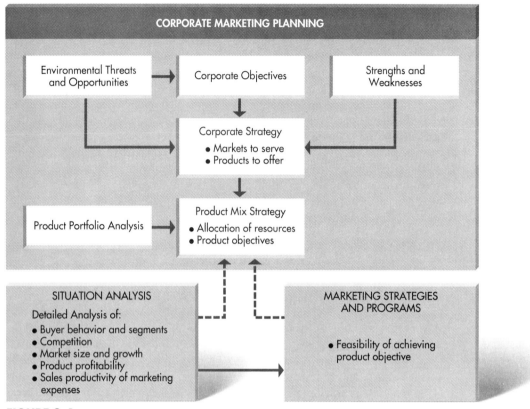

FIGURE 2-4
Relationship between corporate marketing planning and middle-management activities.

that are appropriate for a given strategic focus. In identifying these strategies and programs, it frequently will become apparent that the cost of achieving a product objective will be excessive or that there is no feasible way to achieve the objective because of a lack of resources or because of competitors' strengths or other factors. Consequently, corporate marketing plans may need to be revised once feasibility has been assessed.

Chapters 3 to 13 examine the analytical tools and procedures for performing the situation analysis and for selecting strategies and programs. As we shall see, the starting point for these analyses and decisions must always be an examination of the needs of the marketplace. Accordingly, we will focus on this topic in Chapter 3.

CONCLUSION

Corporate strategies provide the blueprint for the long-term development of a viable, profitable organization by establishing the markets to be served and the goods and services to be offered. In this chapter a variety of corporate strategies were presented, and the reasons for selecting each type of strategy were established. In general, corporate strategies are selected on the basis of an analysis of environmental factors, threats, and opportunities (especially market growth), corporate strengths and weaknesses, and long-run objectives. Further, in deciding which corporate strategy to select, it is important to identify a firm's core competencies. That is, an organization must have the specific resources required to be successful in the specific product and market arenas in which it will compete.

Product mix strategy is an essential element in corporate marketing planning because it forms the bridge between corporate strategy and the development of marketing strategies and programs on a product-by-product basis. The foundation for this bridge is the development of a strategic focus that indicates the objective each product is expected to achieve in contributing to the firm's future growth and profitability requirements. Further, the strategic focus provides a general format for allocating resources among products. In general, a strategic focus and the accompanying product objectives should be determined on the basis of a firm's competitive strength in the market and on the attractiveness of the market as measured by opportunities for growth and profitability.

In order to appreciate more clearly the scope and significance of corporate marketing planning, consider some of the recent developments at Tenneco.

TENNECO: REMAKING A CORPORATION

In 1995, Tenneco spent $1.27 billion to acquire the plastics division of Mobil Corporation. At the time of the purchase, Tenneco already owned Packaging Corporation of America which generated annual sales revenues of $2.2 billion from corrugated, paperboard, and other container products. The purchase of Mobil's plastics business brought product lines such as Baggies, Hefty, and Kordite to Tenneco. As a result, packaging would now represent $4 billion per year in revenues—about 40 percent of all Tenneco sales.

Tenneco's other subsidiaries were Walker exhaust systems and Tenneco Automotive (a maker of parts such as Monroe shock absorbers), Tenneco Gas (natural gas transmission and transport), and Newport News shipbuilding.

Five years earlier, Tenneco had been primarily an oil and gas company but it subsequently divested over $2 billion in assets (including Tenneco Oil). The company retained an interest in the natural gas industry—although it was gradually removing itself from regulated parts of the industry such as pipeline transmission. Increasingly, the firm's emphasis was shifting to global expansion. While the rate of growth in energy demand had leveled in North America, vibrant economies like Chile and Brazil faced dramatically increasing energy needs. Tenneco joined British and Argentine partners in Transgas—a venture that would build a gas pipeline from Argentina to gas-poor Chile. (To help assure demand, Transgas planned on financial assistance to help fifty Chilean industrial plants convert from electricity to natural gas.)

Tenneco's automotive business was also going global. A joint venture in China would make Monroe shock absorbers for a new Jeep assembly plant. Additionally, Tenneco obtained an agreement from Toyota to distribute replacement shocks through the entire 5600 Toyota dealer network in Japan.

1. Was Mobil's plastics business worth more to Tenneco than to Mobil? Explain.
2. What environmental forces and core competencies might be driving Tenneco's corporate strategy?
3. What are the types of corporate strategy that Tenneco has been pursuing?

Sources: Dawn Blalock, "Tenneco Inc. to Buy Mobil's Plastics Unit," *Wall Street Journal,* Oct. 3, 1995, pp. A3–A4; Nelson Antosh, "Tenneco, Japanese Auto Maker Reach Parts Deal," *Houston Chronicle,* Sept. 6, 1995, p. B2; "Alternative in China," *Economist Intelligence Unit,* Oct. 2, 1995; Margaret Orgill, "Gas Companies Vie for Latin American Markets," *European Business Report,* Sept. 17, 1995.

QUESTIONS AND SITUATIONS FOR DISCUSSION

1. In the 1980s Federal Express held a 45 percent share of the domestic overnight delivery market. However, Federal's growth had slowed because of increasing competition from UPS and the boom in facsimile machines. Additionally, price competition had squeezed domestic profits, and the company was actually losing millions on its international business. One response to these events was to acquire Tiger International, the world's largest heavy cargo airline, well known for its Flying Tiger Line airfreight service. Federal Express had not yet cracked the heavy freight business. Additionally, the company looked forward to using Flying Tiger planes for overseas package delivery, reducing the need to subcontract its deliveries to other carriers as they had previously had to do in many countries.

   What corporate strategies was Federal Express pursuing? What do these strategies suggest about Federal's environment, competencies, and objectives?

2. Dunkin' Donuts shops have to be open between 20 and 24 hours a day since part of their appeal is coffee and doughnuts ready whenever they are wanted. However, over 50 percent of sales are between 6 and 10 a.m. If the operating hours cannot be changed, what alternative growth strategies could be pursued?

3. Maytag Company's acquisition of Magic Chef broadened its product line to include brands that serve virtually every segment of the home-appliance market. Maytag's refrigerators are now sold under the Magic Chef, Admiral, Norge, Warwick, and Jenn Air brands. What type of corporate strategy would Maytag seem to be following? What are the problems and limitations of such a strategy?

4. Portfolio management theory suggests that management should assemble a collection of businesses in different industries and with different rates of growth to diversify risk. What would be some of the reasons that these same managements may later have to follow consolidation strategies?

5. After charting your business on the Business Screen matrix, you find the logical strategic focus for each was either "hold" or "harvest." Does a portfolio model tell you where new business should come from?

6. Europe is a growth market for soft drinks. The average European now drinks only 15 gallons of carbonated drinks per year compared to the U.S. consumer's 50 gallons, and European growth is expected to double the rate for the United States in the 1990s. With this growth and the European Union's unified market, Coca-Cola Europe has begun to buy back distribution rights in some countries and form joint ventures with bottlers in others. Previously, Coke had relied upon licensees

and independent regional bottling companies for much of its manufacturing and distribution in Europe. By centralizing bottle filling and distribution, Coke feels it can cut costs and lower its prices to increase sales. In order to do this, Coke standardized on "convenience packaging"—the plastic bottles and aluminum cans that are less expensive, lighter, and easier to transport than bottles. In some European countries, such as Britain, 90 percent of all soft drinks are now sold in cans or plastic. However, in countries such as Germany and Switzerland, most beverages come in reusable bottles. In Germany there are 1100 brewers who also produce soft drinks, and local grocery stores collect and return bottles to local plants. A recent law in Germany discourages the use of plastic beverage containers by putting the equivalent of a 25-cent deposit on each bottle. Discuss the corporate strategy options facing Coca-Cola Europe.

7. In 1995 a number of mergers occurred in the television industry: Westinghouse (owners of fifteen TV and thirty-nine radio stations) purchased CBS; Walt Disney Co. purchased Capital Cities/ABC; and Time Warner (with extensive film libraries and cable TV holdings) merged with Turner Broadcasting (owners of CNN and TNT cable networks and partly owned by TCI cable). Industry observers cited three key environmental forces facing the industry at this time. First, globalization of the television industry is increasing as satellites and cable build growing markets overseas. Second, direct broadcast and digital technology will expand the outlets for programming. Third, federal deregulation was expected to allow broadcast networks to expand ownership of TV stations and to operate several digital channels at each station.

Discuss how these environmental forces create threats and opportunities for the various firms. What are the potential benefits to the various parties from these mergers?

SUGGESTED ADDITIONAL READINGS

Brown, Rick, "Making the Product Portfolio a Basis for Action," *Long Range Planning,* February 1991, pp. 102–110.

Day, George, "The Capabilities of Market-Driven Organizations," *Journal of Marketing,* October 1994, pp. 37–52.

Feldman, Laurence P., and Albert L. Page, "Harvesting: The Misunderstood Market Exit Strategy," *Journal of Business Strategy,* Spring 1985, pp. 79–85.

Hall, George E., "Reflections on Running a Diversified Company," *Harvard Business Review,* January–February 1987, pp. 84–92.

Ohmae, Kenichi, "The Global Logic of Strategic Alliances," *Harvard Business Review,* March–April 1989, pp. 143–149.

Porter, Michael, "Towards a Dynamic Theory of Strategy," *Strategic Management Journal,* Winter 1991, pp. 95–118.

Prahalad, C. K., and Gary Hamel, "The Core Competence of the Corporation," *Harvard Business Review,* May–June 1990, pp. 79–91.

Szymanski, David, Sundar Bharadwaj, and P. Rajan Varadarajan, "An Analysis of the Market Share–Profitability Relationship," *Journal of Marketing,* July 1993, pp. 1–18.

PART TWO

CORPORATE MARKETING PLANNING

SITUATION ANALYSIS

Chapter 3 Market Analysis
Chapter 4 Target Marketing and
Competitive Advantage
Chapter 5 Market Measurement
Chapter 6 Profitability and
Productivity Analysis

MARKETING STRATEGIES AND PROGRAMS

COORDINATION AND CONTROL

SITUATION ANALYSIS

As we demonstrated in Part 1, middle-management decisions should be consistent with the broad decisions that top management makes regarding the long-term purpose and direction of an organization. Specifically, top management is responsible for identifying the role each product should play in achieving an organization's long-run objectives and for effectively communicating what this role is to be through the formulation of a *product objective*.

Essentially, middle managers have the basic task of achieving the product objective. Later on, in Part 3, we will present some fundamental tools and approaches for selecting marketing *strategies* and action *programs* that can be used to achieve the various types of product objectives. However, in order to develop a logical, planned approach to selecting the marketing strategies and programs that are appropriate, managers must not only be aware of the product objective but also understand the specific problems and opportunities confronting a product or a product line.

By performing a *situation analysis,* managers should be able to identify the major problems and opportunities that can be employed to guide the selection of marketing strategies and programs. The chapters in Part 2 are designed to provide the most important and useful analytical procedures and concepts for performing a situation analysis.

Generally, the most significant problems and opportunities are those related to the market demand for a product. Accordingly, in Chapter 3 we examine the process of market analysis. In particular, we identify ways of defining market boundaries and understanding buyers' decision-making processes. These activities are crucial to managers interested in learning how to stimulate market demand.

Not all potential buyers share the same needs or preferences, and the extent of a given market opportunity depends on the competition for each group of customers. Therefore, managers must learn how to assess the segmentation and positioning opportunities in a market. In Chapter 4 we examine ways of identifying market segments and of analyzing the opportunities that various segments present. We also discuss approaches for assessing the competitive environment and for identifying means for achieving a competitive advantage.

In Chapter 5, alternative procedures for measuring the size of a market and for forecasting sales are presented. By understanding the uses, assumptions, and limitations of these procedures, managers will be more capable of identifying the size of a market opportunity and the potential problems that are involved in achieving sales growth.

Chapter 6 examines the relationship between sales and profitability. Because marketing activities cost money, middle managers must know how to determine the sales and profit impact of proposed marketing expenditures. Accordingly, in this chapter we present some basic tools for identifying the problems and opportunities associated with budgeting decisions in marketing.

CHAPTER 3

MARKET ANALYSIS

In our discussion of the marketing concept in Chapter 1, we noted the central importance to an organization of understanding the customer. The ultimate objective of market analysis is to determine which needs of a buyer the firm hopes to satisfy and how to design and target the offer to satisfy these needs. In order to achieve this objective, managers must develop an understanding of the alternative and substitute products available to potential customers and the processes consumers use in deciding among the options.

We begin this chapter with a brief discussion of a technique used to better understand customer needs: the *house of quality.* We then introduce a six-step approach for understanding the competitive nature of markets. The approach is useful for managers concerned either with long-term corporate planning or with short-term marketing strategies. Our approach is designed to clarify the different kinds of demand that managers must consider in strategic decision making. Additionally, it offers a series of diagnostic questions that are designed to guide managers through the process of analyzing demand and establishing targets for marketing strategies and programs (see Figure 3-1).

1. *Define the relevant market.* To analyze a market, managers must first define it. Frequently there are a variety of products and services available for satisfying needs and wants. Most products and services have direct substitutes and alternatives. For example, consider the male shaving market. Bic and Schick disposable razors may be considered substitutes for each other, whereas an electric razor would be considered an alternative. A market can be defined narrowly (to include only products that are very similar to one another) or broadly (for example, to include a variety of different types of products). It is important to remember that the way a market is defined will have a major impact on the specific findings we can expect in the subsequent steps.

2. *Analyze primary demand for the relevant market.* Primary demand involves demand at the product-class level, such as coffee versus tea or the demand for rail versus air travel between two points. In this step managers attempt to profile buyers—that is, define what characteristics the buyers have in common. Managers are also interested in understanding the factors that influence the buying process for all brands and products in the relevant market. Specifically, we provide a series of

questions to help managers diagnose who the buyers (and nonbuyers) in the relevant market are and why they buy (or don't buy).

3. *Analyze selective demand within the relevant market.* In this step we examine the process by which buyers select specific alternative brands or suppliers within the boundary of the relevant market.

4. *Define market segments.* There are few buying situations in which all customers have similar motivations and undergo similar choice processes. The concept of market segmentation explicitly recognizes this reality. This step in the process presents some alternative ways of separating buyers into segments whose members are similar in their response to marketing programs.

5. *Assess the competition.* In this step we examine procedures used by managers to assess their products/brands against competitive offerings. Managers must be aware of how their products/brands are perceived relative to the competition. Competitive intelligence establishes the relationship of the firm to its competitors.

6. *Identify potential target markets.* Ultimately, the goal of market analysis is to identify the best opportunities for creating customers. This final step demonstrates how the information from preceding steps can be used to identify the specific markets (and market segments) managers should consider as targets when selecting marketing strategies.

The first three stages in the framework are presented in this chapter. Stages 4, 5, and 6 are discussed in the next chapter.

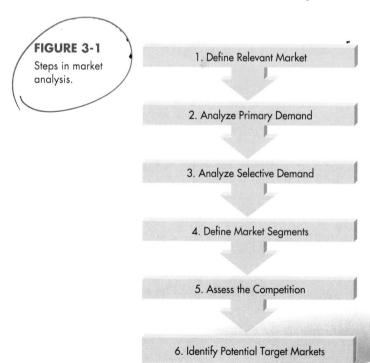

FIGURE 3-1

Steps in market analysis.

1. Define Relevant Market
2. Analyze Primary Demand
3. Analyze Selective Demand
4. Define Market Segments
5. Assess the Competition
6. Identify Potential Target Markets

VOICE OF THE CUSTOMER

As we've emphasized, a thorough understanding of what customers require in products or services to be satisfied is essential to developing effective marketing strategies. This position is consistent with the market orientation discussed in Chapter 1, which preaches success through customer satisfaction. The firm must listen to the *voice of the customer.* Given that consumers have a choice, they will choose what they like the best. The firms offering a product/service that most closely matches the market's product/service requirements will be the ones that survive. One process used to incorporate customer requirements in marketing strategy is quality function deployment.

Quality function deployment (QFD) is a process that originated in 1972 in Mitsubishi's Kobe shipyard. QFD is a practical step-by-step method that incorporates customer needs into the design of new products and/or augmentation of existing products. Using QFD can reduce the design time for new products by up to 60 percent. And, remarkably, the quality of the products is not only maintained but in many instances enhanced.[1] Toyota claims that QFD was responsible for virtually eliminating warranty problems originating from rust.[2] The Ford Motor Company introduced QFD in 1983 as a defensive move against Toyota who had been using the process since 1978. The smashing success of the Taurus/Sable program introduced by Ford is believed to have resulted, at least in part, from QFD.[3] The first step in QFD is to construct the house of quality.

Figure 3-2 provides an abridged illustration of the house of quality for a car door.[4] Four information sources are identified and integrated: customer requirements, engineering characteristics, customer perceptions, and objective characteristics comparisons. Marketing research is used to interview customers to determine what the customers want and expect from products. A very popular technique for identifying customer requirements is a focus group interview. Focus groups involve six to ten people recruited to a central facility to discuss a topic. The focus groups usually last 2 hours. Management can, by way of a one-way mirror, listen to the focus group participants discuss what they expect from a product and what would delight them. These customer requirements are sometimes called the "voice of the customer."

The engineering characteristics, or design attributes, are the technical means available to the company to satisfy the customer requirements. The relationship matrix is based on the association between the engineering characteristics and the customer requirements. The relationship matrix addresses the essential question: How are we fulfilling, or how can we fulfill, customer needs? The house of quality also includes two comparisons. The first compares customers' perceptions of the firm's product

---

[1]John Hauser, "How Puritan-Bennet Used the House of Quality," *Sloan Management Review,* Spring 1993, pp. 61–70.

[2]Abbie Griffin, "Evaluating QFD's Use in the U.S. Firms as a Process for Developing Products," *Journal of Product Innovation Management,* September 1992, pp. 171–187.

[3]Gary S. Vasilash, "Hearing the Voice of the Customer," *Production,* February 1989, pp. 66–68.

[4]John Hauser and D. Clausing, "The House of Quality," *Harvard Business Review,* vol. 66, no. 3, May–June 1988, pp. 63–73.

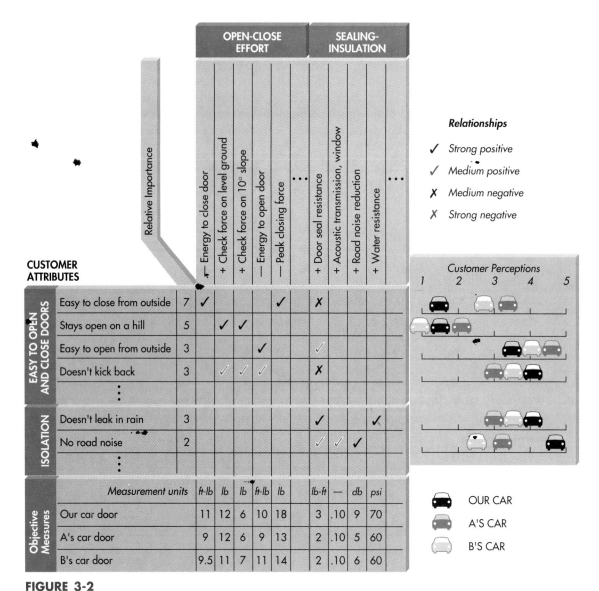

FIGURE 3-2

House of quality. (*Source:* John R. Hauser and Don Clausing, "The House of Quality," *Harvard Business Review,* May–June 1988, p. 69. Reprinted with permission.)

characteristics to those of the competition. The second is an objective comparison between the firm and its competition for the engineering characteristics. Comparisons between customer perceptions and objective measures can highlight image problems faced by the company. The house of quality is one technique used by managers to decide which needs of a buyer the firm hopes to satisfy. Understanding what the market demands, and what choices are available to the buyers, is integral to the development of marketing strategy.

With this goal in mind, we next turn to the first of our six steps.

Step 1

DEFINING THE RELEVANT MARKET

The relevant market is the set of products and/or services (within the total product market structure) that management considers to be strategically important. As we noted in Chapter 2, a product mix strategy can change substantially depending on how the relevant market is defined. For example, a specialized brand of decaffeinated herbal teas may have a relatively large share of that market but a very small share of the total tea market. Moreover, the total tea market is not growing nearly as rapidly as the herbal tea market. Thus, the strategy for this product might be to build if the relevant market is herbal tea but hold or even divest if the relevant market is tea.

Defining the relevant market usually involves two steps. First, management will attempt to describe the structure of the relevant market. Subsequent to the definition of the market, boundaries within the market will be defined. Marketing managers are always concerned about market share. *Market share* is the ratio of a firm's volume to the total volume. How the relevant market is defined will determine the total volume or the denominator in the calculation of market share. Therefore how the relevant market is defined will affect the calculation for the firm's market share.

Describing the Product Market Structure

A market can only exist when both sellers and buyers are present. Consequently, in order to define a market, managers must identify both the needs of the buyers and the goods and services offered by the sellers to meet those needs. A product market structure is a representation of the degrees of substitutability that exist among a set of products and/or services that satisfy similar needs. By describing the product market structure, managers can more readily identify the various ways in which the market for a product might be defined. Specifically, managers can use the product market structure to identify the types of products and services with which they must compete in various need-satisfaction situations.

Managers can classify competing alternatives at three levels.

1. Competing brands (or suppliers) within a product form
2. Competing product forms within a product class
3. Competing product classes serving a generic need

In describing the product market structure, our immediate concern is to classify product forms and classes in order to identify possible ways of defining the market to be analyzed. Because brand or supplier competition can best be analyzed after the relevant market is defined, we discuss the classification of brand alternatives in the third step of the market analysis process. Product markets are classified based on similarities.

A *product market* may be defined by the similarity or dissimilarity of the characteristics or functions of the products capable of satisfying the need. For example, within the generic need "breakfast foods," cereals, pastries, and eggs would be considered distinct product classes based on the different composition and processes used to prepare them. Cereals could be subsequently divided into product forms such as nutritional and presweetened. They are dissimilar cereals but more similar than the alternative product forms.

The market could also be structured based on the similarity or dissimilarity of usage situations. For example, instant coffee and drip coffee may be more similar than coffee and orange juice, but orange juice may be substituted for instant coffee if the usage situation calls for quick preparation.

Several methods are available to identify and classify alternative product forms and product classes.[5] One method is market structure analysis.

Market Structure Analysis

Market structure analysis is a marketing research tool used to determine the degree of substitutability among a set of products or brands. The technique attempts to uncover hierarchical schemes of attributes used by consumers to partition the total set of brands into smaller subsets. The brands in a subset are more similar and therefore more competitive with each other than with any other brands in the product class.[6] Consider Figure 3-3, which presents a market structure for soft drinks. The soft drinks are first partitioned into cola and noncola soft drinks. The soft drinks are then partitioned into diet or regular and then into caffeine or caffeine-free drinks. The lower in the tree, the more similar the brands. The more similar the brands the greater the substitutability. If your favorite soft drink was a caffeine-free diet cola, the brands competing the most for your share of the market would be the other caffeine-free diet colas. If your favorite brand was not available, you would select another brand of caffeine-free diet cola before switching to another type of cola. If no other brands of caffeine-free diet cola were available, you would choose a brand of diet cola with caffeine. The lower in the tree, the greater the probability of switching; therefore, the greater the competition. Market structure studies allow the marketing manager to understand which brands are perceived to be most similar and which attributes are used to cluster brands.

Consumer panel data are used to establish these market structures. Consumer panels record the purchases of families over time. The Nielsen consumer panel, which consists of 40,000 households,[7] captures 85 to 90 percent of packaged goods purchased nationally. The Infoscan household panel operated by Information Resources Incorporated consists of 60,000 families in twenty-seven geographically dispersed markets.

[5]George Day, Allan Shocker, and Rajendra Srivastava, "Customer-Oriented Approaches to Identifying Product Markets," *Journal of Marketing,* Fall 1979, pp. 8–19.

[6]Vithala R. Rao and Darius Jal Sabavala, "Inference of Hierarchical Choice Processes from Panel Data," *Journal of Consumer Research,* vol. 8, June 1981, pp. 85–96.

[7]Anonymous, "The Consumer Quotient Is Up," *Progressive Grocer,* vol. 73, December 1996.

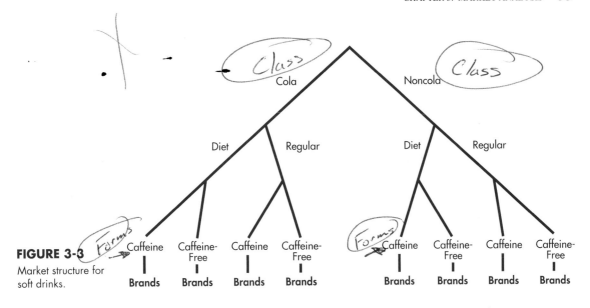

FIGURE 3-3
Market structure for
soft drinks.

These data are used to form tables that record the brand purchased on one occasion and the brand purchased on the next shopping trip. The data show whether the family continued to purchase the same brand or switched to another brand. Statistical models are then used to discover the market structure. One application of market structure analysis[8] used panel data supplied by Market Research Corporation of America (MRCA) on over 155,000 purchases from 8000 families. Two possible structures, shown in Figure 3-4, were tested. The structure that best described the market was the structure shown in panel A of Figure 3-4. Families in the sample were more likely to switch between percolator and drip types of ground coffee than between caffeinated and decaffeinated types of coffee.

Defining Broad Relevant Market Boundaries

Generally, top management will be concerned with identifying long-run growth opportunities (especially through product development) and with identifying potential threats to the firm's growth because of a changing environment. For example, soft-drink manufacturers in the early 1990s were quite concerned with shifts in beverage preferences toward natural and health-oriented products. Fruit-flavored teas, bubbly waters, and concoctions with mystical names like Fruit Integration and Strawberry Passion Awareness were the latest rage in the beverage business. However, "New Age is becoming Old Age says Tom Pirko president of Bevmark Inc., a beverage consulting firm."[9]

[8]Rajiv Grover and William Dillon, *A Probabilistic Model for Testing Hypothesized Hierarchical Market Structures,* The Institute of Management Sciences, 1985, pp. 312–335.

[9]Robert Frand, "Fruity Teas and Mystical Sodas Are Boring Consumers," *Wall Street Journal,* Oct. 9, 1995, p. B1.

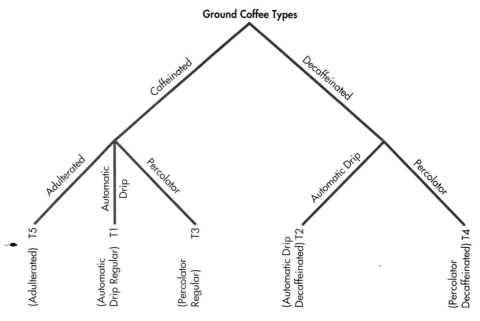

Panel A. Hypothesized Structure

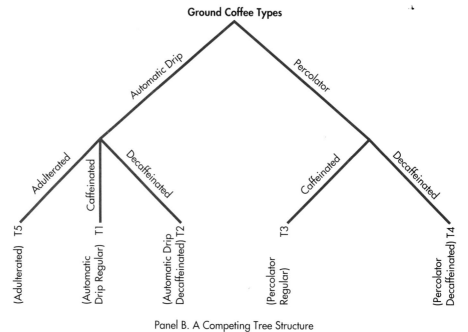

FIGURE 3-4
Competing market structures for ground coffee. (*Source:* Rajiv Grover and William Dillon, *A Probabilistic Model for Testing Hypothesized Hierarchical Market Structures,* The Institute of Management Sciences, 1985, pp. 312–335.)

Panel B. A Competing Tree Structure

Conditions that influence managers (especially at the top-management level) to furnish a broad definition of the relevant market include

- Regulatory and technological changes are expected to create new alternatives on the seller's side of the market. For example, managers of electric utility companies are very concerned with what the industry will look like if the talk about deregulation becomes a reality.
- Economic, demographic, and/or social and cultural changes are likely to change the type or frequency of usage on the buyer's side of the market.
- A company's sales gains and losses are coming increasingly from alternative forms and classes (rather than merely from brand competitors).
- Competitors do not exist at the product-form level (often because the product is an innovative form).

Taking a broad view of the market often leads a firm to shift in and out of product categories. For example, General Mills added a line of oatmeal cereals in 1987 when the U.S. consumer was gobbling up increasing quantities of cholesterol-fighting oat cereals. Four years later, with oatmeal sales declining and ready-to-eat cereal demand continuing to grow, new-product development was focused on the cold cereal side of the market.[10]

Defining Narrow Relevant Market Boundaries

Middle managers are more likely to define the relevant market in terms of a product form rather than a product class. This focus is most likely to be appropriate to the extent that the planning focus is on short-run decisions and in the following situations.

- Brand or company competition is far more significant than competition among forms and classes.
- Major environmental changes are not anticipated or are not expected to lead to major changes in alternative forms or in usage situations. (Although it is often dangerous to assume a no-change situation, the assumption may be reasonable in the short run.)
- The product form or the product class is used for a unique set of usage situations so that there are no easily substitutable products.

In the automotive industry, for example, product-form competition (compact versus subcompact versus luxury) exists as does product-class competition (public transportation versus motorcycles versus recreational vehicles). However, the environmental changes influencing product-form choice are usually gradual, and the cost and time involved in responding to major product changes are extensive. For middle

[10]Fara Warner, "Oatmeal Blues," *Adweek's Marketing Week,* June 24, 1991, pp. 18–19.

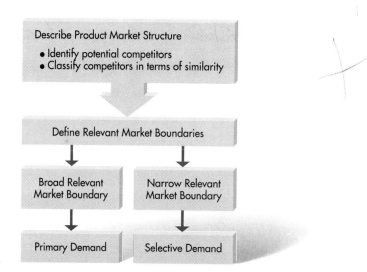

FIGURE 3-5

Elements and implications of the process of defining the relevant market.

managers, then, the primary focus is usually on developing marketing strategies and programs for individual brands and models at the product-form level. On the other hand, top management will be more concerned with long-range strategies reflecting the product mix growth potential of various product forms and of the automobile product class.

Figure 3-5 portrays the major steps involved in selecting a relevant market and the consequences of the choice of broad or narrow boundaries. As suggested in this figure, managers who are concerned with narrow relevant market boundaries will be focusing their attention on brand or supplier choice, otherwise known as selective demand. On the other hand, when management sets broad relevant market boundaries, their concern is the analysis of primary demand. Figure 3-6 identifies some of the issues that managers must consider in analyzing these two forms of demand.

FIGURE 3-6

Analyzing primary and selective demand.

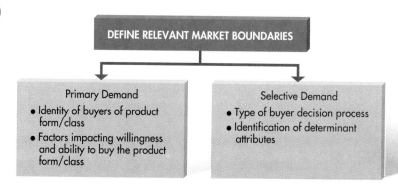

Who buys the product?

ANALYZING PRIMARY DEMAND

By defining the relevant market, a manager will have identified the set of relevant products and services within which the buying process should be analyzed.

Primary demand is the demand for the product form or product class that has been defined as the relevant market. By analyzing primary demand, managers can learn why and how customers buy a product form or class and who the buyers are in the relevant market. For example, if we define the relevant market as herbal teas, the analysis of primary demand should reveal who buys herbal teas (and who does not), and why some people buy and some do not.

Key Elements in Analyzing Primary Demand

The most important reason for analyzing primary demand is to identify the growth opportunities for the product form or class. This information is of special importance to managers of new products. However, it is also important that managers of products in low-growth markets be able to identify possible ways of boosting or revitalizing sales. In fact, new growth opportunities may exist in mature markets. In order to identify growth opportunities and the actions that should be taken to realize these opportunities, managers should attempt to answer a series of diagnostic questions about the buying process. These questions fall into two categories.

- Buyer-identification questions
- Willingness-to-buy and ability-to-buy questions

Buyer Identification

By identifying the existing buyers of a product form or class, managers can obtain insights into the potential growth opportunities in a market and about appropriate means of communicating to the market. Specifically, by identifying the characteristics of current buyers, managers can learn which types of buyers are likely to have a need for the product form or class. To the extent that these buyers can be described in terms of age, location, and similar characteristics, managers can also project changes in primary demand based on population trends for different groups. Additionally, by identifying the heavier users in a product category, managers can select communications media that are efficient in reaching buyers or can identify individuals on whom the sales force should call. Table 3-1 lists the major diagnostic questions that might be used in buyer identification.

BUYER OR USER CHARACTERISTICS

The characteristics of customers provide managers with a variety of insights into what communication programs are appropriate. In particular, three kinds of characteristics are useful for describing buyers of a product form or class: location, demographics, and lifestyle.

TABLE 3-1   DIAGNOSTIC QUESTIONS ON BUYER IDENTIFICATION

1. CHARACTERISTICS OF BUYERS OR USERS

Can buyers of this product category be classified by location, demographics, or lifestyle and psychographics? If so, how?

2. THE BUYING CENTER

Who is involved in the buying process (reference groups; colleagues; family members)?

3. CUSTOMER TURNOVER

Is there a high degree of customer turnover because of mobility or because purchase is tied to age or other demographic factors? If so, why?

Geographics

1. *Location.* Rates of purchase of various product forms may be influenced by climate, population density, cultural traditions, and other factors that vary according to region or urban-suburban-rural distinctions. For example, weather conditions result in a greater demand for ski equipment in New England and in other northern and western states. Accordingly, it may be appropriate for manufacturers of ski equipment to spend a greater share of the advertising budget and to have more retail outlets in those regions.

2. *Demographics.* Age, sex, education, occupation, and family size are among the characteristics that may typify buyers of a product form. Demographics are useful because most advertising media measure these characteristics in describing their audiences and make this information available to prospective advertisers. Consequently, if we know that the majority of buyers are aged 25 to 44, media can be selected to reach these customers efficiently. Similarly, knowing the characteristics of buyers is considered important by many industrial and retail store managers. These managers often believe that buyers will more likely buy from someone who is viewed as similar in age, education, or other demographic traits. Accordingly, they may assign salespeople to accounts partly on the basis of similarity with the buyer.

3. *Lifestyle.* Measures of lifestyle (also called psychographics by some marketers) attempt to reflect the way in which products fit into a consumer's normal pattern of living by examining how people spend their time, what things are important to them, and what opinions they have about themselves and the world around them. In effect, lifestyle measures primarily reflect the influence of social forces on consumption processes. To the extent that lifestyles are related to product-purchase behavior, they may provide clues about why people do or do not use a product regularly. Additionally, the media and advertising setting will be most effective in reaching buyers if it is at least somewhat consistent with customer lifestyles.

One potential problem in relying on buyer characteristics, however, is that this method relies on the past. For example, banks often target men and multiperson households with incomes of $75,000 or more in selling financial services because these kinds of customers have historically dominated demand. But the increasing number of single women in the professions and in management represents a largely ignored market of substantial size.[11]

THE BUYING CENTER

The buying center for a product consists of all the individuals who are involved in the buying decision. In fact, the actual buyer is frequently not the user of a product or service. Accordingly, managers should identify all the individuals who may be involved in the buying process and understand the kind of influence exerted by each one. In the case of some nutritional cereals, for example, advertisements have been directed at parents as well as children, because in many homes both are involved in the decision-making process. Similarly, a manufacturer of sophisticated medical diagnostic equipment found that the sales force was paying too much attention to the purchasing agent and not enough to the chief of surgery, the pathologist, the head nurse, and others with an interest in the product and an influence on the purchase decision. It is important to know who has the most influence for a particular buying situation. Different parties may have different needs. For example, if you are selling fiber-optic cable to independent telephone companies, three parties are generally influential in the purchase: general management, the purchasing agent, and the technical people in the field using the cable. The purchasing agent is probably far more concerned with the terms of the purchase than with the flexibility of the cable. Alternatively, the technical people are concerned with the flexibility and probably don't even know the terms of purchase. It is important to understand the power and influence that each has on the outcome of the final decision.

CUSTOMER TURNOVER

This term refers to the rate at which an organization must replace all or a substantial part of the individuals in its market because of a change in some aspect of the buyer's characteristics. For example, the high rate of geographic mobility in the United States means that a large proportion of the customers of local retail institutions (such as banks) will be newcomers. In other cases, age may be a key factor in customer turnover. For example, buyers of disposable diapers are usually in the market for only a short time. In these situations, managers should recognize that a large part of the marketing effort must be directed toward continually identifying and reaching first-time users or patrons. And because these targets will be less knowledgeable about the product, different marketing strategies and programs must often be designed for them.

A number of major ski resorts such as Vail in Colorado and Waterville Valley in New Hampshire have recognized that as skiers get older, they often decrease their skiing activity. Specifically, skiers in their late twenties and thirties are often parents and have less money for ski vacations, and older skiers often drop out altogether for safety reasons. Accordingly, such resorts have begun to revise their advertising and promotional programs, targeting an increasing proportion of their messages to these demographic groups.

[11]Laura Zinn, Heather Keets, and James Treece, "Home Alone—with $660 Billion," *Business Week,* July 29, 1991, pp. 76–77.

As this example demonstrates, the potential market for a product form is often larger than the current level of demand when some potential customers do not buy the product or service, or do not buy as frequently as they might. But knowing that a market can be expanded because other potential users exist is not sufficient—even if managers can identify such prospects. In addition, managers must understand the factors influencing the willingness and ability to buy the product form or class.

Willingness and Ability to Buy

Customers cannot be created for a company unless potential buyers are first willing and able to purchase the product form or class. To the extent that managers can identify ways of improving the willingness and ability to buy, primary demand can be increased either because potential buyers become actual buyers or because actual buyers increase their rate of use. Table 3-2 lists the major diagnostic questions that might be used to answer these questions.

WILLINGNESS TO BUY

The main determinant of the willingness to buy a product form or class is the buyer's perception of a product's utility for one or more usage situations. A manager's analysis of the product market structure should identify the usage situations to which a product form is potentially applicable. However, in order to determine why some potential buyers do not use the product for one or more of these purposes, several specific questions should be raised.

1. *Related products and services.* Usage may be limited because the related products and services essential to satisfactory usage are inadequate. Manufacturers of personal computers found that the lack of programs for applications that were not job-related served as a barrier to sales growth for in-home computers. In contrast, the market for videocassette recorders was expanded when consumers could rent cassettes of movies rather than having to buy them. Similarly, managers involved in

---

TABLE 3-2	DIAGNOSTIC QUESTIONS ON WILLINGNESS AND ABILITY TO BUY

1. WILLINGNESS TO BUY

Would new or improved related products and services increase utilization?
What usage problems exist or are perceived to exist?
Is the product or service compatible with the values and experiences of the buyer?
What types of perceived risks are significant in the purchase of the product form?

2. ABILITY TO BUY

To what extent do purchase prices and other acquisition or maintenance costs inhibit purchase?
Are product size or packaging factors creating space problems for customers?
Is the product available at a time and place that meets customer needs?

marketing fitness centers are recognizing that related services are important in luring older clients. For example, NutraSweet Co. is opening a series of WellBridge Fitness Centers to serve the over-50 market. This market actually needs fitness training more than the young people typically targeted by health clubs. However, WellBridge centers not only focus on exercise programs designed specifically for this group, but they also offer nutritional counseling.[12]

2. *Usage problems.* Some products are not perceived as performing equally well under all circumstances. It is important to identify situations in which problems occur and to determine whether the problems lie in the product features or in the user's lack of knowledge about how to use the product correctly. In the first case, new product features may have to be designed; in the second, customer training or technical assistance is necessary to overcome perceived deficiencies. To a large extent, the growth of microwave ovens was due to the efforts of manufacturers and retailers to educate consumers about the correct use of the product so that they could avoid overcooking or undercooking various foods.

3. *Value or experience compatibility.* When a new product requires a change in buying or using behavior that conflicts with customers' prior usage experiences or with broader value systems, the rate of adoption will be slower. To overcome this source of resistance, managers should design communications that stress not only the advantages of the product but also the advantages of the change in values or usage experiences that go with the product. A classic study conducted by Maison Haire in the 1950s indicated that the reason households did not adopt instant coffee was that the homemaker would be perceived as lazy.[13] Many frozen and convenience foods met with similar obstacles.

As another example, consider the entry of Miller Lite in the 1970s. Although earlier low-calorie beers were market failures, Miller Lite was extremely successful even though it had essentially the same features. In large part, this success reflected the company's foresight in appealing to the heavy beer drinker by associating a low-calorie count with the positive advantage of a less filling beer. Values are also tied to cultures, so primary demand for some products can vary dramatically across cultures.

> The Japanese penchant for saving is legendary and one byproduct of this attitude is a tremendous demand for life insurance. Per capita life insurance premiums in Japan are now in excess of $1,000 per year and growing. By contrast, per capita premiums in France are less than $300 and in Greece and Spain less than $100. While insurance demand is dependent on income, the primary source of these differences is culture.[14]

When marketers enter multinational markets they must take special care to ensure that the product or service applications do not violate cultural norms. What is accepted in one culture may be rejected in another.

---

[12]Michael Gougis, "NutraSweet Targets Aging Boomers for New Clubs," *Marketing News,* Oct. 14, 1991, p. 15.

[13]Maison Haire, "Projective Techniques in Marketing Research," *Journal of Marketing,* April 1950, pp. 649–656.

[14]Resa King, Larry Armstrong, Steven J. Dryden, and Jonathan Kapstein, "Who's That Knocking on Foreign Doors? U.S. Insurance Salesman," *Business Week,* Mar. 6, 1989, pp. 84–85.

✦ **4.** *Perceived risk.* The willingness to buy a product form or product class will also depend on the types of risks perceived by potential buyers. Perceived risks will exist when buyers believe that there is a strong likelihood of making a poor decision and that the consequences of a poor decision are significant. Specifically, there are six types of risk that may exist when purchasing a product form or class.

  a. Economic or financial risks—if the purchase price, maintenance costs, or operating costs are high

  b. Time or convenience risks—if there is the potential for using up a large amount of time in purchasing or using a product

  c. Performance risks—if there is concern about how well the product performs its basic function

  d. Physical risks—if there is a threat to the health or appearance of the buyer

  e. Social risks—if the purchase or use of the product may affect the attitudes of reference groups toward the buyer

  f. Psychological risks—if the purchase or use of the product may influence the buyer's self-image or self-esteem

By knowing the types of risk perceived by buyers, managers will be able to design marketing programs to reduce these risks and thus enhance the willingness to buy. For example, bottled-water suppliers may offer home delivery to reduce the convenience risk to a consumer not willing to bring home large, heavy jugs of water. Similarly, some firms offer special trial sizes or money-back guarantees to reduce economic risks. Social risks may be reduced if products or services are advertised in a way that emphasizes they are socially acceptable.

ABILITY TO BUY

The ability to buy a product may be limited to a number of factors, many of which are not under the direct control of managers.

1. *Cost factors.* If a product is a discretionary item, or if less expensive product-form alternatives exist, the price and/or associated buyer costs (operating cost, credit cost, installation cost, maintenance cost) are likely to inhibit primary demand. For example, the demand for solar collectors to heat homes has been limited by the large initial investment required of a homeowner, even though solar energy is often very price-competitive when viewed in the long run. Similarly, high interest rates on home mortgage loans and automobile loans were partly responsible for declines in new home and automotive sales during the late 1970s and early 1980s.

2. *Packing and size factors.* Product-form sales may be limited by virtue of space and size requirements. Some potential buyers of home computers, big-screen televisions, and similar products have a space problem in accommodating these items. Many real-estate developments have size limitations on satellite dishes for televisions, if they allow them at all. Also, space limitations may inhibit the purchase of a product in large volumes.

3. *Spatial availability.* The cost of acquiring a product may be a function of locational factors. For example, people in very rural communities have less access to health care and, consequently, visit physicians less frequently. Similarly, the rate of purchase of low-value, postponable purchases can be enhanced by improved access. Consider, for example, the impact on soft-drink sales if vending machines were not available.

Although our discussion of the willingness and ability to buy has focused on the implications for assessing opportunities for building primary demand, these forces can often be important in analyzing selective demand as well. Certainly a firm that gains an advantage on cost or location, or that does a better job of reducing perceived risk or offering related services, will enhance its ability to acquire customers. Indeed, by developing a thorough analysis of primary demand, managers will usually be in a better position to understand the processes determining brand or supplier choice.

ANALYZING SELECTIVE DEMAND

Whereas primary demand is the demand for a product form or class (such as tea, herbal tea, or instant tea), selective demand is the demand for a specific brand or supplier within the relevant market. So if instant tea is chosen as the relevant market, selective demand is the demand for Lipton Instant Tea or Nestea Instant Tea or any other individual brand. Figure 3-7 highlights the difference between primary and secondary demand for transportation during a holiday period. If consumers are interested in traveling to a particular destination during a holiday, they must first determine which alternative (plane, train, bus, or automobile) they most prefer. This decision is at the primary demand level. Selection at this level is primarily based on the factors we discussed: willingness and ability

FIGURE 3-7

Market structure for holiday travel.

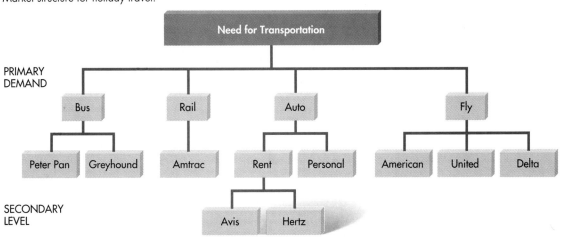

TABLE 3-3	DIAGNOSTIC QUESTIONS ON SELECTIVE DEMAND

1. DECISION PROCESSES

How extensive is the search for information?
Do buyers use personal or impersonal sources of information?
Do buyers seek information about brand or supplier characteristics?

2. DETERMINANT ATTRIBUTES

What are the benefits buyers hope to obtain from usage or ownership of the product?
What product attributes (characteristics) are viewed as providing these benefits?
What is the relative importance of the various benefits desired?
How much variation is perceived among the alternatives on each of the important attributes?

to buy. Once consumers have decided which alternatives they prefer, they must select one of the options within an alternative. For example, if you decide to fly, you must then determine which airline you will use. The factors involved in the decision at the secondary demand level can be different from those important at the primary level.

In analyzing selective demand, managers are primarily interested in understanding how buyers make choices from the alternative brands or suppliers within the relevant market. However, not all buyers are alike in their choices. Rather, choice is a function of buyers' needs (desired benefits) and buyers' perceptions of alternatives in the context of the specific usage situation.

In this section we present an approach for examining selective demand. The first step in this approach is to identify the type of decision-making process likely to be used. The second step is to identify the determinant attributes. Table 3-3 summarizes the diagnostic questions used in analyzing selective demand.

Identifying the Types of Decision Processes

Models of consumer choice are, as a rule, based on the assumption that when faced with a set of options, consumers choose that option considered to deliver the highest level of gratification or satisfaction.[15] In many cases consumers must make complex decisions involving many alternatives. When faced with many alternatives, they use decision rules that narrow down the total number of brands available in the product class to a smaller subset of brands they would consider purchasing.[16] Table 3-4 depicts this sequential process of consumer choice. The total set consists of all brands within the product class available to the consumer. The awareness set is comprised of the brands of which the consumer is aware or can retrieve from memory. The consideration set is the set of brands the consumer would consider buying in the near future.[17]

[15]Robert J. Meyer and Barbara E. Kahn, "Probabilistic Models of Consumer Choice Behavior," in Thomas S. Robertson and Harold H. Kassarjian, eds., *Handbook of Consumer Behavior,* Englewood Cliffs, NJ: 1991.

[16]John A. Howard, *Consumer Behavior in Marketing Strategy,* McGraw-Hill, New York, 1989.

[17]John H. Roberts and James M. Lattin, "Development and Testing of a Model of Consideration Set Composition," *Journal of Marketing Research,* November 1991, pp. 429–440.

Ɨₖₒᴹ/ cʆᴹ

TABLE 3-4	SEQUENTIAL PROCESS OF CONSUMER CHOICE

TOTAL SET BRAND	AWARENESS SET BRAND	CONSIDERATION SET BRAND
Arm & Hammer		
Tide	Tide	Tide
Trend		
Cheer	Cheer	Cheer
Vista		
Sun		
Gain	Gain	
Surf		
Rinso		
All	All	All
Ivory Snow		
Bold	Bold	Bold
Rain		
Dreft		
Oxydol	Oxydol	
Wisk		
Ultra		
Purex	Purex	
Fab	Fab	Fab

Buying decisions are typically categorized into three stages: (1) extensive problem solving (EPS), (2) limited problem solving (LPS), and (3) routinized response behavior (RRB).[18] The stages vary with respect to the time devoted to the decision and the type of information sought.

Extensive problem solving occurs when the consumer is confronted with a radically new decision. For example, consider consumers from a warm climate who decide for the first time that they want to go snow skiing for their vacations. They have not had to make this type of choice before and therefore have no concept formation.[19] *Concept formation* is the process of identifying which criteria or attributes the consumer wants to use to make an evaluation. In extensive problem solving, the consumer not only needs information on brands, but has to decide what information is most important.

Limited problem solving is the process of forming brand concepts. The buyer has a sound knowledge of the product category and the relevant choice criteria but is confronted with a new brand. The amount of time for the decision is less than for extensive problem solving, but is still considerable. The consumers may have to not only

---

[18]*See* William Wilkie, *Consumer Behavior,* 3d ed., New York: John Wiley, 1994, chap. 18, for a detailed treatment of the topic.

[19]Howard, p. 17.

evaluate the new brand but also compare other brands to reinstate their preferences. At this stage the choice criteria are well formed but information on brands is necessary to form an evaluation.

Routinized response behavior is represented by a limited search for information and a speedy decision. The consumers have experience making a choice from the product class and therefore require little, if any, information to make their decisions. In the case of strong brand loyalty the consumers will simply pick their preferred brands if available. If the preferred brand is not available, the consumer may require a small amount of information about those brands in the consideration set, such as sizes available and prices, to make a choice.

Traditionally, these three types of decision processes have been used to describe decisions made by consumers. For organizational buyers, a parallel set of processes (see Figure 3-8) can be identified. The new task is a situation in which extensive problem solving will occur because the product is being purchased for the first time. The modified rebuy is the term used for limited problem solving in organizational purchases. Straight rebuys are essentially routinized response behaviors in that little active search will take place (although for many products in the straight rebuy category, some buyers divide their orders among two or more established suppliers).

There are two reasons why the distinction among types of decision processes is important. First, an understanding of the type of decision process involved in the purchase of a product enables managers to understand buyer search behavior. The more extensive the problem solving required, the greater the amount of search and the more likely customers will be to rely on personal sources of information (including family members, friends, and salespeople). At the other extreme, routinized decision making leads to limited (even perhaps zero) search, with impersonal sources of information likely to play a stronger role than personal sources.

Second, the kind of information required by buyers will vary according to the type of decision process. In routinized decision making, additional information may not even be needed: Buyers may simply respond to those brands or suppliers that have the greatest levels of buyer awareness. In limited problem solving, the key information sought is that which relates to brand or supplier characteristics (attributes). In

FIGURE 3-8

Types of decision processes.

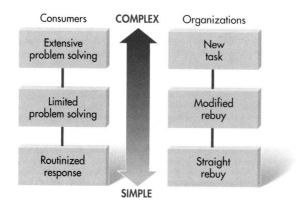

extensive problem solving, it is necessary not only to acquire information on brand or supplier characteristics but to learn what the important considerations should be in making a choice. Stated differently, in extensive problem solving, buyers must learn the determinant attributes.

Determinant Attributes

A traditional psychological or economic view of products and services is that they are bundles of attributes. The consumer forms an overall evaluation of a product by combining perceptions of the product attributes using some rule(s) to weight the information.[20] The first task, which is similar to the cognitive processes that take place in extensive problem solving, is to determine which attributes are most important to the consumer. Once the importance of the attributes is established, the consumer must then search for and evaluate information pertaining to the brands within the product class. These activities are similar to the cognitive processes encountered in limited problem solving. Consider Figure 3-9, which presents the attributes identified as important for purchasing agents selecting vendors.[21] Having identified the choice criteria or important attributes, the next step would be for the purchasing agents to gather information regarding potential vendors on these attributes. The last task is to form rules to integrate the information.

Consumer decision rules or heuristics are procedures used by consumers to facilitate brand choice. These decision rules have been broadly classified as compensatory and noncompensatory decision rules. A unique feature of compensatory rules is that a negative feature of a brand can be overcome by other positive features. Table 3-5 presents four attributes used in the evaluation of fast-food restaurants and their importance ratings.[22] Table 3-6 (page 69) presents ratings for three hypothetical restaurants

| **TABLE 3-5** | **ATTRIBUTES OF FAST-FOOD RESTAURANTS** | |

ATTRIBUTE	IMPORTANCE
Food taste	4.30
Quantity and cost	3.79
Food selection	3.58
Menu alternatives	3.58

1 = unimportant
5 = very important

[20]Meyer and Kahn, p. 88.

[21]R. E. Spekman, "Perceptions of Strategic Vulnerability among Industrial Buyers and Its Effects on Information Search and Suppliers Evaluation," *Journal of Business Research,* vol. 17, no. 4, 1988, pp. 313–326.

[22]Robert L. Armacost and Jamshid C. Hosseini, "Identification of Determinant Attributes Using the Analytic Hierarchy Process," *Journal of the Academy of Marketing Science,* Fall 1994, pp. 383–392.

for each of the four attributes. A simple compensatory rule would average the ratings for each of the restaurants. Following this decision rule, the restaurant with the largest score, in this case restaurant B, is the preferred alternative.

In following a noncompensatory approach, the attributes are first ranked in terms of importance. The brands or objects are then evaluated on the most important attribute and the brand with the best score is the preferred alternative. If there is a tie on the most important attribute, the brands are then evaluated on the second most important attribute. Using this approach, restaurant C would be chosen. Restaurants A and C are evaluated equally on food taste, the most important attribute, but restaurant C was favored with respect to quantity and cost, the second most important attribute.

In many cases, especially where the alternatives and/or attributes are numerous, consumers may use a two-step process. Noncompensatory rules are used to first screen alternatives and then compensatory rules are used to evaluate the brands that passed

FIGURE 3-9

Attributes of vendor selection.

1. *Product*
   Concern for reliability
   Concern for productivity
   Ease of operation
   Product's ease of use
   Vendor's training
      associated with product

2. *Service*
   Response time
   Dependability
   Competence of sales
      representatives
   Prepurchase information
   Vendor's image

3. *Experience*
   Past experience with vendor
   Reputation
   Ability to keep promises

4. *Price*
   Price/performance
   Lower price
   Total costs

5. *Availability*
   Supplier's financial position
   Geographic proximity
   Breadth of product line
   Availability of technical support

| TABLE 3-6 | ATTRIBUTE RATINGS FOR THREE FAST-FOOD RESTAURANTS |

ATTRIBUTE RATINGS FOR THREE FAST-FOOD RESTAURANTS

	RATING OF RESTAURANT		
ATTRIBUTE	A	B	C
Food taste	4	3	4
Quantity and cost	3	5	4
Food selection	3	5	3
Menu alternatives	3	4	3

5 = Excellent
4 = Good
3 = Okay
2 = Fair
1 = Poor

the first screening.[23] It is important that marketing managers understand how their customers use information to form an evaluation. If the customers use a noncompensatory process at any level, then it is imperative that the product is perceived as at least as good as the competition on each important attribute.

Managers should be aware that, often, the attributes governing choice are not attributes of the physical product but, rather, are those of the broader offering. For example, quick, reliable delivery of raw materials is a critically important attribute to many industrial firms. Convenience is generally the most important factor in determining where people have their checking accounts.

Frequently, several products are similar in a large number of attributes. In such cases, it is important to distinguish one or more of the *determinant attributes*—that is, attributes that are most likely to determine the buyer's choice.[24] Two dimensions help make an attribute a determinant attribute: importance and uniqueness. An attribute will be considered important if it provides desirable benefits; however, if all competing alternatives have the same feature, then that attribute will not determine brand choice.

To gain a better understanding of the determinant attribute concept, consider Figure 3-10. Basically, a buyer could evaluate any individual attribute as falling into one of the four categories portrayed in this figure. For example, someone considering alternative brands of lawn mowers would probably consider "easy to start" important. But if most or all competing mowers are equally easy to start, then this becomes a defensive attribute—something that is necessary to avoid being eliminated from consideration but not something that will cause people to choose a product. On the other hand, some attributes may make a product different but are not (currently) considered to be very important. Such attributes are optional attributes (such as a lawn mower steer-

[23]Frank R. Kardes, Gurumurthy Kalyanaram, Murali Chandrashekaran, and Ronald J. Dornoff, "Brand Retrieval, Consideration Set Composition, Consumer Choice, and the Pioneering Advantage," *Journal of Consumer Research,* June 1993, pp. 62–75.

[24]James H. Myers and Mark Alpert, "Determinant Buying Attitudes: Meaning and Measurement," *Journal of Marketing,* October 1968, pp. 13–20.

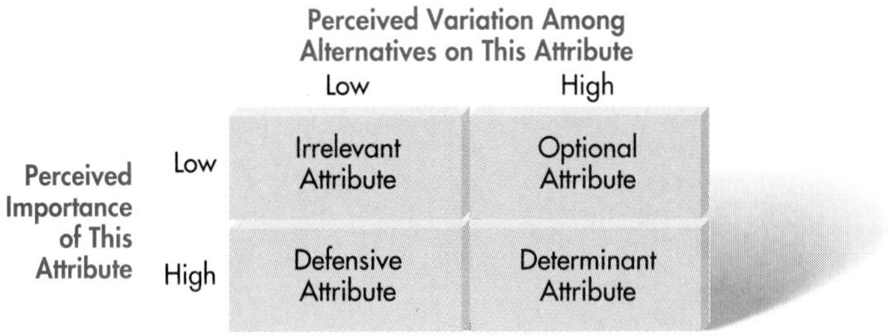

FIGURE 3-10
A framework for assessing whether an attribute is determinant.

Perceived Variation Among
Alternatives on This Attribute

		Low	High
Perceived Importance of This Attribute	Low	Irrelevant Attribute	Optional Attribute
	High	Defensive Attribute	Determinant Attribute

ing wheel that can be tilted at different angles). Of course, optional attributes have the potential to become determinant attributes if they become important. In states with restrictions on the dumping of grass clippings, the first lawn mowers with mulching blades held a temporary competitive advantage because this attribute moved from optional to determinant. Once many competitors offered the mulching blade, this attribute moved from determinant to defensive.

It is especially necessary to consider both dimensions of attribute determinance in the process of new-product development, as the following example demonstrates.

> Procter & Gamble developed a scallop-shaped soap called Monchel with a special fragrance and package to complement its unusual shape. When consumers used the product in blind tests (where the brand was not identified) they indicated a preference for it over other brands. But when the product went to market it flopped. P&G found that they had created a product that was distinctive, but on dimensions that were essentially unimportant to consumers; the product failed to perform better on the attributes that really counted. So when the time came for consumers to spend money, the novelty effects wore off.[25]

CONCLUSION

If an organization is to achieve customer satisfaction, it must first and foremost understand its market. The chapter opened with a brief discussion of the house of quality. The house of quality is a method used by managers to understand what the customer requires to be satisfied and how to design or modify products to meet these requirements. We then identified the first three steps of a six-step approach for analyzing markets that is useful to managers concerned with long-term corporate planning and to those concerned with short-term marketing strategies. Specifically, we examined the process of defining the relevant market—the primary competitive arena of concern to a manager. We also presented diagnostic questions and concepts that managers can employ to analyze primary and selective demand within the relevant market.

These steps are important to the selection of a marketing strategy. However, market analyses should not be performed only when entering a new market. Rather, the diagnostic questions should be examined continuously in order to keep up with changing conditions, a situation confronted by Tupperware.

[25]Zachary Schiller, "Ready, Aim, Market: Combat Training at P&G College," *Business Week,* Feb. 3, 1992, p. 56.

TUPPERWARE: CONFRONTING CHANGING DEMAND CONDITIONS

As refrigerators replaced iceboxes as the primary method of cold-food storage in the United States during the 1920s and 1930s, consumers encountered a new problem—refrigeration caused food to wilt and lose its flavor. Although paper packaging and wrapping could help deal with this problem, paper could leak or tear. In the 1940s, a Massachusetts inventor named Earl Tupper began making lightweight, unbreakable plastic bowls with airtight lids to solve this problem.

Although the product was unique, housewives did not immediately adopt this innovation. They were wary of plastic (still considered a mysterious substance) and saw Tupperware as an expensive, nontraditional solution to food storage problems. Finally, Tupperware distributors thought up the device of home parties to sell the product. A group of women gathered in the home of a friend for lunch or dessert, conversation and games, and a demonstration by a Tupperware salesperson. The hostess received a gift, and the salesperson made some sales.

Throughout the 1950s, 1960s, and 1970s, sales of Tupperware (by then a subsidiary of Dart Industries) grew rapidly—fast enough to entice Rubbermaid to enter the market using the same basic sales approach. But by 1980 there was a noticeable decline in married couples with children, there were fewer children per family, and labor-force participation by women with children was growing rapidly. Although working women have more money to spend, they have less time for parties and are often less concerned about storing leftovers.

Recognizing the significance of this trend, Rubbermaid dropped the home party approach in favor of distribution through grocery stores. Additionally, a number of smaller rivals entered the market, selling low-quality, low-priced bowls through drugstores and other retail outlets. By 1992, Tupperware's unit market share had declined from 60 percent to about 40 to 45 percent while Rubbermaid's share had risen to an estimated 30 to 40 percent. Rubbermaid had been very innovative during this period. For example, in 1983 they designed a seven-piece space-saving set of bowls designed for use in microwave ovens. In the meantime, other competitors challenged Tupperware, mainly on price. As industry observers have noted, it doesn't take a tremendous amount of quality to keep leftover peas fresh in the refrigerator for 5 days.

Back in 1992 Tupperware decided to battle back. They unveiled a new line of "TupperWave" microwavable plastic that is stackable to allow simultaneous cooking of three dishes. They chose to stick with the party sales approach but also began to experiment with catalog sales. Tupperware experienced a loss of $22 million in 1992 but recovered strongly in 1993 showing a profit of $15.5 million. In 1995 Tupperware was considered a good investment by Wall Street analysts—the earnings were increasing and the stock market price rising. Tupperware was facing stiff competition in the United States from discount imitations. However, Tupperware was strong in international markets where good-quality discount imitations were hard to find. In 1995, 80 percent of Tupperware's sales were from international markets.

1. Which diagnostic questions on buyer identification and on willingness and ability to buy are useful in analyzing primary demand in this market?

2. Describe the decision process you would use in buying plastic storage bowls. Would others use a different process?

3. Which attributes are *determinant* in the purchase of plastic storage bowls? Which attributes might be characterized as *defensive* and which as *optional*?

4. Who is Tupperware's target customer? What are some possible reasons why the company chose that target?

Based on Laurie Grossman, "Going Stale: Families Have Changed but Tupperware Keeps Holding Parties," *Wall Street Journal*, July 21, 1992, pp. 1, 4; "After the Party: Tupperware Burps Out Array of New Products," *Adweek*, Sept. 23, 1991, p. 1; "Tupperware to Explore Catalog Sales," *Crain's Chicago Business*, May 31, 1992, p. 78; Bart Greer, "New Tupperware Cookware Resembles Rubbermaid Line," *Plastic News*, Sept. 3, 1990, p. 5; "Get Ready for a Tupperware Party," *Business Week*, May 9, 1994, p. 80; "Heard on the Street: Tupperware Maker Premark Is Poised to Pop the Lid Off Its Stock Price, Some Analysts Say," *Wall Street Journal*, Apr. 3, 1995, sec. C, p. 2.

QUESTIONS AND SITUATIONS FOR DISCUSSION

1. A brand manager was quoted as saying, "You may think you define your relevant market, but you are only kidding yourself, the consumer defines the relevant market." Comment.

2. Although in an attractive market, Dan's product was not doing well. He knew that if he did not become competitive he would be in trouble at the next planning meeting. He wanted first to determine if his product was competitive in the eyes of his relevant market and, if not, he needed to know what he could do to improve his product. The product is composed of six attributes which are, for simplicity, labeled, I, II, III, IV, V, and VI. A team was formed to analyze the product. The team took a house of quality approach and identified six engineering characteristics (A, B, C, D, E, and F) relevant to the production of Dan's product.

   The team submitted the following conclusions to Dan.

   a. It is understandable why you do not have adequate market share, your product is an inferior offering.

   b. Based on our reading of the analyses, we recommend that the product be augmented by increasing characteristic E. This is the most important characteristic and will provide the best differential advantage.

   Do you agree with the team's conclusions?

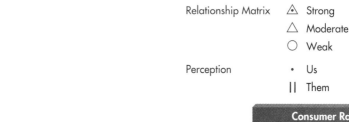

3. Two possible market structures for laundry detergent are presented on page 73. Use the market structures to discuss the following.

   a. For which of the two is brand loyalty greater?

   b. For which of the two will managers most likely want a large product line?

c. For which of the two should a manager's evaluation be relative to the entire market rather than to brands of the same form?

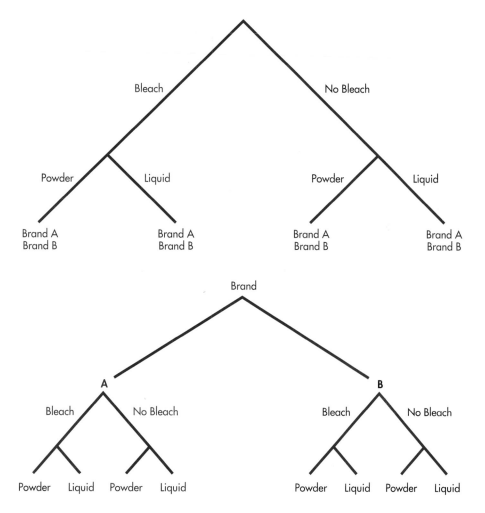

4. Agricultural cooperatives, like Sunkist, combine the produce from many small farmers and market the products collectively. Do marketing co-ops reduce competition at the primary or secondary level?

5. When marketers enter international markets, especially in third world countries, they may be offering a product or service that is quite different from what people are currently using. They are competing at the primary demand level. What factors are likely to cause resistance to the new products?

6. A recent technological innovation in packaging allows entrees that were previously frozen to be packaged and shelved for up to 3 months without refrigeration. This new packaging will allow the introduction of frozen, or what was frozen, dinners in many new countries since refrigeration is no longer an issue.

What information requirements should the marketing manager consider when creating promotional pieces now and in the future?

7. Competitive advantage is a function of the number and degree of determinant attributes claimed by the brand. Comment.

8. The following tables provide ratings of four brands of packaged soup on five attributes and importance rating for those attributes. Use these data to answer the following questions.

   a. If the geographic areas used a non-compensatory decision-making approach, which brand would each area choose?

   b. If the geographic areas used a compensatory decision-making approach, which brand would each area choose?

	BRANDS			
ATTRIBUTES	A	B	C	D
Fat	Low	Low	High	High
Calories	Low	Low	High	High
Taste homemade	Yes	No	Yes	Yes
Cooking time (min.)	Fast	Slow	Medium	Medium
Price	National	Economy	National	National

The following table shows the importance of the attributes to the consumers in each of the five geographical areas. A 1 is the most important and a 5 is the least important.

	GEOGRAPHICAL AREA				
ATTRIBUTE	I	II	III	IV	V
Low fat	1	5	3	4	4
Low calorie	2	4	4	1	5
Taste homemade	5	2	1	3	2
Fast cooking time	4	3	5	5	1
Good price	3	1	2	2	3

SUGGESTED ADDITIONAL READINGS

Davidow, William, and Bro Uttal, "Service Companies: Focus or Falter," *Harvard Business Review,* July–August 1989, pp. 77–85.

Day, George S., "The Capabilities of Market-Driven Organizations," *Journal of Marketing,* October 1994, pp. 37–52.

Day, George S., Allan Shocker, and Rajendra Srivastava, "Customer-Oriented

Approaches to Identifying Product Markets," *Journal of Marketing,* Fall 1979, pp. 8–19.

Griffin, Abbie, "Evaluating QFD's Use in U.S. Firms as a Process for Developing Products," *Journal of Product Innovation Management,* vol. 9, September 1992, pp. 171 –187.

Griffin, Abbie, and John R. Hauser, "The Voice of the Customer," *Marketing Science,* Winter 1993, pp. 1–25.

Holak, Susan, and Donald Lehman, "Purchase Intentions and the Dimensions of Innovation, *Journal of Product Innovation Management,* March 1990, pp. 59–73.

Stanley, Thomas, "Targeting the Affluent Consumer," *Journal of Business Strategy,* September–October 1988, pp. 17–20.

Urban, G. L., P. L. Johnson, and J. R. Hauser, "Testing Competitive Market Structures," *Marketing Science,* Spring 1984, pp. 83–112.

Vithala, R. Rao, and Darius Jal Sabavala, "Inference of Hierarchical Choice Processes from Panel Data," *Journal of Consumer Research,* June 1981, pp. 85–96.

Wells, William, "Psychographics: A Critical Review," *Journal of Marketing Research,* May 1975, pp. 196–213.

CHAPTER 4

TARGET MARKETING AND COMPETITIVE ADVANTAGE

OVERVIEW

The goal of target marketing is to position a brand within a product market so that the brand enjoys a competitive advantage. Products achieve a competitive advantage when they offer attributes that are important to the consumer and are unique. In Chapter 3 a determinant attribute was defined as an attribute that is important and unique. Therefore, to create a competitive advantage, the firm must first understand what is important to consumers. What do consumers prefer? In addition, the firm must determine the degree of homogeneity of preferences within a designated relevant market. Do consumers agree on the importance of attributes or are there segments of consumers that differ from other groups of consumers in their appraisal of attributes? The firm cannot ignore the competitive environment when it is targeting consumers. Management must understand the level and intensity of competitive forces that exist within the relevant market.

In this chapter, we present the final three steps in the six-step process, introduced in Chapter 3, for analyzing markets. These last three steps are: defining market segments, analyzing the competitive environment, and identifying target markets.

Market Segmentation

The concept of market segmentation was introduced by Wendell R. Smith in 1956 in what is now considered a seminal article.[1] He distinguished between bending the will of demand to meet supply and bending the will of supply to meet demand. Mass marketing—one product, one marketing strategy—seeks to bend the will of demand to meet supply. Without doubt, it would be easier, more cost-efficient, and more desirable for a firm to produce one product in one size, one color, and so on. Henry Ford took this approach when he said, "You can have a Model T Ford in any color you want, as long as it is black." Demand for his automobiles far exceeded supply; therefore, he was able to bend the will of demand to that of supply. How well do you think Henry would do with this approach today?

[1] Wendell R. Smith, "Product Differentiation and Market Segmentation as Alternative Marketing Strategies," *Journal of Marketing,* July 1956, pp. 3–8.

Major jean manufacturers changed their focus from a one-size-fits-all approach backed by national media campaigns to a more segmented approach. In the 1960s and 1970s the jean companies were driven by manufacturing. Their goal was to sell what they made to whatever takers were out there. In the 1990s the consumer has a wide variety of choices in jeans. According to Tim Lambeth, president of Lee Corporation, it is now imperative that jean manufacturers hit a responsive chord, that they communicate to specific customers with specialized products and marketing.[2]

Market segmentation capitalizes on differences in consumers' tastes and preferences by targeting segments with a product and marketing strategy consistent with their unique requirements. An article appearing in *The New York Times* in the early 1980s made it clear that no single type of lodging can appeal to the entire traveling public. Ten years after the article appeared, segmentation rules the industry.[3] Marriott Corporation introduced Courtyard by Marriott in 1983. Subsequently, they introduced Marriott Suites, Residence Inn by Marriott, and Fairfield Inn in 1987. The Fairfield Inns are targeted to the economy-minded customer, whereas the Residence Inns and Courtyards are moderately priced.[4]

Three activities are involved in market segmentation: (1) formation and profiling of segments, (2) evaluation of the market segments, and (3) selection of a segmentation strategy. These phases of market segmentation are outlined in Figure 4-1.

FORM AND PROFILE SEGMENTS

A market segment consists of a group of customers whose requirements for satisfaction in a product are similar. To create these segments, market-segmentation studies usually collect four types of data: needs or desired end benefits, purchase behavior, values/lifestyle measures, and classifying characteristics.

Needs/Benefits Sought

Needs and benefits are the characteristics or attributes of a product that consumers seek or consider important. This approach to formation of market segments is sometimes called *benefit segmentation.*[5] Consumers are clustered together on the basis of the benefits they seek. Consider the market for snowmobiles. The benefits desired from snowmobiles may vary with how they are going to be used. Some users, for example, weekend riders, may use their snowmobiles only in groups and close to

---

[2]Susan Reda, "Manufacturers Develop Labels for Different Retail Tiers," *STORES,* January 1994, pp. 35–38.

[3]Ray Schultz, "A Decade of Segmentation," *Lodging Hospitality,* October 1994, p. 20.

[4]Frank E. Camacho and D. Matthew Knain, "Listening to Customers: The Market Research Function at Marriott Corporation," *Marketing Research: A Magazine of Management and Applications,* March 1989, pp. 5–14.

[5]Russell I. Haley, "Benefit Segmentation: A Decision-Oriented Research Tool," *Journal of Marketing,* vol. 32, July 1968, pp. 30–35.

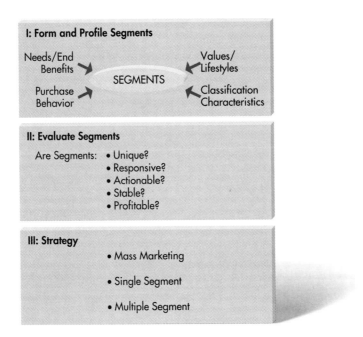

FIGURE 4-1

Market segmentation.

home, whereas other users, say hunters, may use their snowmobiles individually and in remote areas. These two groups are likely to value different aspects of snowmobiles. Both want a snowmobile, but what is required for satisfaction in one group may be unimportant to another group.

MULTI-ITEM SCALE

One approach to formation of needs-based segments is to have consumers indicate how important or unimportant each benefit is to them (see Table 4-1). Statistical methods are then used to form groups of consumers who are seeking the same end benefits. Referring to Table 4-1, do you think hunters and weekend users of snowmobiles would rate the importance of instrument accuracy, styling, or seat for second rider the same? The resulting groups are the market segments. The preferences of consumers within a group are similar to each other but different from other segments. A needs-based approach to market segmentation begins with the identification of needs that customers attempt to satisfy when buying products or services. A competitive advantage, which can also be cost-effective, can be created by forming groups of customers with similar patterns of needs and then targeting product development, marketing, and sales efforts toward the satisfaction of the needs of the groups, or segments, that offer the greatest revenue and profitability potential.[6]

[6]John Berrigan and Carl Finkbeiner, *Segmentation Marketing: New Methods for Capturing Business Marketers,* Harper Business, New York, 1992.

TABLE 4-1

EXAMPLES OF NEEDS/END-BENEFITS CHARACTERISTICS

When you are selecting a snowmobile, how important is each of the following characteristics to you?

	EXTREMELY IMPORTANT	VERY IMPORTANT	SOMEWHAT IMPORTANT	NOT VERY IMPORTANT	NOT AT ALL IMPORTANT
Manufacturer's reputation	5	4	3	2	1
Handling in deep snow	5	4	3	2	1
Appearance	5	4	3	2	1
Cargo capacity	5	4	3	2	1
Acceleration	5	4	3	2	1
Fuel consumption	5	4	3	2	1
Hill climbing	5	4	3	2	1
Instrument accuracy	5	4	3	2	1
Braking response	5	4	3	2	1
Handling on ice	5	4	3	2	1
Styling	5	4	3	2	1
Seat for second rider	5	4	3	2	1

A market-segmentation study conducted for the food industry discovered that a needs-based approach was useful, even for consumers who are very similar in age. The mature market, consumers over the age of 50, can be classified into one of three market segments based on desired end benefits: nutrition-concerned, fast and healthy individuals, and traditional couponers. Table 4-2 provides summaries of the three market segments for people over the age of 50.[7]

TABLE 4-2

SEGMENTS IN THE MATURE MARKET

Nutrition-concerned people make up 46 percent of the over-50 population. This group believes that what you eat affects how you feel. When they shop, they stick to their lists and read labels, but admit that they do consider advertising when buying.

Fast and healthy individuals are also concerned about health and nutrition, but are more interested in convenience. They tend to cook only when the family is together and rely heavily on their microwave ovens.

Traditional couponers show the least interest in nutrition and are the only segment that doesn't worry about eating enough fiber or too much fat. When they shop, they are most interested in using coupons and buying their favorite brands.

[7]Gabrielle Sandor, "Attitude (Not Age) Defines the Mature Market," *American Demographics,* January 1994, pp. 18–21.

CONJOINT ANALYSIS

Conjoint data analysis determines the qualities of a product or service that are most desired by the customer.[8] A conjoint approach to the estimation of consumer preferences requires three stages: identification of relevant attributes, data collection, and data analysis.

1. *Identification of relevant attributes.* Management must first specify which attributes it wants to study. In many cases the attributes to be studied will be those identified as determinant in the decision to choose one product in lieu of another. As an example, consider a fast-food restaurant, such as McDonald's or Burger King, that is deciding whether to expand its menu to include pizza. Five characteristics are identified by management as important to consumers: price, delivery time, price of a second pizza, type of crust, and whether the toppings can be divided. Once the attributes have been identified, the next task is to determine the levels of each attribute to be studied: Should price be assessed at two levels, three levels, or more than three levels? How many types of crust should be considered? and so forth. Table 4-3 contains the five pizza characteristics and the levels of each characteristic to be studied.

    This stage, specification of attributes and levels, is extremely important. If an important attribute is not included, the results can be very misleading. Notice that this study does not measure the value associated with known pizza restaurants such as Dominos or Pizza Hut. If there is loyalty to one chain, this will not be deter-

TABLE 4-3	PIZZA CHARACTERISTICS
Price	$7.45
	$7.90
	$8.35
Delivery	No delivery
	No time guarantee
	Guaranteed in less than 30 min
	Guaranteed in less than 15 min
Price of second pizza	Free
	Half price
	Full price
Type of crust	Regular
	Thick
	Thin
	Pan
Split topping	Yes
	No

[8]Paul E. Green and Yoram Wind, "New Way to Measure Consumers' Judgements," *Harvard Business Review,* July–August 1975, pp. 173–184.

TABLE 4-4	TWO PIZZA SCENARIOS

PIZZA SCENARIO 4

Price	$7.90
Delivery	Guaranteed in less than 15 min
Price of second pizza	Half price
Crust	Pan
Split topping	No
	Rank _____

PIZZA SCENARIO 11

Price	$7.45
Delivery	No guarantee
Price of second pizza	Free
Crust	Thin
Split topping	Yes
	Rank _____

mined by the analysis discussed above. If management wants to assess the value of a name such as "Little Caesar," then brand names have to be included as attributes in the study.

2. *Data collection.* Given the attributes and levels described in Table 4-3, there are $(3 \times 4 \times 3 \times 4 \times 2)$ 288 different possible pizza combinations. It would be too taxing to ask consumers to rate all 288 possible pizza combinations. Computer packages for PCs are available to identify subsets of the 288 combinations that allow marketing managers to estimate consumer preferences for each attribute.[9] For the pizza example described in Table 4-3, consumers would be required to evaluate sixteen pizza combinations. Table 4-4 contains examples of two of the sixteen pizza scenarios to be evaluated. Consumers are usually asked to rank the different scenarios from most preferred to least preferred.

3. *Data analysis.* Conjoint data analysis uses the scenario rank orders provided by the consumers to estimate the amount of value associated with each level of each attribute. A form of regression analysis is often used to determine the value for each level of each attribute. The value associated with each level of the characteristics is referred to as a part-worth utility. The part-worth utility represents the amount of utility or value that would be gained or lost as a result of choosing one level over another. The part-worth utility estimates for the pizza attributes are provided in Table 4-5. Notice that for each attribute one level has been set to zero. The amount of utility provided to the consumer for the other levels of the attribute is determined by comparing the utility for each level to the base. If the restaurant were to offer guaranteed delivery in less than 30 minutes, the amount of utility associated with this is .40 units; if the delivery is not guaranteed, the utility is .10;

[9]J. Douglas Carroll and Paul E. Green, "Psychometric Methods in Marketing Research: Part 1, Conjoint Analysis," *Journal of Marketing Research,* vol. XXXII, November 1995, pp. 385–391.

TABLE 4-5	PART-WORTH UTILITIES	
ATTRIBUTE	LEVEL	UTILITY
Price	$8.25	0
	$7.90	.55
	$7.45	.65
Price of	Full price	0
second pizza	Half price	.35
	Free	.60
Delivery	None	0
	No guarantee	.10
	Less than 30 min	.40
	Less than 15 min	.44
Crust	Regular	0
	Thick	.30
	Thin	.05
	Pan	.25
Split topping	No	0
	Yes	.10

therefore, the restaurant can provide an additional .30 units of utility to the consumers for guaranteeing delivery in less than 30 minutes. Notice that the restaurant would offer virtually no additional utility to the consumer for guaranteeing pizza delivery in less than 15 minutes.

The most desired pizza would be the combination offering the most utility, which, in this case, is a thick crust with split toppings and delivered in less than 15 minutes for a price of $7.45, with a second pizza free. The amount of utility provided by this combination is (.30 + .10 + .44 + .65 + .60) 2.09. Marketing managers can use the results from conjoint analysis to determine the amount of utility associated with any of the 288 possible pizza combinations by adding the part-worth utilities for the levels chosen.

As an example of segmenting markets with conjoint data analysis, assume that a sample of 1000 representatives of the target market ranked ordered the pizza scenarios described above. Part-worth utility values could be calculated for all 1000 consumers. Statistical techniques could then be used to form groups of people with similar likes and dislikes; that is, form segments of people with similar preference functions. Table 4-6 presents three possible segments. The numbers in the table are part-worth utilities and, for convenience, have been scaled to sum to one. Segment 1 is a price segment. The representatives place a lot of value on a low price and receipt of a second pizza free. There is no strong preference for the other attributes. Segment 2 wants quick delivery and either thick or pan pizza; price is not very important. Segment 3 shows a preference for the regular pizza and the split toppings. This segment is also interested in an average-to-lower price.

TABLE 4-6	PART-WORTH UTILITIES FOR THREE CONSUMER SEGMENTS			
ATTRIBUTE	**LEVEL**	**I**	**II**	**III**
Price	$8.25	.05	.30	.10
	$7.90	.10	.35	.40
	$7.45	.85	.35	.50
Price of	Full price	.10	.30	.30
second pizza	Half price	.30	.30	.30
	Free	.60	.40	.40
Delivery	None	.05	.02	.20
	No guarantee	.25	.08	.25
	Less than 30 min	.35	.40	.25
	Less than 15 min	.35	.50	.30
Crust	Regular	.10	.05	.60
	Thick	.30	.35	.20
	Thin	.30	.05	.10
	Pan	.30	.55	.10
Split topping	No	.50	.45	.30
	Yes	.50	.55	.70

Conjoint data analysis is well suited to market segmentation because (1) the focus of conjoint analysis is specifically on buyers' preferences for levels of attributes and (2) the analysis is micro-based; part-worth utilities can be calculated for each respondent.[10] Because the part-worth utilities are calculated for each consumer, they can be used to group consumers who prefer the same levels of each attribute.

Behavioral Measures

Behavioral measures ask consumers to indicate which brands (services) they have purchased over a certain time period. For many product classes, consumers are asked which brands they have purchased in the last month, or the last 3 months. They also may be asked to provide information about their intentions to purchase brands in the future. These data can be used to develop switching patterns among the brands, and the switching patterns can be utilized to form groups of consumers who purchase and switch among the same brands.

In some cases, consumers may be asked to record their purchases in a diary. The Wine Spectrum Company asked a sample of 1150 wine consumers to record all consumption of wine. They recorded consumption as follows.

■ When and where consumed
■ The nature of the situation
■ If at a meal, what type of meal

[10]Paul E. Green and Abba M. Krieger, "Segmenting Markets with Conjoint Analysis," *Journal of Marketing,* vol. 55, October 1991, pp. 20–31.

- The quantity consumed
- Brand, color, and variety of wine
- How many others were present, how many were also drinking wine
- Who decided to have wine, who chose a specific wine[11]

These data were employed to form segments based on the occasion during which the wine was consumed. The largest occasion segment, which accounted for 35 percent of the volume, was called the social segment. Motives associated with this segment were sociability, sharing, celebration, friendship, and fun. The second largest segment, which accounted for 24 percent of the volume, was called introspective. Motives associated with this occasion were thirst, pleasure, sleep, relaxation, indulgence, good feelings, and ease in serving.

Values/Lifestyle Measures

Values and lifestyle measures are used to determine what consumers like and dislike: What are their activities, opinions, and interests? Use of values and/or lifestyle data to segment markets is commonly referred to as *psychographic segmentation.*

The List of Values (LOV) scale is based on a set of values identified by Rokeach.[12] The LOV scale consists of nine values: a sense of belonging, excitement, fun and enjoyment in life, self-fulfillment, being well respected, warm relationships with others, security, accomplishment, and self-respect. To understand a person's choice of vacation spots, marketing researchers administered the LOV scale to approximately 400 English-speaking tourists in Scandinavia. The results indicated that comprehension of a person's values is important to an understanding of what lures a tourist to a particular destination.[13]

The most prevalent use of values and lifestyles in market segmentation is SRI International's values and lifestyles (VALS) program. The VALS approach is based on the notion that people define a social self-image and that the image is reflected in their conduct and consumer behavior. People buy products and services and seek experiences that they see as characteristic of themselves. The products and services help give shape, substance, character, and satisfaction to their lives.[14]

To establish the values/lifestyle segments, respondents are asked to agree or disagree with a battery of items describing different values, attitudes, and lifestyles. Three patterns of response have been identified as effective predictors of consumer behavior.

1. *Principle-oriented.* These consumers are guided by abstract idealized criteria rather than by their feelings or a desire for approval.

---

[11]Joel S. Dubow, "Occasion-Based vs. User-Based Benefit Segmentation: A Case Study," *Journal of Advertising Research,* March/April 1992, pp. 11–18.

[12]Wagner A. Kamakuru and Thomas P. Novak, "Value-System Segmentation: Exploring the Meaning of LOV," *Journal of Consumer Research,* vol. 19, June 1992, pp. 119–132.

[13]Robert Madrigal and Lynne R. Kattle, "Predicting Vacation Activity Preferences on the Basis of Value-System Segmentation," *Journal of Travel Research,* Winter 1994, pp. 22–28.

[14]VALS 2, Values of Lifestyles Program, SRI International.

2. *Status-oriented.* These consumers are heavily influenced by the actions, approval, and opinions of others.
3. *Action-oriented.* These consumers are guided by a desire for social or physical activity, variety, and risk taking.[15]

The Della Femina advertising agency in Pittsburgh used the VALS approach to update the image of Iron City beer. Iron City is a well-known brand in the Pittsburgh area, but it began to lose market share. People in the core markets were getting older and drinking less beer. Younger people were bypassing the brand. The Della Femina agency conducted some research to establish the image of Iron City beer and the VALS profile of beer drinkers.

The respondents pictured Iron City drinkers as "blue-collar steelworkers stopping at the local bar," Mather—director of research at the agency—says. They portrayed themselves as hard-working, but also fun-loving. Like the city, they were gaining economic strength and rejecting the heavy-industry image. Della Femina designed ads that link Iron City beer to the changing self-image of the target group. The ads mix images of Old Pittsburgh with images of the new vibrant city. . . . The soundtrack is the song "working in a coal mine" with the new lyrics—"working on a cold iron." The ads run on radio and TV programs and, in the first month of the campaign, sales of Iron City went up by 26 percent.[16]

Classifying Characteristics

Classifying characteristics represent geographic and/or demographic information. Geographic variables include region, state, county, and city size; urban versus rural communities; climate; and so on. Demographic variables include age, sex, income, education, race, religion, household size, nationality, and so forth. Geodemographic cluster systems such as Claritas's PRIZM, Strategic Mapping's ClusterPLUS 2000, NDS/Equifax's Micro Vision, and CACI's ACORN[17] combine geographic and demographic information to form segments. The clusters are based on the premise that "birds of a feather flock together." Take a look at your own neighborhood. The homes and cars are probably of similar size and value. A check inside the mailboxes and cupboards would probably reveal the same magazines and cereals.[18]

Although any one of the four types of data discussed above could be used as a basis for market-segment formation, for the most part consumer needs or consumer classifying characteristics (demographics) have been employed in segment development. Once the segments have been formed, they are profiled by use of behavioral and values/lifestyle information. If needs are used as the basis of segmentation, consumers are assigned to groups based on their similarity of response to desired end benefits. Once the groups have been formed, the other variables are utilized to estab-

---

[15]Ibid.

[16]Rebecca Piirto, "VALS, the Second Time," *American Demographics,* July 1991, p. 6.

[17]Susan Mitchell, "Birds of a Feather Flock Together," *American Demographics,* February 1995, pp. 40–48.

[18]Ibid.

lish an identity for the group. It would be important for a manufacturer of frozen foods to know that a group of people was more interested in the taste of the frozen entree than the calories. However, to be able to act on the segmentation scheme, the manager must be able to establish a profile for the segment. Are the people

- Young or old?
- Rich or poor?
- Male or female?
- Married or single?
- Educated with more or less than 16 years of school?

The manager should profile the segment with regard to the people's values and lifestyles. Can the segment be characterized as

- Patriotic—buy American?
- Slow to change?
- Seeking variety and excitement?
- Followers or leaders of fashion?
- Impressed by luxuries?

These profiling variables allow the manager to develop a specific strategy for the segment. Once the requirements of the segment have been identified, the product providing the greatest value at a profit can be established. The profiling variables help the manager develop the best message and decide which media should deliver the message. The segment is therefore targeted with a marketing strategy designed specifically for that segment. It is important to know what the segment wants but, in order to target the segment, we must be able to establish a profile.

Table 4-7 outlines the approach taken in a market-segmentation study conducted for the Electric Power and Research Institute (EPRI).[19] The study identified the nine different needs-based segments described in Table 4-8. The segment names are developed by the researchers to illustrate the needs desired by each segment. Figure 4-2 on page 88 shows the differences in response to needs and classifying characteristics for two of the nine segments. Notice that for the "dependents" segment only three needs are greater than neutral: backup generation, flexible billing, and customized service. And, when compared to the "proactives," a significant portion of participants are single-location companies. This information can be used to form product offerings targeted to a specific group.

EVALUATE THE MARKET SEGMENTS

The results of a market-segmentation study are evaluated (see Figure 4-1) against five criteria: uniqueness, responsiveness, actionability, stability, and profitability.

---

[19]John Berrigan and Carl Finkbeiner, *Segmentation Marketing: New Methods for Capturing Business Markets,* Harper Business, New York, 1992.

TABLE 4-7	**SEGMENTING THE ELECTRIC UTILITY MARKET**

EXPLORATORY ANALYSIS

A. One-on-one interviews

Thirty business executives that had just decided whether to purchase new electrical equipment were interviewed. The in-depth interviews uncovered three common influences.

- Senior level
- Executive/staff level
- Energy managers

B. Focus groups

Following the one-on-one interviews, focus groups were used to develop lists of needs within each category.

C. Pilot studies

Two pilot studies were used to filter and refine the needs within each category.

SURVEY

A national survey was completed using a representative sample of commercial establishments throughout the United States.

TABLE 4-8	**NEEDS PROFILES OF SEGMENTS**

Proactives	Actively managed, centralized price competitors who adopt new technologies, supervise energy use, and seek supportive utility relationships
Besieged	Day-to-day managers with low-energy costs who are driven largely by near-term cash concerns
Survivors	Investors in new technologies who strive to improve cash flow by competing on price and learning equipment
Innovators	Risk-taking leaders in quality who develop new products and services, embrace new technologies, and require clean and continuous power
Utilitarians	Multilocational businesses that manage for the long term, prefer to lease equipment, and seek to provide new and superior services
Dependents	Energy managers who require uninterrupted power, want customized services, and need flexibility in billing
Conservatives	Service-oriented, centralized cost controllers who seek clean power, rate stability, and supportive utility relationships
Status quos	Confident managers of mature product lines who have low-percentage energy costs
Self-reliants	Quality-oriented, day-to-day line managers whose businesses do not depend heavily on energy supply or services

Source: Berrigan, John, and Carl Finkbeiner, *Segmentation Marketing: New Methods for Capturing Business Marketing,* HarperCollins Publishers, 1992, p. 73.

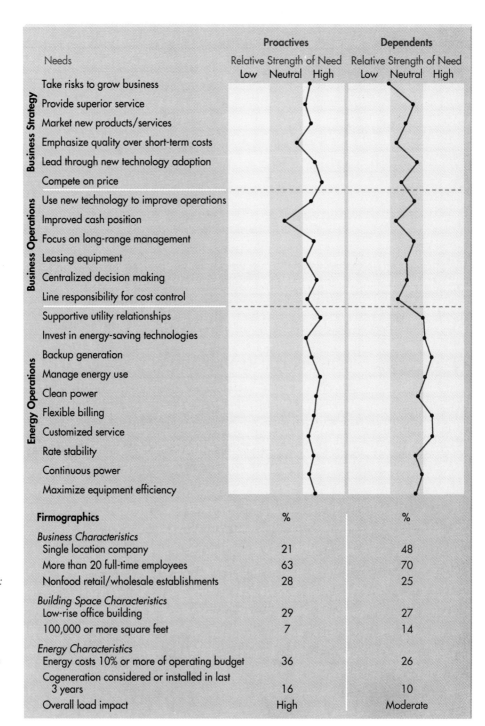

Needs	Proactives Relative Strength of Need	Dependents Relative Strength of Need
	Low — Neutral — High	Low — Neutral — High

Business Strategy
- Take risks to grow business
- Provide superior service
- Market new products/services
- Emphasize quality over short-term costs
- Lead through new technology adoption
- Compete on price

Business Operations
- Use new technology to improve operations
- Improved cash position
- Focus on long-range management
- Leasing equipment
- Centralized decision making
- Line responsibility for cost control

Energy Operations
- Supportive utility relationships
- Invest in energy-saving technologies
- Backup generation
- Manage energy use
- Clean power
- Flexible billing
- Customized service
- Rate stability
- Continuous power
- Maximize equipment efficiency

Firmographics	%	%
Business Characteristics		
Single location company	21	48
More than 20 full-time employees	63	70
Nonfood retail/wholesale establishments	28	25
Building Space Characteristics		
Low-rise office building	29	27
100,000 or more square feet	7	14
Energy Characteristics		
Energy costs 10% or more of operating budget	36	26
Cogeneration considered or installed in last 3 years	16	10
Overall load impact	High	Moderate

FIGURE 4-2

Segmentation marketing. (*Source:* John Berrigan and Carl Finkbeiner, "Segmentation Marketing," *New Methods for Capturing Business Marketing,* HarperCollins Publishers, 1992, p. 72.)

Uniqueness

Uniqueness refers to large between-group differences in the segments. Greater differences in a group's desired benefits render segments that are more unique. The best basis for forming market segments is the one that creates segments that are most unique. The objective of market segmentation is to achieve competitive power by translating the segmentation scheme into integrated strategic and tactical actions.[20] The more unique the segments are, the easier it is to translate the segmentation results into strategic and tactical actions.

Responsiveness

If we design specific strategic and tactical actions for a particular segment, then we would expect that segment to be more responsive to the tactical actions than another segment. Consider the demand for air travel between the United States and Europe. Figure 4-3 contains demand curves for two market segments. The dashed line represents the tactical action of a price change for the segments. Notice that there is little response to a price change in segment A, whereas a significant response to a change in price exists for segment B. These types of responses might be expected for business versus pleasure travelers. The business travelers are not very responsive to a price change, whereas the pleasure travelers are very responsive to a price change. A more precise discussion of price sensitivity is presented in Chapter 9.

Actionability

Actionability is the extent to which the marketing manager can take action on the results of the segmentation analysis. In some cases, segments are formed based on needs, and these needs-based segments are unique; however, no relationship(s) among the needs segments and the other segmentation variables—values/lifestyles, purchase

FIGURE 4-3

Price segments.

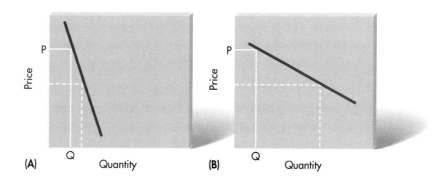

(A)   (B)

[20]Ibid.

behavior, or classifying characteristics—can be formed. Therefore, the marketing manager cannot act on the results produced by the segmentation study. One approach to making the segmentation results more actionable is to simultaneously include classifying characteristics and the other measures. The segments are formed by using both needs and classifying characteristics and, therefore, are as predictive as possible in terms of the behavioral criteria.[21]

Stability

Managers hope that the segments formed are stable over time with respect to desired end benefits and classification factors. It is not necessary that the same people remain in the segment, but people with needs identified by the segment should have the same classification characteristics as the segment. Or, alternatively, people with the same classification characteristics should have the same needs. For example, consider a strategy aimed at a segment of people with children under the age of 5. People who are in the segment now will move out of the segment as their children grow up. They will move into another segment and, if the segments are stable, will then have needs similar to those defined by the next segment in the family life cycle.

Profitability

In Chapter 6 we discuss procedures for analyzing profitability and productivity. These techniques need to be applied to the segments to ensure that they are consistent with the firm's mission and objectives.

SELECT STRATEGY

The last step in a segmentation study is to select a segmentation strategy. Management must first decide whether it wants to take a mass marketing approach, mass producing one product and promoting it to all buyers, or whether it wants to take a segmented approach. If the decision is to target segments, then management must decide whether to target all market segments or only certain market segments. For example, Porsche targets a market segment, whereas Chevrolet targets multiple-market segments. The decision will rely on the number, size, and profitability of the market segments identified in the evaluation stage of the market-segmentation study.

The ultimate segmentation strategy would be to treat each customer as a segment. The use of computer databases is increasing the ability of marketers to tailor their promotion and marketing strategies to individual customers or households. They can send the marketing message directly to the designated households.

[21]W. Fred Van Raaij and Theo M. M. Verhallou, "Domain-Specific Market Segmentation," *European Journal of Marketing,* vol. 26, Nov. 10, 1994, pp. 49–66.

Database Segmentation

It is Valentine's Day and you receive a box of chocolates as a gift, not from a close friend but from the CEO of Talbots, the upscale ladies' apparel, accessories, and shoes retailer. Talbots, through its credit cards, matches data concerning the time of sale, the purchased item, and the size of the order with the name and address of the customer.[22] Dennis Lambert of Tinder Box Tobacco-and-Collectible shops used his database to identify 600 cigar smokers. He sent a postcard to each of these customers to notify them of a shipment he had just received from the Dominican Republic and to explain the characteristics of the West Indian tobacco. Approximately 20 percent of the customers responded with purchases from $3 for one cigar to $75 for a box. Some of the largest consumer packaged-goods marketers, such as Ralston Purina, R. J. Reynolds, Quaker Oats, Gerber, Philip Morris, and Dow Brands, are committed to database marketing. Corporate clubs have risen from 130 in 1992 to 167 in 1994.[23]

Retailers are using point-of-sale (POS) data to target individual households. Vons, a California-based grocery chain, combined check-cashing cards and its own Vons club card to link purchases electronically from its 335 stores to individual households. Its central database can sort purchase history at the household level and by store, department, category, brand, or UPC (Universal Product Code). Vons uses its database to customize the mailing of coupons to households.[24]

Manufacturers such as Quaker Oats see database marketing as the means to treat the household as a segment. Household marketing involves programs where multiple brands are assembled to meet the needs of a single family.[25] Quaker built its own targeted coupon delivery system, Quaker Direct. The program began with the distribution of questionnaires to 50 million households; 18 million households responded to the survey. Quaker used its database to tailor the distribution of coupons. For example, if you do not have a dog, you don't get a coupon for dog food. Quaker abandoned its system in 1991. Quaker did not offer any explanation, but the speculation is that the costs of paper delivery were too high. APT (Advanced Promotion Technologies) attacked the cost problem by using electronic display and receipt of information. Members of the APT *Vision 1000 System* are provided with a smart card that is the size and shape of a credit card. The smart card monitors purchases and records points for items purchased. The points can be redeemed for prizes. The information on the smart card can be used to tailor coupons to individual buyers.[26]

---

[22]"Talbots' Database Pampers Customers," *The Concept, Discount Store News,* May 15, 1995, pp. 55–56.

[23]*Using Databases to Seek Out the (Brand) Loyal Shoppers,* Promo/Progressive Grocer Special Report, February 1995, p. 10.

[24]*How Vons Makes It Work,* Promo/Progressive Grocer Special Report, October 1994, p. 558.

[25]John Deighton, Don Peppers, and Martha Rogers, "Consumer Transaction Databases: Present Status and Prospects," in *The Marketing Information Revolution,* eds. Robert Blatburg, Rashi Glazer, and John Little, Harvard Business Press, Boston, 1994, pp. 58–79.

[26]Ibid.

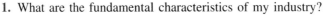

EXAMINING COMPETITIVE MARKET FORCES

Competitive intelligence involves the collection and analysis of data to establish the relationship of the firm to its competitors and business environment. For example, the threat of deregulation in the electric utility industry motivated Duquesne Light Company to study the changing dynamics of the industry in order to position itself better should deregulation become a reality.[27] Competitive analysis focuses on five fundamental questions with emphasis on the first three.[28]

1. What are the fundamental characteristics of my industry?
2. Who are my competitors?
3. What are the current positions of my competitors?
4. What moves are my competitors most likely to make?
5. What moves can we make to achieve a sustainable competitive advantage?

A market-profile analysis is a useful approach to the first question. Perceptual mapping and product positioning techniques can be used to answer the second and third questions.

Creating a Market Profile

A market profile should include sections dealing with industry characteristics and competitor profiles.

INDUSTRY CHARACTERISTICS

To assess the forces that create the competitive environment within an industry, marketing managers need information relating to[29]

- Size and growth rate of the industry
- Substitute products
- Suppliers to the industry
- Principal customers
- Manufacturing and distribution
- Social and economic conditions affecting the industry
- Barriers to entry

The two most heavily used sources for collecting competitive information are trade journals and external databases.[30] IntelliSeek is a CD-ROM database developed by

---

[27]John E. Prescott and Jefrey S. Allenby, "The Role of Competitive Intelligence in Maintaining Strategic Leadership in High-Technology Settings," *Advances in Global High-Technology Management,* vol. 4, part A, 1994, pp. 193–215.

[28]John E. Prescott, "The Evolution of Competitive Intelligence," in *Rethinking Strategic Management,* ed. D. E. Hussey, Wiley, New York, 1995, chap. 3.

[29]Richard E. Combs and John D. Moorhead, "Industry Analysis and Issue Studies," in *The Competitive Intelligence Handbook,* Scarecrow Press: Metuchen, N.J., 1992, pp. 145–149.

[30]John E. Prescott and Gaurab Bhardwaj, "Competitive Intelligence Practices: A Survey," *Competitive Intelligence Review,* vol. 6, 1995, p. 6.

Information Access Company that covers tens of thousands of companies in forty major industries. IntelliSeek provides industry information such as company events, new products, industry trends, new technologies, market size, market shares, and trade opportunities.[31] An excellent reference to sources of industry data is the new book by Leonard Fuld, *The New Competitor Intelligence.*[32]

COMPETITOR PROFILES

One way to summarize the results of a competitor profile is through a competitor strength grid. Figure 4-4 presents a competitor strength grid for the gourmet frozen-food market. The relevant skills and resources in the grid are listed in approximate order of importance. Then the major competitors are positioned on each dimension. Based on this grid, Stouffer's Lean Cuisine would appear to hold the greatest overall position of strength.

In some cases, a strengths, weaknesses, opportunities, and threats (SWOT) analysis of the competitors is also conducted. The objective is to determine where the competitors stand relative to the firm. Table 4-9 shows the results of SWOT analysis for a company in the lawn mower business.[33]

Perceptual Mapping

Perceptual mapping methods can be used to address the second and third questions in competitive analysis: (2) Who are my competitors? and (3) What are the current positions of my competitors? The competitive environment is not defined by the firm

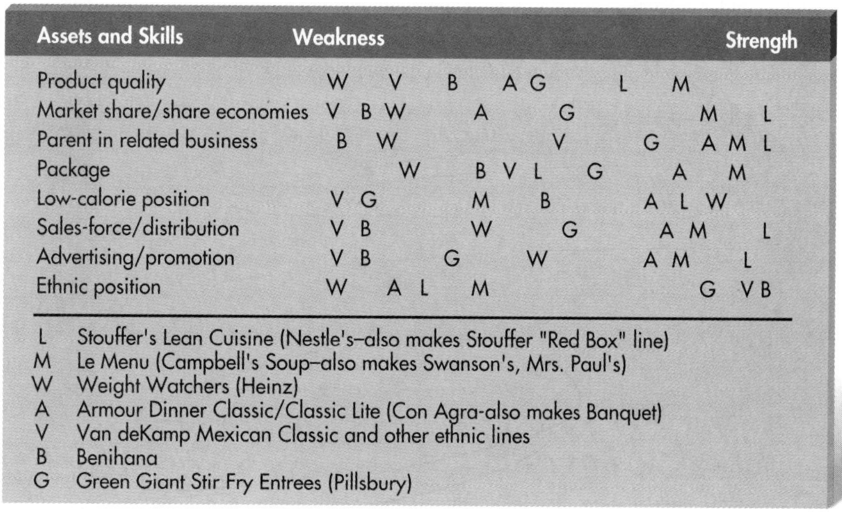

FIGURE 4-4

A competitor strength grid. (*Source:* David Aaker, *Strategic Market Management,* 2d ed., Wiley, New York, 1988, p. 86.)

Assets and Skills	Weakness					Strength
Product quality	W V	B	A G		L	M
Market share/share economies	V B W		A	G		M L
Parent in related business	B	W		V	G	A M L
Package		W	B V L	G		A M
Low-calorie position	V G		M	B		A L W
Sales-force/distribution	V B		W	G		A M L
Advertising/promotion	V B		G	W		A M L
Ethnic position	W	A L	M			G V B

L   Stouffer's Lean Cuisine (Nestle's—also makes Stouffer "Red Box" line)
M   Le Menu (Campbell's Soup—also makes Swanson's, Mrs. Paul's)
W   Weight Watchers (Heinz)
A   Armour Dinner Classic/Classic Lite (Con Agra—also makes Banquet)
V   Van deKamp Mexican Classic and other ethnic lines
B   Benihana
G   Green Giant Stir Fry Entrees (Pillsbury)

[31]"Information Access Company Introduces IntelliSeek," *Information Today,* June 1995, p. 31.

[32]Leonard M. Fuld, *The New Competitor Intelligence,* Wiley, New York, 1995.

[33]Ibid.

TABLE 4-9

SWOT LAWN MOWER DATA

STRENGTHS	RATINGS	DATA	SOURCES
Distribution	A	Lawnsavers acquired four independent lawn equipment wholesalers/servicers in Northern California and two in the southern part of the state.	*San Francisco Chronicle*
Sales	B	Rumors of Lawnsavers' acquisition of Southeastern U.S. distributors.	Green Acres sales manager
	A	Lawnsavers has hired a key salesperson to go after the home center market.	
Management	A	New management team may prove capable of breaking into the home center and other mass markets.	West Coast sales manager
	B	New management team was assembled from senior executives of very successful Fortune 500 companies.	*OPEI Newsletter*
Technology	B	Possibility that Lawnsavers is developing a new, revolutionary, cordless electric mower. Such mowers have failed in the past for lack of cutting power.	Vendor
Capacity	A	The new plant can produce approximately 2000 mowers a day, operating three shifts (or 500,000 mowers per year). This will certainly give them mass-market capability.	Town filings; engineering firm

WEAKNESSES	RATINGS	DATA	SOURCES
Management	C	Old management was recently fired and replaced by new, young management team, possibly inexperienced.	*OPEI Newsletter*
	A	Lawnsavers' owner and CEO is known as a tinkerer and will delay new-product releases until he is satisfied they are free of bugs.	Former employee
Technology	B	This new battery technology is likely to create many manufacturing and service headaches. Many feel that the 4- to 6-month launch date is very optimistic. Unlikely that the Lawnsavers group can bring down costs to develop new technology to an acceptable level for Green Acres profitability guidelines.	Green Acres manufacturing manager
	B	The battery technology was licensed to Green Acres from a Swiss R&D firm for $2 million.	
Costs	A	The new automated factory for building the Go-N-Mow cost $5.2 million, not including soft costs such as parts inventory and training. Soft costs are estimated at $1.2 million. Total = $6.4 million, a relatively large investment for this size firm. This will ikely saddle the company with considerable debt for such a risky venture.	Local newspaper, suppliers
Profitability	A	Gross margin for the new mowers is expected to be only $13 per mower. Parts cost is about $67; labor, about $9; technology license fee, about $5; shipping, $2.	UCC filings, suppliers, newspaper articles

(continued)

WEAKNESSES	RATINGS	DATA	SOURCES
Profitability	A	Cash flow appeared to be positive at a far lower production level than was profitable, indicating that Lawnsavers could hold on for a long time even if not fiscally profitable—as long as it could throw off enough cash to keep operations going and allow it to achieve its apparent goal of expanding its distributor network and penetrating the home center market.	Financial analysis of sources, filings, and interviews with Green Acres management

OPPORTUNITIES	RATINGS	DATA	SOURCES
Customers	A	The fastest growing outlets for lawn mowers have been the home centers.	Trade association
Competitors	A	Other competitors, such as TBL, have already offered less-than-perfect cordless mowers, but are working on newer, more effective models with longer battery life between charges.	Supplier
Trends	B	According to industry studies, all appliances, including lawn mowers, are moving toward smaller, lighter, easier-to-use devices. Overall battery technology, according to the experts, is close to achieving a number of commercial breakthroughs.	Trade magazine

THREATS	RATINGS	DATA	SOURCES
Customers	A	Retailers, such as Wal-Mart, are going to continue to squeeze the whole goods companies, such as Green Acres and Lawnsavers, on price. Margins for most Lawnsavers products will shrink over next 5 years.	Store buyers, magazines, Green Acres salespeople

A Highly important.
B Somewhat interesting.
C Interesting but not necessarily useful.

Source: Fuld, Leonard M., *The New Competitor Intelligence,* John Wiley & Sons (1995).

or its competitors; the competitive environment is defined by the customer. A competitor can be defined as anyone perceived by the customer to offer a similar product/service capable of satisfying a particular need. Product positioning is a procedure that allows marketing managers to determine which brands consumers perceive as similar to theirs. The more similar the brands are in the consumers' minds, the stronger the competition among the brands.

Creating Perceptual Spaces

Two important attributes of an adhesive bandage concern how well it sticks and whether it will irritate the skin. To assess the perceived similarity among four brands of adhesive bandages (Beiersdorf, Curad, Sheerstrip, and Zipstrip), a sample from the

| TABLE 4-10 | HYPOTHETICAL BRAND RATINGS |

	ATTRIBUTE	
	STICK	NONIRRITATION
Beiersdorf	7	1
Curad	7	7
Sheerstrip	6	6
Zipstrip	1	7

target market would be asked to rate each brand on each of the two attributes on a scale from 1 to 7 with 1 being a poor rating and 7 a good rating. Table 4-10 presents hypothetical ratings for the four brands on the two attributes.

The degree of similarity among brands can be measured by the perceived distance between the brands. The distance between any two brands is related to how similar they are rated on the attributes. A common measure of perceived distance is obtained by squaring the difference in perceived ratings for the two brands for each of the attributes and summing these squared distances. For example, the distance between Beiersdorf and Curad is: $(7 - 7)^2 + (1 - 7)^2$ or 36. The distance between each of the other objects is shown in Table 4-11. The goal of perceptual mapping is to place these brands in a space so that the distances are preserved. The perceptual map based on the ratings in Table 4-10 is displayed in Figure 4-5.

The origin is set at the midpoint of each scale. Therefore, as you move to the right in the perceptual space, the brand is perceived as having greater sticking ability. As you move toward the top of the space, the brand is perceived as less irritating to the skin. Notice that Curad and Sheerstrip are located close together in the space. This is because their ratings are very similar and, therefore, the calculated distance between the two is small. If the map is to be an accurate representation of the brand perceptions, these two brands must locate near each other in the space. If two brands had identical ratings, their distance would be zero and they would overlap each other on the perceptual map. To the extent that the brands are dissimilar, they separate in the

| TABLE 4-11 | PERCEIVED DISTANCES |

	BEIERSDORF	CURAD	SHEERSTRIP	ZIPSTRIP
Beiersdorf				
Curad	36			
Sheerstrip	26	2		
Zipstrip	72	36	26	

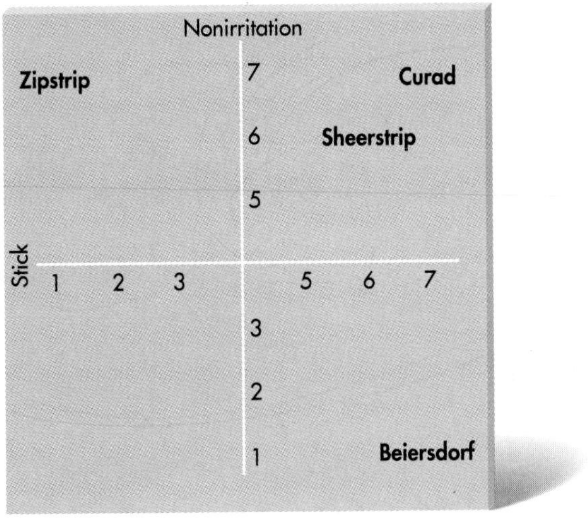

FIGURE 4-5

Perceptual map derived from hypothetical brand ratings.

space. Consequently, the closer they are in the perceptual space, the greater their perceived similarity and, therefore, the greater the competition between the two.

The example described above measured only two attributes and, therefore, the perceptual map shown in Figure 4-5 could preserve the distances (see Table 4-11) between the objects. In fact, they are identical. However, most commercial applications of perceptual mapping would most likely ask consumers to rate brands on more than two attributes.

Table 4-12 provides ratings for restaurants from a sample of business executives for eight attributes considered to be important in the selection of a restaurant for lunch. This is still a modest example; however, assessing the similarities among restaurants is more difficult because now there are eight rather than two attributes. The perceptual map for the four restaurants is displayed in Figure 4-6. Restaurants

TABLE 4-12   **MEAN ATTRIBUTE RATINGS**

	RUSTY SCUPPER	DAVE'S	HILL TOP	WEST VIEW CAFE
High quality	4.91	5.44	3.09	4.54
Low prices	4.04	2.85	5.53	2.94
Pleasant atmosphere	5.12	5.43	3.54	4.46
Large servings	3.75	3.94	4.70	4.09
Wide selection	4.25	3.97	3.93	3.94
Fast service	5.03	3.16	5.04	3.70
Quiet	4.60	5.47	2.37	4.24
Easy to get to	5.07	4.63	1.88	4.94

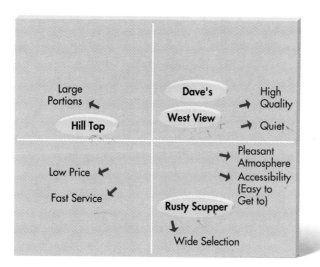

FIGURE 4-6
Perceptual map.

located to the right of the origin appear to contain more of such attributes as quality, quiet, pleasant atmosphere, and accessibility (easy to get to). Alternatively, restaurants located to the left of the horizontal axis are perceived as having larger servings and lower prices. The vertical axis is defined by wide selection; the perception of restaurants located below the origin is that they have wider selection. The results shown on the perceptual map indicate that the restaurants viewed as most similar are Dave's and West View. Hill Top is seen as a restaurant with large servings and low prices but is not high on quality, quiet, or pleasant atmosphere, and is not easy to get to. The Rusty Scupper is regarded as approximately similar to Dave's or West View with respect to quality, quiet, and atmosphere, but appears to offer wider selection.

Ideal Points

By looking at the perpetual map we can determine which brands are perceived as similar. However, we cannot determine where the ideal position is without some additional information. We could have had the respondents rate their ideal restaurant for lunch and locate the ideal restaurant in the perceptual space. Alternatively, market share can be used as a surrogate for the ideal. For example, if most people went to the Rusty Scupper for lunch, then the attributes defining its location in the perceptual space would be the attributes desired.

IDENTIFYING POTENTIAL TARGET MARKETS

The process of market analysis is the first step in designing a marketing strategy for a product or a line of related products. Specifically, a market analysis enables managers to identify potential target markets toward which the marketing effort might be focused. Figure 4-7 portrays the relationship among market analysis and the other sources and types of information that will influence the final selection of a target market and marketing strategy.

CONCLUSION

The greater the choices offered to consumers, the greater the competition among the suppliers offering the choices. Marketing strategy must consider the requirements of the market, the firm's position in the market, and the competitive environment. Market segmentation and product position are two methods used by marketing managers to understand the needs of the market so that they can position products/brands within the market to achieve competitive advantage. As summarized in Figure 4-8, organizations must assess the competitive environment in which they will operate and the competitive advantages (and disadvantages) they will have in a potential target market. Clearly, the process of segmenting and profiling market segments is a critical prerequisite to the selection of a marketing strategy, as the situation at Mobil Corporation suggests.

FIGURE 4-7

The process of identifying target markets.

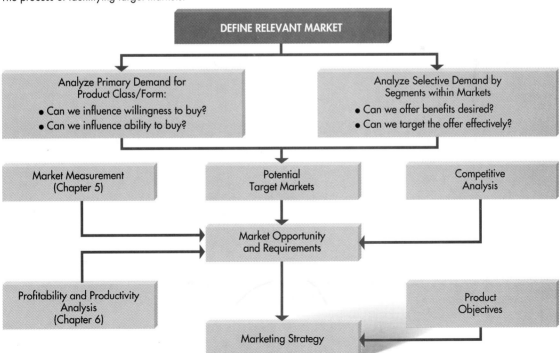

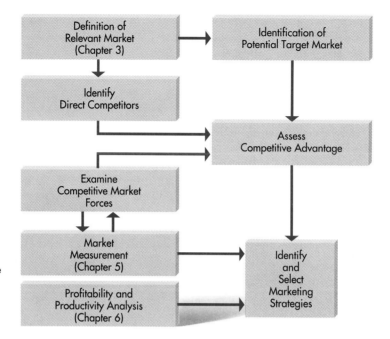

FIGURE 4-8

Steps in competitive analysis and their relationships to other aspects of the situation analysis.

MOBIL: SEGMENTING THE RETAIL GASOLINE MARKET

In the 1950s gasoline companies used giveaways such as glasses, steak knives, trading stamps, and so forth to try to lure customers away from their competitors. By contrast, the recent strategy has been to use low prices to encourage consumers to switch over. These low-price strategies have caused a number of vicious and unprofitable price wars. The emphasis by Mobil Oil is to dazzle the customer with product quality and customer service rather than with low prices. Market research conducted by Mobil identified five segments among gasoline buyers: the "Road Warriors," the "True Blues," the "Generation F3 Drivers," the "Homebodies," and the "Price Driven." The Price Shoppers, who account for about 20 percent of the population, spend on average $700 a year,

whereas the Road Warriors and True Blues, who together account for about 32 percent of the population, spend on average $1200 a year. These two groups of consumers are more interested in classier snacks, human contact, quick service, and attendants who recognize them than in lower prices. They want a competitive price, but this for them is not the most determining factor. For example, one motorist drove into a Mobil station in Orlando, Florida, during a rainstorm; she was not looking forward to pumping her gas in her work clothes in such weather. An attendant at the station offered her superior customer service; he pumped her gas, cleaned her windshield, and took care of the credit card transaction even though she was in a self-service line. The motorist said she would switch from Texaco to Mobil even though Mobil gasoline was two cents more per gallon.

1. Based on the description of the Mobil segmentation study, which approach to segment formation do you think the company used?
2. When evaluating the segmentation study, what criteria should Mobil be concerned with?

3. Since Mobil gasoline will now be about two cents higher than the competition, what can the company do about the Price Shopper segment?

Source: Allanna Sullivan, "Marketing: Mobil Bets Drivers Pick Cappuccino over Low Prices," *Wall Street Journal,* Jan. 30, 1995, B, p. 1.

QUESTIONS AND SITUATIONS FOR DISCUSSION

1. The first stage in market segmentation is to form and profile the segments. Four types of data are typically collected in market-segmentation studies: needs/end benefits, purchase behavior, values/lifestyles, and classifying characteristics. How do you decide which of the four should be used to form the segments and which should be used to profile the segments?

2. On the trip home from a divisional meeting the division manager and you were discussing the merits of conducting a market-segmentation study. During the conversation she asks: Did you understand what the consultant was talking about when he said that the best way to create market segments is with conjoint data analysis? I would really appreciate a summary of conjoint data analysis outlining what it is, how it is used, and why it is so useful for market segmentation. If you could, please give me this summary in the morning. What information would you provide for the division manager's consideration in the morning?

3. The packaged-soup market, although in the mature stage in the United States, is a growing market in the United Kingdom. ACM is a soup company interested in exporting to the United Kingdom. It commissioned a marketing research study to assess (1) the preferences of consumers in the United Kingdom for four characteristics of packaged soup: price, flavor, cooking time, and salt content; and (2) whether the preferences varied for England, Scotland, and Wales. Because of limited shelf space and a lack of relationship with distributors, only one variant could be offered in each market. On page 102 are the results of a conjoint study for each of the three markets. The values represent the part-worth utilities; that is, how much value is associated with each level of the four attributes. In addition, the costs associated with the levels of the attributes are provided. If only one variant were marketed in all three countries, a savings of 10 percent would be realized because of economies of scale. What strategy, mass marketing, or segment marketing would you recommend?

ATTRIBUTE	LEVEL	COST	PART-WORTH UTILITIES		
			ENGLAND	SCOTLAND	WALES
Flavor	Chicken	10 p	.07	.40	.20
	Beef	8 p	.90	.40	.40
	Vegetable	3 p	.03	.20	.40
Cooking time	3 min	15 p	.60	.45	.20
	5 min	10 p	.30	.35	.35
	10 min	0 p	.10	.20	.45
Salt content	None	0 p	.02	.03	.03
	Moderate	1 p	.68	.57	.37
	High	3 p	.30	.40	.60
Price	50 p		.50	.45	.75
	60 p		.40	.40	.20
	70 p		.10	.15	.05

4. In a report to the division manager, with a copy sent to the marketing research department, the brand manager commented that the results of the market-segmentation study were interesting but not actionable. What does the brand manager mean? What would you suggest to make the results actionable?

5. What is the difference between brand marketing and household marketing?

6. The manager of a quick-curing cement company wanted advice regarding long-range planning and strategy formulation. The product is composed of one-third cement, one-third sand, and one-third small stones. The sand and stone are purchased locally. The cement is purchased from one of two possible suppliers in Georgia. Currently, there are five brands in the industry. All companies could increase their sales and distribution by 100 percent with no problem if demand permitted. Three large home centers, like Lowes or Home Depot, represent 85 percent of the market. What recommendations would you make to help the manager become more competitive in the market?

7. The position of each brand in a perceptual space on a product positioning map is a function of the number and degree of determinant attributes the brand has as perceived by the relevant market. Comment.

8. How can you determine the ideal position on a product positioning map?

9. Perceptual maps or product positioning maps may be helpful for products offering intangible attributes; however, perceptual mapping is not very useful in the automotive industry because most of the characteristics such as braking ability, gas mileage, acceleration, warranty, durability, and so forth, are tangible and defined for the consumer. Comment.

10. A sample of 1000 people from Western Europe who had taken a vacation in a U.S. city in the last 3 years were asked to compare five cities for nine attributes. The cities and attributes are listed on page 103. You have been hired by the city of San Antonio to recommend strategies to increase foreign tourism. Use the attached perceptual map (Figure 4-9) and abstract data to formulate your recommendations.

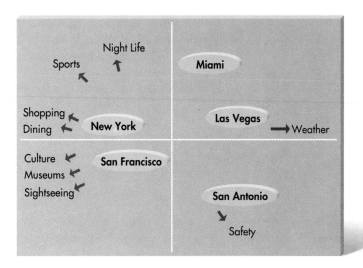

FIGURE 4-9
Perceptual map.

CITY	ATTRIBUTE
Las Vegas	Dining
New York	Night life
San Francisco	Safety
Miami	Culture
San Antonio	Sightseeing
	Shopping
	Weather
	Museums
	Sporting events

CITY	POPULATION	PER CAPITA INCOME	MEDIAN INCOME	FOREIGN TOURISTS
Las Vegas	317,900	$15,997	$34,508	8,756
Miami	362,800	10,410	19,177	2,620
New York	7,386,468	17,453	35,939	17,411
San Antonio	1,134,719	12,604	28,329	840
San Francisco	736,600	20,104	37,125	9,375

SUGGESTED ADDITIONAL READINGS

Bucklin, Randolph E., Sunil Gupta, and Han Sangman, "A Brand's Eye View of Response Segmentation in Consumer Brand Choice Behavior," *Journal of Marketing Research,* vol. 32, February 1995, pp. 66–74.

Cheron, Emmanuel J., and Elko J. Kleinschmidt, "A Review of Industrial Market Segmentation Research and a Proposal for an Integrated Segmentation Framework," *International Journal of Research in Marketing,* vol. 2, no. 2, 1985, pp. 101–115.

Hlavacek, James D., and B. Charles Ames, "Segmenting Industrial and High-Tech Markets," *Journal of Business Strategy,* vol. 17, Fall 1986, pp. 39–50.

Plank, Richard E., "A Critical Review of Industrial Market Segmentation," *Industrial Marketing Management,* vol. 14, May 1985, pp. 79–91.

Prescott, John E., "The Evolution of Competitive Intelligence," *Rethinking Strategic Management,* Wiley, New York, 1995, pp. 71–90.

Prescott, John E., and John H. Grant, "A Manager's Guide for Evaluating Competitive Analysis Techniques," *Interfaces,* vol. 18, no. 3, May–June 1988, pp. 10–22.

Wind, Yoram, "Issues and Advances in Segmentation Research," *Journal of Marketing Research,* vol. 15, August 1978, pp. 153–165.

Wyner, Gordon A., "Segmentation Analysis, Then and Now," *Journal of Marketing Research,* vol. 7, Winter 1995, pp. 40–41.

CHAPTER 5

MARKET MEASUREMENT

OVERVIEW

In Chapters 3 and 4, we discussed some fundamental steps managers should take when analyzing buyers and competitors within markets in order to understand the underlying processes influencing primary and selective demand. Chapter 5 also focuses on primary and selective demand; however, in this chapter our concern is with measuring primary or selective market demand to determine various opportunities within it.

Market measurements are critically important to a number of management decisions. Top management must be aware of the size and rate of growth of markets to shape corporate strategies. Middle-management decisions regarding marketing strategies, programs, and budgets for individual products cannot be made effectively without some estimate of expected levels of industry and company sales. Additionally, to evaluate the performance of a company, a product, a sales territory, or a distributor, some benchmark (such as a sales goal or quota) must be established. Both top management and middle managers will use benchmarks that are based on some estimate of market potential.

Managers need to understand the procedures commonly used to gather and estimate market measurements. Before implementing market measurements, managers should be familiar with the limitations of the measurements and the potential sources of error or bias inherent in them. Market measurements are estimates, and few are so reliable that managers can simply accept a single number as perfectly accurate. By understanding the assumptions used to develop any measure, managers can better evaluate the degree to which such measures are optimistic or pessimistic and the reliability of the measures.

In this chapter, we introduce procedures for measuring absolute market potential (for example, long-distance telephone usage in the United States per month) and relative market potential (long-distance usage per month for the six New England states as a percentage of the United States). We also discuss the methods most commonly used to create sales forecasts. Sales forecasting is an element critical to the formation of marketing plans: based on sales forecasts, budgets, production levels, sales quotas, and so forth, are set. The closer the forecast is to the actual sales level, the more efficient the entire marketing process.

Basic Types of Market Measurements

The market measurements most often requested by managers include

1. *Actual sales.* Managers are concerned with the amount of sales for their products (company demand) and the sales for all the other companies in the market (industry sales).
2. *Sales forecasts.* Industry sales forecasts indicate the level of sales expected to be achieved by all firms selling to a defined market in a defined period of time. A statement such as "Automobile sales in the United States between the years 2000 and 2005 are expected to be 100 million units" is an industry sales forecast. Similarly, company (or product-line or brand) sales forecasts indicate the expected level of sales that will be met by an individual supplier.
3. *Market potential.* The upper limit of demand for a product within a defined period of time is called *market potential.* The maximum sales opportunity that can be achieved by all sellers at the present time is called *current market potential.* The maximum sales that can be achieved during some future period of time is *future market potential.*

Figure 5-1 portrays the relationships among company sales, industry sales, and market potential measurements. As the figure suggests, company sales will generally be lower than industry sales and industry sales will usually be below market potential. (The only exception to this rule is a monopoly. If a firm has no competitors, company sales will equal industry sales.) The ratio of company sales to industry sales is the firm's market share.

Normally, managers should be concerned with the rate of growth in the different measurements over time. If the rate in any of the three measures—market potential, industry sales, or company sales—changes, the gaps will increase or decrease. Changes in the sizes of the gaps have strategic implications.

FIGURE 5-1

Basic kinds of market measurements.

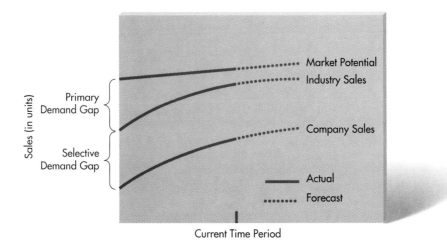

Changes in market potential are usually the result of either more users or current users purchasing more often. Market potential can change because changes in demographic factors cause more users to enter the market. Consider the baby boomers, the oldest of which turned 50 in 1995. This cohort of consumers has affected market potential for many United States industries in the last 50 years and is now creating large sources of demand for industries and companies catering to the mature market. The permanent resident population of Florida is projected to increase from 14.2 million in 1995 to 15.6 million in 2005. People aged 55 to 64 are expected to increase by 54.6 percent.[1] This increase will certainly change the market potential for many products and services.

Industry sales may change over time for several reasons.

- Prices may decrease, improving potential customers' ability to buy.
- Industry marketing efforts (regarding product quality, advertising and selling expenditures, and extent of distribution) may become more extensive, so a greater number of potential customers fully perceive or obtain the product's benefits.
- Environmental factors (such as economic conditions or changing social values) may stimulate the willingness or ability to buy the product.

Pharmaceutical manufacturer Eli Lilly manufactures Prozac, the world's leading anti-depressant drug. When competitors Pfizer and Smith Kline Beecham launched similar so-called "serotonin" anti-depressant drugs, industry experts predicted total industry sales of serotonin drugs would rise. These expectations were based largely on the beliefs about the impact of having three firms aggressively marketing these products. Specifically, it was expected that the efforts of the firms' sales representatives would make more physicians aware of the symptoms of depression (thus decreasing the number of undiagnosed cases) as well as get more physicians to prescribe serotonin-based treatment. Further, as competition heated up, prices were expected to decline, thus making serotonin drugs more price competitive with traditional anti-depressants.[2]

Company sales may change over time for one of two reasons. First, industry sales may change because of a change in market potential. That is, primary demand changes; for example, if more people exercise, the market potential for sports beverages increases. Second, some firms may gain sales at the expense of competitors by offering and promoting superior combinations of benefits and, thus, increase their market share. In 1965, Robert Cade and others at the University of Florida invented a sports drink for athletes that they called Gatorade. Stokely Van Kamp purchased the rights to the drink and built it into a $50 million business. Quaker Oats purchased Stokely Van Kamp and, through aggressive promotion, increased sales of Gatorade to over a billion dollars in 1994.[3]

[1]Shannon Dortch, "Sunshine State Forecast," *American Demographics,* December 1995, p. 4.

[2]Thomas Burton, "Lilly's Controversial Prozac May Benefit from Marketing of Two New Competitors," *Wall Street Journal,* July 17, 1992, pp. B1–B2.

[3]"Can Coke and Pepsi Make Quaker Sweat?" *Fortune,* July 10, 1995, p. 20.

The most important strategic implications of these three measures can be isolated by comparing market potential to industry sales and by comparing industry sales to company sales. If a large difference exists between market potential and industry sales, then a large primary demand gap exists. This means that managers should examine the factors influencing primary demand (discussed in Chapter 3) to determine how industry sales may be increased. If a large difference exists between industry sales and company sales, then a selective demand gap exists. In such situations, managers should examine the buyers' choice processes to identify opportunities that will increase market share.

Defining What to Measure

Managers must clearly specify the relevant market in order to measure industry sales and market potential accurately. The relevant market must be defined in terms of product form, customer segments, and time. For example, a cereal manufacturer could explore market potential for

1. All cereals, or some variant, such as cold cereal (product form)
2. The mass market, or some segment, such as the Southwest or single households (customer segments)
3. The next quarter or the next year (time)

Such choices will affect what is measured and what is estimated.

In the remainder of this chapter, we will examine four basic kinds of market measurements: absolute market potential, relative market potential, industry sales forecasts, and company sales forecasts.

ABSOLUTE MARKET POTENTIAL

Absolute potential is an estimate of maximum potential demand, usually based on two factors: the number of potential users and the rate of purchase. For a given market, absolute potential indicates the total dollar or unit volume that could be sold. There are three kinds of decisions that generally rely on estimates of absolute market potential.

1. *Evaluating market opportunities.* In order to decide what market opportunities to pursue in the future, a firm will want to assess market potential. This is particularly true in the case of new-product-form or new-product-class markets. Consider, for example, the large resource commitments made by companies entering the market for products such as videotape recorders, personal computers, and industrial robots. These commitments could not have been economically justified if the companies had not been able to demonstrate a large potential demand. In the case of existing products, market opportunities can be examined more easily if the market

potential can be measured and compared with industry sales. If the market potential is significantly larger than industry sales, then all suppliers have an opportunity to increase their sales volume by pursuing policies (such as lower prices) to close the primary demand gap. However, if industry sales are already close to market potential, then a firm will know that the only avenue for sales growth is to improve its market share.

2. *Determining sales quotas and objectives.* Market potential is usually considered to establish reasonable objectives for the sales force and distributors. Potential demand in some sales territories may be growing so rapidly that sharp yearly increases in sales objectives are appropriate. However, other territories may be stagnant in the number of potential buyers and purchase rates. Consequently, a fair evaluation of sales-force and distributor performance should be based on the potential for sales in the market.

3. *Determining the number of retail outlets.* Firms that sell through retailers will generally have a desired number of retail distributors for a market of a given size. For instance, an automobile manufacturer may want to have one dealer for every 2000 units per month of market potential in order to assure adequate coverage of the market. Accordingly, the potential in a given retail market area will be a major input into these decisions.

Measuring Absolute Market Potential

There are essentially two components of absolute market potential: the number of possible users and the maximum rate of purchase. In some cases, managers can obtain estimates of absolute market potential by geographic area, industry type, household type, and so on, from trade associations or commercial research firms. However, it is more typical for managers to estimate at least one of these two components of market potential themselves.

ESTIMATING POTENTIAL IN CONSUMER MARKETS

When the characteristics of all potential buyers are known and readily measurable, the easiest way to estimate the number of buyers is to use published data. If potential buyers for consumer goods can be described in terms of basic demographic or locational factors (such as age, county, home ownership, or income), both government and private industry data sources can be employed. For example, the annual *Survey of Buying Power* (published by *Sales and Marketing Management* magazine) provides data on the size and distribution of the population by age group and income category for each county and for metropolitan areas within each county.

To estimate purchasing rates, managers usually use data obtained from trade associations, government, and commercial publications. Particularly in cases where they are estimating current market potential, managers may use the existing ratios of sales per household or sales per person. These kinds of ratios can usually be obtained directly from some secondary sources. The Conference Board, a New York–based, industry-supported organization, publishes a distribution of household expenditures on various product categories. Alternatively, if data on total industry sales are available, average demand per household (or per person) may be calculated by dividing total sales by the number of households.

Although a wide variety of sources of data are used in estimating market potential, the following example is typical of the approach used in estimating potential for consumer markets.

Mr. Bradford, the manager of a 148-store supermarket chain noticed an article about frozen pizza sales in *Frozen Food Age,* "Pizza's Rate of Growth Slows." The first half of 1995 witnessed a halt to the growth of frozen pizza sales. A study by Information Resources Inc. for the Frozen Pizza Institute indicated that pizza, relative to its sales and profits, is underspaced in the frozen-food section. The study also showed that the category experienced a sales increase when it was provided with feature and display activity. Retailers, when questioned, agreed that they shortchanged frozen pizza in terms of space allocation.

Mr. Bradford's supermarket sales for 1994 were $1.7 billion, with 84 percent coming from stores in Colorado and Arizona. Mr. Bradford wanted to update the space allocation and presentation of frozen pizza. He said he would begin with the state (Colorado or Arizona) having the most potential. Research had indicated that 40.5 percent of households purchased frozen pizza in the last 6 months.[4] The most recent population figures indicated that 3,470,000 people live in Colorado and 3,832,000 people live in Arizona. The market potential for the two areas could be estimated to be (.405 × 3,470,000) 1,405,350 households purchasing frozen pizza in Colorado and 1,551,960 households purchasing frozen pizza in Arizona. Based on this analysis, Mr. Bradford would choose to introduce the new program in Arizona. However, these figures are based on the total population. Mr. Bradford's supermarket chain had traditionally targeted the adult population of people from 18 to 54 years of age. Using this target population (18 to 54 years of age), the figures would be revised to 1,967,000 people in Arizona and 1,954,000 people in Colorado. As with most consumer products, however, frozen pizza is not purchased at the same rate by all household segments. Table 5-1 calculates the market potential for Colorado and Arizona, taking into account the different purchase rates for people of different age groups between 18 and 54. Notice, now, that the two states are quite similar and, in fact, the potential is greater in Colorado than in Arizona.

As the previous example suggests, if different buyer types are likely to vary extensively in their purchase rates, total market potential should be measured by summing the potentials for each group of customers. In addition to improving accuracy, this allows the manager to account more readily for the effects of projected demographic changes on future market-potential levels.

This example is typical of many market-potential estimates in that the current average rate of purchase is a good approximation for the maximum rate of purchase. Although this assumption will be valid in many cases, managers should examine the diagnostic questions on willingness and ability to buy (discussed in Chapter 3) to determine whether the current rate of purchase could be increased. For example, the actual rate of frozen pizza purchases may vary across markets because of the relative

---

[4]*Mediamark Research Meat and Prepared Meals Report,* Mediamark Research, Spring 1994, p. 161.

TABLE 5-1

ESTIMATING MARKET POTENTIAL FOR FROZEN PIZZA FOR ARIZONA AND COLORADO (IN THOUSANDS)

AGE GROUP	PERCENT PURCHASING FROZEN PIZZA	POPULATION		POTENTIAL PIZZA SALES	
		ARIZONA	COLORADO	ARIZONA	COLORADO
18–24	10.4	384	341	39.94	35.46
25–34	25.8	634	607	163.57	156.61
35–44	24.3	568	622	138.02	151.15
45–54	14.5	381	384	55.25	55.68
				396.78	398.90

Source: Mediamark Research Meat and Prepared Meals Report, Spring 1994, Mediamark Research, Inc., and Statistical Abstract of the U.S. 1993, U.S. Department of Commerce.

popularity of pizza. If secondary data were available on a statewide basis to adjust the national estimates, then the estimate of potential could be refined. Additionally, it may be possible to increase frozen pizza purchases if manufacturers offer lower prices, more variety, or innovative features. Thus, to the extent that the maximum rate of purchase can be realistically increased, managers should modify this rate to reflect more accurately the gap between actual usage rates and potential usage rates.

ESTIMATING POTENTIAL IN INDUSTRIAL MARKETS

Secondary data sources such as the U.S. Department of Commerce's *County Business Patterns* and the annual *Survey of Industrial Buying Power* are useful in projecting market potential for organizational markets. Each of these two sources is especially useful in identifying the number of buying organizations.

The secondary sources of data utilized to measure purchase rates are usually less useful in organizational markets than in consumer markets. There are two major reasons for this. First, manufacturers sell specialized product lines, but industry sales data are usually available only for broad product categories. A manufacturer of envelopes may not be able to measure industry envelope sales per customer because industry sales will be available only for the broader category "paper products." Second, buyer purchase rates usually vary substantially according to the size of the organization and from one industry to another. This is a point of particular concern if market potential is being estimated for a limited geographic area; that is, a local market may have a smaller number of buyers whose sizes and purchases rates vary widely. Some of these firms may buy much more than the national average sales per customer and some may buy much less than the average simply because of the size of the organization.

Because of the first problem—lack of specific industry sales data—estimates of purchase rates must often be made through primary marketing research. Because of the problem caused by the varying sizes of organizational buyers, managers usually attempt to weigh the potential of each prospective buyer in order to account for differences in size.

Two measures often used to account for size differences are the number of employees and the value of shipments, which measure the value of the production output of a specific industrial plant or facility. The value of shipments and the number of employees are usually closely correlated with the rate of purchase (at least within a given industry). Additionally, these measures are reported annually and are reported for the different industries classified through the Standard Industrial Classification code (SIC code). The SIC code, established by the U.S. Department of Commerce, classifies individual business establishments (such as stores or manufacturing plants) in each county into industry categories. Data on the number of employees and the value of shipments are then aggregated at the county level for each industry code. Government publications (such as *Census of Retailing, Census of Manufacturing, County Business Patterns,* and *U.S. Industrial Outlook*) and commercial publications rely on SIC codes to report such data along various geographic lines. Data are aggregated at what are called two-digit, three-digit, and four-digit levels, as indicated in Table 5-2.

To understand how these types of data can be used to estimate the potential in organizational markets, consider the following example.

Rockmorton Chemical Corporation is a manufacturer of various inks that are used in many types of printing operations. To establish sales quotas for his district, the Midwest sales manager wanted to first determine the market potential for his product line. His five salespeople were located in Pennsylvania, Ohio, Michigan, Indiana, and Illinois. Upon reviewing the sales history for the company, he believed the primary ink-using industries were SIC 2711 (newspapers), SIC 2721 (periodicals), SIC 2732 (book printing), and SIC 2741 (miscellaneous publishing). Close inspection of his sales records, combined with his knowledge of the industry, led him to conclude that the cost of printing ink comprises about 0.1 percent of the value of shipments for the ink-using industries. Basing his estimates on data from the Commerce Department, he calculated the value of shipments in each SIC group for each state as indicated in Table 5-3.

Many of the uses of market-potential information require that management obtain estimates to cover a number of future years. Estimating the number of potential users is

---

| TABLE 5-2 | SOME SIC CODES FOR APPAREL AND TEXTILE PRODUCTS MANUFACTURING |

CODE	INDUSTRY
23	Apparel and textile products
231	Men's and boys' suits, coats
232	Men's and boys' furnishings
2321	Men's and boys' shirts
233	Women's and misses' outerwear
2335	Dresses
2337	Coats and suits
234	Women's and children's undergarments

| TABLE 5-3 | ROCKMORTON CHEMICAL CORPORATION: ESTIMATING MARKET POTENTIAL |

ROCKMORTON CHEMICAL CORPORATION: ESTIMATING MARKET POTENTIAL

	VALUES OF SHIPMENTS (IN MILLIONS OF DOLLARS)				
SIC	ILLINOIS	INDIANA	MICHIGAN	OHIO	PENNSYLVANIA
2711	$1571	$549	$931	$1274	$1558
2721	1296	0	137	389	1280
2732	137	0	158	0	355
2741	573	114	404	250	235
Total	$3577	$663	$1630	$1913	$3428
× .001					

ESTIMATED POTENTIAL (IN MILLIONS)

$3.577	$0.663	$1.630	$1.913	$3.428

For the five-state area, the total value of all shipments was $11,211 million. When this total was multiplied by 0.1 percent, the estimated potential was calculated at $11,211,000.

not generally difficult in the case of consumer goods because projections regarding the number of households, age-group populations, and many other demographic factors are readily available from secondary sources.

In the case of industrial goods, the number of customers may change rather slowly. However, some buying industries may grow more rapidly than others. Further, geographic movements (such as the recent trend in some industries to shift to the Sunbelt) may change the distribution of potential among sales territories. Government publications (such as *Current Industrial Reports* and *U.S. Industrial Outlook*), trade association data, and commercial publications (such as *Predicasts*) are easily obtained and generally provide sufficient information to project the buying industry growth patterns in output and employment.

More difficult is the problem of estimating changes in purchase rates. As a practical matter, management generally assumes that these rates will remain stable. However, managers often project rate changes judgmentally—on the basis of sales-force opinions or recent trends in usage rates.

In the case of durable goods (such as appliances or industrial machines) the future market potential will also depend on the rate at which owners scrap a product because of wear or obsolescence. Managers can estimate scrappage rates either by examining the technical service life of a product or the historical long-term rate of voluntary scrappage. Some products must be scrapped because of technical failure; however, the time until scrappage (or resale) is often a function of economic conditions. For example, new-car lending rates, other economic conditions, or changes in automotive product design (leading to new features, greater efficiency, or improved capability) may influence the voluntary rate of replacement of a durable item. If historical data on scrappage rates can be calculated from a sample of users, managers can use actuarial methods to estimate the replacement potential for products of different ages.

TABLE 5-4

CALCULATING SURVIVAL RATES

YEAR PRODUCT WAS PURCHASED	AGE OF PRODUCT (YEARS)	UNITS SCRAPPED IN 1996 (PERCENT)	ANNUAL SURVIVAL RATE (PERCENT)	UNITS REMAINING AT END OF 1996 (PERCENT)
1992	4	1	99	99
1991	5	5	95	94
1990	6	10	90	85
1989	7	25	75	63
1988	8	50	50	32
1987	9	80	20	6
1986	10	100	0	0

To see how replacement potential for videocassette recorders might be estimated, consider the data in Tables 5-4 and 5-5. Assume that a VCR manufacturer is attempting to estimate replacement market potential for 1997 and is armed with past industry sales data plus data from a consumer survey of VCR owners who purchased their products between 1986 and 1996.

Table 5-4 shows the scrappage rates of VCRs purchased between 1986 and 1992. (Because none of the units bought between 1993 and 1996 had been scrapped as of the end of 1996, the data for those years is not relevant to the calculations of Table 5-4.) The table indicates that 1 percent of those who purchased VCRs in 1992 scrapped their 4-year-old VCRs during 1996. This means that 99 percent of the VCRs

TABLE 5-5

ESTIMATING REPLACEMENT POTENTIAL

YEAR PRODUCT WAS SOLD	INDUSTRY SALES (IN THOUSANDS)	LEFT AT START OF 1997 (PERCENT)	NUMBER LEFT AT START OF 1997 (IN THOUSANDS)	ANNUAL SCRAPPING RATE (PERCENT)	1997 REPLACEMENT POTENTIAL (IN THOUSANDS)
1993	10,300	100	10,300	1	103
1992	10,100	99	9,999	5	500
1991	9,800	94	9,212	10	921
1990	10,700	85	9,095	25	2,274
1989	11,700	63	7,371	50	3,686
1988	13,500	32	4,320	80	3,456
1987	12,000	6	720	100	720
					11,660

purchased in 1992 survived to the end of 1996. Of the VCRs purchased in 1991, 5 percent were scrapped in 1996. If we assume that the scrappage rate for 4-year-old VCRs remained the same, 1 percent of the VCRs purchased in 1991 would have been scrapped during 1995. So, of the original units sold in 1991, the percent surviving to the end of 1996 would be calculated as follows.

Percent of units remaining after 4 years	.99
$\times$ survival rate during 5th year	$\times$ .95
Percent of units remaining after 5 years	.94

Once the scrappage and survival rates are calculated, future replacement potential can be estimated as long as prior industry sales data are available. Table 5-5 demonstrates how this estimate could be developed for 1997. Because we have assumed that no units are scrapped until the fourth year, we begin with 1993 sales data. From Table 5-4, we know that 1 percent of 4-year-old units will be scrapped. So, of the units sold 4 years ago (in 1993), 1 percent will be scrapped during 1997. The VCRs sold in 1992 will be 5 years old in 1997. One percent of these were scrapped in 1996, and 5 percent of the remaining 9,999,000 units are expected to be scrapped in 1997. Total 1997 replacement potential (11,660,000) is calculated by adding the number of units expected to be scrapped from each age group.

RELATIVE MARKET POTENTIAL

Relative market potential is simply the percentage distribution of market potential among different portions of a market (such as geographic areas or customer groups). Measures of relative potential are employed to help management allocate certain resources efficiently. In particular, there are three major applications of relative market potential.

1. *Allocating promotion expenditures.* A national marketer will generally want to allocate the sales promotion and advertising budget among different markets on the basis of the relative importance of each market. For instance, the rate of purchase of room air conditioners or snow tires will vary dramatically among television markets of equal population. By knowing the percentage distribution of market potential among different television markets, management can allocate advertising expenditures in proportion to actual demand.
2. *Allocating salespeople among territories.* A manufacturer or wholesaler will want to assign salespeople in the most efficient manner. If one territory has twice the sales potential of another, it should probably receive twice as many salespeople.
3. *Locating facilities.* In order to minimize transportation costs and maximize the ability to deliver products quickly, most organizations will attempt to locate facilities

closer to markets of larger potential than to markets of lesser potential. Thus, in locating warehouses, production facilities, and district sales offices, the relative potential of the market being served is often a major input.

Measuring Relative Market Potential

When estimating relative potential, managers begin by identifying factors that are measurable and likely to be correlated with market potential. These measures, called corollary factors, can be used to represent market potential.

SINGLE-COROLLARY FACTOR APPROACHES

A manager in an industrial goods firm may know that market potential is directly related to a single, easily measured factor, such as the number of production workers in the industries to which it sells or the total production value of shipments made by such industries.

For example, Pitney Bowes's Business Systems Division makes mail-handling equipment such as postage meters for industrial and commercial customers. In seeking a method to determine the size of the sales force needed in each geographic area, the company found that a single factor—employment growth in the area—seemed to correlate well with sales. Employment growth results from the formation of new businesses and the expansion of existing businesses. These were the two factors that drove the need for new or additional mail-handling equipment. Also, employment statistics are frequently reported and easily available.

Other examples of the single-corollary factor approach might include the number of housing units (for appliances), the number of single-family dwelling units (for home-repair items), disposable-income levels (for financial services), the number of people over 50 (for AARP), average winter temperatures (for solar and other alternative heating), and so on. The goal of the single-corollary factor approach is to find a factor that can be easily obtained, such as demographics, and is related to sales. The relationship between the two variables can be used to predict potential.

MULTIPLE-COROLLARY FACTOR INDEXES

Managers can use more than one corollary factor in estimating relative market potential. In those cases, indexes will be developed to reflect the relative importance of the different factors.

For many frequently purchased consumer goods, a useful index is the Buying Power Index (BPI) provided by Sales and Marketing Management's *Survey of Industrial Buying Power.* A BPI is computed for each county to reflect the percentage of total United States buying power in that county. The index for a market is compiled by weighing three individual factors (each of which is reported separately in the survey) as follows:

$$BPI = .5 \times \text{market's percent of U.S. effective buying income}$$
$$+ .3 \times \text{market's percent of U.S. retail sales}$$
$$+ .2 \times \text{market's percent of U.S. population}$$

To illustrate one use of the BPI, consider the following example.

In 1994, a regional chain of department stores emphasizing middle-quality clothing and other "soft goods" began to look at several alternative new markets with an eye toward expanding the number of stores. Company officials knew that competition would have to be examined in each potential market, but before doing that, they wanted to know which markets had the greatest potential in the five-state market area the company currently served. On the basis of their knowledge of the size of the areas from which their stores drew, potential markets were defined in terms of the counties that would be included, and data were obtained from the *Survey of Buying Power* for each market. Results from four of the markets in the state of Iowa are portrayed in Table 5-6. On the basis of the BPI data, Des Moines was clearly the highest-potential market. Given these comparisons, the company was then able to concentrate its efforts on seeking out specific sites in those markets with the greater relative potential.

In practice, of course, management may also want to project population and buying power changes expected in the future in order to assess the long-run potential of each market.

The Buying Power Index provides marketing managers with standardized measurements of the relevant buying power for geographic areas. However, in some cases the BPI may be too general; the managers may want to define their markets more specifically. In this case, a customized BPI may be used. The manager would select a demographic component (population), an economic component (income), and a distributional component (retail sales) considered relevant to market potential for the product. These measures would then be substituted in the BPI index.[5]

TABLE 5-6

CALCULATION OF BUYING POWER INDEX

STATE	TOTAL POPULATION (THOUS.)	TOTAL EFFECTIVE BUYING INCOME ($000)	RETAIL SALES ($000)	BUYING POWER INDEX
IOWA				
Cedar Rapids-Waterloo & Dubuque	806.1	12,029,332	6,872,185	.3055
Davenport-Rock Island-Moline	775.4	11,318,654	6,289,714	.2860
Des Moines-Ames	938.5	14,835,623	8,363,034	.3705
Ottumwa-Kirksville	106.9	1,302,957	749,699	.0346
Sioux City	403.4	5,590,453	3,069,305	.1427

Source: Calculated from data in *Sales & Marketing Management,* October 28, 1994, p. 32.

[5]"How to Construct a Customer BPI," *Sales and Marketing Management,* Oct. 28, 1994, p. 9.

Targeting High-Potential Markets

In many cases, industry and company sales vary quite sharply across geographic territories. In some territories, per capita purchases of a product (such as powdered lemonade mix) may be very high compared to those in other territories. This suggests that the primary demand gap is somewhat larger in the area with low per capita sales. Similarly, brand-share differences often vary substantially across markets. Country Time lemonade may have a much larger selective demand gap in New Jersey than in Texas, for example.

Marketers frequently construct special indexes to portray these regionally based gaps. A category development index (or CDI) is a measure that helps identify territories in which primary demand gaps are relatively large or small. A brand development index (or BDI) is a measure that can be used to assess selective demand gaps across territories.[6] The process of developing these indexes is demonstrated in Table 5-7.

As Table 5-7 suggests, the same basic procedure is used to calculate a CDI or a BDI. Specifically for a CDI, within each territory the total sales for a product category (such as powdered lemonade) are divided by the number of households in that market. A BDI for Country Time would be calculated by dividing Country Time sales in that same market by the number of households.

Category and brand development indexes are useful as diagnostic tools to help managers identify the markets in which the largest primary demand or selective demand gap exists. For example, the hypothetical indexes in Table 5-8 would enable managers to spot four kinds of variations from average market performance.

- *High CDI/high BDI (Boston):* In these markets, both brand and category consumption are very high. There is little need for additional development activity.
- *High CDI/low BDI (Seattle):* The brand needs support if it is to grow. Distribution and promotional support are probably inadequate.

TABLE 5-7

CALCULATING A DEVELOPMENT INDEX

AREA	ANNUAL CASE SALES (CATEGORY OR BRAND)	÷	THOUSANDS OF HOUSEHOLDS	=	SALES PER 1000 HOUSEHOLDS	INDEX
Total	1,600,000		80,000		20	100
A	22,500		900		25	125
B	13,500		750		18	90
C	52,800		2,400		22	110

Total index = 100. Index for each territory is calculated as:

$$\text{Index} = \frac{\text{sales per 1000 households in territory}}{\text{sales per 1000 households total}} \times 100$$

[6] F. Beavin Ennis, *Marketing Norms for Product Managers,* Association of National Advertisers, New York, 1985, pp. 26–31.

TABLE 5-8 **TYPICAL CATEGORY/BRAND DEVELOPMENT INDEXES**

	CDI	BDI
Total U.S.	100	100
Eastern region		
Boston	144	239
New York	94	137
Baltimore	127	213
Southern region		
Atlanta	87	71
Memphis	74	58
Dallas	92	84
Central region		
Minneapolis	114	101
St. Louis	108	95
Denver	79	139
Western region		
Seattle	118	57
San Francisco	83	84
Los Angeles	73	70

Adapted from F. Beaven Ennis, *Marketing Norms for Product Managers,* Association of National Advertisers, New York, 1985, p. 27.

- *Low CDI/high BDI (Denver):* Opportunities appear to exist to expand primary demand if management can identify why some people are not using the product.
- *Low CDI/low BDI (Memphis):* Neither the brand nor the category has widespread acceptance in this market.

Internal Databases

In many industries, especially those characterized by intensive competition, market leaders are often most concerned with targeting high-potential opportunities within the existing customer base. Specifically, such firms are concerned with focusing marketing efforts on those customers who are likely to purchase in larger volumes or who are likely candidates to purchase additional products from the firm. Internal databases consist of information about the behavior of customers that has been systematically gathered during the course of prior business transactions. Table 5-9 provides a list of some typical data elements that might appear on a marketer's internal database.

Few industries have internal databases that are more useful than those of the financial services industry. Such firms not only have precise transaction histories, but they also obtain extensive additional information when customers apply for credit cards, loans, and so on. Armed with such data, banks could identify, for example, high-income customers who have only a checking account (and thus are good potential customers for certificates of deposit and other investment products). Additionally, the

TABLE 5-9	SOME TYPICAL DATA ELEMENTS IN INTERNAL DATABASES

- Customer identification
- Name and address
- Telephone number
- Dates of promotions to prospect/customer
- Responses to those promotions
- Date of first purchase, of subsequent purchases, of last purchase
- Frequency of purchases
- Item(s) purchased by product ID, category, or department
- Product usage information obtained from records of customer transactions
- Purchase amounts and average purchase amount
- Method of payment (check, cash, type of credit card, etc.)
- Personal information generated by transactions with the company (such as age, income, home value, marital status, ages of children, occupation, and automobile ownership)
- Product and/or purchase information (including reasons for purchase, competitive products considered or owned, intended use of product) obtained from questionnaires packaged with products, which buyers complete and return

Developed from Jack Bickert, *Adventures in Relevance Marketing,* 2d ed., Briefcase Books, Denver, 1990; Ernest Schell, "Lifetime Value of a Customer," *Marketing Insights,* Fall 1991, pp. 85–89; Stan Rapp and Thomas Collins, "The Great Turnaround: Selling to the Individual," *Adweek's Marketing Week,* Aug. 27, 1990, pp. 20–26.

efficiency with which such firms can use marketing resources is improved by the use of databases to identify high-potential targets. Whereas most direct mail solicitations generate responses of only 1 to 2 percent, bank marketers generally cite response rates that are five times larger, thanks to the effective targeting of promotional messages on special certificates of deposit or home equity loan products.[7]

A discussion of the use of internal databases for marketing directly to consumers is presented in Chapter 11.

SALES FORECASTING

Market-potential measures can be of significant value to managers, as the examples in this chapter have indicated. However, because market potential is related to industry and company sales, the usefulness of the market-potential estimates can be enhanced by comparisons with sales forecasts.

Sales forecasts are estimates of future levels of sales. These market measurements can have a tremendous impact on all functional areas of an organization because they are used in making a number of different decisions. There are, however, important differences in the types of sales forecasts and in the methods of sales forecasting, which are discussed in the remainder of this chapter.

[7] Jon Berry, "The Rich and the Worth," *Adweek's Marketing Week,* May 11, 1992, pp. 21–23.

Basic Types of Sales Forecasts

The two major types of sales forecasts are industry sales forecasts and company sales forecasts. Within these two classes, forecasts can be made at different levels of aggregation of sales.

INDUSTRY SALES FORECASTS

Managers may use an industry sales forecast to estimate the total sales that will be achieved by all suppliers in the relevant market. Depending on how the firm has defined the relevant market, industry sales can be measured for a product form, for a product class, or for all competing classes satisfying the same generic need. Indeed, a manager may develop industry sales forecasts for more than one of these levels of aggregation, depending on how the forecast will be used.

There are four basic uses of industry sales forecasts. First, industry sales forecasts indicate the expected rates of growth of alternative markets. Therefore, they are useful elements in corporate marketing planning (as discussed in Chapter 2). Further, to the extent that industry sales forecasts indicate different rates of growth for various product forms or various product classes, decisions on the appropriate relevant market can be made. For example, if one product form (such as nutritional cereals) is growing faster than a competing form (such as presweetened cereals), top management will probably provide greater marketing support to brands in the product-form market with higher growth. Alternatively, if sales forecasts show that industry sales for either a product form or a product class (such as cereals) are growing at a low rate, then strategies to stimulate sales of the product form or class may be examined.

Second, rate of industry sales growth has a major influence on competitive intensity. If the forecast indicates a dramatic decline in the rate of industry sales growth, management will know that future company sales gains must come from increases in market share, a condition that often fosters heavy price and promotion competition.

Third, industry sales forecasts are also important to middle management. Knowing the future level of industry sales enables a firm to calculate the market share required to reach its sales goals. For example, if a product's sales objective is 1 million units with an industry sales forecast of 5 million units, the managers can judge whether or not it is feasible to attain a 20 percent market share based on the company's planned level of marketing effort and on the product's current market-share position. The relationship between industry sales forecasts and marketing budgets is discussed in detail in Chapter 6.

Finally, the rate of industry growth generally has a major influence on company sales growth. Accordingly, an industry sales forecast is often an important input to the company sales forecast.

COMPANY SALES FORECASTS

Just as the industry sales forecast can be developed at any three levels of aggregation, company sales forecasts can also be developed at more than one level. A firm may wish to forecast company sales of a specific item (such as regular-size Tide), a brand (Tide), a product line (Procter & Gamble detergents), or total company sales (all Procter & Gamble sales).

Forecasts at the item level are generally most useful for decisions related to production scheduling and to the transportation of goods to distributors. Forecasts at the highest level of aggregation, company sales, are most useful for overall company financial planning. From a marketing strategy and planning perspective, the most important forecasts are those that focus on brand sales or product-line sales because marketing decisions are most often designed to influence sales at these levels of aggregation.

The initial sales forecast can come from top management or from the field. At Davis and Geck, a medical supply company, the sales forecast was a number given to sales managers that they, in turn, gave to their salespeople. This top-down style was changed in 1993 to a more field-oriented approach to get the salespeople involved in the development of the sales forecast. Dave Jacobs, the national sales director, asked the 120 salespeople and the 13 regional sales managers to come up with a sales forecast they could live with and guarantee.[8] These forecasts were then used to develop regional and national sales forecasts.

United Parcel Services, the Atlanta-based shipping company, uses a two-pronged interactive approach. The corporate marketing group begins the process by assembling an initial sales forecast based on factors such as past sales, economic indicators, Consumer Price Index, and other trends. However, this forecast—"the view from 50,000 feet"—doesn't account for local influences such as Spiegel shutting down a distribution center in Illinois and opening one in Indiana, or the opening of a new automotive plant in South Carolina.[9] The process depends upon the input of local managers who meet with their reps to determine a realistic potential for an area. These territory forecasts are aggregated into district forecasts, and then into regional forecasts that are summed to arrive at a national forecast. These forecasts are negotiated between corporate management and regional directors until there is agreement.[10]

However, not all forecasting approaches are equally useful for marketing decision making. Even when brand or product-line sales are being forecasted, the value of the forecast to managers will depend on the type of approach used to develop the forecast. Time-series methods are generally used to get the best estimate of expected sales. Descriptive forecasts are appropriate to explain how our price and marketing budgets might *influence* future sales.

Basic Forecasting Approaches

Although an extensive array of forecasting approaches exists, there are really three basic types of approaches: time-series models, descriptive models, and judgmental approaches. In a recent survey, a list of forecasting methods was sent to forecasting

---

[8]William Keen, Jr., "Numbers Racket," *Sales and Marketing Management,* May 1995, pp. 64–76.
[9]Ibid.
[10]Ibid.

executives in 500 companies. Based on the responses from over 200 executives who returned the survey, the most familiar sales forecasting techniques are moving averages, exponential smoothing, straight-line projection, and regression analysis. The techniques used most often in a 3-month-to-2-year time horizon were exponential smoothing, jury of executive opinion, sales-force composite, regression, and trend-line analysis.[11] We will discuss moving averages, exponential smoothing, and trend-line approaches under "Time-Series-Based Forecasting Methods." Regression analysis is discussed under "Descriptive Models" and jury of experts is discussed under "Judgmental Approaches." Any one of these approaches can be employed in forecasting either industry or company sales.[12]

TIME-SERIES–BASED FORECASTING METHODS

The basic assumption underlying time-series models is that sales can be forecasted with acceptable accuracy by examining historical sales patterns. These models are relatively easy to use because the only data needed are past sales and these models can be implemented by means of easy-to-obtain "canned" computer programs. A further advantage to these models is that the probable range of the deviation of actual sales from forecasted sales (called the *forecasting error*) can be estimated statistically.

As a general rule, time-series models are most useful when market forces are relatively stable within the forecasting horizon. That is, if sales trends are not likely to vary because of economic changes, marketing actions, or technology, these models are likely to be reasonably accurate. Such conditions are often found when short-run forecast horizons (less than 1 year) are required. They may also be found over longer forecast periods in the case of markets that are technologically mature, are not very susceptible to the effects of economic fluctuations, and are expected to witness few major changes in marketing effort.

Even in the most stable markets, however, seasonal variations, changes in trends, and random fluctuations do occur. Accordingly, a variety of procedures have been developed for "smoothing out" random fluctuations by averaging recent sales levels, giving weights to monthly sales levels to adjust for seasonality, and increasing the importance of more recent sales data to reflect trends.

Consider, for example, Figure 5-2. The dots in this figure portray annual sales for the Tootsie Roll Company from 1984 to 1993. We will use these sales data to compare the three most commonly used time-series models: moving averages, exponential smoothing, and trend-line projections.

[11]John T. Mentzer and Kenneth B. Kahn, "Forecasting Technique Familiarity, Satisfaction, Usage, and Application," *Journal of Forecasting,* vol. 14, 1995, pp. 465–476.

[12]Makridakis Spyros and Steven Wheelwright, "Forecasting: Issues and Challenges for Marketing Management," *Journal of Marketing,* October 1977, pp. 24–38; and David M. Georgoff and Robert G. Murdick, "Manager's Guide to Forecasting," *Harvard Business Review,* January–February 1986, pp. 110–120.

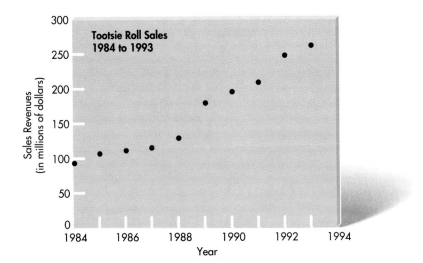

FIGURE 5-2

Tootsie Roll sales
1984 to 1993.

MOVING AVERAGES

As the name indicates, this method is based on the average of some specified historical period to forecast the value of a future period. Table 5-10 provides the sales forecasts for a 3-year moving average. The forecast for 1987 is the average of sales for 1984, 1985, and 1986. The forecast error is the difference between actual sales and the forecasted sales.

EXPONENTIAL SMOOTHING

A limitation to moving averages is that all the years used to create the moving average are given equal weight. In some cases we may want to weight recent years more heavily. Exponential smoothing allows differential weighting of the years. The formula for exponential smoothing is

$$Y_{(t + 1)} = \alpha\, A_t + (1 - \alpha)\, Y_t$$

$Y_{(t + 1)}$ is the forecasted value, α is the smoothing constant, A_t is the actual sales for period t, and Y_t is the forecasted sales for period t. The sales forecast, with a smoothing constant of .5 for 1990 (see Table 5-10), is

$$148.91 = (.5)\, 179.00 + (1 - .5)\, 118.81$$

The smoothing constant is restricted to values between zero and one. The larger the smoothing constant, the greater the emphasis on more recent years.

When the data are characterized by an increasing trend as shown in Table 5-10, both moving averages and exponential smoothing estimates will always be below the actual value.

TABLE 5-10	**TIMES-SERIES FORECAST**

MOVING AVERAGES

YEAR	ACTUAL VALUE	3-YEAR FORECAST VALUE	3-YEAR FORECAST ERROR
1984	93.00		
1985	106.00		
1986	111.00		
1987	114.00	103.33	10.67
1988	128.00	110.33	17.67
1989	179.00	117.67	61.33
1990	194.00	140.33	53.67
1991	207.00	167.00	40.00
1992	245.00	193.33	51.67
1993	259.00	215.33	43.67
1994		237.00	

EXPONENTIAL SMOOTHING (SMOOTHING CONSTANT = .50)

YEAR	ACTUAL VALUE	FORECAST VALUE	FORECAST ERROR
1984	93.00		
1985	106.00	93.00	13.00
1986	111.00	99.50	11.50
1987	114.00	105.25	8.75
1988	128.00	109.62	18.37
1989	179.00	118.81	60.19
1990	194.00	148.91	45.09
1991	207.00	171.45	35.55
1992	245.00	189.23	55.77
1993	259.00	217.11	41.89
1994		238.06	

STRAIGHT-LINE PROJECTIONS

TREND LINE	ACTUAL VALUE	FORECAST VALUE	FORECAST ERROR
1984	93.00	75.29	17.71
1985	106.00	94.92	11.08
1986	111.00	114.54	−3.54
1987	114.00	134.16	−20.16
1988	128.00	153.79	−25.79
1989	179.00	173.41	5.59
1990	194.00	193.04	0.96
1991	207.00	212.66	−5.66
1992	245.00	232.28	12.72
1993	259.00	251.91	7.09
1994		271.53	

STRAIGHT-LINE PROJECTIONS

In cases where pronounced trends exist, random fluctuations are not severe, and managers wish to forecast several periods into the future, line-fitting approaches are often employed to identify the sales time series. In this approach, a computer program is used to determine the equation of the "best-fitting" line—the line or curve that most closely approximates the historical trend. This equation is then used to forecast future sales by projecting that same line or curve into the future. As we can see from Figure 5-2, there is clearly an upward sales trend with modest fluctuations. The trend line for the data is

$$\text{Forecast} = 55.67 + 19.62 \text{ (period)}$$

The results of the trend-line analysis for the data shown in Figure 5-2 are provided in Table 5-10. Sales forecasts for the subsequent years (1995 through 1998) can be made using the formula for periods 12 through 16.

Before using time-series forecasts, managers should answer the questions posed in Table 5-11. Specifically, managers should have a substantial number of data points if they expect a trend to be reliable. Additionally, time-series models represent only the past. Such projections may be too optimistic if industry sales are approaching market potential (and thus likely to have a substantially reduced growth rate). Finally, major changes in future sales often occur because of changes in the demographic or economic environment, the firm's marketing effort, or competitive activity; the potential effects of such changes can be captured only through the use of descriptive models.

DESCRIPTIVE MODELS–BASED FORECASTING METHODS

When environmental changes can be expected to create a shift in the historical pattern of sales, then time-series models are likely to prove unsatisfactory. In such situations, managers are more likely to use forecasting techniques that link sales

---

TABLE 5-11   **QUESTIONS FOR EVALUATING THE RELIABILITY OF TIME-SERIES FORECASTS**

1. Do we have a long enough history of sales data to construct a reliable trend?
2. Can we expect industry growth trends to level off because industry sales are approaching market potential?
3. Is it likely that industry sales will shift because of economic, demographic, or technological factors?
4. Can new competition (including competition from other product forms or classes) be anticipated that will influence industry or company sales?
5. Can we expect major changes in the marketing activity of competitors?
6. Does the industry (company) have the production capacity to fulfill industry (company) sales forecasts?
7. Does our company plan any major changes in its marketing programs?

TABLE 5-12	NEW ZEALAND COOKIE MARKET: MARKET SHARE, RELATIVE PRICE, ADVERTISING, AND DISTRIBUTION FOR A TOP-SELLING BRAND			

PERIOD	MARKET SHARE	RELATIVE PRICE	RELATIVE DISTRIBUTION	RELATIVE ADVERTISING
1	0.518667	0.99596	1.05763	0.83048
2	0.558001	0.99112	1.03970	0.42723
3	0.545538	0.98112	1.04589	0.24783
4	0.493883	1.00633	1.03959	0.55797
5	0.502510	0.98687	1.03284	1.00000
6	0.553169	0.97524	1.04448	1.00000
7	0.561195	0.97223	1.04752	0.97441
8	0.535317	0.99437	1.05605	0.51284
9	0.540326	0.99321	1.05296	0.51284
10	0.522628	0.98322	1.03618	0.56120
11	0.536117	1.00383	1.04714	0.80892
12	0.558861	0.99705	1.04960	1.00000
13	0.524293	1.00225	1.04838	0.22737
14	0.466122	1.00172	1.04868	0.32652
15	0.471938	1.00017	1.02406	0.32546
16	0.497760	0.98295	1.03772	0.80955
17	0.511327	0.97971	1.06260	0.87337
18	0.554894	0.98837	1.09686	0.73084
19	0.590279	0.99098	1.10962	0.95759
20	0.572970	0.98397	1.06835	1.00000
21	0.610783	0.97863	1.11071	0.46047

to one or more factors thought to cause or influence sales. Descriptive models such as multiple-regression models are used when a number of factors have an impact on sales. Multiple-regression forecasts allow managers to incorporate the expected effects of any controllable marketing variables likely to be significant when one is forecasting company sales. The goal is to assess the relationship between these controllable variables and sales. Can the variation in sales for different time periods be explained by levels of price, promotion, distribution, and so on, in those time periods? A multiple-regression model, with sales as the dependent variable and the controllable factors as predictor or independent variables, will address this question.

Consider Table 5-12, which presents data on market shares for a leading brand of cookies in New Zealand.[13] Notice that market share varies from a low of 46.61 percent in period 14 to a high of 61.08 percent in period 21. The factors used to explain the variation in sales are relative levels of price, distribution, and advertising. The

[13]Michael Geurts and David Whitlark, "Forecasting Market Share," *Journal of Business Forecasting,* Winter 1992–1993, pp. 17–22.

relative levels are the ratio of the company's level to the industry average. The multiple-regression model based on the data in Table 5-12 is

$$\text{Market share} = .61 - 1.11 \text{ (relative price)}$$
$$+ .97 \text{ (relative distribution)}$$
$$+ .01 \text{ (relative advertising)}$$

Although many other factors could explain why market share varies from one period to another, the model explains greater than 60 percent of the variation in market share, based solely on relative levels of price, distribution, and advertising.

Additionally, as in any statistical forecast, the company was able to determine the standard error of the forecast—in this case .025; that is, there is always some imprecision in terms of past sales and past forecasts. Two-thirds of the time, the forecast estimate of sales will be within one standard error (in this case .025) of actual market share; 95 percent of the time, forecasted share will be within two standard errors (in this case .05) of the actual market share.

Multiple-regression models allow managers to predict values of the dependent variable (for example, market share) for different levels of the predictor variables (for example, price, distribution, and advertising). If we set the relative price at .95, relative distribution at 1.06, and relative advertising at 1.0, the estimated level of market share, based on the multiple-regression model described above, is

$$\text{Market share} = .61 - 1.11 \, (.95) + .97 \, (1.06) + .01 \, (1.0)$$
$$= .5937$$

When constructing and interpreting multiple-regression models, managers need to address a number of important questions in order to assess the reliability of the regression forecasts. Two of the more important questions regarding multiple-regression models are

- Have any important factors been left out of the model?
- Are the independent or predictor variables correlated among themselves?

The first question deals with the specification of the model. If any factors that have a significant impact on sales have been left out of the model, the impact will not be included in the forecast and, therefore, the forecast can be seriously biased.

The second question deals with the manager's ability to isolate the effects of the predictor variables on the dependent variable. Consider the multiple-regression model for estimating the market shares for the cookie manufacturer. The coefficients for price, distribution, and advertising are -1.11, .97, and .01, respectively. There is a temptation to conclude that distribution is highly related to changes in market share and advertising is not. However, if the two variables, distribution and advertising, are themselves highly correlated, one cannot make this conclusion. The size of the coefficient of each independent variable is affected by the correlation among the variables. When the predictor variables are correlated among themselves, the overall prediction is not affected, but the ability to attribute the effect to any one variable is affected.

JUDGMENTAL APPROACHES

Frequently, it is not possible to rely on statistical approaches to forecasting. Time-series methods may be inappropriate because of wide fluctuations in sales or because of anticipated changes in trends. Regression methods may not be feasible because of a lack of historical data or because of management's inability to determine (or even identify) causal factors. The judgmental approach may be management's only possible avenue for forecasting in these situations.

Even when statistical estimates are available, managers may want to use judgment to supplement these approaches because even the most sophisticated statistical models cannot anticipate all the potential external factors that can influence sales (such as strikes at customers' facilities or major competitive innovations). Two prevalent judgmental techniques are jury of executive opinion and Delphi techniques.[14] The jury of executive opinion invites the input from senior-level executives. In some cases the executives are asked to give an optimistic, pessimistic, and a most probable level of sales for some future period. The forecasting managers first determine a forecast for each executive and then combine the levels of all the executives. The Delphi technique asks members of a team to submit their forecasts and the assumptions behind the forecasts. These are then reviewed by a team leader and given back to the participants, with a summary of the first round, for a second round of forecasts. When an acceptable consensus is reached the process stops.

Interpreting the Forecast

In evaluating the managerial implications of a sales forecast, managers should be fully aware of both the sensitivity of forecast results to slight changes in forecast assumptions or techniques and the costs of forecasting errors.

SENSITIVITY ANALYSIS

If several techniques give essentially the same results, the reliability of a forecast should be greater. Accordingly, some firms develop parallel forecasts based on alternative techniques. Knowing how different techniques or assumptions lead to alternative estimates enables a manager to determine how sensitive the forecast is to a change in these factors. When forecasts are highly sensitive, managers should expect greater imprecision and should closely monitor the environment to find out which model and which assumptions most closely approximate reality.

[14]Norton Paley, "Welcome to the Fast Lane," *Sales and Marketing Management*, August 1994, pp. 65–66.

THE COSTS OF FORECAST ERRORS

Companies that make or sell products with long lifetimes and steady sales are less concerned with the costs of forecast errors, because the forecasts in these cases are likely to be close to actual sales. However, when the sales forecast given to management has a large standard error, managers need to consider the costs of overestimating and underestimating sales. To illustrate this point, assume that a manager has been given a company sales forecast of 200,000 units with a standard error of 10,000 units. Statistical theory tells us that there is a 95 percent chance that the actual level of sales will be within two standard errors. Thus, there is a 95 percent chance that sales will be within the range of 180,000 to 220,000 units. If the manager sets production at the lower end—180,000 units—and demand is higher, the underestimation will lead to stockouts or shortages of the product. If the manager sets production at the high end—220,000 units—and demand is less, the overestimation will lead to excess inventory. Either of these consequences adds to the cost of the products. In some industries characterized by highly volatile demand, like the fashion industry, the costs of stockouts for underestimation and markdowns for overestimation can actually exceed the original cost of manufacturing.[15] There has been a sharp increase in the number of markdowns in the retail industry in the past two decades as shown in Figure 5-3.

As Table 5-13 indicates, different kinds of consequences are associated with overestimating and underestimating company sales. For some firms, the cost of holding excess inventory may be extremely high (perhaps because the product is perishable), whereas the amount of sales lost because of delayed shipments is very low (perhaps because the company has loyal customers). Accordingly, if a firm is in that situation, management will be more willing to risk underestimation than overestimation. This willingness to risk

FIGURE 5-3

Markdowns in the retail industry.

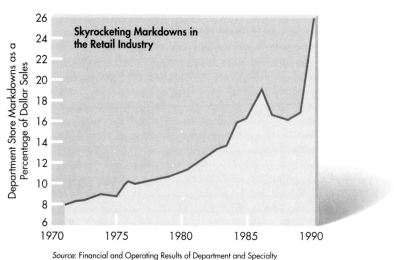

Source: Financial and Operating Results of Department and Specialty Stores, *National Retail Federation*

[15]Marshall Fisher, "Making Supply Meet Demand in an Uncertain World," *Harvard Business Review,* May–June 1994, pp. 83–93.

| **TABLE 5-13** | **POSSIBLE RESULTS OF COMPANY SALES FORECAST ERRORS** |

RESULTS OF OVERESTIMATION

Excess capacity leading to layoffs, loss of skilled labor
Price cuts or additional marketing expenses to move product
Distributor ill will because of excess distributor inventories
Inventory costs:
    Cash flow problems and cost of capital tied up in finished goods, components, raw materials
    Technical obsolescence or damage
    Storage or warehousing costs

RESULTS OF UNDERESTIMATION

Lost sales or customer goodwill
Overtime costs
Costs of expediting shipments
Reduced quality control because of reduced maintenance of machinery at full production capacity
Production bottlenecks because of lack of materials and parts

underestimation occurs because the cost of excess inventory resulting from excess production will outweigh the lost revenue from an inadequate level of production. Because the costs of overestimation are greater for that firm, managers will probably want to base decisions on a forecast that is more conservative than the sales forecast.

CONCLUSION

Market measurement is an activity of critical importance for a wide range of decisions. Market-potential estimates and industry and company sales forecasts are essential for the development of corporate marketing strategies and product objectives. Middle-management decisions regarding the size and allocation of marketing expenditures depend heavily on sales forecasts and on the relationship between forecasts and measures of profitability and productivity. Profitability and productivity analysis is discussed in the next chapter.

In this chapter, we have examined the different kinds of market measurements, their uses, and the various ways in which they can be developed. By understanding the purpose and assumptions behind a given market measurement, a manager will find it easier to specify the kind of information needed in a given situation and to understand the degree of reliability that should be placed on a given market-measurement estimate.

Additionally, managers should be aware of the available data sources that can be used to develop market-measurement estimates. Some of these sources were mentioned in this chapter. However, a more complete listing and description of prominent sources of market information is contained in the Appendix.

The various steps in market measurement and the relationships among these steps are portrayed in Figure 5-4. To gain a better understanding of some of these relationships and become more aware of the challenges involved in market measurement, consider the process used by Sport Obermeyer to forecast demand for skiwear. Obermeyer incorporates formal statistical theory, costs, and judgmental forecast methods to set production.

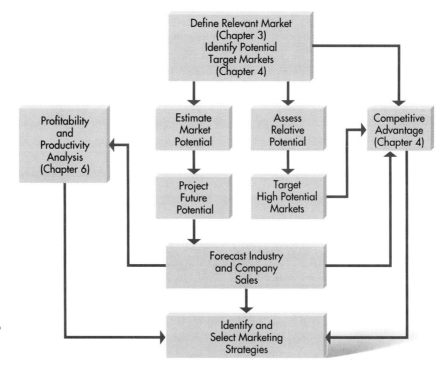

FIGURE 5-4

Steps in market measurement and their relationships to other aspects of the situation analysis.

COPING WITH DEMAND UNCERTAINTY AT SPORT OBERMEYER

Longtime industry player Klaus Obermeyer describes the skiwear market as extremely fickle. With such an unpredictable setting, how could you possibly use formal statistical methods to forecast sales? You'd be surprised. Even though demand for each product varies widely, the overall distribution of demand follows a recognizable pattern.

The management at Sport Obermeyer found that demand data were normally distributed, like the well-known bell curve. This distribution was centered around the mean, or average, demand; the standard deviation, or width of the distribution, defined the level of demand uncertainty. Those figures near the mean were more certain than those numbers on the outside slopes of the curve.

Sport Obermeyer used a buying committee to predict demand for the Pandora parka, and the graph "Probable Sales of the Pandora Parka" (Figure 5-5) shows this forecast distribution. The shaded area represents the probability that demand exceeds 1285 units. The idea behind the distribution curve was to maximize the expected profitability by balancing the risks of overproduction and underproduction.

To balance the costs of overproduction with the costs of sales lost because of underproduction, Obermeyer calculated the marginal profit for each parka sold and the lost profit from each unit produced, but not sold. Economic theory states that the company should keep producing parkas as long as

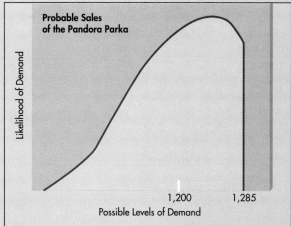

FIGURE 5-5

Probable sales of the Pandora Parka.

it expects its gains to exceed its losses. For example, Sport Obermeyer earns $14.50 on each unit sold, and it loses $5.00 on each parka that it cannot sell. For the parkas the number is 1285. The probability of selling the 1285th parka is 25.7%, whereas the chance of not selling the parka is 74.3%. The expected gain for the 1285th parka is 3.726 (.257 × 14.50), which is about equal to the expected loss of 3.715 (.743 × 5.00) for producing the 1285th parka. Here the company is still earning more money from its sales than it is losing from overproduction. If, however, the company produced 1290 parkas, the probability of selling that many would decrease while the probability of overstocked merchandise would increase, and Obermeyer's losses would be greater than its profits. Thus, the company must accurately assess the probability distribution of demand and compute its costs in order to calculate its chances for profitability.

Typically, sales forecasts use historical demand data, but Obermeyer did not have any predictable measures, so it had to find another suitable estimation technique. Obermeyer started out by asking each member of Sport Obermeyer's buying committee to give individual forecasts for each product. Then, the average forecasts were used as the mean of the demand curve. Next, they used the standard deviation of the predictions to determine the width of the demand curve. Here they had to double the width of the curve because it had found that the standard deviation of actual forecasting errors had typically been twice as large as previous buying committees' forecasts.

It was predicted that forecasts would be more accurate when the buying committee had similar forecasts—that is, when the forecasts had low standard deviations. This prediction was confirmed with actual data from 1992–1993 sales. Thus, the committee discovered that it could go ahead and produce certain products—those for which the buying committee's forecasts had low standard deviations—even before additional sales data were available for guidance.

Sport Obermeyer used basic statistical methods, combined with forecasting techniques, to develop a risk-based production sequence that indicates the link between planning systems and analytic approaches.

1. How is the probability distribution of demand formed?
2. How are the probability of demand distribution, profits, and opportunity costs related to forecast levels of production?
3. In this case, do you think the company is more concerned with overestimation or underestimation?

QUESTIONS AND SITUATIONS FOR DISCUSSION

1. What strategic implications would you be concerned with if you noticed a gap in selective demand?
2. WatchDog manufactures and sells security devices for single-family homes in the New England region of the United States. WatchDog was interested in entering

the Southern market, but wanted to roll out the product one state at a time. Government records indicate that Virginia and North Carolina have approximately the same number of households: 1,218,000 in North Carolina and 1,192,100 in Virginia. Company records indicate that about 1.5 percent of homes valued at less than $150,000 purchased the product, about 3 percent of homes valued at $150,000 or more, but less than $300,000, were users, and about 4 percent of homes valued at $300,000 or more were users. Based on the census data for the value of owner-occupied units provided below, which of the two markets has the greatest market potential?

	OCCUPIED HOUSING UNITS (IN $000)					
STATE	LESS THAN $50,000	$50,000 TO $99,999	$100,000 TO $149,000	$150,000 TO $199,000	$200,000 TO $299,000	$300,000 AND MORE
NC	382.8	575.7	155.2	56.3	33.1	15.0
VA	206.7	466.2	203.9	132.8	116.5	66.0

3. Rockport metal sells an antirust solvent to companies in the 3411 (metal cans) and 3412 (metal barrels) SIC codes. It estimates that the cost of the solvent comprises about .4 percent of the value of shipments. The four largest markets for the SIC codes are California, Ohio, Texas, and New Jersey. The company assigned one salesperson to each of these areas; all other sales were handled by telemarketing. If the rep in Ohio, who is considered a good salesperson, writes about $1.25 million in sales, what should be the quotas for the other salespeople? (Note: You need to use secondary sources to answer this question.)

4. SeaMore, a national travel agency specializing in vacation packages for employees in the construction and manufacturing industries, wants to develop promotion budgets for the Northeastern, Midwestern, Southern, and Western regions of the United States. Past records indicate that 65 percent of SeaMore's business came from employees in construction industries and 35 percent from employees in manufacturing industries. Given a direct mail budget of $5 million, establish budgets for the four regions. Data from the U.S. Bureau of Labor Statistics for the four regions are provided below.

	EMPLOYMENT FIGURES (000)	
REGION	CONSTRUCTION	MANUFACTURING
Northeast	725	3,582
Midwest	1,021	5,414
South	1,714	5,970
West	960	3,107

5. The Tennis Racquet Manufacturers Association has estimated that, for a certain market segment, about 15 percent of users scrap their racquets the first year after they purchase, 25 percent scrap their racquets after 2 years, 50 percent after 3 years, and virtually 100 percent after 4 years. Industry sales (in thousands) for a geographic region are listed below. Based on the sales, what do you estimate the replacement potential will be in the year 1997?

YEAR	SALES
1996	5250
1995	6479
1994	4890
1993	4798
1992	4678

6. What advice would you give to managers who want to develop a multiple-corollary factor index of market potential?

7. To develop media and sales quotas, management needed to rank order the six New England states with respect to their Buying Power Index. Based on the data supplied below, provide the necessary rank ordering.

STATE	POPULATION	RETAIL SALES	EFFECTIVE BUYING INCOME
CT	3,273,900	32,223,567	74,886,978
ME	1,237,700	11,681,170	19,146,000
MA	6,053,000	52,465,985	119,450,956
NH	1,143,000	12,761,493	22,045,996
RI	995,400	7,538,334	16,198,993
VT	582,600	9,011,998	5,125,037
U.S.	262,213,300	2,241,319,080	4,436,178,724

8. What are the differences, with respect to advantages and disadvantages, between a top-down and bottom-up method of developing sales forecasts?

9. The wildlife art exhibit hosted by Charleston, South Carolina, had grown each year for the last 10 years. The chamber of commerce wanted to estimate the number of people likely to attend this year if the same trend held. Based on the data provided on page 136, prepare a forecast using a 3-year moving average, exponential smoothing with a smoothing constant of .6, and trend-line analysis. Compare the forecasts from the three methods and describe why they differ. Also, can you recommend a better way to use any of the three methods?

YEAR	VISITORS
1995	76,890
1994	73,500
1993	67,500
1992	66,780
1991	56,000
1990	54,890
1989	52,765
1988	46,750
1987	42,125
1986	34,400

10. Swing-Rite is one of the leading producers of hinges for garage doors. The product is comparable to any on the market but, if it is not available, contractors will switch to one of three other brands. It is your responsibility to set production levels based on sales forecasts. A multiple-regression model was used to estimate sales. The estimate for 1997 is 14,000,000 units with a standard error of 1,560,000 units. What do you recommend?

SUGGESTED ADDITIONAL READINGS

Bishop, William S., John L. Graham, and Michael H. Jones, "Volatility of Derived Demand in Industrial Markets and Its Management Implications," *Journal of Marketing,* Fall 1984, pp. 95–103.

Dalrymple, Douglas, William Strahle, and Douglas Bock, "How Many Observations Should Be Used in Trend Regression in Forecasts?" *Journal of Business Forecasting,* Spring 1989, pp. 7–10.

Frisbie, Gilbert, and Vincent A. Mabert, "Crystal Ball vs. System: The Forecasting Dilemma," *Business Horizons,* September–October 1981, pp. 72–76.

Georgoff, David M., and Robert G. Murdick, "Manager's Guide to Forecasting," *Harvard Business Review,* January–February 1986, pp. 110–119.

Hagdorn-van der Meijden, Jo, A. E. E. van Nunen, and Aad Ramondt, "Forecasting—Bridging the Gap between Sales and Manufacturing, *International Journal of Production Economics,* 1994, pp. 101–114.

Mahajan, Vijay, Eitan Muller, and Frank Bass, "New Product Diffusion Models in Marketing: A Review and Directions for Research," *Journal of Marketing,* January 1990, pp. 1–26.

Mentzer, John T., and Roger Gomes, "Further Extensions of Adaptive Extended Exponential Smoothing and Comparison with the M-Comparison," *Journal of the Academy of Marketing Science,* vol. 22, no. 4, 1994, pp. 372–382.

Proctor, R. A., "A Different Approach to Sales Forecasting: Using a Spreadsheet," *European Management Journal,* Fall 1989, pp. 358–365.

Schnaars, Steven P., "Situational Factors Affecting Forecast Accuracy," *Journal of Marketing Research,* August 1984, pp. 290–297.

Sobek, Robert, "A Manager's Primer on Forecasting," *Harvard Business Review,* May–June 1973, pp. 6–15.

Wang, George C. S., "What You Should Know about Regression Based Forecasting," *The Journal of Business Forecasting,* Winter 1993–1994, pp. 15–21.

CHAPTER 6

PROFITABILITY AND PRODUCTIVITY ANALYSIS

OVERVIEW

In Chapters 3 and 4, we examined the importance of understanding buyers and competitors when framing marketing decisions. Additionally, in Chapter 5, we considered the relationships among market potential, industry sales, and company sales in the process of market measurement. As a result of performing the analyses in those chapters, managers should be in a position to identify market opportunities and strategies for taking advantage of such opportunities. Before embarking on a marketing strategy, however, middle managers will generally have to do a detailed analysis of what it will cost to implement a strategy and what the expected sales and profit consequences will be.

Productivity analysis is the assessment of the sales or market-share consequences of a marketing strategy. Specifically, a productivity analysis involves the estimation of relationships between price or one or more marketing expenditures (such as advertising budgets) and the sales volume or market share of a particular product or product line. As we show in this chapter, these estimates are generally developed based on insights obtained from market and competitive analyses and from market measurements.

Profitability analysis is the assessment of the impact of various marketing strategies and programs on the profit contribution that can be expected from a product or product line. In considering the role played by profitability analysis, managers should be aware that this analysis is important regardless of the kind of product objective that has been established. Certainly a manager would seldom significantly increase the marketing budget for a cash cow (where the strategic focus is "hold") if the increase would not improve profitability. But even when the primary product objective is volume or market-share growth (rather than profitability), it is still important for a manager to know how much profitability must be sacrificed to achieve a given sales or market-share target.

For an overview of the concepts, tools, and approaches involved in analyzing the impact of marketing expenditures, consider the following situation. Linkster Inc. manufactures a variety of golf umbrellas, golf sweaters, and lightweight water-repellent caps and jackets for golfers. The line is advertised in selected golf magazines and sold by company salespeople (who are paid a salary and commission) to selected pro shops at golf courses and sporting goods stores.

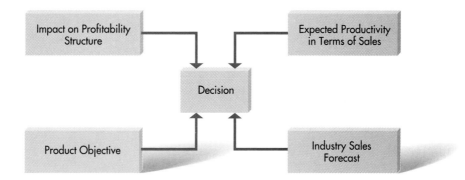

FIGURE 6-1

Factors to be considered in making marketing expenditure decisions.

Linkster is presently reviewing its results for the year just ended. In preparing the budget for the coming year, the firm's marketing manager is considering an increase in the advertising budget for jackets. Specifically, an increase of $100,000 is under consideration.

As Figure 6-1 indicates, Linkster's management must consider four factors in making this decision.

1. The relative importance of market share and profitability as *product objectives* for jackets
2. The *industry sales forecast* for jackets
3. The anticipated *productivity* (that is, the effectiveness) of the increased advertising in increasing jacket sales
4. The various types and levels of cost that determine the *profitability structure* of jackets

In this chapter, we present procedures for measuring product profitability and for estimating the productivity of marketing expenditures. In addition, we illustrate how product objectives, sales forecasts, profitability, and productivity are related to marketing budgeting decisions, using the specific example of Linkster.

MEASURING PRODUCT PROFITABILITY

As most managers know, the income (profit and loss) statement is generally inadequate for analyzing product profitability. Consider the profit and loss statement for Linkster given in Table 6-1.

If Linkster were a single-product organization, the conventional profit and loss statement would provide a reasonably useful measure of product profitability. However, because the firm is a multiproduct organization, management will also be interested in the profitability of each of the various products. Moreover, the conventional profit and loss statement provides few clues to how profitability would be influenced by changes in those costs (such as advertising) that lead to changes in sales volume.

TABLE 6-1	LINKSTER INC.: PROFIT AND LOSS STATEMENT (IN THOUSANDS OF DOLLARS)

Sales		$4640
Less cost of goods sold		2300
Gross profit margin		$2340
Operating expenses:		
Advertising	$600	
Sales salaries	500	
Sales commissions	220	
Designers' salaries	400	
Other (general and administrative costs)	600	
Total operating expense		2320
Net operating profit (loss) before taxes		$ 20

In order to examine these issues, we need to make two kinds of distinctions in types of costs. First, the distinction must be made between *fixed* and *variable* costs. Second, fixed costs should be separated into those that are *direct* or *traceable* to individual products and those that are *indirect* or *nontraceable*.

Variable versus Fixed Costs

Variable costs are costs that vary with sales volume. Sales commissions, material, labor, and packaging are typically variable costs because they go up proportionately with sales; that is, each of these costs is incurred every time a product is produced and sold.

Nearly all other costs are *fixed;* that is, they remain essentially the same regardless of volume levels—at least as long as increases in the size of a production facility or in administrative and clerical staff are not required. Although some of these costs can be *changed* by management (such as advertising budgets and sales-force salaries), they do not vary *automatically* as sales change. For a manufacturer, the cost of goods sold (in the income statement) usually includes both fixed and variable elements; that is, each unit sold is assigned a share of the fixed costs to be added to its variable cost. For a retailer or wholesaler who only resells products made by other firms, the cost of goods sold is only a variable cost because it simply reflects the purchase price of items being resold.

For Linkster, the fixed costs of production (such as supervisory salaries) are considered part of the cost of goods sold (shown in Table 6-1) but not in the *variable* cost of goods sold (shown in Table 6-2). Conversely, Linkster's salespeople earn commissions on each unit sold to their retailers. These costs are variable costs (as seen in Table 6-2) but are not included in the cost of goods sold in Table 6-1.

By separating fixed costs from variable costs (as we have done in Table 6-2), the portion of cost that is sensitive to volume is identified. Out of $4,640,000 in sales, $1,840,000 (that is, $1,620,000 plus $220,000 in commissions) is spent on variable costs. The remaining $2,800,000 is the amount that is contributed to cover all fixed costs and profit after variable costs have been subtracted.

TABLE 6-2	LINKSTER INC.: CONTRIBUTION MARGIN STATEMENT (IN THOUSANDS OF DOLLARS)

Sales		$4640
Less variable cost of goods sold (labor, materials, packaging)		1620
Less other variable selling costs (sales commissions)		220
Variable contribution margin		$2800
Fixed costs:		
Advertising	$600	
Sales salaries	500	
Fixed production costs	680	
Designers' salaries	400	
General and administrative overhead	600	
Total operating expense		2780
Net operating profit before taxes		$ 20

With costs separated in this way, managers can calculate a very useful measure: the *percentage-variable-contribution margin* (PVCM). This measure indicates the percentage of each additional sales dollar that will be available to help the firm cover its fixed costs and increase profits. The percentage-variable-contribution margin can be calculated in either of two ways.

$$PVCM = \frac{\text{variable-contribution margin}}{\text{dollar sales}}$$

or

$$PVCM = \frac{\text{unit price} - \text{unit variable cost}}{\text{unit price}}$$

In the case of Linkster Inc. then,

$$PVCM = \frac{\$2,800,000}{\$4,640,000} = 60.3\%$$

In order to appreciate fully the usefulness of this measure to a marketing manager, it is necessary to understand the distinction between direct fixed costs and indirect fixed costs.

Types of Fixed Costs

When fixed costs are incurred in a multiproduct firm, they are incurred either on behalf of the business as a whole or on behalf of one or more specific products. For example, organizations may design advertisements to communicate a message about a particular product or product line, or they may use *institutional* advertising, which presents a message about the company as a whole and may not even mention the specific products or services sold. Costs, such as product-specific advertising, that are incurred on behalf of a specific product or service are known as *direct fixed* costs. Costs, such as institutional advertising, incurred to support the total business, are *indirect fixed* costs.

In practice, firms recognize that there are really two categories of indirect cost: traceable and nontraceable. *Traceable* costs are indirect costs that can be allocated to various products on some nonarbitrary basis. For example, if a common sales force is used to sell two or more products, the total selling cost is usually allocated between the two products on the basis of some factor such as the percentage of selling time devoted to each one.

The purpose of distinguishing the various types of fixed costs is to provide a basis for evaluating the contributions made by different products or services to the overall profitability of the firm. Thus, firms assign direct and traceable indirect costs to products in order to gauge the costs of supporting each product. But nontraceable indirect costs are not assigned.

Table 6-3 illustrates how the profitability of individual products and services can be measured once management has separated the fixed costs. The bottom line for the

TABLE 6-3

LINKSTER INC.: CONTRIBUTION BY PRODUCT LINE (IN THOUSANDS OF DOLLARS)

	COMPANY TOTAL	UMBRELLAS	SWEATERS	JACKETS	CAPS
Sales	$4640	$840	$2400	$1200	$200
Variable cost of goods sold	1620	400	800	380	40
Gross profit margin	$3020	$440	$1600	$ 820	$160
Other variable costs	220	40	120	60	0
Variable contribution margin	$2800	$400	$1480	$ 760	$160
Direct, traceable fixed costs:					
Sales salaries	$ 500	$ 20	$ 360	$ 120	$ 0
Designers' salaries	400	0	300	100	0
Fixed production costs	680	100	340	230	10
Advertising of specific product lines	300	40	200	60	0
Total	$1880	$160	$1200	$ 510	$ 10
Total contribution	$ 920	$240	$ 280	$ 250	$150
Indirect, nontraceable fixed costs:					
Institutional advertising	$ 300				
General and administrative overhead	$ 600				
Total	$ 900				
Net operating profit	$ 20				

TABLE 6-4	LINKSTER INC.: PERCENTAGE-VARIABLE-CONTRIBUTION MARGINS			
	UMBRELLAS	SWEATERS	JACKETS	CAPS
Number of customers	28,000	40,000	20,000	50,000
Average price paid	$30	$60	$60	$4
Variable cost per unit	$15.71	$23.00	$22.00	$0.80
Variable-contribution margin per unit (Average price−variable cost per unit)	$14.29	$37.00	$38.00	$3.20
PVCM $\dfrac{\text{(Price − VC)}}{\text{Price}}$	47.6%	61.6%	63.3%	80%

individual products and services is no longer net operating profit but *total contribution.* The total contribution is the amount that an individual product or service "contributes" to the coverage of nontraceable indirect costs and to profit.

By examining Table 6-3, we can see that umbrellas and jackets generated total contributions that were nearly as large as the total contribution from sweaters, even though the sales volume from sweaters is much larger. This results from the higher share of direct, traceable fixed costs going to sweaters (sweater sales are twice jacket sales, but the direct costs of design, sales, and advertising are more than twice as high for sweaters).

Additionally, jackets are slightly more profitable than sweaters in terms of the percentage-variable-contribution margin. Table 6-4 summarizes unit price and cost data for the various lines and shows the PVCM calculations. For each $1000 in additional sales of jackets, Linkster will retain about $633 after variable costs are subtracted. For sweaters, $616 would be retained if sales rose by $1000.

IMPLICATIONS OF PROFITABILITY ANALYSIS

By identifying the fixed and variable components of cost and by distinguishing between direct and indirect costs, managers will be able to examine some of the profitability implications of pricing and marketing expenditure decisions. Specifically, by understanding the profitability structure for a product, managers can identify *cost-volume-profit relationships* and *implications for marketing budgets.*

Cost-Volume-Profit Relationships

In many organizations, a large portion of the total operating cost is essentially fixed. In these situations, managers generally will pursue policies that take advantage of *economies of scale.* These economies will exist when a large increase in volume leads to a significant reduction in the average cost of a product.

TABLE 6-5	ECONOMIES OF SCALE FOR SWEATERS	

	ANNUAL SALES VOLUME	
	40,000 UNITS	80,000 UNITS
Unit variable cost	$ 23	$ 23
Multiplied by volume	40,000	80,000
Total variable cost	$ 920,000	$1,840,000
Plus total direct or traceable fixed cost	$1,200,000	$1,200,000
Total direct cost	$2,120,000	$3,040,000
Divided by volume	40,000	80,000
Average unit cost	$ 53	$ 38

Consider, for example, Table 6-5. As sales volume doubles (from 40,000 to 80,000 units), total costs increase by a smaller percentage amount because a high proportion of total costs are fixed. Consequently, the average cost per unit is reduced from $53 to $38.

The existence of strong cost-volume-profit relationships means that managers should be more willing to increase marketing expenses or cut prices if these actions will lead to significant increases in volume. Returning to Table 6-5, we can see that at a price of $53 per unit, the firm will just cover its average costs at a volume of 40,000 units. However, the product could be profitable at a lower price (such as $39) if volume could be doubled as the result of that lower price.

The advantages of employing economies of scale to be price competitive are fundamental to the strategies of low-cost champions. Additionally, fixed costs are often extremely high in high-technology businesses where expenditures on research and development are very large (such as pharmaceuticals) and where manufacturing has become heavily automated. Particularly among global marketers, labor and material costs have declined relative to fixed costs. As a result, firms like Saab have been forced to deal with the issue of economies of scale.

In 1990, General Motors purchased a fifty percent interest in Sweden-based Saab which had lost $300 million the previous year. It quickly became apparent to General Motors' managers that Saab could not remain competitive with its existing cost structure because Saab was a low volume producer in an industry with substantial economies of scale. Accordingly, fixed costs were slashed and labor productivity improved and by 1992 Saab could cover all of its fixed costs at an annual sales volume of 100,000 cars (compared to the 200,000 needed in 1992).[1]

Managers not only must be aware of the opportunities associated with economies of scale, but also need to recognize the potential difficulties they create. When fixed

[1]John Templeman, "Saab: Halfway Through a U-turn," *Business Week,* Apr. 27, 1992, p. 121.

costs are high and industry sales growth is low, intensive competition usually results. This can pose real difficulties for firms that lack established market positions as the following demonstrates.

> IBP Inc. is one of the few meatpacking firms to regularly experience profitability in recent years. Many industry experts attribute this to IBP's aggressive expansion strategy in an industry plagued by excess capacity. Because fixed costs are very high and contribution margins are slim, firms must operate at a high capacity level. By paying top prices for cattle, IBP has been able to ensure that it operates with the best economies of scale in the industry. Essentially, its higher variable costs are offset by economies of scale enabling it to be a price leader in this highly competitive market.[2]

In order to compete with firms that possess such size advantages many firms use strategies that require minimal fixed costs. Specifically, some firms operate in market segments where the fixed costs associated with advertising, selling, or high development costs are very low.

Some firms have also found that variable costs may decline as volume increases. This phenomenon, known as the *experience-curve* effect, has been observed in companies such as Texas Instruments (consumer electronics), Black & Decker (power tools), and Du Pont (chemicals). Generally, these cost reductions occur as a firm becomes more experienced in producing a product for one or more of the following reasons.

- The firm may design more efficient production equipment or processes.
- The firm may improve its ability to obtain discounts or to control inventories, leading to reduced costs for materials and components.
- Production workers may become more efficient (especially in assembly operations) as they become more familiar with the production process.[3]

In sum, when average costs can be dramatically reduced because of economies of scale or experience curves, managers generally have a greater incentive to use competitive pricing or increased marketing expenditures in order to stimulate sales volume.

Semifixed Costs

Semifixed costs (also known as step-variable costs) represent a potential limitation to economies of scale. Essentially, semifixed costs are costs that do not vary automatically on a per unit basis (as variable costs do) but may change if substantial increases in volume occur. For example, a firm may need to set up an additional delivery route,

---

[2]Scott Kilman, "IBP Gobbles Up Weak Rivals in Meatpacking Industry," *Wall Street Journal,* Aug. 31, 1992, p. B3.

[3]See George Day and David Montgomery, "Diagnosing the Experience Curve," *Journal of Marketing,* Spring 1983, pp. 44–58.

TABLE 6-6	EFFECT OF SEMIFIXED COSTS

	ANNUAL SALES VOLUME UMBRELLAS		
	28,000	35,000	40,000
Unit variable cost	$15.71	$15.71	$15.71
Multiplied by volume	28,000	35,000	40,000
Total variable cost	$439,880	$549,850	$628,400
Total direct or traceable fixed/semifixed cost	160,000	160,000	240,000
Plus total variable cost	439,880	549,850	628,400
Total direct cost	$599,880	$709,850	$868,400
Divided by volume	28,000	35,000	40,000
Average unit cost	$21.42	$20.28	$21.71

rent or build new facilities for production or inventory, or hire more salaried supervisory workers or customer service personnel if production output increases dramatically. As Table 6-6 shows, a step-up in certain fixed costs will offset the effects of economies of scale. Whereas fixed costs for umbrellas stay the same as sales volume grows through 35,000 units, average costs decline. But once capacity is reached, large increases in fixed costs will be incurred. In Table 6-6, we see that certain previously fixed costs must be increased from $160,000 to $240,000 in response to the higher sales levels. As a consequence, average costs will edge upward, at least temporarily.

An example of the negative consequences of increased demand is the experience of Arkansas Freightways.

Arkansas Freightways hauls goods across ten states from Texas to Illinois, and in 1991 had sales of about $200 million. In July of 1991, the company's major competitor, Jones Truck Lines, filed for bankruptcy and ceased operations. Arkansas Freightways immediately signed up a number of Jones' customers, and sales volume rose 20% in 24 hours. But the increased volume proved to be very costly, as the company had misjudged its capacity. Employees labored overtime, and five hundred trailers had to be rented to meet demand. While existing trucks were now carrying more goods, packing more into a truck increased loading and unloading time. Finally, greater utilization pushed up maintenance costs. As a consequence of these problems, net income actually fell during the last quarter of 1991.[4]

Special Profitability Issues for Retailers

In addition to evaluating the impact of margins and direct fixed costs on profitability, retailers must assess the amount of space (physical assets) or inventory investment (financial assets) that is appropriate for a given product, product line, or department. Because space and inventory dollars are really the most critical resources for most

[4]Michael Selz, "Benefiting from Rival's Failure May Take Restraint," *Wall Street Journal,* May 19, 1992, p. B2.

retailers, managers involved with retail decision making should also assess profitability in terms of these assets.

Whether measuring profitability on a product, product-line, or departmental basis, retailers typically use four basic measures.

■ Inventory turnover
■ Sales per square foot
■ Gross-margin return on inventory investment
■ Gross-margin return per square foot

Inventory turnover is the ratio of a product's sales to the average dollar value of the inventory held for that product.

Sales per square foot is the ratio of a product's sales to the amount of selling space (measured in square feet) used for the product.

Gross-margin return on inventory investment measures the profit return rather than the sales return on inventory investment. This measure is calculated by multiplying inventory turnover by the gross profit margin percentage.

Gross-margin return per square foot is equivalent to sales per square foot multiplied by gross profit margin percentage.

Table 6-7 summarizes these four measures. In choosing one of them, managers should consider two issues. First, retailers may differ over whether inventory or space is the more critical resource. Some firms have adequate space but limited financial resources for purchasing inventory. Accordingly, these firms should use inventory turnover or gross-margin return on inventory investment, because the most critical decisions will revolve around inventory allocation. However, if space is the scarcer resource, then sales per square foot or gross-margin return per square foot should be used.

A second consideration is whether to use sales or gross margin as a measure of return. Many retailers continue to use sales rather than gross margin because it is simpler to measure sales when product-line or departmental profitability is being

| TABLE 6-7 | MEASURES OF PRODUCT PROFITABILITY FOR RETAILERS AND WHOLESALERS |

Inventory turnover	=	$\dfrac{\text{sales}}{\text{average value of inventory}}$
Sales per square foot	=	$\dfrac{\text{sales}}{\text{square feet of selling space}}$
Gross-margin return on inventory investment	=	$\dfrac{\text{gross margin}}{\text{price}} \times$ inventory turnover
Gross-margin return per square foot	=	$\dfrac{\text{gross margin}}{\text{price}} \times$ sales per square foot

measured. If departments or product lines vary significantly in gross margins, however, using sales as a measure of profitability will definitely be inadequate for comparing profitability.

Implications for Marketing Budgets

As we suggested at the beginning of the chapter, managers should have an understanding of the product objectives and an industry sales forecast in order to develop a budget. Further, managers must have some estimate of the productivity of a proposed price and marketing expenditure level in generating company sales (after taking the industry sales forecast into account). We will examine some procedures for developing these productivity estimates later in this chapter. However, assuming that management has developed these estimates of productivity, the budgeting process can proceed in either of two ways: the *direct* approach or the *indirect* approach.

THE DIRECT APPROACH

In this approach, managers must make specific estimates of the sales that will result from a given price and marketing budget. (The steps in this approach are summarized in Table 6-8.) If data are available for developing industry sales forecasts, managers can obtain an estimate of company sales by estimating the market share they expect to obtain for a given price and marketing budget and then multiplying this market share by the industry sales forecast.

To illustrate, recall that Linkster is considering a $100,000 increase in the advertising budget for jackets. Assuming that no changes occur in price or in other costs, the only elements in the profitability structure that will change are the advertising budget (which also leads to a change in total direct, traceable fixed costs) and variable costs. That is, if the increase in advertising results in increases in sales volume, then *by definition* total variable costs will increase as well.

If total jacket sales in Linkster's market are expected to be 250,000 units, and if Linkster's marketing manager predicts the company's market share to be 10 percent, then projected company sales would be 25,000 units. Assuming the average selling price remains at $60, dollar sales would be $1,500,000. Recalling from Table 6-4 that PVCM for jackets is 63.33 percent of sales, Linkster's variable-contribution margin

TABLE 6-8	STEPS IN THE DIRECT APPROACH TO MARKETING BUDGETING

1. Develop an industry sales forecast (where feasible).
2. Estimate the market share that will result from a given price and marketing expenditure level. (If no industry sales are available, directly estimate company sales instead of market share.)
3. Calculate the expected company sales (market share × industry sales forecast).
4. Calculate variable contribution (company sales × PVCM).
5. Calculate total contribution (variable-contribution margin less direct and traceable fixed costs included in proposed budget).
6. Determine whether the sales, market share, and total contribution levels are acceptable, given the product objectives.

| TABLE 6-9 | LINKSTER INC.: PROJECTED PROFITABILITY FOR JACKETS (IN THOUSANDS OF DOLLARS) |

		CURRENT YEAR		PROJECTED
Sales		$ 1200		$ 1500
× PVCM		.6333		.6333
Variable-contribution margin		$ 760		$ 950
Direct, traceable fixed costs				
Sales salaries	$120		$120	
Advertising	60		160	
Design	100		100	
Fixed production	230		230	
Total direct, traceable		510		610
Total contribution		$ 250		$ 340

will increase by $38 (63.33 percent × $60 selling price) for each additional jacket sold. Table 6-9 summarizes the calculation of the projected profitability of jackets for the proposed budget.

The calculations suggest that the sales increase of $300,000 will result in an increase of $190,000 in the variable-contribution margin (the remainder going to variable costs). Further breakdown of the $190,000 increase in variable-contribution margin shows that $100,000 will be spent on the increase in advertising, leaving a net gain in total contribution of $90,000. The new total contribution of $340,000 must be evaluated (along with the projected market share) against the product objectives. If the projected share and total contribution are high enough to meet top-management expectations, the new advertising budget will be considered adequate. If not, the manager must consider other possible budget levels.

The foregoing example is a rather simple illustration in that we have assumed only one change in projected expenditures. In a more typical case, managers would find that other changes could occur. Sales-force salaries might be increased, variable costs may change, or prices may rise or fall. If such changes are expected to occur, they should be incorporated in the profitability projections. (Note that a change in price or variable cost will require a change in the PVCM and in the variable-contribution margin per unit.)

Further, some degree of uncertainty usually exists in projecting sales and costs. Accordingly, managers who use the direct approach often must calculate several different estimates of total contribution to determine how much the total contribution figures would change if sales or various cost elements turned out somewhat higher or lower. Fortunately, nearly all marketing managers have access to one or more computer spreadsheet programs that allow them to go through the many calculations required by this process very rapidly.

In most cases, the highest degree of uncertainty will rest with the productivity estimates. When managers are very uncertain about these estimates (a situation that is typical of relatively new products), it is often useful to employ the *indirect* approach.

THE INDIRECT APPROACH

In the indirect approach (summarized in Table 6-10), an estimate of the sales productivity of a given price or budget is not required. Rather, managers are required to estimate only whether a benchmark level of sales can be achieved.

Specifically, managers who use this approach must first calculate the level of sales required to achieve the minimum acceptable target contribution for a given budget. This calculation requires three pieces of profitability information.

- The percentage-variable-contribution margin (or the variable-contribution margin per unit) based on the expected prices and variable costs
- The total direct and traceable fixed costs to be incurred (including any expected changes in the marketing budget)
- The minimum target contribution that will be acceptable to top management

Given this information, the *required level of sales* can be calculated using the following formulas.

$$\text{Total dollar sales required} = \frac{\begin{array}{c}(\text{target total contribution})\\ + \ (\text{total direct or traceable fixed costs})\end{array}}{\text{PVCM}}$$

or

$$\text{Total unit sales required} = \frac{\begin{array}{c}(\text{target total contribution})\\ + \ (\text{total direct or traceable fixed costs})\end{array}}{\text{PVCM per unit}}$$

In the case of Linkster, recall from Table 6-4 that the PVCM on jackets is 63.33 percent and that the variable-contribution margin per unit is $38. Given the proposed $100,000 increase in advertising, direct and traceable fixed costs will increase to

| TABLE 6-10 | STEPS IN THE INDIRECT APPROACH TO MARKETING BUDGETING |

1. Establish the target level of total contribution.
2. Calculate the level of sales required to achieve target total contribution for a given price and marketing expenditure level: (proposed total direct and traceable fixed costs plus target total contribution) divided by PVCM.
3. Calculate the required market share: required level of sales divided by industry sales forecast.
4. Based on estimated productivity of the proposed price and marketing expenditures, determine whether the required sales and market share can be achieved.
5. Determine whether the required market share and required sales will be acceptable for the given product objectives. If not, determine whether the sales or market-share objectives can be reached with the proposed budget.

$610,000 (as was shown in Table 6-9). If the owner is satisfied with the *current* total contribution of $250,000, then

$$\text{Total dollar sales required} = \frac{\$250,000 + \$610,000}{.6333}$$

$$= \$1,357,966$$

$$\text{Total unit sales required} = \frac{\$250,000 + \$610,000}{\$38}$$

$$= 22,632 \text{ jackets}$$

Note that if any changes in the target total contribution are made or if prices, variable costs, or other direct or traceable fixed costs are also changed, then the total sales required will change. For example, if Linkster were to reduce prices so that the average price paid was reduced from $60 to $50, the PVCM would be reduced to 56 percent; that is, PVCM would be calculated as ($50 − $22)/$50. Combining the proposed $100,000 increase in advertising with the reduction in price would result in the following calculations.

$$\text{Total dollar sales required} = \frac{\$250,000 + \$610,000}{.56}$$

$$= \$1,535,714$$

$$\text{Total unit sales required} = \frac{\$250,000 + \$610,000}{\$28}$$

$$= 30,714 \text{ jackets}$$

The immediate task now facing the owner is to determine the market share that will be required. As suggested in the previous section, it is assumed that industry sales will climb to 250,000 units in the coming year. Based on the proposal of a $100,000 increase in advertising and a target total contribution of $250,000, the required level of sales was 22,632 units. Therefore,

$$\text{Required market share} = \frac{\text{required level of sales}}{\text{industry sales forecast}} = \frac{22,632}{250,000} = 9\%$$

By determining the required market share, a manager develops a benchmark for evaluating the budget. The manager can now evaluate the proposed budget by addressing the question, "Will a $100,000 increase in advertising allow us to attain a 9 percent market share?" Although this question is not necessarily an easy one to answer, it is usually easier than developing a direct, specific estimate of the sales productivity of the marketing budget.

It should be noted, however, that the required market share calculated through the indirect approach gives only the minimum share needed in order to meet profitability requirements. In some cases, the product objective may call for market-share levels substantially higher than the share required to meet the target total contribution. In such cases, managers will also have to address the question of whether the proposed budget will be sufficiently productive to achieve the market-share objective.

Budgeting for Improved Customer Service and Satisfaction

In Chapter 1, we noted that there is a strong relationship between customer satisfaction and profitability. Satisfied customers are more likely to be repeat (and even loyal) customers. Additionally, satisfied customers are more likely to offer positive opinions about the product to other potential buyers.

Although a firm can take a number of actions to enhance customer satisfaction, one of its most important and effective actions is to improve *customer service.* Customer service activities include any actions that are designed to add value to the customer's product-usage experience. Traditionally, the emphasis in customer service has been on handling complaints or solving individual customer's problems. Today, the term also includes any positive actions that add value, such as keeping an automobile dealer's service department open longer or training airline personnel to be more effective at spotting a customer's unique needs.

Like other marketing activities, customer service costs money. Actions such as training, increasing the number of customer service personnel, providing replacement products at no charge, or establishing toll-free help lines all increase fixed costs. Although the sales payoffs from such actions are often slow to be realized, firms are paying increased attention to their budgetary implications. In particular, many firms (especially in service industries) regularly calculate the incremental profitability that customer service generates through enhancing customer satisfaction and retention.[5] Consider, for example, the case of a hypothetical chain of small resort hotels, Ameresorts.

Ameresorts regularly surveys its guests to measure customer satisfaction. In the most recent year, 1996, the company's research indicated that only 40 percent of its first-time guests were highly satisfied with their experiences at an Ameresorts hotel. By tracking its guests over time in its customer database, management knows that there is a 30 percent chance that a satisfied guest will return and that, on average, these people will return four times in the foreseeable future. The company has also calculated the unit-variable-contribution margin of the average guest stay to be $600. The budgetary questions that Ameresorts management must answer in deciding how much to spend on increased customer service activities are: (1) How much will it cost to improve customer service? (2) What will the impact be on customer satisfaction?

Table 6-11 provides an overview of the elements involved in assessing the profit consequences of Ameresorts' efforts to improve repeat purchasing by enhancing customer service and satisfaction. The table shows that, if Ameresorts can improve the percentage of satisfied first-time guests from 40 to 50 percent, the additional repeat business should generate $8,640,000 in future contributions to profits. (Of course, there will also be some increased business from the positive word of mouth these cus-

---

[5]Peter Dawkins and Frederick Reichheld, "Customer Retention as a Competitive Weapon," *Directors and Boards,* Summer 1990, pp. 41–47.

TABLE 6-11	BUDGETING FOR CUSTOMER SATISFACTION: AMERESORTS	

	1996	
	ACTUAL	**TARGET**
Total guest accounts	200,000	200,000
× Percent first-time guests	× 60%	× 60%
Total new guest accounts	120,000	120,000
× Percent satisfied	× 40%	× 50%
Total satisfied new guest accounts	48,000	60,000
× Probability of repeat	× 30%	× 30%
Expected number of repeaters	14,400	18,000
× Average number of future repeat visits	× 4	× 4
× Unit contribution margin per guest visit	× $600	× $600
Future incremental contribution from repeat purchases by first-time guests	$34,560,000	$43,200,000 − 34,560,000
Expected increased future contribution from improved customer satisfaction		$ 8,640,000

tomers provide to other potential guests.) To calculate the net gain in contribution, Ameresorts management must deduct the costs of the customer service improvement plan from the $8,640,000.

If the cost of the customer service improvement plan is known, management can use a variation on the *indirect method* of budgeting to calculate the increase required in customer satisfaction to maintain the current level of total contribution. For example, if management is prepared to commit $3.6 million for training of personnel and expanding the hours of some resort facilities, the required increase in the number of satisfied customers is

$$\begin{array}{l} \text{Required increase in} \\ \text{number of satisfied} \\ \text{customers} \end{array} = \frac{\text{increase in direct fixed costs for customer service}}{\begin{array}{l}\text{percent of satisfied} \times \text{average number} \times \text{VCM per unit} \\ \text{customers who repeat} \quad \text{of repeat visits}\end{array}}$$

$$= \frac{\$3,600,000}{30\% \times 4 \times \$600}$$

$$= 5000$$

Because Ameresorts had 48,000 satisfied new guests in 1996, the number of satisfied new guests required with the new customer service plan is: 48,000 + 5,000 = 53,000. Assuming that Ameresort has no increase in the number of new guest accounts.

$$\begin{array}{l}\text{Required percentage of satisfied} \\ \text{first-time guests}\end{array} = \frac{53,000}{120,000}$$

$$= 44.17\%$$

Thus, managers should pursue the proposed customer service plan if they believe the plan will increase the percentage of first-time guests who are satisfied from 40 percent to 44.17 percent or higher.

PRODUCTIVITY ANALYSIS

Productivity analysis is the process of estimating the impact on sales of a change in price or in marketing expenditures; that is, the change in sales resulting from a given change in a marketing program indicates how productive that marketing program is. Frequently, the term *sales-response functions* is used to represent relationships between price or a marketing expenditure and sales.

Traditional Methods of Productivity Analysis

Most firms attempt to estimate productivity using one or more of the following approaches.

ANALYSIS OF HISTORICAL RELATIONSHIPS

Frequently, managers look to historical experience in estimating the responsiveness of sales to various expenditures. For instance, internal data may be available to estimate

- The average sales per retail outlet (when an organization is attempting to expand its market coverage)
- The sales increases that have resulted from increases in past advertising budgets
- The sales per sales call on new-prospect accounts
- Historical price elasticity

To the extent that these relationships are applicable to the current situation, they may provide some clues to the impact of proposed expenditures on sales. Although management should not rely too heavily on such observed relationships unless they are supported by extensive sales data, more and more firms are developing computerized databases to track the purchases of customers. If data are also available on the prices buyers paid or on special promotions buyers took advantage of, firms can begin to gauge the effectiveness of these tools. For example, American Express could examine customer account records to determine historically the sales response to direct mail promotions of a luggage product at various prices.

COMPETITIVE PARITY ANALYSIS

This approach also relies on historical experience but is designed to consider relative marketing effort explicitly. For example, when competing products are highly similar in quality, a manager may find a very high correlation between a product's market share and

- Its share of industry advertising expenses
- The number of sales calls made relative to competitors' sales calls
- The relative number of retail accounts that carry the product
- The price of the product relative to the average industry price

To the extent that competitors' actions can be predicted, a competitive parity approach can provide clues to the likely impact of increased expenditures on market share. For example, it has been shown that successful new products maintain an advertising spending level over 2 years such that the brand's share of advertising is about *twice* the target share of market.[6]

MARKET EXPERIMENTS

In a market experiment, a firm tests alternative levels or combinations of marketing effort to see how they compare in terms of sales results. For example, a firm may set different prices in different markets to gauge the impact of a lower or higher price on sales. Or, a firm may compare sales in markets where retailers have been paid to set up special displays with those where there is no display to estimate the incremental sales gain from display. For consumer-goods marketers, an effective way to accomplish such experiments is to use an *electronic test market*. Syndicated marketing research firms A. C. Neilsen and Information Resources Inc. both offer such markets, which work as follows.

- Different sales promotions (such as coupons) are targeted (via mail) or different advertising levels (in terms of number of advertisements) are targeted (via cable television) to a panel of households within a market.
- Each household has a special card, which is scanned along with the household's purchases at supermarket checkout counters.
- Comparisons are made among the groups receiving each ad level or each type of direct mail promotion.

The use of electronic test markets has provided a wealth of information to marketers about the sales productivity of various marketing tools. Firms can assess total sales effects of, say, two types of promotions or two different advertisements and they can also compare these effects within different usage groups. That is, before the experiment begins, the past purchasing behavior of each household is identified so that the impact of the experiment on customers with different brand loyalty patterns or on customers with different usage rates can also be assessed.[7]

---

[6]See Simon Broadbent, *The Advertiser's Handbook for Budget Determination,* Lexington Books, Lexington, Mass., 1988, pp. 131–132.

[7]For a discussion and illustrations of the value of electronic test markets, see Darral G. Clarke, *Marketing Analysis and Decision Making,* 2d ed., Scientific Press, San Francisco, Calif., 1993, chap. 5.

Judgment-Based Productivity Estimates

Unfortunately, most marketing managers do not yet have research opportunities such as electronic test markets to measure the productivity of their marketing expenses. Moreover, even when a firm does have some quantitative evidence about sales response to marketing actions, it is not always certain that the observed relationship will hold up in the future; that is, managers must recognize that there are several limitations when applying observed sales-response relationships.

INTERACTION EFFECTS

Historical relationships may not be valid when two or more major changes take place simultaneously. For example, a firm may have a good understanding of the historical relationship between advertising expenditures and sales. However, if that firm combines a change in advertising with a sharp change in price, the historical advertising-sales relationship may not continue. Unless a firm has an extensive history of combining advertising and price changes, it will be difficult to establish historical relationships among price, advertising, and sales.

COMPETITION

When competitors modify their marketing policies as a reaction to competitive changes, the effectiveness of a given policy is often diminished. For example, a large increase in the advertising budget may lead competitors to respond by matching the increase, thus preventing any relative advantage from being gained.

MARKETING EFFECTIVENESS AND EFFICIENCY

The effectiveness of marketing programs may improve over time and the efficiency with which expenditures are made and allocated may change. In both cases, improvements will mean that the same dollars will yield a larger sales payoff. Thus, advertisements that do a better job of communicating a product's benefits will be more productive on a per dollar basis than less effective advertisements. Similarly, improved selection of media may allow a firm to reach more potential buyers at the same cost. So, to the extent that improvements in effectiveness and efficiency are forthcoming, a given marketing expenditure may be even more productive than would be projected from historical data.

NONLINEARITY

Many marketing phenomena have a changing response function over time or over levels. For instance, promotional efforts may have a pattern of sales effects similar to that presented in Figure 6-2. As this illustration demonstrates, the rate of sales response to an increase in marketing expenditures often changes over time, and thus the relationship is curvilinear. As the figure suggests, sales respond only minimally to low levels of advertising, but after a threshold level is reached, sales increase more rapidly with increases in advertising. Conceivably, at very high levels of advertising,

FIGURE 6-2

Hypothesized relationship between advertising expenditures and sales. (Reprinted by permission from R. L. Ackoff and J. R. Emshoff, "Advertising Research at Anheuser-Busch," *Sloan Management Review,* Winter 1975, p. 4.)

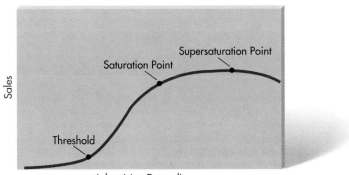

a supersaturation point could be reached. Beyond this point, sales might actually decline if advertising expenditures were to increase further.

In judgment-based productivity estimation, managers use their knowledge of the factors influencing demand, competitors, potential environmental changes, and planned changes in marketing strategies and programs (that is, how marketing dollars will be spent) as supplements to (or even as substitutes for) the other three methods.

One of the most widely publicized approaches to judgment-based estimation is the ADBUDG model developed by John D. C. Little. In Little's approach, managers attempt to quantify their judgments about the relationship between each marketing variable and market share by answering four questions.

1. What level of expenditure is needed to maintain the current market share through the next budget period? (the *maintenance level* of expenditures)
2. What minimum level of market share will result in the next period if expenditures are reduced to zero? (the *zero level* share)
3. What level of market share will result in the next period if expenditures are increased by 50 percent over the maintenance level? (the *plus-fifty level* share)
4. What is the maximum market share that could be obtained in the next period if expenditures were unlimited?[8] (the *maximum* share)

In answering these questions, managers can use any information they might obtain from examining historical ratios, experiments, or competitive parity analysis. However, managers will also consider factors (such as those listed in Table 6-12) that are likely to influence the impact of changes in marketing expenditures or price on market share in the next period.

Given these four estimates, managers can develop a pictorial representation (that is, a *model*) of their productivity judgments. Consider, for example, a situation in

---

[8]See John D. C. Little, "Models and Managers: The Concept of a Decision Calculus," *Management Science,* April 1970, pp. B-466–B-485. An extended version of the model can be found in John D. C. Little, "Brandaid: A Marketing Mix Model," *Operations Research,* July–August 1975, pp. 628–673.

TABLE 6-12	FACTORS TO CONSIDER WHEN MAKING JUDGMENTAL ESTIMATES OF PRODUCTIVITY

1. Stage in product-form life cycle
2. Anticipated prices and expenditures by competitors
3. Likelihood of competitive retaliation if a major increase in expenditures or decrease in prices is made
4. Extent of distribution availability of the product
5. Major improvements in the efficiency with which dollars are spent
6. Major improvements in the effectiveness of strategies and programs that are expected to result in more favorable perceptions on determinant attributes
7. Extent of customer turnover
8. Degrees of customer awareness and preference for our product versus competing products or brands

which a manager is concerned with examining the impact of a change in advertising expenditures on market share. Depending on the answers to Little's four questions, the manager might portray the advertising-market-share relationship in a number of ways. One possible portrayal is presented in Figure 6-3. (This figure was developed by plotting the market shares at the zero, maintenance, and plus-fifty advertising levels; by identifying the maximum share; and by connecting these points with an approximately S-shaped curve to reflect the assumption that the relationship is non-linear.)

FIGURE 6-3

An application of the ADBUDG model.

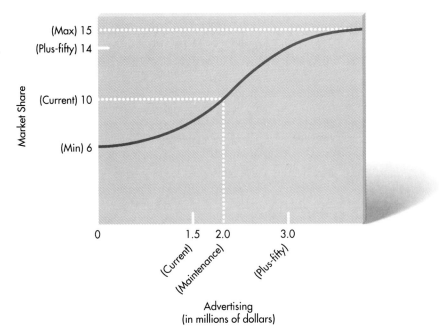

In Figure 6-3, the estimates suggest that an increase in advertising from $1.5 to $2.0 million will be needed simply to maintain market share and that sharp increases or decreases in market share will result from major changes in the budget. These estimates might reflect judgments on several of the factors listed in Table 6-12. That is, market share may be highly sensitive to advertising expenditures if the brand is competing in the early stages of the product life cycle where neither brand awareness nor brand preferences have been strongly established or if the market is characterized by a high degree of customer turnover so that few previous buyers of a brand are still in the market.

Once a manager has developed a model of the productivity relationship, the effect of a proposed expenditure level can be incorporated into the budgeting process. Managers can use this model either to establish direct estimates of market share or, if the indirect method is being used, to determine the likelihood of achieving a required level of market share.[9]

Cross-Elasticity Effects

Earlier, we discussed the concept of indirect costs, indicating that these costs reflect the interdependencies in a multiproduct firm. However, products may also be interdependent in demand. Cross-elasticity effects reflect the interdependencies in demand across a set of products. These effects can be of two types: substitution effects and complementary effects.

Substitution effects take place when two or more products or services are used to perform the same generic function. Thus, eyeglasses and contact lenses are substitutes, and substitution effects will occur when one product receives a relative increase in marketing support: Increases in advertising for contact lenses are likely to have some negative impact on demand for eyeglasses.

Complementary products are those products (or services) that experience a sales increase when related products experience an increase in support. This relationship can occur for a number of reasons.

- *Related use.* When two products are naturally used in conjunction with one another (as are men's suits and ties, or computers and high-speed printers), the purchase of one product may lead to the purchase of the second. Consequently, many firms offer related products to satisfy customer usage needs more completely.
- *Enhanced value.* One product may enhance the value or increase the utilization of another. For example, a new attachment may make a camera easier or more interesting to use.
- *Quality supplements.* Products designed for repair, maintenance, or operating assistance may enable a customer to obtain or maintain a high level of quality performance. For this reason, many industrial and consumer firms today find that service contracts sold with electronics products and other durable goods are often very much in demand.

[9]Ibid.

■ *Convenience.* Products that may be totally unrelated in use may be complementary if they are bought from the same source, because using a common source reduces buyers' search costs.

Thus, when Linkster's jackets are promoted, not only do jacket sales increase, but sales of related-use caps and umbrellas also increase. However, promotion of jackets will likely also lead to a decrease in sweater sales.

To the extent that managers can predict the cross-elasticity relationships among products and services, budgets should be adjusted to account for these effects. Consider, for example, the data in Table 6-13. This table is a simple extension of Table 6-9, which presented a hypothetical projected budget for jackets assuming that a $100,000 increase in advertising resulted in a $300,000 increase in sales.

Given the average price of $60 per jacket, the expected increase is 5000 units. Assume that Linkster knows from its sales records that

■ Ten percent of jacket buyers also purchase a cap and 30 percent purchase matching umbrellas when the jacket purchase is made.
■ Ten percent of jacket buyers would have purchased a Linkster sweater if they did not purchase the jacket.

Given these cross-elasticity estimates and the knowledge of percentage-variable-contribution margins (from Table 6-4), the owner can estimate the net profitability impact of the budget change following the procedure presented in Table 6-13.

TABLE 6-13   **LINKSTER INC.: PROJECTED BUDGET WITH CROSS-ELASTICITY EFFECTS**

	EFFECT OF NEW BUDGET		
	PROJECTED TOTAL		PROJECTED CHANGE
Unit sales	25,000		+ 5,000
Dollar sales	$1,500,000		+$300,000
Total contribution	$ 340,000		+$ 90,000
Plus complementary effects:			
Cap sales			
(5000 × 10% × $4)		$ 2,000	
× PVCM		80%	+$ 1,600
Umbrella sales			
(5000 × 30% × $30)		$45,000	
× PVCM		47.6%	+$ 21,420
Minus substitution effects:			
Sweater sales			
(5000 × 10% × $60)		$30,000	
× PVCM		61.6%	−$ 18,480
Net change in total contribution from budget change			+$ 94,540

CONCLUSION

An understanding of the profitability structure of any product is essential in order to find ways to increase or maintain profitability. As we have seen in this chapter, marketing does cost money. In order to examine the desirability of maintaining, increasing, or decreasing the level of marketing expenses, the variable-contribution margin and other elements of the profitability structure for a product must be known. Moreover, some understanding of the responsiveness of sales to changes in marketing budgets is essential in the planning process. Productivity analysis is the process of determining what the likely sales response will be.

This chapter has examined the difficulties involved in productivity estimation. However, as we have demonstrated, by combining sales-forecast, market-share, productivity, and profitability information, a manager's ability to evaluate proposed expenditures will be improved.

The impact of marketing expenditures on sales and profitability cannot be examined fully by use of the analytical tools presented in this chapter and summarized in Figure 6-4. Because they have some strategic purpose, expenditures must also be examined in the context of the marketing strategies and programs that managers design for a product. That is, these expenditures are more likely to achieve target sales and market-share levels if they support well-chosen strategies and programs.

FIGURE 6-4

Steps in productivity and profitability analysis and their relationships to other aspects of situation analysis.

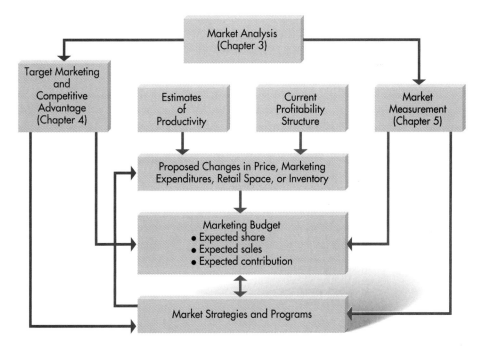

The process of designing effective marketing strategies and programs is the subject of Part 3 of this book. Before continuing on to Part 3, however, consider once again the budgeting issue facing Linkster Inc.

LINKSTER INC.: DEVELOPING A BUDGET

After reviewing Linkster's performance for the past year (as presented in Tables 6-1 through 6-4), the company's chief marketing executive began developing the budget for the coming year. Because the sweater business had been so important in the company's short history, she believed it was important to maintain sales growth for that product. Additionally, competition was more extensive in the sweater business than in the umbrella and jacket businesses. Eight different manufacturers were designing sweaters specifically for the golf market, with Linkster holding an estimated 8 percent share of the market.

Industry sales forecasts were usually made by estimating changes in the number of rounds of golf expected to be played in the coming year, which, in turn, depended on demographic and economic trends. For the coming year, industry sales of golf sweaters were expected to grow by 10 percent to 550,000 units.

Linkster's marketing manager had estimated competitors' total advertising expenditures at $3,100,000 for the most recent year. She also knew that the Linkster line was receiving substantially better acceptance among pro shop owners than most competitors because of the product's quality and up-to-date designs.

The marketing manager wanted to build market share for the sweater line without sacrificing profitability. Before she finalized the budget, however, she wanted to examine the market share and profit consequences of various budget levels. To do this in a thorough manner, she built a judgment-based model, establishing the following parameters for golf sweaters.

Maintenance advertising	= $220,000
Maximum share	= 11.5%
Plus-fifty share	= 10%
Minimum share	= 4%

1. Discuss some of the specific factors the marketing manager would likely have used in making these estimates.
2. Based on these estimates, develop a graph portraying the relationship between Linkster sweater advertising and Linkster sweater market share.
3. Using this graph, estimate the market share that would result and calculate the profit consequences (using the *direct* approach) if the advertising budget is set.

   - At $275,000
   - At $330,000

4. How would the market share and profit estimates in Question 3 change if the industry sales forecast were changed

   - To 520,000 units?
   - To 580,000 units?

QUESTIONS AND SITUATIONS FOR DISCUSSION

1. In what situations would the indirect approach be more useful than the direct approach for evaluating a proposed change in marketing expenditures?

2. **a.** Explain the importance of an accurate industry sales forecast to the budget process.

   b. Can you think of any situations in which the industry sales forecast may change as a result of changes in the marketing budget? Explain your answer.

3. For which of the following companies would experience-curve effects likely be strongest and for which would they likely be weakest? For which would economies of scale be strongest and for which would they likely be weakest?

   a. A firm such as Harley Davidson that assembles motorcycles

   b. A manufacturer of resin-based or durable plastic–based household products such as Rubbermaid

   c. A firm such as Waste Management that collects discarded materials for recycling

4. The Great Lakes Manufacturing Company produces a line of home and garden tools. The company recently introduced a light, but very durable, rake. In the first year the rake achieved a 10 percent share of the market in the region in which Great Lakes competes. Industry sales for the region were 700,000 units last year. Great Lakes sold the rake to retailers at $4 per unit; retailers priced the unit at an average of $7 to consumers. Variable production costs were $1.50 per unit, and direct fixed costs were $200,000.

   a. Calculate Great Lakes' total contribution for last year on the new rake.

   b. Assuming no changes in Great Lakes' costs, price, or in industry sales, what level of market share will be required in order to realize a total contribution of $100,000 on this new product?

   c. How might the Great Lakes manager responsible for this product try to assess the chances of achieving that market share?

5. The AM General Division of LTV Corporation created the Hummer, a four-wheel drive vehicle that could drive in a variety of terrains, for the U.S. military, and the product received many accolades for its performance in the Gulf War. In 1992, the company began producing a commercial version, which they expected would be popular among individuals in construction, ranching, or forestry, or just as an unusual off-road recreation vehicle. Capacity at the Mishawaka, Indiana, plant was 260 units per day—a number far above the requirements of AM General's military business. Assume that at production of 40 units per day (or 10,000 per year), the average cost of producing a vehicle is $30,000, with half of that cost going to variable costs and half to direct fixed costs, and that there are no changes in variable cost required for the new model.

   a. Calculate the average cost of the military version at volumes of 80 and 120 units per day.

   b. How would average costs change (from Question **a.**) if new semifixed costs of $20 million per year were added at a total volume of 80 units?

c. If the variable costs for the commercial version are $10,000 higher than for the military version, how do the answers to **a.** and **b.** change?

6. Midwest Electronics was examining the profitability of two of its cellular phone products. Given below are the cost and revenue figures for 1996.

	AUTO DELUXE	MICRO TALK
Selling price	$150	$200
Unit sales	30,000	20,000
Total variable cost	$75	$100
Traceable promotion expenses	$1,500,000	$1,500,000

Assume that all other costs are indirect.

a. Compare the current profitability of the two products.

b. Given *only* the profitability data, if you had additional funds for promotion, which product should receive those funds?

c. If the price of the Auto Deluxe were reduced by $50, what level of sales would be required to maintain the current level of total contribution?

7. For a standard new compact disc record album, the variable cost of manufacturing and packaging a blank disc is $1.30. A typical royalty to the singer is $1.00 per unit, and the costs of producing the recording session, the video, and the final product could easily run to $2 million.

a. If the manufacturer's price to distributors is $10.70 per unit, what is the variable-contribution margin?

b. At what level of sales will the record break even in terms of profit? (That is, at what sales level will the total contribution be zero?)

c. At what level of sales will the record break even if we add $200,000 for advertising?

d. Assume that Madonna is the artist and that her contract calls for a $20 million advance instead of a royalty. At what level of sales will the album break even?

8. In each of the following hypothetical situations, discuss the major problems that a marketing manager will face in trying to estimate the sales productivity and the profitability of the marketing action being considered, and indicate which method of productivity analysis you would recommend.

a. IBM is considering whether to double its advertising for its line of notebook personal computers.

b. Burger King is going to distribute coupons that can be used to purchase the company's new barbecue sandwich. They need to decide whether the value of the coupons should be 50 cents or 75 cents.

c. Domino's Pizza must decide on its advertising budget for next year. The company can estimate the size of the advertising budgets of its major competitors over time. However, Pizza Hut has been offering home delivery for only a few years, and Little Caesar's has emphasized price specials (such as two pizzas for the price of one), forcing the competition to gradually increase the use of price promotions.

SUGGESTED ADDITIONAL READINGS

Alberts, William, "The Experience Curve Doctrine Revisited," *Journal of Marketing,* July 1989, pp. 36–49.

Ames, B. Charles, and James D. Hlavacek, "Vital Truths about Managing Your Costs," *Harvard Business Review,* January–February 1990, pp. 140–147.

Grant, Alan W. H., and Leonard Schlesinger, "Realize Your Customers' Full Profit Potential," *Harvard Business Review,* September–October 1995, pp. 59–72.

Hoch, Stephen J., Xavier Dreze, and Mary E. Purk, "EDLP, Hi-Lo, and Margin Arithmetic," *Journal of Marketing,* October 1994, pp. 16–27.

Jones, John Philip, "Ad Spending: Maintaining Market Share," *Harvard Business Review,* January–February 1990, pp. 38–43.

Piercy, Nigel, "The Marketing Budgeting Process: Marketing Management Implications," *Journal of Marketing,* October 1987, pp. 45–59.

Rust, Roland T., Anthony Zahorik, and Timothy L. Keiningham, "Return on Quality (ROQ): Making Service Quality Financially Accountable," *Journal of Marketing,* April 1995, pp. 58–70.

Sheth, Jagdish, and Rajendra Sisodia, "Feeling the Heat," *Marketing Management,* Fall 1995, pp. 9–23.

PART THREE

CORPORATE MARKETING PLANNING

SITUATION ANALYSIS

MARKETING STRATEGIES AND PROGRAMS

Chapter 7 Marketing Strategies
Chapter 8 Product-Development Programs
Chapter 9 Pricing Programs
Chapter 10 Advertising Programs
Chapter 11 Sales Promotion and Direct
              Marketing Programs
Chapter 12 Sales and Distribution Programs
Chapter 13 Managing Sales and Distribution

COORDINATION AND CONTROL

MARKETING STRATEGIES AND PROGRAMS

T he primary responsibilities of middle-level marketing managers are to develop and implement marketing strategies and programs for individual products or product lines. In Part 3, we examine concepts and procedures for selecting specific strategies and programs.

It is important to recognize that the concepts and procedures presented in the forthcoming chapters are not independent of those we presented in previous chapters. Indeed, managers will not be able to make sound decisions on marketing strategies and programs without first having an understanding of

- The product objectives to be achieved
- The factors that will influence the responsiveness of primary and selective demand to the marketing offer
- The potential market segments that might be served
- The extent, type, and source of competition
- The size of various market opportunities, as indicated by market potential, industry sales, and company sales trends
- The profitability and productivity implications of making changes in prices or in marketing expenditures

Marketing programs are specific decisions and actions that are the responsibility of middle managers. In Chapters 8 to 13, we examine the decision-making concepts, tools, and procedures for product development, pricing, advertising, sales promotion, direct marketing, and sales and distribution programs. In particular, we will underscore the importance of developing specific program objectives. These objectives can greatly simplify the process of selecting and designing the specific elements of the program. Additionally, we present procedures for understanding the specific budgetary consequences of each of these programs.

Although the development of effective programs is critical to success, different managers are often responsible for designing and executing different programs. Accordingly, some mechanism is necessary to assure that various programs are consistent and work in harmony to achieve the product objective. A *marketing strategy* can provide consistency of direction among programs by identifying the kind of total impact on demand the overall marketing effort is designed to achieve. In Chapter 7, we will discuss the types of marketing strategies that can be employed, the relationship between strategies and programs, and considerations involved in selecting a marketing strategy.

CHAPTER 7

MARKETING STRATEGIES

OVERVIEW

When one considers marketing decisions and how they can affect demand for a firm's products, those actions that change prices, modify advertising campaigns, or establish special promotions come immediately to mind. We call such actions *marketing programs,* and we discuss the various types of marketing programs in subsequent chapters.

Often, several different marketing programs are used jointly. In other situations, managers may need to choose among marketing programs because of budget constraints. To make the best choices of marketing programs in such situations and to assure that the decisions will fulfill management's expectations for the product (as outlined in the product mix strategy, discussed in Chapter 2), marketing managers should first establish and communicate a clear marketing strategy.

Marketing strategies are plans that specify the impact a firm hopes to achieve on the demand for a product or product line in a given target market. As we saw in Chapter 3, firms sometimes perceive the best marketing opportunity to be in expanding primary demand, whereas the best growth opportunity may come from expanding selective demand. The basic options in developing marketing strategies are listed in Table 7-1. That these strategies are not mutually exclusive is important. If Campbell's designs a new marketing campaign promoting consumption of soup for dinner (a

TABLE 7-1

BASIC ELEMENTS OF A MARKETING STRATEGY

Target market selection	All buyers in the relevant market
	Buyers in one or more segments
Type of demand to be stimulated	Primary demand
	Among new users
	Among current users
	Selective demand
	In new served markets
	Among competitors' customers
	In current customer base

primary-demand strategy), the Campbell's brand is likely to benefit from the campaign (thus stimulating selective demand).

In essence, a marketing strategy is the bridge between the corporate strategy and the situation analysis on the one hand and the action-oriented marketing programs on the other. Marketing programs should flow from, and be consistent with, the marketing strategy. In turn, the selection of a marketing strategy should be based on the results of the earlier steps in the planning process. In the remainder of this chapter, we examine the various *types* of marketing strategies that can be chosen, we present a *process* for selecting a marketing strategy, and we discuss some important *dynamic* aspects of marketing strategy.

PRIMARY-DEMAND STRATEGIES

Primary-demand strategies are designed to increase the level of demand for a product form or class. Firms that are pioneers in marketing new product forms (such as Procter & Gamble in disposable diapers or Boeing in jumbo jets) will, by necessity, pursue primary-demand strategies. Additionally, firms with large market shares in established markets (such as Heinz ketchup or Microsoft in personal computer software) often devote at least part of their marketing effort to the expansion of primary demand because, as market leaders, they have the most to gain from expanding the market.

Basically, there are two sources of new demand for a product form or class: nonusers and users who might expand their rate of usage. Primary-demand strategies can, therefore, be categorized in terms of how the strategy is directed.

Strategies for Attracting Nonusers

To increase the number of users, the firm must increase customers' willingness or ability to buy the product.

INCREASING THE WILLINGNESS TO BUY

The willingness to buy may be stimulated by one of three approaches.

1. Demonstrating the benefits already offered by a product form
2. Developing new products with benefits that will be more appealing to certain segments
3. Demonstrating or promoting new benefits from existing products

A focus on demonstrating the basic product-form benefits is often necessary when a new product form is being marketed. For instance, Procter & Gamble had to demonstrate the convenience and performance of Pampers disposable diapers to a market in which washing cloth diapers was a time-honored behavior. Similarly, the popular Miller Lite beer advertisements successfully stimulated the willingness of beer drinkers to try a new product form (light beer) by emphasizing the "tastes great, less filling" attributes.

When new products yield significant additions to the benefits offered by existing product forms, the needs of potential customers are likely to be met. For example, scientists at Minnesota Mining & Manufacturing (3M) Company developed a new type of soap pad for use on nonstick cookware. Such cookware now accounts for about three-fourths of all cookware sales, but conventional soap pads ruin the pans. 3M expected the soap pad category to expand by over 15 percent as a result of this innovation.[1]

Often, industry trade associations undertake primary-demand strategies on behalf of the producers in a market to emphasize benefits that may not be widely known. For example, the American Iron and Steel Institute is campaigning heavily to promote the benefits of using steel in place of lumber for framing houses. The institute argues that steel is a superior alternative because it is durable, stable, maintenance-free, non-combustible, termite-proof, and recyclable. Potentially, the demand for steel framing could be twice as large as the current demand for steel for use in the automotive industry.[2]

The importance of this strategy type is paramount when a new product form or class is introduced, because new products seldom sell themselves. Additionally, this strategy may not be important in advanced economies if a product is well established, but can be critical in bringing a product to a new market in a different culture. Thus, in the United States, Procter & Gamble must focus its marketing strategy for Pampers on acquiring potential customers from competitors but, in developing countries, it will still be emphasizing the basic advantages of disposable diapers in order to stimulate primary demand.

INCREASING THE ABILITY TO BUY

The ability to buy can be improved by offering lower prices or credit, or by providing greater availability (through more distributors, more frequent delivery, or fewer stockouts). For example, reduced prices brought rapid sales increases to the cellular phone market in the late 1980s. Similarly, innovative financing plans can often help stimulate primary demand.

Strategies for Increasing the Purchasing Rate among Users

When managers are concerned with gaining more rapid growth in a sluggish but mature market, the marketing strategy may be geared toward increasing the willingness to buy *more often* or in *more volume,* using one of the following approaches.

BROADENING USAGE

Buyers may expand usage if the variety of uses or use occasions can be expanded. In recent years, a number of advertising campaigns have been conducted to suggest broadened applications for products or services. For example, A1 Sauce has been promoted for use on hamburgers, not just on steak; and Kraft has begun promoting Cheez

---

[1]Eben Shapiro, "Wool Pads of 3M Shake Up Old Business," *Wall Street Journal,* Jan. 13, 1994, p. B6.

[2]J. Linn Allen, "Indiana Project Could Build a Market," *Chicago Tribune,* Oct. 17, 1995, pp. C1–C2.

Whiz as a cheese sauce for nachos. Examples of attempts to broaden usage occasions include Coca-Cola's advertising campaign suggesting "Coke in the morning," and Pizza Hut's increased emphasis on developing its lunchtime business by promising speedy service. Similarly, makers of nutritional drinks and candy bars have recently shifted the focus of their marketing efforts toward the "meal replacement" situation, when some consumers might choose a candy bar. Products like ATP Tour bars and PowerBars were once found only at sports specialty stores but, today, are marketed through grocery, convenience, and drug stores.[3]

INCREASING PRODUCT CONSUMPTION LEVELS

Lower prices or special-volume packaging may lead to higher average volumes and, possibly, to more rapid consumption for products such as soft drinks and snacks. Or, consumption levels may be stimulated if buyers' perceptions of the benefits of a product or service change. This reasoning underlies the efforts of the pork industry to stimulate consumption. A recent industry advertising campaign emphasized pork's similarity to chicken in terms of its health benefits and its status as a white meat. Similarly, American Express expanded the benefits of its card to include automatic insurance of products that are purchased using the card.

ENCOURAGING REPLACEMENT

Product redesign may be thought of as a selective-demand strategy. It is, however, largely a primary-demand strategy in the fashion industry and in other durable-goods industries. Although a refrigerator may well last 20 years, many replacement sales will be made earlier if product convenience, space utilization, and operating costs can be improved.

In sum, primary-demand strategies may be implemented in a number of ways, as shown in Table 7-2. Although these strategies are generally less widely used than selective-demand strategies, they can be extremely useful if market measurements show large gaps between market potential and industry sales. Further, the analysis of

| **TABLE 7-2** | **PRIMARY-DEMAND MARKETING STRATEGIES** |

HOW DEMAND IS IMPACTED	BASIC STRATEGIES FOR INFLUENCING DEMAND
1. Attract nonusers	Increase willingness to buy Increase ability to buy
2. Increase rate of purchase among users	Broaden usage occasions Increase rate of consumption Increase rate of replacement

[3]Kelly Shermach, "Nutrition Drinks: They're Not Just for Athletes Any More," *Marketing News,* Oct. 23, 1995, pp. 1, 3.

TABLE 7-3	SELECTIVE-DEMAND MARKETING STRATEGIES

HOW DEMAND IS IMPACTED	BASIC STRATEGIES FOR INFLUENCING DEMAND
1. Expand served market	Broaden distribution Product-line extension

2. Acquire competitors' customers	Head-to-head competition
	   Superior quality
	   Price-cost leadership
	Differentiation
	   Benefit/attribute positioning
	   Customer-based positioning

3. Retain/expand demand within current customer base	Maintain satisfaction Relationship marketing Complementary products

the buying process may identify the factors limiting the ability or willingness to buy or to adopt a product class or form. If so, managers should have some insights into the kinds of programs that can be used to stimulate primary demand.

SELECTIVE-DEMAND STRATEGIES

As suggested in Table 7-3, selective demand can influence the market in three distinct ways: (1) by expanding the served market, (2) by acquiring competitors' customers, and (3) by retaining and expanding sales within the firm's current customer base.

Strategies for Expanding the Served Market

As we saw in Chapter 3, firms define their relevant market in terms of the product forms or classes in which they compete. The *served market* is that portion of the relevant market that a firm chooses to serve, as reflected by the scope of its product and distribution offerings. When Coca-Cola redefined its relevant market as "soft drinks," it had to decide whether to expand its line to serve product segments such as lemon-lime drinks and root beers. Similarly, Keebler competed in the cookie market, but not on the West Coast until the 1980s. When the opportunities for building market share within already served markets become more limited, firms often pursue sales expansion by broadening the scope of their distribution or by expanding the product line. As we saw in Chapter 2, these marketing strategies are virtually dictated if the corporate strategy emphasizes market development or product development.

BROADENING DISTRIBUTION

A firm's sales and distribution programs are designed to make products available to the target market and, often, to gain effective delivery, display, or promotional support. As firms grow, the increase in their capital may allow them to move into new geographic markets. For example, building-supply retailer Home Depot experienced great success in the Southeast region of the United States several years before it entered the Northeast and then the Midwest. Because the facilities and advertising required for success when breaking into new markets are so very expensive, the company had to proceed gradually and solidify its position in its core markets to generate the funds required.

In other cases, firms may have to move into new channels of distribution in order to serve all portions of a market. Formerly, Levi Strauss sold its men's jeans only in quality menswear stores or in high-quality department stores, but it has now expanded to mass-merchandiser distribution because Levi's realized that a very large portion of its market did not shop for jeans in its traditional outlets. Similarly, IBM began selling personal computers in mass-merchandiser outlets such as Best Buy because many "home computer" buyers were not shopping in specialty computer stores. Compaq used a similar strategy by selling computers through mail order.

PRODUCT-LINE EXTENSION

A firm can expand the line of products it offers within a market through new-product development programs. Specifically, a firm can choose from two main routes when using new-product development to serve new markets.

A *vertical product-line extension* involves adding a new product at a noticeably different price point. Toyota's addition of the Camry staked out a position in the automobile market among buyers with very different price-quality tradeoffs than those of Corolla buyers. On the other hand, Coors introduced Keystone at a lower price point in order to compete more effectively in the "popular" price segment of the beer market.

A *horizontal product-line extension* occurs when a firm adds a new product with different features at more or less the same price level. Liquid Tide detergent and Bud Dry beer are examples. These product-line extensions allow a firm to serve a wider variety of specific tastes or preferences. For example, Coca-Cola extended its soft-drink line to include Fruitopia in response to growing consumer interest in noncarbonated beverages.[4]

In Chapter 8, we will examine in more detail the process for developing these kinds of new products and the considerations involved in making them successful.

Strategies for Acquiring Competitors' Customers

A firm's most direct competitors are those it competes with within the same served market. For General Motors' Saturn the most direct competitors are products such as Chrysler's Neon and Honda's Civic. When buyers make choices within a given served market, those who view the choice process as nonroutine will compare the alternatives in terms of the various attributes. Because choices will largely be based on these

---

[4]Robert Frank, "Fruity Teas, Mystical Sodas Boring Consumers," *Wall Street Journal,* Oct. 9, 1995, pp. B1–B2.

perceptions, customer acquisition strategies will essentially be based on how the product is positioned in the market. That is, a product's *position* represents how it is perceived relative to the competition on the determinant attributes desired by each segment. From a managerial perspective, a firm has two basic strategic options: head-to-head positioning or differentiated positioning.

HEAD-TO-HEAD POSITIONING

With this strategy, a firm offers basically the same benefits as the competition, but tries to *outdo* the competition in some way. One approach to head-to-head competition is to make a *superior marketing effort* (in terms of quality, selection, availability, or brand name recognition). For example, Frito-Lay holds a dominant position in the salty snack, potato chip, and tortilla chip markets, in large part because of its wide variety of flavors, its superior sales force (which assures the widest possible availability), and its extensive advertising effort. In one recent year Frito-Lay's ad budget was $60 million compared to $2 million for its leading competitor, Eagle Snacks.[5]

Alternatively, firms may compete on a *price-cost leadership* basis by offering comparable quality at a lower price. If an industry is characterized by intensive competition (as is the case in the airline industry and long-distance phone service), direct price competition can be expected. Although leading firms often have economies of scale that yield cost advantages (as illustrated in Chapter 6), it is significant that small firms can sometimes succeed on price leadership.

A limitation of head-to-head competition is that, if the similarity among competitors' marketing strategies is very strong, several common marketing problems can result. First, if several brands offer the same price and the same nonprice benefits, they are collectively more vulnerable to aggressive new entrants who offer a unique nonprice benefit. Second, these commonly positioned brands will have a more difficult time standing out in the minds of consumers or distributors. Thus, to gain a competitive advantage, they may have to increase funds spent on marketing communications (advertising, promotion, or personal selling).[6]

DIFFERENTIATED POSITIONING

In differentiated positioning, a firm is trying to distinguish itself either by offering distinctive attributes (or benefits) or by catering to a specific customer type.

In *benefit/attribute positioning,* firms emphasize unique attributes (such as Norelco's rotating electric shaver blades), unique packaging advantages (Lipton Cup-A-Soup), or unique benefits (Gatorade replaces key minerals in the body after exercise). A recent success story in benefit/attribute positioning was Chesebrough-Pond Inc.'s Mentadent toothpaste, which rose quickly to the number 3 market-share position. Dispensed from a bulky pump, Mentadent mixed baking soda with peroxide to

---

[5]Robert Frank, "Frito-Lay Devours Snack Food Business," *Wall Street Journal,* Oct. 27, 1995, pp. B1, B4.

[6]Beaven Ennis, *Marketing Norms for Product Managers,* Association of National Advertisers, New York, 1985, p. 41.

create a fizz (and presumably whiter teeth). Its market success came in spite of a price nearly double that of other brands.[7]

In *customer-oriented positioning* (also known as niching), a firm tries to separate itself from major competitors by serving one or a limited number of special customer groups in a market. Often, niches are defined in terms of particular usage situations or buyer characteristics. Nyquil was the first cold medicine designed to serve a nighttime usage situation. Recently, Taco Bell revised its strategy to concentrate on two customer groups: 18- to 24-year-olds who purchased only the lowest priced offerings and two-income couples interested in speedy service. To reach the first group, Taco Bell expanded its assortment of low-priced (59 cent, 79 cent, and 99 cent) offerings, whereas, to serve the second group, the firm revised its operations away from an orders-on-demand approach to an inventory-based approach.[8]

POSITIONING AND BRAND EQUITY

Products that are successful in implementing a positioning strategy usually develop a high level of brand equity. *Brand equity* is the added value that knowledge about a brand brings to a product offering over and above its basic functional qualities. The foundations of brand equity are (1) extensive brand awareness and (2) strong, unique, and favorable brand associations.[9] Such associations may offer particular benefits (such as between Crest and "fights tooth decay"); provide usage situations (Kodak "for the times of your life") or user characterizations (Coors and "mountain men"); indicate corporate competencies (3M and innovation) or product categories (Rollerblades has become somewhat synonymous with in-line skates). These associations can often be developed if the product consistently delivers satisfactory performance, is backed by extensive promotional efforts, and uses consistent imagery through spokespersons (such as Michael Jordan for Nike) or characters (such as the Marlboro Man).[10]

Brand equity may create a variety of benefits for a firm. Specifically, with strong brand equity a firm can more easily obtain strong promotional support from wholesalers or retailers. Also, a strong brand equity reinforces customer loyalty to a brand. As we discuss in Chapter 8, when a strong existing brand is used on new products, the cost of building market awareness and trial for the new product may be substantially lower. Finally, brand equity often allows a firm to establish a price premium, as in the case of certain personal computers.

Intelliquest Inc., a market research firm specializing in the computer industry, found that customers would be willing to pay $339 more for an IBM PC and $260 more for a Hewlett-Packard PC than for an unbranded "clone." AST computers could only command a $17 pre-

[7]Zachary Schiller, "The Sound and the Flouride," *Business Week*, Aug. 14, 1995, p. 48.

[8]Alan Grant and Leonard Schlesinger, "Realize Your Customers' Full Profit Potential," *Harvard Business Review*, September–October 1995, pp. 65–66.

[9]Kevin Keller, "Conceptualizing, Measuring, and Managing Customer-Based Brand Equity," *Journal of Marketing*, January 1993, pp. 1–22.

[10]Peter Farquhar, "Managing Brand Equity," *Marketing Research*, September 1989, pp. 24–29.

mium. The researchers pointed out that AST has failed to develop any brand identity, while Hewlett-Packard is known for reliability. Similarly, Intel succeeded in building brand equity for its Pentium microprocessor; customers were willing to pay an average of $345 to upgrade to Pentium from a comparably functioning chip made by Advanced Micro Devices.[11]

Strategies for Retaining/Expanding Demand within the Current Customer Base

A 1995 study of 165 businesses by the consulting firm Marketing Metrics revealed that, on average, 53 percent of the marketing budget was directed toward the retention of existing customers versus 47 percent for customer acquisition, reversing the percentages that had been observed in 1991.[12] One reason for the shift is that managers have begun to realize that it usually costs more to acquire new customers than to retain the loyalty of existing ones, so money spent on customer retention is more productive. Consequently, an increasing emphasis is being placed on strategies designed to maximize future sales opportunities from the current customer base. Three such strategic options are:[13]

1. Maintain a high level of customer satisfaction
2. Build a strong economic or interpersonal relationship with the customer
3. Develop complementary products that will appeal to current customers

MAINTAIN SATISFACTION

Loyalty occurs if a customer continues to purchase goods or services from the same source over time. As noted in Chapter 1, customer satisfaction is the main cause of loyalty. In addition, satisfaction and loyalty are enhanced by a strong brand equity. Brands like Coca-Cola (in soft drinks), Campbell's (in soups), Gillette (in razors), and Kellogg's (in cereals) have maintained their leading market shares for three-quarters of a century, in large measure because of their brand imagery.[14] This equity can be maintained and enhanced as long as such firms continue to produce a high level of product quality and invest in their brand associations.

However, even in the best quality-oriented organizations, poor quality of goods or services will occasionally occur. Usually, this results in dissatisfied customers who may or may not complain. One way to maintain satisfaction in those situations is to design a *complaint management* system. In such systems, managers usually categorize customer complaints to determine whether the problem is a product breakdown or can be explained by incorrect usage, inflated expectations, or simple misunderstandings. Whereas complaint management for product breakdowns can usually be

[11]Jim Carlton, "Marketing Plays a Bigger Role in Distinguishing PCs," *Wall Street Journal,* Oct. 16, 1995, p. B4.

[12]Jagdish Sheth and Rajendra Sisodia, "Feeling the Heat," *Marketing Management,* Fall 1995, pp. 9–23.

[13]A descriptive analysis of the strategies used by challengers and defenders is contained in Stanley Stasch and John Ward, "Defending Market Leadership: Characteristics of Competitive Behavior," *Proceedings of the Fall 1992 Educators' Conference,* American Marketing Association, Chicago, pp. 466–472.

[14]*The Value Side of Productivity,* American Association of Advertising Agencies, New York, 1989, p. 18.

handled under warranty policies, a major challenge lies in deciding what policy should govern company response to the other types of complaints. Emerging evidence seems to suggest that firms should liberally accept complaints as valid and should compensate complainants. The arguments for this point of view are:[15]

1. Dissatisfied customers who are persuaded to stay are likely to be more loyal and profitable than before. (One study of 100 firms demonstrated that reducing customer defections by 5 percent resulted in profit increases of 25 to 85 percent primarily because of increased purchases.)[16]
2. Generous complaint management encourages more complaints from unhappy customers who otherwise would simply not repurchase in the future. (A study by British Airways revealed that 50 percent of customers who experienced problems but never complained defected to competitors, whereas 87 percent of customers who complained did not defect.)[17]
3. Consumer complaints can include useful feedback for the design of products and services that better meet the needs of existing customers.

RELATIONSHIP MARKETING

A relationship marketing strategy is designed to enhance the chances of repeat business through development of formal interpersonal ties with the buyer. Long-term relationships are often established through contractual or membership arrangements with customers or distributors. Typically, these arrangements are only successful because of some discount or an economic incentive associated with the cost of purchasing. For example, consumers who buy season tickets for a symphony orchestra series are essentially engaged in a membership relationship. Similarly, annual fees charged by health spas ensure at least a 1-year relationship. In industrial marketing, simplification programs such as long-term protection against price increases or inventory management assistance are frequently so desirable to buyers or to distributors that they will commit themselves to use one supplier as their sole source of supply for a period of time. Another recent development involves the placement of computer terminals (and often, associated software) in customers' offices. These terminals are then hooked into the sellers' terminals, enabling customers to order products instantly (and thus better manage their inventories), check on the progress of deliveries, and obtain technical assistance. In recent years, firms that have experienced success with these systems include Cigna Corp. (assistance on industrial customers' insurance problems), Baxter Health Care (reordering supplies for hospitals), and Benjamin Moore (analyzing color samples provided by paint stores to provide pigment prescriptions).

[15]Claes Fornell and Birger Wernerfelt, "Defensive Marketing Strategy by Customer Complaint Management," *Journal of Marketing Research,* November 1987, pp. 337–346.

[16]Frederick Reichheld and W. Earl Sasser, "Zero Defections: Quality Comes to Services," *Harvard Business Review,* September–October 1990, pp. 105–109.

[17]Charles Weiser, "Championing the Customer," *Harvard Business Review,* November–December 1995, p. 113.

A particular form of relationship marketing that has become increasingly popular is *frequency marketing,* a strategy designed to encourage increased purchases from a firm's best customers. Frequency marketing requires the establishment of customer databases (as discussed in Chapter 5) that permit the targeting of messages and incentives directly to key customers. For example, the Wisconsin-based catalog firm Land's End will examine each household's past purchases and modify the catalogs it sends accordingly. Households that regularly buy crew-neck sweaters or dress shirts may receive catalogs with more displays of those products or even special catalogs devoted to a product category. As the following example illustrates, however, most frequency marketing involves direct economic incentives to encourage more purchasing from the existing customer base.

> Lettuce Entertainment Enterprises owns and manages several Chicago casual, upscale, and fine dining restaurants. Over twenty thousand households are members of the company's *Frequent Diners Program.* Each member completed an application (available in each restaurant) providing basic address information, received a card that is used with each restaurant visit to record purchases, and earns gift certificates at any participating restaurant based on dollar expenditures. Additionally, members with very large expenditures can earn the right to make reservations at certain restaurants that normally do not take them.[18]

COMPLEMENTARY PRODUCTS

In Chapter 6, we discussed the fact that an increase in the sales of one product could lead to increased sales for related complementary products, and we listed the reasons a complementary relationship might occur. Complementary products can often be designed and marketed in a way that helps retain customers. Expanding the number of relationships between a seller and a buyer makes switching to an alternative supplier more expensive for the customer. Many financial institutions try to get checking-account customers to use the institution as a source for their credit cards, loans, and savings accounts. In theory, as consumers concentrate their business in one financial institution, they will be less likely to switch their business for any one product because it would reduce the convenience of one-stop banking.

In other cases, the primary strategic value of complementary products is to apply leverage to the business relationship with current customers in order to sell additional products. Two popular ways of implementing this strategy are bundling and systems selling. *Bundling* involves the development of a specific combination of products sold together (such as personal computers, printers, and software) at a special price. This can be especially effective if some of the products in the bundle are more popular than others; in such cases, some buyers will purchase the full bundle, including the less desirable elements in order to receive the savings. In *systems selling,* a firm designs its products so that they are especially compatible with one another. So IBM will try to design software for networking among IBM computers that is more efficient than competing software.

---

[18]"Frequent Dining—Restaurants Acquire a Taste for Frequency Marketing," *Colloquy,* vol. 4, no. 4, 1994, pp. 1, 4–8.

SELECTING A MARKETING STRATEGY

To choose the best marketing strategy, a manager must consider several kinds of information (see Figure 7-1). First, the marketing strategy must be consistent with the *product objective*. Second, the nature and size of the *market opportunity* should be clearly established based on the market analysis and market measurements. Finally, managers must understand what kinds of competitive advantage and marketing expenditure levels will be necessary to achieve *market success*.

The Role of Product Objectives

Product objectives help determine the basic type of strategy needed. For example, if increased volume or market-share growth are important, managers are likely to use selective-demand strategies that focus on acquiring competitors' customers or expanding the served market. Alternatively, the greater the importance of cash flow and profitability objectives, the more likely a manager will be to focus marketing strategy on the existing customer base; that is, these strategies will, in *general*, be less costly than

FIGURE 7-1

Selecting a marketing strategy.

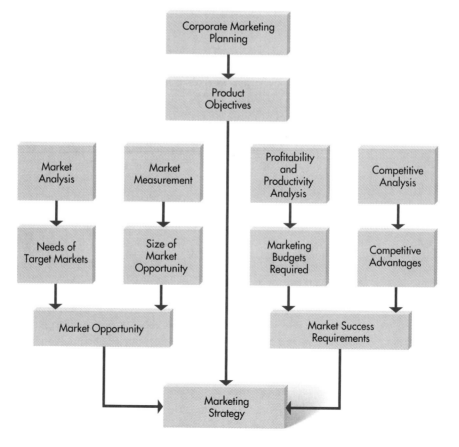

acquisition strategies or strategies aimed at increasing the number of users. (Put simply, it is usually easier to reach and persuade existing brand customers and existing product-form buyers than to convert competitors' customers and nonadopters.)

Additionally, the feasibility of a given strategy depends on the firm's ability to deal with the problems and opportunities identified in the situation analysis. If managers cannot identify a feasible marketing strategy for implementing the product objective, then the objective probably should be modified.

Implications from Situation Analysis

Each of the issues addressed in the chapters on situation analysis (Part 2) has implications for the selection of marketing strategies and programs.

First, market analysis provides information on the person who buys (and who does not buy) the product form, the various situations in which the product is used (or not used), and the factors that influence the willingness and ability to buy. This information can help managers select strategies and programs to increase either the number of users or the rate of use. By analyzing selective demand, managers should gain insights into the alternative segmentation opportunities that exist and the factors that influence buyers' choice processes.

Second, the competitive analysis enables a manager to determine who the competition will be, how intensive the competition will be, and what advantages must be developed in order to compete effectively either against direct brand competitors (in selective-demand strategies) or against indirect product-class competitors (in primary-demand strategies).

Third, market measurements provide information on the size of the *primary-demand gap* between market potential and industry sales. As suggested in Chapter 5, the larger this gap, the greater the opportunity to expand primary demand for a product form or class. Further, the slower the industry sales growth, the more important it will be to find ways of expanding primary demand. Descriptive company sales forecasts can provide insights into the impact of various marketing programs on sales.

Finally, by combining productivity estimates with profitability analysis, managers can determine the profit consequences of the strategies and programs required for achieving market-share objectives.

The Globalization Question

Because an increasing proportion of businesses operate across national boundaries, an important question concerns whether to market a single standardized (and thus globalized) offering or to treat the various nations in the market as segments.

The principle of selling the same product in essentially the same way everywhere in the world is not new. Exxon has been selling motor oil globally since 1911, and Caterpillar adopted a global approach to its marketing after World War II. Caterpillar organized an international network to sell spare parts and built a few large-scale, efficient manufacturing plants in the United States to meet worldwide demand. The product was then assembled by smaller regional plants, which would add those features that were needed for local market conditions. The emergence of global markets has allowed corporations as diverse as Revlon (cosmetics), Sony (televisions), and Black & Decker (power tools) to standardize manufacturing and distribution. Some concessions to cultural differences—such as producing cars with steering columns on the right or left side—are made, but these require only minor modifications, and most other features of the product remain the same.

Some experts argue that advances in communication, transportation, and entertainment technology have brought about more homogeneous world tastes and wants, so companies that fail to adopt a global strategy are seen as vulnerable to global firms that can obtain savings from standardization. Others point out that local tastes and customs are still very important influences on consumers and businesses.

Among the factors favoring globalization the following appear to be most important.[19]

1. *Economies of scale exist.* The greater the economies of scale in production, marketing costs (such as advertising, sales literature), service requirements, and spare parts inventories, the more advantageous a global strategy is. Products like autos, appliances, and construction vehicles are among those where economies are great.
2. *Customers operate globally.* If a firm's customer base is heavily multinational, operating in a variety of countries, it will prefer a standardized offering. Thus, large banks, steel manufacturers, hotels, and computer manufacturers are more likely to offer more standardized products when they serve customers whose operations are global.
3. *Home-country image is valuable.* When a product's appeal is partly a function of its home-country image, that image may be advantageously used by not varying the product. French perfumes, Levi's jeans, Sony entertainment products, and Mercedes automobiles all benefit from home-country images for quality in those particular categories.
4. *Product usage.* Differences in consumption processes or usage conditions can alter the benefits required. European nations differ in the temperatures at which products are cooked and clothes are washed. Condensed soups are historically not as acceptable to Europeans as to Americans.
5. *Government policy.* Local content laws or regulations regarding the labeling of products can restrict globalization efforts. For example, in Italy all "pasta" must be made with durum wheat. In other product categories, tax laws may impede globalization (as in the European practice of taxing automobiles based on engine size).

DYNAMIC ASPECTS OF MARKETING STRATEGY

A firm must usually change the strategy for a product over time because competition, costs, and the nature of demand change. The concept of the *product life cycle* has enjoyed broad acceptance as useful in understanding the strategic implications of these changes.

---

[19]An expanded discussion is available in Vern Terpstra and Ravi Sarathy, *International Marketing,* 6th ed., Dryden Press, Fort Worth, 1994, pp. 264–267.

The Product Life Cycle

The product life cycle represents a pattern of sales over time, with the pattern typically broken into four stages (see Figure 7-2). The four stages are usually defined as follows.

1. *Introduction.* The product is new to the market. Because there are therefore no direct competitors, buyers must be educated about what the product does, how it is used, who it is for, and where to buy it.
2. *Growth.* The product is now more widely known and the sales grow rapidly because new buyers enter the market and, perhaps, because buyers find more ways to use the product. Sales growth stimulates many competitors to enter the market, and the increase of market share becomes the major marketing task.
3. *Maturity.* Sales growth levels off as nearly all potential buyers have entered the market. Consumers are now knowledgeable about the alternatives, repeat purchasers dominate sales, and product innovations are restricted to minor improvements. As a result, only the strongest competitors survive. It is very difficult for weaker firms to obtain distribution and to increase their market share.
4. *Decline.* Sales slowly decline because of changing buyer needs or because of the introduction of new products that are sufficiently different to have their own life cycles.

That the product life cycle reflects the sales pattern of a product form or class—not of a single competitor—is important. Individual brands may come and go at virtually any time. But the concept that sales grow for a while at varying rates, level off, and then are replaced (usually) by some newer form of the product (with a distinct life cycle of its own) is broadly useful.

The product life cycle concept is not without its limitations. For example, it doesn't take into account the specific competencies and resources of the various competitors in a given market. Thus, if competitors have extensive financial resources, the level of marketing expenditure necessary at various stages may be greater than the model suggests. Additionally, competitors that are financially strong because of sales

FIGURE 7-2

Stages of the product life cycle.

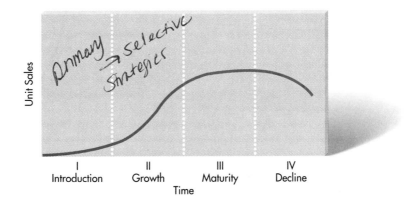

of other products may survive into market maturity even with small market shares. Another limitation is that competitors may mistake a leveling of growth as an indicator of maturity, when the true cause is a lack of industry promotional effort or prices that are too high. Often, the result is a self-fulfilling prophecy: Firms reduce marketing expenditures, which, in turn, retards sales growth.[20]

The Product Life Cycle and Strategy Selection

From a strategic point of view the product life cycle helps managers analyze past and forthcoming changes in their situations. These changes (which are summarized in Table 7-4) can impact both the selection of a marketing strategy and the design of marketing programs that will be used to implement that strategy.

The most obvious impact of the product life cycle is the shift from a primary- to a selective-demand strategy as the life cycle shifts from the introductory stage to the growth and maturity stages. As buyers become more knowledgeable about the product category, and as the primary-demand gap declines, the need for and payoff from primary-demand strategies decline.

A second consideration is that retention strategies should seldom be relied on, even by a market leader, until the life cycle is well into maturity. As long as markets are growing rapidly, acquisition strategies are important.

Third, product-line extensions should be developed as soon as segmentation opportunities arise. Although some marketing consultants have argued that such products should be used to try to reinvigorate life cycles in maturity, the conventional wis-

TABLE 7-4	**HOW THE SITUATION ANALYSIS CHANGES OVER THE PRODUCT LIFE CYCLE**

Market analysis
Buyers become more knowledgeable about the product category and the alternatives
Repeat purchases grow and first-time purchases decline
Segmentation increases

Competitive analysis
Innovators stimulate primary demand
Early followers may imitate or leapfrog
Only the strongest survive shakeout

Market measurement
Primary-demand gap declines
Industry growth rate declines
Differences in penetration of geographic markets accelerate

Profitability/productivity
Marketing costs rise, then level out
Production costs decline with experience
Selective-demand response to price and quality increases
Selective-demand response to advertising and distribution decreases

[20]See Mary Lampkin and George Day, "Evolutionary Processes in Competitive Markets: Beyond the Product Life Cycle," *Journal of Marketing,* July 1989, pp. 4–20.

dom is now changing. Often, line extensions are necessary to move a product through the growth stage because the variation in basic customer needs (for example, personal computers or microwave ovens) is very large. Additionally, market leaders who offer a full product line may preempt competitive opportunities from new entrants or be better able to meet competitive challenges.

The Product Life Cycle and Marketing Programs

As we have suggested, a given type of marketing strategy may be achieved through two or more different marketing programs. For example, acquiring new customers through head-to-head positioning could imply direct competition among price, availability, quality, or brand awareness. However, over the course of the life cycle the productivity of different programs changes. Specifically, as the life cycle moves from introduction toward maturity and decline, the following trends in the response of market share occur.[21]

PRICE The impact of price on primary demand is usually very high during introduction. But the impact of price on market share is relatively low at this stage because of a lack of competitors. As the technology matures, competing products become more alike and buyers become aware of more alternatives. Market share, thus, becomes *increasingly responsive to price.*

PRODUCT QUALITY As buyers gain information from experience and from word-of-mouth communications, they become knowledgeable about the relative quality of various products. Thus, market share becomes *increasingly responsive to product quality.*

ADVERTISING Over time, awareness of a brand and its attributes will grow with cumulative exposure to advertisements. As discussed in Chapter 6, saturation levels may ultimately be reached. In any event, diminishing returns will ultimately set in, so market share will become *decreasingly responsive to awareness-oriented* (as opposed to *price-oriented*) *advertising.*

DISTRIBUTION For consumer goods, the sales force usually focuses on obtaining distribution in large-volume stores initially and then in smaller, less important outlets. By maturity, only the marginal outlets are likely to not carry the product. Thus, money spent on additional salespeople, travel expenses, or incentives to gain additional distribution will have diminishing returns. Market share will, therefore, become *decreasingly responsive to distribution expenditures.*

Competitive Dynamics

One of the most difficult challenges to marketing managers is the prediction of competitors' responses to a marketing strategy. Scholars in marketing and economics have increased their attention to this issue in recent years, developing theoretic "game theory" analyses of a variety of situations involving competitive actions over time.

---

[21]See Gerard Tellis, "The Price Elasticity of Selective Demand: A Meta-Analysis of Econometric Models of Sales," *Journal of Marketing Research,* November 1988, pp. 331–341; and Leonard J. Parsons, "The Product Life Cycle and Time Varying Advertising Elasticities," *Journal of Marketing Research,* November 1975, pp. 476–480.

The best-known scenario involving dynamic competition is the "prisoner's dilemma," which effectively models the situation that often occurs when a small number of largely undifferentiated competitors engage in head-to-head competition in a mature market (where the likelihood of expanding primary demand is small). The resulting outcomes are parallel to those described in Figure 7-3, especially when the competition is based on price.

In Figure 7-3, each competitor has two choices: hold price or reduce price in an attempt to gain market share. Because the competitors are undifferentiated, any difference in price (or advertising expenditures or promotional expenditures) would have a significant impact on buyers' choices. But if the lower price (or the higher advertising and promotional expenditure) is matched, there is no market-share impact.

As the figure shows, neither party can afford to let the other reduce price without matching that price (a scenario that is frequently observed in industries such as airlines, cigarettes, and steel). If each firm maintains its current price, the firms divide the market and earn $100 million. If one firm reduces price and the other fails to follow, the second firm loses $20 million. By matching the lower price the second firm at least breaks even. Logically, neither firm should reduce price if it expects the competitor to follow. But, both firms know they will lose if they fail to act and a rival cuts prices. Once one competitor reduces prices in the (usually mistaken) belief that the rival cannot afford to follow or will exit the market, the rival will match or beat the lower price, and a destructive price war often ensues.

Because this kind of scenario approximates many real-world competitive situations, researchers have sought to find a competitive strategy that is not illegal (that is, does not involve collusion), but can help avoid destructive price wars. The best strategy uncovered is known as the "tit-for-tat" strategy, in which the second firm responds to a price cut by meeting (but not beating) the price cut, and doing so

FIGURE 7-3

An example of outcomes in a "prisoner's dilemma" game.

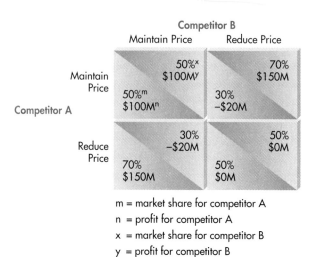

m = market share for competitor A
n = profit for competitor A
x = market share for competitor B
y = profit for competitor B

promptly. Continuing to pursue that strategy signals the price cutter that the second firm is not anxious for a price war but is determined to hold its market share.[22]

CONCLUSION

Although marketing strategies indicate general approaches that can be employed to achieve product objectives, the implementation of these strategies through marketing programs is the most time-consuming part of marketing management.

Marketing programs (such as product-development programs, advertising programs, direct marketing and sales promotion programs, and sales and distribution programs) demonstrate the specific activities that will be necessary to implement a strategy. For instance, if a strategy requires that the firm achieve distributor cooperation, the details of *how* the sales force will achieve cooperation must be worked out in the sales and distribution program. No matter how appropriate a strategy might appear, it will fail if it is not properly implemented. Consequently, clear statements regarding target markets and marketing strategies are necessary to ensure that the correct programs will be developed.

As we have suggested in this chapter, a marketing strategy serves as the major link between corporate marketing planning and situation analysis on the one hand and development of specific programs on the other. Figure 7-4 portrays this relationship.

Perhaps the most important aspect of this relationship is the fact that marketing strategy should be viewed from a dynamic perspective: As the corporate strategy or the situation analysis changes over time, the marketing strategy should change. Consider, for example, the dynamics involved in the market for home-banking services.

FIGURE 7-4

Relationship of marketing strategy to corporate marketing planning, situation analysis, and marketing programs.

[22]See Peter Fader and John Hauser, "Implicit Coalitions in a Generalized Prisoner's Dilemma," *Journal of Conflict Resolution,* September 1988, pp. 553–582.

HOME BANKING: COMPETING FOR THE FUTURE

A number of large U.S. banks, led by Citicorp, began experimenting with telephone-based home-banking systems in the 1980s. Such systems allow customers to check on and transfer checking- and savings-account fund balances and direct the payment of some bills electronically. By 1995, some 700,000 households were active users of home-banking services.

In October of 1995, software maker Intuit released a new version of its popular money-management software Quicken. The new version provides a number of new, sophisticated applications; Internet/World Wide Web connectivity allows users to gain on-line access to information about the cost of loans and credit cards at dozens of banks and permits them to monitor stock and mutual fund portfolios, in addition to the traditional home-banking functions. Over 1 million copies of the new version were ordered even before its release.

Many of the largest banks (including Citicorp) allow Quicken users to access their accounts with those institutions; other banks have similar agreements with Quicken's main competitor, Microsoft Money. However, some banks sought other avenues to accommodate home banking. Wells Fargo of San Francisco and Huntington Bancshares of Columbus, Ohio, began experimenting with direct Internet connections with customers. Still others considered using systems developed by VISA. A major concern of some bankers is that "third parties" like Microsoft and Intuit could interfere with a bank's ability to maintain relationships with its customers. Others wonder about the impact on the demand for branch-banking facilities. With industry analysts predicting that 75 percent of all households will be using some level of home banking by the year 2005, it is no wonder that banks are concerned about the impact of this service.

Meanwhile, Microsoft was not ready to concede market leadership to Intuit. Although Quicken claimed a much larger base of users than Money, Microsoft had released a new version linked to the Windows 95 operating system. Both the Intuit and Microsoft systems were priced similarly in 1995 (about $35 at retail for the software and about $6 a month for up to 20 bill-paying transactions). Quicken had the advantage of being compatible with both Macintosh and IBM-compatible systems, whereas Money was available only to those with Windows systems. Quicken also offered a broader range of functions that appealed to individuals who were very active in managing their investments. Money was simpler and, in the view of some, easier to use for the basic functions of bill paying and account tracking.

1. What primary-demand strategies could be used to build demand for "home banking"?
2. What selective-demand strategies were being used by Intuit and Microsoft in 1995?
3. Are bankers' concerns about possible customer retention problems arising from home banking valid? How would you deal with this threat?
4. How will competition for the home-banking customer change over time?

Developed from Dean Foust, "From In Line to Online," *Business Week*, Nov. 6, 1995, p. 146; Timothy O'Brien, "On Line Banking Has Bankers Fretting PCs May Replace Branches," *Wall Street Journal*, Oct. 25, 1995, pp. A1, A3; Vanessa O'Connell, "Banks Offer Free Personal Finance Software," *Wall Street Journal*, Oct. 25, 1995, pp. C1–C2; "Intuit Confirms Internet Plans for Quicken," *Reuters Business Report*, Oct. 19, 1995; Matt Roush, "Customers Lead Charge to Electronic Bank," *Crain's Detroit Business*, Oct. 16, 1995, p. 36.

QUESTIONS AND SITUATIONS FOR DISCUSSION

1. Explain how market potential and industry sales measures are important in the selection of a marketing strategy.

2. Two leaders in a high-growth industry each have a 20 percent share of the market. One has achieved success through competitive prices, the widest distribution, and the heaviest advertising expenditures. The other has a patented ingredient that enables it to offer a unique, additional benefit. Which of these products would you prefer to manage? Explain your answer.

3. Neutrogena Corp. was a small family-run business, which relied on Neutrogena soap for the majority of company revenues. The soap was positioned as a safe, therapeutic soap offered at a premium price. In the 1980s the company was suddenly confronted with competitive therapeutic soaps such as Johnson & Johnson's Purpose, Noxell's Clarion, and soaps from two Procter & Gamble brands, Oil of Olay and Vidal Sassoon. Suggest some marketing strategies that Neutrogena might have considered.

4. Which of the following is *most* likely to pursue a globalization policy, and which is *least* likely to do so?
   - Nike
   - Prudential Insurance
   - Whirlpool kitchen appliances

5. For each of the following industries, indicate the stage in the product life cycle that best describes the situation for each one, and give your reasoning. (Note that while you may not have direct access to industry sales figures, you may be able to make inferences about the life cycle stage from observing the number and actions of competitors in these markets.)
   - 35 mm cameras
   - Canned spaghetti sauces
   - Internet access services

6. One of the more successful innovations in the telecommunications industry in recent years is voice messaging, a system that allows a person to leave a message in another person's voice mailbox—or in many voice mailboxes simultaneously. Most of the demand in this $2 billion per year market comes from business, government, and other organizational buyers who have found that they can reduce long-distance phone costs substantially by sending succinct messages that do not necessarily require a response. Another advantage of such systems is that, unlike answering machines, voice-mail systems are easily accessed when one is away from a phone. Additionally, voice-mail systems make it easy to respond to callers; often one need only touch one button. By the mid-1990s, eight firms dominated this market with Octel (20 percent share), AT&T (16.5 percent), and Northern Telecom (14 percent) the clear leaders. With demand for business systems beginning to level off, competitors began to turn their attention to developing the residential market. At the time, a typical charge for residential customers was

$6.50 per month plus 20 cents for each message sent out to another person's mailbox.

  a. How does the product life cycle concept apply to the voice-messaging market?

  b. What kinds of marketing strategies would you expect in the business voice-messaging market?

  c. Discuss some appropriate marketing strategies for the residential market. Do the current market leaders have a significant advantage over other potential competitors in this market?

7. Sweet'n Low, the first low-calorie artificial sweetener, was introduced in 1958 and dominated both grocery store and restaurant sales in this market with its distinctive pink packages until the 1980s. In 1981, G. D. Searle introduced a new, patented sugar substitute, aspartame (with the trademark name Nutrasweet) to the marketplace. One of aspartame's first applications was as a packaged artificial sweetener under the Equal brand. Aspartame was over five times more expensive than saccharin, the main ingredient in Sweet'n Low, and was priced three times higher when it reached the market. Equal's marketing effort was backed by a substantial advertising campaign. In a typical year, Equal's ad budget might be five times that of Sweet'n Low's. Although Sweet'n Low was actually sweeter, Equal countered by promoting its "natural" sugar taste. To many, this was a disguised way of questioning the health risks of saccharin, which had been under close scrutiny by many health authorities for years. During the 1980s and 1990s, sales of sugar substitutes grew at a slightly larger rate than before, with Sweet'n Low leading the grocery market in unit sales, whereas Equal (with its higher price) led in dollar sales. In terms of sales to restaurants, Sweet'n Low continued to be the dominant supplier.

  a. What type of marketing strategy best characterizes Equal's strategy?

  b. In your opinion, which of the two rivals has the greater brand equity? Why?

  c. What actions might Sweet'n Low have taken to defend its market share?

  d. Should a primary-demand strategy have been a part of either competitor's marketing effort during this time? Explain why or why not.

  e. Searle's patent on aspartame expired in 1992. How might this change Equal's marketing strategy?

SUGGESTED ADDITIONAL READINGS

Brandenberger, Adam, and Barry Nalebuff, "The Right Game: Use Game Theory to Shape Strategy," *Harvard Business Review,* July–August 1995, pp. 57–71.

Kashani, Kamran, "Beware the Pitfalls of Global Marketing," *Harvard Business Review,* September–October 1989, pp. 91–98.

Keller, Kevin Lane, "Conceptualizing, Measuring, and Managing Brand Equity," *Journal of Marketing,* January 1993, pp. 1–22.

Lambkin, Mary, and George Day, "Evolutionary Processes in Competitive Markets: Beyond the Product Life Cycle," *Journal of Marketing,* July 1989, pp. 4–20.

Lane, Vicki, and Robert Jacobson, "Stock Market Reactions to Brand Extension Announcements: The Effect of Brand Attitude and Familiarity," *Journal of Marketing,* January 1995, pp. 63–77.

McKenna, Regis, "Real-Time Marketing," *Harvard Business Review,* July–August 1995, pp. 87–95.

Ramaswamy, Venkatram, Hubert Gatignon, and David Reibstein, "Competitive Marketing Behavior in Industrial Markets," *Journal of Marketing,* April 1994, pp. 45–55.

Weiser, Charles, "Championing the Customer," *Harvard Business Review,* November–December 1995, pp. 113–116.

CHAPTER 8

PRODUCT-DEVELOPMENT PROGRAMS

OVERVIEW

Constant change in the market environment and in customer needs make it imperative that market-oriented firms continuously improve old products and create new ones if they are to remain competitive and profitable. One recent study of product-development activity concluded that companies that led their industries in sales growth and profitability generated half of all revenues from products introduced within the previous 5 years. In contrast, the least successful firms in those industries derived only 11 percent of their sales volume from such products.[1]

However, although the importance of new products is undeniable, product development is a costly activity filled with uncertainty. Indeed, a review of numerous studies on new-product development concludes that, of those new products that actually reach the marketplace, about 35 percent fail. Additionally, the majority of new products that undergo development never even reach the market.[2] As a result firms are spending a very substantial amount of time and money on new-product development efforts that yield no payoff.

Because of the cost and uncertainty associated with new-product development, an increasing amount of attention has been devoted to designing processes and analytical tools for managing this activity. The primary goal of this chapter is to introduce the most important aspects of typical new-product development processes. Before proceeding, however, it is important to identify various *types of new products* and to examine the implications of their classification for managers involved in new-product development.

TYPES OF NEW PRODUCTS

When we speak of "new" products, it is important to clarify just how new the product is and to whom it is new. More specifically, a product can be *new to the market,* meaning no firm has produced or marketed this product before, and/or *new to the firm.* In the latter case, other firms may already be offering some version of the product. Additionally, *newness* is also a matter of degree. Combining these two types of new-

---

[1]Christopher Power, "Flops: Too Many Products Fail. Here's Why and How to Do Better," *Business Week,* Aug. 17, 1993, p. 76.

[2]See Robert Cooper, *Winning at New Products,* Addison-Wesley, Reading, Mass., 1993, pp. 8–9.

FIGURE 8-1

Types of new
products.

ness and recognizing that there are degrees of newness yield the classification presented in Figure 8-1.[3]

Essentially, all product-development activities will result in one of six types of new product.

1. *New to the world products* are products that create entirely new markets, initiating completely new product life cycles. Such "really new" products (like the Sony Walkman and Pampers disposable diapers) have no direct competition when first launched.

2. *New product lines* are products that represent entries into existing markets that are new to the firm. For example, Hewlett-Packard entered the personal computer market in the mid-1990s when several competitors were already well established. Although the company had been producing printers for personal computers, the two products serve different needs and thus constitute different lines.

3. *Additions to existing lines* (also known as *line extensions*) are new products that allow a firm to extend its served market by offering different benefits or different levels of benefits. General Motors' Saturn and Crest Tartar Control toothpaste are examples. Although both products would appeal to many existing General Motors and Crest customers, it was hoped that they would offer benefits to attract new customers as well.

4. *Improvements to existing products* are usually designed as replacements for existing product offerings. They offer enhanced performance or greater perceived value. Annual model changes made by automobile manufacturers fall into this category as do "new and improved" versions of products such as Microsoft's Windows 95. In some cases, the old version may remain on the market for a time, especially if it occupies a lower price point than the new version.

5. *Repositionings* are very modest technical developments that allow a product to offer new applications and serve new needs. Alka Seltzer is made from the same basic ingredients as Bayer aspirin. But, by adding a fizzing action, it can enjoy the position of a stomach remedy. Similarly, prescription ulcer medicines like Tagamet and Pepcid have been repositioned as over-the-counter stomach-acid blockers.

[3]The six major types were first identified in *New Product Management for the 1980s,* Booze, Allen, & Hamilton, New York, 1982.

6. *Cost reductions* are versions of existing products that provide comparable performance at lower cost. Although not really "new" from a marketing perspective, these products can impact a firm's production operations and competitiveness.

It is important to recognize that decisions to pursue new products with a given type and degree of newness are generally reflections of a firm's corporate strategy or marketing strategy. For example, firms may pursue new-to-the-world products or new product lines to fulfill a diversification strategy. Similarly, line extensions usually reflect a product-development strategy that serves as a response to changes in customer needs or segmentation opportunities. Product improvements, repositionings, and cost reductions would normally be pursued to maintain successful head-to-head or differentiated positioning marketing strategies as competitive and demand conditions change over the product life cycle.

To recognize the various types of new products is important to an understanding of the key uncertainties each will face. Greater newness to the market results in more uncertainty about customers' willingness to buy, the patterns of segmentation, and other demand issues. This uncertainty limits management's understanding of whether potential demand will be adequate and of the precise promotion and distribution requirements for success. Also, the newer a product is to the firm, the greater the uncertainty about a firm's ability to design, produce, and market a quality product in a competitive way; in other words, the concern becomes whether there is a good fit between the product and the firm's core competencies.

However, whereas less newness reduces the risk of poor market response or of a poor company fit, fewer payoffs are also likely. Numerous studies have demonstrated that the earliest entrants to a new market are likely to obtain the highest market shares. This occurs because the first companies or brands in the market can establish brand loyalties before competitors enter, and because late entrants have greater difficulty in gaining distribution.[4] Moreover, products that are not especially new to the firm (for example, those in categories 3 through 6) often draw a substantial portion of their sales from a firm's existing offerings. This effect is known as *cannibalization.*

The role of the product-development process, then, is to help managers assess risks and reduce uncertainties regarding market-demand opportunities (especially in new-to-the-market products), the ability to deliver a competitive product (especially in new-to-the-firm products), and the likelihood of cannibalization (when the degree of newness is lower).

THE NEW-PRODUCT DEVELOPMENT PROCESS

As noted earlier, most firms have developed formal systems and processes for managing the new-product development programs. In large companies that make complex products (such as automobiles or medical instruments), this process may involve

---

[4]Gurumurthy Kalyanaram, William Robinson, and Glen Urban, "Order of Market Entry: Established Empirical Generalizations, Emerging Empirical Generalizations, and Future Research," *Marketing Science,* Summer 1995, pp. G212–G221.

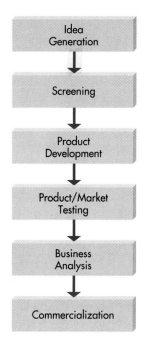

FIGURE 8-2

Stages of the new-product development process.

dozens of specific activities and reviews. In small firms with simple technology, relatively few people may be involved. However, the major activities and analyses are similar in nearly all situations. These activities occur within the stages shown in Figure 8-2. Before examining the individual stages, it is important to be aware of some basic aspects of the overall process.

Stage-Gate Philosophy

A major purpose of a formal approach using sequential stages is to monitor the progress of a new product idea as it proceeds through the various development and testing activities. In each stage, management should be gathering additional information to reduce uncertainty about demand, product-company fit, or cannibalization. At the same time, as a firm proceeds through the process, more time and money are invested.[5]

The concept of a "stage-gate" process involves the maintenance of control over the expenditures involved in new-product development by balancing the firm's investment against the value of additional information. That is, by assessing each idea after each stage based on the information acquired, management can reevaluate the idea's prospects for success. Specifically, in a stage-gate system, managers can "open

[5]For more on stage-gate systems, see Cooper, op. cit., chap. 5.

the gate" to the next stage in the process or elect to kill the new product at that point, thus avoiding further expenditures of time and funds if the demand or profit prospects for the new product seem unfavorable.

Parallel Development

Although the basic new-product development process is structured as sequential groups of activities, there may be a number of operations being performed simultaneously *within* each stage in order to move the process as quickly as possible. Speed is valuable because substantial benefits accrue from being able to bring new products to market quicker. First, the cost of product development is reduced if people involved in the process spend less time on it. Second, as shown in Figure 8-3, firms may be able to increase revenues if (1) earlier entry means the product spends more time in the marketplace during the product life cycle and (2) earlier entry allows the firm to beat some competitors to market and, thus, attain a higher market share than if it entered later.[6] The penalty of being late to market is especially severe in "high-tech" industries like computer software and consumer electronics where technology is changing rapidly.

Parallel development enhances speed to market. This philosophy recognizes that some actions can begin before full information from other activities or tests is available. Thus, marketing managers may begin to develop tentative plans for commer-

FIGURE 8-3

Potential sales gains from early introduction. (*Source:* Preston Smith and Donald Reinertsen, *Developing Products in Half the Time,* Van Nostrand, New York, 1991, p. 4.)

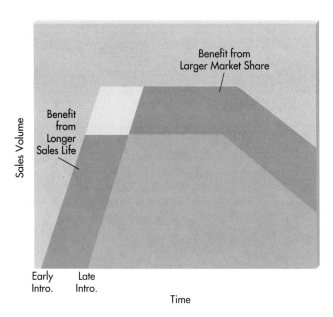

[6]Preston Smith and Donald Reinertsen, *Developing Products in Half the Time,* Van Nostrand, New York, 1991, pp. 3–4.

cialization during the development stage. Similarly, manufacturing managers may begin production planning activities while market testing is in progress. Such efforts can materially affect the total time required between idea generation and launch.[7]

Multidisciplinary Activity

The use of teams is very widespread in product-development programs. Usually, a team is formed once a new product idea has received approval for further analysis. Although the size and structure of teams certainly depend on the size of the project, the technological complexity involved, and the degree of newness of the product, the design of the teams requires that certain general guidelines are followed. These include the following:[8]

- All the key functions (at least marketing, manufacturing, and engineering) are represented.
- Members volunteer to serve on the team.
- Members serve on the team for the duration of the process.
- Members serve full-time on the team.
- Members are physically located close to one another.

Such teams are useful to service providers that design new products, as well as to manufacturers of goods. For example, Union Pacific Railroad uses cross-functional teams to design those products—including rates, schedules, transit times, number of cars provided, and special support services—that are customized to the individual needs of each freight shipper.[9]

Teams oversee the research and development activities, design and engineering processes, marketing research, production planning, and financial analyses as a group. Constant interaction among the members is an essential requirement for and benefit of multidisciplinary teams. Should new technological or marketing opportunities arise during the process, adjustments by the other functions can be accommodated more quickly and at lower cost if a multifunctional team is managing the effort.

STAGE 1: IDEA GENERATION

New product ideas can come from a variety of sources. Especially in technologically oriented firms, a high percentage of new product ideas come from research and development. Other useful sources are dealers, competitors, salespeople, and other employees. Finally, market-oriented firms rely on customers for a large portion of their new product ideas.

---

[7]See Hirotaka Takeuchi and Ikujiro Nonaka, "The New Product Development Game," *Harvard Business Review,* January–February 1986, pp. 137–146.

[8]Smith and Reinertsen, op. cit., pp. 111–112.

[9]Alan Grant and Leonard Schlesinger, "Realize Your Customers' Full Potential," *Harvard Business Review,* September–October 1995, p. 63.

Generally, when ideas come from the technological side of the firm, they are specified in technological terms (for instance, a new drug idea may be based on a new process for manipulating enzymes; a new car idea may be based on improved design for aerodynamics) or physical characteristics (a new cellular phone is lighter and smaller). On the other hand, ideas that are generated from customers or distributors are more likely to be couched in terms of problem-solving benefits (such as a suitcase that fits easily into an airplane overhead compartment). An important multidisciplinary aspect of the product-development process is to develop a precise statement of the *new product concept.* Such statements would include

■ Specification of the *benefits to be received* by potential customers
■ Definition of the *physical attributes or technology* that will provide those benefits

An important part of the team effort at this time is to develop alternative specifications for the product concept. For example, Motorola might specify the product concept for a new cellular phone as "weighs less than 6 ounces and is no more than 3 inches wide so that owners can carry it in a suitcoat pocket." Note that the product concept provides guidance both for technical people and marketing managers; technical people can begin, or continue, their design effort with a clear understanding of their technical goals, and marketers can begin planning the design of the marketing strategy and programs (including the brand name and promotional messages) for introduction of the product to the market.

A variety of methods exist for identifying new product concepts. For industrial products, an effective method is *lead-user analysis.* This is a customer-interviewing approach that focuses on identifying the anticipated future requirements of a company's "lead" customers—those who have the most to gain if some firm provides them with improved products. The assumption is that lead users will provide good ideas about improving the product because they have struggled with and have thought about the product's various problems.[10] For example, IBM might consider salespeople lead users for notebook computers because they travel more than the average user, so portability issues will be more important to them. The application of lead-user thinking can also be seen in Boeing's involvement of key airlines in the design of its 777 jet and in the actions of Harley Davidson's CEO, who spends nearly half his week riding and talking with biker clubs and groups.[11] The experience of firms like Hewlett-Packard, Milliken, and others who use customer visits in their new-product development process suggests that visits should be made by multifunctional teams (not just marketing or engineering personnel), and that it is sometimes valuable to get customer input on the product *support* dimensions of product offerings (such as training, documentation, and customer service), not just on basic features and benefits needed.[12]

A somewhat similar approach that is often used for consumer products is *problem analysis.* In this approach, a firm conducts interviews with heavy users of a cat-

---

[10]Eric von Hippel, *The Sources of Innovation,* Oxford University Press, New York, 1985, chap. 8.

[11]"Producer Power," *The Economist,* Mar. 4, 1995, p. 70.

[12]Edward McQuarrie, *Customer Visits,* Sage, Newbury Park, Calif., 1993, pp. 16, 73.

egory to obtain a list of the problems they have experienced. Users are then asked to rate the *frequency of occurrence* of each problem and the *degree to which it is bothersome* on five-point scales. Problems rated as occurring very frequently and being very bothersome would be identified, and potential new product ideas would be defined as products that would solve those problems.[13]

Focus groups (first discussed in Chapter 3) are slightly less formal ways of conducting problem analyses. Groups of six to ten users of a product category are led by trained moderators in discussions of what people like and dislike about products in that category. They often yield subtle insights about customer problems or opportunities for improvement that might otherwise go unnoticed. For example, the idea that American Express should modify the benefits of its credit card to include extended warranties on products the customer bought with the card was generated in a focus group.

Finally, *direct observation* of customers' usage patterns often provides insights for product development. Braun and Whirlpool videotape customers using their coffee pots and refrigerators, respectively, to identify problems like inconvenient locations for switches or racks that people might not bring up in interviews. Thus, product improvements at these firms focus on providing unanticipated product enhancements. Similarly, United States Surgical sales representatives gain ideas for improving medical instruments by watching surgeons at work in hospital operating rooms.[14]

STAGE 2: SCREENING

Screening can include a variety of activities designed to evaluate a new product concept. In most firms the largest number of new ideas are eliminated at this stage. Although the development process has not proceeded far enough for detailed economic analyses, the information gathered at this stage should allow management to (1) begin projecting the level of potential demand; (2) identify the product's chances of success, as well as the potential barriers to success; and (3) estimate the degree of cannibalization. These judgments are based on information that comes from such activities as market-potential studies, concept tests, and scoring models.

Market-Potential Studies

The various aspects of market-potential estimation were discussed in Chapter 5. In addition to estimating the number of potential buyers and the potential rate of purchase, management will want to assess the competitive environment very closely. Specifically, managers will want to predict who the competitors will be when the new product is launched and the likely degree of price competition in order to forecast dollar sales and profits.

---

[13]Claes Fornell and Robert Menko, "Problem Analysis—A Consumer-Based Methodology for the Discovery of New Ideas," *European Journal of Marketing,* 1981, pp. 61–72.

[14]Jennifer Reese, "Getting Hot Ideas from Customers," *Fortune,* May 18, 1992, pp. 86–87.

Concept Tests

Concept tests are methods of trying to gauge buyer interest in a product before an actual prototype has even been developed. These tests can help a firm gain insight into the specific marketing challenges it will need to overcome when it commercializes the product; they can also help a firm project the degree of cannibalization. If a product prototype has already been developed by engineering, this activity can be excluded. However, when the costs of building a prototype are prohibitive and a large number of competing concepts exist (both of which are possible situations facing automobile manufacturers, for example), then concept testing can be of immense value.

In a typical concept test, potential buyers are shown statements of product features and benefits, sometimes accompanied by visual depictions of the concept. They are then asked for their reactions using structured questionnaires like the one in Table 8-1. Based on analyses of these responses, managers will have insights into the degree to which the product will have a competitive advantage and the potential problems that must be overcome to obtain trial. In addition to this valuable diagnostic information, management will review respondents' estimates of their probability of trial. Although such estimates

TABLE 8-1   **EVALUATING A NEW CLEANING PRODUCT CONCEPT**

Concept statement

A newly developed, nonabrasive, all-purpose cleaner, that not only cleans but also inhibits dirt from adhering to the cleaned surface. By varying the strength of the product, the user can clean windows, vinyl, stainless steel, chrome, aluminum, tires, upholstery, carpet, bathroom fixtures, woodwork, appliances, kitchen cabinets, and counters.

Uniqueness: Which statement best describes this product?

_____ Sounds completely different from any other product now available

_____ Very different from any other product now available

_____ The same as some other product now available

Competition: When people buy a new product, they usually buy it in place of some other product they had been buying. If you were to buy this new product, what item or items would it replace? _____

Need: Does this product solve a problem or need that isn't being satisfied by products now on the market?

_____Yes   What is the problem or need? _____

_____No

Merits: What specific features do you find attractive about this new product?_____

_____

Limitations: What specific features do you find questionable about this new product? _____

_____

Believability: Are there any features or claims about this product that you find hard to believe? _____

_____   _____

Probability of trial: How interested would you be in buying the product described above if it were available at your supermarket?

_____ I would definitely buy

_____ I would probably buy

_____ I might or might not buy

_____ I would probably not buy

_____ I would definitely not buy

are not assumed to be perfectly predictive of actual behavior, management will consider such results in deciding whether to move to the next stage of the process if a very high percentage of the responses is in the top two or bottom two response categories.[15] Finally, insights about potential cannibalization can be obtained by identifying those in the sample who are already users of the firm's other products in the same market and asking them whether they would prefer the proposed concept to the product they currently use. Additionally, the conjoint analysis methods discussed in Chapter 4 are often utilized to determine whether a new product will cannibalize existing offerings.

Scoring Models

Scoring models enable managers to rate the general attractiveness of a new product concept or help rank order competing concepts. The basic procedure is to provide information about each concept to a group of managers and have them independently "score" the concepts on a series of characteristics related to market opportunity, product-company fit, or other factors thought to influence new-product success.

Some very general scoring models are like the portfolio models we discussed in Chapter 2, which focus on factors that influence the overall attractiveness of a market and on whether the firm is likely to have the resources to compete in that market. Typically, firms select those factors that have proven to be most critical in their particular industry. Thus, "likelihood of regulatory problems" might be important in some markets, "patentability" in others, and "sold in grocery stores" in yet others. But, in spite of interindustry differences, there is now evidence that the basic causes of new-product success are somewhat consistent across industries. The NewProd model is a scoring model that has been applied in over 100 companies worldwide. Analysis of the results suggests that there are nine basic factors influencing new-product success; these are listed in Table 8-2.

TABLE 8-2	**FACTORS INFLUENCING NEW-PRODUCT SUCCESS**

1. *Product superiority/quality.* The competitive advantage the product has by virtue of features, benefits, quality, uniqueness, and so on.
2. *Economic advantage to the user.* The product's value for the money for the customer.
3. *Overall company/project fit.* The product's synergy with the company—similarity to established marketing skills, managerial skills, and business knowledge.
4. *Technological compatibility.* The technological synergy with the company—similarity to established R&D, engineering, and production capabilities.
5. *Familiarity to the company.* How familiar the project is to the company (as opposed to entirely new products or projects).
6. *Market need, growth, and size.* The magnitude of the market opportunity.
7. *Competitive situation.* How easy the market is to penetrate from a competitive standpoint.
8. *Defined opportunity.* Whether the product has a well-defined category and established market (as opposed to a true innovation and new category of products).
9. *Project definition.* How well defined the product and project are.

Source: Robert Cooper, "The NewProd System: The Industry Experience," *Journal of Product Innovative Management,* June 1992, pp. 113–127.

---

[15]See Robert Dolan, "Note on Concept Testing," Harvard Business School case 590-063, for a more thorough discussion of concept-testing approaches and limitations.

The NewProd system asks up to twelve managers to evaluate each new product concept on thirty key characteristics (listed in Table 8-3) and to provide their level of confidence in those ratings using a ten-point scale. These characteristics are then combined into indexes to obtain the nine final factors. By answering these questions, managers not only provide insights into the positive and negative aspects of the new product, they also identify issues about which the raters are unsure or divided in their opinions. Such issues are then targeted as areas where more information must be

TABLE 8-3	CHARACTERISTICS EVALUATED IN THE NEWPROD SCORING MODEL

1. Our company's financial resources are more than adequate for this project.
2. Our company's R&D skills and people are more than adequate for this project.
3. Our company's engineering skills and people are more than adequate for this project.
4. Our company's marketing research skills and people are more than adequate for this project.
5. Our company's management skills are more than adequate for this project.
6. Our company's production resources or skills are more than adequate for this project.
7. Our company's sales force and/or distribution resources and skills are more than adequate for this project.
8. Our company's advertising and promotion resources and skills are more than adequate for this project.
9. Our product is highly innovative—totally new to the market.
10. The product specifications—exactly what the product will be—are very clear.
11. The technical aspects—exactly how the technical problems will be solved—are very clear.
12. The potential customers for this product are totally new to our company.
13. The product class or type of product itself is totally new to our company.
14. We have never made or sold products to satisfy this type of customer need or use before.
15. The competitors we face in the market are totally new to our company.
16. Compared to competitive products (or whatever the customer is now using), our product will offer a number of unique features, attributes, or benefits to the customer.
17. Our product will be clearly superior to competing products in terms of meeting customers' needs.
18. Our product will permit the customer to reduce his/her costs, when compared to what he/she is now using.
19. Our product will permit the customer to do a job or do something that he/she cannot do with what is now available on the market.
20. Our product will be of higher quality—however quality is defined in this market—than competing products.
21. Our product will be priced considerably higher than competing products.
22. We will be first into the market with this type of product.
23. Potential customers have a great need for this class or type of product.
24. The dollar size of the market (either existing or potential market) for this product is large.
25. The market for this product is growing very quickly.
26. The market is characterized by intense price competition.
27. There are many competitors in this market.
28. There is a strong dominant competitor—with a large market share—in this market.
29. Potential customers are very satisfied with the products (competitors' products) they are currently using.
30. Users' needs change quickly in this market—a dynamic market situation.

Source: Robert Cooper, "The NewProd System: The Industry Experience," *Journal of Product Innovative Management,* June 1992, pp. 125–126.

obtained. Thus, scoring models like NewProd serve as diagnostic tools that help managers identify the remaining problems and uncertainties associated with a new product concept and decide whether actual development should proceed.[16]

In addition to the use of a scoring model at the screening stage, managers will review a new product idea for its consistency with company priorities, as outlined in the corporate strategy. For example, management in a company that is heavily committed to diversification is likely to be more supportive of an idea that reflects a high degree of newness to the market (even though this may reduce the *probability* of success) than is management in a company that is more committed to existing product lines and markets.

STAGE 3: PRODUCT DEVELOPMENT

Product development is the technical work of converting a concept into a working product. Below, we examine three main activities in this stage: (1) development of the product architecture, (2) application of industrial design, and (3) assessment of the manufacturing requirements.[17] Although marketing managers are not directly involved in the technical work, they are members of the multifunctional team that oversees development, and for good reasons. To be sure, it is important that the architecture and design fulfill (and possibly enhance) the basic product concept. As we discussed in Chapter 3, if a firm applies a quality function deployment process, marketing, manufacturing, and engineering team members will find it easier to discuss the linkages among customer benefits, design features, and manufacturing requirements. Additionally, the manufacturing requirements and performance tests provide information that will be central to pricing decisions and sometimes to other marketing costs.

Product Architecture

The *product architecture* is the specification of the parts, components, assemblies, and technologies and their interrelationships that produces the desired functions. Thus, the architecture is the basic plan for assuring that the product concept will be implemented.

Although marketers are interested in seeing that the concept will, in fact, be realized, a number of key choices about the product architecture that will influence marketing strategy may be required as development proceeds. For example, there may be alternative components or alternative ways to link assemblies that are equally effective in providing a specific benefit, but which differ in terms of facilitating future upgrades, add-on options, or the ability to add different versions. Such choices should

---

[16]See Robert Cooper, "The NewProd System: The Industry Analysis," *Journal of Product Innovation Management,* June 1992, pp. 113–127.

[17]This section draws from Karl Ulrich and Steven Eppinger, *Product Design and Development,* McGraw-Hill, New York, 1995, chap. 7.

be made with input from marketing because they can impact the success of the product in various segments or over time. When Intel introduced its Pentium Pro micro-processor in 1995, some observers were surprised that this product did not offer a huge increase in performance when they used existing personal computing software. But, Intel had chosen to set the architecture in order to accommodate the later development of a large variety of specialized microprocessors for new game and communication applications, thus trading off immediate benefits to one set of applications for a wider set of future applications.[18]

Industrial Design

Industrial design is the process of creating and developing product specifications that optimize the function, value, and appearance of the product. This activity is performed by professional designers (operating within the team environment), but has major implications for the marketing of the product.

Firms such as Braun, Rubbermaid, Chrysler, Reebok, and Motorola acknowledge that most of their important new-product success stories in recent years occurred largely because of the added value created by superior design work.[19] For example, Motorola's immensely successful MicroTAC cellular phone was designed to fit into a shirt pocket. When introduced, it was the smallest and lightest entry in the market. Industrial design was instrumental in helping engineering achieve the technical results. However, the product's immediate success has been attributed more to its ergonomics (that is, its human factor considerations). The product was designed to complement the human face better than existing products through its positioning of the ear-piece and mouthpiece, both of which can be folded up with one hand. The modern, sleek design is also appreciated by users. Thus, industrial design not only helps assure that the basic concept (in this case, a pocket-sized phone) will be implemented, but also substantially adds to the marketability of the product beyond the basic concept. For this reason, designers are increasingly being added to the product-development team at an early stage of the process.[20]

Manufacturing Considerations

Product-development teams often face multiple, possibly conflicting goals. Among the tradeoffs that often must be made is that between delivering all the benefits "promised" in the new product concept and minimizing the variable and fixed costs of manufacturing or operations. Today, firms usually devote a portion of the new-product development process to finding ways of reducing production costs through design modifications, usually by changing the product architecture. A key role of the

---

[18]Don Clark, "Intel Puts Chips under Pentium Brand in Sign Some Won't Reap Its Benefits," *Wall Street Journal,* Sept. 20, 1995, p. B2.

[19]Bruce Nussbaum, "Hot Products: Smart Design Is the Common Thread," *Business Week,* June 7, 1993, pp. 54–58.

[20]Ulrich and Eppinger, op. cit., pp. 152–154.

new-product development team is to assess projected manufacturing costs and determine what tradeoffs in functional performance, if any, will be acceptable in exchange for a given reduction in cost.

STAGE 4: PRODUCT/MARKET TESTING

The broad purposes of product and market testing are (1) to provide more detailed assessments of the new product's chances for success, (2) to identify necessary final adjustments to the product, and (3) to define the important elements of the marketing programs to be used in the introduction of the product to the marketplace. In this section, four product/market testing activities are discussed:

- Technical testing
- Preference and satisfaction testing
- Simulated test markets
- Test markets

Technical Testing

A *product prototype* is an approximation of the final product. Usually, the prototype is expected to be close enough to the final version to be useful in testing one or more key dimensions of product performance at the earliest feasible point in time. A prototype of a new automobile may not incorporate the final engine design, but may be complete enough for technical evaluations of the aerodynamics and for consumer evaluations of the styling and interior roominess. In other cases, the prototype may be sufficiently complete to permit limited usage tests of product performance under different conditions. Such information may be helpful in making final design improvements or in alerting the marketing staff about factors to consider in developing advertising and sales and distribution programs. Specifically, technical testing can provide information on

- Product shelf life
- Product wear-out rates
- Problems resulting from improper use or consumption
- Potential defects
- Appropriate maintenance schedules

Each of these kinds of information may have cost consequences for the marketing of the product. Shelf-life estimates will influence the frequency (and cost) of delivery. The potential for significant usage problems may require additional advertising, labeling, or point-of-sale information. It is important that failure to detect such problems can have a significant negative effect on product trial if there is widespread publicity about them. For this reason, Microsoft distributed 400,000 advance copies of Windows 95 to computer users to help find "bugs" that could be solved by design changes prior to launch.[21] Such advanced prototypes, known as *beta* copies, are usually released when a design is about to be finalized.

Preference and Satisfaction Testing

Whereas technical testing is usually performed on prototypes only, preference and satisfaction testing is normally reserved for the "final" version. Although very poor results in preference and satisfaction tests might lead to a redesign of the product, they are more likely to cause management to abandon the project. The more typical goals of this stage would be to obtain insights about the elements that should be designed into a marketing plan and to make an early sales forecast for the product.

In general, there are two basic approaches to this kind of testing. In one, consumers are asked to use a product for a period of time. In some cases, firms may choose to have a "blind" test so that the brand or manufacturer remains unknown. In the other approach, buyers compare the new product with one or more competing alternatives. (Again, in some cases such as taste tests, the brands are not disclosed.) Subsequently, the potential buyers in the research sample are asked a number of questions depending on the particular goals of the test. Table 8-4 outlines the major purposes of these tests and the specific information sought from those using the product for each purpose.

The significance of the information obtained in this activity should not be underestimated. That is,

- Determining buyer perceptions of a product's specific advantages is important if a firm plans to show superiority over the competition in its promotion; the Federal Trade Commission requires that such claims be substantiated by actual preference tests or by technical tests.
- Estimating repurchase is important in gauging long-term market share. A poor result here would either kill the product or cause management to consider redesign.

TABLE 8-4

PRODUCT PREFERENCE/SATISFACTION TEST PURPOSES AND METHODS

PURPOSE	METHOD
1. Determine which advantages of the product can be cited in making advertising claims.	Compare buyers' ratings of the new product with leading products on key attributes.
2. Determine probability of repurchase of the product.	Ask buyers for ratings of overall satisfaction or ask likelihood of repurchase.
3. Make rough projection of market acceptance based solely on product performance.	Have buyers rank this product relative to other brands known or tried.
4. Predict cannibalization.	Compare rank order preference for the new product versus product normally used.

---

[21]Don Clark, "Amid Hype and Fear, Microsoft Windows 95 Gets Ready to Roll," *Wall Street Journal,* July 14, 1995, p. A1.

- Although new-product market acceptance will be determined by all the marketing programs, not just the product performance, certainly a high ranking on this dimension would suggest that the product should, at least, be carried to the next activity or stage.
- Preference tests probably provide the best early warning signals of a high cannibalization level.

Simulated Test Markets

Simulated test markets (or, as they are sometimes called, *laboratory test markets*) are marketing research procedures designed to provide fast and low-cost ways of obtaining insights into the probable market share a new product can hope to attain. Specifically, these tests are designed to permit the application of models of market response, as portrayed in Figure 8-4. The model assumes that the marketing programs portrayed on the left-hand side cause the consumer reactions in the middle, resulting in the

FIGURE 8-4

Determinants and components of first-year sales volume.

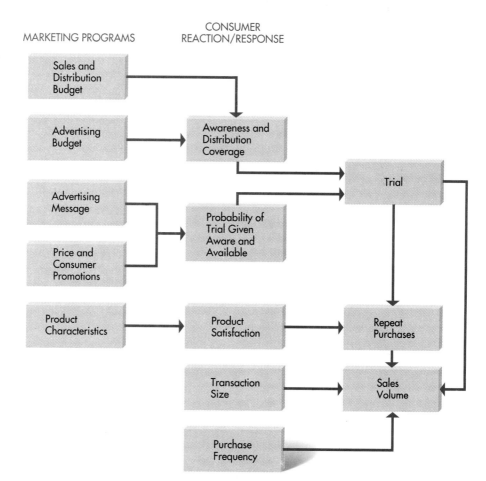

outcomes on the right-hand side. Simulated test-market models incorporate management judgments and market research to give estimates of trial, repeat sales, and total sales or market share for a new product—usually for a limited time horizon, such as 1 year after launch. In general, these models have been applied to nondurable consumer goods marketed through food, drug, and/or mass-merchandise outlets. However, recently, alternative versions have been applied to durable goods.[22]

The most popular of the simulated test-market models are BASES, ASSESSOR, LITMUS, and DESIGNOR. Each model has its own special features and procedures. However, a general description of the basic processes would normally include the following steps.[23]

1. Managers estimate the percentage of the target market that will be made aware of the new product, based on a proposed advertising budget, and the percentage of product availability in retail stores, based on the proposed sales budget.
2. Interviews are conducted with a sample of consumers who use the product category. (Perhaps 300 consumers would be interviewed in each of two or more locations.) The interviews provide information on brand usage, attitudes, and preferences.
3. The consumers in the sample then view a series of concept boards or commercials that include ads for the new product being tested.
4. The same consumers are given cash and are offered the opportunity to purchase one of several alternative products from the category in question in a mock (laboratory) store.
5. People who do not purchase the test product in step 4 are given a free sample.
6. After a period of time sufficient for trial, consumers may be reinterviewed and asked about their attitudes, brand preferences, and intentions to repurchase.

The six steps involved in a simulated test market can provide managers with much of the information needed to apply the model portrayed in Figure 8-4. For example, step 1 provides information on awareness and distribution coverage. Step 4 reflects a trial in a situation where the people have been made aware and given availability. (The trial percentages obtained in this manner are generally reduced by some set amount using the experience of the research firm.) Thus, "trial" can be estimated by combining the information from steps 1 and 4. Repeat is estimated using data from the second interview. This affords management a rough gauge of the product's likely success, as long as the many assumptions of these tests are realistic.

Generally, there is evidence that such tests work fairly well, at least in situations where major changes in consumer behavior are not called for. That is, the models tend to be more effective for new products entering established markets, where buyers can judge the appeal of a new product more readily. However, the best use of simulated

---

[22]See Glen Urban, John Hulland, and Bruce Weinberg, "Premarket Forecasting for New Consumer Durable Goods," *Journal of Marketing,* April 1993, pp. 47–63.

[23]For a comprehensive review and comparison of the leading simulated test-market services, see Kevin Clancy, Robert Shulman, and Marianne Wolf, *Simulated Test Marketing,* Lexington Books, New York, 1994, chap. 4.

test markets is as a screening device to decide whether or not a new product should be brought into a full-scale test market or killed. Research suggests that simulated test markets are very effective at identifying products whose market success prospects are the most questionable.[24]

Test Marketing

In a traditional, full-scale test market, a firm offers a new product for sale in one or more limited geographic areas that are somewhat representative of the total target market and are sufficiently isolated so that *local* network stations and cable systems, radio, and newspapers are the dominant media used by consumers. Special arrangements with retailers assure good distribution. The product is then introduced with a level of local advertising and promotion comparable to what consumers would experience during a national introduction. Sales are then tracked on a weekly basis and, in many cases, parallel marketing research is conducted to analyze who is buying the product.

The decision to use a full-scale test market is not simple. Usually it takes 9 to 12 months of testing to obtain a valid reading of market acceptance. (Early sales can give good insights into the rate of trial, but repeat purchases cannot be assessed until two or three purchase cycles for the product have passed.) The cost of such tests can easily reach $1.5 million for just a single market area.[25] Additionally, when a firm uses full-scale test markets (as opposed to simulated test markets), competitors can observe the test and the firm's marketing strategy. Thus, they can prepare competing products or design retaliatory strategies for their existing products before the firm doing the test is able to introduce its product nationally. Table 8-5 summarizes the considerations involved in deciding whether or not to test-market.

TABLE 8-5	CONSIDERATIONS INVOLVED IN DECIDING WHETHER TO TEST-MARKET

FACTORS FAVORING TEST MARKETING

1. Acceptance of the product concept is very uncertain.
2. Sales potential is difficult to estimate.
3. Cost of developing consumer awareness and trial is difficult to estimate.
4. A major investment is required to produce at full scale (relative to the cost of test marketing).
5. Alternative prices, packages, or promotional appeals are under consideration.

REASONS FOR NOT TEST MARKETING

1. The risk of failure is low relative to test-marketing costs.
2. The product will have a brief life cycle.
3. Beating competition to the market is important because the product is easily imitated.
4. Basic price, package, and promotional appeals are well established.

---

[24]Glen Urban and John Hauser, *Design and Marketing of New Products,* 2d ed., Prentice-Hall, Englewood Cliffs, N.J., 1993, pp. 468–471.

[25]Urban and Hauser, op. cit., p. 495.

An important development that has added to the value of test marketing is the evolution of the electronic test markets discussed in Chapter 6. These systems provide two important additional benefits to test marketers.

1. With respect to the data needed to implement the model in Figure 8-4, electronic test markets allow managers to clearly distinguish trial sales from repeat sales and determine average purchase frequencies and volumes. Such analyses are difficult and unreliable in test markets where scanner-based household purchase data are unavailable.
2. Electronic test markets permit managers to test alternative advertising and sales promotion programs that would introduce new products at less cost and with greater validity because the alternatives can be targeted to individual households within each market.

STAGE 5: BUSINESS ANALYSIS

The purpose of this stage is to obtain the most comprehensive view possible of the financial consequences of introducing a new product. Managers involved in making the financial evaluation will actually perform this activity a number of times as additional information on the manufacturing costs, the marketing costs of launching the new product, and the expected sales and cannibalization levels are provided. Although the basic elements involved in product profitability analysis were presented in Chapter 6, financial evaluations of new products are slightly more complex.

One difference between financial evaluations of new and established products is the time frame involved. The sales and costs for a new product often vary substantially over time. New products are seldom adopted immediately, and the cost of marketing will normally be substantially higher in the first year compared to subsequent years, because of the need to provide awareness of the product and incentives for product distribution and trial. In general, first-year earnings will understate long-term profitability for those products that become successful. Accordingly, a 1-year projection will not be sufficiently informative in most cases.

Additionally, if the new product will cannibalize existing products' sales or will share production or marketing costs with existing offerings, only the incremental sales and costs of the new product should normally be considered in evaluating the profit contribution of the new product. With respect to costs, it is important to distinguish any fixed costs that are assigned to a product as its "share" of the firm's indirect costs. Because such costs would likely be incurred whether or not the new product was added to the line, they probably should not be considered in evaluating the true incremental profit contribution.

Finally, new products may require an additional investment in facilities or equipment. Investments are not costs; they are one-time outlays rather than recurring expenditures. However, because firms have alternative opportunities for investing these funds, and because different products require different amounts of investment capital, managers must consider the size of initial investments in measuring new-product profitability.

The data presented in Table 8-6 illustrate one kind of analysis that might be used in assessing new-product profitability. In this example, test-market results suggest that a new product will achieve sales of 500,000 units. However, 100,000 of these units will reflect sales cannibalized from existing products in the line. So the net sales gain is 400,000 units. Projected sales and distribution expenses (from marketing managers) and estimated production expenses (from the technical tests) provide the data on variable and fixed costs. Of these fixed costs, some (such as the new product's allocated share of sales-force costs and a portion of fixed production costs) are not really incremental. The investment in plant and equipment for the new product is $10 million, to be depreciated over 10 years.

The analysis shows that the projected first-year return on investment is substantially higher when the project is evaluated on an incremental basis. This kind of assessment is important because most firms will evaluate the new product's financial prospects relative to the prospective return on investment from other new-product opportunities. It is also typical for a firm to establish a minimum rate of return (sometimes called a *hurdle rate*) that any new product proposal must satisfy to warrant funding. Additionally, if the firm attempts to project product profitability over a number of years, managers will generally calculate the cash flow (which is equal to net profits after taxes plus depreciation) for each future year and then discount these future cash flows to assess their *net present value.*[26]

TABLE 8-6 FINANCIAL ANALYSIS FOR A NEW PRODUCT

	NEW-PRODUCT PROJECTIONS	INCREMENTAL ANALYSIS
Sales forecast	500,000	400,000
Unit price	$ 22	$ 22
Total revenue	$11,000,000	$ 8,800,000
Variable expense (30% of sales)	−3,300,000	−2,640,000
Advertising and promotion expense	−1,000,000	−1,000,000
Allocated share of sales-force expense	−1,200,000	0
Other fixed expenses	−1,950,000	−300,000
Depreciation	−1,000,000	−1,000,000
Net profit before tax	$ 2,550,000	$ 3,860,000
Investment	$10,000,000	$10,000,000
Return on investment (ROI)	25.5%	38.6%

[26]The present value of future cash flow is calculated as follows:

$$\text{Present value of cash inflow in year } i = \frac{\text{cash flow in year } i}{(1 + d)^i}$$

where d = discount rate (desired percentage return)
    i = year in the planning-period sequence

STAGE 6: COMMERCIALIZATION

Commercialization involves the planning and execution of the *launch strategy* for introducing the new product to the marketplace.[27] Essentially, the launch strategy has three components: (1) deciding on the timing of the introduction; (2) selecting a branding strategy; and (3) coordinating the supporting introductory price, advertising, promotion, and distribution programs.

Timing New-Product Introductions

Timing can be important from both a customer demand and a competitive standpoint. In the case of customer demand, there is some degree of seasonality in every product category. Men's electric razors sell best just before Christmas and beer sales are highest in the summer, for example. It is usually wise to introduce a new product just prior to the peak demand periods for two reasons. First, with a higher level of industry sales, a faster level of new-product sales revenues is likely, which thus helps defray high initial marketing costs. Second, if many buyers have not needed to purchase brands in the category in recent "off-peak" months, they may be less loyal to existing brands and more open to new offerings. An additional consideration is availability. The launch should not be implemented until the firm is certain that distributors can support the launch with high levels of inventory, good customer service, and promotion. The potential scope of this support can be seen in the Windows 95 introduction where, prior to launch, Microsoft trained 15,000 resellers to provide customer assistance in using the software and put up a quarter of a million point-of-purchase sales displays.[28] Thus, coordination among the manufacturing, engineering, and sales and distribution functions is essential even at this late stage of the product-development process.

Timing is also of the essence from a competitive perspective. As we noted above, the earlier a firm enters the market, the greater its chances of gaining consumer awareness and a higher market share. The more similar competing products are, the more important early entry will be. For example, Merck's Pepcid, SmithKline Beecham's Tagamet, and Glaxo's Zantac are very similar acid-blocking medications, and all three received Food and Drug Administration approval to go from prescription-only sale to over-the-counter sale during 1995. In the face of this competition, Merck developed a partnership arrangement to enlist Johnson & Johnson's sales force and marketing expertise. This helped place Pepcid first on the market and, combined with a heavy initial advertising campaign, gave the Merck–Johnson & Johnson partnership the chance to build Pepcid's brand awareness and trial before competitors entered.[29]

---

[27]For a review of research on launch strategy, see Erik Jan Hultink and Henry Robben, "Predicting New Product Success and Failure: The Impact of Launch Strategy and Market Characteristics," in *Bridging the Gap from Concept to Commercialization* by Edward McDonough and Chuck Tomkovick, eds., Product Management and Development Association, Indianapolis, 1994, pp. 108–126.

[28]Kathy Rebello and Mary Kuntz, "Feel the Buzz," *Business Week*, Aug. 28, 1995, p. 31; and Don Clark, "Amid Hype and Fear Windows 95 Ready to Roll," *Wall Street Journal*, July 14, 1995, p. A1.

[29]"Stomach Drugs in New Battle," *Chicago Tribune*, July 17, 1995, sec. 4, pp. 1, 4.

Selecting a Branding Strategy

Customer acceptance of a new product will often be influenced by the image of the brand name. As we pointed out in Chapter 7, firms can often lower the cost of introducing a new product if it carries a brand name with high brand equity. Such brands lower the consumer's perceived risk of trial and increase distributor expectations that the new item will be successful.[30] As a consequence, less marketing effort may be needed to induce trial and obtain selling space from distributors if a firm can *leverage the equity* of existing brands.

The ability to leverage a brand's equity is one of the main sources of value for a brand. Although some leveraging takes place through *brand extensions*—the use of the brand on a new product line (in a new category)—the vast majority of the time it occurs with *line extensions*.[31] In line extensions, the new product is an addition to an existing line (such as Diet Coke or Liquid Tide). Generally speaking, line extensions of a brand are more successful if the brand is strong, it conveys symbolic rather than functional associations, and the entry into the category is relatively early in the product life cycle.[32] Brand extensions appear to have the best chance of success if the new product is perceived as requiring the same production assets and skills as those needed for the brand's original category, or it is perceived as a substitute or complement to the original category.[33] (Crest toothbrushes and Gillette men's toiletries are examples of brand extensions that clearly fit these criteria, while Harley Davidson cigarettes do not.)

On the other hand, sometimes a firm will not want to tie a new product to an existing brand. Many attribute General Motors' decision to introduce Saturn as a separate division with no link to any existing GM brands as an attempt to disassociate the product from the imagery of those brands. In a somewhat similar case, Coors Brewing brought out Keystone beer as a separate brand because, as a "popularly priced" beer, Keystone would carry a lower quality image. Coors did not want a low-price image associated with the Coors' brand name. Finally, people who are loyal to a brand are the customers most likely to try a new product carrying that name—at least when it is an addition to a firm's existing line. Thus, brand leveraging can cause a higher degree of cannibalization. (For example, half the sales of Bud Dry originally came from drinkers of other Budweiser products.) So, a firm may choose to establish a new brand in order to better provide the imagery needed to support the marketing strategy or because management wants to appeal primarily to competitors' customers.

---

[30]A detailed study of the impact of brand extension on market acceptance is Daniel Smith and C. Whan Park, "The Effects of Brand Extensions on Market Share and Advertising Efficiency," *Journal of Marketing Research,* August 1992, pp. 296–313.

[31]David Aaker, *Managing Brand Equity,* Free Press, New York, 1991, p. 208.

[32]Srinivas Reddy, Susan Holak, and Subodh Bhat, "To Extend or Not to Extend: Determinants of Line Extensions," *Journal of Marketing Research,* May 1994, pp. 243–262.

[33]David Aaker and Kevin Keller, "Consumer Evaluations of Brand Extensions," *Journal of Marketing,* January 1990, pp. 27–41.

Coordinating Introductory Marketing Programs

Clearly, the success of any new product will be influenced by the effectiveness of the various marketing programs used to introduce the product to the market. As noted above, these programs need to assure certain levels of awareness and availability. Additionally, in the case of products that are very new to the market, managers should review the factors influencing the willingness to buy (discussed in Chapter 3) to determine whether one or more of these factors (such as relative advantage, complexity in use, or compatibility with values and experiences) need to be addressed in the introductory marketing plan. These issues are the subject of the next five chapters.

CONCLUSION

New products play an important role in the implementation of both corporate and marketing strategy, and the development of these products should involve all elements of the business. Because of the high rate and cost of failure for new products, it is imperative that firms develop systematic procedures for identifying and screening new product ideas and concepts, developing and testing prototypes, and examining profitability.

In this chapter, we have presented a comprehensive approach to guide the product-development process, and we have examined some specific procedures that project market acceptance and profitability of new products. As we noted, however, the efficient implementation of a new product plan requires effective pricing, advertising, and other marketing programs. The relationship among product-development programs, other marketing programs, and corporate and marketing strategy is portrayed in Figure 8-5. Before proceeding to the chapters or these other marketing programs, however, consider the new-product development process for the 1996 Ford Taurus.

FIGURE 8-5

Relationships among corporate marketing planning, marketing strategy, product-development programs, and other marketing programs.

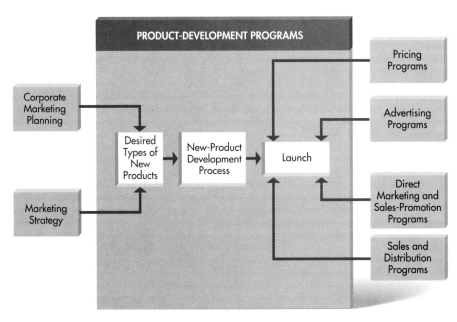

REDESIGNING THE 1996 FORD TAURUS

In the fall of 1995, Ford Motor Company surprised the automotive industry with a major redesign of its most important product, the Taurus. Originally introduced in 1984, the Taurus had become the number 1 source of revenue for Ford and, in 1992, passed the Honda Accord to become the most popular car in America. But, the Taurus had mainly attracted an older market, not the younger, import-buying drivers that Ford would need in the long run.

In 1990, Ford designer Richard Landgraff was assigned to the Taurus. His job was to design the first American car to match the quality and engineering of Taurus's two main Japanese rivals, Accord and Toyota Camry. Ford established a number of "clinics" in 1990 and 1991 at which Taurus and import owners would drive various models, fill out surveys, and discuss their impressions with marketing, design, and engineering personnel. Several themes emerged from this research: customers wanted longer and wider models, but not at the expense of fuel economy; a switch to a more aerodynamic design with better handling would gain more new customers than would be lost; there was a desire for a low-maintenance V6 engine. Ford was also influenced by the continued enthusiasm of Accord and Camry owners for the wide variety of standard equipment they received compared to models made by American firms.

In the fall of 1991, 150 project team members set up offices in Dearborn, Michigan. Ultimately, the Taurus team would include 700 people at one time or another, including supplier representatives and factory workers. Four years and $2.8 billion later, Ford introduced the new Taurus, backed by a $110 million advertising budget. The distinctively elliptical styling was a sharp departure from prior years' models, as were benefits such as taut and precise handling, a quiet interior, and many new standard features like power windows operating with delayed power cutoff (so windows could be rolled up shortly after the engine was stopped).

The design team had worked through seventeen progressively more novel designs. Interior and exterior designers worked together to ensure that the oval external styling was echoed inside in items like rounded radio control panels and air vents. To improve manufacturability, a team of 120 factory workers assembled 200 Tauruses and came up with 700 improvements (like an airbag cover that could be pushed on by hand) to reduce manufacturing time and cost. Still, the new Taurus takes 12 hours to build—one more than the old model—and some observers questioned the high total cost and the extensive investment in new tooling required to achieve the quality goals set by management. Competitive pressures would force Ford to retrench from its initial price point to a level of $19,390 for the most popular model, thus building pressure for higher volume to offset the lower unit contribution margin. However, Ford was quick to note that the Taurus chassis and suspension would be the foundation for five other Ford models in the near future.

1. What evidence is there that a multidisciplinary team is especially useful in the development process for a new automobile?
2. Define the new product *idea* that motivated the decision to make a big change in Taurus and the new product *concept* that guided the development team.
3. Apply the new-product success criteria (from Table 8-2) to the new Taurus concept as it stood in the fall of 1991. Which of these criteria would have been of most concern to management at that time?
4. How important was the role of industrial design in this project? How should the role of industrial design relate to the role of marketing?

Developed from Warren Brown, "Ford Tinkers with Success," *Washington (D.C.) Post,* Jan. 15, 1995, p. H1; Kathleen Kerwin, Edith Hill, and Keith Naughton, "The Shape of a New Machine," *Business Week,* July 24, 1995, p. 60; and "Customer Satisfaction; the Driver at Ford," *PR Newswire,* Feb. 2, 1994.

QUESTIONS AND SITUATIONS FOR DISCUSSION

1. When each of the following new products was first introduced, which types of new products would have best characterized each product?
   a. 3M's Post-it Notes
   b. Hellmann's Low-cholesterol Mayonnaise
   c. Chrysler's first minivan
2. Compile a list of problems that you encounter with products in each of the categories listed below. For each, give your assessment of the frequency with which those problems occur and the degree to which each problem is bothersome. Compare your assessments to those made by your classmates and decide what attributes or benefits should be offered by a new product in each category.
   a. Refrigerators
   b. Car washes
   c. Frozen pizza
3. Consider the following statement: "If a firm were only to develop products that scored very high on the NewProd model, it would never introduce any really innovative products." Do you agree or disagree? Explain.
4. Assemble a list of products for which industrial design efforts are likely to have the most impact in terms of market success. What do these products have in common?
5. Test marketing and customer satisfaction/preference testing are two approaches used to assess the potential success of a new product. Based on the strengths and weaknesses of each approach, which approach (if either) would you recommend for each of the following items?
   a. New, improved detergent
   b. High-definition, flat-screen television
   c. New Nintendo game
   d. New soap pad that can be used on nonstick cookware
6. If the following new products were introduced by leveraging the established brand, for which product would cannibalization most likely be highest? lowest?
   a. Cadillac introduces a minivan.
   b. Prego introduces a tomato sauce for use on homemade pizza.
   c. Schwinn introduces a specially designed bike for people over 50 years of age.
7. Timberland became immensely successful with its line of comfortable, rugged, and water-resistant boots. Subsequently, the company added a line of handsewn leather moccasins similar to the popular Topsider "deck shoe." What other categories might Timberland consider for brand extension opportunities? Discuss the criteria you used in selecting these opportunities.
8. In many industries, research and development is the source of a large portion of new product ideas. Some of these ideas may include benefits and features that customers have not considered or asked for in problem analysis or lead-user surveys. Examples include the Sony Walkman and the microwave oven. What role

should marketing research play in the product-development process for these products? How would it be different from the role it plays in consumer-inspired products?

SUGGESTED ADDITIONAL READINGS

Calantone, Roger, C. Anthony di Benedetto, and Ted Haggblom, "Principles of New Product Management: Exploring the Beliefs of Product Practitioners," *Journal of Product Innovation Management,* June 1995, pp. 235–247.

Cooper, Robert, "The NewProd System: The Industry Experience," *Journal of Product Innovation and Management,* June 1992, pp. 113–127.

de Brentani, Ulrike, "Success and Failure in New Industrial Services," *Journal of Product Innovation Management,* December 1989, pp. 239–258.

Drew, Stephen, "Accelerating Innovation in Financial Services," *Long Range Planning,* August 1995, pp. 11–21.

Guiltinan, Joseph, "A Strategic Framework for Assessing Product Line Additions," *Journal of Product Innovation and Management,* March 1993, pp. 136–147.

Page, Albert, "Assessing New Product Development Practices and Performance," *Journal of Product Innovation and Management,* September 1993, pp. 273–290.

Walker, David, "The Soup, the Bowl, and the Place at the Table," *Design Management Journal,* Fall 1993, pp. 10–21.

Wheelwright, Steven, and W. Earl Sasser, "The New, New Product Development Game," *Harvard Business Review,* May–June 1989, pp. 112–127.

CHAPTER 9

PRICING PROGRAMS

The choice of a product's selling price is one of the most fundamental decisions managers must make. As we observed in Chapter 6, the price has a direct impact on the variable contribution margin of a product and, thus, is a major influence on profitability. Specifically, higher contribution margins allow a firm to achieve the same level of total profitability with a lower unit sales volume or to increase fixed marketing budgets with little or no required increase in sales. But, beyond the margin implications, price can influence demand in a variety of ways and, thus, is an extremely important tool in the implementation of the firm's marketing strategy.

A *pricing program* is the firm's selection of a general level of pricing for a given product relative to the level of the price being charged by competitors. As discussed later in the chapter, the general types of pricing programs are (1) penetration (or, below competitors') pricing; (2) parity (or comparable to competitors') pricing; and (3) premium (or, above competitors') pricing. In this chapter, we examine the process of selecting a pricing program and emphasize that the pricing program should be supportive of the marketing strategy chosen for the product. Subsequently, we examine other factors that must be examined before final prices are selected. These include the anticipated impact of a price on sales of substitutes or complements in the firm's product line, political or legal constraints, and international trade considerations.

To begin, we identify the various *pricing objectives* a firm may pursue with its pricing programs and demonstrate the link between pricing objectives and marketing strategy. We then examine three key elements from the situation analysis that may influence the success of a given pricing program: the elasticity of demand (based on the market analysis discussed in Chapter 3); the nature of price competition (based on the competitive analysis from Chapter 4); and the product's cost structure (as analyzed in Chapter 6).

PRICING OBJECTIVES

As noted above, the primary role of the pricing decision is to help management implement its chosen marketing strategy. In some instances, price will play a minor role in the buying process, either because buyers are more concerned about other attributes and benefits or because the differences in price among competitors are minimal. In other cases, pricing will be a central thrust of the marketing strategy. As Table 9-1

TABLE 9-1	MARKETING STRATEGIES AND POSSIBLE PRICING OBJECTIVES	
	MARKETING STRATEGIES	PRICING OBJECTIVES
	Primary-demand strategies	
	Increase number of users	Reduce economic risk of trial
		Offer better value than competing product forms/classes
	Increase rate of purchase	Enhance frequency of consumption
		Enable use in more situations
	Selective-demand strategies	
	Expand served market	Serve price-oriented segment
		Offer high-end versions of product
	Acquire competitors' customers	Undercut competitors on price
		Use price to signal high quality
	Retain/expand current customer demand	Eliminate competitors' price advantage
		Expand sales of complementary products

indicates, however, there is a potentially important strategic role for price decisions in any type of marketing strategy.

Pricing can be supportive of primary-demand-oriented marketing strategies if the firm believes that lower prices can increase either the number of users or the rate of use or repurchase within the product form or class. Especially in the early stages of the product life cycle, an important goal is to generate new users. A lower price may reduce the risk of trial for a new product or it may enhance the value of a new product relative to an older one. Lower prices on notebook computers have both reduced the risk of a bad decision and increased the relative attractiveness of these products compared to standard-sized PCs. Alternatively, lower prices may be designed to increase the rate of purchase by existing customers. Reducing the price of high-quality cuts of beef or of popular discretionary items like Coca-Cola often results in increases in the rate at which these products are consumed. Southwest Airlines has demonstrated that lower air fares on short-distance flights can encourage people to substitute air travel for automotive or bus transportation.[1]

The use of pricing programs to support primary-demand strategies is somewhat limited. As discussed below, market demand must be price-elastic for such strategies to be successful. Research shows that this is most likely to be the case in the early stages of the product life cycle. Moreover, industry prices tend to decline over the life cycle, leaving less margin available for future price cuts.

With respect to selective-demand marketing strategies, the effectiveness of price depends, in large measure, on the importance customers attach to price in making

---

[1]James Hirsch, "Air Fares Take Leap Backward on Short Hops," *Wall Street Journal,* Aug. 26, 1993, p. B1.

choices within a product form or class and on the nature of demand interrelationships within the product line. For example, firms seeking to expand their served market through line extensions must consider the pricing of a new product in the context of the prices of existing products. Too low a price on an extension targeted at a price-sensitive segment can enhance the probability of cannibalization of existing products' sales. On the other hand, if the line extension is a "high-end" quality-oriented addition, the higher price may signal higher quality.[2] If the firm's strategy is focused on retaining existing customers, the role of price is generally to meet the prices charged by the most direct competitors. Often, price can be used to sell complementary products to existing customers through tactics such as "price leaders" and "bundling." We discuss these tactics later in this chapter. Finally, price may be a critical factor in acquiring competitors' customers, either by becoming the low-price leader or by using a high price to underscore a quality-based differentiation. In most product categories, price differences among competitors decline over time as consumers become more knowledgeable about products and quality differences are harder to maintain.[3] Thus, the pursuit of competitive advantage through pricing programs requires a very thorough understanding of competitive forces.

In the sections that follow, we discuss the specific issues managers must evaluate in their framing of pricing programs. Figure 9-1 offers an overview of these issues.

FIGURE 9-1

Considerations involved in the success of a pricing program.

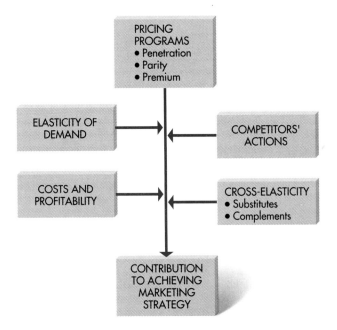

[2]David Curry and Peter Riesz, "Prices and Price/Quality Relationships: A Longitudinal Analysis," *Journal of Marketing*, January 1988, pp. 36–51.

[3]Ibid.

Specifically, the ability to successfully use price to implement a given market strategy will be limited by

■ The price-elasticity of market and company demand
■ Competitors' actions and reactions
■ Costs and profitability consequences
■ Product-line considerations

PRICE-ELASTICITY OF DEMAND

Because the effectiveness of any pricing program depends on the impact of a price change on demand, it is necessary to understand the extent to which unit sales will change in response to a change in price. However, unlike other productivity relationships, a change in price has a twofold effect on a firm's sales revenue: a change in the units sold and a change in revenue per unit. Thus, managers should not be concerned merely with the price-sensitivity of the market; they must also be concerned about the impact of the change on total dollar revenue.

The price-elasticity of demand explicitly takes this into account. That is, price-elasticity is not simply another way to express price-sensitivity. If a change in price causes a change in *units sold,* we can consider demand as somewhat price-sensitive. But when we use the term price-elasticity, we are examining the impact of a price change on *total revenue.*

More specifically, *price-elasticity of demand* is measured by the percentage change in quantity divided by the percentage change in price. Given an initial price P_1 and an initial quantity Q_1, the elasticity of a change in price from P_1 to P_2 is calculated by:

$$e = \frac{Q_2 - Q_1 / \frac{1}{2}(Q_2 + Q_1)}{P_2 - P_1 / \frac{1}{2}(P_2 + P_1)}$$

If the elasticity measure e can be calculated, then management can predict the impact of the price change on revenue, as Table 9-2 indicates.

| TABLE 9-2 | **EFFECTS OF DIFFERENT TYPES OF ELASTICITY** |

EFFECTS OF DIFFERENT TYPES OF ELASTICITY

		EFFECT ON TOTAL REVENUE OF:	
VALUE OF e	TYPE OF ELASTICITY	PRICE INCREASE	PRICE DECREASE
$e > -1$	Inelastic	Increase	Decrease
$e = -1$	Unitary elastic	No change	No change
$e < -1$	Elastic	Decrease	Increase

Note that the important number to keep in mind is -1. If elasticity is -1 or smaller (such as -2 or -3), then demand is very sensitive to price and the change in revenue will be in the opposite direction from the direction (increase or decrease) of the price change. Similarly, if elasticity is greater than -1 (such as $-\frac{1}{2}$ or $+\frac{1}{2}$), then demand is not very price-sensitive, and an increase (decrease) in price will result in an increase (decrease) in revenue. This point is significant because, in practice, it is difficult for managers to develop a precise, reliable estimate of elasticity. But simply being able to determine whether e is greater than -1 or less than -1 will enable managers to understand the general impact of a change in price or revenue.

In making estimates of elasticity, however, managers need to distinguish carefully between elasticity of *market demand* and the elasticity of *company* (or *brand*) *demand* and to recognize that differences in elasticity may exist across segments within a market.

Market, Segment, and Company Elasticity

Market elasticity indicates how total primary demand responds to a change in the average prices of all competitors. Company elasticity indicates the willingness of customers to shift brands or suppliers (or of new customers to choose a supplier) on the basis of price. For a product that offers an example of the significance of this distinction, economists often point to table salt. The market demand for table salt is inelastic, because people cannot consume much more even if all prices are lowered. However, if one producer lowers its price, that producer is likely to gain market share. So, although market demand may be inelastic, company demand, at the same time, can be elastic because buyers may be very sensitive to competitive price differences.

Marketers are not just interested in understanding total market demand, however. Recall from Chapter 4 that, for most products, different buyers have different determinant attributes. Thus, there are often substantial differences in the price-sensitivity of different buyers.

The demand schedules presented in Table 9-3 and portrayed in the demand curves of Figure 9-2 can help to illustrate these points. Assume that these data represent

TABLE 9-3

ILLUSTRATION OF MARKET AND MARKET-SEGMENT DEMAND SCHEDULES

ROUND-TRIP UNDISCOUNTED FARE	WEEKLY MARKET SALES		WEEKLY SALES: BUSINESS FLYERS		WEEKLY SALES: NONBUSINESS FLYERS	
	UNITS	TOTAL REVENUE	UNITS	TOTAL REVENUE	UNITS	TOTAL REVENUE
$350	40,000	$14.0 mill	24,000	$8.4 mill	16,000	$5.6 mill
$325	45,000	$14.625 mill	25,000	$8.125 mill	20,000	$6.5 mill
$300	51,000	$15.3 mill	26,000	$7.8 mill	25,000	$7.5 mill

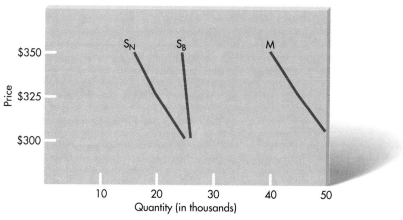

FIGURE 9-2

Illustration of a market demand curve and two market-segment demand curves.

M = market demand curve
S_B = demand curve for business travel segment
S_N = demand curve for nonbusiness travel segment

demand for flights between Chicago and New York at three price levels. For the total market (which includes all air carriers' sales), as the average price declines, total sales *and* total revenues increase, suggesting that demand is elastic. However, demand in this market is the sum of demand from two basic segments: business travel and nonbusiness (pleasure) travel. Within the business travel segment, although sales increase as prices decline, total revenue actually declines: demand in this segment is inelastic. (Of course, demand in the nonbusiness segment is very elastic.) Thus, managers who target the business segment need not use aggressive pricing as the basis for a marketing strategy.

Whether a firm's individual pricing strategy is effective, however, will depend on the *company* elasticity of demand. Even if industry prices decline from $350 to $300, a given firm serving even the elastic nonbusiness travel market might conceivably experience inelastic demand if it could clearly differentiate its flights in terms of some other determinant attribute (such as good flight times or special on-board services). If so, that firm could continue to charge prices higher than its competitors' without reducing profitability.

Managers should note that the distinction between market elasticity and company elasticity is directly related to the two major types of marketing strategies discussed in Chapter 7 and to the pricing objectives discussed earlier in this chapter. Specifically, if a manager's pricing objective is to increase rates of purchase for the product form or to increase demand among users (both of which reflect *primary-demand* strategies), then the manager should determine whether *market demand* is inelastic. On the other hand, if the pricing objectives reflect *selective-demand* strategies (such as the retention or acquisition of customers), then managers should be concerned about the elasticity of *company demand.*

However, it is *not* necessary that demand be elastic in order to achieve a pricing objective. Managers may be very committed to retaining customers or to acquiring

TABLE 9-4	ILLUSTRATION OF A COMPANY DEMAND SCHEDULE	

PRICE	DEMAND	TOTAL REVENUE
$2.00	500,000	$1,000,000
$1.50	600,000	$ 900,000
$1.00	750,000	$ 750,000

new customers when the product objective is to maintain share or to increase market share. Often, this commitment is so strong that managers will be willing to risk some reduction in total revenue in order to maintain (or to establish) a strong position in a market.

To illustrate, consider the company demand schedule in Table 9-4. Demand is inelastic because total revenue declines as the price is reduced from $2.00. However, buyers are still *sensitive* to price: Volume does increase as price declines. Consequently, if the impact of higher volume on total revenue and profitability is acceptable (given the product objective and target total contribution), then a manager may well decide to lower the price, sacrificing some degree of profitability for market share and sales-volume gains.

Factors Underlying Elasticity of Demand

Managers can gain many insights into the elasticity of market and company demand by examining the diagnostic questions discussed in Chapter 3. For example, Table 9-5 indicates some of the buying-process factors that would suggest market demand is likely to be elastic. To the extent that an industrywide price decline results in an increase in the willingness or ability to buy, the gap between market potential and industry sales becomes smaller. For example, price will have an impact on demand for one product form (aluminum) if competing product forms (such as steel) have similar performance characteristics so that the forms may be substituted for one another on a price basis. Similarly, if the number of potential buyers is far above the number who currently buy the product form, lower prices may be one mechanism to gain new buyers.

Table 9-6 presents some of the buying-process factors that would suggest elastic company or brand demand. Economic theory suggests that the greater the number of alternatives about which a buyer is informed, the greater the price-elasticity of

TABLE 9-5	FACTORS SUGGESTING ELASTIC MARKET DEMAND

1. Many alternative product forms or classes exist for which the product can be substituted.
2. Only a small percentage of potential buyers currently purchase or own the product because of the high price and because the product represents a discretionary purchase.
3. The rate of consumption or the rate of replacement can be increased through lower prices.

TABLE 9-6	FACTORS SUGGESTING ELASTIC COMPANY DEMAND

1. Buyers are knowledgeable about a large number of alternatives.
2. Quality differences do not exist or are not perceived.
3. The supplier or brand can be changed easily and with minimal efforts or costs.

demand. Additionally, elasticity will be greater if buyers can rely on observation through their search efforts to make comparisons. Thus, airline competition is price-elastic because the primary nonprice determinant attributes (departure time, flight time) are readily observed. Further, if quality differences are perceived to be minimal, demand will be more elastic. On the other hand, brands that have established a high degree of brand equity are able to charge price premiums because company demand has become price-inelastic.

Finally, if the cost involved in searching out alternatives is low, demand will more likely be elastic. For example, the time and effort involved in shifting a person's banking relationship is much greater than the time and effort involved in selecting a different brand of canned peas. Accordingly, a much larger change in price will generally be required to induce customers to switch banks than to switch brands of canned peas.

ESTIMATING PRICE-ELASTICITY

As we have shown in the previous section, managers should have some estimate of the degree of price-elasticity that exists in order to predict the unit sales volume and total revenues that will result at various price levels. In order to develop this estimate, managers can employ several alternative procedures.

Historical Ratios

In Chapter 6, we indicated that historical ratios may exist to indicate the past effect of changes in a marketing variable (such as price) on sales. Multiple-regression sales forecasting models are often employed to develop the historical relationship between price and sales volume.

When using this approach, managers must have historical data not only on company sales and prices, but also on industry sales and competitive prices. That is, to estimate market elasticity, managers need to determine the historical relationship between *industry* sales and some average of *industry* prices. However, both pieces of information are also needed to estimate company elasticity. That is, the effect of a company's price on selective demand will really depend on how much the company's price differs from the prices of direct competitors. (For example, if, in the past, a firm has consistently raised its price without any loss in sales, management cannot necessarily infer that company demand is inelastic, because competitors may also have been raising prices.) Further, estimates of company elasticity cannot be made without considering changes in industry sales. That is, an increase in company sales may reflect an increase in market share or an increase in industry sales. (In fact, price cutting frequently leads to increases in both primary and selective demand.) Accordingly, managers should examine the historical relationship between a company's relative price (that is, relative to competitors' prices) and market share when attempting to assess company elasticity.

Managers must also recognize that historical ratios will only reveal price-elasticity levels if no changes in other important marketing or environmental variables have occurred. The relationship between airline prices and sales over time will be difficult to understand if a recession has occurred, because such an economic event usually will outweigh the impact of fare levels on demand. Similarly, changes in a firm's advertising or promotional budget may have occurred, the effects of which will be difficult to separate from the effects of pricing.

Field Experiments

In Chapters 6 and 8, we discussed the use of electronic scanner-based consumer panels, noting that firms use such research tools to compare the sales productivity of alternative advertising or promotion spending levels or to track a new product's sales in a test market. Price experiments can also be conducted using the scanner-based panel approach. To do so, a firm would set different prices in selected retail stores and monitor the changes in sales or market share within those parts of the panel shopping at each set of stores.

Table 9-7 illustrates a price experiment for a box of laundry detergent that has been selling at a price of $2.49. Sales are tracked for a period of time to determine the "normal" sales level in the various stores. Then a price of $2.19 is tested in a group of experimental stores. Because weekly changes in sales can occur that are not related to a price change, the sales to those shopping in "experimental" stores should be compared with sales to those shopping in the "control" stores (where normal prices are maintained) to best judge the true impact of the lower price.

As the example in Table 9-7 demonstrates, the price reduction yields an increase in market share. But demand is inelastic because the increase in share is not sufficient to offset the price reduction. That is, since total revenue equals price times quantity, and quantity is equal to market share times industry sales in a specific market, then the total revenue at the normal sales price would have been estimated as:

$$\$2.49 \times 24.65\% \text{ or } \$0.614 \text{ times industry unit sales}$$

whereas the total revenue at the reduced price would have been estimated as:

$$\$2.19 \times 27.25\% \text{ or } \$0.597 \text{ times industry unit sales}$$

Such experiments can be time-consuming to set up and implement, and management must monitor such things as changes in competitive advertising or promotional activities taking place within the market that may have had an impact on the results.

TABLE 9-7	**ILLUSTRATION OF RESULTS OF A FIELD PRICING EXPERIMENT**

| | PERCENT MARKET SHARE | |
WEEK	CONTROL STORES ($2.49)	EXPERIMENTAL STORES ($2.19)
Pretest period		
7/30–8/5	22.0	21.4
8/6–8/12	22.2	21.8
Experimental period		
8/13–8/19	24.4	26.8
8/20–8/26	24.2	27.6
8/27–9/2	25.0	27.1
9/3–9/9	25.0	27.5
Average: pretest period	22.1	21.6
Average: experimental period	24.65	27.25
Increase in share within experimental stores		5.65%
− Increase in share within control stores		2.55%
Net increase attributable to price cut		3.10%

Controlled Choice Experiments

Predictions of what consumers might do in a store environment can often be made from surveys or choice experiments conducted in a controlled setting. The most widely used approach for implementing these experiments is the conjoint analysis method (first discussed in Chapter 4), which analyzes how buyers trade-off attributes in making choices.[4] Because the biggest trade-offs consumers make are usually between various levels of benefits and price, this method is especially relevant to an understanding of price-sensitivity. Additionally, it is especially useful in designing and pricing new products because it allows management to consider the impact of different combinations of price and nonprice attributes in market acceptance.

For example, consider the combination of possible attributes and the levels of each for a personal digital assistant (PDA) like Apple Computer's Newton, shown in Table 9-8. A group of individuals in the target market for this product were asked to rank order their preferences for various combinations of the five attributes. Analysis of the results revealed the utilities for each of these potential customers for the various attribute levels—including the five price levels. As Figure 9-3 demonstrates, there is a very sharp decline in utility when the price is raised above $500. If a firm decided to offer a specific combination of nonprice attributes, conjoint analysis programs can then predict how sensitive the market share or probability of purchase will be to the variations in price. Table 9-9 shows what was learned about price-sensitivity for a fairly simple combination of nonprice PDA attributes.

---

[4]For further insights, see Richard Smallwood, "Using Conjoint Measurement for Price Optimization," *Sawtooth Software Conference Proceedings,* Sawtooth Software, Chicago, 1991, pp. 157–162.

TABLE 9-8	**ATTRIBUTE LEVELS FOR PERSONAL DIGITAL ASSISTANT CONJOINT ANALYSIS**

ATTRIBUTE	LEVELS TESTED
Input method	1. Handwriting 2. Keyboard
Fax capability	1. Yes 2. No
E-mail capability	1. Yes 2. No
Memory	1. 1 meg 2. 2 meg
Price	1. $400 2. $500 3. $600 4. $700 5. $800

FIGURE 9-3

Part-worth utilities of various prices for a new personal digital assistant.

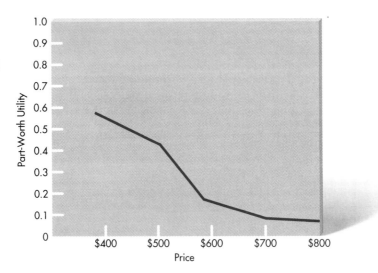

COMPETITIVE FACTORS

Whether a manager is concerned with market or company elasticity, competitors' reactions to a price change must be considered. After all, if the change in price is matched by all competitors, then no change in market share should result. In that event, the price cut will have no effect on selective demand. Accordingly, managers should attempt to determine what competitors' pricing reactions will be.

Usually, it will be useful to examine historical patterns of competitive behavior in projecting price reactions. Some competitors may price their products primarily on the basis of costs. These firms often do not shift their pricing policies over time; instead, they either price very competitively (if they are trying to take advantage of experience curves or economies of scale) or attempt to maintain consistent contribution margins and, thus, avoid direct price competition. Additionally, by analyzing competitors' historical pricing behavior, managers may obtain insights into the likely customer reaction to a price change. Specifically, if an industry has historically been characterized by extensive price cutting, buyers will more likely be price-sensitive because they will have come to expect price differences.

Managers can also use their knowledge of competitive strengths and weaknesses and of the degree of competitive intensity in an industry (as discussed in Chapter 4) when predicting competitors' responses. However, even when price is the decision issue at hand, managers should assess nonprice reactions as well as direct price reactions in a market because competitors' nonprice actions may influence price-elasticity. For example, a number of researchers have studied the influence of advertising on consumer price sensitivities. It is important to note that the conclusions depend on whether the advertising is designed to communicate brand attributes and images or whether it focuses on informing consumers about price. Two generalizations that have emerged from this research are:[5]

1. An increase in price-oriented advertising in a market leads to greater consumer price-sensitivity among consumers.
2. An increase in nonprice advertising in a market leads to lower price-sensitivity among consumers.

TABLE 9-9	EXAMPLE OF CONJOINT ANALYSIS RESULTS: SENSITIVITY ANALYSIS ON PRICE

PRODUCT ATTRIBUTES

Handwriting input
No fax capability
No e-mail capability
1-meg memory

PRICE	AVERAGE PURCHASE PROBABILITY
$400	35.2%
$500	33.9%
$600	13.5%
$700	10.6%
$800	9.9%

[5]See Anil Kaul and Dick Wittink, "Empirical Generalizations about the Impact of Advertising on Price Sensitivity and Price," *Marketing Science,* Fall 1995, pp. 151–160.

COST FACTORS

In Chapter 6, we discussed the pricing implications associated with economies of scale. Specifically, we discussed how lower prices also result in lower average costs if they lead to significant increases in volume: As volume increases, fixed costs are spread over more units. Therefore, the gains from economies of scale are greatest when fixed costs represent a high proportion of total cost. (Of course, if a firm is already producing close to its capacity, the economies of scale are already fully realized; such firms have little to gain from reducing prices.)

In many firms, current or anticipated average costs serve as the primary basis for pricing. Specifically, many firms use the *cost-plus* approach, in which the price is determined by taking the cost per unit and then adding a dollar or percentage-target-contribution margin.

To illustrate one version of the cost-plus approach, consider the data in Table 9-10, which presents the cost structure for a case of a liquid dishwashing detergent brand. In arriving at the manufacturer's price (the price per case paid by the retailer), a firm using cost-plus would usually take the variable costs of producing the detergent and then add on an estimate of each case's share of fixed overhead costs and of estimated advertising and selling costs. Note that in order to estimate the fixed cost per case, the company must have some estimate of the number of cases that will be sold because

$$\text{Fixed cost per case} = \frac{\text{total fixed cost}}{\text{number of cases sold}}$$

Subsequently, a target profit (usually expressed as a percentage of total costs) is added on — hence, the name "cost-plus."

A key issue in using the cost-plus method is the determination of the true unit cost. In many cases, some costs are allocated arbitrarily. For example, fixed costs (such as those shown in Table 9-10) will often include direct fixed costs plus some contribution to company overhead. Additionally, since the amount of fixed costs must be based on some estimate of the number of units sold, the company is implicitly assuming demand will not vary dramatically with any change in the factory price. For

TABLE 9-10   **AN ILLUSTRATION OF COST-PLUS PRICING FOR A LIQUID DISHWASHING DETERGENT**

Variable costs per case (materials, packaging)	$ 6.80
Plus allocated share of manufacturing overhead	1.70
Plus allocated share of advertising	6.50
Total unit cost	$15.00
Plus target profit per case	2.00
Manufacturer's selling price to retailer	$17.00

example, assume that total annual advertising and selling expenses are expected to be $26 million. In order to determine the share of these costs to assign to each case sold, a manager must have some estimate of the expected sales volume, even though the total cost (and thus the final price) has yet to be determined. In our Table 9-10 example, the $6.50 allocation per unit must mean sales are expected to be 4 million cases. That is,

$$\$6.50 = \frac{\$26 \text{ million}}{4 \text{ million cases}}$$

Marketers should recognize, however, that there are two alternative approaches to cost-plus pricing. The previous example illustrated the use of a full-cost approach, in which all costs are considered in setting the minimum price. Alternatively, our detergent manufacturer could also consider a variable-cost pricing approach. As we discussed in Chapter 6, a firm operating in a price-elastic market at less than full capacity may be able to improve total profitability through pricing below the average unit cost; that is, as long as the company is pricing the product above variable cost, each unit sold makes some contribution to fixed costs. Accordingly, if sales stagnate below the expected volume (that is, the volume used to compute average fixed cost), the detergent maker will be better off to lower the manufacturer's price (assuming demand is elastic) below $17 as long as the price exceeds $6.80 per case (the variable cost). However, if managers assume demand is inelastic, they are not likely to pursue this course of action.

TYPES OF PRICING PROGRAMS

Managers can select a pricing program once they have established the pricing objective and the elasticity of demand and once they have assessed their competitive and cost situation. Essentially, there are three basic types of programs for pricing individual products: penetration, parity, and premium.

Penetration Pricing

A pricing program designed to use low price as the major basis for stimulating demand is a penetration pricing program. When using these programs, firms are attempting to increase their product's degree of penetration in the market, either by stimulating primary demand or by increasing market share (acquiring new customers) on price.

The success of a penetration pricing program requires that either market (primary) demand or company (selective) demand be elastic. If market demand is elastic, market demand and total industry revenue will grow with a reduction in industry prices. Thus, even if competitors match our price cut, the increase in market demand will make all competitors better off. If economies of scale exist or the product has many complements, the benefits of increased volume are even greater.

If market demand is inelastic, then penetration pricing can make sense only if company demand is elastic (so buyers will change suppliers on the basis of price) and if competitors cannot or will not match the lower price. The failure of competitors to match the lower price could reflect a lack of competitiveness on costs or a willingness to concede market share (at least for a while) in exchange for higher profits, or because the low price appeals to a minor segment of the market. Often, several of these factors occur simultaneously. Consider, for example, the low-price initiative planned by Compaq Computer.

> Compaq surprised the personal computer industry by announcing that it would introduce a new home PC system (including a monitor) for only $1500, about $500 below the lowest-priced new models at the time. The models were to include the Intel Pentium micro-processor, and other advanced memory and hard drive features sufficient for running the newest multimedia applications. Taiwanese competitor Acer soon followed Compaq's lead but other firms in the industry indicated they would find it difficult to match this price move, arguing that PC margins were already too low.
>
> Compaq management explained that the logic behind this decision was to tap a huge new consumer market among less affluent, price-sensitive households and thus expand industry sales. While 58% of households with incomes over $50,000 owned PCs, the figure was only 14% among households with incomes under $30,000. Moreover, such households were not buying older models which were priced between $1000 and $1500 because these were inadequate for the most widely sought uses. Compaq was also banking on being able to deliver the new PC at a cost advantage relative to other leading firms. In addition to its use of direct sales to consumers (which allowed it to avoid paying margins to retailers for a large portion of sales) Compaq expected to benefit from its economies of scale. Moreover, because of its high volume of purchases, Compaq anticipated receiving discounted prices on microprocessors and hard drives from the manufacturers of these components.[6]

Table 9-11 summarizes the conditions most favorable to penetration pricing programs.

Parity Pricing

Parity pricing means setting a price at or near competitive levels. In effect, parity pricing programs attempt to downplay the role of price so that other marketing programs are primarily responsible for implementing the marketing strategy.

Frequently, this approach will be selected when company demand is elastic, industry demand is inelastic, and most competitors are willing and able to match any price cut. In such situations, managers should avoid penetration pricing because any price cuts will be offset by competitive retaliation (precluding any market-share gains). The resulting lower industry prices will not yield a significant gain in industry sales and, thus, total revenues and profit margins wi'' decline. Table 9-12 summarizes the conditions that generally favor a parity pricing program.

Parity pricing is highly compatible with cost-plus pricing, especially when average costs are based on the full-cost approach. In many industries, cost structures will be

[6]Jim Carlton, "Compaq and Acer Are Slashing Prices on Entry-Level PCs to Expand Market," *Wall Street Journal*, Nov. 11, 1995, p. A3.

TABLE 9-11	CONDITIONS FAVORING A PENETRATION PRICING PROGRAM

1. Market demand is elastic.
2. Company demand is elastic, and competitors cannot match our price because of cost disadvantages.
3. The firm also sells higher-margin complementary products.
4. A large number of strong potential competitors exist.
5. Extensive economies of scale exist, so the variable-cost approach can be used to set the minimum price.
6. The pricing objective is to accomplish either of the following:
   - Build primary demand
   - Acquire new customers by undercutting competition

very similar for the various competitors, especially when similar labor contracts, raw materials, production technologies, and distribution channels are used. In such situations, firms that perceive market demand as inelastic and competitors' costs as comparable are hardly likely to anticipate major volume gains from penetration pricing, because they expect competitors to retaliate. Thus, the potential gains of any economies of scale would go unrealized, meaning a variable-cost price floor is impractical.

Unfortunately, for some manufacturers, there are industries in which the conditions for parity pricing seem to exist, but penetration pricing is the reality. For example, in the markets for television sets, passenger air travel, and salty snacks, there are a few large competitors with significant economies of scale and elastic company demand. But the resources committed in these industries by the leading firms are so great that even firms who have higher costs believe they must meet low competitive prices in order to stay in business. If market demand is inelastic (either because industry sales are approaching market potential or because of recession), penetration pricing results in destructive industry price wars.[7]

Premium Pricing

Premium pricing involves setting a price above competitive levels. (In the case of a new product form or class where there are no direct competitors, premium pricing involves setting a price at a level that is high relative to competing product forms.)

TABLE 9-12	CONDITIONS FAVORING A PARITY PRICING PROGRAM

1. Market demand is inelastic; company demand is elastic.
2. The firm has no cost advantages over competitors.
3. There are no expected gains from economies of scale, so the price floor is based on fully allocated costs.
4. The pricing objective is to meet the competition.

---

[7]See Andrew Serwer, "How to Escape a Price War," *Fortune,* June 13, 1994, pp. 82–90; and Bill Saporito, "Why the Price Wars Never End," *Fortune,* Mar. 23, 1992, pp. 68–71.

TABLE 9-13	CONDITIONS FAVORING A PREMIUM PRICING PROGRAM

1. Company demand is inelastic.
2. The firm has no excess capacity.
3. There are very strong barriers to entry.
4. Gains from economies of scale are relatively minor, so the full-cost method is used to determine the minimum price.
5. The pricing objective is to attract new customers on quality.

This approach will be successful if a firm is able to differentiate its product in terms of higher quality, superior features, or special services, thereby establishing an inelastic company-demand curve at least within one or more target segments. Firms that successfully implement this approach will generate higher contribution margins and, at the same time, insulate themselves from price competition. Consider, for example, a decision made by the British pharmaceutical firm Glaxo.

> When Glaxo first introduced its Zantac ulcer medication as a prescription drug, Tagamet was already in the market and held a strong leadership position. But rather than simply match the price of Tagamet, Glaxo took advantage of some attributes that gave it superior value in the eyes of consumers: It had an easier schedule of doses; fewer side effects; and could be taken safely with other drugs that were not compatible with Tagamet. So, Glaxo set Zantac's price 50% above Tagamet's, and even with this differential Zantac became the market leader within four years.[8]

It is important to note that the advantage that allows a firm to set a premium price may not last forever. Consequently, these programs should be reviewed periodically. Table 9-13 summarizes the conditions that usually favor a premium pricing program.

PRODUCT-LINE CONSIDERATIONS

In a very large number of cases, the pricing decisions a manager makes about one product can influence sales of other products in the firm's mix. *Price cross-elasticities* are the relationships that exist when a change in the price of one product influences the sales volume of a second product (in addition to any impact on the first product's sales). When an increase (decrease) in price on one product results in an increase (decrease) in sales of the second product, the two products are said to be *substitutes;* if the price increase (decrease) results in a decrease (increase) in the second product's sales, the two products are *complements.*

[8]Robert Dolan, "How Do You Know When the Price Is Right?" *Harvard Business Review,* September–October 1995, p. 175.

Pricing Substitutes

In Chapter 7, we noted that a firm may extend its product line in order to expand its served market, and that line extensions could be of two types: vertical extensions and horizontal extensions. With vertical extensions, different offerings provide similar benefits, but at different price and quality levels, whereas with horizontal extensions, each offering has distinctive nonprice benefits. In both cases, cannibalization is a potential problem; if prices are reduced on any one item, much of the sales response could be due to shifts in demand within the firm's own line. Thus, management's major concern in pricing a product that has product-line substitutes is the expected level of cannibalization that will result from changes in the price of one product.

In horizontal extensions, cannibalization that results from price changes is often not very significant because the differentiation among the offerings in the line is related to specialized benefits, usage situations, or preferences that will override price in the choice process. Choosing between Tide in the powdered form and Liquid Tide, between Hellmann's mayonnaise and Hellmann's Light mayonnaise, or between Coca-Cola and the same firm's other soft drinks (such as Sprite and Slice) is not likely to be heavily dependent on modest price differences. That is, in such cases consumers would have a relatively wide range of acceptable prices relative to their reference price. A *reference price* is a psychological standard against which observed prices are compared to judge their reasonableness.[9] When products in the same broad category are evaluated, the reference price range is likely to be wide because the range of actual prices the consumer is aware of is also wide.

In vertical extensions, products within the line are likely to be similar, perhaps differing on only one or two dimensions other than price. For example, Kodak offers three levels of film—Royal Gold, Gold Plus, and Funtime—that presumably differ in quality as well as price. Similarly, Sears offers Craftsman Lawn Tractors in three combinations of horsepower and blade width at prices ranging from $1699 to $2699. In these cases, an important principle is anchoring. *Anchoring* is the effect a price stimulus has on the reference price buyers use to assess prices. When two or more products offer similar types of benefits, buyers evaluate a price in the context of the overall range with which they are confronted. Adding a new price at the high or low end of the range will change the standards by which customers evaluate each item.[10] If Land's End offers mesh knit shirts at $19.50, $21.00, and $23.50, the addition of a new item at $27.50 will raise the price standard by which other shirts will be judged: The perceived quality of the lowest-priced shirt will be somewhat diminished, and some customers will now judge the $23.50 shirt as more reasonable than they did previously. Similarly, the introduction of a new item priced at the low end of the line will enhance the quality image of the products that were formerly at the low end. It is for this reason that grocery stores like to stock generic (nonbranded) products in some categories; the fact that generics are priced below the store's own "private" labels makes the store brand appear less "cheap."

---

[9]Gurumurthy Kalyanaram and Russell Winer, "Empirical Generalizations from Reference Price Studies," *Marketing Science,* Fall 1995, pp. 161–169.

[10]Thomas Nagle, *The Strategy and Tactics of Pricing,* Prentice-Hall, Englewood Cliffs, N.J. 1987, p. 187.

Pricing Complements

In Chapter 6, we discussed the causes of complementarity and the potential impact of complementary relationships on the profitability consequences of marketing decisions. Certainly, the potential impact of price on sales of complementary products can be great. Indeed, the key to successful penetration pricing may be the ability to sell a large volume of add-on or replacement sales items. Pricing for the Gillette Sensor razor and Microsoft's Windows 95 included consideration of the additional sales that would be realized on replacement blades and related software applications.

Analyzing the effect that a price change on one product has on the sales of complementary products can often be difficult. However, managers can attempt to take advantage of complementary relationships through either of two special product-line pricing programs: leader pricing or price bundling.

LEADER PRICING

If the demand for a product is elastic, and if the product has a number of complements that either enhance its value or can be purchased more conveniently by buying from the same source, that product may then be used as a leader. Leader pricing simply involves setting and then promoting a penetration price on the leader. The expectation is that sales of complements to new customers will increase more than enough to offset the reduced profit on the leader.

Table 9-14 lists the major characteristics of a good leader product. Note that in selecting a leader, managers are generally advised to avoid products that customers are likely to stock up on during the special prices or where strong substitution effects will lead to simple shifts in sales from high-margin to low-margin products.

PRICE BUNDLING

In price bundling, two or more products or services are marketed together for a special price.[11] Technically, most firms employ mixed price bundling: Buyers are given the choice of buying two products in a package or buying the products individually.

TABLE 9-14	CHARACTERISTICS OF A GOOD PRICE LEADER

1. The product is widely used by individual buyers in the target market.
2. The product's prevailing market price is well known.
3. The product has a high degree of price-elasticity.
4. The product has many complements, which enhance the value of the leader or are convenient to purchase when buying the leader.
5. The product has few or no substitutes.
6. The product is not usually bought in large quantities and stored.

Adapted from J. Barry Mason and Hazel F. Ezell, *Marketing: Principles and Strategy,* Business Publications, Plano, Tex., 1987, p. 392.

[11]Joseph Guiltinan, "The Price Bundling of Services: A Normative Framework," *Journal of Marketing,* April 1987, pp. 74–85.

Buyers who place a low value on one of the two products will avoid the bundle. However, the economic incentive of a lower price on one item will lead to additional sales of both products to some buyers who otherwise would buy only one. When complementary relationships are very strong, the effects of the special price are even greater.

Mixed price bundling can be accomplished through either of two approaches. In the *mixed leader* form, the price of a lead product is discounted on the condition that a second product be purchased. In *mixed joint* bundling, two or more products or services are offered for a single package price. For example, assume a bank offers a VISA credit card at an annual fee of $15 and a safe deposit box for $25 per year. A mixed leader bundling option would be to discount the VISA to $5 per year on the condition that a customer also rent a safe deposit box at the regular price. The comparable mixed joint bundling option would be "a VISA card and safe deposit box for $30 per year."

Both forms of bundling could be used to achieve the objective of expanding the range of products bought by existing customers. For our bank, the mixed leader option would then make sense if we had a large VISA base and a small safe deposit box base: The discounted VISA would serve as an incentive for renting the safe deposit box. The mixed joint option would be more useful if our customers tended to buy either one or the other product. Safe deposit box holders would then have an incentive to buy a VISA and vice versa.

ADDITIONAL PRICING CONSIDERATIONS

Political-Legal Environment

The political and legal environment can pose significant constraints on pricing decisions. Many of these constraints involve direct regulation of prices. Although the political atmosphere in the United States has evolved toward deregulation, direct regulation is still a factor in monopolistic markets such as cable television and public utilities. Moreover, government regulation of prices remains a significant factor in many other nations around the world.

Government also has an impact on pricing through its taxation policies. State and federal taxation of cigarettes, distilled spirits, luxury automobiles, and boats can have a depressing effect on demand for such products and may heighten the effectiveness of price reductions. Similarly, the federal government's decision to exempt gasoline made with ethanol (a corn-based product) from a portion of the federal gasoline tax provides this product with a competitive price advantage in the markets where it is sold.

In other markets, the role of government and political entities may be more indirect. In the field of health care, there is significant pressure for control of health care costs from the government (which pays a large share of these costs through Medicaid) and from businesses who pay a part of employee health insurance plans. In the early 1990s, the pharmaceutical industry came under verbal attack by the president of the United States and some members of Congress because of the high level of drug prices, and voluntarily reduced the rate of increase for certain categories of medicines. Additionally, Medicaid patients (as well as employees whose insurance is partly paid for by businesses) are increasingly receiving care from large, managed-care organizations that are able to obtain significant discounts on the most widely prescribed drugs.[12]

Finally, managers should be aware of government regulations that are designed to preserve competition and which apply to virtually all industries. Based on the Sherman Antitrust Act, the Federal Trade Commission Act (Section 5), and the Robinson-Patman Act, federal regulations limit pricing behavior in two ways. Collusive behavior (agreements among competitors) is the most fundamental unlawful action in pricing. All the collusive practices listed in Table 9-15 are automatically illegal. Also, companies that distribute through retailers and wholesalers should be aware of the issue of price discrimination if different prices are charged to different resellers. Price discrimination is not automatically illegal. However, it is illegal if these price differences fail to pass at least one of the criteria given in Table 9-16.

International Considerations

The firm's competitive situation and cost structure must also be evaluated in the context of several special international considerations. Even if the firm has no overseas business, foreign firms are likely to be competing in the domestic market, and the ability to compete with foreign-based firms on price is often influenced by nation-specific cultural, political, and economic factors.

Certainly, prices are influenced by the cost of doing business in various nations. Firms that can attract capital, labor, or raw materials at lower cost will have an advantage in pricing. For example, the *cost of borrowing* was significantly lower in Japan than in the United States during the 1980s, allowing Japanese firms to price products slightly lower to get the same profit return as their U.S. counterparts.

Additionally, when firms export products to other nations, they must consider *tariffs* or *import fees*. It is still not unusual to find tariffs of 20 or 30 percent applied to selected imported goods when a nation is trying to protect a domestic industry from price competition.

The most problematic global force for business is the *currency exchange rate*. The rates at which currencies of different nations are exchanged fluctuate over time, and

TABLE 9-15	**EXAMPLES OF COLLUSIVE PRICING PRACTICES**

1. Agreement to reduce prices in order to injure competitors
2. Agreement on selling prices, bids, discounts, or credit policies
3. Agreement on and enforcement of resale prices
4. Agreement to fix price differentials, discounts, or important terms of sale for designated groups of customers
5. Agreement to rotate bids among competitors

---

[12]Elyse Tanouye, "Big Drug Makers Regaining Control over Their Prices," *Wall Street Journal,* July 12, 1995, p. B6.

TABLE 9-16	SITUATIONS IN WHICH DIFFERENT PRICES MAY LEGALLY BE OFFERED TO DIFFERENT RESELLERS

1. The products sold are not of "like grade and quality" in technical content and features.
2. Price differences do not result in injury to competition.
3. Price differences can be justified by variations in the cost of serving the different customers.
4. Price differences are made in good faith to meet equally low prices of competitors in order to retain customers and where a competitor's price is not discriminatory.
5. Discounts and allowances are offered on proportionately equal terms to all competing resellers.

a sharp unexpected change (or even a significant long-term change) can create problems for a firm. For example, a Japanese automobile that sold in the United States in 1985 for $15,000 would have brought the seller nearly 4 million yen at the then-prevailing exchange rate. Ten years later the exchange rate was 102 yen per dollar. Thus, a $15,000 sale would yield the same Japanese firm only 1.5 million yen ($15,000 × 102 = 1,530,000). Thus, even if there were no inflation, the firm would have far fewer yen to purchase components and to pay workers' salaries if it continued to assemble the vehicle in Japan.[13]

Price Elements of Other Marketing Programs

As we have frequently suggested in this book, the various marketing programs are usually interrelated. This chapter has focused on the basic list-price strategy. In subsequent chapters, other programs relating directly or indirectly to price will be addressed. These programs are summarized in Table 9-17.

Although these programs involve modifications of the list price, managers usually employ them to achieve different kinds of program objectives. Decisions regarding the use of these elements are usually made by different managers. Accordingly, these programs will be discussed in subsequent chapters.

TABLE 9-17	PRICE ELEMENTS OF OTHER MARKETING PROGRAMS

SALE-PROMOTION PROGRAMS	SALES AND DISTRIBUTION PROGRAMS
Coupons	Quantity discounts
Cents-off deals	Cash discounts
Promotion allowances	Credit or financing assistance
Rebates	Long-term contracts
	Negotiated pricing

[13]Bill Montague, "Yen Surge Pinches U.S. Customers," *USA Today,* Apr. 20, 1993, p. B1.

CONCLUSION

Management's recognition of the importance of price decisions has increased in recent years. Deregulation, greater international competition, changes in technology, and, occasionally, inflation have all created changes in the pattern of price competition in one industry or another.

However, the process of developing a basic pricing program and arriving at a specific price remains a difficult one. As we have indicated in this chapter, there are no simple rules of thumb managers can use to guarantee a correct price. However, by employing the process this chapter has suggested, managers should be able to devise a pricing program that is consistent with their marketing strategy. Although the pricing program may be modified by sales-promotion programs and by sales and distribution programs, the basic role pricing will play in implementing a marketing strategy should be determined by (1) establishing clear pricing objectives; (2) analyzing price-elasticity, competition, and costs; and (3) considering political-legal and international constraints. Figure 9-4 summarizes these steps and provides an overview of the relationships among them.

Although pricing decisions are not a central element in marketing strategy for many firms, they certainly have had an impact on strategic decisions in the cigarette industry in recent years.

FIGURE 9-4

Relationship of pricing programs to the situation analysis, marketing strategy, and other marketing programs.

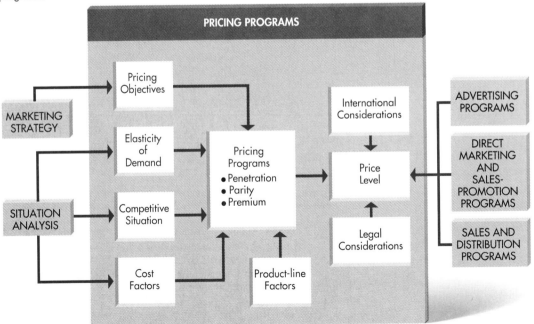

DID COMPETITIVE FIRES BURN SOME
CIGARETTE MAKERS?

For decades, competition in the cigarette industry was characterized by a heavy emphasis on brand proliferation based on minor product differences such as product length, thickness, special filter designs, and taste additives (like menthol). Additionally, brand advertising focused on imagery that associated brands with demographic groups (such as Virginia Slims), characters (like the Marlboro man), or lifestyles (such as Newport).

During the 1980s, a major change occurred in the industry with the introduction of so-called discount brands. As prices of the leading brands rose sharply in that decade, the share of market going to discount brands rose to 40 percent. The two industry leaders were Philip Morris (which sold the industry's top-selling brand, Marlboro, along with brands such as Virginia Slims and Benson & Hedges) and RJR (maker of Winston, Camel, and several other brands). About one-fourth of Philip Morris's unit sales came from its discount business, including the Basic brand, whereas discount cigarettes accounted for half of RJR's business. The other three competitors—American Tobacco, Ligget & Myers, and Brown & Williamson—were even more dependent on discount cigarettes.

Cigarette prices varied widely across the country mainly because of differences in state and local taxes, which often exceeded the 25 cent per pack federal tax. However, a typical price for premium cigarettes was $2.15 versus $1.20 for discount brands. Industry analysts estimated that cigarette makers earned only about a nickel per pack on discount brands compared to 50 cents on premium brands. Sales of cigarettes in the United States had been declining at a rate of about 2 percent per year to a total annual volume of 25 billion packs when, in 1993, Philip Morris shocked the industry with a 40-cent per pack price cut on Marlboro.

The Marlboro price cut was a severe blow to the industry's profit picture. When Philip Morris announced the cut, its management acknowledged that the company stood to lose billions by the move. RJR was carrying a heavy debt burden from a recent leveraged buyout and could ill-afford a price war. Within 6 months, Marlboro's market share climbed from 21.5 to 25.5 percent. After several months of losing market share, however, RJR matched Marlboro's price reduction. Philip Morris also decreased prices on its other premium brands and increased the price of Basic by 10 cents. The rest of the industry followed the lead of the two major competitors.

Over the next 2 years, the price war seemed forgotten. RJR initiated small price increases on both discount and premium brands, and competitors went along with these changes. By the end of 1995, the share of market held by all discount brands was 30 percent. Meanwhile, Marlboro's share had reached 29.7 percent.

1. Discuss the elasticity of demand for cigarettes, considering both the data in the case and the factors discussed in Tables 9-5 and 9-6.
2. Do you think Marlboro correctly anticipated the consequences of its price cut?
3. What pricing objective(s) do you think Philip Morris was pursuing?
4. How might the concepts of "brand equity" and "the prisoner's dilemma," discussed in Chapter 7, be applied to the analysis of pricing in the cigarette market?

Developed from "P-M Prices Hurt Smaller Players," *Brandweek*, July 26, 1993, p. 10; Jay Mathews, "For Tobacco Giants the Future Is Glowing," *Washington* (D.C.) *Post*, July 5, 1994, p. A1; Pamela Moore, "Spoils of War: Analysts Say That Philip Morris' Plan to Cut Price of Marlboro Paid Off Big with Increased Market Share," *Winston-Salem* (N.C.) *Journal*, July 17, 1994, p. E7; Subrata Chakravarty and Amy Feldman, "Don't Underestimate the Champ," *Forbes*, May 10, 1993, p. 106; and "Philip Morris Reports Third Quarter Earnings Results," *Business Wire*, Oct. 17, 1995.

QUESTIONS AND SITUATIONS FOR DISCUSSION

1. A marketing manager for a consumer electronics company is considering a reduction in the price of one of its camcorder models from $698 to $599. Currently, sales of this model are averaging 15,000 units per month.
   a. If sales increase to 17,000 per month, would this imply that demand is elastic or inelastic?
   b. What other factors must the manager consider in determining whether the change in demand truly reflects the degree of price-elasticity?

2. Would the *market* demand for each of the following products be elastic or inelastic with respect to price? Why?
   a. Open-heart surgery
   b. Airline tickets for a vacation
   c. A yacht
   d. Gasoline

3. For each of the following procedures, do you think *company* demand would typically be elastic or inelastic with respect to price? Can there be exceptions to your answer for any of these producers?
   a. A paint manufacturer
   b. A hairstylist
   c. A manufacturer of electric razors
   d. A textbook publisher

4. In which of the following situations would historical ratios be most useful in estimating price-elasticity of demand? Why?
   a. Setting prices on a new line of microwavable frozen dinners
   b. Pricing blank videocassette tapes
   c. Ticket prices for the Boston Celtics basketball team

5. A number of firms around the world are developing sophisticated new high-definition television systems (HDTV) that will offer incredibly improved picture quality. Such systems are now available in Japan at prices on the order of $8000. While much patented technology is involved in the development of HDTV, the federal government will insist that any technology approved for use in transmitting and receiving HDTV signals be available to all potential television set manufacturers.

   Based on this information, what type of pricing program would you recommend to firms who decide to enter this market?

6. In each of the following situations, what type of pricing program would typically be appropriate?
   a. Market demand is inelastic and company demand is elastic.
   b. A firm has a distinct quality advantage.
   c. A firm is not producing at full capacity and company demand is elastic.

7. For each of the following situations, discuss the kinds of product-line issues that should be considered in making pricing decisions.
   a. A publisher offers a book in both hardcover and softcover versions and must set a price on each one.

b. A sporting goods store carrying a wide assortment of goods wants to attract customers who will buy a variety of Christmas presents at the store.

c. A camera manufacturer who also produces and sells the film for its cameras is considering a reduction in the price of its lowest-priced model.

8. British Airways offers a "get-away" vacation package that includes airfare, lodging, and guided tours of historical sights in England for $2600. Ameritech sells a new Motorola cellular phone for the special price of $59 when customers sign up for cellular phone service through Ameritech's mobil phone division.

    a. What type(s) of product-line pricing policies are being used?

    b. In each case, which customers would benefit from the particular offer being made?

    c. Do you think that the demand for the British Airways package is likely to be more elastic or less elastic on price than demand for the Ameritech offer? Explain why.

9. In recent years, the interstate trucking, banking, and long-distance telephone industries have been deregulated, resulting in the rise of new competitors, increased price competition, and the demise of some old competitors.

    a. Which of the conditions favoring penetration pricing do you think are most responsible for these results?

    b. Are there potential negative consequences of deregulation? Explain.

SUGGESTED ADDITIONAL READINGS

Cavusgil, S. Tamer, "Unraveling the Mystery of Export Pricing," *Business Horizons,* May–June 1988, pp. 54–63.

Curry, David, and Peter Riesz, "Prices and Price/Quality Relationships: A Longitudinal Analysis," *Journal of Marketing,* January 1988, pp. 36–51.

Dolan, Robert, "How Do You Know When the Price Is Right?" *Harvard Business Review,* September–October 1995, pp. 174–183.

Farley, John, James Hulbert, and David Weinstein, "Price Setting and Volume Planning by Two European Industrial Companies," *Journal of Marketing,* Winter 1980, pp. 46–54.

Harris, Frederick, and Peter Peacock, "Hold My Place: Yield Management Improves Capacity-Allocation Guesswork," *Marketing Management,* Fall 1995, pp. 34–46.

Prybeck, Frank, and Fernando Alvarez, "How to Price for Successful Product Bundling," *Journal of Pricing Management,* Fall 1990, pp. 5–18.

Tellis, Gerard, "Beyond the Many Faces of Price: An Integration of Pricing Strategies," *Journal of Marketing,* October 1986, pp. 145–160.

Wind, Jerry, "Getting a Read on Market-Defined Value," *Journal of Pricing Management,* Winter 1990, pp. 5–14.

CHAPTER 10

ADVERTISING PROGRAMS

OVERVIEW

As discussed in previous chapters, marketing management entails the development of appropriate products and services for target markets at the right price, and the procedures for making them readily available. However, managers must also develop programs for presenting information about the organization and its products to target markets. Effective marketing communications are essential if prospective buyers are going to be aware of the firm's offerings and motivated to buy its products. Marketing information can be communicated through personal sources—the firm's sales force and distributors—or through impersonal sources—primarily advertising and sales promotion.

Sales Promotion

Sales promotion is an increasingly important aspect of marketing. Sales promotion includes activities such as coupons, samples, multipacks, cents-off, and so forth. Sales promotions, which are discussed in Chapter 11, are short-term actions designed to get immediate responses from consumers, wholesalers, or retailers. When management offers some form of sales promotion to wholesalers or retailers, the expected result is that the product will be pushed to the consumer. For example, assume that Tillotson, a manufacturer of surgical gloves, wants to increase market share. Tillotson offers a 10 percent discount on gloves sold to medical supply companies that sell the product to hospitals. The goal of the sales promotion is to entice medical supply companies to either switch from other glove manufacturers like Johnson & Johnson and Maxxim Medical to Tillotson, or, at least, buy more from Tillotson and then push the Tillotson brand to the hospitals because the margin is greater. If the medical supply rep passes on some of the savings to the hospital, this will make Tillotson gloves even more attractive than the competition. The same process holds for consumer markets. If a grocery store makes an additional 1 or 2 percent margin on a particular brand because of a sales promotion, the grocer is likely to run a sale on the brand to get consumers to buy this brand or the grocer will give it more or better shelf space, and so on.

These actions get quick response, but can have their drawbacks. They increase price sensitivity of consumers as well as the trade (retailers and wholesalers). In addition, sales promotion to wholesalers and retailers can cause them to buy in large quantities when the brand is on sale and simply stockpile the brand for 3 to 4 months. The overall level of sales does not change; it only changes when the product is purchased. The portion of the promotion budget allocated to sales promotion activities in lieu of advertising has been increasing. In the early 1980s, about 65 percent of the promotion budget was allocated to sales promotion activities. This percentage increased to 73.4 percent in 1994.[1]

Advertising

Sales promotion activities may induce trial but do little to enhance long-term brand loyalty. Some companies, such as Procter and Gamble, have decided to invest more in advertising strategies. L. Ross Love, vice president of worldwide advertising for P&G, said that advertising agencies could expect increased budgets in the future. Love believes that advertising is a deposit in the brand equity bank, whereas sales promotions are a withdrawal.[2] Advertising agencies can be used to associate the brand with stronger and more positive perceptions of brand quality, which will lead to increased brand equity. Advertising that communicates a unique and positive message can differentiate the brand from competitive offerings and help insulate the brand from price competition.[3]

Of the various promotion activities, advertising is clearly the most visible. Indeed, many consumers tend to equate the terms advertising and marketing. This is partially explained by the large amount of dollars spent on advertising. For instance, in 1993, advertising expenditures in the United States were expected to exceed $145 billion. Some companies spend in excess of a billion dollars per year. Procter and Gamble's expense in 1993 was $2.4 billion. Other companies spending in excess of $1 billion are Philip Morris (1.8), General Motors (1.59), Sears (1.3), and PepsiCo (1.0).[4] Unfortunately, this preoccupation with advertising sometimes leads people to ascribe a level of effectiveness to advertising that may far exceed the level actually achieved.

Each type of communication program has unique characteristics, and managers must consider these characteristics as well as the effects they hope to achieve from each program. In this chapter we discuss advertising. Subsequent chapters will discuss direct marketing, sales promotion and personal selling, which are other methods of communicating with customers.

---

[1] Terence A. Shimp, *Marketing Communications: Managing of Advertising and Promotions,* 4th ed., HBJ/Dryden, Forth Worth, Tex., 1996.

[2] Sinisi, John, "Love: EDLP Equals Ad Investment," *Brandweek,* Nov. 16, 1992, p. 2.

[3] William Boulding, Eunkyu Lee, and Richard Staelin, "Mastering the Mix: Do Advertising, Promotion, and Sales Force Activities Lead to Differentiation?" *Journal of Marketing Research,* May 1994, pp. 159–172.

[4] Shimp, loc. cit.

ADVERTISING PROGRAMS: DECISIONS AND ORGANIZATION

Decisions regarding the advertising message (what to say and how to say it) and the media (where the message is to be presented and how many times) are fundamental to advertising programs. These decisions generally require highly specialized creative and technical skills such as

- Developing creative copy ideas
- Producing creative artwork and photos
- Testing copy for consumer reactions
- Buying media time
- Researching audience readership or viewing habits

Advertising Organizations

Performance of the advertising tasks involves three basic alternatives. One option is for a company to fund its own in-house advertising department. Unless a company does a large amount of advertising, any benefits of an in-house agency would probably not be offset by the expense.

One alternative to an in-house agency is to contract with an advertising agency. Full-service advertising agencies usually consist of four departments. The creative department is responsible for designing the message and its executional style to match the advertiser's objectives and strategies. The media department is responsible for selecting the various media (for example, television, radio, outdoor, direct, and so on) that will carry the advertising messages. The research department conducts studies such as those involving the purchasing preferences and habits of the advertiser's target market and tests the impact of the ads developed by the creative services people. Account management is responsible for interacting with the advertising agency's clients. It must ensure that the clients' objectives are fulfilled by the agency. Two predominant reasons for contracting with an advertising agency are access to advertising specialists with a knowledge of current and effective advertising techniques and negotiation muscle with media.[5]

Advertising agencies have traditionally charged their clients 15 percent of the gross amount of billing. If an advertisement costs $85,000 to place in a magazine, the agency bills the client $100,000. The agency keeps the 15 percent commission ($15,000) and sends the remaining $85,000 to the magazine. As you might expect, this standard 15 percent commission has been a source of controversy between agencies and their clients, especially clients with large accounts.[6] Agencies and clients have tried a number of alternative compensation systems. Today, only 14 percent of clients pay the standard 15 percent commission.[7]

[5]George Donahue, "Evaluating Advertising Services: Part II," *Marketing Communications,* April 1982, p. 61.

[6]Herbert Zeltner, "Sounding Board: Clients, Admen Split on Compensation," *Advertising Age,* May 18, 1981, pp. 63–76.

[7]"Say Adieu to 15%, But Lower Rates Alive, Kickin'," *Advertising Age,* May 15, 1995, p. 1; Iris Cohen, "Big Profits, Risks with Incentive Fees," *Advertising Age,* May 15, 1995, p. 3.

Another alternative is to purchase advertising services from specialists. These specialists are sometimes referred to as "boutique agencies." In this approach, the advertiser might contract with one agency that specializes in creative services to develop the message and then contract with another agency to schedule and buy the media, and so forth. The advertising functions are performed by a number of independent firms, each specializing in one task. This approach can be cost effective because you only contract for services as needed.[8]

There was a considerable shift toward using in-house agencies and boutiques in the 1970s. The trend today is toward full-service agencies, especially among large advertisers. Traditionally, Procter and Gamble purchased all media using a small in-house media team. P&G in the United Kingdom has chosen two large advertising agencies, Saatchi & Saatchi and Leo Burnett, to handle its media transactions.[9]

Message and media decisions are most effective when advertising agencies, specialists, and in-house departments have some guidance on

- How the advertising program is expected to contribute to the marketing strategy and relate to other programs
- What level of advertising expenditures is consistent with the firm's product mix allocation plan and product profitability

Clearly, specified advertising objectives are necessary to provide guidance on message and media decisions. These objectives should be developed by the managers who are responsible for developing and implementing the overall marketing strategy.

Responsibility for Advertising Programs

Organizations differ on the question of who should serve as the coordinator or liaison with the agency or with other advertising specialists. Because the primary purpose of this chapter is to provide insights and procedures for managing advertising programs (rather than for developing the creative and technical elements of advertisements), it is important to identify, briefly, the marketing positions and organizational approaches involved in advertising management.

The position of advertising manager or advertising director often exists in firms that are organized on a functional basis. In industrial firms, this individual may report to the sales manager because advertising is often a small portion of the marketing effort and because its primary role is to support the sales function. Otherwise, the advertising manager will typically report to a senior marketing manager.

Advertising is supervised by the product or brand manager in firms that are organized on a product basis. When there are a large number of products in a firm, these managers tend to take on considerable responsibility for market analysis, short-run planning, and coordination with the other functions (such as sales and marketing research). In some companies, such as Procter and Gamble, there is an additional layer

---

[8]Donahue, op. cit., p. 64.

[9]Claire Beale, "P&G Makes Media Waves," *Marketing,* Apr. 21, 1994, p. 14.

of management—referred to as the category manager—above the brand managers. This structure is designed to improve and coordinate efforts among groups of product categories.

Although advertising managers and product managers work closely with outside agencies and specialists, their role in advertising management is often shared with the chief marketing executive or the divisional manager. There are two reasons why top management may become involved in these programs rather than delegate all responsibility to middle managers. First, advertising managers are staff personnel. Although they have expertise in selecting the advertising message and media, they are not directly responsible for sales or profits. Second, product or brand managers usually have sales or profit responsibility, but are often seeking increases in advertising budgets—especially if they are responsible for sales volume rather than profitability. However, this varies company by company. For instance, Procter and Gamble has ninety brands and relationships with sixteen advertising agencies. In 1987, P&G eliminated the position of advertising manager for most of its brands in an attempt to coordinate more effectively the activities of brands that were in the same category. In 1989, P&G restored the ad manager position because it discovered that brands with ad managers outperformed brands with no ad managers. At P&G, brand managers usually maintain close contact with the advertising agencies, whereas advertising managers help set overall product-line strategy and approve all advertising and promotions.[10]

Consequently, in order to control the allocation of resources in accordance with product objectives, top management may make the major decisions regarding advertising expenditures, creative policy, or media plans (with the technical support of staff advertising specialists).

Elements of the Advertising Program

As we suggested in the preceding section, message development and media scheduling are not the only elements involved in advertising programs. In fact, as Figure 10-1 indicates, there are a number of decisions involved in the management of the advertising program. Although advertising agencies and other specialists are primarily involved in message design and media decisions, marketing managers in the firm doing the advertising must be somewhat involved in every step of the process.

Given the situation analysis and marketing strategy, these company managers are responsible for defining the objectives of the advertising program and for determining the budget. Subsequently, the advertising agency or outside specialists can develop message and media decisions that are consistent with the objectives and the budget. Additionally, managers should examine the proposed message and media plan for consistency with marketing strategy and product objectives. Finally, managers should evaluate the program to see if objectives are being attained and to determine whether any elements of the program should be revised.

---

[10]Laurie Freeman, "P&G Keen Again on Ad Managers," *Advertising Age,* Sept. 25, 1989, p. 6; and Barry Brown, "P&G Hires 10 Shops," *Advertising Age,* Oct. 21, 1991, p. 38.

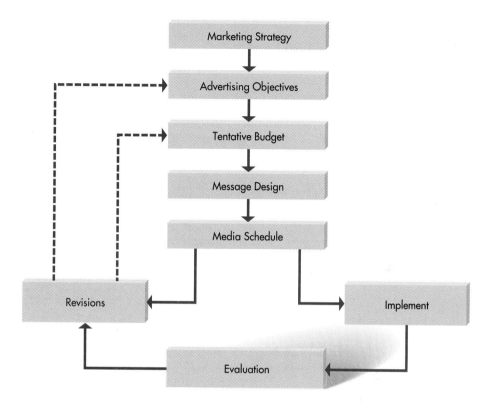

FIGURE 10-1

Basic elements of an advertising program.

ADVERTISING OBJECTIVES

There are two basic reasons to establish objectives for advertising programs. First, advertising objectives can provide guidance for the development of message and media decisions. Second, advertising objectives serve as standards for evaluating the performance of the advertising program. Unless managers have defined what the advertising effort is designed to achieve, there will be no fair way to evaluate the results.

Hierarchy of Effects

Advertising strategies can serve many functions. They can be used to inform consumers, to persuade consumers, and/or to remind consumers.[11] Advertising programs are designed to move consumers from the point where they are unaware of the brand to trial and repeat purchase. One framework that outlines these stages is the hierarchy of effects. There are a variety of hierarchy of effects frameworks. The AIDA model, which stands for attention-interest-desire-action, was first introduced in the

[11]James Webb Young, "What Is Advertising, What Does It Do?" *Advertising Age,* Nov. 21, 1973, p. 12.

TABLE 10-1

EFFECTS OF COMMUNICATIONS AT VARIOUS
STAGES OF RESPONSE

STAGES	SPECIFIC EFFECTS
1. Cognitive stage	Exposure to message Message recall Awareness of product Knowledge of product attributes and uses
2. Affective stage	Willingness to seek more information Interest in product attributes Favorable evaluation of product or brand Intention to try or buy
3. Behavioral stage	Product trial Product purchase

1920s.[12] Two frameworks introduced in the 1960s were the hierarchy of effects model (awareness-knowledge-liking-preference-conviction-purchase)[13] and the innovation adoption model (awareness-interest-evaluation-trial-adoption).[14] These models are very similar. A generally agreed-upon grouping (see Table 10-1) classifies the different effects into one of three levels.

1. *Cognitive responses*—those that indicate receipt of the message
2. *Affective responses*—those that indicate the development of attitudes (liking/disliking) toward the product or company
3. *Behavioral responses*—actual actions taken by the members of the target audience

Figure 10-2 is adapted from a more recent hierarchy of effects framework.[15] Here the consumer moves from being unaware of the brand to forming expectations and then trial. The trial reinforces beliefs about the brand or the image of the brand or company. The beliefs lead to attitude reinforcement, whereas the image leads to brand equity reinforcement. Both attitude and brand equity lead to brand loyalty.

   Of course, over the long run, firms would not spend money on advertising unless they expected that their expenditures would help achieve sales, market-share, and profitability objectives. But sales and profits are generally inappropriate objectives for advertising programs for several reasons. First, sales generally respond rather slowly to advertising. This is especially true for products that are infrequently purchased, but it is also true for frequently purchased products, because most advertisements must be seen more than once before the message is received and acted on. Second, changes in

---

[12]E. K. Strong, "The Psychology of Selling, McGraw-Hill, New York, 1925, p. 9.

[13]Robert J. Lavidge and Gary A. Steiner, "A Model for Predictive Measurements of Advertising Effectiveness," *Journal of Marketing,* October 1961, p. 61.

[14]Everett Rogers, "Diffusion of Innovations," Free Press, New York, 1962, pp. 79–86.

[15]Shimp, loc. cit.

sales and market share are often influenced by environmental factors and competitive actions. An advertising message may be very effective in communicating a particular product benefit about an automobile, but if interest rates rise or if unemployment rises, industry sales and company sales may decline in spite of the advertising effort.

For example, Nissan introduced its luxury Infiniti car with a $60 million campaign. The objectives of the campaign were to create high levels of awareness and interest among prospects for a luxury sports sedan. All of Nissan's measures of awareness, brand identification, and showroom visits indicated that these objectives had been met. However, instead of the 2500-unit monthly sales called for in the marketing plan, only 1700 cars were sold during the first 2 months. Analysts indicated that this occurred because Toyota had introduced its luxury sports sedan Lexus 2 months prior to the Infiniti, and that Nissan had underestimated the competition it would face from other luxury car companies such as BMW, Mercedes, and Volvo.[16]

Additionally, sales and market-share objectives provide very little direction for the development of messages and the selection of media. Motivation of an action (such as a purchase) is only one of the possible effects of communications programs.

What advertising can do, however, is to help implement the marketing strategy for a product or service. That is, managers can establish advertising objectives to guide the selection of messages and media, permit program performance to be evaluated, and make a specific contribution to achievement of the marketing strategy.

FIGURE 10-2

A hierarchy model of how advertising works.

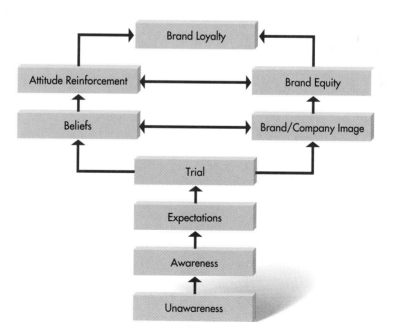

[16]Kenneth R. Sheets, "Infinities Art of Pacific Persuasion," *U.S. News & World Report,* Nov. 13, 1989, p. 67; and Bradley A. Stertz, "Nissan's Infiniti Gets Off to a Slow Start," *Wall Street Journal,* Jan. 8, 1990, p. B6.

Types of Advertising Objectives

Advertising objectives must include a precise statement of generally accepted communication objectives: who, what, and when. The who relates to the audience or target market at whom the message will be aimed. The what relates to the effect we wish to achieve—awareness, attitude change, reminder, and so on. The when relates to the time period during which the object should be obtained. For example, the advertising objectives for a new product launch might first be stated as: Within 3 months of the product launch we expect 75 percent of the target market to be aware of the product.

To be useful, advertising objectives must first be realistic. To the extent possible, advertising objectives should be stated in quantitative terms so that they can be measured and subsequently evaluated. If the objective is not measurable, there is no way to evaluate whether the advertising program achieves its stated objective.

The advertising objectives provide a foundation for subsequent advertising decisions. Therefore, the advertising objectives should be designated before specific decisions of the advertising program, such as the type of message and where the message will be placed, are made. The major reasons why advertising objectives should precede other program decisions include[17]

- Advertising objectives reflect the consensus of management concerning what the advertising should do for the brand.
- Setting the objectives helps set the advertising budget.
- The objectives provide a standard against which the results can be compared.

It is possible to achieve more than one objective during a given campaign, although this can be very difficult and costly. Moreover, each objective is generally most useful for implementing a particular type of marketing strategy. For instance, for the same product, there may be different advertising objectives for different customer groups. Obtaining trial of a particular product or brand may be the objective for nonusers and/or new entrants into the market. For present users, the objective may be to obtain preference or loyalty for the product or brand. In addition, the promotion objective might be to stimulate demand for an entire product class (for example, electric shavers) or for a particular brand (for example, Braun electric shavers). Consequently, if more than one objective is employed, it is important to make certain that the various objectives are compatible with the marketing strategy.

Although no single typology of advertising objectives is considered standard, we can identify eight basic types of advertising objectives.[18] These objectives include

1. Generating awareness
2. Reminding buyers to use

[17]Charles H. Patti and Charles F. Frazer, *Advertising: A Decision-Making Approach,* Dryden Press, Hinsdale, Ill., 1988.

[18]Harper Boyd, Michael Ray, and Edward C. Strong, "An Attitudinal Framework for Advertising Strategy," *Journal of Marketing,* April 1972, pp. 27–33; and Kenneth A. Longman, *Advertising,* Harcourt, Brace, Jovanovich, New York, 1974.

3. Changing attitudes about the use of the product form
4. Changing perceptions about the importance of brand attributes
5. Changing beliefs about brands
6. Reinforcing attitudes
7. Building corporate and product-line image
8. Obtaining a direct response

AWARENESS

Frequently, the primary advertising objective is simply to generate or increase recognition of a brand name, a product concept, or information regarding where or how to buy a product. This can be an important objective in several different situations.

First, when a brand enters the market, buyers will often find it difficult to develop an attitude if the brand and its basic product concept are not known. That is, awareness of the product and comprehension of its basic concept must exist before favorable attitudes toward the brand can be developed.

Second, managers should also employ awareness objectives when customers need to know how to buy, or how to get more information about, a product. Managers of consumer products with highly selective distribution systems may need to emphasize this objective, especially if competing brands have more intensive distribution. Advertisements for John Deere lawn mowers, American Family Insurance, and many other brands usually identify local dealers at the end of the commercials. Similarly, industrial marketers—especially those with small sales forces—may include inquiry slips or toll-free phone numbers in their advertisements to enable interested potential customers to obtain more detailed information, thus providing potential prospects for the sales force.

Finally, awareness and brand name recognition are usually essential objectives in marketing low perceived-risk products when little deliberation or search is involved. In these situations, buyers will make brand selections largely on the basis of brand familiarity. That is, the brands that are most widely recognized will tend to have the largest market shares.

REMINDER TO USE

For discretionary items with irregular usage patterns, an appropriate marketing strategy may be to stimulate primary demand by increasing the rate of usage. The primary role of advertising in implementing this strategy is to remind buyers to use the product or to restock the product. That is, purchases may decline because the product is highly discretionary and consumers have no remaining stock to act as a reminder to use the product.

CHANGING ATTITUDES ABOUT THE USE OF THE PRODUCT FORM

This objective is designed to support primary-demand strategies that attract new users or increase the number of uses. Advertising programs to implement these strategies usually take one of two basic forms. First, advertising campaigns may demonstrate new ways to use the product or new usage occasions. Arm & Hammer has employed advertisements to show that baking soda can eliminate odors in carpets, ashtrays, and refrigerators; and A-1 Steak Sauce has been promoted as an alternative to ketchup for use on hamburgers. Second, some advertising campaigns have been designed to overcome negative perceptions about product categories.

Oldsmobile, realizing that its customer base was getting smaller and older, decided to attack Oldsmobile's fuddy-duddy image directly with its "New Generation" advertising campaign. The "New Generation" ads featured celebrities of the 1950s and 1960s and their children in a series of playful vignettes with Oldsmobile cars. Surveys indicated positive responses to the campaign among consumers aged 35 to 44, which was the target audience Olds desired. Although there was no measurable sales increase after the first year, Oldsmobile marketing executives contend that it takes about 3 years for an advertising theme to work its way down to sales. Nevertheless, Cutlass Supreme buyers who were, on average, 50 years old when the car was introduced in 1987 averaged 45 years of age in 1989. In addition, dealers report a greater number of young people coming into the showrooms.[19]

CHANGING PERCEPTIONS ABOUT THE IMPORTANCE OF BRAND ATTRIBUTES

An effective way to acquire new customers through differentiated positioning is to advertise a "unique selling proposition." For an attribute to be determinant in the buyer's choice process, the attribute must be important and buyers must perceive that alternatives differ in the degree to which they possess the attribute. Therefore, if a brand or supplier has a unique attribute, advertising may be used to stress the importance of the attribute in order to make it determinant. For example, Listerine ads show how the brand helps prevent gingivitis. The objective is to persuade consumers to consider this attribute in forming their attitudes about mouthwashes and make evaluations of Listerine more favorable.

CHANGING BELIEFS ABOUT BRANDS

If an attribute (or benefit) is already considered important, buyers will examine the degree to which each alternative product or brand possesses that attribute or provides that benefit. Accordingly, the advertising objective may be to improve buyers' ratings of a brand on important attributes or to change the relative ratings of competing brands on the attribute. Because the attribute is not unique to a brand, advertising designed to demonstrate this relative superiority would be supporting a marketing strategy of head-to-head competition. For example, ConAgra introduced its Healthy Choice dinners and entrees and illustrated the superiority of its products by attacking the nutritional merits of competitors' frozen dinners. In a $15 million advertising campaign, the company showed that Healthy Choice was healthier in terms of sodium, fat, and cholesterol. Sales of Healthy Choice were $150 million in the first year with more

[19]Joanne Lipman, "New Olds Ad Campaign Updates the Old," *Wall Street Journal,* Aug. 23, 1989, p. 5; Raymond Serafin, "Olds Keeps the Faith," *Advertising Age,* Aug. 25, 1989, p. 50; and Joseph B. White, "New Ads Give a Boost to the Olds Image but Don't Help the Old Sales Woes Much," *Wall Street Journal,* June 19, 1989, p. B1.

than 55 percent of initial purchasers buying the product again. In addition, on average, consumers purchased three boxes of Healthy Choice compared to 1.5 boxes of most frozen meals.[20]

ATTITUDE REINFORCEMENT

Brands or suppliers with a strong market position and with no major competitive weaknesses are more likely to be concerned with customer-retention strategies. By reassuring customers that the brand or supplier continues to offer the greatest level of satisfaction on the most important benefits, advertising can reinforce attitudes and, thus, maintain brand preferences and loyalty. Accordingly, to achieve this kind of objective, Heinz displays the continued high level of thickness and quality of its ketchup by advertising the product's slow-pouring quality, and the Energizer bunny ads remind consumers of the batteries' long life.

CORPORATE AND PRODUCT-LINE IMAGE BUILDING

Frequently, advertising is used to establish or change perceptions of organizations or broad product lines, but without focusing on specific product attributes or benefits. General corporate advertising usually is designed to enhance a corporation's public image, ostensibly to make it more attractive to prospective stockholders. For example, Dow Chemical ran an extensive advertising campaign promoting Dow as a great place for young people to work and emphasizing the corporation's efforts to improve the quality of life. It is possible that such advertising increases awareness about certain corporate attributes, but many experts question its actual effectiveness and value.[21]

In automobiles, computers, most consumer electronics products, and many other categories, many products (each with distinct features and positioning strategies) share a common brand name and a common distribution system. Product-line image advertising is used to provide an umbrella image for the specific attributes and benefits of each item in the line. For example, General Motors' Pontiac automobiles have been marketed under the "We Build Excitement" image, while General Electric products have been linked together by the "We Bring Good Things to Life" theme. Advertising designed to build product-line perceptions will then be augmented by advertising designed to build brand beliefs or attribute importance for individual products and models within the line.

OBTAINING A DIRECT RESPONSE

One of the fastest-growing sectors is that of direct marketing. In direct marketing, the organization communicates directly with target customers with the objective of generating a response or a purchase. Although direct marketing is not solely a part of the promotional mix, it has become an integral part of the communications program.

---

[20]Steve Weiner, "How Josie's Chili Won the Day," *Forbes,* Feb. 5, 1990, pp. 57, 60, 62, 63.

[21]Anne B. Fisher, "Spiffing Up the Corporate Image," *Fortune,* July 21, 1986, pp. 68–70.

Direct response advertising is a method of direct marketing where the product or service is promoted through the advertisement and the customer has the opportunity to buy from, or respond directly to, the manufacturer.

THE BUDGETING PROCESS

Establishing the advertising budget is one of the more difficult tasks facing marketing managers. As we suggested in our discussion of productivity analysis (in Chapter 6), it is extremely difficult to predict the impact of a given level of advertising expenditures on sales for several reasons: The relationship between advertising and sales is not likely to be a direct, linear relationship; competitive actions or environmental factors may offset the effectiveness of advertising efforts; and advertising effects are sometimes offset by changes in price, selling effort, or other marketing programs. An additional problem is that advertising effects tend to be cumulative; that is, expenditures in one year will have some immediate impact on sales, but these expenditures also have a longer-term impact on sales in subsequent periods, as seen in the case of Oldsmobile's campaign. Buyers who have been influenced to purchase a product (or at least to become aware of it or develop favorable attitudes toward it) because of the first-year's advertising effort will often make purchases in subsequent years. A final difficulty revolves around the issue of efficiency. Increased advertising expenditures can never guarantee increased sales; that is, the additional money may be ineffectively spent because of a poor message design or inefficient media scheduling.

In spite of these difficulties, it is important to establish a tentative budget in order to provide some guidance for message designers and media planners. Because these tasks cost money, managers must have some indication of what resources will be available before reasonable message and media alternatives can be identified. (Figure 10-3 explores the development of a tentative advertising budget.)

Although the specifics of the advertising budgeting process will vary among companies, managers can use a general approach that includes the following steps.

1. Establish a baseline budget.
2. Based on the advertising objectives, estimate the message-design and media cost requirements.
3. If time and resources permit, run experiments to obtain a rough estimate of the impact of the proposed program.
4. Revise the budget (or objectives) as necessary on the basis of the costs of the tasks, the results of any experiments, and the costs and expected impact of other marketing programs.

Establishing Baseline Budgets

In most organizations, the total advertising budget does not vary greatly from year to year; thus, a possible approach is to use the previous year's budget, or industry advertising-to-sales ratios, as a guideline (see Table 10-2). More realistically, managers will adjust budgets each year because of a number of factors.

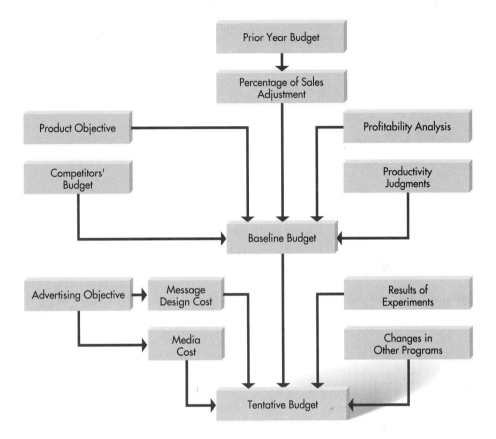

FIGURE 10-3

Developing a tentative advertising budget.

1. Product objectives determine which products should receive increased, sustaining, or reduced support. Accordingly, managers may modify budgets to reflect any changes in product objectives.
2. Product profitability should be a major consideration in budgeting. The greater the contribution margin, the smaller the increase in sales that will be needed to cover the costs of increased advertising budgets.
3. Productivity judgments (especially when combined with profitability analyses) can be useful in determining the effects of changes in budgets. As discussed in Chapter 6, managers may decide that the level of advertising needs to be increased just to maintain the market share at the current level.

Many advertisers believe that it is necessary to keep their advertising budgets (or share of voice) at a consistent ratio of expenditures with the total advertising expenditure of the product category if they are to maintain their market share. This type of competitive parity approach would require that the company increase its "share of voice" to the same percentage level as the desired market share. Firms such as Procter and Gamble, McDonald's, and Wendy's have been reported to use such an

TABLE 10-2

ADVERTISING-TO-SALES RATIOS (BY INDUSTRY), 1991

INDUSTRY	AD DOLLARS AS PERCENT OF SALES	AD DOLLARS AS PERCENT OF MARGIN	INDUSTRY	AD DOLLARS AS PERCENT OF SALES	AD DOLLARS AS PERCENT OF MARGIN
Abrasive, asbestos, misc. minerals	1.1	3.9	Computer communication equipment	1.9	4.0
Adhesives & sealants	2.7	5.9	Computer peripheral equip., NEC	1.9	4.1
Agriculture, chemicals	0.7	3.1	Computer storage devices	1.4	4.8
Agriculture, production-crops	2.2	7.1	Computers & software-wholesale	0.6	5.2
Air cond., heating, refrig. equip.	1.7	6.5	Construction, mining, mat'l handle., equip	4.4	12.9
Air courier services	1.2	9.9	Convert paper, paprbd. ex boxes	2.3	5.2
Air transport. scheduled	1.9	65.5	Dairy products	4.1	11.2
Aircraft & parts	0.6	3.1	Drug & proprietary stores	1.6	5.6
Aircraft parts, aux. equip., NEC	0.8	3.1	Durable goods-wholesale, NEC	3.6	7.6
Auto & home supply stores	2.2	8.9	Educational services	6.9	15.7
Auto rent & lease, no drivers	2.4	3.6	Electrical indl apparatus	2.0	6.2
Automatic regulating controls	3.3	11.5	Electrical measure & test instruments	2.6	5.4
Bakery products	8.0	47.6	Electr. other elec. equip., ex computers	2.2	5.6
Beverages	8.6	14.6	Electric lighting, wiring equip.	2.5	8.5
Books: publ'ng & printing	2.9	6.0	Electromedical apparatus	1.3	2.2
Broadwoven fabric mill, cotton	4.3	21.7	Electronic comp. accessories	0.7	2.3
Business services, NEC	2.7	6.5	Electronic components, NEC	1.0	3.4
Cable & other pay TV services	2.9	6.0	Electronic computers	3.6	7.2
Calculate, acct mach, ex comp	1.7	4.4	Electronic connectors	1.0	4.2
Catalog, mail-order houses	6.9	17.7	Electronic parts, equip.-whsl., NEC	2.0	7.5
Chemicals & allied prods.-whsl.	4.2	18.0	Engineering services	0.4	1.9
Chemicals & allied products	2.3	6.1	Engines & turbines	1.3	6.6
Cmp. programming, data process.	0.2	0.6	Engr. acc. resrch., mgmt., rel. svcs.	1.4	6.7
Computer & comp. software stores	0.6	3.1	Equip. rental & leasing, NEC	0.7	2.4
Computer integrated-system design	1.5	4.1	Fabricated plate work	1.0	3.7
Computer processing, data prep service	1.5	2.9	Fabricated rubber products, NEC	0.7	3.9
Computer programming service	1.7	8.9	Facilities support mgmt. svcs.		11.6
Commercial printing	2.7	10.4	Farm machinery & equipment	1.9 / 1.1	4.5
Communications equipment, NEC	2.1	4.9	Finance-services	0.8	6.9
Communications services, NEC	1.3	3.2	Food & kindred products	6.3	14.9
Computer & office equipment	1.6	3.3			

From *Business Marketing Magazine,* November 1991, pp. 111–113.

approach. This form of budgeting may be misleading for two reasons. First, it ignores the possibility that there may be limits to the market share that is attainable. For example, a brand with a 10 percent share could not reasonably be expected to increase its market share to 50 percent, simply by spending 50 percent of the category's advertising dollars. Second, this approach to budgeting doesn't take into consideration the many other buying behavior factors influencing the brand's sales response function, discussed in Chapter 6.

Message-Design and Media Costs

Given an advertising objective, a manager can estimate message-development costs (for production costs, technical fees, royalties to participants) and media costs (of print space, radio, or television time) fairly quickly. Generally, message-development costs will be a minor proportion of total cost, with media costs constituting the major component. As discussed in detail later in this chapter, media costs are influenced by the size of the target market, the size or length of the advertisement, the number of times the advertisement is presented, and the specific costs of each media vehicle.

Experimentation and Revisions

When feasible, the proposed program should be tested in a limited market area to determine whether the advertising objectives are being achieved and to estimate the sales response. These tests can provide insights into whether historical advertising effects on sales are optimistic or pessimistic relative to the present program. But, experiments usually indicate only the short-run effects of a program because the length of an experiment is usually limited. However, experiments can be particularly useful in determining the effect of alternative copy and media schedules. If different media or different numbers of advertisements are used in different markets, the value of each medium and of different levels of audience exposure to a message can be measured. These measures may enable managers to adjust budgets in order to obtain the most efficient media schedules.

Revisions may also be necessary because of the impact of other programs. To some degree, advertising competes with sales, sales promotion, and product development for funds. Further, price changes will lead to changing contribution margins. Accordingly, changes in the budgets for other programs may force managers to modify the advertising budget to stay within the resources available for a product. For instance, Sprint reduced its ad spending from $81 million to $68 million in 1991, whereas its competitor, MCI, increased its ad budget from $56 million to $94 million. MCI's market share increased from 14.2 percent to 16 percent; Sprint's decreased from 9.7 percent to 9.5 percent.[22]

[22]Terry Lefton, "The Man from Mars' Game Plan for Sprint," *Adweek's Marketing Week,* May 25, 1992, p. 12.

DESIGN

The advertising message includes two basic elements: the appeals (or copy claims) that represent the central idea of the message and the method of presentation (or execution style) used to present the copy claims. Although message design is primarily the responsibility of the advertising agency or other creative specialists, the advertising director or product managers can provide significant input to help determine whether the message design is appropriate for the marketing strategy and advertising objectives. In particular, information regarding the demographic and lifestyle characteristics of the target audience is useful in deciding the kinds of individuals to portray in the advertisements.

Contents of an Effective Message

Information on the buying process can help the agency or specialists deal with the three major requirements of an effective message: desirability, exclusiveness, and believability.[23] Desirability and exclusiveness criteria are simply a firm's means to emphasize those determinant attributes that provide an advantage. If desirability is a problem, the usefulness of the product in solving a usage problem might be portrayed. Exclusiveness may be demonstrated through comparisons (direct or indirect) once the real and perceived product differences are known. Believability is important in those situations where the product benefit or attribute is difficult to demonstrate or is highly subjective, or where it requires a major change in usage patterns. For example, Del Monte foods scrapped a new shelf-stable yogurt, Little Lunch, after consumer research revealed that yogurt buyers refused to accept the idea that yogurt could be kept unrefrigerated. Early research indicated that the concept was viewed as desirable and unique, but the cost of achieving believability was finally judged too high after lengthy test marketing with various types of messages.[24]

Copy-Claim Alternatives

The copy claims (or basic appeals of the message) are the motivational arguments or descriptive statements contained in the message. These claims can be of three types:

- Claims that describe the physical attributes of the product
- Claims that describe the functional benefits that can be obtained from the product
- Claims that characterize the product in terms of the types of people who use it, the results of obtaining the functional benefits or moods

[23]Dik Warren Twedt, "How to Plan New Products, Improve Old Ones and Create Better Advertising," *Journal of Marketing,* January 1969, p. 53–57.

[24]Sally Scanlon, "Calling the Shots More Closely," 1978, *Sales and Marketing Plans, Sales and Marketing Management,* 1979, p. 90.

In choosing the type of copy claim for a given advertising program, creative specialists should, initially, be guided by the statement of the firm's advertising objective. That is, the advertising objective should clearly state the specific features that generate buyer awareness or the specific attributes or benefits on which perceptions are to be changed or reinforced. In addition, some advertising objectives may focus on exclusiveness, whereas others may emphasize the desirability (importance) of an attribute. Given the advertising objective, creative specialists can then select a copy approach that will support the desirability, exclusiveness, or believability (or any combination of these) of the attribute or benefit being featured.

When creative specialists develop the copy, they must consider the type of brand concept involved. Products can be classified in terms of one of the following needs:[25]

1. *Functional needs*—products that resolve consumption-related problems brought on by the individual's environment (lawn mowers, for example)
2. *Symbolic needs*—products that fulfill internally generated needs, such as self-enhancement or ego identification (automobiles, for example)
3. *Experiential needs*—products that provide sensory pleasure, variety, or other kinds of stimulation (such as food or entertainment)

Clearly, characterization becomes an important element of the copy when symbolic or experiential needs are involved. In addition, the type of need often has significant influence on the selection of an execution style.

Execution Style

Execution style is the manner in which copy claims are presented to the target audience. Below, we present a brief discussion of the more common execution styles. The details of the selection of an execution style are beyond the scope of this book.[26]

Symbolic associations provide a means of dramatizing intangible attributes or benefits by associating the product or service with a certain type of individual (usually the case in automobile advertisements) or a tangible object. (Note the symbols of assurance used by insurance companies: sentries, shields, the Rock of Gibraltar, and so forth.)

Functional benefits of the product can be communicated in a variety of ways. *Testimonials* are employed to support the believability of product benefits by using celebrities who have some association with the product category; for example, the sports beverage Gatorade is using images of Michael Jordan on its web site http://www.gatorade.[27] *Product demonstrations* or recipes show how a particular

[25]C. Whan Park, Bernard Jaworski, and Deborah MacInnis, "Strategic Brand Concept-Image Management," *Journal of Marketing,* October 1986, pp. 135–145.

[26]An extended discussion is available in George E. Belch and Michael A. Belch, "Introduction to Advertising and Promotion," Irwin, Homewood, Ill., 1993, pp. 351–382.

[27]Gerry Khermouch, "Jordan Goes On-Line for Gatorade," *Brandweek,* Feb. 19, 1996, p. 14.

buyer problem can be solved to enhance desirability. *"Slice of life"* sequences portraying buyers in problem-solving situations are similar to demonstrations that show product benefits. *Case histories* documenting the benefits of a product (such as flashlight batteries that burn all night) provide both credibility and a demonstration of product benefits.

When copy focuses on functional product attributes, documentation of the product's attributes (by presumably unbiased organizations) can be beneficial. More recently, *comparison advertising* formats (in which two or more brands are compared on one or more attributes) have enjoyed wide utilization as a means of demonstrating the uniqueness or believability of a product-attribute claim.

One of the most successful U.S. comparative ad campaigns has been the "Pepsi Challenge"—comparing the taste of Coke and Pepsi. However, in Japan, where commercials showing Japanese consumers taking the "Pepsi Challenge" were shown, the networks made Pepsi cover up Coke's name, diminishing the impact of the advertisement. Japanese consumers consider it arrogant to compare one product against another, and most Japanese businesspeople believe that openly challenging competition is unethical. Later, when Japan's Fair Trade Commission lessened restrictions against comparative advertising, Pepsi aired a comparative spot using rap singer M. C. Hammer. In the 2 months during which the spot aired on the five major commercial stations, Pepsi sales increased 50 percent. This was attributed to the popularity of M. C. Hammer and the heavy soft-drink–consuming youth population. However, additional spots were rejected by TV stations, and the future of comparative advertising in Japan is uncertain.[28]

Pepsi has continued to have problems with advertising that compares Pepsi to other brands. A recent ruling in England may force Pepsi to change its comparison with Coke to a comparison with "Brand X."[29] When Pepsi tried the Pepsi challenge approach with the English brand Virgin Cola, Virgin accused Pepsi of damaging its brand name. Management at Virgin is asking the authorities to make Pepsi change its commercials or pull them.[30] Advertising watchdogs from the European Union have historically been against the use of comparative advertising. However, after many years of debate, comparative advertising is about to become Eurolaw, which means that countries like Belgium and Germany will have to scrap their generalized prohibition of comparative advertising.[31]

One common and, often debated, execution style is *humor.* As early as 1923, Claude Hopkins, a famous advertising copywriter, suggested that advertising should never seek to amuse because the humor would draw attention away from the message content. In 1963, another famous advertising executive, David Ogilvy, issued a caveat

[28]"Pepsi, Coke Spar in Japan over Comparative TV Ad," *Wall Street Journal,* Mar. 8, 1991, p. B6; Yukimo Ono, "Pepsi Challenges Japanese Taboo as It Ribs Coke," *Wall Street Journal,* Mar. 6, 1991, p. B3; and David Kilburn, "Pepsi's Challenge: Double Japan Share," *Advertising Age,* Dec. 10, 1990, p. 36.

[29]"Pepisco Has to Change TV Campaign," *Marketing Week,* Feb. 10, 1995, p. 7.

[30]Rose Snowdon, "Virgin Challenges Pepsi's Claims," *Marketing,* Sept. 14, 1995, p. 1.

[31]Lionel Stanbrook, "Comparison Is a Liberty Which We Must Still Defend," *Marketing,* Nov. 30, 1995, p. 16.

against the use of humor; however, in 1982, he amended his original caveat to suggest that humor may be useful in certain circumstances.[32] A survey of advertising executives from the top 150 U.S. agencies indicated that humor is an effective way to gain attention. Humor works best for nondurable products and when it is directly related to the product. The vehicles best suited to humorous advertising are television and radio.[33] The results of an advertising study that included hundreds of advertisements in radio, television, and magazines indicated that humor was best suited for low-risk products such as snack foods, desserts, beer, and so forth. Humor was least suited for higher-risk functional products such as appliances, equipment, insurance, tires, and, especially, higher-risk expressive products like fashion goods and jewelry.[34]

As the preceding discussion has indicated, a great many options are available to creative specialists. However, they are more likely to select effective copy and execution styles if they understand the advertising objective and the buying process. Accordingly, it is important that managers state these objectives and provide specialists with insights they gained through buyer analysis.

MEDIA SCHEDULING

Media scheduling decisions are extremely important for two reasons. First, purchases of radio and television time and of newspaper and magazine space represent the largest element of cost in the advertising budget. For instance, the cost of a 30-second advertisement during the National Football League's 1995 championship Super Bowl game could cost over $1,000,000. A full-page ad in the national edition of *The Wall Street Journal* costs $123,591 per day; a similar ad targeting the New England region would cost $15,700 per day.[35]

Second, an advertisement's success in achieving the advertising objectives depends largely on how well each show or magazine reaches buyers in the target market segment. Because the cost, audience size, and characteristics of each media alternative are generally known, managers can employ some quantitative tools in media scheduling. However, as we will demonstrate, managers must also employ judgment in media scheduling decisions because some of the attributes of media are not easily measured.

In this section, we will present the major steps involved in developing the media schedule. In particular, we examine each of the following kinds of decisions:

- Selecting the type of medium to use
- Selecting specific vehicles for consideration

[32]Marc G. Weinberger, Harland Spotts, Leland Campbell, and Amy L. Parsons, "The Use and Effect of Humor in Different Advertising Media," *Journal of Advertising Research,* May–June 1995, p. 44.

[33]Thomas J. Madden, and Marc G. Weinberger, "Humor in Advertising: A Partitioner View," *Journal of Advertising Research,* 24.4, 1984, pp. 23–29.

[34]Weinberger, loc. cit.

[35]*Marketer's Guide to Media,* Spring–Summer 95, Adweek Publishing.

■ Determining the size, length, and position of an advertisement
■ Determining the desired reach and frequency distribution of messages

After these decisions have been made, one or more media schedules can be developed. Managers should then examine the media schedule to determine if it will be adequate to achieve the objective desired and if revisions of the tentative budget will be needed.

As in the case of message design, advertising managers and product managers may not make each of the detailed decisions involved in this process. However, these managers should review and analyze those decisions to make certain that they are consistent with the type of advertising objective desired and will be appropriate for the target market and the message design. We provide some guidelines for making these reviews and evaluations in this section of the chapter.[36]

Selecting the Type of Medium

Each medium (TV, radio, newspaper, magazine) has unique characteristics that may or may not be appropriate for the kind of message to be presented and for the kind of target segment to be reached. For instance, when using direct-mail advertising, a firm usually relies on a mailing list containing the names of individuals with some common characteristic such as age (for example, senior citizens), occupation (student or doctor, for example), geographic area (such as suburban locations), or product ownership (such as homeowners).

Often, where to promote is related to geographic considerations. Advertising expenditures may be allocated according to the market potential of an area if sales vary from one area to another. Advertising expenditures may be allocated to those areas where the product is already a leader in order to help maintain market share or where there is more potential for growth. Media planners often use indexes to help make these decisions. In addition to indexes such as the Survey of Buying Power, Brand Development Index (BDI), and Category Development Index (CDI) discussed in Chapter 5, firms may rely on secondary information such as that provided by Simmons Market Research Bureau (SMRB) or Mediamark Research, Inc. (MRI). These sources provide syndicated data on audience size and composition for approximately 100 publications, as well as data on broadcast exposure and usage of over 800 consumer products and services. In addition, they provide lifestyle information as well as media usage characteristics of the population. Table 10-3 is an example from Mediamark Research, Inc., for freshwater fishing and golf. Notice, using the index, that *New York Magazine* is useful for golf, but not fishing. As you might expect, *North American Fisherman* would be selected to reach a freshwater fishing audience.

Because the audience is narrowed down, this tends to be an economical way to communicate complex messages to specific target segments. Alternatively, managers

---

[36]Dennis Gensch, "Media Factors: A Review Article," *Journal of Marketing Research,* May 1970, pp. 216–225; and Leo Bogart, "Mass Advertising: The Message, Not the Measure," *Harvard Business Review,* September–October 1976, pp. 107–116.

TABLE 10-3

SPORTS: PARTICIPATED IN PAST WEEK

BASE: ADULTS	TOTAL U.S. '000	FISHING (FRESH WATER)				GOLF			
		A '000	B % DOWN	C % ACROSS	D INDEX	A '000	B % DOWN	C % ACROSS	D INDEX
All Adults	187756	5356	100.0	2.9	100	5719	100.0	3.0	100
Money	10634	292	5.5	2.7	96	608	10.6	5.7	188
Motor Trend	4939	225	4.2	4.6	160	238	4.2	4.8	158
Muscle & Fitness	6842	335	6.3	4.9	172	345	6.0	5.0	166
National Enquirer	20315	836	15.6	4.1	144	319	5.6	1.6	52
National Geographic	31769	986	18.4	3.1	109	1377	24.1	4.3	142
National Geographic Traveler	3744	108	2.0	2.9	101	226	4.0	6.0	198
Natural History	1771	55	1.0	3.1	109	22	.4	1.2	41
Newsweek	22143	719	13.4	3.2	114	967	16.9	4.4	143
New Woman	3977	72	1.3	1.8	63	57	1.0	1.4	47
New York Magazine	1839	8	.1	.4	15	83	1.5	4.5	148
New York Times (Daily)	3099	14	.3	.5	16	103	1.8	3.3	109
New York Times Magazine	4443	66	1.2	1.5	52	105	1.8	2.4	78
The New Yorker	3985	113	2.1	2.8	99	144	2.5	3.6	119
North American Fisherman	3098	421	7.9	13.6	476	147	2.6	4.7	156
North American Hunter	3150	414	7.7	13.1	461	155	2.7	4.9	162
Omni	3310	77	1.4	2.3	82	137	2.4	4.1	136
Organic Gardening	4259	94	1.8	2.2	77	76	1.3	1.8	59
Outdoor Life	7151	816	15.2	11.4	400	301	5.3	4.2	138
Outside	1681	70	1.3	4.2	146	55	1.0	3.3	107
Parade	80074	2431	45.4	3.0	106	2966	51.9	3.7	122
Parenting	5669	203	3.8	3.6	126	77	1.3	1.4	45

Source: Mediamark Research Sports & Recreation Report, Spring 1994.

may use media such as billboards, posters, and advertising on mass-transit vehicles when short, clear messages are presented to a (typically) nonselect audience.

Selecting Possible Vehicles

A vehicle is a specific magazine, newspaper, radio, or television program. When selecting a specific set of vehicles, managers should understand each vehicle's ability to reach the target market segments. Rating services and special research provided by the vehicles or by advertising agencies provide information on the audience size and demographics for each vehicle. Some magazines provide separate editions to reach specific demographic groups. *Time* magazine provides separate editions containing special advertising for doctors, educators, business executives, and students.

Vehicles should be evaluated on their likely effectiveness for the specific product and message. For instance, the editorial climate of a vehicle such as *Time* or *Newsweek* may enhance the credibility of an appeal because the vehicle is perceived as trustworthy. Similarly, a vehicle recognized for its prestige or expertise on a given subject may be an excellent choice for certain products (for example, *Sports Illustrated* for athletic equipment). A vehicle's ability to deliver messages with special technical needs involving color, size, and so on, may influence the selection of a specific vehicle.

Media availability and conflicting national regulations vary dramatically around the world. In certain countries, advertisements on television or radio are not available, or are limited in use. There are conflicting national regulations that may include limits on the amount of time available for advertisements on television, ranging from complete prohibition to 15 to 20 minutes a day in blocks of 3 to 5 minutes. As we have seen, different nations have varying restrictions on the use of comparative claims.

By examining audience characteristics and effectiveness, managers can reduce the number of potential vehicles to a more manageable number for subsequent analyses. Cost is usually an important consideration in the selection of the final media schedule. The cost per insertion in various media can be obtained from direct contact with media personnel, from media buying specialists (who are often able to obtain discounts on these rates), and from Standard Rate and Data Service publications.

The actual cost per insertion will depend on the size, length, and position of the advertisement.

Determining Size, Length, and Position

The cost of an insertion is influenced by the size, length, and position of the advertisement. After determining the particular size, length, and position of an advertisement, managers can calculate the cost in terms of the number of people reached by each vehicle.

The most common method used to measure the cost of an advertisement is the cost per thousand, abbreviated CPM. The CPM is calculated by dividing the cost of an advertisement by the number of people it reaches. For example, assume a manufacturer of women's golf shoes wanted to use magazine advertising to introduce its new line. The cost for a four-color full-page ad in *Golf* is $65,560, whereas the cost for the same ad in *Golf Digest* is $78,380. The circulation for *Golf* is 2,740,000 and the circulation for *Golf Digest* is 4,260,000. The CPM for the two magazines is:[37]

$$\text{CPM } (Golf) = \frac{\$65,560 \times 1000}{2,740,000}$$
$$= \$23.93$$
$$\text{CPM } (Golf\ Digest) = \frac{\$78,380 \times 1000}{4,260,000}$$
$$= \$18.40$$

[37]*Marketer's Guide to Media,* loc. cit.

The total expense of the ad is greater in *Golf Digest,* but the cost to reach each person is less.

In some cases, agencies use a targeted CPM; that is, the cost per thousand for members of a specific target market. The manufacturer advertising a line of women's golf shoes would most likely be interested in the cost to reach female readers of the magazines. The CPM targeted to the female audience is

$$\text{CPM } (Golf) = \frac{\$65,560 \times 1000}{700,000}$$
$$= \$93.66$$
$$\text{CPM } (Golf\ Digest) = \frac{\$78,380 \times 1000}{1,050,000}$$
$$= \$74.65$$

The cost to run the ad remains the same but, because the readership is primarily male, the cost to reach a female audience has increased.

The basic measure used to estimate CPM for television is a rating point. The most common source used for television ratings is the Nielsen Television Index. Figure 10-4 presents Nielsen television ratings for the week ending April 7, 1996. The rating is calculated by dividing the number of households viewing the program by the total number of households. In 1996, there were approximately 97 million households in the United States; therefore, $.305 \times 97,000,000 = 29,585,000$ households watched *Seinfeld.*

MEDIA OBJECTIVES

For a given planning period, advertising expenditures can be distributed in different ways: according to the timing of the expenditures or according to reach and frequency.

Timing of Expenditures

Timing reflects the manner in which expenditures are distributed over the course of the planning period. Many products and services have highly seasonal sales patterns. Toy sales peak in November and December, cold tablet sales peak in winter, and greeting card sales soar before major holidays. To the extent that seasonal patterns are known, managers can schedule advertising so that the bulk of the dollar expenditures coincides with (or slightly leads) the peak sales period.

Advertisers have three alternatives to the timing of the message. With a *continuous schedule* they allocate approximately an equal amount of money for each time period. If the yearly budget is $3 million, $250,000 would be spent in each of the 12 months. With a *pulsing schedule,* a certain portion is spent each month; however, the size can change. For example, a soup manufacturer may want to advertise throughout the year, but allocate more during the colder months. In this case, with a $3 million

FIGURE 10-4

Nielsen ratings. (*Source:* Nielsen Ratings, *USA Today,* April 10, 1996, p. 3c.)

NIELSEN RATINGS

Legend:
- Ratings point = 959,000 TV households
- Share = percentage of sets in use
- Number of viewers in millions

(*) = a Nielsen ratings tie.
(r) = a repeat episode.
(s) = a special broadcast.
•Source: Nielsen Media Research

Network ratings

For the week:			Season to date:		
NBC ... 10.3	Fox 6.5		NBC ... 11.8	Fox 7.5	
ABC ... 10.0	UPN ... 2.6		ABC ... 10.9	UPN ... 3.2	
CBS 9.7	WB 2.3		CBS 9.7	WB 2.5	

Time	Program	Viewers	Rating	Share	Rank	Last Week
Monday, April 1, 1996						
8:00	The Nanny (CBS) (r)	15.1	10.9	18	*25	
	Melrose Place (Fox)	13.3	9.3	15	39	
	Fresh Prince of Bel-Air (NBC) (r)	13.3	9.0	14	*42	*27
	Second Noah (ABC)	12.6	8.2	13	*51	
	Star Trek: Voyager (UPN) (r)	5.1	4.0	6	90	90
8:30	Almost Perfect (CBS)	13.4	9.7	15	*32	
	Brotherly Love (NBC)	12.1	7.9	12	*56	*47
9:00	Prelude to a Championship (CBS) (s)	20.1	14.1	22	8	
	Untamed Heart (NBC)	15.1	10.9	17	*25	
	High Incident (ABC)	13.3	8.9	14	44	
	Ned and Stacey (Fox)	10.6	7.5	11	60	
	Nowhere Man (UPN) (r)	2.9	2.1	3	*99	106
9:15	NCAA Basketball (CBS) (s)	26.7	18.3	39	5	
9:30	Partners (Fox)	8.3	6.0	9	*73	
10:00	Murder One (ABC)	12.0	8.7	14	*46	
Tuesday, April 2, 1996						
8:00	Roseanne (ABC) (r)	17.5	11.6	20	17	*12
	Wings (NBC) (r)	13.8	9.7	17	*32	*30
	John Grisham's The Client (CBS)	10.0	7.1	12	62	62
	Kindred: The Embraced (Fox)	7.5	5.4	9	81	
	Moesha (UPN) (r)	4.1	3.1	5	91	91
8:30	Coach (ABC)	18.8	12.6	20	*10	18
	3rd Rock From the Sun (NBC)	17.6	11.7	19	16	17
	Minor Adjustments (UPN)	3.5	2.4	4	98	*99
9:00	Home Improvement (ABC)	38.0	23.0	36	1	10
	Frasier (NBC) (r)	14.9	10.5	16	*28	11
	Never Give Up:					
	Jimmy V. Story (CBS)	9.3	6.7	11	*66	
	The Paranormal BorderLine (UPN)	2.9	2.1	3	*99	104
9:30	The Dana Carvey Show (ABC)	19.7	12.6	21	*10	*21
	The John Larroquette Show (NBC) (r)	16.4	11.3	18	21	19
	Tales From the Crypt (Fox)	6.1	4.4	7	*85	
10:00	NYPD Blue (ABC)	19.7	13.9	25	9	16
	Dateline NBC (NBC)	15.1	11.1	20	*22	20
Wednesday, April 3, 1996						
8:00	Ellen (ABC)	15.6	10.7	19	27	*37
	JAG (NBC)	12.3	9.0	15	*42	35
	Beverly Hills, 90210 (Fox)	12.8	8.6	15	48	
	Dave's World (CBS)	9.5	6.9	12	65	*63
	Sister, Sister (WB) (r)	4.0	2.9	5	93	*94
	The Sentinel (UPN)	3.9	2.8	5	*94	*99
8:30	The Faculty (ABC)	13.8	9.6	16	*34	*44
	My Guys (CBS)	7.8	5.8	10	76	
	The Parent 'Hood (WB) (r)	3.9	2.7	5	96	*92
9:00	Grace Under Fire (ABC)	18.9	12.5	21	13	24
	Dateline NBC (NBC)	15.9	11.5	19	18	15
	Summer of Fear (CBS)	11.1	8.1	14	*53	
	Kindred: The Embraced (Fox)	7.9	5.5	9	80	
	The Wayans Bros. (WB) (r)	4.5	3.0	5	92	*94
	Swift Justice (UPN)	2.6	2.0	3	102	101
9:30	Ellen (ABC) (r)	17.3	11.4	19	*19	
	Unhappily Ever After (WB) (r)	3.6	2.5	4	97	102
10:00	PrimeTime Live (ABC)	17.6	12.3	22	15	*21
	Law & Order (NBC) (r)	14.1	10.5	19	*28	23
Thursday, April 4, 1996						
8:00	Friends (NBC)	27.4	18.4	31	4	4
	Murder, She Wrote (CBS)	12.0	8.7	15	*46	40
	Before They Were Stars (ABC) (r)	9.7	6.7	11	*66	
	Living Single (Fox)	9.3	6.0	10	*73	*77
8:30	Boston Common (NBC)	23.3	15.3	25	7	7
	Martin (Fox)	10.7	6.7	11	*66	*63
9:00	Seinfeld (NBC)	30.5	20.0	32	3	3

Time	Program	Viewers	Rating	Share	Rank	Last Week
	Bermuda Triangle (ABC)	12.2	8.2	13	*51	
	Rescue 911 (CBS)	10.3	7.0	11	*63	60
	New York Undercover (Fox)	10.9	7.0	11	*63	*72
9:30	Caroline in the City (NBC)	26.7	17.8	29	6	5
10:00	ER (NBC)	33.2	22.3	37	2	2
	48 Hours (CBS)	11.4	8.1	14	*53	53
Friday, April 5, 1996						
8:00	Family Matters (ABC) (r)	15.1	9.4	18	*37	*30
	Unsolved Mysteries (NBC) (r)	11.9	8.4	16	*49	41
	Due South (CBS)	11.2	7.6	14	*58	*63
	Sliders (Fox)	8.3	5.6	10	79	81
8:30	Muppets Tonight! (ABC)	14.2	7.9	14	*56	61
9:00	Dateline NBC (NBC)	13.9	9.8	17	31	25
	The X-Files (Fox) (r)	14.3	9.4	18	*37	36
	America's Funniest Videos (ABC) (r)	16.3	9.2	16	40	
	Diagnosis Murder (CBS)	13.0	9.1	16	41	46
10:00	20/20 (ABC)	18.5	12.6	24	*10	*12
	Nash Bridges (CBS)	14.4	9.5	18	36	*37
	Homicide: Life on the Street (NBC)	11.4	8.1	15	*53	52
Saturday, April 6, 1996						
8:00	Dr. Quinn, Medicine Woman (CBS)	15.3	9.6	19	*34	
	Cops (Fox)	9.4	6.0	12	*73	79
	Real Funny (ABC) (s)	7.4	4.7	9	*83	
	Malibu Shores (NBC)	5.9	4.3	9	*87	*82
8:30	Cops 2 (Fox) (r)	10.5	6.6	13	*69	*72
9:00	Touched by an Angel (CBS) (r)	16.3	10.4	20	30	
	Brothers of the Frontier (ABC)	10.9	6.6	13	*69	
	America's Most Wanted (Fox)	10.2	6.6	12	*69	75
	Hope & Gloria (ABC)	6.2	4.3	8	*87	87
9:30	Home Court (NBC)	6.0	4.4	8	*85	85
10:00	Walker, Texas Ranger (CBS)	17.7	11.1	22	*22	
	Sisters (NBC)	7.4	5.7	11	*77	76
Sunday, April 7, 1996						
7:00	60 Minutes (CBS)	17.9	12.4	25	14	8
	The Ten Commandments (ABC) (r).	18.1	11.1	20	*22	
	World's Funniest Outtakes (Fox) (r).	7.2	4.7	10	*83	
	Pinky & the Brain (WB) (r).	2.0	1.4	3	104	105
7:30	The Parent 'Hood (WB) (r)	1.9	1.2	2	105	103
8:00	Cybill (CBS) (r)	12.1	8.4	16	*49	26
	The Simpsons (Fox) (r).	9.0	5.7	11	*77	*63
	Sister, Sister (WB) (r)	3.3	1.9	4	103	*94
8:12	Mad About You (NBC) (r)	11.7	7.6	14	*58	*42
8:30	Bonnie (NBC) (r)	10.3	7.2	13	61	*50
	The Show (Fox)	6.7	4.3	8	*87	*82
	Kirk (WB) (r).	3.4	2.1	4	*99	98
8:42	*Sommersby* (NBC)	13.3	8.8	15	45	
9:00	To Sir, With Love II (CBS)	16.0	11.4	19	*19	
	Married . . . With Children (Fox) (r)	9.3	6.3	11	72	*68
	Savannah (WB)	4.0	2.8	5	*94	*94
9:30	Local Heroes (Fox)	6.8	4.8	8	82	84

The Top 20

1	Home Improvement (ABC)	14	60 Minutes (CBS)
2	ER (NBC)	15	PrimeTime Live (ABC)
3	Seinfeld (NBC)	16	3rd Rock From the Sun (NBC)
4	Friends (NBC)	17	Roseanne (ABC)
5	NCAA Basketball (CBS)	18	Dateline NBC (Wed) (NBC)
6	Caroline in the City (NBC)	19	*To Sir, With Love II* (CBS)
7	Boston Common (NBC)	*Ellen (ABC)	
8	Prelude to a Championship (CBS)		
9	NYPD Blue (ABC)		
10	Coach (ABC)		
	*Dana Carvey Show (ABC)		
	*20/20 (ABC)		
13	Grace Under Fire (ABC)		

Evening News

For the week:		Last week	
ABC 9.0		ABC 9.2	
NBC 8.3		NBC 8.6	
CBS 7.4		CBS 7.6	

budget, the soup manufacturer may allocate $100,000 for the months of April through September and $400,000 for the months of October to March. A *flighting schedule* is similar to a pulsing schedule except that, with a flighting schedule, some periods receive no funds. The soup manufacturer may allocate $500,000 for November to February, $250,000 for March, April, September, and October and nothing for the months of May to August.[38]

Measuring Reach and Frequency

Reach is the percentage of a target audience that is exposed to the advertising message at least once in some defined time period (usually 4 weeks). *Frequency* is the average number of times a member of the target audience is exposed to the message in the 4-week time period. If an advertiser places his or her ad in a magazine that is only published every 4 weeks and has only one ad in each issue, the reach and frequency are rather straightforward. The reach would be the number of people reading the magazine and the frequency is one. Now consider the more likely case where an advertiser uses multiple media. For example, an advertisement for the product is shown on two prime-time television shows, the audio version of the commercial is aired during drive-time radio, and, finally, an ad is placed in a major newspaper. Reach is the probability that a person will be exposed to the message at least once through one or more of these vehicles. Frequency is the average number of times a person is exposed to the message. For example, if the commercial is aired on *Seinfeld* every Thursday for a 4-week period and you watch *Seinfeld* all 4 weeks, the frequency is four. When multiple media are used, frequency is estimated as the average number of times an individual is exposed to the message. For example, if 40 percent of the target audience were reached once, 30 percent were reached twice, and 10 percent were reached three times, 80 percent of the target audience were reached, and the average frequency would be

$$\frac{(.4 \times 1) + (.3 \times 2) + (.1 \times 3)}{.80} = 1.63$$

Therefore, 80 percent of the target population would be exposed to the message an average 1.63 times.

Advertising reach and frequency are easily defined but, in practice, are rather complicated to calculate. Probability distributions are needed to indicate the likelihood that a member of the target market will be exposed to the message. Media directors usually rely on computerized models for estimates of reach and frequency.

Gross Rating Points

Managers often use measures such as *gross rating points* (GRPs) to set media goals or evaluate alternative vehicles or media schedules. GRPs are calculated by

[38]Shimp, loc. cit.

multiplying reach times frequency. Given that a particular media schedule will reach 80 percent of the target audience with a frequency of 2.5 times, the GRP is

$$GRP = reach \times frequency$$
$$= 80 \times 2.5$$
$$= 200$$

An increase of either reach or frequency will increase GRPs. Figure 10-5 illustrates the relationship of reach, frequency, and GRPs for different media. A manager might ask: What will it cost to achieve 200 GRPs per month for the first 6 months of a product introduction? or, How many GRPs can I get for $2,000,000? One criticism of GRPs is that each exposure is considered to have the same effect.[39] Advertiser and media analysts are turning to effective reach as a guideline for media scheduling. *Effective reach* is based on the notion that an advertisement is only effective if it reaches the target audience the correct number of times: neither too few nor too many.[40]

FIGURE 10-5

Relationship of reach, frequency, and GRPs. (*Source:* Michael L. Rothschild, *Advertising, from Fundamentals to Strategies,* Heath, Lexington, Mass., 1987, p. 381.)

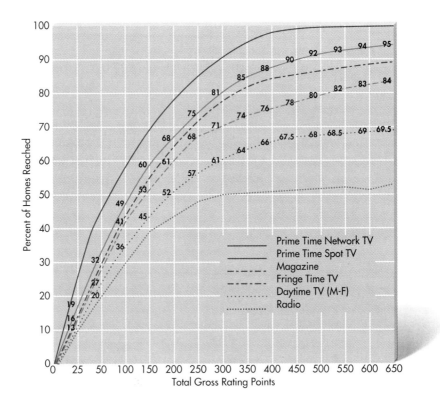

[39] A quote from advertising consultant Alvin Achenbaum, cited in B. G. Yovovich, "Media's New Exposures," *Advertising Age,* Apr. 13, 1981, sec. S, p. 7.

[40] Shimp, loc. cit., and one study found that over 80% of advertising agencies use "effective reach" as a criterion in media planning. See Peggy J. Kreshel, Kent M. Lancaster, and Margaret A. Toomey, "How Leading Advertising Agencies Perceive Effective Reach and Frequency," *Journal of Advertising,* no. 3, 1985, pp. 32–38.

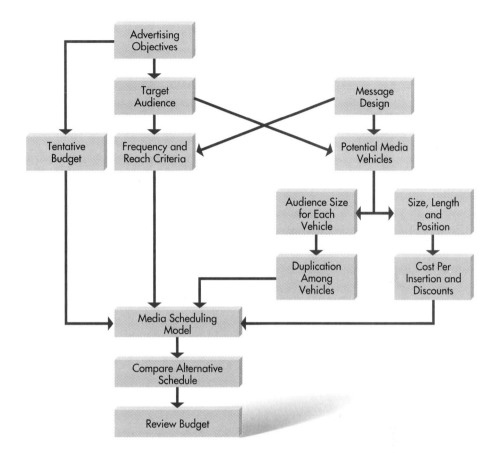

FIGURE 10-6
Developing the media schedule.

Based on a 1979 publication by the American National Advertisers (ANA), the rule for effective reach is 3. This rule has recently been challenged. The conclusions of a new study, "Advertising Reach & Frequency: Maximizing Advertising Results through Effective Frequency," published by the ANA, dispels the 3-plus rule. A lot of advertising is simply reminding consumers about products familiar to them; therefore, two exposures are probably an effective reach.[41]

SETTING THE MEDIA SCHEDULE

As indicated in Figure 10-6, the preceding steps provide the basic management inputs to the media scheduling decision. Computer routines, based on budget limitations, target audience for the commercial, desired frequency and reach, cost per insertion for a given length and position, and audience size and demographics for each acceptable

[41]Joe Mandese, "Revisiting Ad Reach, Frequency," *Advertising Age,* vol. 66, iss. 48, Nov. 27, 1995, p. 46.

TABLE 10-4   MEDIA PLAN FOR A MAN'S GIFT PRODUCT

		MEN 25–49	
MONTH	MEDIUM	REACH	FREQUENCY
March	Television	78	3.1
	Magazines	69	2.1
	Combined	93	2.4
April	Television	78	3.1
	Magazines	33	1.3
	Combined	84	3.4
May	Magazines	34	1.3
June	Magazines	34	1.3
	Radio	38	5.3
	Combined	59	4.1
July	Radio	38	5.3
September	Magazines	35	1.3
October	Magazines	59	1.7
November and			
December	Television	81	3.5
	Magazines	32	1.2
	Radio	38	5.3
	Combined	92	5.7

vehicle, are typically used to allocate the budget among the acceptable vehicles. Generally, these routines will yield a set of media schedules that provide the largest number of GRPs for the given budget.

Table 10-4 provides an example of a media schedule for a man's gift item. In examining the table, we can see that advertising tends to be heaviest during the Easter, graduation, and Christmas periods. Reach and frequency levels are provided for each month.

Although a number of media scheduling models have been developed by using a variety of mathematical procedures,[42] it is important to recognize that the use of such models does not serve as a substitute for managerial judgment. Rather, these models merely serve to display the best schedules, based on the budget and on prior management decisions, regarding message and objectives and size, length, and position. In fact, even the most sophisticated models available to advertisers require very extensive inputs by advertising or product managers.[43]

[42]Dennis Gensch, *Advertising Planning: Mathematical Models in Advertising Media Planning,* Elsevier Scientific, Amsterdam, 1973.

[43]John D.C. Little and Leonard M. Lodish, "A Media Planning Calculus," *Operations Research,* January–February 1969, pp. 1–35.

EVALUATING EFFECTIVENESS

Advertising expenditures frequently represent a significant proportion of the marketing budget and are often an essential ingredient to the success of a product. Accordingly, managers want to know whether the advertising expenditures are being well utilized. Measuring the effectiveness of an advertising program is often difficult and expensive. However, the results of advertising research inform managers whether the advertisement is achieving its goals and, if not, what needs to be corrected.

The role of advertising managers and product managers in the evaluation process is critical—especially in monitoring the achievement of objectives. Advertising agencies and creative specialists are likely to be skilled and very objective in evaluating individual messages to determine the most effective copy. But advertising managers, product managers, and top-level marketing managers should attempt to determine whether the message is creating the desired effect on awareness or attitudes. Advertisements well liked by the ad industry and recalled by viewers do not necessarily move product. For instance, Pepsi's 1991 "chill out" campaign achieved very strong results in terms of memorability and consumers' strong liking of the ads. However, Pepsi's sales during this period grew at a significantly lower rate than did those of Coke.[44]

Further, advertising and product managers should be primarily responsible for evaluating the effectiveness of the total program, for two reasons. First, it is nearly impossible for agencies to be perfectly objective. Second, even when clearly specified communications-oriented objectives have been established, awareness and attitude may still be influenced by other factors (such as changes in distribution availability, prices, and competitors' actions). Only the marketing managers in the firm doing the advertising can properly assess the impact of those factors.

When possible, advertising research results should be diagnostic. That is, the research should not merely indicate which of two alternative messages is superior, or how well some advertising objective is being achieved; the research should provide insights into any remedial actions, if needed.

Procedures

As indicated in Table 10-5, a number of alternative procedures for evaluating advertising effectiveness are available.[45] Some of these procedures must be implemented by the advertiser or its agency, whereas others are available from commercial advertising research services.

It is important to recognize that different procedures are used for different kinds of evaluations. In particular, three kinds of effectiveness evaluations can be made.

[44]"Pepsi: Memorable Ads, Forgettable Sales," *Business Week,* Oct. 21, 1991, p. 36.

[45]Joanne Lipman, "Single Source Ad Research Heralds Detailed Look at Household Habits," *Wall Street Journal,* Feb. 16, 1988, p. 35; D. Dalbey et al., *Advertising Measurement and Decision-Making,* Allyn and Bacon, Boston, 1968; also see Bernard Ryan, Jr., *It Works! How Investment Spending in Advertising Pays Off,* American Association of Advertising Agencies, New York, 1991, pp. 1–63.

TABLE 10-5	PROCEDURES FOR EVALUATING ADVERTISING PROGRAMS

PROCEDURES FOR EVALUATING SPECIFIC ADVERTISEMENTS

1. Recognition tests:
   Estimate the percentage of people claiming to have read a magazine who recognize the ad when it is shown to them.
2. Recall tests:
   Estimate the percentage of people claiming to have read a magazine who can (unaided) recall the ad and its contents.
3. Opinion tests:
   Potential audience members are asked to rank alternative advertisements as most interesting, most believable, best liked.
4. Theater tests:
   Theater audience is asked for brand preferences before and after an ad is shown in context of a TV show.

PROCEDURES FOR EVALUATING SPECIFIC ADVERTISING OBJECTIVES

1. Awareness:
   Potential buyers are asked to indicate brands that come to mind in a product category. A message used in an ad campaign is given and buyers are asked to identify the brand that was advertised using that message.
2. Attitude:
   Potential buyers are asked to rate competing or individual brands on determinant attributes, benefits, and characterizations using rating scales.

PROCEDURES FOR EVALUATING MOTIVATIONAL IMPACT

1. Intentions to buy:
   Potential buyers are asked to indicate likelihood they will buy a brand (on a scale from "definitely will" to "definitely will not").
2. Market test:
   Sales changes in different markets are monitored to compare effects of different messages, budget levels.

■ Evaluating individual advertising messages (copy and format) in order to choose the best of two or more alternatives or to measure the degree to which the message is being received by the audience

■ Evaluating awareness and attitudes

■ Evaluating the motivational impact of the advertising program as reflected in sales or intentions to buy

Note that when managers measure awareness, attitudes, intentions to buy, and sales, they should make these measurements before a campaign begins and, again, at intervals during the campaign.

AT&T ran a series of advertisements that portrayed angry or frightened business-people coping with telephone and computer problems. These ads portrayed business-people who were not always nice and polite when they purchased a phone system. The ads were developed and monitored using a variety of research methods. Focus groups were conducted and these led to the original concept. Later, in-house tests were conducted to measure persuasion and recall of the advertisements. Prior to launching the ad campaign, additional focus groups were conducted to see if they supported the results of the in-house testing of the advertisements. Throughout the campaign, results were monitored and research was conducted with salespersons.[46]

A procedure such as that of AT&T enabled management to catch problems and think of possible modifications to message design or media scheduling at as early a time as possible. Further, those tests that provide diagnostic information are generally most useful to managers in their determination of which specific modifications are necessary. For example, recall tests help diagnose weaknesses in a message by indicating which copy claims are not recalled. Additionally, differences in recall among vehicles can reveal differences in the effectiveness of vehicles (or in the effects of size, length, and position factors, if these differ). Similarly, attitude tests can serve to tell whether the copy is effective in changing perceptions and whether unintended changes in perception have resulted from the copy.

GLOBAL ADVERTISING

The global approach has received considerable attention; it views the world as one market rather than as a collection of many national or regional markets.[47] This orientation employs a uniform marketing approach and standardized products. The advantages of this highly standardized approach include lower production costs, higher quality products, a consistent worldwide image, and more efficient marketing.

Some advertising executives believe global advertising, because of the necessity to appeal to a multicultural audience, constrains creativity. "You end up with the lowest common denominator in advertising when going around the world—it usually works as long as you get down to an incredibly easy-to-understand level."[48] In response to a global brief for a shampoo with the target audience consisting of "every woman in the world who has ever washed her hair" an account director included the following directions to the creators: "No dialogue. No lip sync. No humor. No sex. No chance of an award."[49]

Mr. Volpi, the senior vice president for creative services of J. Walter Thompson, suggests that global ads should focus on feelings, that, in many cases, may be universal. He cites the agency's 1988 "True Colors" campaign for Kodak, which aired

---

[46]Thornton C. Lockwood, "Behind the Emotion in Slice of Death Advertising," *Business Marketing,* September 1988, pp. 87–93.

[47]Robert D. Buzzell, "Can You Standardize Multinational Marketing?" *Harvard Business Review,* November–December 1968, p. 102. Professor Buzzell was one of the first persons to raise the question of how much multinational marketing could be standardized. Theodore Levitt, "The Globalization of Markets," *Harvard Business Review,* May–June 1983, pp. 92–96, declared the approach appropriate for all firms. See also, "Differences, Confusion Slow Global Marketing Bandwagon," *Marketing News,* Jan. 16, 1987, p. 1. In a study of 100 advertisers selling products overseas, only 9 percent used a global marketing approach.

[48]Roberta Lawrence, "Global Advertising: Maximum Mileage," *SHOOT,* Feb. 24, 1995, pp. 35–38.

[49]John Kelly, "Globaldiary," *Adweek,* Eastern edition, vol. 36, no. 29, July 17, 1995, p. 43(1).

in the United States, Europe, and Asia, and is still running. One example, which was aired in Latin America, Europe, North America, and Asia, depicted an emotional exchange between a father and a daughter on her wedding day. The father looked into her eyes as they were dancing and it triggered memories of the things they did. "The emotional cloud it hits rings true whatever your culture."[50]

The biggest hindrance to global marketing may still be cultural differences. There is little evidence to support the contention that world consumers are becoming more alike. In fact, as people become more affluent and better educated, their tastes diverge, and it may become necessary to make greater adjustments for local culture and conditions. The Grey Advertising Agency has identified three questions that companies should ask when selling products in foreign markets. A negative answer to any one of these would suggest that a global advertising program is not appropriate.[51]

- Are consumer targets similar in different nations? For instance, Kentucky Fried Chicken may be viewed as an ordinary meal in the United States while considered a treat in another nation.
- Do consumers share the same wants and needs around the world? General Foods successfully positioned Tang as a substitute for orange juice at breakfast but found that, in France, people drank little orange juice and almost none at breakfast.
- Has the market developed in the same way from country to country? For instance, Kellogg's Pop-Tarts failed in the United Kingdom because toasters are not widely used, whereas a toaster is a common household appliance in the United States.

Swatch has produced a five-spot campaign that will air in more than sixty-four countries. For example, "Tattoo" shows the styling of the watch against the wrist of a tattooed woman; "Car Wash" shows the watch is better able to survive a top-down car wash than the women driving.[52] Global advertising may be an answer to shrinking production budgets: it allows maximum reach for the commercial, using a minimum of production dollars.[53]

However, advertisers must be sensitive to differences among countries that may require a promotional effort tailored to reflect local considerations. Sara Lee's best-selling herbal bath soap in Great Britain is Radox. However, many Europeans confuse this name with Raid, the bug killer, and Radox comes across as an unsuitable product for skin. In place of Radox, Sara Lee promotes Sanex, a Spanish soap perceived by Europeans as a brand that lathers nicely and kills germs. However, in the big British market it sounds like "sanitary" and has the wrong connotations. Other names such as L'eggs do not translate for many European markets. For instance, the word for L'eggs in France would have to be Les Oeufs (the eggs).[54]

---

[50]Lawrence, loc. cit.

[51]Ronald Alsop, "Efficacy of Global Ad Projects Is Questioned in Firm's Survey," *Wall Street Journal,* Sept. 13, 1984, p. 1.

[52]Lawrence, loc. cit.

[53]Lawrence, loc. cit.

[54]Steve Weiner, "How Do You Say L'eggs in French?" *Forbes,* Nov. 27, 1989, pp. 73–77.

CONCLUSION

Although the process of developing and implementing advertisements is often the primary responsibility of an advertising agency, it is critical that advertising managers, product managers, and top-level marketing management personnel take an active part in this process. In particular, it is essential that managers set advertising objectives that are (1) consistent with the marketing strategy, (2) specific enough to provide guidance to the copy and media people, and (3) measurable, so managers can effectively evaluate the program's effectiveness.

The importance of taking an active role in the development of an advertising program seems obvious. But far too many firms, especially smaller ones, allow their agencies too much freedom in developing a program. In effect, creative concerns often receive more attention than managerial concerns. Of course, agencies or other specialists are essential to the advertising process. But, by taking an active role in specifying the marketing strategy, the target market, the advertising objectives, and the basis for evaluating effectiveness, managers can assure that advertising programs are viewed as part of the marketing effort (rather than vice versa) by the agency.

In this chapter, we have presented several guidelines and procedures for developing effective advertising programs. Additionally, we have presented a process within which these guidelines and procedures can be most effectively used. Figure 10-7

FIGURE 10-7

Relationship of advertising programs to situation analysis, marketing strategy, and other marketing programs.

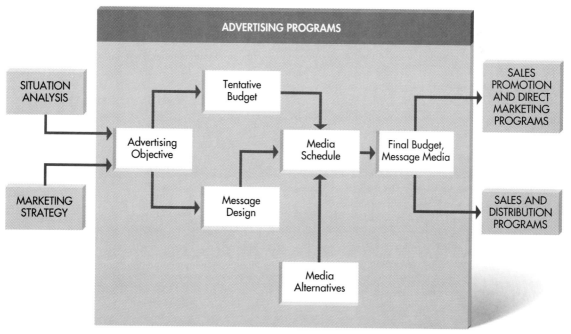

summarizes this process and indicates the relationship between the advertising programs and the other elements of the planning process. As this figure illustrates, advertising programs are closely related to the other kinds of marketing programs. Sales-promotion programs must often be communicated through advertising. Further, sales promotions and advertising should be closely coordinated, for reasons discussed in Chapter 11. Advertising and personal selling efforts should be coordinated as well, because advertising often paves the way for the sales force. This relationship will be discussed in greater detail in Chapter 12.

RENAMING NEW COKE

For 20 years, the Coca-Cola Company and Pepsi-Cola have competed for leadership in the soft-drink market. These two companies account for 70 percent of industry sales and spend hundreds of millions of dollars on advertising each year. Each percentage point of market share is equal to $460 million in retail sales in the $44.4 billion soft-drink industry.

In April 1985, Coca-Cola changed the formula of its product and introduced New Coke. This resulted in a strong protest from loyal customers of the old brand and led to the reintroduction of the original Coke as Coca-Cola Classic a short time later. In addition, New Coke never attained the market-share goals that had been established and was relegated to obscurity, although it continued to be distributed in markets where Pepsi was strong, such as Spokane, Washington, and southern California. Coke marketers, exploring ways to obtain younger drinkers who prefer a sweeter flavor, decided to revive New Coke and reintroduce it as Coke II.

The city of Spokane, Washington, was chosen as a test market to research reintroduction of this brand. Spokane was selected because of its relatively isolated media market with sophisticated market-research facilities and high Pepsi market share. In the test, Coke countered Pepsi's rap ads with its own, as well as with special 16 oz. cans at 12 oz. prices. Coke II advertising emphasized its "real cola taste—plus the sweetness of Pepsi."

Pepsi responded to Coke advertisements with ads aimed at consumer confusion about what seemed like three types of Coke. Before and during the ads Coca-Cola conducted focus groups, weekly phone surveys, man-in-the-mall surveys, and studies of comparative local ads for Coke II and Pepsi. This research was designed to learn what it would take to convert a loyal Pepsi fan to the new Coke formula.

When the test began in March 1990, New Coke had a 1.3 percent share in Spokane. A month after the test began, Coke II had a 4.7 percent share, which by May was 2.4 percent. During this same time, New Coke's national share was 0.6 percent. In addition, both Coke's and Pepsi's overall sales increased, in large part because of price cuts.

After the tests, Coke decided to reposition New Coke as Coke II nationally. TV ads, showing a can of Coke II with a voice-over informing viewers that New Coke is now called Coke II and has a real cola taste with the sweetness of Pepsi, were run. These ads suggested that those drinking Pepsi should give Coke II a try and reminded the viewer that Coca-Cola Classic hadn't changed.

Research Systems Corp. (RSC) found that 24 percent of the viewers of these ads were able to play back the new name message. The research was conducted in four geographically dispersed markets and involved 832 soft-drink purchasers. RSC investigated how persuasive these ads were. This was done by measuring the change in brand preference that resulted from being exposed to the ad. RSC's experience with similar studies led it to conclude that the ads alone would not generate the share increase desired. Interviews were conducted with those soft-drink purchasers participating in the persuasion tests 3 days later. By that time, only 57 percent of the respondents were able to recall the key message of the ad. This led RSC to conclude that Coke would need to use a number of different ads so that they could replace each spot as its recall declined. This would maximize the persuasion level for the GRPs under Coke II's media budget.

1. What seem to be Coca-Cola's objectives for the Coke II advertising spots?
2. What would be the advantages/disadvantages of testing the Coke II campaign in Spokane?
3. How would reach and frequency be important in scheduling the Coke II campaign?

This case was developed from Laura Bird, "Coke II: The Sequel," *Adweek's Marketing Week*, July 30, 1990, pp. 6–7; "Coke II Spot Goes Flat on Persuasion," *Advertising Age*, Sept. 7, 1992, p. 9; Patricia Winters, "Jury Still Out on Future of Coke II," *Advertising Age*, July 16, 1990, p. 44; Patricia Winters, "Pepsi Yawning over Relaunch Plans for Coke II," *Advertising Age*, March 1990, pp. 3, 77; John Lippman, "Coca-Cola Pours More Energy into Ads," *Los Angeles Times*, Sept. 5, 1991, pp. D1, 7.

QUESTIONS AND SITUATIONS FOR DISCUSSION

1. What competitive factors would lead to different allocations of the promotion budget for advertising and sales promotion?
2. In which of the following cases would it be most reasonable to use sales volume as a primary advertising objective? What, if any, are the possible long-term disadvantages to the use of a sales program in these instances?
   a. A small software firm is planning an advertising program in leading business magazines.
   b. Kellogg's is introducing a new anticholesterol cereal product to the market.
   c. Marshall Fields is advertising its private-label line of men's sports coats.
3. Upjohn Company had taken a low-key approach to advertising its hair-loss remedy, Rogaine. The advertisements did not mention either Rogaine or Minoxidil, its active ingredient. The U.S. Food and Drug Administration prohibits the mention of drugs in advertisements unless there is full disclosure of any warnings and side effects. The ads appeared in male-oriented magazines such as *Golf Digest, Sports Illustrated,* and *Gentlemen's Quarterly.* In addition to not using the name, the treatment in the ad isn't even referred to as a drug. The result is that the audience does not know if the treatment is a hair weave, a transplant, or a drug. The message is, "If you're concerned about hair loss you should see your doctor." What are the advertising objectives Upjohn seems to have for its campaign for Rogaine? What are the advantages of advertising in magazines, as opposed to broadcast media, for a high-involvement product such as Rogaine?
4. You are a member of the account management team for a large advertising agency. On a recent visit to the client's office, she told you that the objective for the advertising program for her category for the next planning period was to

increase brand awareness. She asked: "Before leaving, do you have any questions?" How would you respond?

5. Some executives see advertising as a necessary cost of informing the target audience, whereas some executives argue that advertising can add value to the product. What, do you think, can advertising add as value to the product?

6. What makes advertising effective?

7. You have recently been hired by U.S. Health, a nationwide fitness club syndication. It wants to be to fitness clubs what Best Western is to hotels. U.S. Health has decided to launch an advertising campaign using national magazines and has asked for your opinion of the top ten to fifteen magazines. Your answer is expected in the morning.

8. Assume that the cost to produce a television ad is $200,000. Further, assume that the cost to air the ad on *Seinfeld* is $420,000 for a 30-second commercial and on *Rescue 911* is $195,000 for a 30-second commercial. The product manager states that he cannot afford to advertise on *Seinfeld;* he would rather advertise twice on *Rescue 911.* How would you respond? (*Hint:* You may wish to review Figure 10-4).

9. Is maximizing reach or maximizing frequency more important?

10. How do flighting and pulsing affect GRPs for the same budget when compared to continuous schedules?

SUGGESTED ADDITIONAL READINGS

Cannon, Hugh M., and Edward A. Riordan, "Effective Reach and Frequency: Does It Really Make Sense?" *Journal of Advertising Research,* March–April 1994, pp. 19–28.

Dickson, Peter R., "GRP: A Case of a Mistaken Identity," *Journal of Advertising Research,* February–March 1991, pp. 55–59.

Erwin, Ephron, "More Weeks, Less Weight: The Shelf-Space Model of Advertising," *Journal of Advertising Research,* May–June 1995, pp. 18–23.

Gronhaug, Kjell, Olan Kvitastein, and Sigmund Gronmo, "Factors Moderating Advertising Effectiveness as Reflected in 333 Tested Advertisements," *Journal of Advertising Research,* October–November 1991, pp. 42–58.

Hite, Robert E., and Cynthia Fraser, "International Advertising Strategies of Multinational Corporations," *Journal of Advertising Research,* August–September 1988, pp. 9–17.

Jones, John P., "Ad Spending: Maintaining Market Share," *Harvard Business Review,* January–February 1990, pp. 38–42.

Kashani, Kamran, "Beware of the Pitfalls of Global Marketing," *Harvard Business Review,* September–October 1989, pp. 91–98.

Lodish, Leonard M., et al., "How T.V. Advertising Works: A Meta-Analysis of 389 Real World Split Cable T.V. Advertising Experiments," *Journal of Marketing Research,* May 1995, pp. 125–139.

Ogilvy, David, *Confessions of an Advertising Man,* Atheneum, New York, 1986.

Peltier, James W., Barbara Mueller, and Richard G. Rosen, "Direct Response versus Image Advertising: Enhancing Communication Effectiveness through an Integrated Approach," *Journal of Direct Marketing,* Winter 1992, pp. 40–48.

Plummer, Joseph T., "The Role of Copy Research in Multinational Advertising," *Journal of Advertising Research,* October–November 1986, pp. 11–15.

Schroer, James C., "Ad Spending: Growing Market Shares," *Harvard Business Review,* January–February 1990, pp. 44–48.

Schumann, David W., Jan M. Hathcote, and Susan West, "Corporate Advertising in America: A Review of Published Studies on Use, Measurement, and Effectiveness," *Journal of Advertising,* vol. 20, September 1991, pp. 35–56.

Zaltman, Gerald, and Christine Moorman, "The Management and Use of Advertising Research," *Journal of Advertising Research,* December 1988–January 1989, pp. 11–18.

CHAPTER 11

SALES-PROMOTION AND DIRECT MARKETING PROGRAMS

OVERVIEW

In Chapter 10, we examined advertising programs. More specifically, our coverage was focused on advertising through the mass media—television, radio, newspapers, magazines. Such advertising can be an efficient way to address a substantial audience of potential buyers with a common message about the product. As we pointed out when we discussed advertising objectives and evaluation of advertising effectiveness, mass media advertising is primarily designed to build awareness, influence perceptions and preferences, or reinforce brand equity. Ultimately, such programs should also result in sales to those who receive the message, but their immediate impact will usually be confined to nonbehavioral responses. This chapter focuses on two kinds of marketing programs used to obtain immediate, easily measurable behavioral responses—sales promotion and direct marketing.

Sales promotion is any short-term offer or incentive directed toward buyers, retailers, or wholesalers that is designed to achieve a specific, immediate response. The two basic classifications of sales promotion are *consumer promotions,* including coupons, free samples, premiums, and special exhibits; and *trade promotions,* in which cash, merchandise, equipment, or other resources are awarded to retail or wholesale firms or to their personnel. Consumer sales promotions are often communicated through, or coordinated with, advertising programs. Consequently, they may assist advertising by increasing awareness or by changing or reinforcing attitudes. But the main value of both consumer and trade promotions lies in their effectiveness in stimulating *behavioral responses.*

Direct marketing is an *interactive system* of marketing that uses a variety of communication media to achieve specific, measurable responses.[1] Prominent among the direct marketing methods are direct mail, including catalogs; telephone marketing; direct response television (such as Home Shopping Network); direct response ads in newspapers; and the Internet. Because direct marketing programs often incorporate

---

[1]Mary Lou Roberts and Paul Berger, *Direct Marketing Management,* Prentice-Hall, Englewood Cliffs, N.J., 1989, p. 2.

special incentives, sales-promotion activities can often be implemented through a direct marketing system. However, direct marketing is distinctive in certain respects. First, the system is interactive, meaning that marketers not only communicate to buyers, but also measure the success of the communication, because *each* buyer has an opportunity to respond to that communication. Second, the system is characterized by a database on which marketers record both the history of communications directed to each customer and the sales or other responses received. Thus, direct marketing can tailor messages to *individual* buyers—not just to *segments* of potential buyers in the audiences of particular mass media vehicles.

In the remainder of this chapter, we examine both sales promotion and direct marketing. Specifically, we identify (1) the specific kinds of objectives one could pursue with each program, (2) key considerations in designing a program, and (3) the profitability issues that must be considered in evaluating specific programs.

SALES-PROMOTION PROGRAMS

During the 1980s, sales promotion's share of total marketing expenditures in the United States grew steadily and, by the early 1990s, the amount of money firms spent on consumer promotion alone had equaled expenditures on mass advertising. Although a number of explanations have been offered for this development, five basic forces seem to be most responsible.[2]

1. Slow population growth has intensified the competition for market share in packaged-goods industries where promotions are most widely used.
2. Increased audience segmentation (especially with the growth of cable television networks) and rising mass media costs have made advertising less cost effective for those firms catering to broad customer targets.
3. More products have reached the maturity stage of the life cycle so that opportunities for differentiation are decreasing and price has become increasingly important in brand choice.
4. Large retailers and wholesalers have placed increasing demands on manufacturers for promotions because special cash and merchandising allowances are a significant contribution to their profits.
5. Price promotions have usually been more reliable than advertising in boosting short-term earnings, which appeals to firms whose stock prices are under pressure to show bottom-line results.

Today, numerous signs suggest that promotion budgets may have passed their peak. For example, Procter & Gamble has decided to phase out most trade promotions and is eliminating coupons in selected trial markets in favor of a policy of "everyday low prices" (or EDLP). General Mills has also attempted to all but eliminate consumer

[2]Robert Buzzell, John Quelch, and Walter Salmon, "The Costly Bargain of Sales Promotion," *Harvard Business Review*, March–April 1990, pp. 141–149.

promotions.[3] Nevertheless, many firms will continue to spend relatively large amounts of their marketing budgets on promotion in those cases where these programs can accomplish key objectives that are essential to the marketing strategy.

SALES-PROMOTION OBJECTIVES

The array of specific sales-promotion ideas, tactics, and activities that have been used is enormous, and it seems to grow weekly as creative marketing minds generate still more new promotions. As was the case with advertising programs, however, a sales-promotion program should not be designed until the objective is clearly understood. Moreover, the sales-promotion objective should be consistent with the marketing strategy.

Although the number of possible specific sales-promotion objectives is very large, there are a limited number of basic types of objectives that may be established. Tables 11-1 and 11-2 list these objectives and indicate some typical programs that can be used to achieve each objective.

| TABLE 11-1 | SALES-PROMOTION OBJECTIVES AND ALTERNATIVE PROGRAMS DIRECTED AT FINAL BUYERS |

OBJECTIVE	ALTERNATIVE PROGRAMS
Inquiries	Free gifts
	Mail-in coupons for information
	Catalog offers
	Exhibits
Product trial	Coupons
■ New products	Cents-off specials
■ Related products	Free samples
■ Brand switchers	Contests
	Premiums
	Demonstrations
Repurchase	On-pack coupons
	Mail-in coupons for rebate
	Continuity premiums
Traffic building	Special sales
	Weekly specials
	Entertainment events
	Retailer coupons
	Premiums
Increased rate of purchase	Multipacks
■ Inventory building	Special price on twos
■ Increased usage rate	Information on new usage situations

---

[3]Tim Triplett, "Cereal Manufacturers Await Reaction to General Mills' Coupon Decision," *Marketing News,* May 9, 1994, pp. 1–2; and "Procter's Gamble," *The Economist,* July 25, 1992, pp. 61–62.

TABLE 11-2	SALES-PROMOTION OBJECTIVES AND ALTERNATIVE PROGRAMS DIRECTED AT THE TRADE

OBJECTIVE	ALTERNATIVE PROGRAMS
Inventory-building	
■ New-product acceptance	Returns allowances
■ Increased space allotment	Merchandise allowances
	Slotting allowances
Promotional support	
■ Local ad feature	Promotional allowances
■ Displays	Cooperative promotions
■ Price special	Reusable display cases
	Sales contests
	Merchandise allowances

Objectives Directed at Final Buyers

Five basic types of buyer actions can be stimulated by sales promotions: inquiries, product trial, repurchase, traffic building, and increases in rate of purchase.

STIMULATING INQUIRIES

Inquiries can include returning a form requesting additional information about a product or service or visiting an exhibit at a trade association meeting. Managers can generate inquiries by offering such things as a free catalog or some premium or prize. (Often, the incentive is offered in the context of some advertising message designed to introduce the product's benefits. Accordingly, such promotions must be closely coordinated with advertising programs.) A manager will often select this objective when attempting to identify and attract new prospects for a product or service. This objective is especially important when clients or customers must be periodically replenished (a problem facing colleges and the military). In addition, it is often important to attract only high-interest prospects, especially when the potential buyers are few and hard to identify. In these cases, firms that are effective in stimulating inquiries will be able to focus their follow-up sales and other marketing activities on high-interest prospects. Further, when new models or versions of a product or service are being offered, sales promotions may be designed to stimulate inquiries from past customers in order to maintain contact with prospects.

GENERATING PRODUCT TRIAL

A product trial objective is certainly appropriate in marketing new products. Free samples and coupons are usually useful in stimulating trial for low perceived-risk products because they generate a usage experience that, if positive, may lead to favorable attitudes faster than advertising. For more complex, higher-priced products (such as durable goods or many services), in-store demonstrations appear to be most useful.

For houseware items, demonstrations have been known to increase sales by 80 to 300 percent during the week of the demonstration.[4]

Additionally, firms that market a number of different products (such as product-line extensions or complementary products) may use techniques such as cross-couponing to build trial for these other products. Thus, a package of Gillette razor blades might contain a coupon for a new Gillette Foamy shaving cream line extension.

ENCOURAGING REPURCHASE

To the extent that habit building will lead to brand loyalty (especially for low perceived-risk products), promotional incentives that "tie" a buyer to a seller may be desired. For example, coupons contained in a package that can be redeemed on the next purchase can have this type of impact and will be especially valuable in implementing retention strategies. Similarly, retailers may encourage store loyalty (or at least continued visits to the store) through special sales offered to charge-account customers or through continuity promotions. *Continuity promotions* include trading stamps, games, and contests that run over a period of weeks, or gifts distributed in increments over time (such as sets of dishes). These promotions stimulate repurchase from a retail store because customers must continue to return to the store to obtain the full value of the program.

TRAFFIC BUILDING

Retailers employ sales promotions as vehicles to stimulate store traffic from new buyers as well as for the repurchase objectives already cited. Special entertainment events (such as having authors autograph copies of their books) and special attractions placed in shopping malls may attract customers, who will then make some purchases. Additionally, by establishing price specials on so-called *leader* products (as we discussed in Chapter 9), retailers may draw customers who purchase the leader plus complementary products (at nonsale prices).

INCREASING RATES OF PURCHASE

Often the major desired effect of a promotion is to get more purchases from existing buyers. But there are two alternative strategic purposes underlying this objective: consumer loading and increased consumption rate. *Consumer loading* reflects a retention-oriented marketing strategy in which the main goal is to get buyers to stock up on the product. A buyer who is carrying above-normal stocks of a product is not likely to buy competing products. Thus, multipacks and similar promotions may be used just before new competing products are introduced or in anticipation of increased competitor promotional activity. Alternatively, the promotion may stimulate primary demand if the lower prices encourage a higher rate of consumption (often the case with products such as soft drinks or some meat products).

Additionally, a well-known method of increasing purchase rates is the use of in-store displays. By examining scanner data for periods covering both the use and

---

[4]Elaine Appleton, "Houseware Companies Are Convinced that Seeing Is Believing," *Adweek's Marketing Week*, Oct. 9, 1989, pp. 20–21.

nonuse of displays, Information Resources Inc. reports that displays are especially effective for snack foods, soft drinks, and apple juice. However, the company also reports weekly sales gains of 100 to 200 percent for other products, including soups and laundry detergents.[5]

Trade Sales-Promotion Objectives

The fundamental purposes of trade promotions are (1) to *push* the product through the marketing channel by getting resellers (retailers and wholesalers) to market the product aggressively and (2) to help ensure the success of consumer promotions designed to *pull* the product through the channel. These two purposes are reflected in two types of sales-promotion objectives.

ENCOURAGING TRADE INVENTORY BUILDING

Marketers who are developing extensive consumer-oriented promotions will nearly always want to pursue this objective simultaneously. If the consumer promotion is expected to build short-run demand, retail stockouts must be avoided. Thus, manufacturers may offer special margins or extra merchandise at no extra cost to induce an increase in retailer or wholesaler inventories. In addition, special returns allowances—higher-than-usual prices paid to retailers for unsold goods they return—may also be used to encourage retailers to risk higher inventories.

With respect to building acceptance for new products, manufacturers have increasingly encountered retailer demands for so-called *slotting allowances.* These are cash payments given to retailers in exchange for stocking a new product for a specified period of time. According to one source, it can easily cost $70,000 to get a truckload's worth of a new product line accepted into a chain with fifty stores. The cause of the rise in slotting allowances is the proliferation of new grocery products. About 10,000 new items are introduced each year in grocery stores.[6] Retailers seeking these slotting allowances argue that most new products fail, whereas others merely draw sales from established products within the store. In either case, the retailer anticipates little gain in profits from adding the new product.

OBTAINING DISTRIBUTOR PROMOTIONAL ASSISTANCE

As we discuss in Chapter 12, the objective of obtaining distributor promotional assistance must usually be implemented by the sales force. However, the personal selling effort is easier if sales-promotion incentives are available. Sales contests and special cash or merchandise allowances may be offered in return for distributor agreements to provide special display space or additional selling or advertising effort. If effective, these programs may help ensure the success of a consumer promotion. For example, retailers may have a limited amount of space to devote to special displays. Consequently, trade-promotion incentives (usually in the form of free cases of the product being displayed) are essential to gain retailer support.

---

[5]Kathleen Deveny, "Displays Pay Off," *Wall Street Journal,* Oct. 15, 1992, p. B1.

[6]Jim Bessen, "Riding the Marketing Information Wave," *Harvard Business Review,* September–October 1993, p. 152.

Relationship of Sales-Promotion Objectives to Marketing Strategy

As we have indicated, different types of sales promotions serve different sales-promotion objectives. In turn, each of the sales-promotion objectives is more appropriate for some marketing strategies than for others.

With respect to promotions directed toward final buyers, inquiries and product trial are generally more effective when the marketing strategy is used either to attract nonusers or to acquire new customers. Repurchase-oriented promotions support a strategy directed at retention of current customers. Promotions to increase the rate of purchase may support a primary-demand strategy (through increasing the rate of usage) or a retention strategy, as we discussed above. Traffic building is a broad objective and may serve any of the basic strategies, depending on the specific nature of the promotion: Weekly specials tend to stimulate retention, whereas unique exhibits may attract new customers. Finally, trade promotions must be viewed as a means rather than an end. The basic purpose of trade promotion is to support advertising or consumer sales promotions. Thus, the different trade-promotion objectives may ultimately serve any of the marketing strategies.[7]

CONSIDERATIONS IN PROGRAM DESIGN

As we suggested in the previous section, managers should establish the sales-promotion objective before selecting a specific type of sales-promotion incentive. Further, the sales-promotion objective should support the marketing strategy for the product. However, managers involved in the design of these programs need to consider (1) the factors that will influence the nature of short-term market response and (2) brand-specific factors related to a firm's long-term positioning.

Factors Influencing the Nature of Market Response

Many experts in the marketing of packaged goods believe that firms waste a large amount of money on promotions. Specifically, these people argue that many promotions are ineffective and too costly for one of the following reasons.

- Consumer response to the promotion (especially the coupon *redemption* rate) is very small.
- The sales resulting from promotions are largely *displaced sales,* that is, sales to regular buyers who would have purchased the product anyway.
- A large portion of the sales increase is simply due to *stocking-up,* thus borrowing sales from future periods.

[7]Kenneth Hardy, "Key Success Factors for Manufacturers' Sales Promotion in Package Goods," *Journal of Marketing,* July 1986, pp. 13–23.

One complicating factor is that size loyalty may exist in some product categories, so a promotion on one size may not attract competitors' customers who prefer other sizes. This would imply that if size loyalty exists, a firm should offer the incentive on the size in which it has the *lowest* market share if the purpose of the promotion is to induce trial. By focusing on its lowest market-share sizes, the firm will reduce the proportion of coupons used by its regular customers and will likely attract competitors' customers.

Consumer response to sales promotions will, in large part, depend on the amount and type of search effort required of the consumer. For example, in-pack or on-pack coupons generally have the highest redemption rate because regular users don't have to exert much effort to acquire these coupons and because these customers are already favorably disposed to the product. Of course, this approach will not be effective in gaining trial from nonusers or buyers of competing brands. For those objectives, weekly cents-off specials and "free-standing insert coupons" in newspapers or magazines are highly popular with manufacturers. But these promotions are not focused at all on a target market. For example, in one recent year, packaged-goods firms spent $6.1 billion on 300 billion coupons, but only 1.8 percent were redeemed and of these nearly 80 percent were used by people who would have bought the product anyway.[8] Consequently, increased emphasis is now being devoted to focusing promotions more precisely.

One of the most successful ways to improve the targeting of coupons is through the use of *in-store promotion systems* (such as Catalina Marketing's checkout Coupon System or Vision Value Club). These systems provide coupons or other incentives in the store, based on actual purchases. For example, in the Catalina system, as checkout scanners read bar codes, a Catalina computer spits out coupons for competitive or complementary products, or even for the same product, depending on the objective of the manufacturer using the system. Catalina reports that it attains an average redemption rate of 9 percent.[9]

Finally, as noted above, the effect of some promotions is that regular buyers "stock up" on the product at promotional prices. Logically, this building up of consumer inventories should result in a drop in sales at some time in the future (when prices are at "normal" levels). However, this effect is not likely to be strong in all situations. In general, stock-up effects are likely to be greatest when

- Buyers will not have a large amount of space or money tied up in inventory.
- The risk of spoilage or obsolescence is low.
- Promotions are directed toward regular buyers.
- No limits on volume (such as two to a customer) are established.

It is important to note that coupons and in-store price promotions have been shown to change stock-up rates differently. A price promotion is only temporary and usually

---

[8]Matt Walsh, "Point-of-Sale Persuaders," *Forbes,* Oct. 24, 1994, pp. 232–233.
[9]Ibid., p. 233.

applies to multiple purchases, so stock-up effects are generally high. By contrast, coupons usually do not have short-term expiration dates and are only good for one purchase, so the incentive to stock up is less.[10]

Brand-Specific Considerations

There is an increasing amount of research available on sales promotions—especially on those involving direct price incentives—and much of this research has been focused on the competitive effectiveness of sales promotions.[11]

One finding that is well documented is that, within a given market, promoting high-quality brands impacts weaker brands (and private-label products) disproportionately. That is, promoting higher-price-tier brands generates more switching from lower-price-tier brands than promoting lower-price-tier brands generates from higher-price-tier brands. Presumably this effect is due to the higher brand equity enjoyed by premium brands.

However, it is also important to recognize the dynamic effects of using price promotions. For example, one of the biggest concerns of marketers is that heavy price promotion will lead to a reduction in a firm's brand equity. To date, there is conflicting evidence about the long-term effect of promotion. However, there is evidence that the higher the frequency of price "deals" the more sensitive consumers are to price. Thus, an increase in the frequency of price deals will reduce the amount of the price premium a national brand may be able to command in the marketplace. Over the long term, therefore, a premium brand that continues to fight regular or discount brands with price promotions may gradually undermine its position of advantage.

In addition to considering a brand's equity in formulating sales-promotion programs, managers should also consider the brand's market-share position. Although the leading brands usually have the most loyal customers, thus partially insulating them from the effects of competitive promotions, they have the most customers to lose and the fewest to gain from engaging in promotional battles. Also, because they have the most customers, the lost profitability from selling to regular buyers at promotional prices is a more significant one for the high-share brand than for small-share brands; because regular buyers will be the ones most attracted to a price special, the larger the share, the higher the percentage of coupons redeemed, and the greater the percentage of promotion-priced sales that will come from the brand being promoted.

Promotions to Resellers

As discussed earlier, trade promotions (those directed at retailers or wholesalers) are designed to achieve either inventory building or promotional support. Indeed, it may be necessary to achieve both objectives to ensure the success of consumer promotions.

---

[10]See Robert Blattberg, Gary Eppen, and Joshua Lieberman, "A Theoretical and Empirical Evaluation of Price Deals for Consumer Nondurables," *Journal of Marketing,* Winter 1981, pp. 116–129.

[11]This section draws heavily from Robert Blattberg, Richard Briesch, and Edward Fox, "How Promotions Work," *Marketing Science,* Fall 1995, pp. G122–G132.

Unfortunately, many trade promotions are not achieving these objectives. Specifically, evidence of three major problems with trade sales promotions exists.

- Many trade buyers respond to promotions by purchasing for normal inventory. In some cases, buyers buy in large volume during deals to avoid buying at normal prices.
- Trade buyers often accept the incentive but fail to perform the promotional requirements expected.
- Some retailers make purchases beyond their own requirements during price "deals" and then resell the discounted merchandise to other retailers at a profit.[12]

Although these problems are not easily resolved, managers can take several steps to reduce their severity.

First, managers must understand the distributor's needs with respect to the product category. For example, price-oriented promotions (such as merchandise allowances) may be more effective in gaining support from retailers who are volume-oriented (such as warehouse clubs and discounters), whereas cooperative advertising promotions that help build a retailer's image on quality may be more important for high-margin, high-service retailers (such as leading department stores).[13] As we discuss in Chapter 12 in more detail, managers should also recognize the profit impact of a sales promotion on a dealer's space and inventory constraints and on the retailer's assortment of products. Because resellers are likely to vary along these and other dimensions, most experts now believe greater flexibility should be provided in the promotional performance requirements expected of retailers.

The advent of electronic scanning has certainly improved the ability of firms to assess the impact of consumer promotions on retailer performance as well as on the performance of the brand. Thus, managers are increasingly knowledgeable about the payoffs from various kinds of trade support to both manufacturers and retailers. If manufacturers can show how a given promotion affects *total* sales for a given retailer, they will find it easier to gain trade acceptance.

PROFITABILITY ISSUES

The answer to the question, "How much should be spent on sales promotion?" is an elusive one. But the importance of answering that question cannot be overstated. Firms that regularly use sales promotion know that it is tremendously expensive. General Mills, for example, estimated that the 50-cent coupons its customers redeemed cost the firm as much as 75 cents for printing, distribution, handling, and redemption.[14] However, the sales and profit consequences are difficult to predict.

In this section, we will review the basic elements that should be considered in

---

[12]John Quelch, "It's Time to Make Trade Promotion More Productive," *Harvard Business Review,* May–June 1983, pp. 130–136.

[13]Rockney Walters, "An Empirical Investigation into Retailer Response to Manufacturers' Coupons," *Journal of Retailing,* Summer 1989, pp. 253–272.

[14]Triplett, op. cit., p. 1.

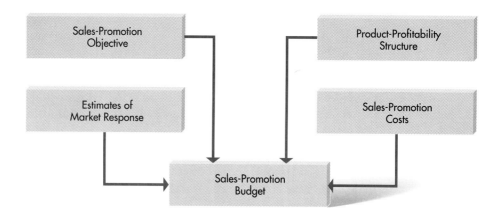

FIGURE 11-1

Factors to be considered in developing the sales-promotion budget.

the budgeting process. These elements are depicted in Figure 11-1. Additionally, we illustrate the approaches that can be used in developing the budget. Because consumer promotions are those most widely used, and because they are generally the most complex from a budgeting perspective, our discussion will focus on the budgeting process for those types of promotions.

Determining Costs

Most promotions will incur direct fixed costs and variable costs. Among the direct fixed costs are the costs of physically distributing samples; mailing coupons; and placing advertisements carrying coupons, inquiry slips, and premium offers. Additionally, contribution margins may be reduced because the value of the coupon or cents-off special is effectively a price reduction. Further, when coupons are used, retailers must be remunerated for each coupon redeemed (usually at the rate of about 8 cents each), and this represents an increase in the variable cost per unit.

One key problem in estimating costs is that contribution margins are reduced only on those items actually purchased at promotional prices. Therefore, some estimate of sales response will be necessary to determine the actual reduction in contribution margins.

Additionally, when coupons are used, some retailers will redeem coupons even when the product is not actually purchased; they then redeem the face value of the coupon and receive the 8-cent handling charge. Although this procedure (called *misredemption*) is a fraud, it is believed to be very extensive and is highly costly to manufacturers. Thus, some provision for estimating the level of misredemptions should be considered in projecting costs.

Estimating Market Response

In Chapter 10, we suggested that managers must have some estimate of sales response in order to set the tentative advertising budget. Specifically, managers need to have some projections of the market response discussed earlier—redemption rates, displacement rates, and stock-up effects. In developing these projections, managers have historically relied on judgment and on their experience from similar past promotions. Additionally, managers may use experiments to estimate market response. In particular, electronic scanner data results (as discussed in Chapter 6) are extremely useful in predicting the level of response, discovering who responds, and tracking the volume of purchases.

In addition to redemption, displacement, and stock-up, managers would like to know three other market response factors: acquisition rates, conversion rates, and product-line effects. The *acquisition rate* is the percent of coupons redeemed by nonregular buyers, and the *conversion rate* is the number of future purchases of the brand by those nonregular buyers attracted by the promotion. These are especially important factors when the strategic objective of the program is to attract new customers because they, in essence, determine the success of the promotion. Of course, if we can reliably forecast the displacement rate (the percentage of sales to regular buyers), estimating acquisition is fairly simple. But conversions are hard to forecast (although they can be tracked after the fact by observing data from electronic scanner–based panels). *Product-line effects* (discussed in Chapters 6 and 9) are also of interest if the item being promoted has close substitutes or complements.

Figure 11-2 summarizes the relationships among these various market response factors.

FIGURE 11-2

Relationship among types of market responses to sales promotions.

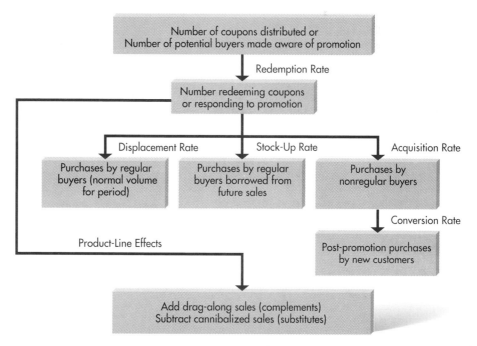

Assessing Profitability Implications

If managers can identify the direct costs associated with a sales promotion and can develop some rough estimates of market response, the profitability implications of a given promotion can be assessed by comparing the "normal" contribution over the period of the promotion with the expected promotional contribution. As Figure 11-3 indicates, there are three steps involved in assessing profitability implications: (1) estimate the reduced contribution from displaced and stock-up sales; (2) estimate the increased contribution from incremental sales to new buyers; and (3) subtract the direct costs of the sales promotion. These steps are illustrated in the following example.

Linkster (introduced in Chapter 6) produces a line of golf apparel and accessories. In trying to expand sales of its specially designed golf sweaters (currently selling at a rate of 40,000 per year), the company is taking out a full-page advertisement in *Golf Digest* (circulation 1.4 million). The total cost (including artwork) of the ad is $96,000. Part of the advertisement contains a $20 coupon on any Linkster sweater.

As indicated in Chapter 6, the normal unit contribution on a sweater is $37. Linkster will reimburse its dealers for the $20 coupon plus 25 cents for the expense of handling the redemptions. Thus, Linkster's contribution margin on coupon sales will be:

$$\$37.00 - \$20.00 - \$0.25 = \$16.75$$

Based on information from *Golf Digest* and industry experience, Linkster's marketing manager anticipates that 0.5 to 1 percent of the coupons will be redeemed and

FIGURE 11-3

Assessing the profitability of a sales promotion.

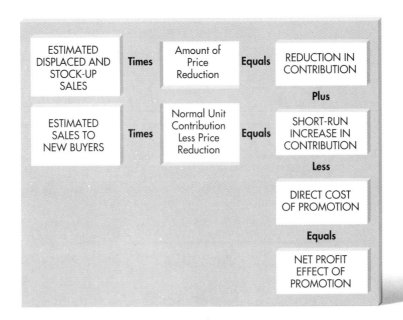

TABLE 11-3

ESTIMATING THE LIKELY PROFIT CONSEQUENCES OF LINKSTER'S PROMOTION

	0.5% REDEMPTION		1% REDEMPTION	
	15% DISPLACED	20% DISPLACED	15% DISPLACED	20% DISPLACED
Total redeemed	7,000	7,000	14,000	14,000
■ New buyers	5,950	5,600	11,900	11,200
■ Displaced sales	1,050	1,400	2,100	2,800
Increased contribution on sales to new buyers (at $16.75)	$99,663	$93,800	$199,325	$187,600
Minus lost contribution on displaced sales (at $20.25)	$21,263	$28,350	$42,525	$56,700
Minus increase in direct costs	$96,000	$96,000	$96,000	$96,000
Net impact on total contribution	($17,600)	($30,550)	$60,800	$34,900

that 15 to 20 percent of the redemptions will be displaced sales. Given these estimates, the estimated sales resulting from the coupon promotion will be between

$$1.4 \text{ million} \times .005 = 7000$$

and

$$1.4 \text{ million} \times .01 = 14,000$$

The profitability consequences of this promotion can be identified in Table 11-3. While each sale to a new buyer generates $16.75 in incremental contribution, each displaced sale reduces Linkster's contribution by $37.00 − $16.75, or $20.25. Subtracting the direct costs of $96,000 and the lost contribution on displaced sales from the incremental revenue from new buyers, yields the expected net impact in total contribution. As we can see, the consequences are quite sensitive to our estimates of redemption rate and displacement rate. Under the best conditions, the promotion generates a $60,800 gain, but under the most pessimistic estimates (that is, lower redemption and higher displacement), the promotion results in a $30,550 decrease in contribution.

It is important, however, that this (or any) promotion not be judged solely on the profit consequences. Some reduced profitability may well be acceptable to management if the promotion has achieved its primary objective of acquiring new customers.

In this particular case, nonregular buyers are expected to purchase between 5600 and 11,900 sweaters during the promotion, and many of these new customers are likely to purchase additional sweaters in the future. Of course, Linkster's marketing manager should also examine the company's experience and the buying process to determine whether the promotion will cannibalize sales of other products or create any drag-along sales from complementary products.

DIRECT MARKETING PROGRAMS

Direct marketing programs like mail-order catalog selling have existed for more than a century. In recent years, in the United States, this approach to marketing has become widely adopted and very diverse in its application. One reason for this growth is the expanded ownership of credit cards, which facilitates the completion of transactions stimulated by mail, telephone, television, or Internet-based marketing communications. (Additionally, an increasing number of vending machines accept credit cards.) A second factor is the increased computing power available for storing and analyzing large customer databases. (The cost of holding a customer's name, address, and purchase history on-line fell by a factor of 1000 between the 1970s and the 1990s.)[15] But, most significantly, direct marketing has grown because of the realization among marketing managers that there are great benefits from treating each customer as an individual. Indeed, most direct marketing program objectives reflect this orientation toward the customer as an individual.

Direct Marketing Objectives

A given direct marketing program can be designed to achieve a variety of specific objectives. Table 11-4 provides a list of these objectives. Many direct marketing programs will, in fact, be able to achieve more than one of these objectives, as we shall demonstrate below.

GENERATING LEADS OR TRIAL

Like traditional mass marketing, direct marketing can be used to expand a firm's customer base by attracting nonusers to a category or by acquiring competitors' customers. In some cases, direct marketers will solicit new customers through *direct response* advertising or telemarketing. Marketers acquire lists of people who appear to be prospects, based on factors such as their geographic location, age group, or readership of certain magazines. Direct sales efforts are then made through telemarketing or direct mail. For example, Fingerhut, which has seventy-five specialty catalogs covering specialty areas such as outdoor living, juvenile apparel and toys, and house-

---

[15]Robert Blattberg and John Deighton, "Interactive Marketing: Exploiting the Age of Addressability," *Sloan Management Review,* Fall 1991, p. 6.

TABLE 11-4	DIRECT MARKETING OBJECTIVES AND ALTERNATIVE PROGRAMS

OBJECTIVE	ALTERNATIVE PROGRAMS
Generate leads or trial	Direct response solicitation Point-of-purchase coupons Referral programs Inquiry generation through direct response
Expand customer relationships	Cross-selling programs based on purchase histories Upgrade programs
Retain customers	Frequency programs Targeted discounts
Reactivate former customers	Targeted discounts

wares, uses lists sold by magazines, financial companies, and other retailers. Customers are mailed a series of offerings with merchandise of progressively higher value to establish the creditworthiness and volume potential of each customer.[16]

A variation on this approach that can be implemented by manufacturers of packaged goods is *point-of-purchase coupons* targeted to users of competing brands. For example, earlier in this chapter we discussed the Catalina system, which programs store check-out registers to emit coupons, based on a shopper's scanned purchases. Many firms elect to provide such coupons only to people who purchase competing products—a practice that reduces displaced sales and the cost per coupon redeemed by new customers by two-thirds.[17]

For some complex products, such as expensive vacation homes or mutual funds, the marketing of a product involves the dissemination of extensive information. In such cases, the time and costs involved in communicating to customers are quite high, so direct marketers are more likely to use a two-step approach, first designing programs to build up leads (that is, lists of prime prospects), then applying the direct response program.[18] One approach is the *referral program* in which a firm's current customers receive incentives in exchange for providing the names of friends who ultimately become customers. Alternatively, managers may use *inquiry generation through direct response* to encourage prospects to call an 800 number for more information. For example, some discount stock brokers deal with only selected high-volume clients; they use television ads on business-related programming (such as cable network CNBC) to make investors aware of their low rates and encourage inquiries. Prospects who respond are later "qualified" to make certain their business volume will justify the firm's low rates.

---

[16]Bessen, op. cit., pp. 156–157.

[17]Walsh, op. cit., p. 234.

[18]Martin Baier, Henry Hoke, and Bob Stone, "Direct Marketing—What Is It?" in *Readings and Cases in Direct Marketing,* eds. H. Brown and B. Buskirk, NTC Publishing, Lincolnwood, Ill., 1992, pp. 8–10.

EXPANDING CUSTOMER RELATIONSHIPS

Because direct marketing involves the development of databases with customer pur-chase histories, managers are often able to obtain insights into the level and type of additional business that might be generated from individual customers.

Cross-selling programs are designed to call the customer's attention to and estab-lish a desire for complementary products. One such application is actor Robert Red-ford's *Sundance* catalog, which sells American handicrafts over the Internet. Cus-tomers can browse the catalog electronically and "click" on items they wish to order. An electronic order form is then produced on the screen. The system then suggests complementary products—such as a handmade scarf to go with a fringe jacket.[19]

Upgrading programs apply the same principle to move customers from less expen-sive to more expensive merchandise. The Women's Specialty Retail Group of U.S. Shoe operates Casual Corner, Petite Sophisticate, and several other women's clothing chains that incorporate a variety of direct marketing programs by using personalized incentives. Their upgrade programs are designed to focus on customers who have high long-range sales potential. They know, for example, that two customers may purchase the same dollar volume over a 6-month period, but if one customer's purchase includes a suit, the potential future sales of high-value merchandise to that customer is much greater.[20]

RETAINING CUSTOMERS

As noted in Chapter 7, more firms are recognizing the paramount importance of retain-ing customers. Accordingly, this objective is usually a dominant one for any estab-lished organization. Two main types of programs for achieving retention are targeted discounts and frequency programs.

Targeted discounts are the simplest approach. A firm simply provides existing cus-tomers with coupons or other incentives that can be used on future purchases. Some firms, however, prefer to focus these rewards on their best customers. Von's Super-markets, a leading California chain, has upgraded the traditional check-approval card into an electronic checking card that allows the chain to capture the sales histories of its customers across product categories. The store's best customers—those whose gro-cery bills are 2½ times that of the average Von's Supermarkets shopper—earn instant electronic discounts on all regular promotional items when their cards are swiped by checkout scanners. This assures the customer of receiving all applicable specials with-out the need to clip coupons. Additionally, these customers also receive many targeted coupons from manufacturers, based on their purchases.[21]

---

[19]John Verity and Robert Hof, "The Internet: How It Will Change the Way You Do Business," *Business Week,* Nov. 14, 1994, p. 84.

[20]"Building 'Share-of-Customer' Becomes a Priority at U.S. Shoe's Women's Specialty Retailing Group," *Colloquy,* vol. 4, no. 1, 1993, pp. 3–5.

[21]Larry Armstrong, "Coupon Clippers, Save Your Scissors," *Business Week,* June 20, 1994, pp. 164–165.

Frequency programs also provide incentives to keep customers coming back, but generally avoid couponing activities. Typically, these programs are presented in the context of some "membership" arrangement where benefits are gradually built up from repeat purchases. Airlines' "frequent flyer" programs are examples. Similarly, casinos have established "slot clubs" for customers who are heavy slot-machine players, rewarding heavy players by giving points good for free dinners and shows.[22] Fast-food retailer Arby's also uses this approach. Customers join "Club Arby's" by completing a free enrollment application giving their name, address, education level, occupation, and menu preferences. Members' personalized club cards are scanned at the register and they earn points for various Arby's food awards or for non-Arby's products such as theme park admissions. Arby's management believes the program has been more effective and less expensive than traditional couponing to customers, perhaps doubling repeat business in the stores using it at a cost of about 35 to 40 cents per repeat visit.[23]

REACTIVATING FORMER CUSTOMERS

Although management's attention is usually focused on current or new customers, many firms have found that time spent on lapsed customers can be productive. In many product categories, some loss of customers is to be expected over time because of the customers' desire for variety. In other cases, customers may have had a poor service experience. Reactivation programs can be designed to target both groups of customers with incentives.

For example, the Women's Specialty Retail Group of U.S. Shoe surveys former customers to find out why they have stopped shopping at a given store. Whether the shopper's decision was due to poor service, a desire for variety, or other reasons, these former customers are offered $10 coupons good on any merchandise worth $20 or more. The company finds this often leads to sales that match or exceed the $75 that the average shopper spends in one of these stores per trip.[24]

Relationship of Direct Marketing Objectives to Marketing Strategy

As with sales-promotion objectives, the different direct marketing program objectives will serve different types of marketing strategy. Generating leads and trial will be the objective when the marketing strategy is targeted toward creating new category users or acquiring competitors' customers. Reactivation will also serve as an objective for strategies directed toward acquiring competitors' customers, but only in those situations where a firm is trying to bring back former customers (as opposed to buyers who have never been customers). The special strengths of direct marketing lie in its

---

[22]Bruce Orwall, "Like Playing Slots? Casinos Know All about You," *Wall Street Journal,* Dec. 20, 1995, pp. B1–B3.

[23]"Club Arby's: 'Different Is Good,'" *Colloquy,* vol. 4, no. 3, 1993, pp. 12–13.

[24]"Building 'Share-of-Customer,'" op. cit., p. 4.

ability to use knowledge about past customer behavior. Thus, the other two types of direct marketing objectives support the basic strategy of retaining and expanding demand among current customers.

CONSIDERATIONS IN PROGRAM DESIGN

The effectiveness of a direct marketing program depends on (1) how *effective* it is in generating the desired response (that is, in achieving the direct marketing objective) and (2) how *efficient* it is as measured by the cost and profit consequences. The profitability issues will be examined in a later section of this chapter. The effectiveness of a direct marketing program depends very much on two key issues: the design of the marketing database and the process of using the database to select target customers (or potential customers).

Developing the Marketing Database

To be effective, a marketing database should enable managers to identify the best prospects for a given marketing offer. This means that managers should be able to identify past purchasing behavior and also predict how individuals will respond to specific offers. To achieve this, there are a number of guidelines that managers should follow in designing or modifying databases.[25]

1. Managers should use separate databases for existing customers and for prospects because different data will be needed for the two groups.
2. Both the customer database and the prospect database should contain records of all marketing initiatives that have been targeted to each household or business in the past.
3. The customer database should track purchase histories to show the *recency, frequency,* and *monetary value* of past purchases.
4. In addition to the above information, firms should add "profile" information, such as demographic, psychographic and lifestyle, and financial information about customers, either by surveying customers directly or by purchasing external databases such as those listed in Table 11-5.

USING PURCHASE HISTORY TO FORECAST RESPONSE

One major advantage of direct marketing is its ability to deliver specific offers efficiently by focusing the firm's effort on those customers who are most responsive. To accomplish this, direct marketers segment their customer base with respect to purchase history, with the most useful data being that pertaining to recency, frequency, and monetary value. *Recency* is usually measured by the amount of time since the customer's last purchase or by the number of consecutive offerings without a

---

[25]See Robert Blattberg and John Deighton, op. cit., pp. 13–14, for a comprehensive discussion of these points and other recommendations.

TABLE 11-5	**LEADING U.S. CONSUMER DATABASES**

Dun & Bradstreet—Fast Data
  Demographic data and some purchasing behavior on households

Equifax
  Individual financial and purchasing data based on credit card histories

R. R. Donnelly—Metromail
  Demographic, lifestyle, purchase data on most U.S. households

TRW
  Data on credit transactions

response. *Frequency* is most widely measured as the percentage of solicitations in some recent period that resulted in an order or by the number of orders in some recent period of time. *Monetary value* is the average order amount within some recent period of time.[26]

A typical traditional process for using these data is portrayed in Figure 11-4. A catalog firm has segmented a mailing list of 240,000 customers into high and low recency, high and low frequency, and high, medium, and low monetary value levels. Each customer is put into the group that characterizes his or her purchase history. By looking at historical records, or through experiments with a planned offer, the firm

FIGURE 11-4

Database segmentation by recentness, frequency, and monetary value: response rate by RFM group.

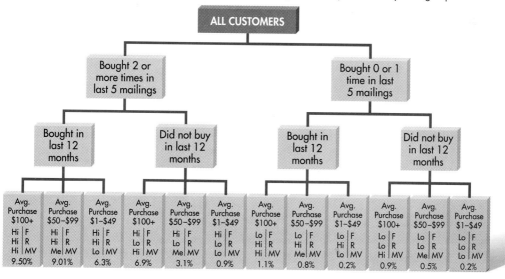

[26]See Mary Lou Roberts and Paul Berger, *Direct Marketing Management*, Prentice-Hall, Englewood Cliffs, N.J., 1989, pp. 105–107, for further discussion.

TABLE 11-6

RESULTS OF RECENCY/FREQUENCY/MONETARY VALUE SEGMENTATION

SEGMENT	NUMBER OF CUSTOMERS	RESPONSE RATE	TOTAL SALES
Hi F/Hi R/HiMV	12,000	.095	1,140
Hi F/Hi R/MeMV	20,000	.090	1,802
Hi F/Hi R/LoMV	10,000	.063	630
Hi F/Lo R/HiMV	8,000	.069	552
Hi F/Lo R/MeMV	8,000	.031	248
Hi F/Lo R/LoMV	13,000	.009	117
Lo F/Hi R/HiMV	24,000	.011	264
Lo F/Hi R/MeMV	21,000	.008	168
Lo F/Hi R/LoMV	25,000	.002	50
Lo F/Lo R/HiMV	18,000	.009	162
Lo F/Lo R/MeMV	38,000	.005	190
Lo F/Lo R/LoMV	43,000	.002	86
Total	240,000	.022	5,409

can estimate the response rate for each segment. When differences in response rates and differences in segment size are taken into account (as demonstrated in Table 11-6) we see how the database can enhance efficiency. Our firm can send the offer to all 240,000 customers and realize 5409 responses for an aggregate response rate of 2.2 percent, or decide to target only the best segments (for example, the five segments in which response exceeds 3 percent) and realize 4372 customer responses out of 58,000 solicitations (for a response rate of 7.5 percent), while incurring one-fourth the mailing costs. Of course, recalling our discussion of direct marketing objectives, there will also be times when a reactivation objective or an upgrade objective are established. In such situations, the firm may decide to select low recency or low frequency customers for special promotions. The most typical use however, is to apply the firm's direct marketing dollars in a way that targets the best customers.

In recent years, direct marketers have become more sophisticated in their applications of statistical techniques for the segmentation of databases. Additional purchase history data (such as the type of product purchased) can now be added to the segmentation process. New techniques can determine with greater precision just how to split the customer base to identify the most homogeneous segments.[27] Nevertheless, RFM data are still the most valuable predictors of response.

INTEGRATING PROFILE INFORMATION WITH PURCHASE HISTORIES

The integration of profile information with the customer database can serve two functions. First, knowing a customer's age or preference for certain activities can assist managers in the design of incentives. Earlier, we saw how such information was used

---

[27]David Shepard Associates, "The Role of Modeling in the New Direct Marketing," in *The New Direct Marketing,* Irwin, Homewood, Ill., 1995, pp. 271–314.

by Fingerhut in its selection of prospects for certain types of specialty catalogs. Similarly, Arby's can select non-Arby's merchandise incentives for various Arby's Club members by using such information. (Senior citizens are likely to be less responsive to incentives for amusement parks than families with young children.)

A second use of the external database is to help select new prospects that share common features with best customers. For example, a firm may have data on its best customers, based largely on purchase histories. To find new prospects who are likely to be similar in purchase patterns, some firms will search for common characteristics that provide clues to why some individuals are better customers. These are likely to be demographic or lifestyle characteristics in the case of consumer products and perhaps firm size or type of product line in the case of business customers. An external database that contains such data can be analyzed to determine the characteristics of the best customers. Consider the hypothetical example presented in Table 11-7. In this illustration, a business that sells new books directly to members of its "club" at a discount has bought one of these external lists. Searching for its own customers among those in the external database, it finds three of its high-value customers and three of its lesser-value customers. (Of course, most people on such lists will be noncustomers.) As the table shows, the three "best" customers share three characteristics in common: they are between 45 and 60 years of age, have incomes between $30,000 and $70,000, and have no children at home. Low-value customers do *not* share those characteristics, but at least one noncustomer does—C. Stengel. Thus, that customer (and others sharing such key characteristics) would be considered for the prospect list.

| TABLE 11-7 | **COMBINING INTERNAL AND EXTERNAL DATABASES** |

NAMES	INTERNAL DATA	EXTERNAL DATA				
		AGE	INC	CHI	SPO	LIM
M. Ciccone	B	45–60	$30–70K	0	Y	$10K
R. Jackson	B	45–60	$30–70K	0	N	$15K
G. Nash	B	45–60	$30–70K	0	N	$4K
G. Bush	N	60+	$70K+	3+	Y	$4K
C. Chase	N	45–60	$70K+	3+	N	$15K
C. Stengel	N	45–60	$30–70K	0	N	$3K
T. Aikman	O	25–44	$70K+	1	Y	$6K
J. Canseco	O	25–44	Under $30K	0	Y	$10K
S. Stone	O	60+	Under $30K	2	Y	$6K

Key
B = high-value customer
N = noncustomer
O = low-value customer
AGE = age of household head
INC = total household income
CHI = number of children at home
SPO = does household head enjoy outdoor sports?
LIM = household credit card limit

In practice, the process just described is a simplified example of a "scoring model." Usually there are a number of characteristics that can be used to profile customers and prospects. Moreover, the statistical analyses involved in selecting the characteristics to use are somewhat complex. The most basic approach would use a multiple regression approach like that discussed in the sales forecasting section of Chapter 5. The various techniques are designed to help managers find the combination of characteristics that best predict high-value purchasing behavior.[28]

PROFITABILITY ISSUES

The basic profitability concepts presented in Chapter 6 are directly applicable to the development of direct marketing budgets. However, in applying these concepts, it is important to understand (1) the distinctive economics of direct marketing and (2) the concept of lifetime value.

The Distinctive Economics of Direct Marketing

As discussed earlier, the uniqueness of direct marketing lies in its philosophy of targeting communications and product delivery directly to individual customers. Two consequences of this are (1) the elimination of distributors (and, thus, of the need to pay for their services) and (2) the opportunity for more efficient application of the marketing budget.[29]

Consider, for example, the situation at Linkster—the manufacturer of golf sweaters and other apparel discussed both in Chapter 6 and earlier in this chapter. Linkster has been selling its line through retail golf shops, using a sales force to call on these firms and contacting potential consumers through magazine advertising. The first column of Table 11-8 summarizes the economics of marketing Linkster sweaters through its traditional indirect channel to the consumer (using the price, cost, and contribution data for Linkster sweaters from Tables 6-3 and 6-4).

Alternatively, Linkster could use direct marketing by, for example, soliciting sweater orders by mail from purchased lists of subscribers to golf magazines and shipping direct to the consumer. The economics of this approach differ in two respects. First, elimination of the retailer allows Linkster to receive the full retail price of the product as opposed to the price paid by the retailer to Linkster. Assuming retail golf shops were pricing the product to consumers at $90, this becomes the new manufacturer's selling price. (Note: our analysis assumes that consumers also pay the cost of delivery in addition to the retail price.) Partially offsetting this gain is the additional

---

[28]For an introductory view of the various methods, see Behram Hansotia, "List Segmentation: How to Find Your Best Prospects," in Brown and Buskirk, eds., op. cit., pp. 103–113.

[29]For more detailed discussion see Pierre Pasavant, *The Dollars and Sense of Direct Mail,* Dependable Lists, New York, 1981.

| TABLE 11-8 | PROFITABILITY STRUCTURE OF DIRECT MARKETING VERSUS INDIRECT CHANNELS FOR LINKSTER SWEATERS |

	INDIRECT CHANNEL	DIRECT MARKETING
Manufacturer's selling price	$60	$90
Less variable costs per unit		
Cost of goods sold	−20	−20
Sales commissions	−3	−0
Fulfillment	−0	−4
Variable-contribution margin per unit	$37	$66
Times unit sales	×40,000	×40,000
Dollar variable-contribution margin	$1,480,000	$2,640,000
Less fixed costs		
Sales force	−360,000	−0
Mass advertising	−200,000	−0
Design and production	−640,000	−640,000
Mail (@$400 per 1000)*	−0	−800,000
Total contribution	$ 280,000	$1,200,000

*At a 2% response rate, Linkster will need to solicit 2 million potential buyers to sell 40,000 units. That is, 2 million × 2% = 40,000. The mail cost is therefore: (2,000,000 ÷ 1,000) × $400 = $800,000.

cost of *fulfillment* (that is, of processing each customer's order and preparing it for shipment). Second, while some direct marketing (such as direct response ads on television or in magazines) remains geared toward mass audiences, targeted telephone and direct mail marketing typically lead to reduced sales force and mass advertising costs.

These economic consequences can be observed from Table 11-8. In this table, Linkster can contrast the profitability of direct and indirect marketing by estimating the number of direct mail solicitations required to generate the 40,000 units of sales volume currently generated through indirect channels. For example, if Linkster expects a 2 percent response rate, the firm needs to solicit 2 million prospects (that is, 2,000,000 × .02 = 40,000). Inspection of Table 11-8 reveals why direct marketing is so appealing to many firms. Even with the large direct mail cost, Linkster's profitability will increase dramatically through the elimination of advertising and selling costs and because of the higher variable contribution per unit from eliminating the retailer. Additionally, as Linkster develops a customer database that allows management to identify frequent or high-value customers, its efficiency will increase even more. For example, if Linkster could increase its response rate to 5 percent (using the database analysis approaches discussed in the preceding section of this chapter), the number of solicitations required to generate sales to 40,000 customers would then be:

$$\frac{40,000}{.05} = 800,000 \text{ prospects}$$

At a mailing cost of $400 per thousand, the total cost of solicitation would be:

$$\frac{800,000}{1,000} \times \$400 = \$320,000$$

This represents a fixed cost reduction (and, therefore, an increase in total contribution) of $480,000 when compared to a mailing that would solicit 2 million prospects.

Lifetime Value of a Customer

When the primary objective of a direct marketing program is either new-customer acquisition or customer reactivation, managers should attempt to estimate the *lifetime value* of each of these customers. Essentially, the lifetime value of a customer is what acquisition of that customer is worth, taking into account future purchases as well as initial purchases. Solicitations for products like *Sports Illustrated* magazine and Columbia House Video Club often include seemingly exorbitant incentives to motivate purchases. Understanding the lifetime value allows managers in such firms to determine how much can be profitably spent to acquire new customers or reactivate old ones.[30]

Returning to our Linkster sweaters example, recall from earlier in this chapter that Linkster is considering a $20 coupon offer to prospective buyers. By considering the lifetime value of acquiring a new Linkster customer, managers may find that a larger incentive may be appropriate—especially now that Linkster is selling direct and receiving a higher unit variable-contribution margin.

The process of estimating lifetime value is very similar to the approach (discussed in Chapter 6) used to estimate the benefits of repeat purchases that result from programs designed to improve customer satisfaction. The major difference is that, here, we are estimating the potential value of *future* rather than *existing* customers. To determine lifetime value, a firm normally analyzes the customer database to estimate the average repeat purchase rate and the average dollar purchase. Additionally, managers will need to know the average variable-contribution margin on all products. (Recall from Chapter 6 that Linkster's percentage variable-contribution margin varies across its different products.)

Table 11-9 offers a simplified example of how lifetime value might be calculated. Based on the firm's historical data, 38 percent of new customers never repurchase a product from Linkster, but a small percentage repeat several times. Weighting the number of repeats by the percent of buyers displaying each purchasing pattern allows Linkster to calculate that 1.55 repeats can be expected from the "average" new customer. Combining this with the information on the average dollar amount of a sale and the average variable-contribution margin allows the firm to forecast lifetime value. Linkster can then assess how much it can afford to spend to acquire each average customer. (Based on Table 11-8, Linkster plans on spending $800,000 to attract 40,000 new customers—or $20 per customer. Adding the proposed $20 incentive gives a total "acquisition cost" per customer of $40. This is well below the lifetime value of $177.60.)

---

[30]Other examples of lifetime value calculations are available in Arthur Hughes, *The Complete Database Marketer,* Probus Publishing, Chicago, 1991, chap. 10.

| TABLE 11-9 | **LIFETIME VALUE OF A NEW LINKSTER CUSTOMER** |

LIFETIME VALUE OF A NEW LINKSTER CUSTOMER

NUMBER OF REPEAT PURCHASES	×	PERCENT OF LINKSTER CUSTOMERS	=	WEIGHTED AVERAGE
0		.38		0
1		.21		.21
2		.15		.30
3		.10		.30
4		.08		.32
5		.06		.30
6		.02		.12
		1.00		1.55

Average number of repeats	1.55
Times average dollar sale	× $120
Times average variable-contribution margin	× .60
Total variable-contribution margin on repeat sales	$111.60
Plus variable contribution on initial sale (from Table 11-8)	66.00
Lifetime value	$177.60

The examination of the lifetime value concept reinforces a point made several times in this book in various ways. That is, managers should avoid thinking of customers in terms of individual transactions and, instead, focus on continuing relationships. Additionally, managers should also focus on the segmentation opportunities provided by analysis of the customer database. Clearly, lifetime value is based on frequency and monetary value. So, if the solicitation can be targeted to prospects likely to have high RFM scores (as discussed earlier), the lifetime value of the new customers (and, thus, the amount a firm should be willing to spend) can be much larger.

CONCLUSION

High rates of growth in sales-promotion and direct marketing activity appear to reflect the effectiveness of these marketing programs in influencing demand. However, some cautionary notes are in order to managers using these programs.

First, as noted earlier, the long-term impact of sales promotions on brand equity is not certain. Some believe that promotion can damage the brand image, especially if it is not combined with advertising or other programs that build brand-benefit linkages. So, managers should attempt to develop a high degree of coordination between advertising and sales-promotion programs and should involve advertising agencies in the sales-promotion decision process.

Second, sales promotions and direct marketing must often be coordinated with advertising programs (to communicate the offer) and with personal selling programs (to follow up on customers' inquiries and trade support). This means clearly defined objectives and logically developed and integrated programs will be essential if these programs are to work in a synchronized way to implement the marketing strategy.

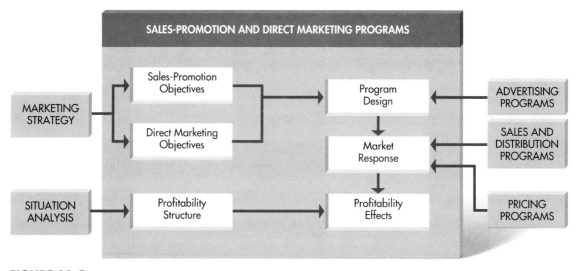

FIGURE 11-5

Relationship of sales-promotion and direct marketing programs to marketing strategy, situation analysis, and other marketing programs.

In this chapter, we have presented several concepts and tools managers can use to develop effective sales-promotion and direct marketing programs. In addition, we have shown how specific programs and program objectives can and should be linked to the marketing strategy and the product's profitability requirements. This process is summarized in Figure 11-5.

To review some of these elements and their relationships to one another, consider the sales-promotion and direct marketing programs being considered by LapCom Computer.

LAPCOM COMPUTER

LapCom is a manufacturer of sophisticated laptop computers and currently sells its product line through specialty computer stores. The company caters to the knowledgeable computer user in the business community, offering an unmatched combination of power, compactness, and versatility, as well as built-in software and interfaces for fast Internet access and fax capability.

LapCom's retailers purchase the machines at a price of $2550 and retail them at a price of $3000, on average. The variable cost to LapCom is $1800 per machine, and LapCom's total sales and advertising budget is $25 million. Sales in 1996 were 100,000 units, a very small share of the industry, and management is attempting to identify ways to expand the sales base. (While customers are loyal, the repurchase interval for laptops is fairly long for most customers.)

One option being considered is a $200 rebate offer during a 2-month period. Buyers of new Lap-Com computers would receive a check for that amount by sending in proof of purchase (warranty cards plus sales slips). The marketing manager has estimated that the offer would result in sales of between 20,000 and 30,000 units with a displacement rate of 40 to 60 percent.

Alternatively, LapCom is thinking about initiating a direct marketing program. Using the mailing lists from selected computer magazines plus the company's internal database (which has been built up over the years from warranty cards), LapCom would solicit orders directly, offering the computers at a price of $2600. The cost of direct mail will run about $500 per thousand and fulfillment costs will be $50 per order. Other fixed marketing costs will be about $10 million.

1. Evaluate the proposed rebate program in terms of the potential profitability consequences.
2. What other considerations should LapCom take into account in deciding on the rebate plan?
3. If LapCom were to achieve a 1 percent response, would the total contribution from direct marketing be more or less than the current total contribution from the indirect channel?
4. What additional considerations should LapCom take into account in deciding on the direct marketing plan?

QUESTIONS AND SITUATIONS FOR DISCUSSION

1. What sales-promotion objective and program would be most appropriate for each of the following? Why?
   a. A leading brand of spaghetti
   b. A new substance-abuse health care facility
   c. A lawn-care company
   d. A sports magazine
2. Giorgio of Beverly Hills decided to introduce a perfume called *Red* for a slightly older and wealthier target market than those targeted by the firm's other perfumes. Giorgio's research had revealed that, if a woman wore a fragrance at least three times, she was likely to buy it. The company obtained mailing lists of department stores' preferred charge customers and mailed them a 3-day sample supply of *Red* in red tubes along with announcements that the product would be available at their department stores in 2 weeks. *Red* achieved a $90 million sales volume in its first year, and became the leading seller.

   Discuss how the design of this program would have influenced the nature of the market response.
3. For which of the following are stock-up effects likely to be greatest? Explain your reasoning.
   a. Coca-Cola
   b. Jell-O instant pudding
   c. Maxwell House ground coffee
   d. Alpo dog food (40-pound bag)
4. Earlier in this chapter, it was noted that promotions on premium-priced brands are more effective in attracting customers from lower-priced brands than promotions on lower-priced brands are in attracting customers who normally buy pre-

mium brands. Does this mean that, when the leading market-share brand is a premium brand, managers should always be aggressive in using sales promotion? Explain.

5. In general, which of the following kinds of sales responses do you think would be most *difficult* to predict for a firm with extensive experience in sales promotion?

   a. Displacement rates

   b. Conversion rates

   c. Coupon redemption rates

6. Some direct marketers rely very heavily on direct response advertising that is targeted at demographic groups, lifestyle groups, or viewers of specific types of television shows, rather than at individuals. For example, marketers of exercise equipment and of compact discs containing the "top tunes of the '80s" often use ESPN2, whose viewers are interested in athletics and are fairly young. Given all the advantages of targeting messages to the individual buyer that we discussed in this chapter, what conditions would lead a firm to use these other forms of direct marketing?

7. In 1996, a woman sued Victoria's Secret, accusing the company of charging different prices to different recipients of its catalog. Specifically, she claimed that she received an offer of a $10 discount on a purchase of $75 from the winter catalog, whereas another person (who was male and wealthier) received a $25 discount offer with the same catalog.

   a. If the allegation were true, why would Victoria's Secret pursue such a policy?

   b. Is such a policy unfair to consumers? Why or why not?

8. The Quaker Oats Company launched Quaker Direct, a system that delivers coupons for Quaker products to households that are individually targeted, based on a database developed by Computerize Marketing Technologies of New York. With this system, Quaker can be certain that only households with dogs receive coupons for Gaines Burgers. Moreover, coupon values can be varied by household. Finally, because each coupon is coded, Quaker can track redemptions by households. The system also allows Quaker to design surveys that would detect changing customer needs. To attract and retain these households, Quaker might run sweepstakes and contests for participants.

   The cost of Quaker Direct is about $27.50 per 1000 households reached. This is four times the cost of distributing free-standing insert coupons in newspapers. Given this higher cost, what offsetting benefits might such a system provide for Quaker?

SUGGESTED ADDITIONAL READINGS

Basu, Amiya, Atasi Basu, and Rajeev Batra, "Modeling the Response Pattern to Direct Marketing Campaigns," *Journal of Marketing Research,* May 1995, pp. 204–212.

Bawa, Kapil, and Robert Shoemaker, "Analyzing Incremental Sales from a Direct Mail Coupon Promotion," *Journal of Marketing,* July 1989, pp. 66–78.

Bessen, Jim, "Riding the Marketing Information Wave," *Harvard Business Review*, September–October 1993, pp. 150–160.

Blattberg, Robert, Richard Briesch, and Edward Fox, "How Promotions Work," *Marketing Science*, Fall 1995, pp. G122–G132.

———, and John Deighton, "Interactive Marketing: Exploiting the Age of Addressability," *Sloan Management Review*, Fall 1991, pp. 5–14.

Fader, Peter, and Leonard Lodish, "A Cross-Category Analysis of Category Structure and Promotional Activity for Grocery Products," *Journal of Marketing*, October 1990, pp. 52–64.

Farris, Paul, and John A. Quelch, "In Defense of Price Promotion," *Sloan Management Review*, Fall 1987, pp. 63–69.

Jones, John Philip, "The Double Jeopardy of Sales Promotions," *Harvard Business Review*, September–October 1990, pp. 145–152.

CHAPTER 12

SALES AND DISTRIBUTION PROGRAMS

OVERVIEW

Sales and distribution programs include all activities that involve direct personal contact with final buyers or with wholesale or retail intermediaries. Principally, these activities focus on three functions.

- Communicating individually tailored sales messages
- Providing customer service—information or assistance regarding product features, order status, or complaints for individual customers
- Creating value for customers by coordinating the scheduling and methods of product/service delivery to provide convenience, reliability, and support

These activities are of paramount importance in executing a marketing strategy when individual buyers or distributors have highly complex and varied needs and wants. In such circumstances, personal interaction is critical to properly understand and respond to each customer's buying situation or problem.

Although the range of activities involved in sales and distribution programs seems rather broad, in reality, these activities are all part of the sales function in a typical organization. Indeed, individual salespeople often spend more time on the many customer service activities than on *selling* per se. Additionally, as we discuss later in this chapter, salespeople may find that customers' logistics needs associated with the frequency, size, and timeliness of product shipments are as important as product quality or list price in making a sale.

Essentially, every product or service must be communicated and distributed to the customer through a marketing channel. These same basic activities take place whether a firm is selling directly to final buyers or through an extensive number of intermediaries. In small industrial firms, in particular, the same salespeople or sales managers may have the responsibility for both direct sales to buyers and for working with intermediaries in the marketing channel. The emergence of marketing intermediaries results from either buyers or sellers working with others to assist them in communicating or distributing the product to complete the transaction. The involvement of other parties beyond the buyer and seller means that the value associated with transactions that normally would exist between the buyer and seller must now be shared with these intermediaries in exchange for the services they provide, or additional value must be created for these services and shared among the participants as well as the buyer. Normally, this is accomplished through the pricing programs that exist among the participants in the marketing channel.

Because the topics of personal selling, customer service, distribution-channel relationships, and physical distribution policy are so highly integrated, they must be viewed as parts of comprehensive sales and distribution programs. In some companies, employees from other areas of the company such as marketing, finance, distribution, and operations have been assigned to coordinate with sales and work with key buyers to facilitate such coordination and integration.

In addition, an outside service provider such as a warehousing company or rail carrier may provide an integral part of the sales and distribution strategy and program. In this chapter and the next, we examine the process for developing and evaluating these programs. Four major steps are required in this process.

1. Defining sales and distribution *objectives* designed to implement the firm's marketing strategy
2. Identifying the most appropriate sales *appeals* to be used in accomplishing objectives
3. Determining and assigning the human and financial *resources* required for the program
4. Evaluating the program *performance* in order to adjust the program as necessary

The first two of these steps are examined in this chapter. In particular, we will present the kinds of objectives that can be used to guide the sales and distribution effort and the kinds of appeals the firms can employ. Subsequently, we will discuss the factors to be considered in selecting the best appeal and the best approaches that the sales force can use in presenting and gaining acceptance of the sales appeal. Finally, we will examine some of the unique considerations involved in selling through distributors.

Before examining sales and distribution objectives, however, it is important to understand the basic types of *sales and marketing channel systems* that can be employed by organizations. An understanding of these types of systems is important because the specific role of the sales force in implementing a marketing strategy will vary across these types of systems. (Figure 12-1 shows the main elements of a sales and distribution program.)

TYPES OF SALES AND MARKETING CHANNEL SYSTEMS

In addition to direct marketing systems (discussed in Chapter 11), marketers can employ three other basic types of sales and distribution systems. As summarized in Table 12-1, each of these systems differs in terms of the role played by personal selling.

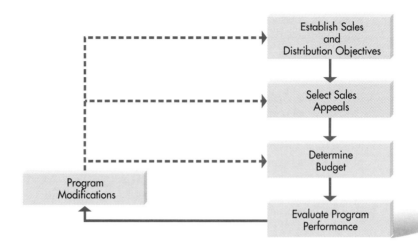

FIGURE 12-1

Elements of a sales
and distribution
program.

Direct Personal Selling Systems

As with direct marketing systems, in direct personal selling systems products are shipped directly to the customer. However, unlike direct-marketing systems most sales messages are delivered face to face. Note that this direct selling may be performed by a manufacturer's own sales force or by commissioned sales representatives. Technically, such representatives are agent wholesalers, but they perform only selling activities, so if they call only on final buyers they function as a direct sales force. Direct personal selling is used when the role of the sales force is more complex than the presentation of a simple sales message and asking for the order. Specifically, these salespeople focus their efforts on helping customers solve selected purchasing problems by demonstrating how a product (or service) can be used or adapted to fit customer needs. Additionally, they may also be responsible for identifying new products that might be developed to satisfy these needs. (Du Pont developed a flexible sales team recruited from all executive ranks to develop and sell new products. In 1990, this group identified the need for a new herbicide that corn growers could apply less often than existing herbicides and created a product that had $57 million in sales its first year.[1]) Finally, they may also perform *customer service* activities such as following up on customer complaints; providing maintenance, repair, and operating (MRO) services; assuring reliable delivery; providing information on inventories and order processing; and assisting customers in managing spare parts inventories.

Trade Selling Systems

When organizations employ wholesalers and/or retailers to physically distribute products to final customers, a major role for the sales force is to assure that distributors are willing and able to support the marketing strategy. Accordingly, the sales force is usually called on to demonstrate to distributors how they can benefit from following

[1]"Smart Selling," *Business Week,* Aug. 3, 1992, p. 48.

specific policies that also enhance a manufacturer's sales. These policies can include promotion, service, space allocation, inventory, and production-assortment decisions. Additionally, this sales force may be responsible for providing distributors with the same kinds of customer service support that the direct sales force provides for the final buyer.

For example, RJR's Nabisco Biscuit runs a "direct store delivery" distribution system. Instead of shipping to central warehouses, company trucks deliver to 105,000 stores about three times a week. Nabisco's 400 merchandisers build store displays and organize shelves. The 2800 Nabisco sales reps use handheld computers to collect sales data for individual stores and help retail buyers configure their shelf space most productively. This system led to a change in Nabisco's new-product strategy so that new products with high demand don't outstrip the bakery's ability to fill orders in a timely fashion.[2]

Missionary Selling Systems

Missionary selling also involves activities that enhance distributors' sales. However, these activities are primarily directed toward final buyers or toward individuals who influence the buying decision rather than toward distributors. For instance, a

TABLE 12-1	**TYPES OF SALES AND MARKETING CHANNEL SYSTEMS**

TYPES	KEY CHARACTERISTICS
	DIRECT SYSTEMS
1. Direct personal selling systems	Products distributed directly to final buyer
	Sales message delivered to individual buyers by face-to-face contact (Telephone selling may be used for order taking.)
	Primary functions are to provide product information, technical advice, customer service; identify changing customer needs
	INDIRECT SYSTEMS
1. Trade selling systems	Products distributed through wholesalers or retailers who usually buy for resale to final buyers
	Sales message delivered by face-to-face contact (Telephone selling may be used for order taking.)
	Primary functions are to obtain distributor support, provide product information, provide sales training and assistance to distributors
2. Missionary selling systems	Products distributed through wholesalers or retailers who usually buy for resale to final buyers
	Sales message delivered by face-to-face contact
	Primary function is to provide product information and customer service directly to final buyer or to those who influence buyers

[2]"This Cookie Is Tops in Food Sales," *Fortune,* May 4, 1992, p. 100.

hospital-equipment manufacturer may use a wholesaler, but will rely on its own missionary sales force to provide product information to key hospital personnel. Similarly, publishers use their own sales force to call on college professors, who influence students' purchases of textbooks, even though a local bookstore is used to distribute the product. These kinds of sales forces are employed when distributors' salespeople are inadequately trained or insufficient in number to provide the technical information required. Additionally, when distributors carry extremely wide and diverse product lines and when new products are developed at a high rate (as happens in the pharmaceutical industry), the missionary sales force will be especially useful.

The foregoing characterization suggests that there are significant differences in the role of the sales force across sales and distribution systems. However, there are also many differences in the role of the sales force *within* each type of system, as each selling organization has different products, customers, competitors, and strategies. Moreover, some organizations will employ more than one type of system. For example, in marketing personal computers IBM uses both direct marketing and direct personal selling systems, as well as selling to the trade. Companies will use different distribution systems depending on their size as shown in Table 12-2. Finally, when selling through distributors, the type of system used will have a bearing on the design of sales and distribution programs. We examine some distribution channel alternatives in the next section of this chapter.

DISTRIBUTION CHANNEL STRUCTURE

A *distribution channel* is a set of organizational participants that performs all the functions required to get a product from a seller to the final buyer. The distribution system could include "primary" channel participants (wholesalers and retailers who take title and risk) and "specialized" channel participants (freight companies, freight forwarders, public warehouses, and brokers who market and move the product). In addition, "facilitating" channel members (banks, communication firms, market research firms, retail merchandising companies, and so on) could also be participants in the

TABLE 12-2

COMPANIES USING DIFFERENT DISTRIBUTION ALTERNATIVES (by percent)

SIZE OF COMPANY (SALES IN MILLIONS)	TELEMARKETING	MFG. REPS.	DISTRIBUTORS/ WHOLESALER	MAJOR NATIONAL ACCOUNT REPS
Less than $5	34.5	20.7	32.8	5.2
$5–25	21.6	52.6	48.5	5.2
$25–100	24.5	36.7	51.1	12.2
$100–250	44.0	20.0	48.0	16.0
$250+	25.0	8.3	58.3	29.2

Adapted from "Twenty-Sixth Survey of Sales Force Compensation," The Dartnell Corp., Chicago, 1990.

distribution channel. The structure of the channel is determined by three elements: the *tasks* and activities to be performed by intermediaries, the *type* of distributor to be used, and the *number* of each type of distributor.[3]

Tasks

Firms use channel participants to perform those marketing tasks that a seller cannot perform as effectively or efficiently or is not willing to perform. The most widely executed tasks include maintaining availability through local delivery or by having the product at locations convenient to the customer, providing customer financing and maintenance or repair services, and local selling and advertising of the product's benefits. These tasks are most likely to be carried out by one or more channel participants rather than the supplier when

- There are large numbers of buyers, each of whom purchases in small dollar amounts so that the cost of making personal sales calls on each one would be very high if performed by a manufacturer.
- A detailed knowledge of local market conditions and buyer needs is important because customers vary dramatically in their needs.
- Special emergency service is important.
- Competitors provide a high level of availability, and therefore convenience or speed of delivery is necessary to be competitive.
- Buyers purchase a wide assortment of related products in small volumes while the manufacturer provides only a narrow assortment and, thus, cannot meet the buyer's full range of needs.
- Participants seek to benefit from the synergy of working together to provide customer satisfaction and loyalty.

In other words, the tasks that must be performed will depend on what is needed to competitively meet customer needs and on the relative economic efficiency of performing or delegating the task.

Type of Wholesale-Level Distributor

A manufacturer considering the use of wholesale-level distributors has a variety of options. The major differences among types of wholesalers are in the type and number of functions they perform. Whereas all wholesale-level intermediaries provide a selling function, only merchant wholesalers assume the risk associated with taking title to goods as they move toward the final buyer. Not surprisingly, these wholesalers also receive the largest margins on the sales they make—as high as 25 percent compared to 3 to 7 percent for most agents and brokers who do not take title to the goods. This distinction in functions between merchant wholesalers and agents (or brokers) is the reason why merchant wholesalers are part of a trade selling system, whereas

---

[3]For a comprehensive examination of distribution channels, see Louis Stern, Adel El-Ansary, and James Brown, *Management in Marketing Channels,* Prentice-Hall, Englewood Cliffs, N.J., 1989.

agents are basically just substitutes for a manufacturer's sales force. Thus, when agents call on other intermediaries (as is the case with food brokers), they are part of a trade selling system. If they call on final buyers, they are part of a direct selling system.

Type of Retailer

Retailers differ in terms of three major factors: the extent of the product lines they carry, the type of consumer search effort they cater to, and the level of service offered. The type of retail intermediary employed will depend upon the firm's target markets. For example, in catering to a price-oriented market, stores that are classified as shopping goods–oriented are more likely to be chosen. In attempting to reach a market that is concerned with personal service and an image of quality, specialty stores are generally more appropriate.

At both the wholesale and the retail level, sales managers should target their efforts toward distributors who will perform the required tasks and who are of the type desired to reach the target market.

Number of Distributors

Channels may have an *intensive* pattern of distribution (in which a relatively large number of distributors exist for a given area) or a *selective* pattern of distribution (in which only a few distributors exist for a given area). At the extreme, a distributor may be designated the *exclusive* representative in an area. In general, the more functions a distributor is expected to perform, the more likely an exclusive or selective pattern of distribution will be necessary as a protective measure to provide the incentive for holding large inventories, for offering service, and for aggressive promotion. Selective distribution has other advantages for a supplier as well. When a firm has fewer distributors, the selling costs, delivery costs, and costs of monitoring distributor performance are usually lower. These advantages exist because fewer sales personnel are needed and because fewer points of delivery (normally with more economically sized loads) are required.

However, traditional exclusive distribution systems may be inappropriate if consumer shopping patterns and market conditions change. Goodyear Tire and Rubber in March 1992 announced plans to sell Goodyear brand tires through Sears as well as its own exclusive network of 2500 independent dealers. Goodyear's decision was based on its continual study of other distribution alternatives and the growth of large super retailers such as Sears, Kmart, Wal-Mart, and others. Since that announcement, hundreds of Goodyear dealers have adopted private brands, which offer them higher margins and lower their incentive to sell Goodyear Tires.[4]

---

[4]Dana Milband, "Independent Goodyear Dealers Rebel: Decision to Sell through Sears Proves Unpopular," *Wall Street Journal,* July 8, 1992, p. B2; and "And Fix That Flat before You Go Stanley," *Business Week,* Jan. 16, 1995, p. 35.

On the other hand, to the extent that convenience in buying is very important to the buyer (especially for low-involvement consumer goods), more intensive distribution will be required. Accordingly, managers should be certain that the desired number of accounts in each market is considered before stating the specific number of new accounts to be developed.

Vertical Marketing Systems

The increased recognition of the importance of selling *through and not just to* the distributor led many firms to develop highly coordinated channels. The term *vertical marketing system* is generally used to describe types of channels in which distributor actions are very highly coordinated with the manufacturer's marketing strategy because a strong, continuing, formal relationship has been established. These systems can be of three types: corporate, contractual, and administered.

Corporate systems are channels in which some degree of vertical integration has taken place. That is, if a retailer is owned by a supplier (or vice versa) then a corporate system exists. Today, many oil companies, tire companies, and clothing companies own at least some of their retail outlets. Although the cost of owning distribution outlets may be great, the sales representatives are generally assured that the distribution outlets will fully support the marketing strategy.

For instance, France is the only major market in the world where Coke owns the bottling business. Previously, Pernod-Ricard, a large spirits producer, controlled Coke's bottling in France for 40 years. France had the lowest per capita consumption of Coke in the European community, and Coke attributes this to Pernod-Ricard's promotion of its own brands at the expense of Coke and Coca-Cola's other products. After Coke's purchase of bottling operations, unit volume in France rose 23 percent the first year. This was the largest increase on the continent.[5]

Contractual systems include franchising programs and voluntary associations in which legally binding contracts are established that specify the tasks which each party will perform. Specifically, *franchise* programs are contractual arrangements between a manufacturer and a retail- or wholesale-level distributor that specify what assistance suppliers will provide as well as the obligations of distributors. In recent years, these programs have been dominant in such retail businesses as automobile sales, fast-food restaurants, automotive supplies and services, and in some wholesaling businesses (including soft-drink bottling). These lines of trade are similar in several respects: distributors rely primarily on one supplier, extensive capital investment is required of the distributor, and maintenance of quality service standards is important. Because of these features, the franchisors and franchisees are highly dependent on each other.

When this does not occur, such distribution arrangements deteriorate rapidly, as in the case of Burger King. A series of misdirected advertising campaigns and lack of new products led to franchisee revolts. Under new leadership now, store design,

---

[5]Patricia Sellers, "Coke Gets Off Its Can in Europe," *Fortune,* Aug. 13, 1990, p. 70; and "Fizzing," *The Economist,* Sept. 4, 1993, pp. 63–65.

product development, and food research report to the CEO. This reorganization is designed to accelerate the introduction of new products and services that have been suggested by franchisees.[6]

Voluntary associations, on the other hand, are contractual systems organized by wholesalers or retailers to provide comprehensive merchandising and promotional programs to independent retailers. These programs are primarily designed to help wholesalers' customers maintain competitive posture in relation to franchised or vertically integrated chain retailers. IGA food stores and Western Auto stores are among the organizations falling into this category.

Administered systems are channels in which distributors have no contractual or ownership dependency on a supplier. Essentially, these manufacturers provide a wide range of incentives in exchange for extensive promotional support and for carrying large inventories and a full line of products. These systems are employed by firms such as O. M. Scott and Sons (lawn and garden products) and Kraft (food products) to provide distributors with comprehensive merchandising advice, protective provisions (such as exclusive distributorships), and direct financial assistance.

SALES AND DISTRIBUTION OBJECTIVES

Given a marketing strategy, managers can define one or more basic objectives for the sales and distribution program. Further, these objectives should be defined in specific terms in order to provide direction to the sales force and establish a basis for evaluating program success.

Of course, the most specific kind of objective that can be set and the easiest to measure is a dollar or unit-sales objective. And indeed, sales volume is an important program objective and a widely used basis for evaluating salesperson, sales-territory, and program performance. However, in most cases, sales volume will not be adequate as a program objective, for several reasons.

First, sales and distribution programs cost money. In many cases distribution costs, including selling costs, have been estimated to be as much as 30 to 40 percent of a product's cost.[7] Efforts designed to increase sales may not lead to increased profitability, for reasons discussed in Chapter 13. Accordingly, a sales objective may not be consistent with a product objective of increased profitability. Second, sales results are often determined by competitors' actions, environmental forces, or other marketing programs outside the control of the sales force. Third, the primary role of a marketing program is to implement a marketing strategy. Because the marketing strategy defines target markets and the kind of impact on demand to be achieved, program objectives should reflect the marketing strategy, and simply establishing a sales or profit objective will not reflect the strategy very precisely. Fourth, and finally, a sales objective does not provide the sales force with any guidance on *how*

---

[6]"Sid Fettenstein Is Having It His Way," *Business Week,* Nov. 23, 1992, p. 64.
[7]Rita Koselka, "Distribution Revolution," *Forbes,* May 25, 1992, p. 58.

to increase (or maintain) sales volume. Managers should be responsible for providing direction to the sales force by helping identify the best opportunities for sales development.

In sum, although sales-volume objectives are useful, managers should also establish sales and distribution objectives that

- Reflect the marketing strategy
- Contribute to customer satisfaction and loyalty
- Provide a focus for sales-force activities
- Identify the targets from which future sales volume will come
- Can be used to evaluate sales-force efforts as well as results

In general, four kinds of sales and distribution objectives can be employed (each of which should be stated in specific terms): account development, distributor support, account maintenance, and account penetration.

1. *Account-development* objectives are designed to emphasize the acquisition of new distributors or customers. Preferably, managers should identify specific targets for new accounts depending on the marketing strategy. For example, managers might identify specific user groups or industries in a direct selling system or specific types of retail outlets in a trade selling system.

2. *Distributor-support* objectives apply to trade selling and are designed to gain the cooperation of retail or wholesale distributors in implementing the marketing strategy. Specifically, manufacturers may seek a variety of types of support, such as distributor participation in cooperative advertising or special sales promotions, aggressive selling of the product, or provision of extensive customer service. Distributor support is generally viewed as essential in indirect systems because the distributor is a key partner in the marketing effort. Indeed, when products are in the mature stage of the product life cycle, distributor support may well be the major marketing element in sales success because technically similar products may be broadly available.

3. *Account-maintenance* objectives typically take up the bulk of a salesperson's time in direct personal selling systems and in trade selling systems. These objectives are emphasized when management is concerned with maintaining an effective selling position through regular sales calls designed to provide information about new products, acquire information on changing customer or distributor needs, and perform customer service activities. (For instance, Kraft's sales reps no longer limit their efforts to devising promotions in supermarkets. They now offer research and advice for improving a store's profits.)

4. *Account-penetration* objectives are designed to increase total sales volume or to increase the sales of more profitable products or complementary products to existing distributors or buyers. For instance, Agco increased revenues from $274 million in 1991, its first full year, to $1.4 billion in 1994 by purchasing declining brands like White Tractor, Hesston hay tools, and tractor giant Massey-Ferguson. The company can now offer its 6600 dealers the opportunity to sell multiple Agco

brands. Each time a dealer adds a new brand, it generates an additional $150,000 in sales for that dealership.[8]

Industrial firms often share the business of some customers with one or more competitors. (For instance, some automobile manufacturers will purchase tires from two or three suppliers.) An attempt by such firms to increase their share of a buyer's purchase volume reflects an account-penetration objective. Finally, firms that are attempting to get distributors to carry more inventory or allocate more selling space to a product are also pursuing account penetration.

Selecting an Objective

Managers should select a sales and distribution objective that is based on the marketing strategy for each product or product line, because the purpose of sales and distribution programs is to help implement these strategies. This means that managers should identify the needs of the target buyers or distributors and the marketing strategies to be implemented when selecting sales and distribution objectives.

Note that being able to "type" a product according to a portfolio model will not, in itself, enable a manager to select a sales and distribution objective. Although account development is typically an important objective for new products, account penetration may also be employed in those cases. Similarly, reseller support may be an objective sought by managers of any of these types of products. Table 12-3 sum-

TABLE 12-3   **SALES AND DISTRIBUTION OBJECTIVES AND RELATED MARKETING STRATEGIES**

SALES AND DISTRIBUTION OBJECTIVES	HOW THEY IMPLEMENT MARKETING STRATEGIES
1. Account development	Increasing availability relative to competitors Gaining access to new segments Increasing ability to buy
2. Distributor support	Increasing availability (inventory) Increasing consumption rate Reducing competitive opportunities Increasing promotional support relative to competition
3. Account maintenance	Assuring user satisfaction Reducing competitive opportunities
4. Account penetration	Simplification Increasing consumption rate and purchase volume Increasing ability to buy Head-to-head competition Complementary product sales

[8]Geoffrey Brewer, "Wheeler Dealers: What the Hell Was Robert Ratliff Thinking?" *Sales and Marketing Management,* June 1995, pp. 39–44.

marizes the marketing strategies that are typically associated with the various sales and distribution objectives.

Once the program objective has been established, management can then turn its attention to the question of how to achieve the objective. Specifically, managers must identify the kinds of appeals that will be most effective in satisfying the benefit desired by the buyer or distributor.

SALES APPEALS

Sales appeals are the basic elements of the marketing offer that the sales force will communicate. That is, appeals reflect the benefits that a seller will offer in order to obtain the type of customer or distributor response stated in the program objective. Because the sales force communicates directly with final buyers and channel participants, it is possible to particularize the appeal to a much greater degree than is possible with advertising. This attribute of selling is distinctly important because distributors may differ in the benefits they desire and because organizational buyers often differ in the criteria they use for selecting a supplier.

In general, six types of appeals may be employed in sales and distribution programs.

- Product appeals
- Logistical appeals
- Protective-provisions appeals
- Simplification appeals
- Price appeals
- Financial-assistance appeals

Product Appeals

Product appeals are the specific product-related benefits that buyers will gain from using a product or that distributors will gain from having the product in their assortments. The benefits of the product will almost always be important to the buyer or distributor. Accordingly, they will almost always be included in the sales message. However, in many cases, a number of competing firms will be able to match product attributes or benefits. In those situations, other appeals are more likely to be determinant.

Product appeals are more likely to be determinant when noneconomic perceived risks are high. For example, if an industrial buyer purchases a component that is a major element in the quality of the final product, product quality and reliability will be the most critical attributes. For consumer goods, product appeals will be more important when social or psychological risks are paramount as the following example shows.

BeautiControl Cosmetics has become the third largest direct selling women's cosmetics business, primarily by focusing on reaching career-oriented and professional women. The key appeal in the BeautiControl marketing plan is that the company offers free color analysis. This technique involves determining a woman's skin tone and then identifying what color cosmetics will look best.[9]

In the case of industrial products, product appeals generally include quality control, reliability, distinctive performance features, the ability to meet computer specifications, or compatibility with existing products and systems. In the case of selling to distributors, product appeals are those which demonstrate the impact that carrying the product has on total distributor sales. For example, some products may help build store traffic, provide prestige to the distributor, or enable the distributor to offer a more complete product line. Of course, not all these product benefits can be easily demonstrated. As we shall discuss at the end of the chapter, the ability of the sales force to effectively and credibly communicate these benefits will be a major factor in the success of product appeals.

Logistical Appeals

Distribution logistics is the management of the flow of products from the point of origin to the point of consumption to meet customer needs. The customer will benefit by receiving products on time, in the right place, in the right quantity, in the right condition, and at the lowest total cost. The total cost of physical distribution has been often estimated at about 8 percent of sales revenues. The main components of total physical distribution costs consist of transportation, inventory carrying, and order processing/customer service/distribution administration. In addition, opportunity costs associated with inadequate parts or service levels or missed volume discounts must also be considered. As a result, physical distribution must be viewed not only as a cost, but also as a tool to attract and retain customers by offering better service or lower prices.

In recent years, the cost of holding inventory has risen sharply because of an increase in the number of models and lines offered and because of the higher cost of borrowing money. For instance, it has been estimated that the grocery industry could save $30 billion annually by streamlining logistics. Because of duplication and inefficiency, a typical box of breakfast cereal takes 104 days to get from the factory to the supermarket through a series of wholesalers, distributors, brokers, and consolidators, each having its own warehouse.[10] Accordingly, logistical appeals have become increasingly effective in dealing with distributors and industrial buyers. These appeals include providing fast processing of orders, providing frequent delivery, and offering expedited delivery.

On-time delivery has become a key competitive advantage in most industries. In Europe, for instance, Nissan guarantees its dealers 10-day delivery, and Caterpillar delivers replacement parts within 72 hours 99.7 percent of the time. Logistics has become central to marketing strategy; it can provide a distinctive competitive advantage because consumers value convenience, reliability, and support not just the prod-

---

[9]William Barrett, "See Dick and Jinger Sell," *Forbes,* Aug. 7, 1989, p. 48.
[10]Ronald Henkoff, "Delivering the Goods," *Fortune,* Nov. 28, 1994, pp. 64–78.

uct alone. For direct response companies like Dell Computers, on-time delivery is a key element of their competitive strategy. Dell's promise of product shipment within 5 days of an order and 2-day delivery has been a key factor in its being rated first in its industry in customer satisfaction.[11] On the other hand, Compaq's computers reach the customer only 40 percent of the time on schedule. In addition, Compaq estimates it lost $500 million to $1 billion in sales in 1994 by not having computers available when and where customers were ready to buy them.

Additionally, some manufacturers offer inventory-management appeals. For example, a buyer may guarantee a supplier that it will buy a minimum amount of a product over the course of a year. In exchange, the seller is responsible for providing very quick delivery (often within 24 hours) and also inherits the inventory-holding cost burden.

The primary effect of logistical appeals, therefore, is to help buyers or distributors reduce the amount of inventory they carry. In the case of Kmart, the company was able to reduce the inventory carried in distribution centers by 20 percent while at the same time increasing sales by 15 percent through the addition of new information systems and distribution programs. This benefit to downstream intermediaries is extremely important when any of the following conditions occur.

- The cost of borrowing money to finance inventories causes a significant drain on profits.
- Demand for a product is difficult to predict, perhaps because demand is very sensitive to changes in economic conditions.
- The rate of productoobsolescence is very high because of fashion changes, technological changes, or spoilage.
- Space constraints limit the amount of inventory that buyers or distributors are willing to carry.

For instance, Wal-Mart stores use only about 10 percent of their square footage for inventory, compared to the average store, which has 25 percent for nonselling uses.

A variety of techniques are available to help customers with inventory problems. Some of these can be seen in the actions taken by A. M. Castle & Co.

A. M. Castle is an Illinois-based distributor of steel, aluminum, and other metal products to 30,000 industrial customers in a wide variety of industries and locations. During the 1990s, A. M. Castle will reduce from 18 to 12 the number of its regional warehouses. The surviving warehouses will be larger, however, and will stock more inventory to improve customer product selection. Additionally, improved locations for the warehouses will assure next-day delivery for the entire continental United States. At the same time, the company has linked its computer systems with those of customers to exchange information that enables Castle to help its customers track and manage inventory levels.[12]

Although logistical appeals may be very effective, the cost of these appeals can

[11]Rita Koselka, op. cit., p. 59; and Anil Kumar and Graham Sherman, "We Love Your Product, but Where Is It?" *Sloan Management Review,* Winter 1992, pp. 93–99.

[12]Flynn McRoberts, "Castle Fortified Metal Operations," *Chicago Tribune,* Aug. 7, 1989, p. B1.

be very high. Accordingly, managers who wish to consider using these appeals should closely examine the profit impact that will result. Some procedures for evaluating this impact are discussed in Chapter 13.

Protective-Provision Appeals

Protective provisions represent specific policies designed to reduce buyer and distributor risk in accepting a product. An example is a supplier that may offer *exclusive distributorships;* for instance, Haggar Corporation sells its "Brickerton by Haggar" line of men's slacks only to Dillard's Department Stores.

To protect resellers against the risk of poor sales, manufacturers may offer the product on *consignment.* In this procedure, the title and the inventory risk remain with the seller until the distributor actually sells the product, or, the seller may provide liberal *return allowances.* For instance, in Japan, most department stores and other traditional retailers generally buy merchandise on the condition they can return whatever doesn't sell.

To protect buyers against price increases, sellers may offer *long-term contracts* that specify future price levels in exchange for a minimum order volume. To an increasing extent, buyers are becoming willing to accept such contracts even when specific *escalator clauses* are included. These clauses permit the seller to add certain kinds of cost increases (such as labor or material cost increases) to the contracted price.

Finally, *private branding* may be the appeal employed for protective provisions offered to distributors. A private brand is a product manufactured by one firm yet sold under a brand name controlled by a distributor (such as Wal-Mart's Sam's American Choice cola and chocolate chip cookies, which are made by Loblaw Co., the Canadian grocery chain). Frequently, manufacturers of products with high market shares in low-growth industries will offer to produce private brands as a means of using excess capacity without incurring the cost of supporting a brand through heavy promotion. Distributors may be successful with a private brand in the maturity stage of the life cycle if a large segment of the market is price-sensitive. Additionally, by having a brand with no direct comparisons available, a distributor's risk of facing heavy price competition is reduced.

In many product categories, an issue of major importance to retail and wholesale distributors is the existence of *gray marketers,* unauthorized outlets that sell branded products far below list price and often offer no service. Gray markets can come about when large buyers take advantage of discounts of 30 to 40 percent and then resell the products to unauthorized dealers at less than what small retail outlets might pay. IBM has protected its dealers from such unauthorized competitors by insisting that dealers and large customers sign contracts agreeing not to resell to unauthorized dealers and by eliminating dealers who violate these contracts.

Simplification Appeals

Simplification appeals are designed to enable the buyer or distributor to reduce the costs of handling, using, or promoting the product.

Manufacturers who sell to distributors often "preticket" merchandise (to save labor costs on the distributor's part) or provide specific promotional aids (sales training or displays). In some cases, big retailers demand that the manufacturer put price stickers on individual packages. Totes, Inc., for instance, was warned by one large retailer it would impose a $30,000 fine for errors in bar coding on products.[13]

Some manufacturers offer distributors a complete plan for merchandising the product, providing inventory and space-allocation guidelines and promotional programs specifically tailored to the distributor's market. Manufacturers of packaged-goods products offer a variety of simplification appeals to enhance sales of the product. Some, such as Kraft and Campbell Soup, help grocers rearrange shelves and displays to maximize profits. Others redesign products, packages, and delivery methods specifically for such wholesale clubs as Costco, Price, and Sam's. For example, Heinz bundles condiments like ketchup and relish into a single package and ships 64-ounce bottles on customized display pallets that are easy for stores to handle.[14]

In the case of industrial buyers, the provision of special maintenance, repair, and operating (MRO) services and inventory assistance constitutes a parallel to such merchandising plans. This approach simplifies a customer's problems in using the product. As a result, the seller may be able to develop greater buyer or distributor loyalty, because these programs may enable the buyer to use the product more satisfactorily or because they may lead to an increased dependence on the supplier.

Price Appeals

As suggested in Chapter 9, basic price-level decisions are developed by product managers or marketing managers on the basis of cost, demand, and competitive considerations, and on the basis of the marketing strategy. The sales force often has an important impact on the final price paid by each buyer, however.

In the case of industrial goods, price *shading* is a commonly used appeal for closing a sale—especially when new accounts are being sought. That is, the sales force will often have some latitude on the actual price to be charged and may price "below list" if necessary. This practice is widespread among industrial goods firms. Additionally, under inflationary pressures, many firms develop price lists reflecting possible cost increases that might be incurred, and then systematically offer prices "off list" until cost increases catch up with the original list-price levels. In so doing, firms avoid the cost of frequent price-list revisions and also reduce buyer displeasure over rising prices.

Shading is not always an available option when manufacturers sell to distributors because of the Robinson-Patman Act restraints on price discrimination discussed in Chapter 9. However, *quantity discounts* provide a mechanism for justifying lower prices to some distributors, and they also provide significant benefits to industrial buyers. The rationale for quantity discounts lies in the fact that buyers who order in large quantities do not require proportionately larger sales force, credit, or delivery costs to

---

[13]"Clout: More and More, Retail Giants Rule the Marketplace," *Business Week,* Dec. 21, 1992, p. 68.
[14]Patricia Sellers, "Winning Over the New Consumer," *Fortune,* July 29, 1991, pp. 113ff.

service the account. An additional possible benefit of quantity purchases to the seller is the reduction in inventory cost that results from shifting large volumes to the distributor or industrial buyer.

Financial-Assistance Appeals

In some cases, a buyer's working-capital, investment, or direct-expense requirements will be sharply increased as a result of a purchase. *Credit and cash discounts* are often provided when inventory requirements are large. Credit terms may range from 30 to 120 days (and often longer) and are designed to allow the distributor time to complete the resale of the product or to allow a buyer time for the production and sale of the final product in order to pay for the order. Cash discounts are designed to permit savings to firms that pay invoices quickly.

Additionally, sellers may offer special equipment free or at substantial savings to distributors in order to defray equipment and facilities investments. Signs, tools, service equipment, storage equipment, and many other inducements fall into this category.

More recently, new forms of financial assistance have been initiated that are designed to achieve special cooperation in stocking new products or building distributor sales support. On the consumer packaged-goods side, the dominant new appeal in recent years is the slotting allowance, which is generally requested by supermarkets when a decision about stocking new products comes up. Slotting allowances are viewed by retailers as a way of recouping part of the cost of setting up, handling, and stocking new products. In a typical supermarket, the number of items carried doubled between 1979 and 1995. Because many of these new items are line extensions or competing versions, the net gain in retailer revenue is usually modest. For instance, one study found that buyers at supermarket chains listened to about twelve presentations about new products weekly and rejected about two-thirds of them.[15] Often, this rejection is based on the lower return on investment associated with brands other than the leading one or two items. Accordingly, retailers began to require slotting allowances—up-front payments of $1000 to $5000 or more per store for each store in a chain to underwrite costs.

In addition to slotting allowances, trade promotional support from manufacturers may be in the form of display fees to cover space costs, discounts, and other short-term incentives. By the late 1980s, U.S. consumer-goods manufacturers spent more on trade promotions than on advertising as a percentage of the marketing budget. It has been estimated that manufacturers offered the average U.S. grocery retailer twenty times more trade promotions than could be accommodated within the available store display space.[16] However, inducing wholesale and retail customers to buy more product than they can promptly resell creates production problems and increases inventories and costs. As retailers and wholesalers buy on trade deals and discounts, wide

---

[15]Edward W. McClanglin and Vithala K. Rao, *Decision Criteria for New Product Acceptance: The Role of Trade Buyers,* Quorom Books, Westport, Conn., 1991, pp. 59–61.

[16]John A. Quelch, *Sales Promotion Management,* Prentice-Hall, Englewood Cliffs, N.J., 1989, p. 33.

price swings are passed on to consumers in unpredictable patterns. These consumers then buy only when the product is on sale and load up with whatever item is on promotion.

The Relationship Between Appeals and Objectives

As summarized in Table 12-4, a large number of appeals can be used as the focal point of the sales-force effort. Indeed, managers may elect to use several of these appeals simultaneously.

In general, nearly any type of appeal can be used to attempt to achieve a given sales and distribution objective. However, for a given type of objective, certain appeals do merit special consideration. For example

- Protective provisions, shading, and product appeals are very widely used for account development, especially if the buyers or distributors have limited knowledge of the seller's product.
- Simplification and financial-assistance appeals are widely utilized to build distributor support because these appeals are effective in stimulating cooperative attitudes on·the part of distributors.
- Logistical and simplification appeals are widely used in achieving account maintenance, especially if product features and prices do not vary a great deal among competing suppliers.

TABLE 12-4	TYPES OF SALES APPEALS

TYPE OF APPEAL	EXAMPLES
Product	Technical features
	Performance features
	Impact on distributor sales
Logistical	Speed of delivery
	Inventory management
Protective provisions	Exclusive distributorships
	Consignment selling
	Return allowances
	Long-term contracts
	Private branding
Simplification	Preticketing
	Merchandising assistance
	MRO services
Price	Price shading
	Quantity discounts
Financial assistance	Credit and cash discounts
	Slotting allowances
	Special equipment

■ Quantity discounts and long-term contracts are often effective for achieving account-penetration objectives because they focus most directly on the issue of increased volume.

However, in selecting specific appeals for a customer or a market segment, it is important that sales managers and sales-force personnel understand what motivates a buyer or distributor. As we suggested earlier, one advantage of using a sales force is the ability to adapt the marketing offer to meet particular buyer or distributor requirements. Additionally, the success of a given appeal will depend on the type of power or influence relationship that exists between a seller and a buyer or distributor. Buyer-distributor requirements and power relationships are both discussed in the next section of this chapter.

SELECTING AND IMPLEMENTING APPEALS

As we suggested at the outset of this chapter, the distinctive feature of sales-force activities is the personal interaction between the sales force and the buyers and distributors. This personal interaction has two basic functions.

■ To develop an understanding of buyer or distributor requirements so that management can select appropriate appeals. (Figure 12-2 shows the process of selecting a sales appeal.)
■ To maintain an influence relationship with buyers or distributors in order to successfully *implement* the appeals.

FIGURE 12-2
The process of selecting a sales appeal.

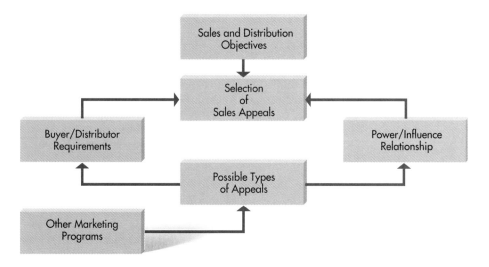

Buyer or Distributor Requirements

Requirements here refers to the various benefits that organizational buyers or distributors desire from a seller to satisfy the needs of their businesses. In Chapter 4, several kinds of benefits were identified. However, these can be expected to vary on a segment-by-segment basis, and often on a customer-by-customer basis—especially when a number of individuals are involved in the buying center. For instance, motor oil was traditionally sold primarily by service stations, but today it is marketed through outlets such as Quality Farm and Fleet stores, Discount Auto Parts, Albertson supermarkets, Sam's warehouse clubs, Wal-Mart, 7-11, Jiffy-Lube, and a variety of other distribution outlets. This requires the need to understand and customize marketing programs for each distinctive trade channel. Accordingly, sales and customer service personnel must assess how their products and services fit the needs of each account if they are to create value for customers and a competitive advantage for themselves. In order to do this, they need to understand the different channel participants' price-value positioning strategies, merchandising requirements, delivery/inventory needs, advertising and promotion methods, packaging needs, and the importance of the product in their total mix.[17]

Additionally, the salespeople who call on buyers or distributors must understand not only the buyer/distributor *product* requirements but the customer's sales process as well. That is, each buyer is likely to have individual preferences or be in special situations that condition the amount and kind of information needed to make a purchase. Some may desire a short sales presentation while others may need extensive information and materials to use in gaining approval from their managers.[18]

Sales and Distribution Relationships

The relationship among the various participants in a distribution channel will vary across industries and from company to company. In most cases, the extent to which one company can influence the actions and decisions of another is based on the different types of power each holds. Power is significant in the selection of appeals because it reflects the degree to which sellers have real control over what appeals to offer. Some buyer or distributor requirements may be met in full simply because the supplier needs their selling support or buying volume. In such cases, the buyer or distributor can be viewed as more powerful than the seller. Alternatively, buyers or distributors may be willing to accept a seller-determined appeal because of various sources of power possessed by the seller. Theoretically, five bases of power exist. See Table 12-5 for a summary of the power bases available.

Some guidelines for selecting appeals can be developed to indicate the extent to which a supplier can measure the amount of power it holds relative to the amount

[17]Allan J. Magrath, "One Size Doesn't Fill All," *Sales and Marketing Management,* July 1994, pp. 27–28.

[18]David Szymanski, "Determinants of Selling Effectiveness: The Importance of Declarative Knowledge to the Personal Concept," *Journal of Marketing,* January 1988, pp. 64–77.

TABLE 12-5	ALTERNATIVE POWER BASES AVAILABLE TO MANUFACTURERS, DISTRIBUTORS, AND BUYERS	

POWER BASE	TO A MANUFACTURER	TO A BUYER OR DISTRIBUTOR
Reward	Ability to offer products with low prices, quantity discounts, high margins	Ability to offer large buying volume
Coercive	Ability to withdraw product (with little loss in sales) when no comparable alternative is available to buyer or distributor	Ability to reject offer (with little loss in sales volume) when no equivalent distributors or buyers are available to seller
Expert	Ability to offer superior or needed technical assistance	Ability to provide unique distribution support
Referent	Ability to offer prestige brand name or represent an established well-known company	Ability to offer image of quality retail outlet or to serve as prestige example of satisfied buyer
Legitimate	Contractual provision that requires distributor to carry full line	Contractual provision that requires seller to provide warranty, repair, exclusive distribution

buyers hold. For example, if a supplier knows that it is perceived as having a unique technological advantage, management should emphasize its expertise by using product appeals. If a supplier has the ability to significantly reduce a buyer's costs or increase a distributor's profit by offering lower prices, management should use reward power by employing price appeals.

It is also important to recognize that power relationships can change over time. The recent growth of vertical and multichannel marketing systems has brought about the need for sales and distribution relationships based on more cooperation, partnership, or distribution programming than solely on the basis of power. Channel participants have different needs, problems, strengths, and weaknesses. For this reason, companies realize the need to develop long-term partnerships with distributors and avoid the use of coercive power. Indeed, it appears that the relative power of manufacturers is in decline in many industries (both domestic and overseas) for a variety of reasons.

- In wholesale distribution, larger professionally managed firms are displacing smaller family businesses at a rapid rate. Moreover, these larger wholesalers are establishing strong ongoing, long-term contractual relationships with final buyers, making it difficult for manufacturers to avoid dealing with them from a coercive power base.[19]

[19]James C. Anderson and James Narus, "A Model of Distributor Firm and Manufacturer Firm Working Partnerships," *Journal of Marketing,* January 1990, pp. 42–58.

- Large-scale retailers are also gaining a larger share of consumer-goods sales. This has enabled them to build their economic power base. But additionally, their expertise power is growing because of information technology. Expanded electronic scanning and computing capabilities combined with new statistical models for doing productivity analyses are allowing retailers to assess the profit performance of manufacturer brands more closely and to rely less on manufacturers' sales forces for advice on space allocation and in-store merchandising tactics.[20]

In Europe, grocery chains are merging and building stores outside their home countries, and buying decisions have been shifted to the home office. The establishment of the EU has led retailers to work together through alliances to buy a single product at the lowest cost. In the United States, there has been a consolidation of retailers, which has led to giant "power retailers" who use sophisticated information systems, tight inventory management, and competitive pricing to squeeze out weaker stores. The growth of these powerful retailers has brought about a power shift in the traditional relationship between manufacturer and retailer. Today, retailers such as Wal-Mart, Kmart, Target, Toys 'R' Us, and others dictate to even the largest manufacturers what goods to make and in what colors and sizes. In addition, shipping quantities and just-in-time deliveries, as well as discounts for new store openings and payments of fines for shipping errors, are being demanded. Because of these developments, vendors have had to reconsider their customer base and the pricing and promotion of their products. In many cases, this shift of power has led to a restructuring of the organization on the part of suppliers.

In addition to requiring on-time delivery and minimizing inventory, large power retailers are in a position to demand a variety of other special requirements from suppliers (see Table 12-6).

Large discount retailers find that the most efficient way to buy is at one low price. In this way, they are avoiding inventory buildups from special promotion programs and can maintain consistent low-price policies. The practice of pricing up and then discounting back through a variety of sales promotions has become more and more inefficient for manufacturers and retailers. As a result, companies such as Procter and Gamble, Kraft, and General Mills are moving toward everyday low pricing. For instance, General Mills, in April 1994, announced that it planned to reduce spending on inefficient cereal couponing and price promotions by more than $175 million annually. Instead, General Mills cut prices of its top brands by an average of 11 percent.[21] Kraft now tailors its offering not only to each supermarket chain, but to individual stores within the chain. Working in partnership with the supermarket chain, it developed merchandising programs appropriate for each store. Programs such as Kraft's require close working relationships throughout the supply chain on such operational factors as average inventory levels, delivery times, treatment of damaged and lost goods, and cooperation in promotional programs.

---

[20]Brent Belgner, "Retailers Grab Power, Control Marketplace," *Marketing News,* Jan. 16, 1989, pp. 1–2.

[21]Tim Triplett, "Cereal Makers Await Reaction to General Mills' Coupon Decision," *Marketing News,* May 9, 1994, pp. 1–2.

TABLE 12-6	REQUIREMENTS AND PRACTICES OF MAJOR RETAILERS

RETAILER

Wal-Mart	Computerized reordering and electronic linkups with 5000 suppliers Wants to eliminate independent brokers and manufacturing reps and deal directly with suppliers Desires everyday low prices and avoids price promotions On-time delivery of defect-free merchandise
Kmart	Electronic links with 2600 of 3000 suppliers Provides major vendors with point-of-sale data that allow for automatic restocking of inventory
Toys 'R' Us	Involved in early design of new products Requires exclusive rights to some products
Home Depot	Requires lumber industry to place bar-code stickers on all wood pieces Provides input into supplier's new-product development—colors, names, warranties
Costco	Requires special package sizes and shipping procedures to minimize handling
Dillard's	Develops "hybrid exclusive labels" with suppliers

Source: Patricia Sellers, "How to Remake Your Sales Force," *Fortune,* May 4, 1992, pp. 98–103; and "Clout: More and More, Retail Giants Rule the Marketplace," *Business Week,* Dec. 21, 1992, pp. 66–73.

Historically, manufacturers have held a strong power advantage in Japan because of the dominance of small retailers. In that nation, 1.6 million small stores control 53 percent of sales. (In contrast, only 3 percent of sales go through small stores in the United States.) In large measure, this power is a result of legislation that allowed small retailers to determine whether large stores could be introduced in their trading areas. But in spite of this tradition, large-scale retailing now appears to be gaining ground in Japan.[22]

Relationship Building

As the power of a manufacturer declines relative to the power of strong distributors or large buyers, there is a greater tendency to pursue long-term *relational exchanges.* These kinds of exchanges occur when both parties have a high degree of dependence on the other and when they operate in highly uncertain environments (such as those dominated by fast-paced technological change or extensive competition). A high degree of joint planning, well-coordinated activities, and mutual trust characterize these exchanges.[23] As a consequence, sales and distribution programs in these settings are geared toward implementing relationship marketing strategies (as we discussed in Chapter 7). Illustrative of the need for such programs is the one developed at Snapple.

[22]Bruce Hirobayashi, "Winds of Change," *Age of Information Marketing,* A. C. Nielsen Co., Chicago, 1989, pp. 9–12; and Emily Thornton, "Revolution in Japanese Retailing," *Fortune,* Feb. 7, 1994, pp. 143–146.

[23]See F. Robert Dwyer, Paul Schurr, and Sejo Oh, "Developing Buyer-Seller Relationships," *Journal of Marketing,* April 1987, pp. 11–27, for a discussion of how these relationships develop.

After the acquisition of Snapple by Quaker Oats, Quaker Oats attempted to take supermarket accounts from Snapple distributors and give them to Gatorade. Snapple distributors would then concentrate on convenience and mom-and-pop accounts. Snapple distributors refused and marketing plans for 1995 were delayed. This resulted in a financial loss and 5 percent decrease in sales. Snapple's distribution system was completely different from Gatorade's. For example, Snapple's 300 distributors deliver directly to stores whereas Gatorade's distributors deliver to warehouses. After this initial conflict, Quaker worked closely with Snapple distributors to develop a closer relationship. This has led to a reduction in delivery time to distributors from 3 weeks to 3 days. Distributors have been able to reduce inventory costs by 50 percent and still deliver to stores within 2 days. Quaker is planning a computer hook up with top distributors to replenish their inventory automatically. In addition, working with distributors, Quaker has reduced the number of flavors Snapple carried from 50 to 35, and has improved packaging and distributor relations through better communications.[24]

Regardless of the nature of the relationship, however, a power base cannot be effectively employed and a relational exchange cannot be established except through the sales force. To a large extent, the salesperson is the personification of the company. If a given salesperson demonstrates a lack of expertise, the company's image on this potential power base will suffer. Thus, both in selecting and in implementing appeals, the individual members of the sales force have a major role to play.

The Critical Role of the Sales Force

In selling to organizations (whether distributors or final buyers), it is important to maintain effective relationships with each account. That is, the salesperson generally faces the same buyer over and over, selling the same type of merchandise each time and becoming the major link between a supplier and its customer or distributor.[25]

Furthermore, the salespeople generally have a dual role. They are not merely the company's representatives to the customers (providing product information), they are also the customers' or distributors' representatives to the supplier because they help buyers obtain on-time delivery, special services, or special product designs.

These relationships are more or less continuous and involve the development of interpersonal relationships in which each individual (salesperson and buyer) is somewhat dependent on the other. Accordingly, the effectiveness of the salespeople is often dependent on the degree to which they are successful in communicating power.

TYPES OF SALESPERSON POWER

The primary bases of power available to the salesperson are expert power, referent power, and reward power.

Expert power exists to the extent that buyers or distributors believe that the salesperson has knowledge or skills that can be valuable to the buyer. Forms of salesperson

---

[24]Zina Moukheiber, "He Who Laughs Last," *Forbes,* June 1, 1996, pp. 42–43.

[25]Benson Shapiro, "Manage the Customer, Not Just the Sales Force," *Harvard Business Review,* September–October 1974, p. 130.

expertise that may be valuable to buyers or distributors include knowledge of how a product can be effectively used, the ability to set up an effective display, and a knowledge of the products and models that will appeal to a distributor's customers. Consequently, appeals that employ the expertise of the salesperson may provide that salesperson with a basis for influencing the buyer.

Referent power exists when the buyer is attracted to the salesperson out of friendship or a feeling of shared identity because the salesperson is viewed as having similar values or interests.[26] Because shared identity often leads to an increase in the buyer's willingness to trust the salesperson, referent power will provide the sales force with a source of influence that is useful even when a high degree of technical expertise is not needed.[27]

Reward power can also be employed by the sales force. Entertainment or special favors performed for the buyer (especially those related to the salesperson's role as the customer's representative to the supplier) are illustrative of the use of reward power. When reward power is used over a period of time, the salesperson may, as a result, develop a referent power base as well, because the buyer will be more willing to trust the salesperson.

WHICH POWER BASE TO USE

Individual customers are likely to differ in their frequency of interaction with the salesperson, the size of their order, the amount of risk they perceive in a given buying situation, and the kind of decision process employed (as was discussed in Chapter 3). Accordingly, the selection of a type of appeal and a type of power should depend heavily on the specific selling situation confronting the salesperson. Additionally, the technical skills and personal characteristics of salespeople will vary. Whereas one may be adept at using expert power, another may rely on referent power. Accordingly, no single approach may be superior. Rather, a given salesperson is likely to be most successful by adopting a behavior that is appropriate for his or her characteristics and skills as well as for meeting the buyer's or distributor's requirements.[28]

In sum, the salespeople must develop their own plan for the accounts they call on. A situation analysis should be performed for each customer, depending on that customer's requirements. An objective should be established for each account based on the current sales and distribution objective and on the salesperson's assessment of the opportunities for achieving that objective in each account. (This assessment will rely on competition, on the past level of success, and on whether the salesperson's

[26]See Gilbert Churchill, Robert Collins, and William Strang, "Should Retail Salespersons Be Similar to Their Customers?" *Journal of Retailing,* Fall 1975, pp. 29–42.

[27]Paul Busch and David Wilson, "An Experimental Analysis of a Salesman's Expert and Referent Bases of Social Power in the Buyer-Seller Dyad," *Journal of Marketing Research,* February 1976, pp. 3–11.

[28]See Barton Weitz, "Effectiveness in Sales Interactions: A Contingency Framework," *Journal of Marketing,* Winter 1981, pp. 85–103; and Thomas Leigh and Patrick McCraw, "Mapping the Procedural Knowledge of Industrial Sales Personnel: A Script-Theoretic Investigation," *Journal of Marketing,* January 1989, pp. 16–34.

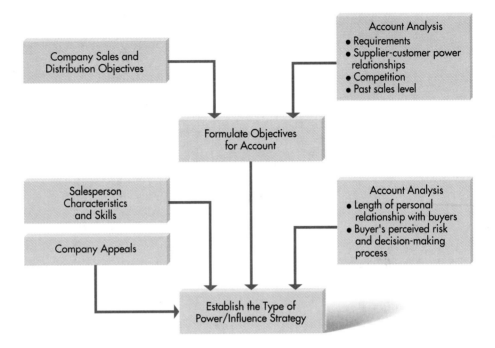

FIGURE 12-3
The salesperson's planning process.

company has the power to offer the necessary appeals.) Finally, the salesperson must adopt an influence strategy for each account based on his or her own capabilities and on the existing relationship with the buyer. Figure 12-3 portrays some of the elements involved in developing the individual account plan.

CONCLUSION

Sales and distribution programs provide the fundamental linkages between a firm and its buyers or distributors. The type of sales and distribution system a firm selects determines whether a product is sold directly or through wholesale or retail intermediaries and specifies the basic communication and customer service roles the sales force will play.

More specific direction for sales-force activities is provided by the program objectives that are established. These objectives should reflect the firm's marketing strategy and provide a basis for selecting the critical appeals offered to buyers or distributors. Additionally, managers must consider buyer requirements and the existing power relationships among manufacturers, distributors, and buyers in selecting appeals.

Although sales managers have an important role to play in designing the sales and distribution program, it will be up to the salespeople as well as sales managers to

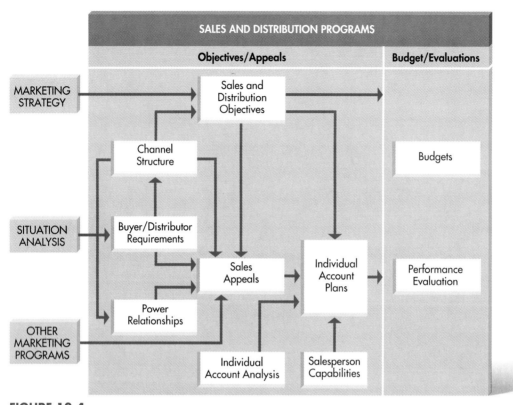

FIGURE 12-4

Relationship of sales and distribution objectives and appeals to maketing strategy, situation analysis, and other marketing programs.

identify achievable objectives and to select appeals that will be effective in each buying situation. In effect, the sales-force members may become marketing strategists for their market areas. However, in order to assure consistency among salespeople, managers should set the overall program objectives and determine the range of appeals that can be offered before individual sales-force members design their own plans and tactics for influencing customers. In this chapter, we have examined the types of objectives and appeals that managers may choose, the process for selecting objectives and appeals, and some of the major considerations involved in implementing appeals. Figure 12-4 summarizes the relationship among the topics in this chapter and their relationships to the preceding and following chapters.

As with any marketing program, sales and distribution activities cost money and do not always lead to the achievement of objectives. Accordingly, it is important to understand the mechanisms for budgeting, allocating, and evaluating expenditures on these activities. These are the major topics in Chapter 13. However, before proceeding to the next chapter, consider the following example to review some of the major elements of a sales and distribution program.

PROCTER & GAMBLE: RESPONDING TO SHIFTING RETAIL CHANNELS

The growth of membership warehouse clubs such as Costco and Sam's and discount stores such as Wal-Mart has led Procter & Gamble to convert to every-day low prices (EDLP) rather than maintain high list prices with frequent, irregular promotional discounts. Retailers such as Wal-Mart and Costco are less interested in price promotions than in low day-to-day prices, truckload quantities delivered directly to them rather than warehouses, and minimal inventories. However, many supermarkets and wholesalers still want case allowances, cooperative advertising dollars, and other discounts. In 1970, manufacturers offered retailers promotional discounts averaging about 4 percent. By the 1990s, promotional discounts had grown to 10 to 15 percent and accounted for 44 percent of every dollar spent on advertising and promotion by manufacturers. P&G claimed that only 30 percent of these trade-promotion monies meant lower consumer prices. In addition, it estimated that 35 percent are lost in inefficiencies and 35 percent remain with the retailer. This occurred because many distributors practice forward buying, the process of stocking up with more deal goods than they plan to sell during the promotion. When the promotional period is over, these goods are sold at regular prices or diverted either to a supermarket where the discounts weren't offered or to an intermediary who diverts them.

At one point, 17 percent of all P&G products—and in some categories 100 percent—were sold on promotional deals. This resulted in plant inefficiency and fifty-five price changes a day across its thirty-four product categories and seventeen pricing brackets. Trade loading resulted in ups and downs in shelf prices—Tide at $1.99 one week and $2.99 the next. This induced consumers to increasingly buy only promotional goods or switch to private-label products. Such practices also led to increased costs, because wholesalers often kept much of the discount and there were big swings in production as specials came and went. Keeping track of all the trade promotional deals also contributed to billing errors and numerous adjustments.

P&G's EDLP strategy was to reduce trade promotional spending from 17 percent of sales to approximately 5 percent of revenues. By withdrawing trade promotional money, forward buying would be discouraged, production smoothed out, and list prices reduced. By 1994, P&G reduced prices from 12 percent to 24 percent on nearly all brands. P&G has made the distribution system linking supplier, wholesaler, retailer, and consumer more efficient by replacing the old piecemeal ordering system with continuous product replenishment (CPR). By using scanners at retail stores linked directly to the factory, P&G can determine when and where to replace inventory. This will minimize mistakes and credit adjustments, reduce inventory, minimize out-of-stocks, and improve cash flow. Price changes have been reduced to one a day and inventory turns at customer warehouses rose from seventeen to twenty-seven a year. Even though only 25 percent of orders fall under CPR, factory efficiency has improved and North American inventories are down 10 percent and estimated to be down by up to 20 percent within a year.

1. P&G cannot deliver everyday low prices without incurring everyday low costs. How does the EDLP program lead to cost reductions?
2. Why would some supermarkets and wholesalers prefer case allowances, cooperative advertising dollars, and other discounts to everyday low prices?
3. What would be the advantages and disadvantages of P&G's new EDLP program on new-product development and introductions?

Bill Saporito, "Behind the Tumult at P&G," *Fortune*, Mar. 7, 1994, pp. 74–82; "Ed Artzt's Elbow Grease Has P&G Shining," *Business Week*, Oct. 10, 1994, pp. 84–86; Patricia Sellers, "The Dumbest Marketing Ploy," *Fortune*, Oct. 5, 1992, pp. 88–93; and "Not Everyone Loves a Supermarket Special," *Business Week*, Feb. 17, 1992, pp. 64–68.

QUESTIONS AND SITUATIONS FOR DISCUSSION

1. Black & Decker's U.S. Power Tool business established Wal-Mart and Home Depot divisions to cater to these large accounts. A vice president oversees a group composed of salespeople, a marketer, an information systems expert, a sales forecaster, and a financial analyst. This team is responsible for creating specially designed packaging for drills and drill bits for the retailer. In addition, prior to introducing a new line of power tools, Black and Decker works closely with retailers for 9 months obtaining input about the name, color, and development of a 30-day no-questions asked return policy. What advantages are there for Black and Decker to cater to large accounts in this way? Are there any disadvantages?

2. Wal-Mart accounts for over 20 percent of the sales of Mr. Coffee, Royal Appliance, and Gitano apparel. What advantages/disadvantages are there for both Wal-Mart and these suppliers to have such a heavy concentration of sales with one account?

3. Both firms that use trade sales forces and firms that use missionary sales forces employ distributors. Explain how these types of sales forces differ. Explain how the tasks performed by the distributors differ among channels in which the manufacturer uses each type of sales force.

4. Which type of sales and distribution objective would be most appropriate for each of the following firms?
   a. A computer manufacturer operating at full capacity
   b. A women's hosiery manufacturer with a product that is carried by a relatively small number of department stores
   c. A bottler that wants to set up in-store retail displays for a new line of soft drinks
   d. A manufacturer of automobile seat belts that is only one of several suppliers used by automobile manufacturers

5. What are the trade-offs that managers who are responsible for inventory need to consider when reordering merchandise?

6. In 1991, Wal-Mart's president sent a letter to manufacturers stating: "We have decided that our dealings should be directly with the principals of your company." This will lead to the elimination of manufacturer's representatives. What are the advantages/disadvantages for Wal-Mart and manufacturers?

7. National brand suppliers may agree to manufacture private-label items for large supermarket chains. What are the advantages and disadvantages to such suppliers of private labels?

8. Duracell has relied heavily on short-term promotions and discounts in selling batteries. These promotions and discounts occurred during 32 weeks of the year and accounted for 90 percent of company volume. Duracell has eliminated the majority of these deals and discounts and replaced them with new displays and store events to draw customers. What factors would cause Duracell to change its previous sales promotions and discounting strategy? What reaction to this change would you expect from retailers?

9. Gus is an account representative for a major computer manufacturer and is responsible for all sales and customer service activities at a major New York bank. Besides Gus, two sales managers, four salespeople, two trainees, and thirteen technical service reps are assigned to this account by the computer firm. When major acquisitions are being contemplated, the decision-making process in this bank may well take a year.

   a. What are the probable reasons for selecting a direct personal selling system in this case?

   b. Which sales and distribution objective will Gus and his team likely emphasize most?

   c. Which appeals do you think will be most effective in this situation?

   d. Discuss the most important factors a salesperson should consider in this type of selling situation.

SUGGESTED ADDITIONAL READINGS

Calantone, Roger J., and Jule B. Gassenheimer, "Overcoming Basic Problems between Manufacturers and Distributors," *Industrial Marketing Management,* August 1991, pp. 215–221.

Fites, Donald V., "Make Your Dealers Your Partners," *Harvard Business Review,* March–April 1996, pp. 84–95.

Fuller, Joseph B., James O'Conor, and Richard Rawlinson, "Tailored Logistics: The Next Advantage," *Harvard Business Review,* May–June 1993, pp. 87–98.

Ganesan, Shankar, "Determinants of Long-Term Orientation in Buyer-Seller Relationships," *Journal of Marketing,* April 1994, pp. 1–19.

Gaski, John F., "The Theory of Power and Conflict in Channels of Distribution," *Journal of Marketing,* Summer 1984, pp. 9–29.

Gassenheimer, Jule B., and Rosemary Ramsey, "The Impact of Dependence on Dealer Satisfaction: A Comparison of Reseller-Supplier Relationships," *Journal of Retailing,* Fall 1994, pp. 253–266.

Kalwani, Manohar U., and Narakesar Narayandas, "Long-Term Manufacturer-Supplier Relationships: Do They Pay Off for Supplier Firms?" *Journal of Marketing,* January 1995, pp. 1–16.

Leigh, Thomas, and Patrick McGraw, "Mapping the Procedural Knowledge of Industrial Sales Personnel: A Script-Theoretic Investigation," *Journal of Marketing,* January 1989, pp. 16–34.

Magrath, Allan, and Kenneth Hardy, "Avoiding the Pitfalls in Managing Distribution Channels," *Business Horizons,* September–October 1987, pp. 29–33.

Quelch, John A., and David Harding, "Brands versus Private Labels: Fighting to Win," *Harvard Business Review,* January–February 1996, pp. 99–109.

Shapiro, Benson P., V. Kasturi Rangan, and John J. Sviokla, "Staple Yourself to an Order," *Harvard Business Review,* July–August 1992, pp. 113–122.

CHAPTER 13

MANAGING SALES AND DISTRIBUTION

OVERVIEW

In Chapter 12, we pointed out the importance of establishing sales and distribution objectives that would provide guidance for the design of specific sales and distribution appeals. We also discussed the importance of selecting appeals that would best satisfy the benefits being sought by the buyer-distributor. Those appeals should be based on careful analysis of buyer-distributor requirements as well as existing power relationships. It is important to remember that in today's competitive marketplace, a program that only maximizes sales or some other program objective (such as new-product sales) may not be optimal from a profit perspective.

In today's world, companies not only sell products, but also must provide added value throughout the supply chain. This means that it is necessary to not only satisfy the next link in the distribution system, but also meet the complex needs of the end user. These needs may be technical, operational, or financial. This has resulted not only in increased emphasis on improving efficiency throughout the sales and distribution system, but also in reduced costs. Like all other marketing programs, sales and distribution activities cost money. With the average cost per sales call for *senior* salespeople being $513, sales managers must operate within a budget that is consistent with overall marketing and profit objectives.[1] It is the task of sales management not only to establish the budget necessary to support the expenses of the selling operation, but also to match the available resources to the requirements of the markets.

In addition to assessing the cost of various programs, sales managers are responsible for evaluating program performance on both sales-volume and non-sales-volume dimensions. These evaluations usually are made at various levels: The performances of individual salespeople, distributors, or sales territories are examined in addition to overall program performance. Such evaluations are then used to identify possible program modifications for improving performance.

---

[1]The Gallup Organization surveyed 301 senior salespeople from Fortune 1000 companies in an exclusive study for *Sales and Marketing Management*. In addition to the average cost of a sales call, they found that 56 percent of those surveyed spend more than $500 monthly on travel with the average travel cost being $2045 and the cost of entertainment $600 per month. See Allison Lucas, "Leading Edge," *Sales and Marketing Management,* June 1995, p. 13.

In this chapter, we provide procedures for establishing the program budget as we examine the relationship between sales and distribution appeals and sales and distribution costs. Later in the chapter, we also present a number of methods for evaluating sales and distribution performance. In Chapter 14, we will discuss some of the sales management actions that are directed toward enhancing the performance of individual sales-force members.

ESTABLISHING THE SALES AND DISTRIBUTION BUDGET

In designing a program to achieve a sales and distribution objective, sales managers should attempt to estimate the budgetary consequences of the program. Specifically, managers should examine the costs a specific program will incur and the expected impact of the program on profitability. The importance of this can be illustrated by the general manager of the Health Care Division of Johnson & Johnson, who stated, "If [the departments] fail to meet the profit objectives of the division, the departmental budgets are reworked until they are brought in line."[2]

Managers can then determine if the budget is consistent with the product objectives. That is, a sales and distribution budget that will lead to increased sales and market share may be appropriate for a "build" objective even if a decline in total contribution is expected in the short run. For instance, with those types of products and services, it is not unusual for companies to pay additional incentives to open new accounts in order to increase market share. In addition, travel and entertainment expenses associated with the sale of low-share products in high-growth markets often are higher because of increased competitive activity. Alternatively, sales and distribution budgets for high-share products in low-growth markets should normally result in an increase in total contribution.[3]

Figure 13-1 summarizes the elements in the budgeting process. As Figure 13-1 suggests, if the expected results of the proposed budget are inconsistent with the product objectives, revisions in objectives or in the appeals may be appropriate.

The first step in this process is to estimate the impact of the appeals on the profitability structure. As seen in Figure 13-1, sales and distribution programs can influence the direct costs of marketing a product or product line and the variable-contribution margin. This requires that sales managers have timely information about different markets, specific accounts in these markets, and needs of channel participants at these accounts. However, in most companies, accounting systems track costs primarily by product categories rather than by customer or distribution-channel participant. This can often lead to a lack of management understanding of the costs associated

---

[2]"At Johnson & Johnson, the Sales Budget Gets the Best of Care," *Sales Management,* May 19, 1975, p. 10; and Nigel Pierey, "The Marketing Budgeting Process," *Journal of Marketing,* October 1987, pp. 45–59.

[3]The relationship between marketing budgets and their effect on market share is discussed in Robert D. Buzzell and Frederick E. Wiersma, "Successful Share-Building Strategies," *Harvard Business Review,* January–February 1981, pp. 135–144.

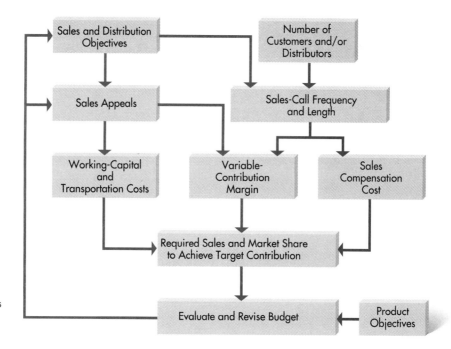

FIGURE 13-1

Establishing a sales and distribution budget.

with reaching and servicing different types of buyers and different types of distribution channels.[4] Nevertheless, major budgetary factors that must be considered are

- Sales-force compensation costs
- Working-capital costs for credit and inventory
- Physical distribution costs
- Prices and discounts (variable-contribution margin)

Sales-Force Compensation Costs

The salaries of sales and customer service personnel and the travel expenses necessary for supporting them are a major expense category for firms that employ company sales forces. Table 13-1 gives a more complete indication of the average cost per sales call associated with personal selling. The primary determinant of these costs is the size of the sales force.[5]

There are several ways in which one can determine the number of salespeople that will be needed. Probably the easiest approach is to divide the dollars available by the costs necessary to support one salesperson. Although this method is simple to apply, it

[4]H. Thomas Johnson and Robert S. Kaplan, *Relevance Lost: The Rise and Fall of Management Accounting,* Harvard Business School Press, Boston, 1987, p. 245.

[5]For a useful review of techniques for estimating the appropriate size of a sales force, see Arthur Median, "Optimizing the Number of Industrial Salespersons," *Industrial Marketing Management,* February 1982, pp. 63–74.

ignores the market conditions that should influence sales-force size. For instance, one would expect that early in the product life cycle it may be desirable to have more sales staff than would be necessary in the decline stage. Some firms hire as many salespeople as possible as long as the gross profit on the new business they generate equals the costs associated with the additional salesperson. This policy can readily lead to over-staffing, with too many salespersons calling on too few customers. In addition, both economic and market conditions are overlooked when such an approach is followed.[6]

A more logical and systematic approach is to determine the size of the sales force necessary by considering the number of customers or prospects and their requirements. A basic estimate of the number of salespeople needed can generally be made as follows:

$$\text{Size of sales force} = \frac{\text{number of accounts in target market} \times \text{required number of calls per year per account}}{\text{number of calls each salesperson can make}}$$

Note that managers may have to develop separate sales-force size estimates for different parts of the sales force. For example, when distinct selling tasks are required for different customers, specialized sales forces may exist. Managers may need to calculate separately the sizes of

- The sales force and the customer service force
- The new-prospect sales force and the sales force calling on established accounts

TABLE 13-1 AVERAGE COST OF A SALES CALL

	TYPE OF SALES FORCE		
	CONSUMER GOODS	INDUSTRIAL GOODS	SERVICE
Median direct costs			
Compensation	70,500	68,500	71,500
Expenses	16,600	24,000	15,600
Total	87,100	92,500	87,100
Average calls per year*			
High-frequency areas or policies	841.5	748.0	1122.0
Low-frequency areas or policies	561.0	561.0	654.5
Average cost per call			
High-frequency areas or policies	144.03	155.97	110.03
Low-frequency areas or policies	216.05	230.62	217.49

*Assumes 187 selling days per year.
Developed from "1993 Sales Manager's Budget Planner," *Sales and Marketing Management,* June 28, 1993.

[6]Leonard M. Lodish, "A User-Oriented Model for Sales Force Size, Product, and Market Allocation Decisions," *Journal of Marketing,* Summer 1980, pp. 70–78.

■ The sales forces that call on accounts in different industries (when a specialized knowledge of industry production processes or technologies is important)
■ The sales force for each territory

Whatever the relevant sales-force definition, the staffing plan must consider the number of accounts, the required sales-call frequency, and the call capacity of the sales and service representatives.

Estimating Required Call Frequency

Managers should consider each of the following factors in estimating the required number of calls per account.

■ The size of the various buyer or distributor accounts
■ The sales and distribution objectives
■ The need for unplanned calls
■ The estimated sales effects of increasing or reducing the number of calls per account

ACCOUNT SIZE

An important consideration in estimating the required number of calls is the size of the account, because the sales manager will want to minimize the risk of losing large accounts. Large accounts, moreover, may be more profitable because of lower physical distribution costs such as order inputting, invoicing, order picking and packing, consolidating, and transporting.

The ABC rule of account classification holds that the first 15 percent of a firm's customers will account for 65 percent of the firm's sales, the next 20 percent will yield 20 percent of the sales, and the last 65 percent will produce only 15 percent of sales.[7] A recent study of 192 firms found that the top 20 percent of accounts produced 75 percent of the sales volume.[8]

It is a common practice of many firms to divide distributor or buyer accounts into account-size categories similar to the breakdown given in Table 13-2. As the table indicates, a small number of large accounts (the A accounts) generally represent a very large portion of sales. This is true whether the accounts are final buyers or distributors. Mergers, acquisitions, and strategic alliances require that suppliers put more emphasis on key accounts. Large retail chains require specialized services and a coordinated approach from their suppliers in such areas as logistical support, inventory management, customized applications, and merchandising support. Accordingly, those

---

[7]Henry Porter, "The Important Few—The Unimportant Many," *1980 Portfolio of Sales and Marketing Plans,* Sales and Marketing Management, New York, 1980, pp. 34–37.

[8]William A. O'Connell and William Keenan, Jr., "The Shape of Things to Come," *Sales and Marketing Management,* January 1990, pp. 36–41.

| TABLE 13-2 | AN ILLUSTRATION OF SALES-CALL FREQUENCIES BY ACCOUNT SIZE |

ACCOUNT GROUP	VOLUME PER MONTH	NUMBER OF ACCOUNTS	PLANNED FREQUENCY PER ACCOUNT	TOTAL CALLS
A	2000	100	24/year	2400
B	600	300	12/year	3600
C	50	600	6/year	3600
				9600

accounts will be called on more frequently than medium and small accounts, as seen in the case of Dictaphone.

> Dictaphone grouped its five-year historical sales data by the type of business sold to and the number of employees working in those businesses. Using the Dun & Bradstreet Market Identifiers database of 8.8 million U.S. businesses and Dictaphone's sales by type of business vs. number of employees at that business, they created values based upon what had historically been sold to each type and size of business. This provided Dictaphone with the potential dollar value that could be assigned to any size business. After eliminating businesses that offered too little potential, they created separate profile cards for each business, separated by territory. These were assigned to sales reps with rankings based upon sales potential. The company suggested that A accounts be called every two weeks, B accounts once a month, and C accounts once a quarter.[9]

An important issue in examining account size is whether to use *actual* sales or *potential* sales as the basis for classifying accounts. Firms that classify accounts on the basis of current sales are implicitly assuming the company has reached its maximum level of achievement in each account. Yet, for most firms, some of the C accounts may likely become A accounts if additional effort is applied. Development of key accounts demands a resource commitment from the supplier. The costs for such development require that the firm carefully establish an account selection process based upon both the near-term potential and the longer-term resources required to profit from the account relationship.[10]

SALES AND DISTRIBUTION OBJECTIVES

The sales and distribution objectives for a specific program may force a modification of the basic call-frequency pattern, however. Although the frequency patterns given in Table 13-2 may be appropriate for account maintenance, if managers establish other

[9]Bob Attanasio, "How PC-Based Sales Quotas Boost Productivity, Morale," *Sales and Marketing Management,* September 1991, p. 150.

[10]For a discussion of account selection and the account selection process, see Frank V. Cespedes, *"Concurrent Marketing: Integrating Product Sales and Service,"* Harvard Business School Press, Boston, 1995, pp. 189–198.

objectives, then revisions in call frequency may be necessary. For example, if an account-development objective is established, sales calls on new accounts must be included in the staffing plan. For instance, Goodyear requires that each salesperson open five new accounts a year and gives bonuses according to the size of the new accounts.[11] Similarly, some sales or customer service calls to existing accounts are designed to fulfill a specific objective (such as demonstrating a product's superiority in order to increase sales penetration in key accounts, or stimulating special reseller support on special programs).

UNPLANNED CALLS

Emergency repairs or follow-up of an order may require unplanned calls. Usually the ratio of unplanned-to-planned calls can be established from historical sales-call reports. However, in developing a staffing plan, the number of unplanned calls should be considered, because they take additional time from the sales force.

ESTIMATED SALES EFFECTS

As a final consideration in determining the required number of calls, managers should attempt to estimate the change in sales that will result from increasing or decreasing the current sales-call frequencies on each account. This analysis (which is incorporated in many computer-based systems for territory management) must usually be made on the basis of the joint judgment of the salesperson and the sales manager.[12] For example:

> Turner Warmack, Vice President of Sales and Marketing at Ziegler Tools, holds an annual meeting with each of his 18 salespeople to discuss previous year's sales, key accounts, account growth, and possible areas for new business. Warmack and his salespeople categorize accounts and decide how often to call upon them. If the salesperson believes he or she can get more business from an account by calling on that account more frequently, he or she is encouraged to increase the call frequency.[13]

As was the case with the judgmental estimates we discussed in Chapter 6 (response of sales to advertising) and in Chapter 9 (price-elasticity), managers should seek to answer certain specific questions to gain insight into the relationship between sales calls and sales volume. Among these questions are the following.

- How frequently are buying decisions made?
- Is there a significant opportunity for account penetration?
- How frequently do competitors call on this account?

---

[11]Bill Kelley, "How Much Help Does a Salesperson Need?" *Sales Management,* May 1989, p. 35.

[12]Leonard Lodish, "Vaguely Right Approach to Sales Force Allocations," *Harvard Business Review,* January–February 1974, pp. 199–214. The impact of sales-call length and frequency is also examined in Raymond LaForge and David Cravens, "A Marketing Response Model for Sales Management Decision Making," *Journal of Personal Selling and Sales Management,* Fall/Winter, 1981–1982, pp. 10–16.

[13]Kelley, op. cit., p. 32.

- Are new competitors, new products, or new technologies anticipated?
- How important is it to maintain referent power through frequent contact?
- How difficult or time-consuming will it be for buyers or distributors to change suppliers?
- How frequently do buyers or distributors need customer service support?
- What is required to develop a cooperative relationship, rather than a series of transactions?

ESTIMATING SALES-FORCE CALL CAPACITY

In most organizations, it is not usually a difficult task to estimate the average length of a sales call. However, the length of a sales call may differ significantly from new to existing accounts and from large to small accounts and will also vary if the purchase decision is made by a buying committee rather than an individual. In addition to selling effort requirements, nonselling time considerations (telephone, paperwork, planning time, and so on) should be considered in the analysis. Further, the possible number of calls will depend on the time required to travel between accounts.

For instance, Diesel Supply Co. (DSC) has a seven-person national sales force, which calls on natural gas pipeline and refinery accounts. DSC salespeople can only make about four sales calls per day because accounts are seventy to eighty miles apart. To assist field sales, DSC uses mapping software to construct sales-call routing maps based upon highly specific client data.[14]

Accordingly, the sales-force call capacity will be significantly affected by the way the sales force is allocated to territories and to accounts. In turn, the number of salespeople and their travel costs will be determined by the allocation system.

Studies show that as many as 80 percent of the firms in the United States have imbalanced sales territories. By having too many salespeople in one territory and too few in another, companies experience 2 to 7 percent in sales losses each year. Decisions regarding the allocation of the sales force to territories should be modified when management expects different territories to experience different rates of growth in potential, or market conditions have changed. As an example, consider the changes made by Hoescht Roussel, the pharmaceutical branch of Hoescht Celanese.[15]

Traditionally, pharmaceutical industry salespersons sold to as many private-care physicians as possible. However, the increasing influence of managed care has brought more decision makers into the purchasing process. Industry studies reveal that more than 90 percent of doctors belong to at least one third-party managed-care plan. This requires that territory alignment and allocation of salespersons be based not only on where physicians are located, but also on which physicians belong to which plan. In addition, managed-care companies need to be marketed to as well. Hoescht Roussel decided it was necessary to realign its sales force to reflect the changes in the marketplace. In order to do this, factors such as which salespeople

---

[14]Richard Lewis, "Putting Sales on the Map," *Sales and Marketing Management,* August 1992, p. 29.

[15]Melissa Campenelli, "Reshuffling the Deck," *Sales and Marketing Management,* June 1994, pp. 83–90.

would be put in which regions, how customers would respond, what training would be necessary, and what costs would be associated with such a realignment needed to be considered.

Hoescht's sales force of 640 people was assigned on the basis of where physicians and hospitals were located. The sales force operated on the assumption that 65 percent of physicians wrote 94 percent of the prescriptions. Research was conducted into which of these 65 percent should be targeted and the influence of managed-care companies in specific geographic areas in order to divide the sales force geographically around the following customer segments: primary-care physician's offices, managed-care companies, and hospitals. A software program called MapPix was used to factor in geographic variables such as mountain ranges, rivers, and roadways, and other factors that would affect a salesperson's travel time.

The result of such analysis was a reduction in regions from nine to six and the addition of six regional operations managers. These operations managers are responsible for salesperson deployment and training at the regional level. Managers are responsible for managing more salespeople per region, and 125 reps who mostly sold directly to physicians were eliminated. The sales force was aligned on the basis of high-volume/low-volume customers within each segment. Sales costs were reduced by approximately 15 percent, or a savings of more than $10 million annually. Calls were reduced overall by 200,000, but Hoescht will make 100,000 more calls to high-volume customers. Lower-volume customers will be reached by direct mail and telemarketing.[16]

Special Compensation Costs

Special compensation includes sales commissions, bonuses, and special incentives (such as merchandise and travel awards). These incentives are offered in order to achieve some specific type of performance on the part of sales-force members or distributors.

In the case of sales commissions, the incentive is directed toward sales-volume gains. Because the level of commission earned is determined as a percentage of sales or a fixed amount per unit of sales, the cost of this incentive is a *variable cost.* However, most special compensation costs represent increases in fixed direct costs and generally are tied to specific sales and distribution objectives. For example, bonuses or travel awards may be provided to salespeople who achieve a certain level of new-account openings or a certain level of retailer participation in a sales promotion. In addition, an increasing number of companies are now using measures of customer satisfaction as a basis for special compensation.

Because of the high cost of having a company sales force, a great many firms use manufacturer's representatives to perform the direct selling function. Manufacturer's representatives are independent businesses. Approximately 50,000 U.S. manufactur-

---

[16]Ibid.

ers use independent representatives; in 1995 there were over 38,000 representative firms in operation.[17]

These firms usually sell the product lines of a number of manufacturers within a specific industry and operate on a percent-of-sales commission basis. A study of the Manufacturer's Agent National Association showed that the typical independent agency represented an average of 10.1 different manufacturers and employed 5.6 salespeople. Table 13-3 gives some examples of the level of percent commission paid on net sales to manufacturer's reps in some selected industries.

From a cost perspective, the decision to use a company sales force or a manufacturer's rep revolves around the company's total sales volume. A company sales force is a fixed cost with respect to sales volume, whereas the manufacturer's rep commission is a variable cost. Thus, at very low sales volumes, the manufacturer's rep is the lower cost alternative. As sales volume (within a specific territory or market) grows, the fixed cost of the company sales force is gradually spread over more units.

Table 13-4 provides a comparison of direct sales and sales agencies costs. Figure 13-2 demonstrates how the costs of the two alternatives behave as sales volume increases. If the cost of a company sales force is $200,000 for a given territory, and if a manufacturer's representative charges 5 percent of sales, the costs are equal when sales are equal to $4 million. The point of equal costs is derived as follows:

$$\text{Cost of manufacturer's rep} = \text{cost of company sales force}$$
$$0.5 \times \text{company sales} = \$200,000$$
$$\text{Company sales} = \$4,000,000$$

| TABLE 13-3 | AVERAGE MANUFACTURERS' REPRESENTATIVES COMMISSIONS IN SELECTED LINES |

PRODUCT OR SERVICE	AVERAGE COMMISSION PAID
Advertising products and services	16.17
Building materials and supplies	7.65
Computers	9.99
Electronic consumer products	5.64
Food products and services	15.00
Marine	9.81
Paper industry	11.16
Plastics	6.18
Sporting goods supplies and accessories	8.18

Source: Manufacturers' Agents National Association, *Survey of Sales Commissions,* as reported in *1987 Survey of Selling Costs, Sales and Marketing Management,* Feb. 16, 1987, p. 59.

[17]Lois C. DuBoise and Roger H. Grace, "The Care and Feeding of Manufacturer's Reps," *Business Marketing,* December 1987, p. 56; and Michael Marshall and Frank Siegler, "Selecting the Right Rep Firm," *Sales and Marketing Management,* January 1993, p. 46. Also see Melissa Campenelli, "Agents of Change," *Sales and Marketing Management,* February 1995, p. 72.

TABLE 13-4	DIRECT SALES VERSUS SALES AGENCIES: A COST/RATIO ANALYSIS

NUMBER OF DIRECT SALESPEOPLE	TERRITORY VOLUME			
	$250,000	$500,000	$1M	$2M
1	$ 50,000 20%*	$ 50,000 10%	$ 50,000 5%	$ 50,000 2.5%
2	$100,000 40%	$100,000 20%	$100,000 10%	$100,000 5%
3	$150,000 60%	$150,000 30%	$150,000 15%	$150,000 7.5%
4	$200,000 80%	$200,000 40%	$200,000 20%	$200,000 10%

SALES AGENCY COMMISSION	TERRITORY VOLUME			
	$250,000	$500,000	$1M	$2M
5%	$ 12,500 5%*	$ 25,000 5%	$ 50,000 5%	$100,000 5%
7.5%	$ 18,750 7.5%	$ 37,500 7.5%	$ 75,000 7.5%	$150,000 7.5%
10%	$ 25,000 10%	$ 50,000 10%	$100,000 10%	$200,000 10%

*Cost as a percent of total sales.

Notes: Annual cost figures for direct sales are based on a salary of $39,000 plus $11,000 expenses per salesperson. This doesn't include the cost of branch office facilities and personnel or fringe benefits normally paid to direct salespeople. The number of agency people covering the same territory may vary, but commissions as a ratio of sales would remain the same.

Source: Edwin E. Bobrow, "The Question of Reps," *Sales and Marketing Management,* June 1991, p. 34.

In this example, therefore, the cost of a manufacturer's rep is lower at sales volumes below $4 million, but the cost of a company sales force is lower at sales volumes above $4 million. In addition to cost, other factors must be considered in the choice between a company sales force and a manufacturer's representative. Among the major arguments made on behalf of the two alternatives, the following points are the most widely accepted.[18]

■ Two critical advantages of manufacturers' reps are that they may have a better knowledge of customer or distributor needs and they may provide better coverage of small accounts. They are able to achieve these advantages because they com-

[18]See Erin Anderson, "The Salesperson as Outside Agent or Employee: A Transaction Cost Analysis," *Marketing Science,* Summer 1985, pp. 234–254. For another view, see "Wal-Mart's War on Reps," *Sales and Marketing Management,* March 1987, pp. 41–43.

bine the lines of several suppliers and, thus, can justify more calls on such accounts.

■ The critical advantage of the company sales force lies in control over performance. While manufacturers' reps do not get paid unless they make a sale, a company sales force can be motivated to perform nonselling or sales-development activities designed to build long-term growth or emphasize account maintenance. For instance, in Germany, industrial salespeople seldom prospect, infrequently expedite orders, and rarely follow up on orders. However, the Germans excel at training their clients' employees, as well as helping install what they sell.[19] Nevertheless, the focus of manufacturers' representatives has changed. Many representatives and agencies are now working closely with the strategic planning departments of major manufacturers and providing field input to developing new products. Some agencies are hiring customer support service personnel and offering marketing services such as telemarketing and direct mail programs.[20]

Working-Capital Costs

Until recently, the costs associated with providing credit to buyers and distributors and with inventory incentives were seldom related to sales budgets. However, inventory and credit appeals have become more important to buyers and distributors. As a result, more organizations have begun to evaluate the additional working-capital costs that are incurred because of the use of these appeals.[21]

FIGURE 13-2

Relationship between sales volume and the cost of either a manufacturer's representative or a company sales force.

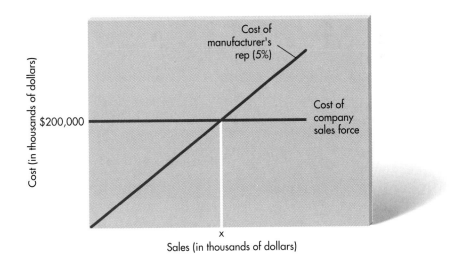

[19]"How the Germans Do It," *Sales and Marketing Management,* Nov. 19, 1989, p. 25.

[20]Melissa Campenelli, "Agents of Change," op. cit., pp. 71–75.

[21]R. D. Rutherford, "Make Your Sales Force Credit Smart," *Sales and Marketing Management,* November 1989, pp. 50–55.

CREDIT COSTS

In examining the costs of offering a credit appeal, managers must consider each of the following factors.

- An estimate of the sales volumes generated under alternative credit policies
- The annual rate of turnover of accounts receivable
- The annual cost of providing trade credit (usually, the firm's cost of borrowing short-term capital plus costs of credit administration)
- The variable-contribution margin

For example, assume a firm offers 30-day credit, a variable-contribution margin of 20 percent, and an annual cost of credit of 12 percent of the average amount of credit outstanding. If all credit customers pay their bills every month, and if expected credit sales under this policy are $20 million, then the annual rate of turnover is 12 (that is, 12 months in a year divided by 1 month), and the annual cost of credit is

$$\frac{\$20 \text{ million}}{12 \text{ turns}} \times .12 = \$200,000$$

Now, assume the same firm believes it can generate an additional $4 million in sales if customers are given 2 months to pay. Because the same credit terms must generally be offered to all customers, we can expect all credit customers to take the full 2 months to pay. Therefore, the accounts receivable turnover is now six per year (12 months divided by 2 months), and the cost of this credit policy is

$$\frac{\$24 \text{ million}}{6 \text{ turns}} \times .12 = \$480,000$$

Thus, credit costs will rise by $280,000 under the new policy. However, at a variable-contribution margin of 20 percent, the added $4 million in sales will increase the firm's dollar variable contribution by

$$\$4 \text{ million} \times .20 = \$800,000$$

Therefore, the net effect of the change in the credit policy will be

$$\begin{aligned} &\$800,000 \text{ (increased variable contribution)} \\ -&\underline{\$280,000} \text{ (increased working-capital cost)} \\ &\$520,000 \end{aligned}$$

Salespeople need to know the direct cost of delayed payment terms. When salespeople are paid commissions based on sales orders rather than on paid-up sales, they do not appreciate the direct cost to the company of delayed payment terms. However, many companies pay their salespeople when payment for the goods is received. In this way, salespeople quickly become as concerned about cash flow and the effect of credit terms on profitability as top management. Geolograph-Pioneer furnishes its salespeople with two statements each month. One shows collections from customers received during the prior month and the second shows all billings not paid. These two statements show each sales representative the status of each account every month, which leads to a closer working relationship between sales and credit.[22]

INVENTORY COSTS

Managers can employ a procedure similar to that used to examine the cost of credit appeals when they wish to identify the budgeting implications of inventory appeals. The major differences in the two analyses are that the annual rate of inventory turnover will be used in place of the annual accounts receivable turnover, and the annual cost of carrying inventory is used in place of the annual cost of providing trade credit. That is, for a given inventory policy

$$\text{Inventory cost} = \frac{\text{annual sales}}{\text{inventory turnover}} \times \text{inventory carrying cost}$$

where

$$\text{Inventory turnover} = \frac{\text{annual dollar sales}}{\text{average dollar value of inventory held by the firm}}$$

Carrying costs generally incorporate short-term borrowing costs, administrative costs, product obsolescence, and breakage. Today these costs are being watched more closely than ever. For instance, 3M Corporation not only looks at inventory costs as they impact its performance but also that of its customers. By affixing logistics labels that position 3M office items located in their customer Boise Cascade's warehouses, 3M was able to reduce inventory by 5 percent or $500,000 for this customer.[23]

As in the case of accounts receivable, increases in inventory costs that result from sales and distribution appeals should be considered direct expenses, and managers should consider the amount of these expenses in evaluating the profitability consequences of the program.

As we suggested earlier, many firms do not yet incorporate these costs when developing sales and distribution budgets. However, as product obsolescence becomes more significant (a particular problem in fashion and high-technology industries), more firms begin to consider the impact of these costs. Consider, for example, the problems experienced by Dynascan.

Dynascan was originally a manufacturer of electronic testing equipment but moved into consumer and office products with its Cobra-brand citizens band radios in the 1970s. Subsequently, the company produced lines of cordless telephones, radar detectors, answering

[22]Ibid.
[23]Rahul Jacob, "Why Some Customers Are More Equal than Others," *Fortune,* Sept. 19, 1994, p. 218.

machines, and other electronics products. While the company was highly successful with all of these products from a sales standpoint, it had severe profit problems with the CB radio and cordless phone products: When sales leveled off, the company was awash in inventory. The company then recognized the impact of working-capital costs on its profits: $4 of working capital was needed to support every $10 of sales. So the company set up a system to analyze all sales programs continually for their impact on working-capital costs.[24]

Physical Distribution Costs

The objective of the physical distribution system should be to minimize total distribution costs and, at the same time, reach a target level of customer service. Because physical distribution activities involve trade-offs, it is necessary to develop systems that take into account the fact that costs often interact in an adverse way. For instance, sales and distribution programs may cause increases in transportation costs when

- The sales force agrees to offer expedited (fastest-way) shipment of rush orders (requiring the most expensive transportation methods).
- More frequent delivery schedules (often entailing less-than-truckload or less-than-carload quantities) are offered.

However, transportation costs are closely linked with customers' inventory policies. Many manufacturers are adopting just-in-time inventory policies. These policies minimize the volume of inventory that needs to be kept on hand for the production process. Usually, the ability to help a customer implement a just-in-time policy is a prerequisite to obtaining a sale.

To the extent that transportation-cost increases result from sales or customer service programs, the increased direct cost should be charged to the sales and distribution budget. Moreover, because transportation costs usually represent a large portion of total costs for products that are bulky or have a high package-to-product weight ratio, it is difficult to pass the increased transportation costs on to customers who require these appeals. Frequently, however, a change in the structure of the sales and distribution system may be useful in providing improved delivery at the same (or lower) prices. As an example, consider the changes initiated by National Semiconductor.

National Semiconductor produces chips at six different fabrication plants; four in the U.S., one in Britain, and another in Israel. The company then ships finished goods to such customers as IBM, Ford, Compaq and Siemens, each with factories located around the world. To reach these customers, National utilized twelve airlines, 20,000 different routes and ten warehouses. National delivered ninety-five percent of its products to customers within forty-five days from the time they were ordered. The remaining five percent took as long as ninety days for delivery, so customers required ninety days' inventory of everything, not knowing which five percent would be late. To reduce costs, they eliminated almost one-half of their products which were in most cases poor revenue contributors. Finished chips were then sent

[24]David Henry, "Death Wish," *Forbes,* Oct. 20, 1986, pp. 50–51.

to a central facility in Singapore operated by Federal Express. FedEx stores, sorts and ships National chips. National now moves product from factory to customer in four days or less and distribution costs have fallen from 2.6 percent of revenues to 1.9 percent.[25]

The total cost of physical distribution is a combination of transportation costs, order-processing costs, and inventory costs. However, these costs are not mutually exclusive and are often complicated because different individuals have responsibility for controlling different components of the costs of physical distribution. For instance, when the traffic manager utilizes rail shipment to reduce transportation costs, the decision may tie up working capital for a long period, delay customer payment, and result in poor customer satisfaction. The same effect on total distribution costs would occur if inappropriate containers were used to minimize shipping costs and led to a high rate of damaged goods and eventual loss of customers. Because decisions on warehousing, inventory, and transportation require close coordination, many firms have centralized control over their physical distribution activities. It is important to recognize that a total cost/customer service level must be considered in physical distribution rather than minimization of each cost component.

Variable-Contribution-Margin Effects

Managers often use price appeals (such as cash and quantity discounts or price shading) to achieve the program objectives. However, each of these appeals results in a reduction in the variable-contribution margin. Accordingly, to the extent that sales personnel have a role in setting prices, the profitability impact of price appeals should be closely evaluated.

CASH DISCOUNTS

Firms in most industries employ cash discounts as sales appeals. In fact, cash discount policies are often established more by industry tradition than through analysis. A wide variety of terms are available. Liz Claiborne, for instance, has terms of 10/10 EOM: Retailers get a discount of 10 percent if they pay for merchandise in the first 10 days after the month in which they receive the goods. Full payment must be made by the end of the month after the goods are received.[26]

Although cash discounts may encourage faster payment of invoices (thus reducing working-capital costs), the costs of the discount often exceed the working-capital costs. For example, a firm that offers a 2 percent discount to buyers or distributors who pay in 10 days rather than 30 days is really paying 2 percent to get its cash 20 days sooner. This translates into an annual interest rate of about 36 percent (that is, 2 percent times 365 days divided by 20 days equals 36 percent). Because most firms can borrow money at rates well below 36 percent, the cash discount policy really increases total cost.

---

[25]Ronald Henkoff, "Delivering the Goods," *Fortune,* Nov. 28, 1994, pp. 70–74.

[26]"An SA Surprise: Claiborne Hikes Trade Discount," *Women's Wear Daily,* July 30, 1990, pp. 1, 19.

QUANTITY DISCOUNTS

The seller may save in many ways through quantity discounts.[27]

- A possible shifting of inventory burdens and costs to the buyer or distributor
- Reduced sales-contact and order-processing costs
- More economical shipping costs because of increases in volume per shipment
- Improved production scheduling because larger, more economical production runs can be made

For instance, assume a firm has a buyer that orders 1200 units per year in monthly orders of 100 units each. Also assume the seller's sales-contact and processing costs per order are $400, the inventory-carrying cost is 20 percent, the unit-variable-production cost is $80, and the price is $100 per unit. Further assume the buyer will purchase in orders of 200 units if the price is lowered to $98 per unit. This means the firm must obtain and process only six orders per year (1200 units divided by 200 units per order). From the seller's viewpoint the two alternatives can be compared in terms of margin reductions and order costs, as indicated in Table 13-5.

The reduced direct cost of obtaining and processing orders offsets the lost contribution margin in this example. Note that this analysis does require several key assumptions.

- That order rates are fairly constant over the year
- That order-processing costs are actually lowered (that is, the sales calls are reduced and reductions in order-processing costs are actually made)

TABLE 13-5 **EVALUATING THE PROFIT IMPACT OF A QUANTITY DISCOUNT**

	AT NORMAL PRICE	AT QUANTITY DISCOUNT
Price	$100/unit	$98/unit
Variable cost	$80/unit	$80/unit
Unit variable-contribution margin	$20/unit	$18/unit
Sales volume	1200	1200
Dollar contribution margin	$24,000	$21,600
Order cost	$400/order	$400/order
Number of orders	12	6
Total order cost	$4800	$2400

Reduction in margin	$24,000 − $21,600 = $2,400
Savings in order cost	$ 4,800 − $ 2,400 = $2,400
Net profit impact	$ 0

---

[27]An analytical approach to establishing quantity discounts is available in James P. Monahan, "A Quantity Discount Pricing Model to Increase Vendor Profits," *Management Science,* June 1984, pp. 720–726.

■ That buyers will perceive a gain from the lower prices that exceed their increased carrying costs

However, the seller is very likely to obtain additional benefits from reduced transportation costs and, in some cases, from reductions in the amount of inventory that must be held by the seller in order to satisfy customer requirements.

CUMULATIVE QUANTITY DISCOUNTS

These discounts (also known as *volume rebates*) are given on the basis of the total volume of purchases over a period of time (usually 1 year) regardless of average order size. Some firms justify these discounts by showing that selling costs for large-volume accounts are proportionately less than for smaller accounts. However, the motivations for employing volume rebates are usually competitive. Customers may demand volume rebates because competitors offer them. However, firms may offer the rebates because the rebates give better account penetration: With volume rebates, there is more incentive for a buyer or distributor to reduce the number of sources of supply.[28]

PRICE SHADING

Price shading appeals are used when a lower price will enable the sales force to close a sale to a particular customer. Frequently, the lower price results in additional sales that otherwise would not be made. This is true especially when opening a new account or attempting to gain a larger share of the business of an existing account (account penetration). In those cases, price shading will increase profitability as long as excess capacity exists and as long as the price exceeds the variable costs plus the cost of delivery. However, the excessive use of price shading may mean the sales force is not emphasizing other nonprice appeals to an adequate extent. By employing price shading on a broad scale, managers may ultimately find dollar-contribution margins begin to decline and competitors begin to expand their use of price shading. Accordingly, some firms have begun to eliminate shading except for new accounts or very large buyers, and others have put greater limits on the sales force's authority regarding price in order to ensure that minimally acceptable margins are realized. For instance, Nucor Corporation, a North Carolina–based steel manufacturer allows no flexibility in pricing by the sales force. Prices are based on how much it costs to run the mill to capacity 24 hours a day. Although salespeople can work with customers in improving delivery times and advising on freight rates, they can't deviate from the price schedule.[29]

---

[28]See Ashak Rao, "Quantity Discounts in Today's Marketing," *Journal of Marketing,* Fall 1980, pp. 44–51, for a more extensive discussion.

[29]In one study, researchers found that salespeople with the greatest degree of pricing authority generated the lowest sales and profit performance. See P. Ronald Stephenson, William L. Cron, and Gary L. Frazier, "Delegating Pricing Authority to the Sales Force: The Effect on Sales and Profit Performance," *Journal of Marketing,* Spring 1979, pp. 21–28; and Melissa Campenelli, "The Price to Pay," *Sales and Marketing Management,* September 1994, pp. 96–102.

Finalizing the Budget

After a manager has identified the costs and margin reductions associated with providing a given set of appeals, a sales budget can be established. As indicated in Figure 13-3, several steps are involved in developing this budget.

1. Determining the required levels of sales and market share needed based on (a) increases in direct costs, (b) changes in variable-contribution margins, (c) the target contribution desired, and (d) the industry sales forecast
2. Determining whether the required sales and market share can be achieved on the basis of productivity judgments
3. Making revisions, if necessary, to the program objectives (such as the level of achievement required) or to the appeals in order to develop a more realistic budget
4. Assigning specific levels of achievement, if appropriate, for program objectives and sales quotas to individual sales territories, salespeople, and, perhaps, to indi-

FIGURE 13-3

Finalizing the sales and distribution budget.

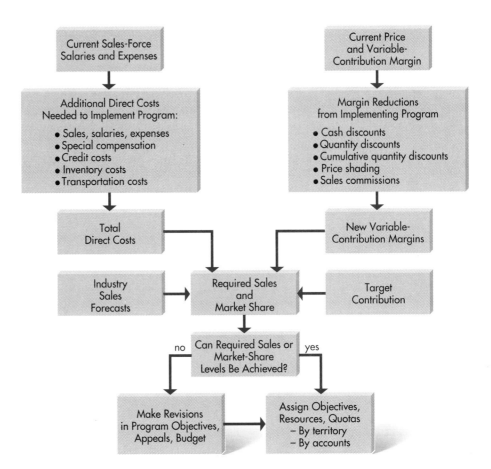

vidual accounts, and allocating human and financial resources to each sales territory in a manner consistent with territorial potential, objectives, and quotas

Note that steps 1 through 3 deal with the total sales and distribution budget. In assessing the likelihood that the required sales and market-share levels will be reached, the impact of other programs (such as advertising) must be known.

Consequently, the sales managers may not be the only managers involved in making the assessment about the reasonableness of the budget. (The process of coordinating program budgets is discussed in detail in Chapter 15.)

Managers may also have to develop separate budgets for different portions of the sales force. For example, a number of organizations separate the sales and customer service functions and budgets. That is, in some firms, customer service is viewed as a separate profit center—particularly, when direct service charges are made to customers receiving maintenance, repair, and operating services.

Finally, as indicated in step 4, separate budgets may be established for individual sales territories and for specific customer or distributor accounts. Sales quotas may be established to indicate specifically the share of required sales that must be achieved in each territory or account in order to meet the budget requirements. Human and financial resources may be allocated to territories or to accounts to reflect differences in the potential for achieving the program objectives or for achieving sales-volume gains.

As the budget becomes finalized, then, the sales manager has effectively established a number of standards for monitoring and evaluating performance.

EVALUATING PERFORMANCE

In order to measure the effectiveness of sales and distribution programs and to identify opportunities for improved resource utilization, managers must employ some procedure for performance evaluation. Of course, measures of sales volume and total profit contribution are useful in evaluation of performance, but these measures may reflect the overall effectiveness of the marketing effort.[30] In evaluating sales and distribution performance, sales managers need measures and procedures that focus on the specific objectives, activities, and costs for which they are responsible. Further, sales managers usually need to evaluate performance at one or more of the following levels.

- Individual salesperson performance
- Individual distributor performance
- Sales territory performance
- Sales segment performance

---

[30]Robert J. Freedman, "For More Profitable Sales, Look beyond Volume," *Sales and Marketing Management,* August 1989, pp. 50–53.

By examining performance at these various levels (as well as total performance), sales managers will be better able to understand the reasons for the overall total program results. Specifically, they will be able to identify the sales segments, territories, salespeople, and distributors that are strong and weak performers. Additionally, if the evaluation procedure is sufficiently detailed, managers should be able to understand the reasons for differences in performance and prescribe some corrective actions.

Individual Salesperson and Distributor Performance

Managers must evaluate the performance of individual sales and customer service personnel and individual distributors with several purposes in mind.

- Awarding incentives and bonuses
- Identifying personnel or distributors who may need additional training
- Identifying *problem* accounts or *problem* geographical areas covered by individual salespeople or distributors
- Determining whether new or additional distributors are needed

To be as widely useful as possible, measures of salesperson or distributor performance should help managers determine whether the performance is due to individual or distributor actions or noncontrollable market forces. This means performance evaluation should include *results-oriented* and *effort-oriented* measures. Tables 13-6 and 13-7 present some of the typical performance measures that are widely used by sales managers.[31]

When results-oriented measures are being used, the measure should have a logical and equitable basis. For example, if dollar-sales volume is being used, individual quotas should be established only after the sales potential in each distributor's or salesperson's account has been considered. Similarly, if the number of new accounts

TABLE 13-6	RESULTS-ORIENTED MEASURES FOR EVALUATING DISTRIBUTORS OR SALESPEOPLE

1. Sales volume (total or by product or model)
2. Sales volume as a percentage of quota
3. Sales profitability (dollar gross margin or contribution)
4. Number of new accounts
5. Number of stockouts
6. Number of distributors participating in programs
7. Number of lost accounts
8. Percentage volume increase in key accounts
9. Number of customer complaints
10. Distributor sales-inventory ratios

---

[31]The frequency with which managers use these various measures is examined in Donald Jackson, Janet Keith, and John Schlacter, "Evaluation of Selling Performance: A Study of Current Practices," *Journal of Personal Selling and Sales Management,* November 1983, pp. 43–51.

TABLE 13-7	EFFORT-ORIENTED MEASURES FOR EVALUATING DISTRIBUTORS OR SALESPEOPLE

1. Number of sales calls made
2. Number of MRO calls made
3. Number of complaints handled
4. Number of checks on reseller stocks
5. Uncontrollable lost job time
6. Number of inquiries followed up
7. Number of demonstrations completed

opened is the performance measure, then the number of potential accounts in each salesperson's or distributor's territory should be considered in evaluating performance.

The most appropriate effort-oriented measures are those most directly related to the sales and distribution program. For example, the number of inquiries followed up will be the most appropriate effort measure to use if the sales and distribution objective is to increase the number of accounts. However, the number of complaints handled will be a more appropriate measure of effort when an accounts-maintenance objective has been established.

In general, however, management's primary concern is with results. Effort-related measures are primarily useful for diagnosing why performance is above or below average. That is, by comparing efforts and results, managers should be better able to assess whether poor performance is due to inadequate effort or misdirected effort. For instance, a salesperson or distributor may have a low performance measure in terms of account development because of a rush of customer complaints that had to be handled or because an inadequate number of sales calls were made. In the latter case, management can ascribe poor performance to a weak effort. But in the former case, the effort may have merely been misdirected because of circumstances beyond the distributor's or salesperson's control. Many companies are in the process of attempting to develop customer satisfaction measures that can be used in measuring individual salesperson performance. Nevertheless, because the customer may be unhappy for reasons out of the salesperson's control (such as prices, competition, or credit policies), performance and effort measures relating to customer satisfaction have not been widely used.[32] By combining results-oriented and effort-oriented measures, therefore, sales managers can better diagnose the reasons for variations in performance and take the necessary remedial actions.

Sales-Territory Performance

Individual sales territories will differ in terms of sales potential and in terms of the resources they require for the firm to remain competitive. For example, some territories will have several well-established, high-volume accounts concentrated in a small

[32]"Taking Aim at Tomorrow's Challenges," *Sales and Marketing Management,* September 1991, pp. 66–80.

area (so sales volume will be high and travel costs low). But other territories may have a large number of small accounts that are widely dispersed geographically, leading to a lower sales potential and higher travel costs. Because of these kinds of differences, managers cannot easily compare performance in several territories. However, each territory can be evaluated in terms of the degree to which sales and distribution objectives are achieved and in terms of profitability measures.

ACHIEVEMENT OF OBJECTIVES

Measures of the achievement of objectives compare the level of performance of each territory with the objectives specified in the sales and distribution program. As we suggested earlier in this chapter, sales managers will usually assign specific levels of the program objective (such as the number of new accounts opened) to each sales territory.

Although managers often use these measures for awarding bonuses and other incentives, they also use them as diagnostic devices for identifying low-performance territories. Once the low-performing territories have been identified, the sales manager can attempt to determine the causes of low performance. For instance, Frito-Lay found sales declining in its South Texas market. Closer analysis revealed that this was occurring because a competitor had gained more shelf space at Frito-Lay's expense in specific Houston and San Antonio supermarkets. Based on this discovery, a head-to-head strategy using computerized analysis and inventory planning to regain shelf space was developed by the district sales manager.[33]

In some cases, the territory objectives may have been set arbitrarily without adequate consideration of market potential and competitive conditions. Alternatively, inadequate effort, unexpected changes in local economic conditions, or a lack of necessary resources may be the cause of poor performance. On the other hand, some territories may have reached their sales and distribution objectives simply because of excessive reliance on price appeals or delivery appeals, which may have resulted in negative profitability. Accordingly, sales-territory performance should also be evaluated from a profitability perspective.

PROFITABILITY

Measures of profitability at the sales-territory level can take several forms. Managers may compare territories to identify any variations in margins and traceable fixed selling costs as a percentage of sales. Additionally, margins and fixed selling costs may be related to sales and distribution objectives. For example, managers may want to measure the total dollars of selling cost per new account.

In addition to margins and selling costs, certain assets may be managed at the sales-territory level. Accordingly, territorial profitability may also be measured in terms of the return generated on those assets. Return-on-assets-managed ratios for dif-

---

[33]Jeffrey Rothfeder, Jim Bartimo, Lois Therrien, and Richard Brandt, "How Software Is Making Food Sales a Piece of Cake," *Business Week,* July 2, 1990, pp. 54–55.

ferent territories can be compared to find opportunities to improve allocation procedures regarding assets and direct expenses or to modify territorial budgets. Typically, accounts receivable, inventories, and warehouse assets are the assets that might be employed for calculating *assets managed*. To the extent that the sales territory determines credit policy and has its own warehouse for holding inventory, the assets managed may be substantial enough to warrant using this measure. Sales and cost analysis identifies the results achieved and the costs of obtaining those results. However, it is also necessary to consider the assets that are necessary to obtain those results. The formula for return on assets managed (ROAM) considers both the contribution margin for a given level of sales and asset turnover.

$$ROAM = contribution\ as\ percentage\ of\ sales \times asset\ turnover\ rate$$

Table 13-8 provides an illustration of the use of territorial profitability measurement.

By comparing profitability results and levels of achievement of program objectives in different territories, managers can obtain several insights on territorial performance. For example

- A low percentage-variable-contribution margin may indicate excessive reliance on price appeals.
- A high ratio of shipping costs-to-sales or a low ratio of sales-to-average inventory may indicate excessive reliance on logistical appeals.

TABLE 13-8

CALCULATING TERRITORIAL PROFITABILITY MEASURES

Sales	$1,500,000
Less variable costs	900,000
Variable-contribution margin	$ 600,000
Less direct costs	
Salaries of sales and customer service personnel	$ 200,000
Travel expense	50,000
Point-of-sale material	30,000
Expediting of shipments	20,000
Contribution to indirect costs and profit	$ 300,000
Assets managed	
Accounts receivable	$ 140,000
Warehouse	600,000
Finished-goods inventory	160,000
Total assets managed	$ 900,000
Contribution as a percentage of sales	$\dfrac{\$300,000}{\$1,500,000} = 20\%$
Asset turnover	$\dfrac{\$1,500,000}{\$900,000} = 1.667$

$$ROAM = 1.667 \times 20\%$$
$$= 33\tfrac{1}{3}\%$$

■ A territory in which account-development objectives are not being met may have a high ratio of new accounts per dollar of salary expense. The current sales force is doing an adequate job of generating new accounts, but is failing to capitalize on the total market opportunity, indicating that the territory may be understaffed.

In sum, the combined use of profitability-performance measures with a measure of the achievement of program objectives will enable managers to evaluate sales territories more fairly and will permit managers to diagnose the problems and opportunities in each territory more effectively.

Sales-Segment Performance

Frequently, managers find major differences in sales and profitability patterns when comparing different types of distributors and different types of customers. By recognizing these differences, managers can often identify possible improvements in the allocation of sales and customer service resources. For example, call frequencies, delivery policies, and discount policies may be adjusted for different types of sales segments. Two approaches can be used in examining these segment differences: sales analysis and distribution cost analysis.

SALES ANALYSIS

Sales analysis is a term that covers a variety of procedures for examining sales performance and sales opportunities across various territories, customer groups, or distribution channels. There is no one best measure of sales and distribution effectiveness. Because of multiple goals and objectives, any performance evaluation needs to consider several factors. Typically, managers use sales analysis to answer questions such as

■ How are sales distributed across sales segments?
■ In which segments did sales exceed or fail to meet expectations?
■ How effectively are sales resources being allocated to sales segments?
■ Which products are being sold to which segments?

Essentially, sales analysis is the process of aggregating the sales reports of individual salespeople in a variety of ways. Consider, for example, the data in Table 13-9.

In this sales analysis report, each salesperson's unit sales results for the period October–December 1995 are aggregated by one of three model types and by customer group. (Note that this company sells directly to some customers, such as government agencies and banking and financial institutions, and indirectly through distributors to other buyers.)

The managerial value of sales analysis can best be examined by first inspecting the total sales figures for each model for the three customer groups and then exam-

TABLE 13-9

EXAMPLE OF A SALES ANALYSIS REPORT

	UNIT SALES OF HIGH-SPEED PRINTERS				
CUSTOMER GROUP AND COMPUTER SERIES	ACTUAL OCT.–DEC. 1995	PLANNED OCT.–DEC. 1995	PERFORMANCE* INDEX	ACTUAL OCT.–DEC. 1994	PERCENT† CHANGE
1. Government agencies					
Series 60	8,000	6,000	133	4,000	100
Series 90	2,000	5,000	40	4,000	−50
Series 99	2,000	4,000	50	4,000	−50
Total	12,000	15,000	80	12,000	0
2. Banking and finance					
Series 60	3,000	3,500	86	3,000	0
Series 90	4,000	2,000	200	2,000	100
Series 99	1,000	1,500	67	1,000	0
Total	8,000	7,000	114	6,000	33
3. Distributors					
Series 60	23,000	18,000	128	18,000	28
Series 90	13,000	16,000	81	10,500	24
Series 99	4,000	2,000	200	1,500	167
Total	40,000	36,000	111	30,000	33
4. Total for 3 groups					
Series 60	34,000	27,500	123	25,000	36
Series 90	19,000	23,000	83	16,500	15
Series 99	7,000	7,500	93	6,500	8
Total	60,000	58,000	104	48,000	25

*Calculated as: (actual 95 ÷ planned 95) × 100

†Calculated as: (actual 95 − actual 94) ÷ (actual 94) × 100

ining the figures within customer groups. For example, Series 99 sales grew by only 8 percent over the preceding year and fell just shy of expectations. (Note that the performance index is just below 100, a level at which planned and actual sales would be equal.) However, these results mask some important sales results. When Series 99 sales are compared across customer groups, it is apparent the sales of this model were well below expectations in the government and banking and finance groups. Similarly, the banking and finance customer group is decidedly different from the other two in the sales performance for the Series 60 and Series 90 models.

This type of information permits management to readily identify areas in which performance is distinctly different from expectations or from past trends. Armed with such information, managers can focus their attention on these particular sales segments to determine whether changes in objectives, appeals, or sales-force effort should be considered. For example, the manager using the data in Table 13-9 would likely be concerned with determining why banking and finance customers are shifting from the Series 60 to the Series 90 whereas government agencies seem to be moving in a different direction.

It is important to recognize, however, that sales analysis provides information on only one dimension. As we suggested at the outset of this chapter, managers must also examine the costs involved in generating these sales and the profit implications of using alternative sales appeals. The most comprehensive approach for analyzing sales and distribution costs is known as *distribution cost analysis.*

DISTRIBUTION COST ANALYSIS

Distribution cost analysis is a procedure that compares the profitability of sales segments and identifies possible approaches for improving profitability. The emphasis in distribution cost analysis is on assessing the costs incurred to generate the achieved level of sales. Specifically, distribution cost analysis can be used to identify changes in sales and distribution appeals and budgets or in the structure of sales and distribution systems that may enhance the profitability of one or more sales segments. Although this procedure can be used to examine the profitability of sales territories, it is more widely employed when the sales segments to be analyzed are

- Alternative systems (for example, direct response versus direct personal selling versus trade selling)
- Alternative distribution channels (for example, department store versus discount chains or wholesale versus direct to retail channels)
- Alternative customer types (for example, buyers in different industries)
- Alternative account-size (sales-volume) classes

The basic procedure employed in performing a distribution cost analysis is to identify the sales revenues and costs attributable to each sales segment. Typically, managers allocate three types of costs to the various sales segments.

- Variable costs associated with manufacturing or selling the product (including sales commissions)
- Direct fixed costs that would not be incurred if a given sales segment were eliminated. (For example, if one or more salespeople sold only to a given sales segment, the salaries and travel expenses of those salespeople would be directly assignable to that segment.)
- Traceable indirect costs that can be allocated (traced) to various segments on some logical, nonarbitrary basis. Operationally, firms will only allocate those indirect costs for which the level of costs can be influenced by the sales and distribution effort or appeals assigned to each sales segment.

The procedures and uses of distribution cost analysis can be illustrated by the analysis developed by Classic Apparel, Inc.

Classic sold a line of fashion-oriented lace blouses through quality department and specialty stores, using a small sales force. Each member of the sales force called on both large department store buyers and small independent women's apparel stores in a given geographic area. In 1995, Classic also began selling blouses via a direct response campaign in which mail-in order forms were distributed through a direct mail service targeted to higher-income households. Classic paid for shipments made to its retail distributors. However, direct response customers paid for the shipping costs of their orders. Table 13-10 presents a distribution cost analysis of Classic's sales and distribution systems.

The analysis revealed some significant differences in the relative profitability of the various systems.

■ The percentage-variable-contribution margin on manufacturer sales for the direct response system was 60 percent, as opposed to 50 percent for the indirect channels, reflecting the elimination of retail margins in the direct response channel.
■ Shipping, selling, and order-taking costs as a percentage of manufacturer sales were much higher for specialty stores than for department stores. A major reason for this was that specialty stores were large in number but purchased in smaller volumes. Department stores were able to order in quantities that were large enough to ship economically.

On the basis of these results, Classic's sales manager was able to identify some possible actions to take in order to improve profitability.

1. Classic could establish minimum order volumes for free delivery or impose delivery charges for small orders.
2. Classic could require cash payments on small orders to reduce credit costs.

TABLE 13-10

DISTRIBUTION COST ANALYSIS: CLASSIC APPAREL, INC.
(sales in thousands)

	DEPARTMENT STORE CHAINS	SPECIALTY APPAREL STORES	DIRECT RESPONSE SALES	BASIS FOR ALLOCATION
Sales	$12,000	$ 4,800	$1,500	Sales receipts
Labor	−2,000	−800	−200	Unit cost
Material	−4,000	−1,600	−400	Unit cost
Variable contribution	$ 6,000	$ 2,400	$ 900	
Shipping	−800	−600	0	Delivery records
Order taking/billing	−10	−30	−60	No. of orders
Personal selling	−400	−800	0	Sales-call reports
Direct mail	−0	−0	−50	Invoices
Credit	−300	−200	−50	Average amount outstanding
Total contribution	$ 4,490	$ 770	$ 740	
Total contribution per $ sales	$ .374	$ .160	$ .493	

3. Classic could reduce the frequency of sales calls on smaller accounts and thereby either reduce the size of the sales force or shift more selling effort to department store chains.

4. The fact that percentage-variable-contribution margins are identical for the two indirect channels suggests that no quantity discounts are being offered. Classic might elect to raise prices but offer quantity discounts to large-volume buyers.

5. Classic might attempt to hire manufacturer's representatives to sell to specialty stores. Currently, personal selling, order taking, and credit costs account for over 20 percent of specialty store sales. If these functions could be performed at a lesser cost by using a second intermediary, profitability could be enhanced.

6. Classic could separate the specialty apparel segment into multiple subsegments based on purchase volume levels. This analysis might reveal that some accounts should be eliminated. It is important to note that a distribution cost analysis is useful in diagnosing where the profitability problems are but not necessarily in choosing the actions to be taken; that is, each of the alternatives under consideration would reduce or eliminate a sales and distribution appeal. Accordingly, before implementing any of these actions, Classic's marketing manager must analyze the sales consequences as well as the cost consequences. In other words, Classic must review the importance of these appeals in the context of distributor requirements and power relationships (as discussed in Chapter 12) in order to determine how specialty apparel stores will respond.

The sales budget is used as the benchmark for evaluating costs. The general approach is to compare the actual costs incurred with those planned as defined in the budget. The ultimate purpose of selling costs is to generate sales. The objective is not to minimize selling costs but to see that a specified relationship between sales and those selling costs is maintained. It is useful to calculate various selling costs as a percentage of sales achieved. This provides a means for evaluating whether the cost-sales relationship has been maintained even when actual costs may exceed the level provided for in the selling budget.

In our discussion of distribution cost analysis we have not taken into consideration what it costs to replace a lost customer. For instance, banks lose about $80 in unrealized revenue every time they lose a customer. Other studies have shown that companies can increase profits by almost 100 percent by retaining just 5 percent more of their customers.[34] In Chapter 7, we noted the importance of customer satisfaction and retention and its impact on the firm. For these reasons, some companies use "number of lost accounts" as a measure of sales performance.[35] Development Dimensions International (DDI) has gone so far as to eliminate sales bonuses for bringing in new clients. This has been done because they believe such bonuses motivate salespersons to develop new business rather than service the existing customer base.

---

[34]Frederick F. Reichheld and W. Earl Sasser, Jr., "Zero Defections: Quality Comes to Services," *Harvard Business Review,* September–October 1990, pp. 105–111.

[35]"How Much Is a Customer Worth?" *Sales and Marketing Management,* May 1989, p. 23.

CONCLUSION

Sales and distribution programs incorporate a variety of activities linking the sales force, the customer service force, and distributors. Further, a number of different objectives and appeals may be employed by sales managers, and these objectives and appeals will affect the firm's cost and profitability structure in many ways.

The complexity of these programs does not mean they are unmanageable, however. The purpose of Chapters 12 and 13 was to present a logical approach for developing and implementing these programs and to identify some of the conceptual and analytical approaches managers can use to achieve effective sales and distribution efforts. The relationship among these conceptual and analytical approaches and the relationship of sales and distribution programs to the other chapters in this book are summarized in Figure 13-4.

Because most marketing jobs fall into the sales and customer service categories, and because the cost and effectiveness of these programs are critical to marketing success, an understanding of these approaches, concepts, and tools is of paramount importance not only to sales managers, but also to the members of the sales force as well. It is vital that managers recognize and use the various tools and concepts discussed in this chapter, as the Alpha One situation demonstrates.

FIGURE 13-4

Relationship of sales and distribution programs to situation analysis, marketing strategy, other marketing programs, and coordination and control activities.

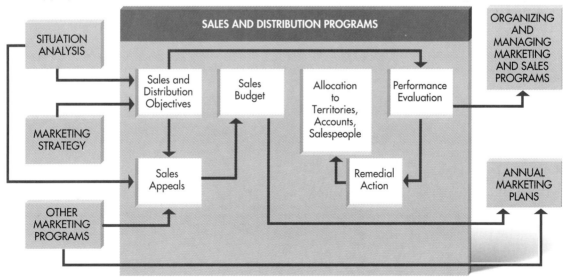

ALPHA ONE:
OUTSOURCING SALES AND MARKETING

Sales Mark was founded in 1904 as a food brokerage. The company operated as a traditional food broker in the state of Arkansas until 1980. Recognizing the trend of consolidation in the food industry, Sales Mark acquired food brokers in Memphis, Tennessee, and Jackson, Mississippi. It then began to offer its services on a regional basis, which meant that a manufacturer could hire one organization for several markets and achieve considerable savings and efficiencies. As manufacturers reduced fees for brokerage services, traditional food brokers expanded into new markets in order to grow and gain market share.

Sales Mark continued to expand to other regions with the goal of becoming the first national food broker. In January 1996, Sales Mark signed a letter of intent to merge with the Gordon Company of Texas and the Phillips Company of Alabama. This was the largest merger to ever take place in the food brokerage industry. With the trend of consolidation likely to continue, it is Sales Mark's goal to have an office in every market where there is a top twenty food wholesaler or chain.

In 1979, the company started providing retail merchandising services for Wal-Mart. Sales Mark had served as a manufacturer's representative for Peter Paul Cadbury, Heath candy, and other confectionery companies and each year these companies requested that, after Halloween, Sales Mark visit all Wal-Mart stores and pick up out-of-date products. Initially, Sales Mark utilized people in the food brokerage business to cover Wal-Mart stores on a once-a-year basis. In 1982, it developed an exclusive retail force to provide ongoing retail merchandising support for Wal-Mart. Recent college graduates were recruited and trained to make effective store calls. Sales Mark provided this service for the manufacturers they represented and offered this as a value-added service. Many manufacturers were beginning to develop teams to work with mass merchandisers such as Wal-Mart, Kmart, and Target at the headquarters level, but they could not afford to dedicate special teams to call upon individual stores to ensure compliance with shelf placement, point-of-sale material, and displays and other implementation of their marketing programs.

In 1987, Sales Mark started a new division with the mission of providing headquarters selling and retail store–level merchandising for the mass merchandise class of trade. Since then, they have expanded their services to over twenty retailers throughout the United States and Canada. Companies like Colgate, Dial, Bristol Myers, Schering Plough, and Procter & Gamble utilized their own direct sales force for store-level merchandising 5 years ago but, today, all use third-party merchandise providers either exclusively or as part of a hybrid organization. In 1995, Sales Mark's Special Market Division was given its own identity as Alpha One because of its rapid growth and acceptance.

Manufacturers have outsourced their retail merchandising services in order to achieve cost reduction and productivity improvement. Third-party providers are specialists and have developed experience and systems to achieve greater results than many manufacturers obtain with their own direct sales forces. Today, major food retailers are reducing labor by eliminating store personnel who often lack the expertise and time to respond to the manufacturer's specialized needs in an environment of cost containment. An organization like Alpha One is viewed as a cost-efficient alternative to staffing an internal organization.

By 1995, Alpha One had $30 million in revenues and 1340 associates. A small sample of its clients includes Coke Foods, Del Monte, Ocean Spray, Fuji, Kal Kan, Mr. Coffee, Bausch & Lomb, Bristol-Myers, Clairol, Dial Corp., and Dow Brands. Retailers serviced include such companies as Wal-Mart, Kmart, Target, Price/Costco, Walgreens, PharMor, Revco, Eckerds, and category superstores. Accounts are classified and coverage may range from weekly to a maximum of quarterly, depending on manufacturer and retail outlet needs and requirements. Alpha One's retail responsibilities may include the following.

- New-item distribution
- Out-of-stocks/voids corrections
- Creation of tags
- Shelf-placement
- Modular changes that sell theme events
- Discretionary display sales
- Major category resets
- IRC placement
- Point-of-sale material placement
- Displays
- Regional projects
- Communication of headquarter trends
- Communication of competitive activity penetration of account
- Audits
- Sample and coupon distribution

Territory sales managers are full-time, salaried, and college-educated employees. They focus on selling and they interface with store management and are able to direct the completion of a variety of complex tasks through the use of approximately 1200 merchandisers who are part-time, hourly employees focused on merchandising. An extensive array of communication systems, including voice mail, interactive response systems, notebook computers, retail reports, and conference calls, are used by Alpha One.

Manufacturers outsourcing their retail merchandising services have been able to reduce their cost of sales from around 5 percent on average to less than 2 percent. In addition, on average, Alpha One is able to increase the rate of products available for sale and on the shelf by 12 percent within the first 6 months it begins servicing the manufacturer. In some cases, out-of-stocks on the shelf have decreased by over 62 percent, with 28 percent corrected immediately with backroom inventory.

1. More companies are trimming inefficiencies and costs by outsourcing internal operations, including some in sales and marketing. Are there any reasons why a company would not utilize retail merchandising services by a third party such as Alpha One?
2. How can Alpha One contribute to lower working-capital costs for both the manufacturers they represent and the retailers?
3. If you were a manufacturer using the services of Alpha One, what measures would you use to evaluate its performance?

Developed with the cooperation of Mr. John N. Owens, president, Alpha-One.

QUESTIONS AND SITUATIONS FOR DISCUSSION

1. If you were to ask ten sales managers what the cost of a sales call is, you would likely get ten different answers. These might range anywhere from $100 to $1000. What do you think would explain such wide disparity in their estimates?
2. After completing an analysis of its accounts, the M&N company found that many of its small accounts were unprofitable. Under what conditions would you recommend that M&N stop selling to these accounts and instead concentrate its resources on the more profitable medium and large customers?
3. Alpha Corporation sells $50 million worth of industrial repair parts to manufacturing companies each year, earning a 50 percent variable-contribution margin.

Recently, customers representing 10 percent of Alpha's sales told Alpha that it must guarantee delivery in 2 days on all parts if it wants their business. Alpha's managers have figures that indicate it will have to increase inventory levels at the regional warehouses from an annual average of $12.5 million to $20 million in order to provide this service. Currently, Alpha's cost of carrying inventory is 25 percent of average inventory.

a. Determine Alpha's inventory cost at both average inventory levels.

b. Should Alpha submit to this request?

4. A manufacturer is reviewing its policy of offering discounts of 1 percent to distributors who pay invoices within 10 days rather than within the normal 30-day period. What specific issues should the manufacturer consider before making this decision?

5. "Computers and communications networks are changing long-standing supplier-buyer relationships." Arthur D. Little predicts that by the year 2000, methods such as desktop computers and interactive television networks (that allow consumers to book flights, hotels, and even entire vacations) will cannibalize 20 to 30 percent of travel agent sales. What effects will this have on both suppliers (airlines, hotels, and so on) and travel agents? What are some ways travel agents can respond to this change?

6. Some companies, such as Nucor, prohibit salespeople from shading prices. Others, such as Canton Analytical Laboratory, Inc., give salespeople pricing authority. What are the factors a company should consider when determining how much flexibility the sales force should have in price negotiations?

7. The national sales manager for your company has asked you to begin evaluating working-capital requirements in assessing the performance of sales territories. You have received the following data for the year just ended for two territories, A and B.

a. Compare the two territories in terms of return on assets managed.

b. Assume the firm's cost of carrying inventory and accounts receivable are 15 and 10 percent, respectively. Treating inventory and accounts receivable as direct costs, compare the total contribution of the territories.

c. Which territory performs best, and what factors account for the differences in performance?

	TERRITORY	
	A	B
Sales	$5,500,000	$6,800,000
Variable costs	3,300,000	4,488,000
Direct selling costs	300,000	350,000
Average inventory	2,040,000	2,125,000
Average accounts receivable	440,000	450,000

SUGGESTED ADDITIONAL READINGS

Cespedes, Frank V., "Channel Management Is General Management," *California Management Review,* Fall 1988, pp. 98–120.

Finkin, Eugene F., "Expense Control in Sales and Marketing," *Journal of Business Strategy,* May–June 1988, pp. 52–55.

Gates, Michael, "New Measures of Sales Performance," *Incentive,* November 1988, pp. 45–52.

Grant, Alan W. H., and Leonard A. Schlesinger, "Realize Your Customers Full Profit Potential," *Harvard Business Review,* September–October 1955, pp. 59–72.

Jackson, Donald, and Lonnie Ostrom, "Grouping Segments for Profitability Analysis," *Business Topics,* Spring 1980, pp. 39–44.

Kaplan, Robert S., "One Cost System Isn't Enough," *Harvard Business Review,* January–February 1988, pp. 61–66.

Lambert, Douglas M., and Jay U. Sterling, "What Types of Profitability Reports Do Marketing Managers Receive?" *Industrial Marketing Management,* November 1987, pp. 295–304.

Levy, Michael, and Michael Van Breda, "A Financial Perspective on the Shift of Marketing Functions," *Journal of Retailing,* Winter 1984, pp. 23–42.

Lodish, Leonard M., "A User-Oriented Model for Sales Force Size, Product, and Market Allocation Decisions," *Journal of Marketing,* Summary 1980, pp. 70–78.

Monahan, James P., "A Quantity Discount Pricing Model to Increase Vendor Profits," *Management Science,* June 1984, pp. 720–726.

Piercy, Nigel, "The Marketing Budgeting Process," *Journal of Marketing,* October 1987, pp. 45–59.

Schiff, J. S., "Evaluating the Sales Force as a Business," *Industrial Marketing Management,* April 1983, pp. 131–137.

Wotruba, Thomas P., and Pradeep K. Tyagi, "Met Expectations and Turnover in Direct Selling," *Journal of Marketing,* July 1991, pp. 24–35.

PART FOUR

CORPORATE MARKETING PLANNING

SITUATION ANALYSIS

MARKETING STRATEGIES AND PROGRAMS

COORDINATION AND CONTROL

Chapter 14 Organizing and Managing
Marketing and Sales Programs
Chapter 15 The Annual Marketing Plan

COORDINATION AND CONTROL

In Part 3 we examined the various marketing strategies and programs that managers use to achieve product objectives. More specifically, we noted that product development, price, advertising, sales promotion, direct marketing, and sales and distribution programs can be used jointly or individually to stimulate demand in the desired fashion.

Because a variety of programs may be employed to carry out a marketing strategy and because more than one individual may be involved in managing these programs for a product or product line, some method of coordinating the programs is necessary. Further, the effectiveness of marketing strategies and programs will depend on how well they are executed. Nevertheless, even a well-designed, closely coordinated, and properly executed plan may fail to achieve the product objectives because of uncontrollable factors such as economic forces or competitors' actions.

In Chapters 14 and 15 we provide tools and procedures for

- Improving the coordination and execution of strategies and programs
- Monitoring results
- Modifying strategies and programs as necessary on the basis of performance or because of major environmental changes or both

Specifically, in Chapter 14, we present alternative approaches for structuring the organization and for managing human resources in order to achieve effective coordination and execution of strategies and programs. In Chapter 15, we demonstrate how managers can use annual marketing plans to coordinate the allocation of resources among marketing programs, monitor performance, and adjust the plan in response to gaps between planned and actual levels of performance.

CHAPTER 14

ORGANIZING AND MANAGING MARKETING AND SALES PROGRAMS

OVERVIEW

A central theme of this book is that managers should select strategies and programs that are consistent with the situation analysis and are designed to achieve specific objectives. However, a well-chosen strategy will still be ineffective if it is not properly executed. It is much easier to think up marketing strategies than it is to make them work under company, competitive, and customer constraints.[1]

As will be shown in Chapter 15, by coordinating the various marketing programs through annual plans, managers can improve the likelihood that the marketing strategy will be properly implemented. However, though the strategy may have been the appropriate one, given the situation, poor execution may have resulted in poor market performance. Therefore, it is important to coordinate and control marketing practices as well as the persons responsible for implementing these decisions.

Additionally, the success of the marketing effort will depend in large part on the degree of coordination achieved between marketing and the other functional areas of a business.

Over the past two decades, a number of important changes have had a major impact on the role of marketing within the company. New forms of business organizations have developed in response to competitive and market conditions. This has led to a transformation of the marketing function and its traditional role within the organization. Accordingly, the organizational structure a firm uses to achieve coordination and the effectiveness of interpersonal relationships among managers in the various functional areas will have a major influence on the success of the firm's strategies.

In this chapter, we will examine some of the problems associated with executing marketing strategies. Because organizational design may be one of the key factors in determining the effectiveness of people in the firm, we will examine some of the

---

[1]The importance of paying attention to execution is discussed in Thomas V. Bonoma, "Making Your Marketing Strategy Work," *Harvard Business Review,* March–April 1984, pp. 68–76.

types of organizational structure as well as factors considered in selecting the most appropriate type. Subsequently, we will examine the relationships among other functions of the business and discuss some ways of managing interfunctional conflict to improve coordination. We then discuss some of the factors bringing about the need to integrate sales and distribution programs in a more efficient way. Additionally, because the successful execution of marketing strategies is determined at the level of the individual salesperson, some of the actions managers can take to improve salesforce execution and effectiveness will be discussed.

The role of the sales force is particularly important in the execution of strategy. As we indicated in Chapter 12, the sales function will be effective only if appropriate sales appeals are communicated and if the sales force is structured for maximum efficiency in calling on customers or distributors. Accordingly, management must be certain that these human resources are effectively used if the strategy is to be properly executed.

EXECUTING MARKETING STRATEGY

Marketing practitioners know successful performance depends both on strategy and on the execution of that strategy. Consider, for example, the case of IKEA:

IKEA is one of Europe's largest furniture retailers. This Swedish firm distributes ready-to-assemble furniture and decorating accessories through a transnational distribution system. IKEA uses an innovative flat-pack technology that saves storage space and cuts shipping costs. This flat-pack technology allows IKEA to display more than 10,000 products in large warehouse stores. Most of its furniture is sold as knock-down kits which customers take home and assemble themselves. A global sourcing network of 1500 suppliers in 67 countries ship to a central warehouse in Amhult, Sweden. This warehouse is staffed by only three people using computerized fork lifts and thirteen robots. IKEA has a thirty percent price advantage over competitors due to the economies of scale from the size of each store and long production runs made possible by selling the same furniture around the world.

However, this successful and flexible system had problems in the United States. In 1985, IKEA opened a 169,000-square-foot warehouse store outside Philadelphia. By 1991, six additional stores were opened, but as early as 1989, IKEA's American operation was in trouble. Many people visited IKEA warehouses but did not purchase. Customers complained of long queues and non-availability of stock. IKEA's American expansion had broken several of the rules of international retailing such as enter a market only after careful study, cater to local tastes as much as possible, and gain local expertise through acquisition, joint ventures, or local franchising. For instance, Swedish beds were narrow and measured in centimeters, matching bedroom suites were unavailable and kitchen cupboards were too narrow for large dinner plates.

IKEA adapted by introducing king and queen sized beds, deeper drawers, and wider shelves. New cash registers that improved throughput by twenty percent, altered store layouts, more generous return policies than in Europe, and next-day delivery service were implemented. In addition, forty-five percent of the furniture in American stores is produced locally, allowing IKEA to cut prices. However, the American experience raises two questions: whether costs can be controlled if the uniformity of products is diluted and whether it is possible to manage effectively the increasingly complex global supply chain.[2]

Marketing strategy and the execution of this strategy have a reciprocal effect on each other. Thomas Bonoma, a former professor at the Harvard Business School, has concluded that strategy obviously affects actions; and execution also affects marketing strategies over time.[3] Problems in implementation can often disguise a good strategy. If the execution of the strategy is poor, it may cause marketing management to attribute the failure to a poor strategy and permanently change its approach. However, at the other extreme, one may find inappropriate strategies compensated for by excellent execution. In this situation, management may have time to recognize its strategic mistakes and adjust its strategy. At other times, it is possible that good execution of a poorly designed strategy can accelerate failure. Because poor execution may disguise whether the strategy was appropriate or inappropriate, it is necessary that managers look to marketing practices before immediately making strategic adjustments. These problems and practices can occur with either marketing functions, programs, systems, or policy directives.

Often, poor execution is the result of the failure of management to pursue marketing fundamentals or to follow up on their implementation. Another cause of problems or failure comes about from the lack of a clear focus or from trying to concentrate on too many functions at one time, resulting in what Bonoma has called "global mediocrity." In contrast, successful execution often derives from excellence in performing one function well. Leading companies drive the market by raising the value that customers expect from everyone. Research shows that no company today can succeed by being all things to all people. Instead, companies must offer unique customer value in operational excellence (Wal-Mart), product leadership (Nike), or customer intimacy (Cable & Wireless Communications).[4]

Marketing programs often require the coordination of marketing and nonmarketing activities. Management attempts to blend functions such as sales promotion and production to sell a particular product or penetrate a target market. The combining of these various functions into effective marketing programs is often done poorly. Poorly executed programs may result when a company tries to go beyond its functional capabilities or if it lacks direction. Pepperidge Farm's decision to introduce Star Wars cookies, which didn't fit their upscale, high-quality image, was a strategy that didn't match either marketing identity or product direction.

---

[2]Barbara Soloman, "A Swedish Company Corners the Business Worldwide," *Management Review,* April 1991, p. 10-B; Bill Saporito, "IKEA's Got 'Em Living Up," *Fortune,* Mar. 14, 1991. p. 72; Jeffrey A. Tracktenberg, "IKEA Furniture Chain Pleases with Its Prices, Not with Its Service," *Wall Street Journal,* Sept. 17, 1991, pp. A1, A5; and "Furnishing the World," *The Economist,* Nov. 19, 1994, pp. 79–80.

[3]Professor Bonoma has argued that more often than not it is poor implementation rather than poorly designed strategies that results in failure to achieve marketing objectives. This section is based on Bonoma's investigations as described in Thomas V. Bonoma, "Making Your Marketing Strategy Work," *Harvard Business Review,* March–April 1984, pp. 69–76; and in Thomas V. Bonoma, *Managing Marketing,* Free Press, New York, 1984, p. 552.

[4]Michael Treacy and Fred Wersema, "How Market Leaders Keep Their Edge," *Fortune,* Feb. 6, 1995, pp. 88–98.

Poor marketing practice may be due to errors in formal organization, inadequate resource commitment, or failure to depart from tradition. For instance, a few years ago IBM was one of the world's most profitable companies, and reputedly one of the best managed. IBM's success had been built upon market domination for large mainframe computers. These machines were built to proprietary standards so they didn't work with those of other manufacturers. Once a customer was committed to IBM, there was little payoff in scrapping millions invested in hardware and customized software to switch to an unfamiliar supplier. However, in the mid-1980s the increasing power and falling prices of personal computers transformed the industry. In the late 1980s, new integrated circuits and a new variety of desktop machines (workstations) made it possible to tie these units together in a network as a cheap alternative to minicomputers and mainframes. IBM failed to see the threat that PCs and workstations posed to its mainframe business. This resulted in losses of $16 billion for IBM between 1991 and 1993.[5]

The lack of adequate information may also result in poor execution. Too frequently, marketing managers lack the necessary information to determine profitability by segment, product, or individual account—even though such information is requested from other functional departments.

Several distinct characteristics seem to differentiate companies that execute marketing effectively from those that do not. First, the best organizations seem to have a sense of identity and direction. A clear theme and vision are present, and there is little uncertainty as to what the company represents and where it is going. For instance, Mag Instruments manufactures and markets state-of-the-art flashlights. Mag has been built on a philosophy and strategy of pushing quality to the limit. Premium quality permeates every aspect of the company's operations, from its uniquely designed products to its manufacturing process and entire marketing effort. As a result, the company can sell its best-selling flashlight for a retail price of $16.95, double the price of most flashlights. Mag products consistently appear in lists of best American-made products as well as on those that illustrate the finest in American design.[6]

Second, concern for customers, including retail and wholesale distributors, exists with those firms that consistently execute their strategies effectively. These firms view end users and distributors as partners and expect them to profit in terms of the value they receive as well as the lasting partnership that develops. For instance, Black & Decker Corp. has divisions with people from a variety of functions, such as logistics and finance, that are dedicated to serving such customers as Home Depot. In developing its new heavy duty professional power tools, Black & Decker executives spent 3 months visiting more than 200 retailers to solicit feedback.[7]

Finally, in those companies that consistently seem to execute marketing well, employees are encouraged to challenge and question upper management.[8] For exam-

[5]"What Went Wrong at IBM?" *The Economist*, Jan. 16, 1993, pp. 23–26; and Carol J. Loomis and David Kilpatrick, "The Hunt for Mr. X: Who Can Run IBM?" *Fortune*, Feb. 22, 1993, pp. 68–72; and "The View from IBM," *Business Week*, Oct. 30, 1995, pp. 142–152.

[6]Paul B. Brown, "Magnificent Obsession," *Inc.*, August 1989, pp. 79–84.

[7]"New Selling Tool: The Acura Concept," *Fortune*, Feb. 24, 1992, p. 88.

[8]Thomas V. Bonoma, "Market Success Can Breed Market Inertia," *Harvard Business Review*, October 1981, p. 115.

ple, lower-level managers are encouraged to provide suggestions for improvements to existing methods of operation. Delta Airlines, for instance, is known for its open-door policy for employees and its willingness to make substantial policy changes as a result of employee suggestions.

Factors Influencing Marketing Organization

Marketing as a management function was centralized well into the 1970s. Marketing was related to the other functions of the business primarily through the budgeting and financial reporting process. This centralization provided for specialized expertise as well as economies in the purchase of marketing services. In addition, it was useful for maintaining control of marketing efforts for individual product groups and brands as well as the sales effort.

In the 1980s, more and more organizations found it necessary to downsize and become more flexible in responding to changing competition and market conditions, including advances in telecommunications, transportation, and information. In addition, global competition led to better alternative products at lower costs for consumers. In most companies, these changes resulted in pressures to reduce costs through technological improvements in products, better manufacturing processes, and reorganization.

The new organizations took on a variety of forms to respond to changes in technology, competition, and consumer demands. One trend was the emphasis on partnerships between previously competing firms, such as General Motors and Toyota, Ford and Mazda, and IBM and Apple Computer. Other responses were to develop multiple types of ownership and partnering within the organization, such as IBM displayed in reorganizing itself into more autonomous operating units (such as Lexmark International, its former desktop printer and typewriter business). Others, such as Nike and Reebok, whose strengths are in design and marketing, farm out the production of their shoes to efficient, low-cost factories in the Far East. Regardless of the form, these new organizational responses are characterized by flexibility, specialization, and an emphasis on managing relationships rather than just market transactions.[9] Although market forces are a major factor in conducting business and determining prices, equally important are ongoing relationships and negotiation.

These relationships take the form of either a strategic alliance, a joint venture, or a network. A strategic alliance takes place in the context of a company's long-term strategic plan and seeks to improve or dramatically change a company's competitive position. Joint ventures are a kind of strategic alliance, but unique in that they create a new firm with its own capital structure where members share other resources. Networks result from multiple strategic alliances and are usually combined with other forms of organization either within or outside the existing company. Although there is no single best way to organize, the presence or absence of certain conditions can influence the effectiveness of a given organizational structure.

---

[9]For an excellent discussion, see Frederick E. Webster, Jr., "The Changing Role of Marketing in the Corporation," *Journal of Marketing,* October 1992, pp. 1–17.

Corporate Strategy

A major purpose of structure in an organization is to assist in the implementation of corporate strategies. Accordingly, one type of structural form may be superior or inferior, depending on the strategic situation. A market-development strategy might require a functional or customer-oriented organization if new markets are to be effectively developed. For example,

> Digital Equipment Corporation (DEC) was organized by product line for nineteen years. Product managers were responsible for profitably developing and marketing one product line. However, introducing the VAX superminicomputers, which were intended to be capable of automating entire corporations, required a highly unified and coordinated marketing effort. To accomplish this marketing effort DEC dismantled the product-line organization and organized along functional lines. The development of the VAX 9000, which directly competes with IBM mainframes, brought additional organizational changes in 1989. In an effort to target specific industries, regional managers were put in charge of all employees—programmers, system engineers, and salespeople—who serve a given industry.[10]
>
> In 1992, the company reorganized into nine business units, focusing on specific industries and product markets. In addition, DEC is seeking a partner to help design future processors for its Alpha AXP line of computers based on a reduced-instruction-set computing chip.[11]

Note that DEC's structure changed as its strategy changed. Consequently, management should allow the strategy to dictate the structure rather than the reverse. For instance, Sony is working with Panavision, Inc., on a lens for a high-definition TV; with Compression Labs, Inc., on a new video conferencing machine; and with Alphatronix, Inc., on rewritable optical disk storage technologies. In none of these cases has Sony assumed equity or formed a joint venture. They simply share staff, production facilities, engineering concepts, and marketing research and plans.[12]

Needs of Target-Segment Customers

A firm's organizational structure should provide management with the most effective way to meet customer needs quickly. Oracle Corporation reorganized its marketing for this reason. Oracle produces large and small databases and applications programs and operates the fourth largest consulting business in the world. In the 1980s, Oracle dominated the high-end database market and sales had reached $1 billion in 1990. However, in 1990, Oracle was close to bankruptcy. Products were being sold before developers had finished making them, marketing efforts were inconsistent, and, by the time a product was finished, it often took several months before it reached the field

---

[10]Peter Petre, "America's Most Successful Entrepreneur," *Fortune,* Oct. 27, 1986, pp. 24–32; and "DEC Has One Little Word for 30,000 Employees: Sell," *Business Week,* Jan. 18, 1993.

[11]Gary McWilliams, "DEC's Comeback Is Still a Work in Progress," *Business Week,* Jan. 18, 1993, pp. 75–76.

[12]Allan J. Magrath, "Collaborative Marketing Comes of Age—Again," *Sales and Marketing Management,* September 1991, p. 62.

sales force. Product groups passed new products to a product marketing group, which then passed the product to the corporate marketing group. Corporate marketing then passed the product to field marketing and from there to the 2000 Oracle salespersons. Reorganization was undertaken starting in 1993 and, after restructuring, the only exchange is from product marketing to the field group. In 1995, sales were up 50 percent over the previous year and ten major new products were introduced.[13]

Customer considerations are the major focus at Sony Medical, which makes printers and other peripherals used with medical imaging equipment. Sony personnel spend lots of time with doctors and HMOs and constantly search the rest of Sony for technologies that might serve these customers. When they find a possible technological application, they start a new group of about ten people from different disciplines to develop the idea. In 1992, using Sony's Touchscreen and laser-disc technology, they created an interactive system that helps patients learn about their afflictions. Sales are projected to total $40 million within 4 to 6 years. Sony Medical is constantly creating, and then eventually destroying, the organization as the market demands.[14]

In sum, to the extent that customer needs differ among products and customers, the organizational structure should enable the firm to develop and execute marketing strategies to meet the needs of target customers. Further, the more dynamic a firm's markets, the greater the importance of being able to respond to customers' needs.

Management Philosophy and Resources

Management attitudes regarding concepts such as participative decision making, decentralization, and innovation will also influence the effectiveness of an organizational design. For example, in discussing Henry Ford II's decision to retire as chief executive officer of the Ford Motor Company, *Business Week* emphasized his desire to build a decentralized management structure similar to that of General Motors.[15] However, because of the strong personality of Henry Ford and his inability to relinquish control over certain decision areas, this effort was less than successful.

Unilever, which was formed in a 1930 merger of Britain's Lever Brothers Ltd. with Holland's Margine Union Ltd., was one of the first true global marketers. Most of Unilever's United States business is done by Lever Brothers. Unilever's unusual Anglo-Dutch structure gave it a multinational culture, which resulted in a highly decentralized management. For the most part, Unilever's top management let local executives of its 500 subsidiaries in 75 countries run things as they chose. However, in the United States, the company set unrealistic profit objectives that led Lever Brothers managers to reduce advertising spending at the same time competitors were increasing expenditures and introducing new brands.

After Lever Brothers lost a total of $100 million from 1981 to 1986, Unilever took a more active role in the U.S. operations. One of Unilever's top executives came to the United States and essentially dismantled Lever Brothers, leaving it with only

---

[13]Allison Lucas, "Zack Attack," *Sales and Marketing Management,* December 1995, pp. 46–50.

[14]Brian Dumaine, "The New Non-Manager Managers," *Fortune,* Feb. 22, 1993, pp. 83–84.

[15]"Ford after Henry II: Will He Really Leave? Absolutely," *Business Week,* Apr. 30, 1979, pp. 62–72.

household products. The personal products division was shifted to Chesebrough-Ponds Inc., and the food division was made into a separate unit called VanderBurgh Foods. Each division now reports directly to Europe. This eliminated several layers of management and resulted in faster adoption of new ideas. Subsequently, Unilever's share of the U.S. household products market rose from 15 percent in 1980 to 25 percent in 1989. In addition, overall operating profit increased 69 percent during this period.[16]

To summarize, the marketing organization must be structured so that corporate and marketing strategies can be effectively and efficiently carried out to meet customer needs. In addition, top management must be aware that both its philosophy and attitudes about the role of marketing and the availability of qualified middle managers can lead to the choice of an improper structure.

However, the structure of the total organization and of the marketing organization can never ensure the successful execution of strategies and programs. Organization charts do not coordinate activities—people do. And because of marketing's integrative role with the other functional areas, the ability to manage interorganizational relationships is essential, especially for product and market managers.

TYPES OF ORGANIZATIONAL STRUCTURES

Essentially, an organizational structure accomplishes two things.

1. It defines the formal allocation of work roles in order to identify the members of the organization who will perform each activity.
2. It establishes the lines of authority in order to integrate and coordinate activities.

In this section, our major concern is with the impact of traditional organizational structure on the execution of marketing activities. Specifically, we examine the ways in which a given structure can enhance or limit the coordination of marketing activities.

Firms have organized along one of three dimensions: the *functions* performed, the *products* and product lines offered, or the *markets* to be served. Although certain combinations of these forms can be used to fit the specific situation facing an individual firm, the primary basis for organization will be along one of these three dimensions.

Organizing by Function

The functional organization structure is a common approach to grouping marketing activities, especially among companies that offer a limited variety of products or services. In this type of structure, marketing activities are organized according to the type of duties performed, and decision-making authority and coordination are highly centralized. Because all functions are centralized, this structure is most applicable

---

[16]Walecia Konrad, "The New, Improved Univeler Aims to Clean Up in the U.S.," *Business Week,* Nov. 27, 1989, pp. 102–106.

when the product line is relatively limited; when the products have similar manufacturing, research, and advertising requirements; and when the same sales force and distributors can easily be used for all the firm's products.

Although the centralization of the marketing effort reduces problems in coordinating marketing programs, it places a major responsibility on the chief marketing executive to coordinate marketing with the other functional areas. Additionally, when all decisions are centralized, decision making is often slow. Further, in large firms, the chief marketing executive may have difficulty in keeping abreast of market developments for every product. As a result, many firms have found that, as product lines expand, a completely centralized functional organization becomes unwieldy. For example, consider the changes initiated by Xerox.

> When Japanese producers introduced low-price copiers in the mid-1970s, Xerox was unprepared to compete for this market segment. Because of this competition, Xerox's share of U.S. copy revenues declined from 96 percent in 1970 to less than 45 percent in 1983. Product planning, design, service, and manufacturing had reported to separate executives at corporate headquarters, and no one had the primary responsibility for seeing that new products were completed and introduced. To correct this, Xerox reorganized the copier business into four strategic business units. General managers of each unit set long-range strategy and oversaw product development while reporting to the head of the Reprographics Business Group, who in turn answered to only one executive at headquarters. This resulted in an immediate 10 percent productivity gain. Further, engineering cycles for some new products were shortened by 10 percent.[17]

Essentially, decentralization can be accomplished by organizing on the basis of products or markets. The previous Xerox organizational form was in place until 1992, when Xerox created nine businesses aimed at markets such as small business systems, engineering systems, and office document systems. Each business now has its own profit responsibility and an identifiable set of competitors. Manufacturing layouts have been reorganized to be dedicated to specific businesses. A new Customer Operations Group, consisting of sales, shipping, installation, service, and billing, has been created. Businesses negotiate contracts with Customer Operations to ensure that information about market forces and customers extends into all areas of each business.[18]

Organizing by Product

To the extent that a firm has a large array of products, and to the extent that the products are dissimilar in terms of their marketing requirements (so that each product requires specialized attention), a product-oriented organization can be structured in two ways: through product-manager systems or through autonomous product divisions.

[17]"How Xerox Speeds Up the Birth of New Products," *Business Week,* Mar. 19, 1984, p. 38; and "The New Lean, Mean Xerox: Fending Off the Japanese," *Business Week,* Oct. 12, 1981, pp. 126–132.

[18]Thomas A. Stewart, "The Search for the Organization of Tomorrow," *Fortune,* May 18, 1992, pp. 92–98.

THE PRODUCT-MANAGER SYSTEM

In a product-manager system, individual managers are assigned to coordinate the marketing programs of one or more products or brands. The key to the successful use of this form of organization is the effectiveness with which the product manager coordinates marketing programs with manufacturing and logistics. The product manager will develop and administer marketing programs; analyze and report on a business's progress; administer budgets; oversee sales, product development, and manufacturing functions; and train personnel. Although product managers have no line authority over the field sales force, they work closely with them to accomplish the necessary sales goals for their products. Although the product-management job differs from organization to organization, frequently, the product or brand manager is given a budget for the marketing of the brand and then is expected to purchase sales support, advertising, marketing research, or other services the brand requires from the company.

The product-manager organization is not without its deficiencies, however. For example

■ The product manager may be knowledgeable about the product while lacking the expertise needed to make appropriate decisions in the technical areas of product research, manufacturing, and even sales and media.

■ Product managers generally lack the authority commensurate with their responsibilities. For example, they must attempt to coordinate sales promotions with sales-force and manufacturing schedules, but they have no authority over either activity. Accordingly, they must rely on their persuasive capabilities to gain the necessary cooperation.

■ Many product managers find little time to perform the planning activities so critical to success because of the extensive time and effort involved in their daily interactions with other functional areas.

■ Product managers spend considerable time on research and analysis, refining and executing minor changes, and balancing quarterly marketing expenditures, but much of this activity deals with issues on which they can have only limited impact.

■ If the product or brand manager has profit responsibility and is rewarded based on the profit performance of the brand, there may be no incentive to invest to build market share, because this may reduce short-term profits.

Product management is undergoing a fundamental change for several reasons. Technology has provided brand managers with increasing amounts of information, and mass markets are becoming more fragmented. The advent of tracking technology has changed brand marketing's focus from broad national programs into numerous regional and subregional campaigns. Perhaps, more important, has been the growth of the retailer's influence, as we discussed in Chapter 12. Retailers want companies to talk to them with one voice rather than several. This has led to the development of category management in companies like Procter & Gamble, Clorox, and Ralston Purina. At Ralston Purina, category managers set the trade promotion budget and calendar, and the trade marketing organization controls day-to-day decisions in the field, including how the budget is spent. At some companies, such as Coca-Cola Foods in Houston, brand managers have been eliminated and replaced by regional trade and consumer marketing groups.[19]

THE MULTIDIVISIONAL PRODUCT ORGANIZATION

Firms with a very large number of products that differ in their manufacturing and R&D requirements, as well as in their marketing requirements, often employ a multidivisional product organization. In this organizational structure, separate divisions are formed, with products grouped into divisions containing similar products. Each division will have its own functional organization and, very frequently, will contain a product-management system.

In many firms, each division will be treated as a unique, autonomous business. Additionally, a recent study indicates that in well-managed companies, divisional managers are usually given responsibility for replenishing the new-product array and are usually allowed to reinvest earnings from the division's own products within the division. Although this practice appears inconsistent with the product portfolio approach, managers can still use the product portfolio concept to determine allocations of resources and product objectives among products within each division. More important, many of these firms believe managers will not develop entrepreneurial skills in corporations that "give the fruits of one manager's labor to someone else."[20]

This organizational approach has some limitations. In some cases, divisional lines can inhibit coordination and increase costs. But Sara Lee avoided this problem.

> Sara Lee made its first European acquisition in 1962 when it obtained a Dutch producer of canned foods. Since that time, Sara Lee has made numerous other international acquisitions, including Douwe Egberts (Dutch coffee, tea, and tobacco company), Nicholas Kiwi Ltd. (the Australian maker of shoe polish), Akzo N.V. (consumer products division), and DIM (French hosiery and underwear). Cornelius Boomstra, chairman of the company's main European unit, in preparation for the European Union after 1992, initiated a program of standardization and reorganization. Douwe Egberts coffee was previously sold under different brand names in seven countries. Standardized packaging sizes and colors and a global advertising campaign was initiated to develop a European identity. By integrating the management structures of Akzo, Douwe Egberts, and other European units, Sara Lee expected profits to improve by $40 million a year. To avoid interdivisional disputes with existing megabrands, specialty products have been emphasized for Eurobranding. For instance, instead of expanding *Prudent,* its top selling Benelux brand, Sara Lee selected *Zendium,* a Danish enzyme toothpaste that cost more. By combining administration and developing a coordinated approach, Boomstra anticipates Sara Lee will be better prepared to develop the European market and at the same time save enormous amounts of money.[21]

[19]Laurie Peterson, "Brand Managing's New Accent," *Adweek's Marketing Week,* Apr. 15, 1991, pp. 18–22.

[20]Thomas J. Peters, "Putting Excellence into Management," *Business Week,* July 21, 1980, p. 200.

[21]Steve Werner, "How Do You Say L'Eggs in French?" *Forbes,* Nov. 27, 1989, pp. 73–77.

Organizing by Market

When customer groups have dramatically different needs, and when these groups are large enough to justify individual attention, the organizational structure often includes market managers and separate sales forces. Note that the various market managers may share common manufacturing and research facilities because, essentially, the same product is being sold to different markets. However, there may be major differences in the quantities purchased, the appropriate channels of distribution, or the technical usage needs of the various customer groups. Accordingly, different packaging and pricing programs, sales forces, and customer service activities may be needed for each group. In these situations, many firms have begun to adopt these market-based organizational structures.

For example, Procter & Gamble has assigned employees from other areas of the company—marketing, finance, distribution, operations—to coordinate with sales and work with key buyers. A group of P&G executives was moved to Arkansas to work every day with Wal-Mart, P&G's largest account. Borden, Inc., at one time had twenty-eight different people calling on Wal-Mart to sell a variety of snack-food brands. Borden has combined its eight sales organizations, six distribution operations, and five information systems into one to deal with large customers.

As in the case of product managers, market managers seldom have authority over all the functional areas that are essential for implementing the marketing programs. Rather, market managers are responsible for planning and coordination, and sales managers are responsible for implementation. Mergers of large retailers have created a number of regional giants with immense distribution power. These large retailers require specialized attention, such as Gillette's Safety Razor Division provides. Gillette chose to concentrate on the regional level rather than expand their national accounts department. Regional key account managers not only call upon headquarters but also upon chain division offices, even if they are outside the region. The regional sales manager's job expanded into that of a business unit manager. This was accomplished by putting merchandising and sales planning under the regional sales manager. Salespeople, as a result of this restructuring, are now prepared to talk to their accounts about pricing, distribution, promotion, and display.[22]

A recent study of American consumer-goods firms by the Boston Consulting Group found that 90 percent of those surveyed had restructured their marketing departments.[23] For instance, in 1994, Lever Brothers eliminated the position of marketing director. Lever combined the marketing and sales departments and reorganized them as a series of business groups. These groups focus on consumer research and product development. In addition, Lever has established "customer development" teams that are responsible for relations with retailers for all the company's brands. The traditional marketing department at Pillsbury has been replaced by multidisciplinary teams for different product groups. These teams include managers from production, sales, and marketing. Pillsbury has reduced its product-development team by 30 percent under this new structure.

[22]"Gillette Hones Salespower to a Fine Edge," *Sales and Marketing Management,* June 1987, p. 59.

[23]"Death of the Brand Manager," *The Economist,* Apr. 9, 1994, pp. 67–68.

MANAGING ORGANIZATIONAL RELATIONSHIPS

In Chapter 1, we discussed the various ways in which marketing was related to the other functional areas of the organization. Because of these interrelationships, marketing managers must develop interpersonal skills to be successful in dealing with managers over whom they have no direct authority. Managers consistently cite the importance of their interactions with others, especially in coordinating efforts with other departments. In particular, marketing activities must be closely coordinated with R&D, manufacturing, physical distribution, and finance. We will now discuss the importance of achieving coordination with each of these functions.

Research and Development

In most product-development programs, marketing and R&D must work closely together. Accordingly, marketing managers should have an understanding of the technical problems and processes involved in the various stages of product development. Additionally, managers must be aware of the inevitable frustrations and exacting nature of the R&D activity and should share fully their knowledge of the needs of the market to provide useful guidelines for the work of R&D. Consider, for example, the experience of Colgate.

In 1985, Colgate started to adopt a system whereby managers of product categories would have direct profit responsibility. To provide them with the necessary authority, these category managers were given some control over other functions such as research, finance, and manufacturing. This system was designed to promote better planned and faster new-product introductions. A. Courtenay Shepard, Colgate's president in the United States, says, "by surrounding the marketing people with these multidisciplinary skills we make them instantly effective." This approach has been attributed as the reason the company could take FAB 1 Shot detergent and fabric softener from the idea stage to national introduction in only 11 months.[24]

But these two functions often don't share knowledge. One author has suggested four reasons for the lack of coordination between marketing and R&D.

1. *Product-oriented company philosophy:* In many companies the orientation is an inward-looking one, dominated by products, properties, and processes. This attitude leads to the development of products that are designed around the organization's technological capability rather than around market needs.
2. *Deference toward R&D:* Marketing managers' lack of knowledge regarding the tools and techniques of the "scientists" may lead to permissiveness or great deference to R&D. As a result, some R&D efforts may lead to products that have little chance for commercial success.
3. *Search for perfect products:* R&D often attempts to achieve product perfection. But a technically perfect solution to the problem may be more than the market

---

[24]Zachary Schiller, "The Marketing Revolution at Procter & Gamble," *Business Week,* July 25, 1988, p. 76.

desires. Technically superior products may be unmarketable because the complexity of these products may preclude high reliability or ease of maintenance. Alternatively, such products may have to be priced too high because of excessive production costs.

4. *Science versus art:* Although market satisfaction is derived from *benefits* (which are usually intangible), R&D is concerned with the tangible *attributes* of products.[25]

Because marketing and R&D in many companies tend to view their jobs as very different from one another, it is difficult to get them to cooperate. However, in a study of German small and midsize companies having world market shares in the range of 70 to 90 percent, it was found that these firms viewed the market and technology as equal driving forces. These companies believe that when technology dominates, engineers become remote from customers. Likewise, when marketing dominates, technology suffers. The ideal would be for technical people to have a thorough understanding of consumer needs. Direct contact by people in R&D with consumers is critical. Wurth & Company, for instance, requires all its managers to see a customer at least once a month.[26] Physically locating departments next to one another and holding combined departmental meetings has worked for some firms. The key is having someone coordinate the effort—someone who has the necessary authority to get the two groups to cooperate. In Chapter 3 we discussed the "house of quality" as a way of getting marketing and research and development to work more closely with each other. QFD encourages better communication between functions, because manufacturing, R&D, and engineering each have their own uses and demands for information from the customer.[27]

Manufacturing

Probably the most frequent conflicts between functions are those between marketing and manufacturing. Areas of potential conflict may be present in such areas as capacity planning, sales forecasting, production scheduling, logistics, quality assurance, and new-product introductions. For instance, in 1995, General Electric introduced its first fundamentally new washing machine in 42 years. GE spent an estimated $10 million on advertising and marketing, and orders from retailers far exceeded GE's expectations. Retailers' floor samples were delayed and production schedules were 3 weeks behind schedule. This production delay resulted in risking the brief marketing advantage GE had anticipated for the Maxus line.[28]

[25]Mack Hanan, "Effective Coordination of Marketing with Research and Development," in *Handbook of Modern Marketing,* ed. Victor Buell, McGraw-Hill, New York, 1970, pp. 3-17 to 3-28.

[26]Herman Simon, "Lessons from Germany's Midsize Giants," *Harvard Business Review,* March–April 1992, p. 120.

[27]Michael Duerr, *The Commercial Development of New Products,* The Conference Board, New York, 1986; Abbie Griffin and John R. Hauser, "The Voice of the Customer," *Marketing Science,* Winter 1993, pp. 2–3.

[28]"GE Has a New Washing Machine," *Business Week,* Nov. 20, 1995, pp. 97–100.

Although these conflicts can seldom be fully resolved, the level of conflict between these two groups can be made more manageable so that greater cooperation is achieved. Among the actions managers may employ to manage these conflicts are the following.

- Clearly specified corporate strategies and marketing strategies should be developed to provide a common set of rules for both functions. For example, when the markets to be served are clearly specified, the number of models or product lines to be produced can be agreed upon more easily.
- Management can modify the evaluation and reward system to include interfunctional performance. For instance, marketing managers may be evaluated on sales forecasting performance and manufacturing managers on order response time as well as on inventory levels. Marketers must be made aware that process-development capabilities can help differentiate products. The manufacturing process for Gillette Sensor not only makes possible a distinctive product, but also is a major barrier to entry for competitive blades and razors.[29]
- By having manufacturing personnel attend sales meetings or marketing managers do "internships" in manufacturing positions, managers in each functional area may gain better insights into the problems facing managers in the other functional areas.[30]

Physical Distribution

An effective and well-integrated physical distribution system can provide a firm with a significant competitive marketing advantage. Because a substantial share of the final price of a product is accounted for by physical distribution costs, any reduction in price resulting from more effective coordination will lead to more competitive prices or higher margins. In addition, companies are finding that the speed with which they respond to changes in the market is the most crucial element in being more competitive.

Allegheny Beverages' computerized order-entry system provides this type of advantage for its field sales force and production scheduling system. Allegheny's Desk and Furnishings Division's sales representatives are each equipped with a Hewlett-Packard Portable Plus laptop computer that allows them to dial into the headquarters' HP 3000 mainframe. Individual salespeople can check on the order status as well as shipment schedule for any customer. In this way, they can assure customers of delivery dates or suggest alternatives. In addition, they can reserve inventory as well as place orders almost instantaneously.[31]

[29]Gary P. Pisano and Steven C. Wheelwright, "How Manufacturing Can Make Low-Tech Products High-Tech," *Harvard Business Review,* September–October 1995, p. 98.

[30]Benson Shapiro, "Can Marketing and Manufacturing Coexist?" *Harvard Business Review,* September–October 1977, pp. 111–113.

[31]Thayer C. Taylor, "Laptops and the Salesforce: New Stars in the Sky," *Sales and Marketing Management,* April 1987, pp. 50–55.

As we noted in Chapters 12 and 13, logistical appeals are becoming more desirable to customers, but the cost of providing these appeals is also increasing. Just about every business is looking for ways to cut distribution costs. Accordingly, coordination between sales programs and physical distribution is essential to building profitable sales-volume levels. Helene Curtis's Suave shampoo cut its price to the consumer by 10 percent over a 2-year period. Over one-half of that cut was made up by savings in distribution and inventory costs. Helene Curtis's overall distribution costs were cut by 40 percent, in large part because of its modern automated and computerized distribution warehouse. This facility has no paper order tickets or shipping tags and uses computer-controlled forklifts to place packages on conveyors. Once they are on the conveyor, lasers read bar codes and sort the packages by destination. This one facility can handle twice as many goods as the six older warehouses it replaced. On the other hand, Sun Microsystems has outsourced its distribution system to Federal Express, because Sun wanted distribution to be primarily a variable rather than fixed cost in the manufacturing process.[32]

Finance

The marketing plan includes major financial inputs, such as the cost and profit history for the business, pro forma financial statements, budgets, and the related marketing strategies. In developing and selecting the appropriate marketing strategies, management requires certain financial inputs. Many marketing decisions should be viewed as investment decisions. For instance, as discussed in Chapter 8, new product alternatives should include a financial evaluation of the required investment and revenue stream. However, this shouldn't be limited to new products, as the financial aspects of promotion, distribution alternatives, and pricing decisions must be considered by marketing management as well. In addition, financial considerations can often act as a significant constraint on the strategic options open to the marketer.

Frequently, marketers fail to recognize the impact their decisions have on such variables as inventory level, working-capital needs, financing costs, debt-to-equity ratios, and stock prices. Too often these are thought of as purely the responsibility of finance. Marketing management needs to be particularly sensitive to the impact various marketing strategies can have upon the financial well-being of the company. The development of financial plans involving capital requirements, cash flow, and credit policies all require that marketing input work effectively with the finance department. It may be necessary for marketing to provide alternative strategies and environmental-condition scenarios to assist in financial planning. In addition, marketers must be willing to make the trade-offs necessitated by various financial considerations. This requires close cooperation and contact with the finance function, as well as an understanding of the concepts and approaches utilized.

In sum, although an effective organizational structure can assist managers in the execution of corporate and marketing strategies, the development of interorganiza-

---

[32]Rita Koselka, "Distribution Revolution," *Forbes*, May 25, 1992, pp. 54–61.

tional coordination ultimately will depend on the attitudes and actions of the managers of the firm. For example, Rockwell International managers coordinate with their counterparts in other business units to use their technologies, skills, and competencies to develop new products. Marketing and sales benefit from such cooperation by having new and innovative products to sell, as well as modified products for existing markets. Cross-functional teams, new organizational configurations, and extensive use of communication devices have facilitated this cooperation among diverse departments. However, as one Rockwell executive points out, "The first place a marketing person has to sell is on the inside—and that's the hardest of all."[33] To be effective in performing this task, an understanding of the needs and aspirations of other managers and an awareness of the constraints limiting their actions (such as the reward system they face) are essential. If marketing managers can develop this kind of understanding, they are likely to develop programs that will receive support from managers in other functional areas.

INTEGRATING SALES AND DISTRIBUTION PROGRAMS

In the last few years, several developments have taken place that require firms to better integrate their sales and distribution programs. Much of the pressure for such change came from companies that were cutting their costs and their payrolls. The result was that many firms reduced the number of suppliers to those that help them improve their operations. For instance, Manco, Inc., a retail supplier of tapes, weather stripping, and mailing supplies helps manage the inventory of its thirty products for customers like Wal-Mart and Kmart.[34] In addition to cost reduction, developments in technology, flexible production processes, more customer information, and globalization make better integration of sales and distribution activities a prerequisite for effective marketing. These changes have altered how customer value is created and delivered. Frank Cespedes, in his book *Concurrent Marketing: Integrating Product Sales and Service* summarizes how these changes affect the nature of the product mix, the market, the sales and distribution system, and competition.[35]

Today, a firm must tailor its products to meet the needs of its customers, and also to add value throughout the sales and distribution system. Product offerings often require additional services such as cooperative development, distribution logistics, merchandising, customized package sizes, delivery terms, and so on. These services become a major part of the value added and require close participation by all participants. In addition, computer-integrated manufacturing allows for broader lines without lowering quality or inflating costs. Point-of-sale systems provide information about categories, brands, sizes, prices, and merchandise activity, which has led to the customization of products and increased emphasis on smaller market segments.

[33]"All for One," *Sales and Marketing Management,* January 1996, pp. 22–23.

[34]Susan Gould, "The Art of Selling," *Inc.,* June 1993, pp. 72–80.

[35]Frank V. Cespedes, *Concurrent Marketing: Integrating Product, Sales and Service,* Harvard Business School Press, Boston, 1995, pp. 3–28.

The emphasis on quality has resulted in a reconsideration of supplier relationships by many companies. Fewer suppliers require less monitoring, and long-term relationships based on factors other than price are becoming routine across industries. In developing long-term relationships, suppliers find it necessary to work closely in partnership with their customers to increase profitability. Competition has reduced the length of most product life cycles. This has resulted in more substitutes, increased price pressures, more new-product development, and less time to make more profits. These changes will require a greater emphasis on cross-functional leadership and strategic thinking if a company is to maximize its long-term profitability. This means that the role of both sales managers and the individual salespersons will continue to evolve as these changes occur.[36]

MANAGING THE FIELD SALES FORCE

Managing human resources is an important task in all functional areas but, within marketing, this task is primarily important for sales managers. This is true for three reasons. First, the largest number of marketing personnel are in sales positions. Second, the cost of personal selling is extremely high because sales salaries and other compensation are usually relatively high and because of the expenses associated with travel, training, and sales demonstrations. As shown in Table 14-1, these selling expenses as a percentage of total sales range from 10.5 percent for consumer goods to as high as 15.3 percent for services.

Finally, effective sales-force management is important because the responsibility for execution of sales and distribution is highly decentralized; that is, the effectiveness of these programs depends on the performance of a large number of people. In

TABLE 14-1

SALES-RELATED COSTS BY INDUSTRY

INDUSTRY GROUP	SELLING EXPENSES* AS PERCENT OF TOTAL SALES	ADV. PROMO. EXPENSES[†]	MEDIAN SALES BY INDUSTRY[‡]
Consumer goods	10.5%	4.5%	$25,000,000
Industrial goods	11.0%	3.0%	$24,000,000
Services	15.3%	3.4%	$18,000,000

*Selling expenses include compensation, benefits, travel and entertainment expenses, meeting costs, recruiting and training costs, support materials, staff and administrative expenses, and commissions to outside reps and distributors.

†Advertising and promotional expenses include direct costs of materials and media (print, radio, TV, and so on), as well as any associated costs related to research, preparation, and execution.

‡Median sales by industry is calculated by examining the entire range of responses to this year's survey and selecting the midpoint in each set of ranges (that is, half the responses were above, and half below, this figure).

Source: "1993 Sales Manager's Budget Planner," *Sales and Marketing Management,* June 28, 1993, p. 65.

[36]"Brand Managers Give Way to Integrators," *Sales and Marketing Management,* June 1995, pp. 35–36.

contrast, other marketing programs (such as advertising) are normally executed by a relatively small number of people who have the opportunity to work closely with the managers responsible for the programs. Accordingly, sales managers must generally be far more concerned with human resource management than other middle-level marketing managers.

In Chapter 13, we reviewed some of the considerations involved in determining the number of sales calls, the size of the sales force, and sales-force allocation. In the remaining portion of this chapter, we examine sales-management actions that are directed more toward enhancing the performance of individual members of the sales force—especially regarding the quality of the sales call. These sales-management actions take on increased importance in light of the changes taking place in business today. Diverse customer requirements, intense competition, and a rapidly changing marketplace have brought about the need for companies to redesign their selling strategies and manage their sales forces accordingly. The sales force is a key contributor to the sales, profit, and customer satisfaction performance of many companies. Salespeople are being asked to assume new responsibilities and perform sales management activities to reflect these changes.

Selecting Salespeople

In many firms, efforts to recruit, select, and train sales-force members are almost continuous because of market expansion, promotions of salespeople into management, and resignations or retirements. A large investment of time and money is required to recruit and train new salespeople. Accordingly, it is important to develop selection procedures that enable a firm to hire people who will be successful. An improper selection can cost an organization $150,000 or more when all the efforts involved in selecting, training, developing, and managing are calculated. For example, consider the case of Dow Chemical.

> Dow Chemical recruits almost exclusively from college campuses. Over the years, Dow has selected a group of about thirty-five colleges and universities, primarily in the Midwestern and Southern parts of the United States. The company has developed relationships with these institutions similar to those of a business partner. All recruits are processed through a year-long program, followed by actual field selling. Dow calculates that after about four years with the company, the investment in each recruit is in the hundreds of thousands of dollars.[37]

Selecting salespeople would not be a difficult task if the characteristics that made a good salesperson could be readily identified. Moreover, each sales job has its own unique requirements. Many companies are making long-term relationships the major focus of their marketing and sales strategy. This has altered the traditional role of the salesperson from merely making transactions to working with other business functions in a team capacity. Highly specialized sales forces are being merged to reduce

[37]"Dow Makes It Big by Thinking Small," *Sales and Marketing Management,* September 1991, p. 46.

duplication and improve customer coordination. Philip Morris has combined all its food operations into one division. Previously, 3500 specialized salespersons represented Kraft, General Foods, Oscar Mayer Foods, and Maxwell House products and called upon 26,000 stores. Now, one representative is responsible for a store instead of several. Instead of focusing on one brand, sales managers have been reorganized into 300 marketing support teams, each assigned to a chain of stores. The salesperson is now responsible for a wide range of grocery products rather than a narrow line. This will place different demands on the salesperson and mistakes made in the selection process will be costly.[38] Formal tests, extensive interviews, and weighted applications are finding increasing use as firms attempt to improve their recruiting processes. Increasing use is being made of psychological assessment services in an attempt to reduce turnover.

In 1991, turnover was greater than 20 percent for 24 percent of the companies in services industries.[39] Acme Fabrication estimates that they lose about $25,000 in salary, training, and recruiting cost each time they have to replace a salesperson. Each year, they interview approximately 500 persons and hire 100 of them. Of these 100, about 20 will be terminated during the first year, resulting in a loss of $500,000. In an attempt to improve this performance, Acme has started to utilize a psychological assessment service. After preliminary interviews are conducted, they refer the best 200 candidates to an assessment firm for review at a cost of $150 a candidate. Acme believes that if the assessment service can reduce turnover by 2 percent, they get full payback in three-fifths of a year: two people times $25,000 (turnover cost) equals $50,000 as opposed to 200 times $150 equals $30,000 (cost of assessment).[40]

Training Programs

To the extent that training provides the salesperson with product knowledge, customer knowledge, and special skills, the expert power of the salesperson can be enhanced. Similarly, training in interpersonal relations can improve a salesperson's ability to use referent power. Additionally, training sessions may help salespeople manage their time better and, thus, be more productive. With rare exceptions, those companies switching to value-added strategies and relationship building are finding that training takes on more importance in their organizations. As selling cycles become longer and presentations are made at higher levels, personal selling is less about overcoming objections or closing techniques and more about production processes, inventory controls, and product and customer knowledge. Training can be costly and time-consuming, but more and more companies are recognizing the importance of this activity. For example:

> IBM has reduced its worldwide sales and marketing salesforce by fifty percent since 1990. As part of this downsizing, IBM created a new organization that is a cross between a con-

---

[38]"Will So Many Ingredients Work Together?" *Business Week,* Mar. 27, 1995, pp. 189–191.

[39]"1992 Sales Manager's Budget Planner," *Sales and Marketing Management,* June 22, 1992, p. 71.

[40]Lester L. Tobias, "Making Tests Pay," *Sales and Marketing Management,* Aug. 12, 1985, p. 80.

sulting business and a conventional sales operation. IBM has developed a year-long certification program for 300 heads of client teams. A classroom component at Harvard for three weeks is followed by work on case studies and a thesis on their particular client. During the three weeks at Harvard, participants spend one week on general business knowledge, one week on consulting, and one on the industry they specialize in.

Every member of Hewlett-Packard's sales staff receives basic training in strategic selling and account management, using custom-training videos. H-P also uses interactive TV/satellite training sessions to train sales groups on specific projects or on regional groups whose customers would benefit from specific H-P products. Industry-specific training that relates new technologies to customer needs has become a major component of H-P's training and development effort.[41]

Standard Operating Procedures and Selling Tools

Standard operating procedures are used to develop routines for those aspects of the sales function that lend themselves to standardization. If managers can routinize certain aspects of the sales function, more of the salesperson's time can be freed for the creative part of the selling task. Increasingly, firms are using automation and computerization for this purpose.

A variety of audiovisual sales aids and literature can be used to increase the communications effectiveness of the salesperson. In addition, technology is providing new ways of performing many selling activities. This has led to increased efficiency and improved quality of the selling function. Videodisc players, compact portable computers, telemarketing, and other electronic tools are becoming widely used in an effort to boost sales productivity.

Physician sales and service (PSS) is a distributor of medical supplies and equipment and pharmaceuticals located in Jacksonville, Florida. PSS's 362 sales representatives work out of forty-six service centers and call on office-based physicians at 40,000 sites in forty-four states. The typical sales representative has 200 accounts and is expected to call on each account once every 2 weeks. In 1993, PSS gave its field sales force Compaq Notebook computers, provided them with wireless communications, and developed a sophisticated management information system. The company spent $1.5 million, but says the investment paid for itself in less than 1 year. This has made it easier for order entry and now customers get same-day delivery rather than the previous 2 to 3 days. The wireless processing cycle has resulted in 8 hours of additional selling time per week for the average representative. This additional time can be used to develop consultative relationships with customers. The service center database provides reps with account history, product price, availability, and backorder status, and can confirm delivery.[42]

---

[41]Jaclyn Fierman, "The Death and Rebirth of the Salesman," *Fortune,* July 25, 1995, pp. 80–91; and "Hewlett-Packard Strives to Connect with Its Customers," *Sales and Marketing Management,* September 1991, p. 48.

[42]Thayer C. Taylor, "Sales and Automation Cuts the Cord," *Sales and Marketing Management,* July 1995, pp. 110–114.

All of Nabisco's 2800 sales reps carry handheld computers, used to collect sales data for individual accounts. In addition, two-thirds use laptop computers to help retail buyers configure their shelf space in the most productive manner. Computer models then tell the salesperson the best display method for each account for each Nabisco product. This focus on the clients' needs helped Nabisco double its profit over a 3-year period, while at the same time winning recognition as the best customer-focused sales organization in the packaged-goods industry.[43]

Motivation and Compensation

A central concern of any top- or middle-level manager is how to motivate people to achieve the desired level and type of performance. Unfortunately, research on motivation has not provided management with simple guidelines for selecting the best way to motivate the sales force.

In fact, most studies indicate that performance does not depend solely on motivational devices such as bonuses, awards, and promotions. Rather, performance also depends on factors such as quality of supervision, the realism of the selling objectives and quotas, the salesperson's need for achievement, the type of selling task (such as new-account development or account maintenance), and the type of sales job (such as trade selling versus missionary selling). Accordingly, the effectiveness of incentives will differ among industries, firms, and even salespeople within a firm.

It is clear that noncompensation-related forms of motivation should be a part of the motivational package in most firms. Recognition is critical and, after a fair level of compensation, is a major motivational tool in many companies.[44]

Compensation-based incentives are also widely employed and are extremely effective in many industries. However, when incentive compensation plans are to be used, they should be designed to support the firm's particular sales-program objectives. An incentive based on dollar volume alone may encourage the sales force to emphasize low-margin products and may also lead to inadequate attention to any customer service or account-development objectives that have been established. In an attempt to overcome such problems, many firms in a variety of industries have moved away from straight commission schedules and fixed salaries.

In a study of compensation plans, it was found that the most frequently used was some combination of base salary plus incentive pay in the form of commissions, bonuses, or both. Only 14.8 percent of the companies studied used only salary, and only 7.5 percent of the compensation plans were based on full commission.[45]

In order to serve customers better, many firms have worked to increase teamwork and collaboration both within the sales force and between the sales force and other functions of the company. This has led to difficulties in determining compensation, and companies are starting to test and implement new forms. There is a growing trend tying customer satisfaction to a salesperson's compensation. Companies desiring to create lasting relationships with customers are more frequently using sales-force

---

[43]Patricia Sellers, "How to Remake Your Sales Force," *Fortune,* May 4, 1992, p. 100.

[44]"Rewarding the Troops," *Inc.,* October 1991, p. 156.

[45]"Compensation: How Do You Pay Your Sales Force?" *Inc.,* August 1991, p. 82.

incentives based on customer satisfaction. For instance, Appleton Papers, Inc., determines its fifty salespeople's end-of-year bonuses on the basis of 30 percent for volume, 30 percent for profit, and 40 percent for objectives, with customer satisfaction being the leading objective. Formerly, IBM adjusted the compensation plan every January to increase sales of specific products or raise market share in certain areas. However, in 1994, it tied 60 percent of the sales-force commissions to the profits they bring in. To ensure that sales reps don't just push fast-turnover, high-margin products, IBM bases the remaining 40 percent of their commissions on customer satisfaction.[46]

CONCLUSION

Essential to success in any business, government, or other type of organization are the individuals (and groups of individuals) who make and execute plans. Accordingly, if people are to be effective, managers must design an environment that will facilitate   not hinder   the efforts of individuals and enhance the coordination of efforts. Marketing strategy and the execution of this strategy have a reciprocal effect on each other. Inappropriate strategies can sometimes be compensated for by excellent execution. On the other hand, good strategies can often fail because they are poorly implemented. Several distinct characteristics differentiate those companies that seem to do a good job of implementation from those that do not. A well-defined direction, concern for customers' needs, and managers who encourage subordinates' ideas are among those major characteristics.

In this chapter, we discussed the impact of the organizational structure in facilitating the execution of strategies and programs. But, we also recognized that no structure will ensure coordination. Interpersonal skills and cooperative attitudes must be developed to ensure effective coordination. Further, managers must learn to understand the factors that can hinder the performance of people within their own functions. In marketing, this problem is most critical with respect to sales-force performance because, if programs are to be effectively implemented, the sales force usually has a major role to play. Although there is no "magic formula" for effective sales-force management, managers must consider the issues discussed in this chapter in order to build and maintain a quality sales effort.

It is important to be aware that organizing and managing human resources are essential parts of the planning process. Different organizational structures, different approaches for coordinating activities, and different devices for directing the sales-force effort will be necessary depending upon the types of strategies and programs selected. The relationships between these decisions and the other elements of the planning process are summarized in Figure 14-1.

It is particularly important to recognize that the corporate strategy and the product objectives have a special relationship to decisions regarding organization and human resources management. In fact, some managers believe that products require different managerial skills at various stages of the product life cycle.

---

[46]"IBM Leans on Its Sales Force," *Business Week,* Feb. 7, 1994, p. 100; and Andy Cohen, "Right on Target," *Sales and Marketing Management,* December 1994, pp. 59–63.

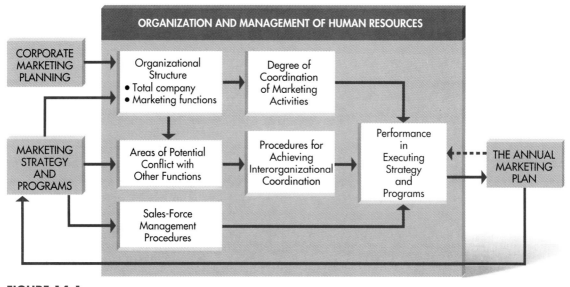

FIGURE 14-1

Relationship of organizing and managing human resources to the other elements of the marketing planning process.

In sum, an effective organizational structure and sound human resource management procedures can be of immense value in executing a marketing strategy. However, because a complex array of marketing programs are often employed to implement the marketing strategy, annual marketing plans should be developed to define and coordinate program plans. As we indicate in the next chapter, the specific type of plan will depend, in part, on the organizational structure selected. Before proceeding to the chapter, however, consider the following situation in light of the issues discussed in the present chapter.

AGCO: AN INNOVATIVE
DEALER MARKETING STRATEGY

In 1985, the U.S. tractor maker Allis-Chalmers was sold to a German farm-equipment company. Within 2 years, the new U.S. division was losing $80 million yearly on revenues of $200 million. The wheelbase of its line of tractors was too wide for standard U.S. planting methods, which resulted in the destruction of a row of crops every time a trac-

tor crossed the field. When he tried to rectify this problem, the American manager Robert Ratliff was told, "There's no problem with the tractor   change the farmer." Ratliff decided it was time to buy the company; he named it Agco Corporation.

Agco was founded in mid-1990 and, in 1991, Agco's revenues were $274 million with earnings of $8.7 million. At this time, agriculture was depressed and manufacturers were overproducing machinery. Much of this machinery would sit on the dealers' lots for a lengthy period until price cuts substantial enough to move it were made. For instance, Case Corporation dealers held 11-month inventory with supplies during this period.

From the beginning, Agco's focus was on marketing rather than manufacturing. Aware of the importance to farmers of established brand names, Agco bought several farm-equipment brands, such as Massey Ferguson tractors and Hesston Hay balers. The company's growth strategy was developed around building a large network of loyal dealers. Agco's dealer philosophy was in Ratliff's words, "In a mature market, all of the manufacturing smarts and marketing savvy in the world won't necessarily move your product. The distributor is king, and must be managed as the pivotal player on your team."

Agco would purchase a farm-equipment manufacturer, keep the brand's well-known name, and purchase the dealer contracts. Agco's dealer network is now approximately 7000 with 2600 in North America. Dealers are offered the opportunity to sell other Agco brands. These crossover contracts added $130 million in revenues in 1994. Other farm-equipment manufacturers like John Deere and Case Corporation have exclusive distributors. Agco pays a volume bonus to its dealers based on all Agco product sales. In addition to increasing their gross margins, dealers are provided with noncash incentives as well.

However, incentives alone did not build dealer loyalty. One of the major problems in the farm-equipment industry has been overcapacity. As a result, manufacturers would load up dealers with more inventory than they could sell. Agco recognized this problem and, instead, concentrated on working to minimize dealer inventories. For instance, Agco's field sales force is paid on 50 percent commission and 50 percent salary. However, unlike John Deere, Ford, and Case, the commission is only paid when the dealer makes a sale. This eliminates the incentive of pushing inventory on the dealer and provides Agco's 100 salespeople with the motivation to help the dealer make the final sale to the farmer. In addition, Agco's salespeople (who work with twenty-five dealers each) help dealers develop business plans and assist them in forecasting. They serve in a consultative capacity in the development of each dealer's marketing strategy. Agco will not ship a dealer more than a 6-month supply and closely monitors its dealers' sales. For instance, during growing season, if a dealer hasn't sold a combine in 30 days, Agco will shift this inventory to another dealer to reduce the dealer's interest costs.

In addition, Agco salespeople conduct a minimum of two training sessions per year per brand in their regions. Agco offers extensive training for dealers in such topics as service, retail selling skills, and financial management. Agco has also established a hot line for dealers who need to locate a part or product or who seek the answer to a technical question. Open meetings with dealers are held in each region. Dealer panels are held twice yearly. Agco says that 85 percent of the policies and decisions it makes originate from interface meetings, dealer panels, and direct dealer one-on-one contact. In the past 15 years the number of farm-equipment dealers in the United States has shrunk from 15,000 to 6000 but, at the same time, Agco had increased its dealer network. The dealer network has been the primary factor in Agco's growth in revenues to $1.4 billion in 1994. Analysts are projecting that Agco will double its market share in the next 5 years.

1. Most Agco dealers sell more than one of its brands. Each time a dealer adds an Agco brand it generates $150,000 additional revenue. However, a few dealers have chosen to sell only one line. What factors would explain a dealer's decision to sell just one line rather than several?

2. How would you expect the job of a sales manager for Agco to differ from that of one using exclusive distributors like John Deere?

3. What type of organizational structure would seem appropriate for Agco given the importance it places on its distribution system?

Developed from "Plant Pals," *Forbes*, May 8, 1995, pp. 130–131; "Case Digs Out from Under Way," *Business Week*, Aug. 14, 1995, pp. 62–63; and Geoffrey Brewer, "Wheeler Dealers: What the Hell Was Robert Ratliff Thinking?" *Sales and Marketing Management*, June 1995, pp. 39–44.

QUESTIONS AND SITUATIONS FOR DISCUSSION

1. Pioneer Hi-Bred International produces and markets hybrid seeds that are hardier and more productive than varietal seeds. Pioneer's 4500 commissioned salespeople in the past called on every farmer in a sales area. Now they concentrate on sophisticated, large-scale farmers who plant 1000 acres or more. Agronomists and specialists are called in to provide preferred customers with detailed information on new kinds of seeds or assist those having crop problems. This "customer focus" marketing approach is credited with Pioneer's recent market-share increases. What compensation problems would you expect with such an approach?

2. A Bain and Company study estimates that a decrease in the customer defection rate by 5 percent can increase profits by 25 to 95 percent. Why would such a small improvement in reducing customer defections result in such a large increase in profitability?

3. A leading marketing manager recently said, "as markets become more fragmented and companies keep developing multiple products, the key technical, manufacturing, and sales issues will become line-oriented rather than brand-oriented, making the involvement of product managers inefficient." Why would these factors prompt such a prediction?

4. James River Corp. has reorganized its sales force. Previously, three or more salespeople would call on a client: one with plates, one with Dixie cups, and one with toilet paper. To obtain the lowest price, a client would have had to buy three full truckloads, one for each product. Today, a unified team calls upon the client and a mix of products will be shipped at the lowest price. What are the advantages to James River and its clients of such a shift in sales strategy? Would there be any disadvantages?

5. "As retail customers become fewer and more sophisticated, the balance of power is shifting to the customer's favor." How would you expect this to affect the job of sales management?

6. A medium-sized manufacturer of machine tools uses a top-management group for all major decisions. This group consists of the president and vice presidents of finance, marketing, manufacturing, personnel, and research and development. Assume that you are the vice president of marketing and the top-management group is considering the following issues:

   a. Whether to expand warehouse capacity for finished goods at the existing home manufacturing facility or to establish four regional warehouses across the United States.

   b. Additional requests have been made for increasing staff by the research and development manager and by the sales manager. The vice president of finance indicates that only one of these requests can be funded at this time.

   c. A new alloy that is cheaper and more compatible with manufacturing processes has been proposed for use in a majority of products in the existing product line.

   Would there be any difference(s) in the position you took if you approached these issues from the best interest of the company as a whole as opposed to those of your own function? Explain.

SUGGESTED ADDITIONAL READINGS

Avlonitis, George J., Kevin A. Boyle, and A. G. Kouremenos, "Matching Salesmen to the Selling Job," *Industrial Marketing Management,* vol. 15, February 1986, pp. 45–54.

Cespedes, Frank V., "Channel Management Is General Management," *California Management Review,* Fall 1988, pp. 98–120.

Cravens, David W., "The Changing Role of the Sales Force," *Marketing Management,* Fall 1995, pp. 49–58.

Griffin, Abbie, and John Hauser, "Integrating R&D and Marketing," *Journal of Product Innovation and Management,* May 1996, pp. 191–215.

Lorange, Peter, and Johan Roos, "Why Some Strategic Alliances Succeed and Others Fail," *Journal of Business Strategy,* January–February 1991, pp. 32–35.

Lyons, Michael Paul, "Joint Ventures as Strategic Choice   A Literature Review," *Long-Range Planning,* August 1991, pp. 130–144.

McAdams, Jerry, "Rewarding Sales and Marketing Performance," *Management Review,* April 1987, pp. 33–38.

McKenna, Regis, "Real-Time Marketing," *Harvard Business Review,* July–August 1995, pp. 87–95.

Ruekert, Robert W., and Orville C. Walker, Jr., "Marketing's Interaction with Other Functional Units: A Conceptual Framework and Empirical Evidence," *Journal of Marketing,* January 1987, pp. 1–19.

Simon, Herman, "Lessons from Germany's Midsize Giants," *Harvard Business Review,* March–April 1992, pp. 115–123.

St. John, C. H., and E. H. Hall, Jr., "The Interdependency between Marketing and Manufacturing," *Industrial Marketing Management,* August 1991, pp. 223–229.

Vaccaro, Joseph P., "Organizational Issues in Sales Force Decisions," *Journal of Professional Services Marketing,* vol. 6, no. 2, 1991, pp. 69–80.

Webster, Frederick E., Jr., "The Changing Role of Marketing in the Corporation," *Journal of Marketing,* October 1992, pp. 1–17.

Yovovich, B. G., "Partnering at Its Best," *Business Marketing,* March 1992, pp. 36–37.

CHAPTER 15

THE ANNUAL MARKETING PLAN

OVERVIEW

For virtually all organizations, the most basic planning mechanism is an annual plan that describes the goals or objectives the organization expects to achieve in the coming year and the budget required to realize these objectives. As we have indicated at several points in this book, many corporate and marketing strategies will take a long time (at least more than a year) to be implemented fully. Nevertheless, because the financial results for the total organization must be presented annually, budgets and the rationale for these budgets must also be developed within this time frame.

In this chapter, we examine the annual *marketing* plan, which is the mechanism by which the objectives, activities, and budgets for the various marketing programs (discussed in Chapters 8 through 13) are integrated.[1] These plans serve three basic purposes.

- Like the various program plans, annual plans serve as a communications device. They indicate clearly to the personnel involved in marketing what the planned objectives and programs are, and thus should provide guidance to personnel on what activities to pursue.
- In an organization with multiple products, markets, or other divisions, annual plans serve as important inputs to the resource allocation process. Top management usually will review each annual plan within an organization, assess the corporate resources available, and approve or modify budgets based on an assessment of each unit's needs and contributions.
- Finally, once approved, the annual plan serves as a mechanism for control. That is, the annual plan establishes standards of performance against which the organizational unit's progress can be evaluated. Periodic checks of the performance-evaluation gap can be useful in making timely modifications to the plan. Additionally, the overall achievement of the unit is assessed largely on annual performance relative to the plan.

The major goal of this chapter is to identify the basic elements of a typical annual marketing plan, to demonstrate the use of the marketing plan for purposes of control,

---

[1]Hal Goetsch, "Are Marketing Plans Passe?" *Marketing News,* Dec. 5, 1994, pp. 4–5.

and to present some of the most important organizational issues associated with effective planning. Because managers must also assess the impact of environmental factors in setting standards and in evaluating performance, we also examine the process of environmental monitoring and its relationship to the marketing planning process. Before examining these concepts and procedures, however, we distinguish three major types of annual marketing plans, and we indicate the various types of objectives that can be selected for the annual plan.

TYPES OF ANNUAL MARKETING PLANS

Organizations may have one annual marketing plan or several annual marketing plans. Additionally, the scope of the annual plan is not the same for all companies. Basically, the number of plans and the scope of the plans will depend on the diversity of the firm's products and markets and on the firm's organizational structure.

The Business-Level Annual Marketing Plan

Often, an organization with a single product or a single line of highly related products sells through a sales force responsible only for that product or line. Not only is this situation typical of many small- and medium-sized manufacturing firms, but it also may typify strategic business units or business categories within a large diversified firm. In such cases, a single annual marketing plan is developed for that particular "business" (whether the business is an entire company, a division, or some other strategic unit). Usually, such plans are designed by the general sales manager or by the marketing manager for the business. Similarly, limited-line retailers who specialize in a product category may develop a single storewide plan under the guidance of a merchandise manager or a store manager. Finally, a total marketing plan may be developed by a marketing director of a consumer services company (such as a bank or a health maintenance organization). These firms offer a large number of highly related services and do not normally employ sales forces.

Annual Product or Department Plans

Firms organized by product lines may require separate plans for each product (or, in retailing, for each department). In these situations, the number of programs included in the scope of the plans is limited. For instance, a product manager typically develops the advertising and sales-promotion elements of a plan. But, if a common sales force is used for several separately managed products, the product manager often has no control over the size of and expenses incurred by the sales force. In such cases, the sales budget may not be a part of the annual product plan. Finally, large service companies (such as large banks) may employ product plans if some products require special attention. For example, many banks develop separate annual plans to market services used only by corporate customers (such as certain pension trust services).

When individual product plans are developed, these plans must be integrated into other plans at higher levels in the organization. For example, in an organization with several divisions, each of which has several products, a divisional manager must develop plans reflecting the sum of the product plans. Subsequently, corporate plans and divisional plans must be consistent with the corporate marketing planning objectives discussed in Chapter 2.

Annual Sales Plans

A third type of plan is the annual sales plan. If a sales force is responsible for several products in a division, a separate plan and budget covering only sales-force responsibilities may be developed by the sales manager. Sales-force salaries, commissions, and expenses will typically be the major elements in such budgets. However, to the extent that the sales force has decision-making power regarding discounts, credit, special-delivery terms, warranties, and merchandise returns, these may also be included in the scope of the plan. The annual sales plan will then be integrated with the various product plans in the divisional plan.

Because sales plans have already been discussed in Chapter 13, our discussion of the annual plan will center on the total marketing plan and the product plan. However, it is important to recognize that in multiproduct companies, each annual plan will be reviewed at the divisional or corporate level, or both.

Figure 15-1 indicates how the various types of middle-management-level marketing plans may be integrated at higher organizational levels. As we suggested in Chap-

FIGURE 15-1

Relationship of annual marketing plans, product plans, and sales plans to divisional and corporate-level planning.

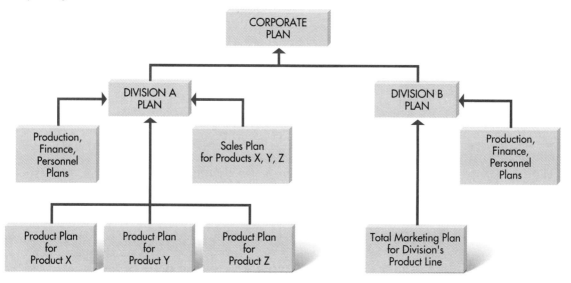

ter 2, these product plans must be consistent with the product objectives established at the top-management level. However, the plans must also be developed in a way that reflects the situation analysis. In the next section, we briefly review the major considerations influencing the marketing plan.

DEVELOPING THE PLAN

There is no single format or formula that is universally agreed on for every annual planning situation. In practice, each firm will develop a method, outline, or form that seems to fit its own needs best. However, there are two basic kinds of inputs to the planning process that should be a part of every plan: (1) a comprehensive situation analysis and (2) a statement of overall performance objectives.

Comprehensive Situation Analysis

As we discussed in the early chapters of this book, a firm should perform a situation analysis before designing its marketing strategy and programs. Specifically, we argued that a marketing strategy should be based on a detailed market analysis, a competitive analysis, market measurements, and profitability and productivity analysis.

For an annual plan, it is not usually necessary to repeat each of these analyses (unless the annual plan will present a new marketing strategy). Assuming a firm is continuing with its basic marketing strategy, the emphasis of the annual plan will be on the choice of, and funding for, individual marketing programs. Consequently, the situation analysis for an annual plan will focus on competitors' activities, industry trends (such as shifts in industry sales growth), and the productivity of the most recent marketing programs.

Consider, for example, Figure 15-2, which portrays a process that has been used at Procter & Gamble. In this figure, we see that the annual planning process begins about 12 weeks before approval with a review of the sales performance of a given brand and of competitive activity. Over the following weeks, the product manager develops estimates of the level of budgetary commitment required to achieve various unit sales volume and market-share levels. These productivity estimates (which are based largely on the analysis of historical ratios and judgments of competitive activity) are critical inputs to the budgeting process. In addition, however, managers involved in the planning process must have a clear sense of the objectives they are expected to achieve.

Annual-Plan Objectives

In Chapter 2 we examined *corporate objectives* and the process of establishing corporate strategies. On the basis of these corporate strategies and the product portfolio analysis, *product objectives* are used to provide guidance to middle managers who develop the marketing strategies and programs that are needed to achieve the product objectives.

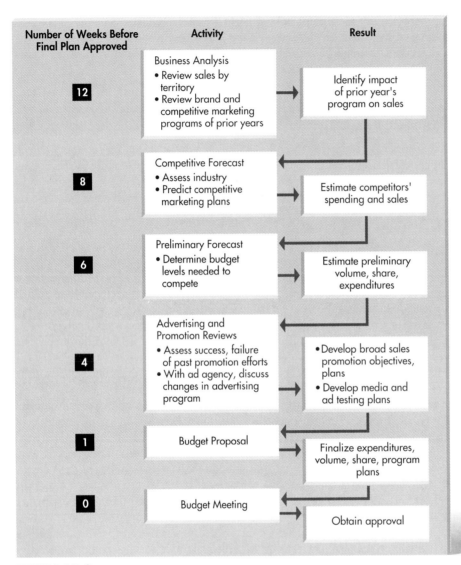

FIGURE 15-2
An example of the annual planning process.

Because an annual plan must be developed for each product or product line, the plan must be consistent with the product objective. However, product objectives are usually stated in general terms (such as "increase market share"). Because a marketing plan must be expressed in detail, management must express the annual marketing-plan objective (or the annual product-plan objective) in specific terms regarding *time* and *level*. For example, a product objective stated as "increase the market share of product X" might be specified in an annual plan as "increase the market share of product X from 17 to 20 percent in 6 months, and to 22 percent in 1 year." When stated in this way, the objectives can provide more specific guidance on budget development and more measurable standards for evaluating achievement.

Essentially, there are three types of objectives managers can establish for an annual plan: market-share objectives, sales-volume objectives, and profitability objectives.

Market-Share Objectives

When management believes a high market share will mean high profits, market-share objectives will be established. As suggested in Chapter 2, market-share growth is typically an objective for a product categorized as a "question" in a product portfolio model. If the markets are growing rapidly, an increase in market share will lead to rapid sales growth and long-run profitability for these products. Further, growth in market share may be essential in order to achieve or maintain adequate distribution because distributors may prefer to carry only the best-selling brands.

For those products in the "build" category, the objective may be to maintain the current level of market share. Because these types of products already have high shares and the markets in which they compete are attractive to competitors, it may be costly, if not impossible, to achieve major additional share gains. If the market growth rate for these products is high, however, profitability can be increased over time simply by maintaining the current share.

Sales-Volume Objectives

Sales objectives are clearly related to market-share objectives. That is, if a firm has a market-share objective and an industry sales forecast, then a sales objective can be calculated by multiplying the industry sales forecast by the market-share objective. The primary reason for converting a market-share objective into a sales-volume objective is that a unit sales-volume objective is needed to develop a complete budget. Without some estimate of the units to be sold, production costs cannot be calculated and, therefore, profitability cannot be estimated. Accordingly, when a market-share objective is established, the sales volume that reflects that market-share objective should also be determined. Additionally, sales-volume objectives are appropriate when market share cannot be reliably measured because of a lack of industry sales data, as well as when the annual plan is for a new product form (where the market share is 100 percent).

Profitability Objectives

As noted earlier, products in the "question" category must receive extensive marketing support if management hopes to build their sales volume and market share. The same is true for new products. In the short run, this means that profitability may have to be sacrificed for such products in order to achieve a stronger market position and long-run profitability. For products in the "hold" and "harvest" categories, however, the long-run sales-growth opportunities are presumed to be few. Thus, profitability objectives are usually paramount in such cases. Additionally, products in the "build" category are usually expected to contribute a certain level of profitability. Moreover, even with new products and questions, profitability cannot be totally ignored. There will be limits to the losses management is willing to take on these products. In general, then, some level of profitability will be either a primary objective or a secondary objective on all products. Therefore, in any annual plan, managers should expect to set some minimum target contribution (or some maximum negative contribution in the case of new products or "questions") to overall divisional or company profitability.

Returning to Figure 15-2, it is important to recognize that, in this particular process, all preliminary forecasts are submitted to top management so that the sum total of budget requests are known and can be prioritized before final budget meetings are held. Significant differences of opinion on budget levels between top management and the brand manager could well result in a directive to provide substantially revised goals or plans in the final budget proposal prior to the budget meeting.

To illustrate the development of an annual plan, we will return to the case of Linkster, Inc., first discussed in Chapter 6.

An Annual Product Plan: Linkster, Inc.

Linkster's marketing manager has developed an annual product plan for jackets. Table 15-1 summarizes the basic elements of the plan. (As indicated in Chapter 6, this plan is likely to have some influence on umbrella and sweater sales. Those effects might

---

TABLE 15-1   **LINKSTER: 1997 PRODUCT PLAN FOR JACKETS**

ANNUAL PERFORMANCE OBJECTIVES

1. Increase unit sales of jackets to 28,000 (from 20,000 in 1996)
2. Increase total contribution on jackets to $300,000 (from $250,000 in 1996)

MARKETING STRATEGY

Acquire new customers from differentiated positioning (warm and rain repellent; designed just for golfers).

MARKETING PROGRAMS

PROGRAM	OBJECTIVES	BUDGET
1. Magazine ads: Jan.–Mar.	Achieve 40 percent awareness among readers of golf magazines by March 30.	$176,000 for 4 insertions in a golf magazine plus production costs of $8000.
2. September promotion: $15 savings in golf course pro shops	Achieve sales of 8000 units.	$10,000 in point-of-purchase displays; $15 discount on 3000 displaced sales.

TABLE 15-2

CALCULATION OF LINKSTER'S REQUIRED ADVERTISING BUDGET

Size of target audience	1,000,000
$\times$ 1%	$\times$ 1%
Number of people to be reached for 1 gross rating point (GRP)	10,000
$\times$ Number of GRPs required	$\times$ 800
Total impressions required	8,000,000
$\div$ 1000	$\div$ 1000
Thousands of impressions required	8,000
$\times$ Cost per thousand (CPM)	$\times$ \$22
Required media budget	\$176,000

be captured in the overall business plan, which would also incorporate marketing plans for other Linkster products.)

The essence of Linkster's plan is to build volume through a price promotion during April and a magazine advertising campaign. The advertising campaign will emphasize two distinctive benefits: the jackets (1) are warm as well as rain repellent and (2) were designed by golfers specifically for golfers. The price promotion will involve a \$15 discount on any Linkster jacket at all golf course pro shops. The promotion will be announced in the magazine advertisements. The plan suggests that the combined effects of these programs will yield a 40 percent increase in jacket sales.

Specific features of the plan merit special discussion:

- Total promotional sales are expected to be 8000 units, with 3000 of these expected to be displaced sales. (Without the price promotion, management's expected gain in sales from the advertising campaign alone was 3000.)
- Because Linkster's prior advertising has been modest, the company's goal for 1997 is to begin building greater brand awareness as a base for the future. The target audience will be golfers who subscribe to a golf magazine, which has a circulation of about 1 million. Linkster's ad agency believes it must generate 800 GRPs by the end of March to establish 40 percent awareness. Because the target audience is 1 million, and because one GRP is achieved by reaching 1 percent of the target audience one time, it takes 1 percent times 1 million or 10,000 impressions to generate one GRP. (Refer back to Chapter 10 to review the relationship between gross rating points and gross impressions.) The agency thinks it can purchase space in a golf magazine at a cost per thousand of \$22. Therefore, Linkster can obtain the required GRPs for \$176,000, as calculated in Table 15-2.

The process of putting the annual plan together is not a simple one because a variety of combinations of prices, program budgets, and costs may have to be considered. Consequently, managers will often go through a number of tentative plans before coming up with one that is satisfactory. However, the complexity and time involved in this process are substantially reduced if a manager uses one of the popular interactive electronic spreadsheet programs (such as Lotus 1-2-3) available on personal computers.

Finally, the plan should not assume results will be achieved at a constant rate throughout the year. Seasonality of demand and variations in the timing of alternative programs are likely to exist in most plans. Where possible, therefore, monthly or quarterly breakouts should be established to let all managers know when the various results are expected to be achieved and to facilitate control. (Table 15-3 provides monthly benchmarks for Linkster's product plan.)

USING THE PLAN FOR CONTROL

If managers were simply to forget about a plan once it was adopted, they would be failing to take full advantage of the planning process. That is, the annual plan serves not merely as a tool for coordination, but also as a control device.

In fact, seldom will results go precisely according to plan. Changes in competitive actions, in buyers' willingness and ability to buy, or in other environmental factors may occur. Also, managers can seldom be absolutely certain of how productive the marketing programs will be in influencing sales—even in the absence of competitive reactions or other environmental changes. Finally, even costs are sometimes difficult to project.

Managers should recognize that there are at least two approaches to control. *Postaction* control can be used at the end of the planning period to review the degree of success achieved and to isolate the causes of any gaps between planned and actual

TABLE 15-3

LINKSTER, INC.: BIMONTHLY PROJECTIONS FOR 1997 FOR JACKETS

	JAN.– FEB.	MAR.– APR.	MAY– JUN.	JULY– AUG.	SEPT.– OCT.	NOV.– DEC.	BUDGET TOTAL
Jacket sales at regular prices	2,000	6,000	4,000	2,000	3,000	3,000	20,000
VCM (Variable contribution margin)—regular sales	$76,000	$228,000	$152,000	$ 76,000	$114,000	$114,000	$760,000
Jacket sales at promotion prices	0	0	0	0	8,000	0	8,000
VCM—promotion sales	0	0	0	0	$184,000	0	$184,000
Total sales (cumulative)	2,000	8,000	12,000	14,000	25,000	28,000	28,000
Total VCM (cumulative)	$76,000	$304,000	$456,000	$532,000	$830,000	$944,000	$944,000
Advertising expense (cumulative)	$52,000	$184,000	$184,000	$184,000	$184,000	$184,000	$184,000
Promotion expense (cumulative)	0	0	0	0	$ 10,000	$ 10,000	$ 10,000
Other direct expense (cumulative)	$75,000	$150,000	$225,000	$300,000	$375,000	$450,000	$450,000
Total contribution (cumulative)	($51,000)	($ 30,000)	$ 47,000	$ 48,000	$261,000	$300,000	$300,000

performance. For example, at the end of 1997, Linkster could review its results, compare these to the planned sales and profit objectives, and try to determine why any performance-plan gaps resulted. The major purpose of this type of control system is to use the knowledge obtained from this analysis in developing future plans.

As an alternative, organizations can adopt *steering-control* models. This approach assumes that if performance deviations from the plan can be identified sufficiently early, managers can take corrective actions—that is, the plan can be adjusted (steered) to meet the original objectives.[2] From a marketing management standpoint, the steering-control approach certainly has important short-run advantages because the effectiveness of marketing programs in producing sales is always somewhat uncertain. Consequently, managers would prefer to have the opportunity to make adjustments to the marketing plan as soon as possible when it becomes apparent that annual objectives may not be achieved.

In order to implement the steering-control approach, managers must take the following steps:

1. Select the performance measures to be monitored.
2. Compare actual and planned performance at appropriate time intervals.
3. Specify the acceptable degree of deviation.
4. Identify implications of the deviations.
5. Modify the plan to steer it toward the objectives.

Selecting Performance Measures

Because the primary objectives of a marketing plan are stated in terms of sales, market share, or profitability, managers would naturally want to monitor these performance measures. However, managers are likely to find that these measures are inadequate for a steering-control model for two reasons. First, information on these measures may not be available quickly enough. For example, manufacturers who sell through distributors often experience a lag between the timing of retailer sales and retailer purchases. Additionally, information on market shares may not be available on a regular basis. Second, and more important, managers who use the steering-control approach need information on *how* to change the plan to meet sales, market-share, or profit objectives. Consequently, it is important to monitor program performance because deviations in program performance may serve as indicators that annual objectives are not being achieved. Table 15-4 lists some of the more common performance indicators that managers should monitor.

In many companies, the kind of information portrayed in Table 15-4 is also not available in a timely manner. In such cases, experienced managers often resort to developing their own measures using whatever data are available. For example, one consumer-goods manager devised a weekly "Gimme Index," which was computed as the ratio of trade-promotion expenditures to consumer-promotion expenditures. The index served as a warning either of increased competitive activity to get shelf space

TABLE 15-4	SOME POSSIBLE PERFORMANCE MEASURES TO BE MONITORED FOR CONTROL

OVERALL PERFORMANCE MEASURES

1. Unit sales
2. Dollar sales
3. Sales in specific market segments
4. Marketing costs
5. Production costs
6. Market share
7. Customer ratings of product quality
8. Customer ratings of servicing provided

PROGRAM PERFORMANCE MEASURES

1. New-product programs	a. Rate of trial
	b. Repurchase rate
	c. Cannibalized sales
	d. Number of customer returns
2. Pricing programs	a. Actual price charged
	b. Price relative to industry average
3. Advertising programs	a. Awareness levels
	b. Attribute ratings
	c. Actual expenditures
4. Sales-promotion programs	a. Redemption rates
	b. Displacement rates
	c. Stock-up rates
5. Sales and distribution programs	a. Direct response rates
	b. Number of sales calls
	c. Number of new accounts
	d. Number of lost accounts
	e. Number of distributors carrying the product
	f. Number of customer complaints
	g. Travel costs

(when the ratio is very high) or of weakening consumer sales (when the ratio declines). As a result, it signaled the manager that there was likely to be a deviation between planned and actual performance on either the level of distribution achieved or on sales.[3]

As we noted in Chapter 1, customer satisfaction is now recognized as a critical aspect of performance. Many firms are learning that boosting satisfaction can lead to higher levels of customer retention and profitability. Some firms are measuring satisfaction and perceived quality directly.[4] Others rely on indicators of satisfaction (such

---

[3]Thomas Bonoma, "Marketing Subversives," *Harvard Business Review,* November–December 1986, pp. 113–118.

[4]For a discussion of measurement scales, see Tom Brown, Gilbert Churchill, and J. Paul Peter, "Research Note: Improving the Measurement of Service Quality," *Journal of Retailing,* Spring 1993, pp. 127–139.

as the number of reported problems or the probability of repurchasing the product in the future). Changes in these indicators over time tell management whether performance is improving or deteriorating.

Comparing Actual Performance with Planned Performance

Performance comparisons should be made as frequently as possible so that managers can have the greatest opportunity for steering the plan. However, the intervals used to compare performance should be long enough to be meaningful. For example, because advertising programs generally work slowly, it will be more difficult to get useful indicators of advertising performance in a short period of time. On the other hand, sales promotion and direct response marketing work more quickly and can meaningfully be monitored on a monthly basis (or even more frequently if desired). Additionally, effort-based performance measures (such as the number of sales calls or product demonstrations) can also be measured frequently. Finally, differences do exist across industries in terms of customer purchase frequencies. Consequently, sales performance may be meaningfully measured on a monthly basis in some markets, whereas in others quarterly comparisons may be more reasonable.

Specifying Acceptable Degrees of Deviation

The annual plan should also specify the acceptable degree of deviation from the performance standards. As noted earlier, managers do not really expect every performance standard to be fully attained. However, managers do want to identify significant deviations from the sales, market-share, and cost standards that have been set. Accordingly, it is generally useful to specify the acceptable range of performance in advance, so that management attention can be focused on the most important deviations. (For example, one firm may consider a 5 percent deviation in actual sales from planned sales acceptable, whereas another may consider only 1 percent acceptable.)

Additionally, the acceptability of a deviation should be considered in the context of the degree of reliability of the performance standard. For example, if managers want to impress their superiors, there is always the chance they will set performance standards in too pessimistic a fashion so that the likelihood of achieving a standard (and any resulting bonus) is enhanced. On the flip side, some high-level managers push planners to set unrealistically high performance expectations. This may occur because top management is hoping for a good result (perhaps to justify an earlier decision) and, thus, is too optimistic, or because these managers believe the middle managers doing the product and sales plans have been setting conservative sales and profit goals so they can more easily meet them. While this problem is not easily solved, it can sometimes be made more manageable by getting managers to articulate their degree of certainty about various performance levels. For example, managers might be asked: "For a given budget, what share of market is 50 percent likely? 80 percent likely? 100 percent likely?"[5]

[5]For a discussion of these and other issues related to goal setting on marketing plans, see Thomas Bonoma, "Marketing Performance—What Do You Expect?" *Harvard Business Review,* September–October 1989, pp. 44–47.

Identifying Implications of Deviations

Depending on the specific performance indicators being monitored, managers will be faced with analyzing deviations in sales performance, program performance, or cost performance.

Observed deviations from planned sales performance may be due to uncontrollable factors, such as changing market conditions that lead to a decline in industry sales or unanticipated competitive actions.[6] But, if managers find no evidence that either type of uncontrollable factor is responsible for performance deviations, then the logical next step is to analyze the performance of the marketing programs. (Additionally, as noted earlier, managers may want to examine indicators of program performance even before useful sales results are available.)

Program performance should be examined at two levels, where possible: the degree to which program *objectives* are being achieved and the degree to which planned program *effort* is being achieved. If levels of effort (such as actual sales calls or advertising coverage) are not being achieved as planned, then neither program objectives nor sales-performance objectives are likely to be achieved. However, if the planned level of effort is being achieved but program objectives (for example, number of new accounts or brand awareness levels) are not being achieved, then either the *design* of the program (for example, sales appeals, price level, advertising copy, value of coupon, and so on) is ineffective or the *budget* is inadequate. Further, managers may find that the performances of the various programs are all proceeding according to plan, but sales performance is still below the planned level. Assuming the manager has ruled out uncontrollable factors as a cause of sales deviation, the manager must conclude that the sales productivity of the various programs has been overestimated. (Figure 15-3 summarizes the steps involved in analyzing sales deviations.)

Finally, the actual direct marketing costs and variable costs may deviate from planned costs. Accordingly, reasons for these deviations should be identified. These reasons may include cost increases dictated by suppliers, inadequate estimates of the cost of reaching program objectives, or simply, faster achievement of program objectives than anticipated. For example, the sales force may call on some customers earlier or more frequently than planned. If so, sales costs may exceed the budget during the early periods of the plan.[7]

Regardless of the type of deviation being examined, managers must be able to distinguish environmental causes from controllable causes of poor performance. This is often very difficult because not all environmental changes are immediately recognized. Accordingly, a system for monitoring environmental trends and forces will assist managers in identifying uncontrollable effects and in attempting to make modifications to the plan. Some procedures and approaches to environmental monitoring are discussed later in this chapter.

---

[6]For examples, see Joan Delaney, "Crafting a Marketing Plan that Works," *Black Enterprise,* November 1994, pp. 120–124.

[7]Methods for identifying the sources of cost variance are presented in James Hulbert and Norman E. Toy, "A Strategic Framework for Marketing Control," *Journal of Marketing,* April 1977, pp. 12–20.

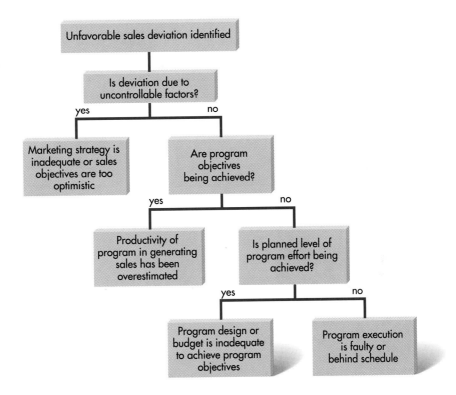

FIGURE 15-3

Analyzing sales
deviations.

Making Modifications to the Plan as Needed

Managers should make any marketing program modifications that are needed to get the firm back on track toward achieving the annual-plan objectives. If deviations between the plan and actual performance are relatively minor, then this is usually the only type of remedial action managers must take. However, if the deviations are fairly large and if the likelihood of making up for these deviations during the rest of the year is relatively small, management may have to revise the annual-plan objectives. (Of course, if actual performance exceeds planned performance, it may be desirable to revise objectives upward.) Finally, in the case of serious unanticipated competitive, cost, or other environmental changes, the entire marketing strategy and even the product objectives may have to be revised.

To illustrate the process of controlling the marketing plan, let us return to the case of Linkster, Inc. Table 15-5 summarizes the overall performance of the product plan as of the end of June. Halfway through the year, Linkster is lagging far behind its sales and profit plan.

In assessing the reasons for the failure to meet performance standards, management discovered the following:

■ *Uncontrollable factors:* The spring weather was unusually warm in the South and unusually wet in the North. Thus, demand for jackets was lower than usual

TABLE 15-5	LINKSTER, INC.: ACTUAL VERSUS PLANNED PRODUCT PERFORMANCE—JANUARY–JUNE 1997		

PERFORMANCE MEASURES	ACTUAL	PLANNED
Total jackets at regular price	9,500	12,000
Total jackets at promotion price	0	0
Total jackets	9,500	12,000
Total VCM	$361,000	$456,000
Advertising expense	$197,000	$184,000
Other direct costs	$220,000	$225,000
Total contribution	($ 56,000)	$ 47,000

in the South and many Northern golfers were forced to delay the start of their season.

■ *Program objectives not achieved:* By tracking brand awareness, management was able to determine that only 25 percent of the target audience was aware of the brand by mid-June. The program execution was on schedule, leaving poor advertising strategy or inadequate spending as the problem.

■ *Cost overruns:* Initial estimates of advertising design costs proved to be low, resulting in a modest overrun in the advertising budget. This was partly offset by lower-than-planned fixed production costs.

Based on this analysis, Linkster's management decided on the following actions.

■ The annual sales goal for jackets at nonpromotion prices was revised downward by 2000 units in recognition of the sales lost because of weather conditions.

■ Advertising spending of $45,000 was added for September to coincide with the promotion. Management hoped this would increase promotion sales in September by 2000 units (from 8000 to 10,000) and also stimulate an extra 500 units in sales during the postpromotion period.

Table 15-6 presents the revised plan. Note that if Linkster can achieve the levels of performance stipulated in the revision, the company will make up all of the shortfall in sales and part of the shortfall in total contribution. In other words, management will have begun the process of steering the plan toward the original objectives. Although the initial profit objective is no longer viewed as achievable, the process at least enabled management to spot the effects of uncontrollable factors and an ineffective program before the entire year was wasted. Clearly, the earlier the detection of such problems, the more effective a steering-control system will be.

It is also important to note that the effectiveness of steering control will depend, in part, on the degree to which a firm can be effective in making modifications. If deviations are primarily due to noncontrollable environmental factors, managers cannot modify their strategies without thorough consideration of the effects of further

TABLE 15-6   **LINKSTER, INC.: REVISED PLAN FOR JULY–DECEMBER 1997**

	ORIGINAL JULY–DEC.	REVISED JULY–DEC.	NEW TOTAL* FOR 1997
Total jackets at regular price	8,000	8,500	18,000
Total jackets at promotion price	8,000	10,000	10,000
Total jackets	16,000	18,500	28,000
VCM—regular price	$304,000	$323,000	$684,000
VCM—promotion price	$184,000	$230,000	$230,000
Total VCM	$488,000	$553,000	$914,000
Advertising expense	0	$ 45,000	$242,000
Promotion expense	$ 10,000	$ 10,000	$ 10,000
Other direct costs	$225,000	$225,000	$445,000
Total contribution	$253,000	$273,000	$217,000

*Includes January–June actual and July–December revised plan.

environmental changes. Thus, the process of environmental monitoring is an important adjunct to the process of steering control.

ENVIRONMENTAL MONITORING

Environmental monitoring consists of searching for, and processing information about, changes in an organization's environment. Although some analysis of the environment is a prerequisite for the development of corporate and marketing strategies, the marketing environments faced by most firms are dynamic. Thus, in order to analyze deviations in performance from the basic plan and in order to make any necessary adaptations in strategy, managers should have access to systems that continually monitor the environment.

Strategic Environmental Monitoring Systems

Strategic environmental monitoring systems are formalized approaches for monitoring change on a continuous and systematic basis. Such a system can be effective if management has clearly defined its purpose to ensure that crucial information will not be overlooked.

Montgomery and Weinberg have proposed three kinds of purposes for such systems.[8]

1. *Defensive:* This intelligence is obtained in an effort to avoid surprises. That is, the purpose of environmental monitoring is simply to determine if the implicit and explicit assumptions upon which current strategies are based will remain valid.

[8]David B. Montgomery and Charles B. Weinberg, "Toward Strategic Intelligence Systems," *Journal of Marketing,* Fall 1979, p. 42.

2. *Passive:* This intelligence is used to provide benchmark data for an objective evaluation of a firm's policies. For example, a firm might gather industry sales compensation data in order to reward sales performance in a manner comparable to the firm's competitors.

3. *Offensive:* This kind of intelligence is designed to *identify* opportunities.

By establishing the purpose of a strategic environmental monitoring system, management can make certain it collects the kinds of information it requires and avoids what is irrelevant. Once the information sources and needs have been established, the participants who need this environmental information must be identified. Since a variety of individuals and departments are involved in providing the necessary strategic information, definite assignments for the acquisition of specific types of intelligence must be made.[9] Figure 15-4 summarizes the major elements that would be necessary in a strategic environmental scanning system.

Environmental Information Sources

In establishing a formal environmental monitoring effort, managers must identify the information sources likely to be of most use for its stated purposes. In Chapter 5 we identified some sources for general market-measurement data. Additional useful sources are presented in the Appendix.

Perhaps the most important development in recent years with regard to environmental monitoring is the on-line information bank. Some of the better-known organizations and the data they make available are listed in Table 15-7. Additionally, as more people have achieved access to the Internet through universities, commercial organizations such as America On-line or Compuserve, or directly through other servers, an enormous variety of market intelligence and raw data have become available, ranging from trade statistics to data on competitors (such as new-product announcements or marketing strategies) to recent political and economic developments in countries around the globe. With respect to government statistics, a vast array of data are available through the Bureau of the Census. The gateway to these databases can be reached in any of the following ways.[10]

FIGURE 15-4

Organizing a strategic environmental scanning system.

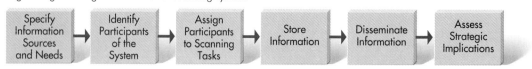

[9]David B. Baker, "Organizing a Strategic Information Scanning System," *California Management Review,* January 1983, pp. 76–83.

[10]Jackson Morton, "Census on the Internet," *American Demographics,* March 1995, pp. 52–54.

TABLE 15-7	MAJOR DATABASE DISTRIBUTORS OF BUSINESS INFORMATION
SERVICE AND DISTRIBUTION	**DESCRIPTION**
DIALOG Information Services	More than 200 databases containing over 55 million records; article indexes and financial data; annual reports of publicly held U.S. corporations
Dow Jones News Retrieval	Business and economic news, stock quotes, investment information, complete and unabridged articles from *The Wall Street Journal, Barron's,* and Dow Jones News Service.
Lexis/Nexis	Access to over 650 full-text business information sources including U.S. and international wire services, newspapers, magazines, journals, and newsletters.
Compuserve Information Service	Financial information, banking, encyclopedia, newspaper abstracts.
Data Resources	Business and economic data and Japanese Economic Information Service.
PROMPT	Citations and abstracts on new products, technology, markets from over 2000 U.S. and foreign publications.
DRI-VisiCorp	Fifty-eight databases, economic forecasts, foreign exchange, individual industries.

Via e-mail: ftp@census.gov (Type "help" in the message body to receive instructions.)

Via World-Wide Web: http://www.census.gov

Via AOL or any "gopher" server select Census from the gopher menu, then select "Access Our Other Information Services," then select "Census Bureau Anonymous FTP."

Other Sources of Intelligence

In addition to data-based sources of intelligence, there are several sources that are reliant on the skills and expertise of human experts.

TECHNOLOGICAL FORECASTING

Technological forecasting includes a variety of procedures managers may use to predict the probability, timing, and significance of future technological developments regarding products or processes. Among the procedures firms use for technological forecasting are Delphi probes, scenarios, and trend extrapolation.

The *Delphi probe* is a systematic method for analyzing independent expert opinion. A panel of experts are questioned individually about some future event or trend. All responses are combined and summarized, and the results are returned to the participants. After the results have been communicated to all participants, the experts are asked to respond again to these questions. This process is repeated for three or more rounds until a consensus is reached. The Delphi method may be used not only for identifying relevant changes, but also for identifying the most appropriate actions the firm should take.

Scenarios are composite descriptions of possible future technological events or conditions that may have an effect on the decisions made by an organization. Usually multiple scenarios are developed to represent possible alternative environments. In effect, scenarios are "what if" exercises that force managers to consider certain technological challenges they may face. Given a set of alternative scenarios, strategic planners can then develop and evaluate the alternative strategic responses the firm should be prepared to make if a given technological development materializes.

Another method of technological forecasting is to *extrapolate historical trends.* The primary assumption is that the trend of technological advances in the past will remain fairly constant in the future. Particularly in very high technology industries such as electronics, past rates of advance (such as cost per bit of information processed) can be projected into the future with some degree of reliability.

SOCIAL TREND ANALYSIS

Individuals, groups of individuals, and society at large are constantly changing in terms of what is considered a desirable and acceptable way of living and behaving. These changes can have a profound impact on individuals' attitudes toward products and toward marketing activities. In particular, it is important for managers to understand and predict changes in consumer values and changes in the social issues that groups within society believe are important. To track such changes, several independent research firms measure social and value trends on issues such as materialism, sexual freedom, and religion. Organizations, such as Arthur D. Little's Impact Service, Predicasts, Inc., and The Future Group, also provide subscription services for monitoring social trends and related economic trends.[11]

ORGANIZING FOR PLANNING

Because the annual marketing plan may involve different program elements in different organizations, there is no single best way to assign responsibility for the annual marketing plan for an individual product.

Although a number of larger firms have planning staffs, these individuals are primarily involved in long-range planning and in providing information regarding short-run forecasts and market conditions. Thus, the role of a planning staff in developing the annual plan is to provide basic inputs into the short-run situation analysis and objective setting. Additionally, these individuals may participate in the process of reviewing proposed plans to ensure that key market assumptions (and sometimes the manufacturing cost assumptions) are reasonable.

Most planners seem to believe that planning should be delegated as far down the organization as possible, so that one person is responsible for achieving each program

---

[11]Myron Magnet, "Who Needs a Trend Spotter?" *Fortune,* Dec. 9, 1985, pp. 51–56.

objective. The reasoning behind this view is that the manager most closely involved with a program is in the best position to estimate the costs and productivity of the program and to identify possible changes in market conditions.

However, in many firms, this means that planning for an individual product rests in the hands of more than one person. That is, unless the plan is confined strictly to one marketing program (such as sales), some organizational mechanism is needed to coordinate program plans into the overall annual plan. In firms with a broad product line, the product manager or brand manager will typically assume this role, and that manager's plans will be reviewed by a higher-level marketing manager. In other firms, the sales manager may perform this role—especially when selling costs dominate the budget, when the sales manager is responsible for sales promotions (often the case in industrial marketing), and when advertising focuses on the corporation as a whole rather than on individual products and, thus, is managed at the corporate level. Finally, the senior marketing manager may perform this role when program responsibilities are widely dispersed among a number of managers.

It is clear, however, that in the modern, large organization the marketing planning process is bidirectional. Research on how firms develop marketing plans indicates that it is rare to find a situation where the total marketing budget is developed simply by summing the requests of various product or sales managers. More typically, these requests are reviewed and revised to fit total corporate needs. In still other cases, the total marketing budget is decided centrally (usually with excessive influence by the finance department) and allocated to individual products or departments.[12]

CONCLUSION

Because of the array of different programs that managers may employ to implement the marketing strategy for a product or a line of related products, the annual plan is a critical element in coordinating activities and budgets. Further, because the marketing environment is dynamic and because the effectiveness and costs of marketing programs are always somewhat uncertain, annual plans are necessary for monitoring results and directing corrective actions. Individual programs must also be monitored because, in most cases, each program makes only a partial contribution to product objectives such as sales or market share or total profitability. Consequently, the annual plan is necessary in order to evaluate the total marketing effort as well as the contributions of the various program elements. (Figure 15-5 shows the relationship of annual planning to other aspects of the marketing planning process.)

Moreover, because program performance is heavily influenced by environmental changes, an effective control system cannot be developed unless managers have access to strategic intelligence regarding customers, competitors, or other relevant environmental forces.

---

[12]Nigel Piercy, "The Marketing Budgeting Process: Marketing Management Implications," *Journal of Marketing,* October 1987, pp. 45–59.

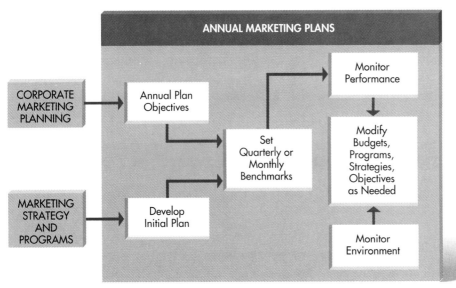

FIGURE 15-5

Relationship of annual marketing planning to other elements of the marketing planning process.

Ultimately, the effectiveness of the annual marketing planning process depends on the quality of the efforts made by those who do the plans. But the degree to which the organization facilitates market-driven planning is also important. In organizations that are truly market-oriented (as discussed in Chapter 1), the annual marketing plan is likely to be viewed as a very important management activity and is also likely to be primarily designed by the manager most knowledgeable about the market. To gain additional insights into the process of developing an annual marketing plan, consider the task facing management at Microsoft in 1995.

PLANNING FOR WINDOWS 95

Microsoft launched its new operating system for desktop personal computers, Windows 95, in August of 1995. At the time, Microsoft's Windows 3.1 operating system was already the industry leader. In fact, in the prior year, 60 percent of desktop operating systems were Windows 3.1 systems. The new system promised simplified processes for such things as setting file names, using CD-ROM diskettes, and accessing on-line services. Additionally, Windows 95 could load a far larger number of programs simultaneously. The system had been tested with over 400,000 customers. However, management knew that the complexity caused by a system with 15 million lines of computer code was bound to result in some incompatibility problems or limitations for some users, depending on the particular configuration of hardware and software they might be using. Indeed, Microsoft had limited control over these issues; much of the software that would run on Windows 95 was designed by other firms. So, in addition to its own in-house experts, Microsoft attempted to train 15,000 retailers and a number of service contractors to handle questions from users. Historically, Microsoft had achieved customer service response goals of 95 percent—that is, 95 percent of all calls for technical assistance were handled the same day. With the huge volume of sales anticipated, management was concerned about maintaining that level of customer service.

The launch of Windows 95 was backed by $200 million for advertising and promotional programs. It was estimated that Microsoft's ads for Windows 95 would create 3 billion gross impressions in the United States in the first 6 months. Microsoft hoped to obtain retail distribution in some 25,000 outlets, far more than carried Windows 3.1. Initial sales forecasts called for 30 million copies to be sold by the end of December 1995 and 63 million in 1996.

1. Which measures (from Table 15-4) would be most useful to Microsoft in tracking the performance of the Windows 95 plan? (Be certain to discuss whether or not it would be very important from a marketing point of view to track customer service problems in this particular case.)

2. Following Figure 15-3, lay out the list and sequence of questions Microsoft should have been prepared to ask.

3. What uncontrollable factors might have an impact in the success of the Windows 95 plan?

Developed from Don Clark, "Amid Hype and Fear, Microsoft Windows 95 Gets Ready to Roll," *Wall Street Journal,* July 14, 1995, pp. A1, A4; Kathy Rebello and Mary Kuntz, "Feel the Buzz," *Business Week,* Aug. 28, 1995, p. 31; Kathy Rebello, "Start Me Up—Just Try," *Business Week,* Sept. 25, 1995, p. 114; and Dick Satran, "Microsoft's Win 95 Enters Critical Period," *Reuters European Business Report,* Sept. 19, 1995.

QUESTIONS AND SITUATIONS FOR DISCUSSION

1. Explain why a market-share growth objective should be accompanied by a sales-volume objective and a target-contribution objective.
2. Explain the difference between postaction control and steering control.
3. In each of the following situations, would you tend to establish performance benchmarks at short intervals (such as weekly or monthly) or at long intervals (such as quarterly)? Explain your answers.
   a. A consumer-goods firm relies heavily on sales-promotion programs to achieve a sales-volume objective for its line of cookies.
   b. A manufacturer of copy machines is introducing a new line of products for its commercial and industrial buyers. Advertising in industrial magazines and personal selling are the primary programs being used to achieve a sales-volume objective.
   c. A food company is attempting to improve the profitability of the product line it sells to institutional customers. The marketing effort is primarily designed to increase the volume purchased by large, existing accounts through more frequent sales calls and the use of quantity discounts.
4. What differences, if any, are there between a strategic environmental monitoring system and marketing research?
5. In some firms, marketing budgets are primarily determined by top management and in others by middle managers. In what circumstances should top management

be the initiator of the budget as opposed to acting primarily as a reviewer of the budgets submitted by middle management?

6. In February of 1990, Time Warner Inc. launched *Entertainment Weekly,* a magazine designed to review movies, videos, records, books, and television shows. In addition to reviews, several in-depth features on the entertainment business were to be part of each issue.

After 2 years of direct mail testing, the company was able to identify the market to which it had the greatest appeal. The expected profile of the readership was 36.8 years of age, equally divided between male and female, 72 percent college educated, with a median income of $41,800. The magazine was priced at $1.95 per issue or $51.48 for an annual subscription. Because magazine revenues come from two sources—subscriptions or newsstand sales and advertising sales—Time Warner needed to develop two separate, yet consistent, plans. The size of the circulation base (which was targeted at 600,000 per week for the first year) would obviously have an impact on magazine sales revenue. But the circulation base, along with the profile of the readers and the actual number of readers (which might be five times the circulation), would all be important to prospective advertisers.

To get subscribers, Time Warner offered a sales promotion involving four free issues of the magazine. The promotion was bolstered by $30 million in advertising through television and Time Warner's other magazines. Simultaneously, the advertising sales force was making calls on potential advertisers and advertising agencies, with a goal of signing up 100 advertisers to 2-year commitments.

a. Develop a list of the annual performance objectives that could have been included in the annual plan(s).

b. What program performance measures should Time Warner have used for control?

7. Discuss the kinds of environmental variables that managers in each of the following product categories would most want to monitor on a frequent basis, and discuss where they would likely seek information.

a. High-definition television (HDTV)

b. Running shoes

c. Minivans

d. Frozen yogurt

e. College textbooks

8. The National Broadcasting Corporation (NBC) counted heavily on revenue from pay-per-view television of the Triple Cast to offset the costs of broadcasting the 1992 Summer Olympics.

In January of 1992, NBC established a sales target of 3.5 million homes on the assumption that cable systems would make pay-per-view technically accessible to 35.9 million households. The costs for the Triple Cast were expected to be $40 million in promotion and $55 million in production costs, split among the local cable companies and NBC.

NBC actually began its promotional campaign in December 1991, 8 months before the Olympics were to be held, even though previous cable company experience with pay-per-view sports broadcasts suggested that 90 percent of all orders for a special event are placed in the final week before the event. Christmas season ads were placed on NBC and through the cable channels, and NBC marketing officials claimed these generated 100,000 inquiries. Further, NBC was planning monthly promotions beginning in February for each month prior to the Olympics. For example, a free remote control was to be offered for each purchase of the complete pay-per-view package (priced at $125 for the full 15 days) in February, and a free VCR plus for each sign-up made in March.

Industry observers noted that the extensive promotional campaign was designed to build a level of consumer demand that would overcome the resistance of cable operators who needed to clear their channels to provide Triple Cast coverage.

a. What program performance measures could NBC have used for control?

b. Given that pay-per-view customers tend to wait until the last minute to order, would there be any point in tracking sign-ups for purpose of control?

c. Following the general format presented in Figure 15-3, lay out the list and sequence of questions NBC should have been asking when it became obvious that sales would be below expectations.

SUGGESTED ADDITIONAL READINGS

Bonoma, Thomas, "Marketing Performance—What Do You Expect?" *Harvard Business Review,* September–October 1989, pp. 44–47.

Chebat, Jean-Charles, Pierre Filiatrault, Amon Katz, and Schlomo Mai Tal, "Strategic Auditing of Human and Financial Resource Allocation in Marketing," *Journal of Business Research,* October–November 1994, pp. 197–208.

Daniells, Lorna, "Sources on Marketing," *Harvard Business Review,* July–August 1982, pp. 40–43.

Georgoff, David, and Robert Murdick, "Manager's Guide to Forecasting," *Harvard Business Review,* January–February 1986, pp. 110–120.

Jaworski, Bernard, Vlasis Stathakopoulos, and H. Shankar Krishnan, "Control Combinations in Marketing: Conceptual Framework and Empirical Evidence," *Journal of Marketing,* January 1993, pp. 57–69.

Piercy, Nigel, "The Marketing Budgeting Process: Marketing Management Implications," *Journal of Marketing,* October 1987, pp. 45–59.

Stasch, Stanley, and Patricia Lanktree, "Can Your Marketing Planning Procedures Be Improved?" *Journal of Marketing,* Summer 1980, pp. 79–90.

Wack, Pierre, "Scenarios: Unchartered Waters Ahead," *Harvard Business Review,* November–December 1985, pp. 73–89.

APPENDIX

Source Description Code

A General industry conditions, competitors, trends
B Consumer market characteristics/buying power
C Consumer purchasing patterns
D Advertising and promotion statistics
E Sales tracking and marketing effectiveness studies

ABI/INFORM: (A)
> UMI/Data Courier, Inc.
> 620 S. Third St., Louisville, KY 40202-2475; (502) 582-4211
>> On-line service. Provides access to business information. Contains abstracts of articles on accounting, economics, information science, marketing, and other related subjects. Magazine express, periodical abstracts.

ADTRACK: (D)
> Corporate Intelligence, Inc.
> P.O. Box 16073, St. Paul, MN 55116
>> A computerized index to advertising appearing in major consumer and business magazines. Advertisements of $\frac{1}{4}$-page size or larger are indexed by fourteen data items. Data coverage includes company name, product name, description, color, data, page number, magazine name, and spokesperson.

Advertising Age—100 Leading National Advertisers: (D)
> Crain Communications
> 740 Rush St., Chicago, IL 60611; (312) 649-5200
>> Marketing reports for each company provide useful facts about their marketing operations, such as sales and earnings, leading product lines and brands, how they rank nationally, share of market, advertising expenditures; also names of marketing personnel and agency account executives, both for print company and for principal divisions (found in the mid-September issue).

431

Advertising and Marketing Intelligence (AMI): (C, D)

New York Times Information Service, Inc., and J. Walter Thompson Co.

Mt. Pleasant Office Park, 1719 Route 10, Parsippany, NJ 07054

Includes abstracts from advertising, media, and marketing covering new products, consumer trends, people, research, media planning and buying, and sales promotions. Each entry consists of a brief statement on the subject, product, or person with the relevant bibliographic citation.

Adweek's Marketer's Guide to Media: (B)

ASM Communications, Inc.

1515 Broadway, New York, NY 10036; (212) 536-5336

Quarterly. Includes audience data for various kinds of media.

American Profile: (B)

Donnelley Marketing Information Services

P.O. Box 10250, 70 Seaview Ave., Stamford, CT 06904;

(203) 353-7266; FAX (203) 353-7276

Profiles over 70 million households. Coverage includes household population, income, dependents, and other demographic variables. This database also maintains an excellent array of socioeconomic data including number and type of businesses, number of employees in area, banking activity, and other demographic area profiles.

American Statistics Index: (A, B)

Congressional Information Service, Inc.

4520 E-W Highway, Bethesda MD 20814; (800) 638-8380,

(301) 654-1550

This is a comprehensive guide and index to the statistics published by all government agencies, congressional committees, and statistics-producing programs.

Annual Study of Advertisers: (D)

Provides information on the 100 U.S. firms that spend the most on advertising. For each advertiser, provides estimates of total advertising and promotional expenditures, total sales, and total earnings. Contains extensive descriptions of each firm's products, markets, corporate planning, and strategy. Ranks the top 100 advertising spenders, and includes general descriptions of trends in advertising spending, strategy, and techniques of these firms.

BAR (Broadcast Advertising Reports): (D)

BAR, Inc. (owned by ARBITRON)

142 W. 57th St., New York, NY 10019; (212) 887-1300

Maintains monthly data on network television commercial activities and expenditures by product, network, parent company, and mean estimate per commercial minute. Includes the relationship between a particular commercial and the others aired in the preceding and succeeding time slots.

Brand Preference Change Measurements: (E)

Audience Studies, Inc. (ASI)

The ASI measurements are made during and after exposure of the test commercials to a recruited, captive audience gathered in a theater. Various aspects of viewer response to television commercials are measured.

CACI Marketing Systems: (B)

1100 N. Glebe Rd., Arlington, VA 22201; (800) 292-2240; FAX (703) 243-6372

This service provides demographic information and is accessible on nine time-sharing networks. Offers a sales potential system that measures consumer spending in any area of the United States. Information can be used for site selection, market-entry planning, market-share and penetration decisions, promotional planning, store performance analysis, and so forth. Updates U.S. Census data regularly and provides many specialized reports.

Consumer Economic Service Data: (B, C)

Data Resources, Inc.

24 Hartwell Ave., Lexington, MA 02173; (617) 863-5100

Offers vast amount of detailed demographic and economic data in five report areas: (1) Current Population Survey Annual Demographic File; (2) Consumer Expectations Survey—a diary and interview of 40,000 households; (3) TGI-Brand specific purchasing and media penetration data; (4) Longitudinal Retirement History Survey; and (5) Consumer Markets Services—personal consumption, retail sales, and associated prices.

Consumer Expenditure Study: (C)

Bureau of Labor Statistics, Department of Labor

2 Massachusetts Ave., NE, Washington, DC 20212; (202) 606-7808

Bulletins and/or reports. Annual. These studies are based on personal interviews from a sample of 20,000 consumer units and record keeping by a sample of 23,000 consumer units. These samples offer income and expenditure analysis by income class, family size, and several other demographic parameters.

Consumer Expenditure Survey: (B)

National Technology Info. Service, U.S. Dept. of Commerce

5285 Port Royal Rd., Springfield, VA 22161; (703) 487-4600

Report. Eight volumes. Covers seven demographic parameters and presents consumer expenditure statistics for each area by demographic type. Coverage includes family income, size, age, race, education, tenure, and composition.

Demographic Research Company: (B)
233 Wilshire Blvd., Suite 995, Santa Monica, CA 90401; (310) 452-7587; 451-8583

This database provides demographic, marketing research, and multi-variate analysis assistance as well as a ZIP code data base that organizes U.S. Census data in terms of income, occupation, and housing in ZIP code areas.

DIALOG: (A, B)
3460 Hillview Ave., Palo Alto, CA 94303-0993; (800) 334-2564; (415) 858-3785; FAX: (415) 858-7069

This on-line service covers more topics than almost any other database. The DIALOG Business Connection is a menu-based information service that offers quick and easy access to high-quality business information from a collection of respected sources. Available information includes share of market data, analysts' reports on industries, sales prospecting, and much more.

Dow Jones News Retrieval
Dow Jones and Company
Box 300, Princeton, NJ 08543-0300; (800) 522-3567, Ext. 141

Comprehensive Company Reports: (A)
On-line service that provides detailed financial and business information on public companies.

Dun & Bradstreet Financial Profiles and Company Reports: (A)
In-depth historical, financial, and operational reports for public and private companies.

Statistical Comparisons of Companies and Industries: (A)
Offers comparative stock prices, volume, and fundamental data on companies and industries.

Editor and Publisher's Market Guide: (B, C)
11 W. 19th St., New York, NY 10011; (212) 675-4380

Useful for market planning and selection, setting sales quotas, planning advertising and merchandising programs, and selecting store/plant/warehouse locations; this guide contains standardized fourteen-item surveys of market data for over 1500 daily newspaper markets in the United States and Canada. Also includes estimates of total and per household disposable income and offers current retailing data for nine sales classifications based on U.S. Census of Retail Trade. Published annually.

Industry Reports: (A)
U.S. Dept. of Commerce, Superintendent of Documents,
    U.S. Government Printing Office
Washington, DC 20402; (202) 783-3238
    Reports. Quarterly. Presents summaries on selected industry trends.

Information Access Corporation
362 Lakeside Dr., Foster City, CA 94404; (800) 227-8431

America Buys: (C)
Annual book. Indexes information on over 40,000 products, including evaluations, brand name references, consumer buying information, and brand comparisons.

Business Index: (A)
This database indexes and abstracts information from more than 300 business periodicals, *The Wall Street Journal* (cover to cover), *Barron's* (cover to cover), *The New York Times* (Financial Section), business articles from more than 1000 general and legal periodicals, and business books from the Library of Congress's MARC database. It provides extensive special indexing of information on corporations, their divisions, executives, and profits.

International Media Guide
Directories International, Inc.: (D)
150 Fifth Ave., Suite 610, New York, NY 10011; (212) 807-1660
Comprehensive source of rate lists for business publications, newspapers, and consumer magazines. Complete set includes six volumes: IMG Business Publications—Europe, Latin America, Middle East/Africa, and Asia/Pacific; IMG Newspaper Worldwide; IMG Consumer Magazines Worldwide.

Leading National Advertiser, Inc. (LNA)
11 W. 42 St., New York, NY 10036; (212) 789-1440

Company Brand Report: (D)
Records the advertising expenditures of national advertisers. Lists parent companies alphabetically, showing total advertising expenditures by brand along with expenditures in each of the following

media: magazines, newspaper supplements, network television, spot television, network radio, and outdoor advertising. Also lists the leading national advertisers, the top-ranking spenders in each of the six media, media tools for the 10 previous years, magazine totals by group, total industry class expenditures, and industry class expenditures in each of the six media.

Multi-Media Report Service: (D)
   Quarterly. Analyzes advertising expenditures of about 15,000 companies.

Publishers Information Bureau: (D)
PIB/LNA Magazine Advertising Analysis
   Three volumes (monthly service). This is a service that provides detailed month-by-month advertising expenditures and lineage by brand and by name of specific magazine. It is arranged in the following sections: volume 1 contains data for apparel, business/finance, and general/retail; volume 2 lists drug/toiletries, food/beverages, home building, transportation, and agriculture; volume 3 gives magazine totals, class totals, and an index.

Market Profile Analysis: (B)
   Dun & Bradstreet, Inc.
   299 Park Ave., New York, NY 10171; (212) 593-6800
      Annual. Loose-leaf. Detailed profiles of U.S. metropolitan areas.

Market Statistics, Inc. (B)
   355 Park Ave. South, New York, NY 10010; (212) 592-6250
      This database includes demographic and retail sales information on each of 3100 American counties, including data on income, buying power, demographic profiles, and more. Four basic data packages are available: (1) Demographic Data Base I (basic demographic information); (2) Demographic Data Base II (basic demographic information plus ethnic characteristics); (3) County Commercial and Industrial Data Base (covers industrial and business characteristics); and (4) Planner's Data Base (includes television, geographic, and market information necessary for strategic planning and forecasting).

Mead Data Central, Inc.: (A, B)
   P.O. Box 933, Dayton, OH 45401; (800) 227-4908; (513) 865-6800
      Through Lexis, one of its two main database families, Mead Data Central provides electronic access to the full text of hundreds of business databases. Available information includes wire services, company annual reports, investment firm reports, periodicals, newsletters, and selected newspapers.

Media Market Guide: (B, D)
>
> 322 East 50th St., New York, NY 10022; (212) 832-7170
>
>> Published by Conceptual Dynamics, Inc. Provides marketers, media sellers, media buyers, and advertising executives with a description of the physical dimensions, population characteristics, and major media opportunities in each of the top 100 metro markets.

Merrill Lynch Economic Regional Database: (A, B)
>
> Merrill Lynch Economics, Inc.
>
> One Liberty Plaza, 165 Broadway, New York, NY 10080;
>> (212) 449-1000
>
>> Maintains demographic and economic data for individual statistics and SMSAs on labor-force trends, population, tax payments, individual profiles, retail sales, construction, income, and housing starts.

MRI: (C, D)
>
> Mediamark Research, Inc.
>
> 708 Third Ave., New York, NY 10017; (212) 599-0444
>
>> This is a syndicated research organization that compiles information showing relationships among media use, product use, and demographics. Advertising agencies, magazines, and other media utilize the information to guide strategy and target markets. Reports include those on magazine audiences, multimedia audiences, and product volumes.

NEXIS
>
> Mead Data Central, Inc.
>
> 9393 Springboro Pike, P.O. Box 933, Dayton, OH 45401; (800) 227-4908
>
> Marketing: (A, B, C)
>
>> Information from trade publications and other sources on advertising, marketing, marketing research, and public relations. Also consumer attitudes, product announcements, demographics, and reviews.
>
> Promt/Plus: (A, E)
>
>> Presents overview of markets and technology. Analyzes specific companies and industries, tracks competitors, identifies and monitors trends. Various advertising and promotional technologies are assessed and summarized.

Nielsen, A. C
>
> Nielsen Plaza, Northbrook, IL 60062-6288; (708) 498-6300
>
> Retail Index: (C)
>
>> This index measures the buying patterns of consumers by store type, brand/product, sales area or region, and price. Data are indexed by

major media advertising expenditures, in-house advertising support, retailer's gross profits, and retail inventory profiles.

Station Index: (B)

This index keeps track of family viewing habits by tracking the results of each family's diary. The results are used by advertisers in buying time and stations for program evaluation.

TV Index: (B)

The Nielsen Television Index measures the number of homes in which television sets are in use, the channels to which these sets are tuned, and reports these measures in terms of total homes and percentage ratings and shares. Data are developed for those demographic characteristics that reflect household data such as geographic area, county size, household size, household income, and presence of nonadults. The NTI reports measurements of 4-week cumulative program audience and frequency, in addition to many other breakdowns and analyses.

NPD Research: (C)

9801 W. Higgins Rd., Rosemont, IL 60018; (312) 692-6700

Offers four syndicated research services: (1) The CREST Report (Consumer Reports on Eating Share Trends) on consumer buying habits in restaurants; (2) The Gasoline Market Index on national and regional gasoline and allied products; (3) Textile Apparel Market Index on household textile, apparel, and home sewing markets; and (4) The Toy Market Index of the national toy market.

Online Site Evaluation System (ONSITE): (B, C)

Urban Decision Systems, Inc.

2040 Armacost Ave., P.O. Box 25953, Los Angeles, CA 90025; (310) 820-8931

Provides trade-area demographic data of more than 600 aggregate data items. Coverage includes such demographics as consumer expenditures, updated income, population, and household equipment and figures.

Predicasts

Predicasts, Inc.

11001 Cedar Ave., Cleveland, OH 44106; (800) 321-6388

Basebook: (A)

Comprehensive, loose-leaf volume containing approximately 29,000 time series, arranged by modified 7-digit SIC code; and including statistics for economic indicators. The industry statistics usually include production, consumption, exports/imports, wholesale price, plant and equipment expenditures, wage rate.

PROMT: (A)

Monthly. Quarterly and annual cumulation. Abstracts of market information grouped into twenty-eight major industry sections. International coverage.

Terminal System (PTS): (A)

This database contains over 3 million summaries of information taken from over 2500 U.S. and foreign trade journals, newspapers, and general business publications. It offers article summaries, statistical data, and one- or two-line indexing services to provide users with background information on companies, products, industries, or marketing trends.

Prospects: (B)

The Futures Group

80 Glastonbury Blvd., Glastonbury, CT 06033; (203) 633-3501

A database for consumer forecasting. Sample data coverage includes households, families, marriage, divorce, education, labor-force, population, and lifestyle indicators. Forecasts are accompanied by a list of projected events based on historical trends and related events. Forecasts may contain over 100 indicators used to describe American consumers and their behavior. Also used for forecasting the hospital supply and pharmaceutical industries.

Rand McNally's Commercial Atlas and Marketing Guide: (B, C)

Rand McNally & Company

8255 Central Park Ave., P.O. Box 127, Skokie, IL 60076;

(800) 284-6565; (708) 673-9100

Of particular use in allocating sales efforts, this volume presents detailed maps of the United States and provides information about population, households, retail sales, auto registration, sales for consumer goods, food stores, drugstores, and other census statistics for counties, principal cities, and Standard Metro Statistical Areas. Published annually.

Rezide/1980 Update: (B)

Claritas Corp.

1911 N. Fort Meyer Dr., Arlington, VA 22209

1981. National edition (ten volumes). For each ZIP code in the United States, shows population, number of households, household income in seven intervals, and median household income.

Sales Manager's Budget Planner: (E)

Sales and Marketing Management Magazine

633 Third Ave., New York, NY 10017; (800) 554-2754; (212) 986-4800
Presented in the June issue, this guide contains information on compensation and expenses by industry, salesperson and sales-support personnel average compensation, media cost per call by industry, trade show exhibit costs, and automobile operating expenses. Also profiles metro markets giving meal and lodging costs, hotels, and conference centers with telephone numbers and rates.

Simmons Study of Media and Markets: (B, C)
Simmons Market Research Bureau
420 Lexington Ave., 8th Floor, New York, NY 10170; (212) 916-8900; FAX: (212) 916-8918
Consists of detailed descriptions of the characteristics of users of individual products, brands, and services, and of audiences of individual media. Descriptions include detailed information regarding age, sex, education, occupation, income, geographic location, household description, lifestyle, and psychographic data (including hobbies, recreational and leisure activities), respondent self-concept, buying style, and social position.

Site Potential: (B, C)
Caci, Marketing Systems
1100 N. Glebe Rd., Arlington, VA 22201; (800) 292-2240; FAX: (703) 243-6272
Provides estimates of the demand (consumer expenditures) by residents within a defined area for approximately 140 product and service items. This database generates reports covering sixteen different retail stores and three financial institutions. Coverage includes apparel stores, appliance stores, auto service stores, department stores, drugstores, footwear stores, grocery stores, hair salons, home improvement stores, ice cream stores, optical centers, commercial banks, financial companies, and savings and loan associations.

Social Indicators: (B)
Government Printing Office, Washington, DC 20402
Triennial. Charts and tables on population; the family; housing; social security and welfare; health and nutrition; public safety; education and training; "work," income, wealth, and expenses; culture, leisure, and the use of time; social mobility; and participation. International data are provided for comparison. Extensive technical notes accompany each section. Includes references for further reading and a subject index.

SRI Values and Lifestyles (VALS): (E)
>SRI International
>333 Ravenswood Ave., Menlo Park, CA 94025; (415) 326-6200
>>SRI International–VALS is a research service that tracks marketing-relevant shifts in the beliefs, values, and lifestyles of a sample of the American population. The VALS system divides the population into segments consisting of three major groups of consumers, in turn divided into nine specific segments. Tracking the shifts in the values and behavior of these segments can help in understanding the target segment to which one is appealing.

Standard & Poor's Industry Surveys: (A)
>Standard & Poor Corp.
>25 Broadway, New York, NY 10004; (212) 208-8000
>>Separate pamphlets for thirty-three industries, updated quarterly and annually. This is a valuable source for basic data on thirty-three industries, with financial comparisons of the leading companies in each industry. For each industry, there is a "Basic Analysis" (about forty pages) revised annually, and a short "Current Analysis" (about eight pages) published three times per year. Received with this is a four-page monthly on "Trends and Projections," which includes tables of economic and industry indicators, and a monthly "Earnings Supplement," giving concise, up-to-date revenue, income, and profitability data on over 1000 leading companies in these thirty-three major industries.

Starch Recognition Tests of Print Advertisements: (E)
>Starch INRA Hooper, Inc.
>566 E. Boston Post Rd., Mamaroneck, NY 10543; (914) 698-0800
>>Starch Readership Studies make three basic measurements among persons who claim readership of specific magazine issues: the noting score, the seen associated score, and the read most score.

Statistical Abstract of the United States: (A, B)
>U.S. Bureau of Census, Department of Commerce, Public Info. Office, Federal Office Bldg., 3 Silver Hill, Rm. 2705, Suitland, MD 20233; (202) 482-3263
>>This guide provides a general overview of statistics collected by the federal government and other public and private organizations. Some of the topics covered include geography and environment, labor force, communications, population, employment and earnings, business enterprises, vital statistics, transportation, energy manufacturers, foreign commerce and aid, standard metro area statistics, and more.

Statistics Reference Index
    Congressional Information Service, Inc.
    4520 E-W Highway, Suite 800, Bethesda, MD 20814; (301) 654-1550;
      (800) 638-8380
        Monthly in two parts, with annual cumulations. A comprehensive,
        selective guide to American statistical publications available from
        sources other than the United States government, such as trade, profit,
        and other nonprofit associations and institutions; business organiza-
        tions; commercial publishers (including trade journals); independent
        and university research centers; state government agencies.

Survey of Buying Power: (B)
    Sales and Marketing Management Magazine
    633 Third Ave., New York, NY 10017; (800) 543-3000; (212) 986-4800
        Presented in the July issue, this guide contains information on all
        Standard Metropolitan Statistical Areas in the country and covers
        population, households, effective buying income, retail sales, and a
        "Buying Power Index" useful in allocating marketing and promo-
        tional efforts. Also includes national and regional summaries; and
        metro areas, county, and city rankings. Published annually.

Survey of Current Business: (A)
    Bureau of Economic Analysis, Department of Commerce,
    Tower Bldg., 1401 K Street, NW, Washington, DC 20230
        This publication presents monthly and quarterly statistics on several
        business indicators for national income, from income and marketing,
        inventories, industrial production, commodities, advertising, and
        wholesale and retail trade by product category. Published monthly.
        Order from U.S. Government Printing Office, Superintendent of
        Documents, Washington, DC 20402.

Survey of Media Markets: (B, D)
    Sales and Marketing Management Magazine
    622 Third Ave., New York, NY 10017; (800) 544-2754; (212) 986-4800
        Presented in the October issue, this guide contains population,
        income, and retail sales data for Media Markets as well as projec-
        tions. Breakdowns of Media Markets (ADIs) ranking as well as 1996
        projections for states and regions and U.S. totals. These are given for
        population, EBI, Retail Sales, and Buying Power Index.

Target Group Index: (B, C)
    Axiom Market Research Bureau, Inc.
    666 Fifth Ave., New York, NY 10103; (212) 541-3811
        Report. Supplies sample demographic data for users and nonusers of
        various products and services. Includes market shares for such things
        as product brands, TV programs watched, and magazines read.

ACKNOWLEDGMENTS: FIGURES, TABLES, AND FOOTNOTE REFERENCES

Chapter 1

Fig. 1.3 Reprinted with permission from the American Marketing Association. Adapted from Lynn Phillips, Dae Chang, and Robert Buzzell, "Product Quality, Cost Position, and Business Performance: A Test of Some Key Hypotheses," *Journal of Marketing,* vol. 47, p. 29, Spring 1983. **Fig. 1.4** Reprinted with permission from Harvard Business School Press. From *Product Juggernauts* by Jean-Philippe Deschamps and P. Ranganath Nayak, Boston, MA., 1995, p. 6. Copyright © 1995 by the President and Fellows of Harvard College; all rights reserved.

Table 1.1 Reprinted with permission from the American Marketing Association. From "Market Orientation: Antecedents and Consequences" by Bernard Jaworski and Ajay Kohli, *Journal of Marketing,* July 1993, pp. 65–66.

Fn. 1 *Chicago Tribune*, June 22, 1995. **Fn. 2** *Harvard Business Review*, July-Aug. 1994. **Fn. 3** *Consumer Behavior*, Wiley, 1994. **Fn. 4** *Harvard Business Review*, Nov.-Dec. 1987. **Fn. 6** *Well-Made in America: Lessons from Harley-Davidson*, The McGraw-Hill Companies, Inc., 1990. **Fn. 7** *Product Juggernauts*, Harvard Business School Press, 1995. **Fn. 8** *Journal of Marketing*, July 1993. **Fn. 9** *Research and Technology Management,* Sept.-Oct. 1994; *Quality*, Jan. 1994. **Fn. 10** *Harvard Business Review*, Nov.-Dec. 1988. **Fn. 11** *Harvard Business Review*, Sept.-Oct. 1995. **Fn. 12** *Wall Street Journal*, Sept. 25, 1995.

Chapter 2

Fig. 2.3 Adapted from "Make the Product Portfolio a Basis for Action" by Rick Brown, *Long-Range Planning*, vol. 24, Feb. 1991, p. 104. Copyright © 1991 with permission from Elsevier Science Ltd., Kidlington, England.

Fn. 2 *Wall Street Journal*, Sept. 22, 1995. **Fn. 3** *Wall Street Journal*, Oct. 6, 1995. **Fn. 4** *Wall Street Journal*, July 28, 1995. **Fn. 5** *Wall Street Journal*, July 14, 1995. **Fn. 6** *Business Week*, Aug. 14, 1995. **Fn. 7** *Wall Street Journal*, Aug. 29, 1995. **Fn. 8** *Chicago Tribune*, Aug. 9, 1995. **Fn. 9** *Wall Street Journal*, Sept. 13, 1995. **Fn. 10** *Reuters Business Report*, May 16, 1995. **Fn. 11** *Business Week*, June 8, 1992; *Chicago Tribune*, May 15, 1992. **Fn. 12** *Business Week*, Aug. 14, 1995. **Fn. 13** *PIMS Letter on Business Strategy*, Strategic Planning Institute, 1977. **Fn. 14** *Harvard Business Review*, May-June 1987.

Chapter 3

Fig. 3.2 Reprinted with permission from *Harvard Business Review*. From "The House of Quality" by John Hauser and Don Clausing, May-June 1988, p. 69. Copyright © 1988 by the President and Fellows of Harvard College; all rights reserved. **Fig. 3.4** Reprinted with permission. *A Probabilistic Model for Testing Hypothesized Hierarchical Market Structures* by Rajiv Grover and William Dillon. Copyright © 1985 by the Institute of Management Sciences and Operations Research Society of America (INFORMS), Providence, RI.

Fn. 1 *Sloan Management Review*, Spring 1993. **Fn. 2** *Journal of Product Innovation Management*, Sept. 1992. **Fn. 3** *Production*, Feb. 1989. **Fn. 4** *Harvard Business Review*, May-June 1988. **Fn. 5** *Journal of Marketing*, Fall 1979. **Fn. 6** *Journal of Consumer Research*, June 1981. **Fn. 7** *Progressive Grocer*, Dec. 1996. **Fn. 8** *Model for Testing Hypothesized Hierarchical Market Structures*, The Institute of Management Sciences, 1985. **Fn. 9** *Wall Street Journal*, Oct. 9, 1995. **Fn. 10** *Adweek's Marketing Week*, June 24, 1991. **Fn. 11** *Business Week*, July 29, 1991. **Fn. 12** *Marketing News*, Oct. 14, 1991. **Fn. 13** *Journal of Marketing*, April 1950. **Fn. 14** *Business Week*, March 6, 1989. **Fn. 15** *Handbook of Consumer Behavior*, 1991. **Fn. 16** *Consumer Behavior in Marketing Strategy*, The McGraw-Hill Companies, Inc., 1989. **Fn. 17** *Journal of Marketing Research*, Nov. 1991. **Fn. 19** *Consumer Behavior in Marketing Strategy*, The McGraw-Hill Companies, Inc., 1989. **Fn. 20** *Handbook of Consumer Behavior*, 1991. **Fn. 21** *Journal of Business Research*, vol. 17, no. 4, 1988. **Fn. 22** *Journal of the Academy of Marketing Science*, Fall 1994. **Fn. 23** *Journal of Consumer Research*, June 1993. **Fn. 24** *Journal of Marketing*, Oct. 1968. **Fn. 25** *Business Week*, Feb. 3, 1992.

Chapter 4

Fig. 4.2 From "Segmentation Marketing" by John Berrigan and Carl Finkbeiner, *New Methods for Capturing Business Marketing.* New York: HarperCollins, 1992, p. 72. **Fig. 4.4** From *Strategic Marketing Management* by David Aaker. New York: John Wiley, 1988, p. 86.

Table 4.8 From "Segmentation Marketing" by John Berrigan and Carl Finkbeiner, *New Methods for Capturing Business Marketing.* New York: HarperCollins, 1992, p. 73. **Table 4.9** From *The New Competitor Intelligence* by Leonard M. Fuld. New York: John Wiley, 1995.

Fn. 1 *Journal of Marketing*, July 1956. **Fn. 2** *Stores*, Jan. 1994. **Fn. 3** *Lodging Hospitality,* Oct. 1994. **Fn. 4** *Marketing Research: A Magazine of Management and Applications*, March 1989. **Fn. 5** *Journal of Marketing*, July 1968. **Fn. 6** *New Methods for Capturing Business Marketers*, Harper Business, 1992. **Fn. 7** *American Demographics*, Jan. 1994. **Fn. 8** *Harvard Business Review*, July-Aug. 1975. **Fn. 9** *Journal of Marketing Research*, Nov. 1995. **Fn. 10** *Journal of Marketing*, Oct. 1991. **Fn. 11** *Journal of Advertising Research*, March-April 1992. **Fn. 12** *Journal of Consumer Research,* June 1992. **Fn. 13** *Journal of Travel Research*, Winter 1994. **Fn. 14** Values of Lifestyles Program, SRI International. **Fn. 15** Values of Lifestyles Program, SRI International. **Fn. 16** *American Demographics*, July 1991. **Fn. 17** *American Demographics*, Feb. 1995. **Fn. 18** *American Demographics*, Feb. 1995. **Fn. 19** *Segmentation Marketing: New Methods for Capturing Business Markets*, Harper Business, 1992. **Fn. 20** *Segmentation Marketing: New Methods for Capturing Business Markets*, Harper Business, 1992. **Fn. 21** *European Journal of Marketing*, Nov. 10, 1994. **Fn. 22** *The Concept*, Discount Store News, May 15, 1995. **Fn. 23** *Using Databases to Seek Out the (Brand) Loyal Shoppers*, Promo/Progressive Grocer Special Report, Feb. 1995. **Fn. 24** *How Vons Makes It Work*, Promo/Progressive Grocer Special Report, Oct. 1994. **Fn. 25** *The Marketing Information Revolution*, Harvard University Press, 1994. **Fn. 26** *The Marketing Information Revolution*, Harvard University Press, 1994. **Fn. 27** *Advances in Global High-Technology Management*, vol. 4, part 4, 1994. **Fn. 28** *Rethinking Strategic Management*, John Wiley, 1995. **Fn. 29** *The Competitive Intelligence Handbook*, Scarecrow Press, 1992. **Fn. 30** *Competitive Intelligence Review*, vol. 6, 1995. **Fn. 31** *Information Today*, June 1995. **Fn. 32** *The New Competitor Intelligence,* John Wiley, 1995. **Fn. 33** *The New Competitor Intelligence,* John Wiley, 1995.

Chapter 5
Fig. 5.3 Reprinted with permission from *Harvard Business Review,* May-June 1994. Copyright © 1994 by the President and Fellows of Harvard College; all rights reserved.
Table 5.8 Reprinted with permission from the Association of National Advertisers. Adapted from *Marketing Norms for Product Managers* by F. Beaven Ennis. New York: Association of National Advertisers, 1985, p. 27. **Table 5.9** Reprinted with permission. Developed from *Adventures in Relevance Marketing* by Jock Bickert. Denver: Briefcase Books, 1990; "Lifetime Value of a Customer," *Marketing Insights,* Fall 1991, pp. 85–89; "The Great Turnaround: Selling to the Individual" by Stan Rapp and Thomas Collins, *Adweek's Marketing Week,* Aug. 27, 1990, pp. 20–26.
Fn. 1 *American Demographics*, Dec. 1995. **Fn. 2** *Wall Street Journal*, July 17, 1992. **Fn. 3** *Fortune*, July 10, 1995. **Fn. 4** *Mediamark Research Meat and Prepared Meals Report*, Mediamark Research, Spring 1994. **Fn. 5** *Sales and Marketing Management*, Oct. 28, 1994. **Fn. 6** *Marketing Norms for Product Managers*, Association of National Advertisers, 1985. **Fn. 7** *Adweek's Marketing Week*, May 11, 1992. **Fn. 8** *Sales and Marketing Management*, May 1995. **Fn. 9** *Sales and Marketing Management*, May 1995. **Fn. 10** *Sales and Marketing Management*, May 1995. **Fn. 11** *Journal of Forecasting*, vol. 14, 1995. **Fn. 12** *Harvard Business Review*, Jan.-Feb. 1986. **Fn. 13** *Journal of Business Forecasting*, Winter 1992-1993. **Fn. 14** *Sales and Marketing Management*, Aug. 1994. **Fn. 15** *Harvard Business Review*, May-June 1994.

Chapter 6
Fig. 6.2 Reprinted with permission from "Advertising Research at Anheuser-Busch" by R. L. Ackoff and J. R. Emshoff, *Sloan Management Review,* Winter 1975, p. 4. Copyright © by Sloan Management Review Association; all rights reserved.
Fn. 1 *Business Week*, April 27, 1992. **Fn. 2** *Wall Street Journal*, Aug. 31, 1992. **Fn. 4** *Wall Street Journal*, May 19, 1992. **Fn. 5** *Directors and Boards*, Summer 1990.

Chapter 7
Fn. 1 *Wall Street Journal*, Jan. 13, 1994. **Fn. 2** *Chicago Tribune*, Oct. 17, 1995. **Fn. 3** *Marketing News*, Oct. 23, 1995. **Fn. 4** *Wall Street Journal,* Oct. 9, 1995. **Fn. 5** *Wall Street Journal*, Oct. 27, 1995. **Fn. 6** *Marketing Norms for Product Managers*, Association of National Advertisers, 1985. **Fn. 7** *Business Week*, Aug. 14, 1995. **Fn. 8** *Harvard Business Review*, Sept.-Oct. 1995. **Fn. 9** *Journal of Marketing*, Jan. 1993. **Fn. 10** *Marketing Research*, Sept. 1989. **Fn. 11** *Wall Street Journal*, Oct. 16, 1995. **Fn. 12** *Marketing Management*, Fall 1995. **Fn. 14** *The Value Side of Productivity*, American Association of Advertising Agencies, 1989. **Fn. 15** *Journal of Marketing Research*, Nov. 1987. **Fn. 16** *Harvard Business Review*, Sept.-Oct. 1990. **Fn. 17** *Harvard Business Review*, Nov.-Dec. 1995. **Fn. 18** *Colloquy*, vol. 4, no. 4, 1994.

Chapter 8
Fig. 8.3 From *Developing Products in Half the Time* by Preston Smith and Donald Reinertsen. New York: Van Nostrand, 1991, p. 4.
Table 8.2 Reprinted with permission. From "The NewProd System: The Industry Experience" by Robert Cooper, *Journal of Product Innovative Management*, June 1992. Copyright © 1992 by Elsevier Science, Inc. **Table 8.3** Reprinted with permission. From "The NewProd System: The Industry Experience" by Robert Cooper, *Journal of Product Innovative Management*, June 1992. Copyright © 1992 by Elsevier Science, Inc.
Fn. 1 *Business Week* Aug. 17, 1993. **Fn. 4** *Marketing Science*, Summer 1995. **Fn. 6** *Developing Products in Half the Time*, Van Nostrand, 1991. **Fn. 8** *Developing Products in Half the Time*, Van Nostrand, 1991. **Fn. 9** *Harvard Business Review*, Sept.-Oct. 1995. **Fn. 10** *The Sources of Innovation*, Oxford University Press, 1985. **Fn. 11** *The Economist*, March 4, 1995. **Fn. 12** *Customer Visits*, Sage, 1993. **Fn. 13** *European Journal of Marketing*, 1981. **Fn. 14** *Fortune*, May 18, 1992. **Fn. 17** *Product Design and Development*, The McGraw-Hill Companies, Inc., 1995. **Fn. 18** *Wall Street Journal*, Sept. 20, 1995. **Fn. 19** *Business Week*, June 7, 1993. **Fn. 20** *Product Design and Development*, The McGraw-Hill Companies, Inc., 1995. **Fn. 21** *Wall Street Journal*, July 14, 1995. **Fn.**

24 *Design and Marketing of New Products*, Prentice-Hall, 1993. **Fn. 25** *Design and Marketing of New Products*, Prentice-Hall, 1993. **Fn. 28** *Business Week*, Aug. 28, 1995; *Wall Street Journal*, July 14, 1995. **Fn. 29** *Chicago Tribune*, July 17, 1995. **Fn. 31** *Managing Brand Equity*, Free Press, 1991. **Fn. 32** *Journal of Marketing Research*, May 1994. **Fn. 33** *Journal of Marketing*, Jan. 1990.

Chapter 9

Table 9.14 Adapted from *Marketing: Principles and Strategy* by J. Barry Mason and Hazel F. Ezell. Business Publications: Plano, TX, 1987, p. 392.

Fn. 1 *Wall Street Journal*, Aug. 26, 1993. **Fn. 2** *Journal of Marketing*, Jan. 1988. **Fn. 3** *Journal of Marketing*, Jan. 1988. **Fn. 6** *Wall Street Journal*, Nov. 11, 1995. **Fn. 8** *Harvard Business Review*, Sept.-Oct. 1995. **Fn. 9** *Marketing Science*, Fall 1995. **Fn. 10** *The Strategy and Tactics of Pricing*, Prentice-Hall, 1987. **Fn. 11** *Journal of Marketing*, April 1987. **Fn. 12** *Wall Street Journal*, July 12, 1995. **Fn. 13** *USA Today*, April 20, 1993.

Chapter 10

Fig. 10.4 Reprinted with permission. Copyright © 1996 *USA Today*, April 1996, p. 3. **Fig. 10.5** Reprinted with permission of Houghton Mifflin Company. From *Advertising: From Fundamentals to Strategies* by Michael L. Rothschild. Copyright © 1987. Lexington, MA: D. C. Heath, 1987, p. 381.

Table 10.2 Reprinted with permission. Copyright © Crain Communications, Inc. From *Business Marketing Magazine*, Nov. 1991, pp. 111–113. **Table 10.3** From *Sports and Recreation Report*, Spring 1994, Mediamark Research.

Fn. 1 *Marketing Communications: Managing of Advertising and Promotions*, HBJ/Dryden, 1996. **Fn. 2** *Brandweek*, Nov. 16, 1992. **Fn. 3** *Journal of Marketing Research*, May 1994. **Fn. 5** *Marketing Communications*, April 1982. **Fn. 6** *Advertising Age*, May 18, 1981. **Fn. 7** *Advertising Age*, May 15, 1995. **Fn. 8** *Marketing Communications*, April 1982. **Fn. 9** *Marketing*, April 21, 1994. **Fn. 10** *Advertising Age*, Sept. 25, 1989, and Oct. 21, 1991. **Fn. 11** *Advertising Age*, Nov. 21, 1973. **Fn. 12** *The Psychology of Selling*, The McGraw-Hill Companies, Inc., 1925. **Fn. 13** *Journal of Marketing*, Oct. 1961. **Fn. 14** *Diffusion of Innovations*, Free Press, 1962. **Fn. 16** *U.S News & World Report*, Nov. 13, 1989. **Fn. 17** *Advertising: A Decision-Making Approach*, Dryden, 1988. **Fn. 18** *Journal of Marketing*, April 1972; *Advertising*, HBJ, 1974. **Fn. 19** *Wall Street Journal*, Aug. 23, 1989; *Advertising Age*, Aug. 25, 1989; *Wall Street Journal*, June 19, 1989. **Fn 20** *Forbes*, Feb. 5, 1990. **Fn. 21** *Fortune*, July 21, 1986. **Fn. 22** *Adweek's Marketing Week*, May 25, 1992. **Fn. 23** *Journal of Marketing*, Jan. 1969. **Fn. 24** *Sales and Marketing Plans, Sales and Marketing Management*, 1979. **Fn. 25** *Journal of Marketing*, Oct. 1986. **Fn. 27** *Brandweek*, Feb. 19, 1996. **Fn. 28** *Wall Street Journal*, March 6 and 8, 1991; *Advertising Age*, Dec. 10, 1990. **Fn. 29** *Marketing Week*, Feb. 10, 1995. **Fn. 30** *Marketing*, Sept. 14, 1995. **Fn. 31** *Marketing*, Nov. 30, 1995. **Fn 32** *Journal of Advertising Research*, May-June 1995. **Fn. 33** *Journal of Advertising Research*, 24.4, 1984. **Fn. 34** *Journal of Advertising Research*, May-June 1995. **Fn. 35** *Marketer's Guide to Media*, Adweek Publishing, Spring-Summer, 1995. **Fn. 36** *Journal of Marketing Research*, May 1970. **Fn. 37** *Marketer's Guide to Media*, Adweek Publishing, Spring-Summer, 1995. **Fn. 39** *Advertising Age*, April 13, 1981. **Fn. 41** *Advertising Age*, Nov. 27, 1995. **Fn. 42** *Advertising Planning: Mathematical Models in Advertising Media Planning*, Elsevier Scientific, 1973. **Fn. 43** *Operations Research*, Jan.-Feb. 1969. **Fn. 44** *Business Week*, Oct. 21, 1991. **Fn. 45** *Wall Street Journal*, Feb. 16, 1988; *Advertising Measurement and Decision-Making*, Allyn and Bacon, 1968. **Fn. 46** *Business Marketing*, Sept. 1988. **Fn. 47** *Harvard Business Review*, Nov.-Dec. 1968. **Fn. 48** *Shoot*, Feb. 24, 1995. **Fn. 49** *Adweek*, July 17, 1995. **Fn. 50** *Shoot*, Feb. 24, 1995. **Fn. 51** *Wall Street Journal*, Sept. 13, 1984. **Fn. 52** *Shoot*, Feb. 24, 1995. **Fn. 53** *Shoot*, Feb. 24, 1995. **Fn. 54** *Forbes*, Nov. 27, 1989.

Chapter 11

Fn. 1 *Direct Marketing Management*, Prentice-Hall, 1989. **Fn. 2** *Harvard Business Review*, March-April, 1990. **Fn. 3** *Marketing News*, May 9, 1994; *The Economist*, July 25, 1992. **Fn. 4** *Adweek's Marketing Week*, Oct. 9, 1989. **Fn. 5** *Wall Street Journal*, Oct. 15, 1992. **Fn. 6** *Harvard Business Review*, Sept.-Oct. 1993. **Fn. 7** *Journal of Marketing*, July 1986. **Fn. 8** *Forbes*, Oct. 24, 1994. **Fn. 9** *Forbes*, Oct. 24, 1994. **Fn. 11** *Marketing Science*, Fall 1995. **Fn. 12** *Harvard Business Review*, May-June 1983. **Fn. 13** *Journal of Retailing*, Summer 1989. **Fn. 14** *Marketing News*, May 9, 1994; *The Economist*, July 25, 1992. **Fn. 15** *Sloan Management Review*, Fall 1991. **Fn. 16** *Harvard Business Review*, Sept.-Oct. 1993. **Fn. 17** *Forbes*, Oct. 24, 1994. **Fn. 18** *Readings and Cases in Direct Marketing*, NTC Publishing, 1992. **Fn. 19** *Business Week*, Nov. 14, 1994. **Fn. 20** *Colloquy*, vol. 4, no. 1, 1993. **Fn. 21** *Business Week*, June 20, 1994. **Fn. 22** *Wall Street Journal*, Dec. 20, 1995. **Fn. 23** *Colloquy*, vol. 4, no. 3, 1993. **Fn. 24** *Colloquy*, vol. 4, no. 1, 1993. **Fn. 27** *The New Direct Marketing*, Irwin, 1995.

Chapter 12

Table 12.2 Reprinted by permission of the Dartnell Corporation, Chicago, IL. Adapted from "Twenty-Sixth Survey of Sales Force Compensation," 1990. **Table 12.6** From "How to Remake Your Sales Force" by Patricia Sellers, *Fortune*, May 4, 1992, pp. 98–103; "Clout: More and More, Retail Giants Rule the Marketplace," *Business Week*, Dec. 21, 1992, pp. 66–73.

Fn. 1 *Business Week*, Aug. 3, 1992. **Fn. 2** *Fortune*, May 4, 1992. **Fn. 4** *Wall Street Journal*, July 8, 1992; *Business Week*, Jan. 16, 1995. **Fn. 5** *Fortune*, Aug. 13, 1990; *The Economist*, Sept. 4, 1993. **Fn. 6** *Business Week*, Nov. 23, 1992. **Fn. 7** *Forbes*, May 25, 1992. **Fn. 8** *Sales and Marketing Management*, June 1995. **Fn. 9** *Forbes*, Aug. 7, 1989. **Fn. 10** *Fortune*, Nov. 28, 1994. **Fn. 11** *Sloan Management Review*, Winter 1992. **Fn. 12** *Chicago Tribune*, Aug. 7, 1989. **Fn. 13** *Business Week*, Dec. 21, 1992. **Fn. 14** *Fortune*, July 29, 1991. **Fn. 15** *Decision-Criteria for New Product Acceptance: The Role of Trade Buyers*, Quorum Books, 1991. **Fn. 16** *Sales Promotion Management*, Prentice-Hall, 1989. **Fn. 17** *Sales and Marketing Management*, July 1994. **Fn. 18** *Journal of Marketing*, Jan. 1988. **Fn. 19** *Journal of Marketing*, Jan. 1990. **Fn. 20** *Marketing News*, Jan. 16, 1989. **Fn. 21** *Marketing News*, May 9,

1994. **Fn. 22** *Age of Information Marketing*, A. C. Nielsen, 1989. **Fn. 24** *Forbes*, June 1, 1996. **Fn. 25** *Harvard Business Review*, Sept.-Oct. 1974. **Fn. 27** *Journal of Marketing Research*, Feb. 1976.

Chapter 13
   Table 13.1 Reprinted with permission of *Sales and Marketing Management*, June 1993. Developed from "1993 Sales Manager's Budget Planner," *Sales and Marketing Management*, June 28, 1993. **Table 13.3** Reprinted with permission of *Sales and Marketing Management*, Feb. 1987. **Table 13.4** Reprinted with permission of *Sales and Marketing Management*. From "The Question of Reps," *Sales and Marketing Management*, June 1991, p. 34.
   Fn. 2 *Sales Management*, May 19, 1975; *Journal of Marketing*, Oct. 1987. **Fn. 4** *Relevance Loss: The Rise and Fall of Management Accounting*, Harvard Business School Press, 1987. **Fn. 6** *Journal of Marketing*, Summer 1980. **Fn. 7** *1980 Portfolio of Sales and Marketing Plans*, Sales and Marketing Management, 1980. **Fn. 8** *Sales and Marketing Management*, Jan. 1990. **Fn. 9** *Sales and Marketing Management*, Sept. 1991. **Fn. 11** *Sales Management*, May 1989. **Fn. 12** *Harvard Business Review*, Jan.-Feb. 1974. **Fn. 13** *Sales Management*, May 1989. **Fn. 14** *Sales and Marketing Management*, Aug. 1992. **Fn. 15** *Sales and Marketing Management*, June 1994. **Fn. 16** *Sales and Marketing Management*, June 1994. **Fn. 17** *Business Marketing*, Dec. 1987; *Sales and Marketing Management*, Jan. 1993. **Fn. 19** *Sales and Marketing Management*, Nov. 19, 1989. **Fn. 20** *Sales and Marketing Management*, June 1994. **Fn. 21** *Sales and Marketing Management*, Nov. 1989. **Fn. 22** *Sales and Marketing Management*, Nov. 1989. **Fn. 23** *Fortune*, Sept. 19, 1994. **Fn. 24** *Forbes*, Oct. 20, 1986. **Fn. 25** *Fortune*, Nov. 28, 1994. **Fn. 26** *Women's Wear Daily*, July 30, 1990. **Fn. 30** *Sales and Marketing Management*, Aug. 1989. **Fn. 32** *Sales and Marketing Management*, Sept. 1991. **Fn. 33** *Business Week*, July 2, 1990. **Fn. 34** *Harvard Business Review*, Sept.-Oct. 1990. **Fn. 35** *Sales and Marketing Management*, May 1989.

Chapter 14
   Table 14.1 Reprinted with permission of *Sales and Marketing Management*, June 1993. From "1993 Sales Manager's Budget Planner," *Sales and Marketing Management*, June 28, 1993, p. 65.
   Fn. 2 *Management Review*, April 1991; *Fortune*, March 14, 1991; *Wall Street Journal*, Sept. 17, 1991; *The Economist*, Nov. 19, 1994. **Fn. 3** *Harvard Business Review*, March-April 1984; *Managing Marketing*, Free Press, 1984. **Fn. 4** *Fortune*, Feb. 6, 1995. **Fn. 5** *The Economist*, Jan. 16, 1993; *Fortune*, Feb. 22, 1993; *Business Week*, Oct. 30, 1995. **Fn. 6** *Inc.*, Aug. 1989. **Fn. 7** *Fortune*, Feb. 24, 1992. **Fn. 8** *Harvard Business Review*, Oct. 1981. **Fn. 10** *Fortune*, Oct. 27, 1986. **Fn. 11** *Business Week*, Jan. 18, 1993. **Fn. 12** *Sales and Marketing Management*, Sept. 1991. **Fn. 13** *Sales and Marketing Management*, Dec. 1995. **Fn. 14** *Fortune*, Feb. 22, 1993. **Fn. 15** *Business Week*, April 30, 1979. **Fn. 16** *Business Week*, Nov. 27, 1989. **Fn. 17** *Business Week*, March 19, 1984, and Oct. 12, 1981. **Fn. 18** *Fortune*, May 18, 1992. **Fn. 19** *Adweek's Marketing Week*, April 15, 1991. **Fn. 20** *Business Week*, July 21, 1980. **Fn. 21** *Forbes*, Nov. 27, 1989. **Fn. 22** *Sales and Marketing Management*, June 1987. **Fn. 23** *The Economist*, April 9, 1994. **Fn. 24** *Business Week*, July 25, 1988. **Fn. 25** *Handbook of Modern Marketing*, The McGraw-Hill Companies, Inc., 1970. **Fn. 26** *Harvard Business Review*, March-April 1992. **Fn. 27** *The Commercial Development of New Products*, The Conference Board, 1986; *Marketing Science*, Winter 1993. **Fn. 28** *Business Week*, Nov. 20, 1995. **Fn. 29** *Harvard Business Review*, Sept.-Oct. 1995. **Fn. 30** *Harvard Business Review*, Sept.-Oct. 1977. **Fn. 31** *Sales and Marketing Management*, April 1987. **Fn. 32** *Forbes*, May 25, 1992. **Fn. 33** *Sales and Marketing Management*, Jan. 1996. **Fn. 34** *Inc.*, June 1993. **Fn. 35** *Concurrent Marketing: Integrating Product, Sales, and Service*, Harvard Business School Press, 1995. **Fn. 36** *Sales and Marketing Management*, June 1995. **Fn. 37** *Sales and Marketing Management*, Sept. 1991. **Fn. 38** *Business Week*, March 27, 1995. **Fn. 39** *Sales and Marketing Management*, June 22, 1992. **Fn. 40** *Sales and Marketing Management*, Aug. 12, 1985. **Fn. 41** *Fortune*, July 25, 1995; *Sales and Marketing Management*, Sept. 1991. **Fn. 42** *Sales and Marketing Management*, July 1995. **Fn. 43** *Fortune*, May 4, 1992. **Fn. 44** *Inc.*, Oct. 1991. **Fn. 45** *Inc.*, Aug. 1991. **Fn. 46** *Business Week*, Feb. 7, 1994; *Sales and Marketing Management*, Dec. 1994.

Chapter 15
   Fn. 1 *Marketing News*, Dec. 5, 1994. **Fn. 2** *Journal of Marketing*, Spring 1982. **Fn. 3** *Harvard Business Review*, Nov.-Dec. 1986. **Fn. 8** *Journal of Marketing*, Fall 1979. **Fn. 9** *California Management Review*, Jan. 1983. **Fn. 10** *American Demographics*, March 1995. **Fn. 11** *Fortune*, Dec. 9, 1985. **Fn. 12** *Journal of Marketing*, Oct. 1987.

INDEX